Master

ISDA Master Agreements

(1992 and 2002)

Mastering the ISDA Master Agreements

(1992 and 2002)

A Practical Guide for Negotiators

PAUL C. HARDING

with a chapter on Legal Issues by Simon J. Leifer and Christian A. Johnson

FT Prentice Hall
FINANCIAL TIMES

An imprint of Pearson Education

London • New York • Toronto • Sydney • Tokyo • Singapore
Hong Kong • Cape Town • Madrid • Paris • Amsterdam • Munich • Milan

PEARSON EDUCATION LIMITED

Head Office:
Edinburgh Gate
Harlow CM20 2JE
Tel: +44 (0)1279 623623
Fax: +44 (0)1279 431059

Website: www.pearsoned.co.uk

First published in Great Britain in 2004

ISBN-13: 978-0-273-66395-9

British Library Cataloguing in Publication Data
A CIP catalogue record for this book can be obtained from the British Library.

10 9 8 7 6

Typeset by Pantek Arts Ltd, Maidstone, Kent.
Printed and bound in Great Britain by Ashford Colour Press Ltd, Gosport, Hants
The Publishers' policy is to use paper manufactured from sustainable forests.

CONTENTS

ABOUT THE AUTHOR

Paul Harding is a graduate of London University and has worked in several UK and foreign banks in London in credit, marketing and documentation roles. Since 1990 he has been involved with derivatives documentation and was a well-known negotiator in the City of London with Barclays Capital Securities Limited and Hill Samuel Bank Limited where he was head of Treasury Documentation.

In February 1997 he founded Derivatives Documentation Limited, a derivatives consultancy and project management company based in the City of London and providing negotiation, recruitment and in-house training services in derivatives documentation. Its clients include many of the world's leading banks.

In November 2001 Paul's book, *Mastering the ISDA Master Agreement* was published by Financial Times-Prentice Hall. This was followed by his *Mastering Collateral Management and Documentation* in conjunction with Christian Johnson, also in this series, which was published in November 2002.

DISCLAIMER

This book is intended to provide an informational and illustrative overview of its subject mainly to non-lawyers and is not at all intended to provide legal or tax advice in respect of any particular situation, contractual relationship or contemplated transaction. The laws and regulations applicable to over the counter derivatives transactions are complex and subject to frequent change. Users of this book should consult their legal and other advisers as they deem appropriate in the preparation and negotiation of over the counter derivatives documentation.

The authors of this book regard the examples given herein as illustrative only and assume no responsibility for any use to which ISDA standard documentation or any definition or provision set forth in this book may be put.

ACKNOWLEDGEMENTS

I should like to thank my wife, Sheila, for all her encouragement in getting this book completed to time. She taught me the simple lesson that if you wanted to write a book you needed to sit down and actually write it and not just talk about it. Sheila knew when to urge me to press on and when to stand back and I thank her for all her patience and sacrifices over the past few months.

My grateful thanks are due to my daughter, Abby, for much excellent emergency typing and technical assistance.

I should like to thank the International Swaps and Derivatives Association, Inc for kindly permitting the reproduction of the 1992 and 2002 ISDA Master Agreements and Amendment: Close-out Amount as Annexes 1–3 of this book.

I would like to thank all those who kindly read first proofs and made comments, in particular:

Richard Atkinson, Merrill Lynch Europe plc
Sybrand de Vries, ABN AMRO Bank NV
Wilfried Schütte, Landesbank Hessen-Thüringen Girozentrale
Keith Spiller, Executive Director, UBS Investment Bank
Svend-Erik Walther, Danske Bank A/S

I should like to thank the editorial staff at Financial Times-Prentice Hall for all their excellent editing and support. Special thanks are due to Laurie Donaldson, Linda Dhondy, Andrew Devine and Lisa Reading. Readers have more diagrams to break up the text through their efforts.

Special thanks are also due to Mia Franks of Bradford & Bingley plc for her useful revisions to the text of the Building Societies section in Chapter 9.

Last but not least, it has been a real pleasure working again with Simon Leifer who kindly revised his excellent distillation on English law relating to derivatives in Chapter 5 and Christian Johnson who wrote knowledgeably and clearly on US law in the same chapter and provided input and suggestions that helped me to develop the section on US Schedule provisions in Chapter 8. Christian also supplied part of the commentary on the new US Payee Tax Representations in Part 2(b) of the 2002 Agreement Schedule in Chapter 4.

I could not have worked with two nicer people throughout.

AUTHOR'S FOREWORD

There is an old ISDA story.

Dante and Virgil decided to visit ISDA Heaven and ISDA Hell.

First they went to ISDA Hell. There they saw large numbers of ISDA negotiators sitting in comfortable offices, happily negotiating ISDA Master Agreements with telephones, faxes and e-mail links.

Next they went to ISDA Heaven. There they saw large numbers of ISDA negotiators sitting in comfortable offices, happily negotiating ISDA Master Agreements with telephones, faxes and e-mail links.

Dante was puzzled and said to Virgil "But ISDA Heaven seems to be the same as ISDA Hell?"

"Ah yes", Virgil replied, "but with one big difference. In ISDA Heaven the Agreements get signed."

This book aims at ISDA Heaven.

It is primarily written for relatively new ISDA Master Agreement negotiators. It is not full of negotiation tips nor does it outline, even if that were possible, how to become the perfect ISDA negotiator. What it does advocate is the importance of gaining a good knowledge base from which to negotiate confidently and, I would add, on a "win-win basis".

Differences arise in Schedules because institutions want to protect themselves and while one provision is vitally important to one it could be a matter of indifference to another.

As a negotiator I have found that reasonableness, knowledge, decisiveness, organisation and persistence when combined will result in numerous Agreements being completed quickly and thoroughly. That creates job satisfaction and a certain "buzz".

ISDA Hell is where you can find those negotiators who nitpick on trivial matters and some who make Al Qaeda look like reasonable people. The most extreme example of delaying a negotiation I know was when a City lawyer asked for a new final draft because a comma was missing from one clause and then took two weeks to confirm that he would accept execution copies! That type of delay is inefficient and in that case was more costly for his client.

This book is not just a second edition of *Mastering the ISDA Master Agreement* which appeared in November 2001.

Instead it covers the new 2002 ISDA Master Agreement comprehensively in Chapter 4; includes a new US law section in Chapter 5 and offers many new and revised examples of Schedule provisions in Chapters 8 and 9. Moreover, 75% of the New Developments in Chapter 10 are new to this book.

Since 2001 a number of interesting things have happened. One purchaser bought three copies and used them as a doorstop. It has been reported that several copies of *Mastering the ISDA Master Agreement* have been stolen from desks in various institutions. This surprises me given the reasonable price charged by the publishers. Some, I am told, have even been sold second hand on ebay. I hope they were not the same ones!

There is even the story of the counterparty who was surprised after signing an ISDA Master Agreement and waiting for a few weeks that a swap deal did not automatically appear.

Finally, an individual counterparty got his plumber and carpenter to witness his signature on page 18 of a 1992 Agreement. For some the ISDA Master Agreement will always be an unfathomable mystery.

This book comprises ten chapters and nine Annexes.

Chapter 1 sets the scene and describes the market in general and how a deal is done from start to finish and where the documentation process fits into this.

Chapter 2 describes the evolution of ISDA documentation including the general and product Definitions, Confirmations and the various incarnations of the Agreement itself.

In Chapter 3, I hope to escape Byron's condemnation of Coleridge:

Explaining metaphysics to the nation.
I wish he would explain his explanation.

Chapter 3 is, I hope, a clear but detailed commentary on the individual sections and provisions of the 1992 ISDA Master Agreement. At the end of the chapter there is a simple glossary of terms which becomes simpler if you read the chapter first.

Chapter 4 is a repeat of the elements of Chapter 3, but in respect of the new 2002 ISDA Master Agreement. The 2002 Agreement contains new concepts and new clause references – just when we had finally grasped the last lot!

Chapter 5 covers the main legal issues surrounding the Agreement and OTC derivatives in general both from UK and US law perspectives. The English law section is written by Simon Leifer, a director of Dresdner Kleinwort Wasserstein's Trading and Derivatives-Legal Services Department and an English qualified solicitor. I am very grateful to Simon for this concise and lucid section of the chapter. The second part of the chapter on US legal issues relating to derivatives is written by Christian Johnson, Associate Professor at the School of Law at Loyola University, Chicago. I thank Christian for a very clear explanation of US law in this area.

Chapter 6 covers the many credit issues arising from the negotiation of ISDA Master Agreements and points out the drawbacks if you do not put an Agreement in place.

Chapter 7 looks at the impact of operational issues on the Agreement's provisions.

Chapter 8 presents a sample 1992 Schedule, comments on its provisions and provides variants and other examples seen in the market. The various examples are illustrative only and for information purposes. They are not meant to be imported wholesale or piecemeal into Schedules you are negotiating but could be seen as a starting point to develop wording which will fit your precise requirements in a negotiation.

Chapter 9 reviews some special Schedules including those for building societies, insurance companies, hedge funds and sovereign entities. My comments in the last two sentences of the previous paragraph apply at least as strongly here.

I have not commented on Schedules involving commodities at all in this book as I regard them as a subject in themselves.

The final section of Chapter 9 deals with provisions seen in US Schedules which often face non-US negotiators. Christian Johnson has kindly provided much input for this section and I should like to thank him for developing a very clear commentary on why US counterparties ask for these provisions. It certainly helps to reduce the "fear of the unknown" in this respect for those of us who are non-US negotiators.

Chapter 10 highlights a few new developments relating to the ISDA Master Agreement mostly in connection with various Amendments issued by ISDA to bring the new Close-out Amount mechanism into existing 1992 Agreements to avoid the need to amend these Agreements between parties wholesale.

Finally the nine Annexes are meant to provide useful information in one place. They are:

Annex 1

A facsimile of the Multicurrency-Cross Border version of the 1992 ISDA Master Agreement and its Schedule (reproduced with the kind permission of the International Swaps and Derivatives Association, Inc).

Annex 2

A facsimile of the 2002 ISDA Master Agreement and its Schedule (reproduced with the kind permission of the International Swaps and Derivatives Association, Inc).

Annex 3

A facsimile of the Amendment: Close-out Amount (reproduced with the kind permission of the International Swaps and Derivatives Association, Inc).

Annex 4
A list of the 39 jurisdictions where ISDA has obtained netting opinions in respect of the 1992 Agreement as at October 2003, and a separate list of 36 jurisdictions where ISDA has obtained netting opinions in respect of the 2002 Agreement, also as at October 2003.

Annex 5
A checklist for the constituents of a guarantee governed by New York law.

Annex 6
A checklist for the constituents of a guarantee governed by English law.

Annex 7
A list of credit ratings from major credit ratings agencies.

Annex 8
A sample Board resolution for UK corporates.

Annex 9
Useful website addresses.

Once when talking to a management consultant, I was told I was in danger of making the ISDA Master Agreement understandable. I hope above all that this may be the case with this book.

Any opinions expressed are those of the authors themselves and do not necessarily reflect those of their employers.

I hope you enjoy this book and find it useful.

Paul Harding

Introduction

1

WHAT ARE DERIVATIVES?

First of all what is a derivative apart from something which appears in news headlines about spectacular financial collapses?

A derivative is a financial product which *derives* from an underlying market.

So for instance, a currency derivative derives from the foreign exchange market; an equity derivative derives from a stock market and an interest rate derivative derives from a cash or money market.

Derivatives can be used to protect against adverse movements in interest rates, exchange rates or market prices. This use of them is called "hedging". They can also be used for speculation and when that goes wrong in a big way, it can make the headlines.

As the *Financial Times* put it in March 1995: "A derivative is like a razor. You can use it to shave yourself and make yourself attractive to your girlfriend. Or you can slit your throat with it."

Straightforward standard derivatives are called "plain vanilla" derivatives. More complex derivatives are called structured or exotic derivatives.

Derivatives are traded on regulated exchanges (like the London International Financial Futures and Options Exchange (LIFFE)) and then not surprisingly are called exchange-traded derivatives. Futures are an example of exchange-traded derivatives. Exchange-traded derivatives are in standard amounts and for standard periods. Over-the-counter ("OTC") derivatives are tailored to the specific requirements of customers. This book focuses on OTC derivatives.

DIFFERENCES BETWEEN THE OTC AND EXCHANGE-TRADED DERIVATIVES MARKETS

The main differences between the exchange-traded markets and the OTC derivatives markets for derivatives may be summarised as follows:

Regulation

Exchange-traded derivatives are highly regulated both in terms of the operation of the exchange itself and the products traded there. Regulation of the OTC derivatives markets is often piecemeal and performed by the individual regulators of the parties, e.g. bank or securities firm regulators.

Counterparty risk

For all exchange-traded transactions, the exchange itself becomes the counterparty for each transaction once the initial trade has been done and it ensures all payments for margin and top-up margin are made. This is not the case in the OTC market where each party focuses carefully on the other's creditworthiness and ability to perform its obligations throughout the life of the trade. The main worry here is, will the counterparty default?

Standardisation

Exchange-traded products are standardised, e.g. in contract size, tenor, expiration date and approved products. OTC derivatives products are designed for the individual customer and may be based upon any amount, tenor, maturity date or product.

Price risk

Exchange-traded contracts can be closed out because the markets are liquid, but it may not be possible to obtain a representative price if an OTC derivative is exotic as few other investors may be interested in it.

Legal risk

Exchange-traded transactions are generally subject to a very detailed legal framework. With OTC derivative transactions this is not always the case and legal opinions are often required which slows down trading.

Settlement risk

Exchanges ensure that parties comply with their obligations within strict time limits. This is not the case with OTC derivative markets where settlements can be delayed and payment netting not be recognised by the laws of some countries. Despite these drawbacks, OTC derivatives are far more flexible than exchange-traded ones.

Let's look briefly at the main products.

MAIN PRODUCTS

Swaps

Interest rate swaps

An interest rate swap is an agreement between two parties to exchange interest payments on their debt over a period of years. One party will pay fixed rate interest and the other floating rate interest. The swap is therefore said to have two legs – a fixed and a floating leg. There is no exchange of principal as there is in a currency swap. Interest payments are in the same currency and are normally made every three or six months and are linked to a notional principal amount. Payments are made net, i.e. being the difference between what is owed by the fixed rate payer and the floating rate payer.

The purpose of an interest rate swap is for both parties to reduce their borrowing costs or to match their interest payments to their expected income.

Essentially, one party who may be able to borrow more cheaply in the fixed rate market (e.g. via a bond issue) actually wants to borrow at a floating rate like LIBOR (London Interbank Offered Rate), while another party wants to do the opposite. The total savings each party can make in each market are calculated and netted off against each other and the answer, say 30 basis points (i.e. 30/100ths of 1%) is shared out between them in a deal structured by a bank, with the bank taking a fee of, say, 5 b.p. for organising the swap. So everybody benefits.

That's how things work in theory. Normally the bank will enter into one side of the deal and then find a counterparty for the other side later. In other words it warehouses the deal until it can find the other party.

There are other interest rate products/variations viz:

Basis swaps

With a plain vanilla interest rate swap, there is a fixed leg linked to a fixed interest rate, e.g. 5% and a floating leg. With a basis swap, both legs are linked to different floating interest rates. A typical basis risk swap might be for payments based on US$ LIBOR against US$ Treasury bill rates, both of which are floating rates.

Asset swaps

Asset swaps can take the form of plain vanilla interest rate swaps or basis swaps. Interest rate swaps are linked to debt obligations of the parties and are also called liability swaps. With an asset swap, one of the parties is swapping the interest payments on an asset it holds, e.g. a bond it has invested in.

Interest rate caps

Companies who have floating rate loans and are concerned that interest rates may rise can buy a cap for a premium which will put a ceiling on the maximum interest they will have to pay on their loans. For instance, if they pay 7% on their loans at present they could buy a cap for 8% for five years. Every three or six months, the bank will review the interest rate. If it is over 8%, it will pay the company the difference. If it is below 8%, nothing happens. The company pays the floating rate concerned. As a result the company's borrowing cost is fixed at 8% for five years.

Interest rate floors

A floor is the same in principle as a cap, except that it guards against interest rates falling too low. This might be useful for a company with high deposit balances in a market where interest rates are falling. The company will pay a premium and if rates fall below a certain level, the bank will pay the company the difference.

Collars

These are a combination of a cap and a floor and guarantee that interest rates will not move outside a chosen band, e.g. 5–8%.

Currency swaps

A currency swap involves an exchange of interest liabilities in two different currencies and normally consists of three stages:

- **a spot exchange of principal (spot settlement is two business days after the rate fixing);**
- **a continuing exchange of interest payments during the swap's life. This is essentially a series of forward FX trades during the term of the contract;**
- **a re-exchange of principal at the maturity of the contract, normally at the same spot rates used at the start.**

The aim is to obtain amounts of foreign exchange at a lower funding rate over a period of years. Currency swaps are particularly useful in hedging project finance currency risk.

Payments under currency swaps cannot be netted.

Options

An option is a contract between a buyer and a seller *giving the right but not the obligation* to buy or sell a given instrument or asset on or until a certain date ("the exercise date") at a predetermined price (the "exercise" or "strike price").

The seller of the option (known as "the writer") receives a premium from the buyer and keeps it whether the option is exercised or not.

A call option gives the buyer the right to call for or buy the asset or instrument from the option seller at the agreed strike price.

A put option gives the buyer the right to put or sell the asset or instrument to the option seller at the agreed strike price.

The main options are either American, i.e. they can be exercised at any time during the option term or European where they can only be exercised on the last day of the option period.

Options are said to be:

- **"in the money" if prices have moved so that it is profitable for the buyer to exercise them;**
- **"out of money" where it is not profitable to exercise them; or**
- **"at the money" where the market price equals the strike price.**

OTC options may be purchased for a wide variety of financial instruments or assets, e.g.:

- **interest rates (interest rate options);**
- **currencies (currency options);**
- **shares (equity or equity index options);**
- **commodities (commodity options);**
- **bonds (bond options).**

When exercised, options are normally settled by a cash payment but sometimes equity and commodity options, for instance, are settled by physical delivery of the share or commodity concerned.

It is also possible to buy a swaption – an option to enter into a swap at a given future rate, date and maturity.

Equity derivatives

This is a fast growing OTC market. Equity derivatives are swaps and options on single stocks or indices like the FTSE 100, Nikkei 225, or Dow Jones Index or on baskets of stocks and indices. They aim to protect against market price movements.

An equity index option gives the buyer the right but not the obligation to buy or sell an agreed amount of an equity index at a specific price on or before a specific date. The buyer pays the seller a premium for this. Index options are usually cash settled, but may be physically settled where a basket of shares reflects the composition of the index concerned. Where a single stock option is concerned, upon exercise it is normally physically settled by delivery of the stock concerned or by a cash payment.

An equity index swap is an agreement between two parties to exchange cash flows based on a percentage change in one or more stocks or stock indices for an agreed period. It will be cash settled. One side of an equity swap will involve a floating reference rate. Equity swaps may be structured with individual equities or baskets of several different shares or indices.

In all cases payout is linked to the performance of an equity or equity index.

Credit derivatives

Credit derivatives are used to hedge the potential risk that borrowers might fail to repay their outstanding bonds or loans. They allow banks to hedge their credit risk without selling or transferring the underlying bond or loan.

The first credit derivative transactions were done in New York in 1992. By the end of 2002, the British Bankers' Association forecast a US$ 1,952 billion market for credit derivatives in notional amount terms. The latest ISDA figures published on 19 March 2003 for the six months to 31 December 2002 gave a total notional outstanding volume figure of US$ 2,150 billion, a 37% increase on the preceding half year figure.

There a no standard dictionary definition of what credit derivatives are, partly because the term covers a number of products. However, a possible definition is:

Credit derivatives are customised contracts between two parties under which one party agrees to make a payment to the other party if an observable credit event occurs or there is a change in a credit spread.

Credit derivative contracts assume or lay off credit risk on loans or bonds or in relation to particular borrowers or issuers or countries in return for either swap or premium payments.

Under a credit default option contract a protection seller undertakes to pay out an agreed sum if a particular borrower or issuer defaults on one, some or all of its obligations (in a specified way). The seller receives a fixed premium from the buyer periodically during the life of the option for assuming this risk.

Credit derivatives have been used by:

- **commercial banks wanting to change the risk profiles of their loan books and offload some risk to free up lines for more profitable business;**
- **investment banks wanting to hedge huge bond and derivatives portfolios;**
- **manufacturing companies over exposed to a single customer;**

- **equity investors in project finance deals with unacceptable sovereign risk;**
- **institutional investors with unusual or speculative risk appetites; and**
- **employees (in some early cases) worried about the safety of their bonuses and wanting to hedge against the bankruptcy of their employer.**

This has necessarily been a very brief description of the main OTC derivatives products and there are many books that describe them more fully and diagrammatically. One of them is Francesca Taylor's *Mastering Derivatives Markets* also in this series. All these derivatives products may be covered under an ISDA Master Agreement.

SIZE OF THE GLOBAL DERIVATIVES MARKET

Every half year the International Swaps and Derivatives Association, Inc ("ISDA") publishes estimated figures for the size of the global OTC derivatives market based on survey answers from its primary members.

The latest figures for the half year ended 31 December 2002 showed a volume measurement based on notional principal amounts of currency swaps and interest swaps and options of just under US$ 100 trillion (US$ 100,000 billion). This was a 45% increase on the position as at 31 December 2001 (i.e. US$ 69 trillion).

What does this measurement mean? Well, first of all swaps and other derivatives are assigned notional principal amounts. These are not the same as the principal amount of a £1 million loan which is £1 million. Dealers decide on the notional principal amount at the start of each transaction and all calculations are linked to it. Normally, the notional amount of a swap remains the same throughout its life but it can also be reduced or increased. However, consultants have estimated that the real risk is 1–2% of the notional amount. This is what it is estimated it would cost to replace derivatives transactions that have to be closed out. On the US$ 100 trillion figure above this would equate to US$ 1,000 billion–2,000 billion on a gross basis before netting of transactions between common counterparties. Assuming the lower figure, this is the equivalent to about 20 times Bill Gates's fortune. So a lot is at stake.

About 90% of the US$ 100 trillion figure is represented by interest rate swap or interest rate option contracts. The main currencies are US dollars, Euro, Yen and Sterling.

The main market users for derivatives are banks, corporates, insurance companies, hedge funds, mutual funds, building societies, sovereign and semi-sovereign institutions and pension funds. The market is therefore well diversified.

There are other measurements of market volume. In May 2003, the Bank for International Settlements ("BIS") issued gross volume figures for the global

OTC derivatives market again based upon notional amounts of nearly US$ 142 trillion as at 31 December 2002, an 11% increase from 30 June 2002. The BIS includes a broader range of products than ISDA in its general figure, e.g. foreign exchange, forward rate agreements and commodity derivatives as well as interest rate contracts.

The first swap was a currency swap between the World Bank and IBM in 1981 and so the market is still relatively young and has grown rapidly especially over the past five years. This being the case, it is vital that derivatives transactions are documented comprehensively, both at the Confirmation and Master Agreement level.

HOW A DEAL IS DONE FROM START TO FINISH

To set things in context, it might first be useful to describe how a typical swap deal is done from start to finish. Before any deals are done a credit line has to be applied for.

Before the deal

Normally, a marketer will visit a prospect, e.g. a company and discuss the types of derivatives business they would like to do together. If this is possible, the marketer will discuss the specifics with a trader who may provide the prospect with indicative quotations and/or sample structures for the transactions. If all is agreed in principle, the marketer will write a paper to the credit department requesting a dealing line of a certain amount for a certain type of product and for a certain period.

The credit department will probably obtain the prospect's audited accounts for the past three years from the marketer and will:

- **check if there is any existing Group relationship with the prospect – are they a customer already?; and**
- **seek any further information either direct from the prospect or via the marketer.**

They will also take into account any formal credit rating the prospect has received from the major credit rating agencies. Assuming the result of the credit department's initial analysis is positive, a credit application is then prepared and forwarded to the relevant sanctioning officer/committee. This may be local or overseas (e.g. a foreign bank's Head Office) depending upon the size of the line applied for.

Once approval comes through, the credit department tells the marketer and marks the limit on the system together with any conditions for use. The marketer now contacts the customer and together with the trader discusses the timing and structure of specific deals. Usually the marketer and the trader are different people, but in smaller organisations they can be the same person.

The deal

One day the customer and the trader will deal. This is normally done over the telephone and confirmed in writing. *The Conduct of Business Rules* (2001) issued by the Financial Services Authority ("FSA") recommend that a Confirmation is sent no later than the following business day (COB 8.15 (2)(a)).

The oral deal is legally binding until both parties sign the Confirmation. The telephone call will have been taped and banks generally hold the tapes for three to six months. One of the parties will be nominated as Calculation Agent. The trader will probably hedge the deal by entering into a mirror image deal with another counterparty.

When the deal is done it is marked against the limit. If the trader knows that the limit will be breached, he will telephone the credit department for clearance and request a temporary increase. If he does not realise this, it will show up on an excess report the next day and will be investigated by the credit department. Most deals are done within limits. In the UK, the professional behaviour of traders is governed by the FSA's *Interprofessional Conduct* chapter and the Bank of England's *Non-Investment Products Code.*

When the deal is done, the marketer will advise the customer's details to a static data person in the back office. They will record their name, address, payment instructions and any other standard relevant information.

The trader or marketer would normally send the customer necessary regulatory information which was probably originally drafted by the legal department. With a new counterparty this will include any anti-moneylaundering checks required by the compliance department. They will also ask the legal department or the Documentation Officer to send out a draft ISDA Master Agreement Schedule to the customer for review.

The Confirmation

In the past a bank might have sent a customer a pre-Confirmation (sometimes called an interim Confirmation). This used to take two forms:

- **a Confirmation showing details of a particular deal usually a complex one (nowadays Terms Sheets are used for this purpose);**
- **a Confirmation which showed the deal details but which also contained detailed provisions and selections from the ISDA Master Agreement. The aim was to bind the customer to these before negotiating the Agreement.**

Nowadays, people often consider it better to move straight to negotiating the Agreement. Indeed one of the problems with pre-Confirmations was that discrepancies could arise between them and the Agreement, when eventually negotiated, which could cause problems given the supremacy of the Confirmation in respect of individual Transactions. Another practical difficulty was that normally, different people with different expertise negotiate Confirmations and Master Agreements in banks, so pre-Confirmations did not usually save any time in the overall documentation negotiation process. Pre-Confirmations have largely fallen into disuse.

As mentioned above, the FSA's *Conduct of Business Rules* recommends that Confirmations are exchanged no later than the following business day. With plain vanilla deals this is not always achieved due to high volumes. With complex transactions it rarely happens.

Normally in a Confirmations section, one person drafts the Confirmation from the trader's deal ticket or trading system details. Another person checks it and it is then sent to the trader and/or marketer for approval, whereupon it is signed by different people who are authorised signatories. It is then faxed to the customer who may also fax you their Confirmation. With particularly complex Confirmations it would be normal for the Legal Department to review and approve them before despatch.

Many Confirmations departments process a high volume of deals and there will normally be someone allocated to check receipt of Confirmations and chase any which are slow in being returned.

Sometimes the customer's payment instructions may be incorrect, so the customer would revise these and raise any other points where he disagrees.

Assuming these points are resolved satisfactorily, the Confirmations department will fax an amended Confirmation to the customer who would sign it and fax it back. It would be deleted from the outstandings list and filed in a Confirmations run of files. Some banks scan signed Confirmations directly into their systems. Any revised payment instructions or other standard information would be advised to the static data person so that they could amend their records.

Payments (also called Settlements)

Most interest rate swap transactions will have a fixed rate leg and a floating rate leg (probably linked to LIBOR or EURIBOR). The interest rate on the floating rate leg needs to be reset periodically, e.g. every three to six months. This is the job of the Calculation Agent (i.e. usually one of the two parties to the

Transaction is chosen as Calculation Agent). A short time before the date when the floating rate needs to be reset, the Payments section will fax or e-mail the customer details of the amount of floating rate interest it expects to receive on the Scheduled Payment Date for the current period and the fixed interest it will be paying and will also repeat standard payment instructions. Sometimes these will change during the Transaction's life. If payment netting has been agreed, only the net amount due (i.e. the difference between the fixed and floating rate interest payments in the same currency) will be transferred on the Scheduled Payment Date. The Payments section (if the bank is Calculation Agent) will also reset the floating rate leg for the next three or six months at the agreed time (e.g. 11 a.m. London time) and send a rate fixing notice to the other party.

The Payments section will check from its reports on the day after the Scheduled Payment Date if the payment was actually received. If it was not, it will immediately contact the customer to find out why.

Terminations

Even without Events of Default, not all deals run to maturity. Most derivatives transactions are done for hedging or protective purposes. Where one of the parties considers, for example, that the need for the protection has disappeared or it is becoming more and more unprofitable for it to hold its position because of market rate movements (e.g. it has to pay a high fixed rate for five years and all the time floating rates are going down), it may decide to terminate or unwind the swap. In that case both traders will agree a termination price, date and fee which will reflect the cost of maintaining the remaining party's hedge elsewhere. These matters are confirmed in writing in a short termination Confirmation. It is also possible for only part of the Transaction to be terminated.

THE PEOPLE INVOLVED

This is a basic structure and may obviously differ between banks.

Marketer

He gets the business, writes up the credit application and interfaces with the customer.

Credit officer

He performs the risk analysis of the application, obtains credit approval and marks the limit. He will also investigate limit excesses.

Trader

He runs the dealing book, transacts with the customer and hedges his positions where necessary.

Static data person

He maintains all relevant customer information on a database which is constantly updated.

Confirmations section

This section is responsible for drafting Confirmations from deal tickets or trading systems and having them independently checked before signing and despatch. It is also responsible for tracking their return.

Payments or settlements section

This section is responsible for sending notices of payments due and monitoring their timely receipt and chasing late ones. It is responsible for remitting payments owed by the bank. It will also usually be responsible for rate fixings and resolving any disputes. This is the Calculation Agent role.

Legal department or documentation officer

The legal department or the Documentation Officer will negotiate the ISDA Master Agreement with the customer. The legal department often reviews and approves complex Confirmations.

Compliance department

The Compliance department will perform regulatory checks on counterparties including anti-moneylaundering checks and will review information received in this respect.

Collateral management

This section will manage the collateral position with any customer ensuring that the bank is secured.

Other features of a back office

- **Everything is normally computerised.**
- **Biggest management concerns are unsigned Confirmations and missed payments.**
- **Most back offices deal with very high volumes, are understaffed and heavily reliant on temps.**
- **A typical structure for a small bank might be one manager, one rate fixing person, one payments person, two or three Confirmations people and a static data person. There would be some understudying of each other's jobs or temps would be used.**
- **Nowadays most back office people have degrees. School leavers are rare.**
- **Functionally, the back office is often classified under Operations.**

THE DOCUMENTATION PROCESS

Before the negotiation starts, the negotiator should receive or obtain credit terms from the credit department for inclusion in the Schedule to the Agreement which is the document negotiators negotiate.

Normally, the negotiator will only have limited discretion to make concessions to the counterparty on points in the Schedule. Usually they need to be referred to Credit, Legal, Tax or the trader depending upon their nature. It is good practice for a negotiator to advise a counterparty from which department he is seeking approval on outstanding matters and, if possible, an estimate of the timescale before he will revert.

Sometimes, because of volume pressures or staff shortage in a bank or lack of in-house expertise in a corporate, negotiation is outsourced to an external law firm. Here it is important for the law firm to be fully aware of its client's policies and what issues they need to refer back to the client. Time consuming arguments on minor issues can then be avoided.

Negotiation departments are most effective where three factors or items are present:

- **a clear, regularly updated, written negotiation policy;**
- **a computerised negotiation tracking system which is regularly updated and incorporates a diary system giving deadlines for the next move;**
- **well informed credit officers conversant with the nature and impact of the type of credit issues which regularly arise in negotiations. (These are featured in Chapter 6.)**

Negotiations typically go through several rounds but eventually agreement is reached and final drafts sent which, if approved, trigger execution copies. Supporting documents (e.g. signing authorities, legal opinions etc) are also requested. When the documentation is signed and complete it is archived and usually details are entered into a database which specifies the important constituent elements of the Agreement.

It is best to enter into an ISDA Master Agreement before an OTC derivatives transaction is done because if an imminent deal is in prospect, a counterparty is never more interested in negotiating the Agreement. It is important to prioritise and "strike while the iron is hot".

Many Credit Departments will stipulate that with certain entities (e.g. corporates credit rated below certain levels, building societies, insurance companies, pension fund trustees and other specialised entities) an ISDA Master Agreement must be completed before trading commences. However, banks regularly trade with each other before an Agreement is completed. Where this happens backlogs can arise which entail counterparty credit risk and documentation risk.

Generally speaking, negotiation of Schedules with traders' marketing prospects where no deals are imminent receive low priority because negotiation sections are normally short staffed and attention has to be focused on negotiations where deals are outstanding. The same usually applies to upgrades of old Agreements.

In the UK, Section 107 of the old *London Code of Conduct* reissued by the FSA in June 1999 recommended that master agreement documentation should be completed within three months of the date of the first trade. In 1995 the Bank of England conducted a survey that found that only one in three master agreements were completed in this timescale. The situation is probably not much better today. Nonetheless, completion of the ISDA Master Agreement well within three months should be the goal so that documentation risk may be minimised.

2 The Evolution of the ISDA Master Agreement

How ISDA documentation has evolved

Inefficient documentation of trades in the market's early days

The ISDA documentation architecture

The ISDA Master Agreement

HOW ISDA DOCUMENTATION HAS EVOLVED

This chapter deals with three types of ISDA documentation:

- **Product Definitions**
- **Confirmations**
- **Master Agreements.**

The International Swaps and Derivatives Association, Inc ("ISDA") is the major issuer of these in the market and I should first like to describe that organisation.

INEFFICIENT DOCUMENTATION OF TRADES IN THE MARKET'S EARLY DAYS

ISDA was formed in New York in 1985 with ten members (it now has over 600) to standardise market practice and documentation. In this it has been a resounding success because previously there was little standard documentation in the market and high legal fees abounded as lawyers Concorded across the Atlantic to complete individual deals. With more complex Transactions this wide variety of documentation caused legal uncertainty.

In 1985 and 1986 ISDA published two Swap Codes to cover US$ interest rate swaps only. These were followed in 1987 by an Interest Rate Swap Agreement again only covering US$ swaps.

However, the first major breakthrough was the Interest Rate and Currency Exchange Agreement (a multi-currency, cross-border agreement) which was also published in 1987. This 1987 Agreement only covered interest rate and currency swaps. For currency swaps it covered 15 currencies. Addenda were issued in 1989 and 1990 to cover caps, floors, collars and options. The terms of these addenda were largely incorporated into the 1992 Agreement which updated the 1987 Agreement and is called the ISDA Master Agreement.

In 1987, ISDA also issued its first Definitions to help in the composition of more standardised interest rate and currency swap Confirmations.

The 1987 Agreement was revised into the 1992 Agreement to:

- **expand the Agreement's product range and to promote netting across products.**
- **take account of changes in laws since 1987, particularly bankruptcy laws.**
- **take account of alterations sought by ISDA members due to market practice changes.**

The revision process took two years.

In December 2001 ISDA started a review and redrafting of the 1992 Agreement which involved over 100 of its member firms. This resulted in the publication of the 2002 ISDA Master Agreement on 8 January 2003. This is the subject of Chapter 4.

ISDA DOCUMENTATION ARCHITECTURE

Product Definitions

Since 1991, ISDA has issued 11 sets of product definition booklets.

Figure 2.1 represents what ISDA calls its documentation architecture. It shows the interconnection between the product Definitions, Confirmations, the ISDA Master Agreement and the ISDA Credit Support Annexes used in collateralised (i.e. secured) transactions.

In July 2000 the *2000 ISDA Definitions* (the *"2000 Definitions"*) were published. This was the first major consolidation of ISDA's general Definitions in almost ten years. It consolidated the *1991 Definitions*, *1998 Supplement* and part of the *1998 Euro Definitions* into the *2000 Definitions*. It then transferred information on rate options, day count fractions and currencies into a separate Annex which can be updated and reissued as necessary. The Annex forms part of the *2000 Definitions*. If a Confirmation incorporates the *2000 Definitions*, it will automatically include the latest version of the Annex unless the parties agree otherwise.

Most Definition booklets are about 40 pages long and describe terms in use in the various product confirmations. The idea is that the terms of each relevant set of Definitions are incorporated by reference in the Confirmation so that they do not need to be spelt out in full every time a deal is done. The Confirmations just tend to concentrate on the economic details of the particular trade. Until July 1999, the average length of a credit derivatives Confirmation was about 15 pages and it was very complex. Now it is between three to five pages long and even has some tick boxes!

The product Definitions themselves are not very easy to read and include frequent cross references, but on the whole they work well provided they are used critically.

The ISDA definitions booklets are mainly used in connection with Confirmations, although you may sometimes see references to them in ISDA Master Agreement Schedules particularly in provisions concerning inconsistencies between general and product specific Definitions or among Definitions, a Confirmation, the Schedule or the Agreement itself. There is an example of this in Chapter 8 (page 565).

FIG. 2.1

ISDA Agreement Structure (2003)

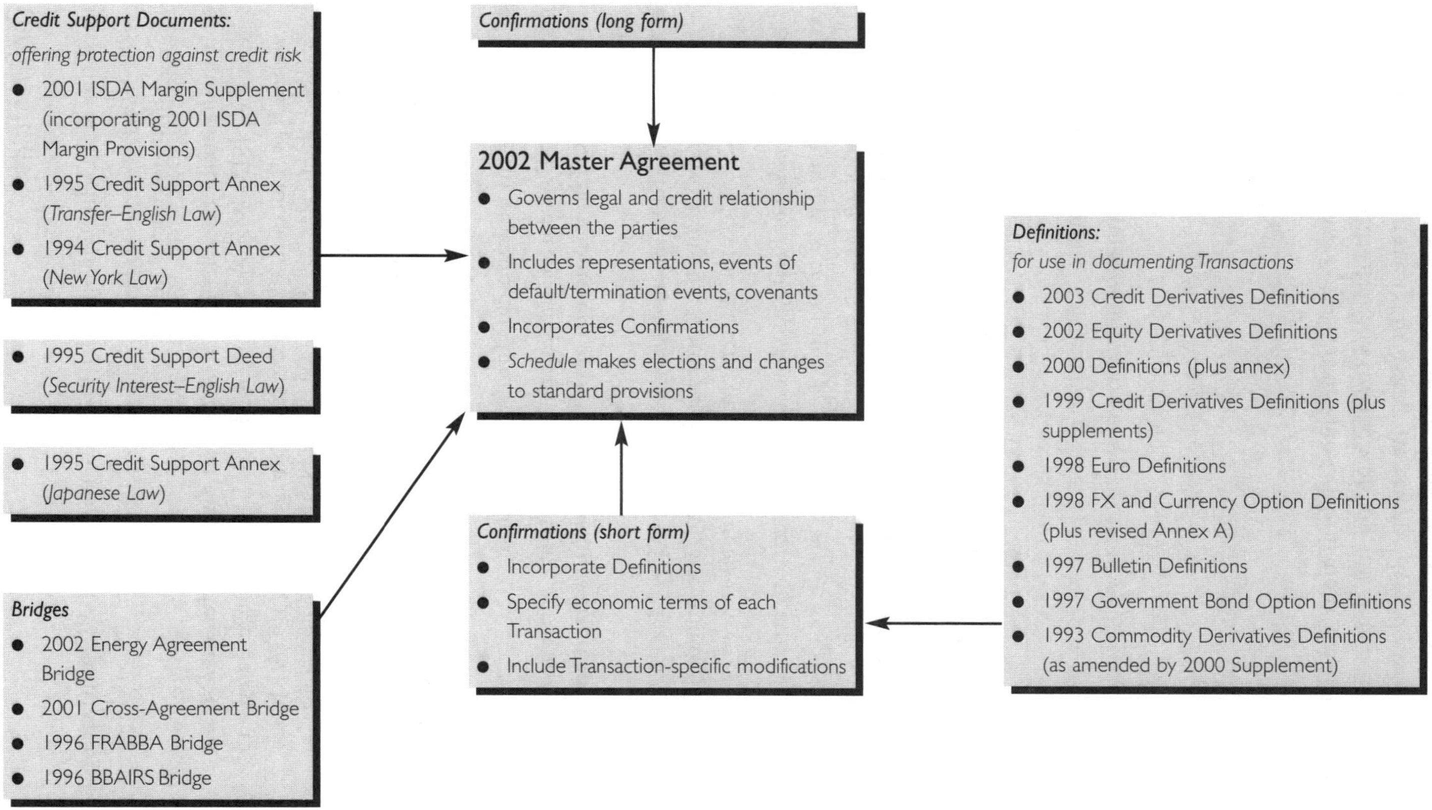

Confirmations

Each product Definitions booklet provides examples of a Confirmation for the specific product. By and large the market tends to use these templates.

A Confirmation does the following:

- **it incorporates the relevant ISDA Definitions and references to any executed ISDA Master Agreement. If this is not yet negotiated and signed it will include an undertaking to negotiate an ISDA Master Agreement. In the meantime a "vanilla ISDA" is considered by lawyers to exist (see Chapter 6 pages 392–3 for an explanation of this term);**
- **it specifies the economic terms of a transaction (e.g. trade, effective and maturity dates; payment calculation terms, timing and mechanics and offices through which payments are to be made);**
- **it includes any amendments for the specific deal;**
- **with the ISDA Master Agreement it forms a single agreement between the parties. The importance of this is explained in Chapter 3 (page 35); and**
- **where there is any inconsistency between the ISDA Master Agreement or the Confirmation, the Confirmation prevails for an individual Transaction (unless the Agreement Schedule states otherwise).**

The FSA's *Conduct of Business Rules (2001)* provides that parties should aim to send Confirmations to each other by the business day following the trade. This does not often happen even with plain vanilla product Confirmations where Confirmations are sent by fax and SWIFT. It is hardly ever achieved with structured and complex trades. One credit derivative Confirmation I came across before the *1999 Definitions* came out took 57 weeks to negotiate!

There are a few more things I should like to say about Confirmations in relation to:

- **pre-Confirmations;**
- **long-form Confirmations;**
- **break clauses.**

Pre-Confirmations

In the past, some market players issued pre-Confirmations, i.e. Confirmations stating the terms of the deal and specific wording and choices for provisions that would appear in the ISDA Master Agreement. The idea was to commit counterparties to this wording before the Agreement was signed.

Pre-Confirmations can cause confusion and are now seldom used. Nowadays dealers issue terms sheets when negotiating Transaction terms and parties prefer to move directly to negotiating ISDA Master Agreements rather than negotiating the terms of a pre-Confirmation. Delays often occurred with the latter approach as Confirmations staff do not usually negotiate ISDA Master Agreements and the document had to be sent to another department anyway.

In addition, paragraph 114 of the Bank of England's *Non-Investment Products Code (2001)* discourages the sending of more than one Confirmation by each party for a trade in order to avoid confusion.

Long-form Confirmations

Before the publication of the various ISDA product Definitions booklets, long-form Confirmations were the norm. I have already mentioned the 15–20 page credit derivative Confirmations which were common before the *1999 ISDA Credit Derivatives Definitions* were published. Long-form Confirmations are still used in the rare circumstances where a transaction is not to be subject to any master agreement or market terms.

Some banks use them where they know that their counterparty will not sign an Agreement, e.g. a small corporate which lacks the in-house expertise or resources to pay external lawyers for advice on entering into an Agreement. However, in these circumstances, it is advisable to use them only for relatively short dated, straightforward deals, typically one-off deals.

Long-form Confirmations are also used even where they state that they incorporate the relevant ISDA Definitions. This is because a trade may be so complex that its terms need to be spelt out in great detail.

Break clauses

The purpose of a break clause is to give the parties to a Transaction the option to terminate it before its final maturity.

Traders try to influence credit departments to extend dealing lines to weaker counterparties on the basis of break clauses. For example, a credit department may be happy to extend a five-year swap line to a UK corporate but not a ten-year line. However, the UK corporate and the bank trader only want to transact seven-year interest rate swap deals. So the dealer suggests a seven-year line with a break clause after five years. There are two problems with this arrangement:

- **monitoring by the back office;**
- **hedging.**

Hedging is the more serious problem because mismatches could occur in long-dated Transactions with a break clause offering early termination on the fifth anniversary of the Transaction and every anniversary thereafter upon an agreed number of days' notice. How do you hedge that most economically?

Break clauses can appear in Confirmations or in the Agreement or in both. In the last case, it is necessary to check that the clause is identical to avoid inconsistencies.

If a break clause appears in an Agreement, it will normally feature in Part 1(h) of the Schedule as an Additional Termination Event. Clauses vary, but either both parties calculate the deal's close-out figure (a "no fault termination"), or the party not wanting to terminate the Transaction does so.

Finally, you should remember that a *Confirmation* documents a *single* trade while an *Agreement* covers *all* Confirmations and trades.

THE ISDA MASTER AGREEMENT

After two years' deliberation by lawyers and market practitioners, the ISDA Master Agreement was published in January 1993, together with a *User's Guide.* Since then it has become the pre-eminent, market standard *multiproduct* Master Agreement for parties who plan to enter into a series of OTC derivatives transactions with each other.

The products covered under it are:

- **interest rate swaps**
- **currency swaps**
- **forward rate agreements**
- **commodity swaps**
- **equity/equity index swaps**
- **options (e.g. interest rate, bond, currency, equity, equity index, commodity)**
- **foreign exchange transactions**
- **caps, collars, floors**
- **credit derivatives**
- **bullion**
- **weather derivatives.**

It is an extremely versatile agreement. However, it is not a unique beast because its structure and components are similar to other financial documentation (some of which copied the Agreement) even if some of its terms differ. What is distinctive about the Agreement is that much of it is a pre-printed agreement which can be amended through its Schedule or via Amendment Agreements.

With an ordinary loan, the lender lends money to the borrower at the start of the loan and the borrower has an obligation to repay the lender on an agreed date or dates. With an OTC derivatives transaction, this is less predictable and market rate or price movements can change the roles of the parties several times during the life of a deal. Because of this the Agreement's provisions are mutual and apply to each party unless otherwise agreed.

The Master Agreement structure

The ISDA Master Agreement is an internationally agreed document. It is divided into the following 14 Sections:

- **Interpretation**
- **Obligations**
- **Representations**
- **Agreements**
- **Events of Default and Termination Events**
- **Early Termination**
- **Transfer**
- **Contractual Currency**
- **Miscellaneous**
- **Offices: Multibranch Parties**
- **Expenses**
- **Notices**
- **Governing Law and Jurisdiction**
- **Definitions.**

A Schedule amends the standard terms of the ISDA Master Agreement and this is what negotiators negotiate. This is usually divided into six Parts:

- **Part 1 – Termination Provisions**
- **Part 2 – Tax Representations**
- **Part 3 – Agreement to deliver Documents**
- **Part 4 – Miscellaneous**
- **Part 5 – Other Provisions**
- **Part 6 – Foreign Exchange Transactions and Currency Options.**

Please note: an ISDA Master Agreement covers all types of OTC derivatives transactions between the parties but a Confirmation only covers a single Transaction.

If a bank executes an ISDA Master Agreement it may do so on a single branch basis, e.g. X Bank AG Frankfurt or on a multibranch basis, e.g. X Bank AG Frankfurt, London, New York and Tokyo meaning that each bank branch may separately do deals under the same Agreement.

While the vast majority of market players use the Multicurrency Cross-Border version of the Agreement, there is also a single jurisdiction version known as the Local Currency-Single Jurisdiction Master Agreement also dated 1992. This can be used where both parties are located in the same jurisdiction and do transactions in one currency (usually the local currency). So if both parties were in the UK and only wanted to transact sterling interest rate swaps they could use a Local Currency Master Agreement.

The main difference between the two Master Agreements is that the Local Currency Master Agreement excludes the following provisions:

- **Provisions relating to tax matters**
  - **Section 2(d): Deduction or Withholding for Tax**
  - **Sections 3(e) and (f): Payer and Payee Tax Representations**
  - **Sections 4(a)(i) and (iii): Agreements to provide tax forms or documents**
  - **Section 4(d): Tax Agreement**
  - **Section 4(e): Payment of Stamp Tax**
  - **Sections 5(b)(ii) and (iii): Tax Event and Tax Event Upon Merger**
  - **Section 11: Stamp Tax reference**
  - **Part 2 of the Schedule: Tax Representations.**
- **Provisions relating to currency issues**
  - **Sections 6(e)(i) and (ii): references to Termination Currency Equivalent**
  - **Section 8: Contractual Currency.**
- **Other provisions**
  - **Section 6(b)(ii): Transfer to Avoid Termination Event**
  - **Section 10: Offices; Multibranch Parties**
  - **Section 13(c): Service of Process**
  - **Section 14: deletion from some Definitions of matters raised above.**

All these provisions are unnecessary where both parties are doing business in the same jurisdiction and currency. For example, it might be worth considering using the Local Currency Master Agreement if you are dealing with a small UK corporate who only wanted to transact a few sterling swaps, caps or options. However, once foreign currency or cross-border Transactions are being considered, you would need to revert to the normal Multicurrency Cross-Border version of the ISDA Master Agreement.

The full text of the 1992 ISDA Master Agreement (Multicurrency Cross-Border version) and its Schedule is reproduced in Annex 1 by kind permission of the International Swaps and Derivatives Association, Inc which has also kindly consented to the reproduction of the full text of the 2002 ISDA Master Agreement in Annex 2.

The provisions of the 2002 ISDA Master Agreement and how they differ from those of the 1992 ISDA Master Agreement are discussed in Chapter 4.

The 1992 ISDA Master Agreement

3

Section by section analysis of the 1992 ISDA Master Agreement

Glossary of most terms in Section 14

When I first came across an ISDA Master Agreement in 1990 (it was a 1987 style Agreement) I had three thoughts:

- **Where's my magnifying glass?**
- **Help!**
- **God so loved the world He didn't send a Committee.**

However, when I became more familiar with it, I found some similarities to provisions in loan agreements although the terminology differed. By and large, the main difference between ISDA documentation and loan agreements is the two-way application of many of the provisions in the Agreement.

SECTION BY SECTION ANALYSIS OF THE 1992 ISDA MASTER AGREEMENT

The main interpretative document for the 1992 ISDA Master Agreement is the *User's Guide to the 1992 ISDA Master Agreements* (the *User's Guide*) published by ISDA in January 1993. This describes:

- **how the ISDA Master Agreement evolved;**
- **gives technical interpretations and reasoning for the provisions; and**
- **mentions areas where agreement was not reached by the Working Group.**

The *User's Guide* has a wealth of information but its language can at times be complex and, as it is likely that many of its users may not be legal or tax technicians nor speak English as their first language, I thought it might be useful to provide a section by section interpretation of the 1992 ISDA Master Agreement which is clear but not oversimplified.

ISDA®

International Swap Dealers Association, Inc.

MASTER AGREEMENT

dated as of ....

.... and ....

have entered and/or anticipate entering into one or more transactions (each a "Transaction") that are or will be governed by this Master Agreement, which includes the schedule (the "Schedule"), and the documents and other confirming evidence (each a "Confirmation") exchanged between the parties confirming those Transactions.

Preamble

The ISDA Master Agreement starts by being expressed as "dated as of". It is customary to date the Agreement and its Schedule as of the date of the first trade between the parties, even if the Agreement is not signed until some months later. This is based on US practice where the words "as of" mean "with effect from" a specified date. This is contrary to best English practice where it is normal to date an agreement on the day it is signed. Under English law you cannot create a contract retrospectively through backdating it. If you do, you run the high risk of it being considered a forgery. To avoid misleading any court, the preamble to the signing block on page 18 makes it clear that the "as of" date is merely the effective date. The signing block records the date upon which the Agreement is actually signed.

The two parties then enter their full legal names and can add details of the jurisdictions where they are incorporated. If cited, this would also be repeated on the first page of the Schedule. Then there is a statement that the parties have entered or propose to enter into Transactions under the Agreement which includes its Schedule (used to add to or amend the basic Agreement provisions and which is what negotiators negotiate) and any Confirmations exchanged between the parties. This is the basis for the parties' contractual relationship and is important for the single agreement concept as we shall see shortly in Section 1(c). It is made clear that the Agreement can cover transactions entered into before it was executed.

Market practice is not to make changes directly on to the pre-printed Agreement text (although this was sometimes done in the early days of the market) but rather in the Schedule. This avoids the need to search the preprinted text for changes when reviewing it at a later date.

Accordingly, the parties agree as follows:-

1. Interpretation

(a) *Definitions.* The terms defined in Section 14 and in the Schedule will have the meanings therein specified for the purpose of this Master Agreement.

(b) *Inconsistency.* In the event of any inconsistency between the provisions of the Schedule and the other provisions of this Master Agreement, the Schedule will prevail. In the event of any inconsistency between the provisions of any Confirmation and this Master Agreement (including the Schedule), such Confirmation will prevail for the purpose of the relevant Transaction.

(c) *Single Agreement.* All Transactions are entered into in reliance on the fact that this Master Agreement and all Confirmations form a single agreement between the parties (collectively referred to as this "Agreement"), and the parties would not otherwise enter into any Transactions.

Section 1 – Interpretation

Section 1(a)

Defined terms in Section 14 and the Schedule will have their relevant meanings for the purpose of the Agreement.

Section 1(b)

Where there is any inconsistency between the Agreement text and the Schedule, the Schedule will prevail. Where there is a conflict between a Confirmation and the Agreement and its Schedule, the Confirmation will prevail in respect of the relevant Transaction. This gives the Confirmation supremacy in respect of individual deals.

Section 1(c)

The single agreement concept is vitally important and is the basis of close-out netting. Section 1(c) states that all Transactions are entered into relying upon the fact that the Agreement and all Confirmations under it form a single agreement between the parties and they would not have entered into these Transactions otherwise. What this means is that in a close-out situation, the values of all Transactions between the parties are calculated and netted off against each other so as to produce a single figure payable one way or the other. In an insolvency situation, this prevents a liquidator cherrypicking, i.e. making payments on those Transactions which are profitable to his insolvent client and refusing to do so on other Transactions which are not profitable to them. A liquidator cannot do this if all the Transactions are collapsed into a single payment due to one party or the other. In other words there is only one cherry. The single agreement concept reinforces this position.

2. Obligations

(a) ***General Conditions.***

(i) Each party will make each payment or delivery specified in each Confirmation to be made by it, subject to the other provisions of this Agreement.

(ii) Payments under this Agreement will be made on the due date for value on that date in the place of the account specified in the relevant Confirmation or otherwise pursuant to this Agreement, in freely transferable funds and in the manner customary for payments in the required currency. Where settlement is by delivery (that is, other than by payment), such delivery will be made for receipt on the due date in the manner customary for the relevant obligation unless otherwise specified in the relevant Confirmation or elsewhere in this Agreement.

(iii) Each obligation of each party under Section 2(a)(i) is subject to (1) the condition precedent that no Event of Default or Potential Event of Default with respect to the other party has occurred and is continuing, (2) the condition precedent that no Early Termination Date in respect of the relevant Transaction has occurred or been effectively designated and (3) each other applicable condition precedent specified in this Agreement.

(b) ***Change of Account.*** Either party may change its account for receiving a payment or delivery by giving notice to the other party at least five Local Business Days prior to the scheduled date for the payment or delivery to which such change applies unless such other party gives timely notice of a reasonable objection to such change.

Section 2 – Obligations

Section 2(a)

(a)(i) This is a simple statement that each party will make each payment or delivery required from it under the relevant Confirmation unless other terms of the Agreement (e.g. Early Termination provisions) intervene. The numerous references to "delivery" in the Agreement cover Transactions which are settled by physical delivery (i.e. delivery of a share or commodity instead of cash) which can also be covered by the Agreement. However, the Agreement itself cannot fully document physically settled Transactions, which is why Confirmations for them are very detailed.

(a)(ii) This is a general statement to the effect that payments and deliveries will be made promptly, in freely transferable funds and in the customary manner in the place of settlement, unless otherwise agreed in a Confirmation or elsewhere in the Agreement.

(a)(iii) This means that normal payments or deliveries under Section 2(a)(i) will stop if an Event of Default or Potential Event of Default (an event which could lead to an Event of Default if it develops) occurs to one of the parties or if an Early Termination Date (when close-out calculations are made) is designated whether for a Termination Event (see page 67 for an explanation of this latter term) or if any other condition precedent (e.g. the provision of credit support) in the Agreement is unfulfilled. Please note that under (1), the default could be outside the Agreement, e.g. non-payment of indebtedness under another agreement which might trigger the Cross Default clause in this Agreement.

Any payments withheld because of the events in section 2(a)(iii) will be treated as Unpaid Amounts under the Section 6 close-out calculations if Market Quotation is chosen as a payment measure (see commentary on Section 6, pages 77–9 or one of the components of Loss (if that is chosen as the payment measure).

Section 2(b)

One party to the Agreement may give the other at least five Local Business Days' notice of a change in its account for payments or deliveries. The *User's Guide* clarifies that this notice period is to be calculated in the Local Business Days of the place where the new account is to be located. The other party may object to this (there is a reasonableness standard) by giving notice to the first party. It might do this if such a change of account is to an overseas Office of the first party and a withholding tax charge might arise. It might also object to an overseas transfer of account if there was a risk of exchange controls being imposed.

(c) ***Netting***. If on any date amounts would otherwise be payable:-

(i) in the same currency; and

(ii) in respect of the same Transaction,

by each party to the other, then, on such date, each party's obligation to make payment of any such amount will be automatically satisfied and discharged and, if the aggregate amount that would otherwise have been payable by one party exceeds the aggregate amount that would otherwise have been payable by the other party, replaced by an obligation upon the party by whom the larger aggregate amount would have been payable to pay to the other party the excess of the larger aggregate amount over the smaller aggregate amount.

The parties may elect in respect of two or more Transactions that a net amount will be determined in respect of all amounts payable on the same date in the same currency in respect of such Transactions, regardless of whether such amounts are payable in respect of the same Transaction. The election may be made in the Schedule or a Confirmation by specifying that subparagraph (ii) above will not apply to the Transactions identified as being subject to the election, together with the starting date (in which case subparagraph (ii) above will not, or will cease to, apply to such Transactions from such date). This election may be made separately for different groups of Transactions and will apply separately to each pairing of Offices through which the parties make and receive payments or deliveries.

Section 2(c)

Section 2(c) of the Agreement is about payment or settlement netting and aims to reduce settlement risk – sometimes called daylight risk.

Payments can be made net if they are in the same currency, for the same Transaction and payable on the same date. This means that both parties do not have to make payments to each other but the one who owes the most pays the difference between the two amounts to the other party. This avoids the inconvenience of each party making a gross payment to the other and also reduces settlement risk (i.e. that one party will fail to make its payment after the other party has done so).

The basic payment netting position is single Transaction netting, i.e. same Transaction, same currency and same value date. By making a choice in the Schedule that single Transaction netting will not apply, parties can net payments due under two or more Transactions in the same currency and on the same date both for the same and different products.

For multiple Transaction netting they can net different groups of Transactions (e.g. interest rate swaps only) and/or apply this separately to each pairing of their Offices. These arrangements can also be applied to deliveries. The provisions are very flexible, but you should only really agree to what you can actually do operationally or you could incur operational risk.

Figure 3.1 should help to illustrate this.

FIG. 3.1

Single Transaction payment netting:
- same Transaction
- same currency
- same value date

(d) ***Deduction or Withholding for Tax.***

(i) ***Gross-Up.*** All payments under this Agreement will be made without any deduction or withholding for or on account of any Tax unless such deduction or withholding is required by applicable law, as modified by the practice of any relevant governmental revenue authority, then in effect. If a party is so required to deduct or withhold, then that party ("X") will:-

(1) promptly notify the other party ("Y") of such requirement;

(2) pay to the relevant authorities the full amount required to be deducted or withheld (including the full amount required to be deducted or withheld from any additional amount paid by X to Y under this Section 2(d)) promptly upon the earlier of determining that such deduction or withholding is required or receiving notice that such amount has been assessed against Y;

(3) promptly forward to Y an official receipt (or a certified copy), or other documentation reasonably acceptable to Y, evidencing such payment to such authorities; and

(4) if such Tax is an Indemnifiable Tax, pay to Y, in addition to the payment to which Y is otherwise entitled under this Agreement, such additional amount as is necessary to ensure that the net amount actually received by Y (free and clear of Indemnifiable Taxes, whether assessed against X or Y) will equal the full amount Y would have received had no such deduction or withholding been required. However, X will not be required to pay any additional amount to Y to the extent that it would not be required to be paid but for:-

Section 2(d)

(i)

This is a complex clause on withholding tax but it becomes clearer if you see X as the payer and Y as the payee or recipient. Please note that under ISDA, a withholding tax only applies in cross-border transactions.

The ISDA Master Agreement is an international agreement and where cross-border Transactions occur, tax authorities may impose taxes called withholding taxes on payments made under those Transactions. Where this happens and you were due to receive a payment as payee, you would receive less than you expected. Section 2(d) provides an indemnity that a payer has to increase his payment if a withholding tax is charged so that the payee receives what he expected to receive. Generally speaking, the burden of withholding taxes usually falls on the payer.

Withholding taxes can arise in three ways:

- **incorrect initial analysis that no withholding tax applied;**
- **a change in Tax Law or similar legal development;**
- **a change of facts relating to either the payer or payee which occurs after a Transaction is entered.**

This could arise through a change of status or business resulting in the party being no longer eligible for tax treaty benefits. If a withholding tax is levied because of a change of facts the responsible party will need to pay it or suffer it but will have no right to call a Tax Event Termination Event (see commentary on Section 5(b)(ii)).

Going through the various points, if a withholding tax is levied on a payer, it must:

- **promptly notify the payee of this;**
- **promptly pay the withholding tax calculated or assessed to the tax authorities;**
- **promptly send the payee satisfactory documentation evidencing the tax payment to the authorities; and**
- **pay the equivalent of the withholding tax together with the net payment to the payee so that it ends up with the amount it originally anticipated.**

(A) the failure by Y to comply with or perform any agreement contained in Section 4(a)(i), 4(a)(iii) or 4(d); or

(B) the failure of a representation made by Y pursuant to Section 3(f) to be accurate and true unless such failure would not have occurred but for (I) any action taken by a taxing authority, or brought in a court of competent jurisdiction, on or after the date on which a Transaction is entered into (regardless of whether such action is taken or brought with respect to a party to this Agreement) or (II) a Change in Tax Law.

Please note that an Indemnifiable Tax arises in a cross-border situation and is not a domestic income, capital or sales tax. It aims to indemnify a party adversely affected by it, usually a payee. It arises because the payer has decided to do business with a foreign payee.

However, (A) and (B) (in the text opposite) provide two exceptions to this.

The payee will not receive a payment grossed up for withholding tax where it has failed to provide any tax documentation necessary to the payer or a Payee Tax Representation it has made has becomes false, unless this has happened because of tax authority or court action or a Change in Tax Law.

Let's take an example to illustrate this. Suppose that a US payer has to pay a foreign payee US$1,000,000 under the terms of a Confirmation. Assume further that the US levies withholding tax at 30% on this payment and under the terms of the Agreement the payer has to gross up the payment. The payer's total grossed up payment would be US$1,428,571.

This is calculated as follows:

Confirmation Payment/1–Withholding Tax rate = Grossed up payment
US$1,000,000/0.70 (i.e. 100%–30%) = US$1,428,571.

The amount of the gross up payment as a percentage of the Confirmation payment is greater than the 30% withholding tax rate because it also applies to the additional gross up payment the payer is required to make. This is because the obligation to indemnify applies to gross payments.

Similar provisions are common in loan agreements where cross-border payments have to be made.

(ii) ***Liability***. If:-

(1) X is required by any applicable law, as modified by the practice of any relevant governmental revenue authority, to make any deduction or withholding in respect of which X would not be required to pay an additional amount to Y under Section 2(d)(i)(4);
(2) X does not so deduct or withhold; and
(3) a liability resulting from such Tax is assessed directly against X,

then, except to the extent Y has satisfied or then satisfies the liability resulting from such Tax, Y will promptly pay to X the amount of such liability (including any related liability for interest, but including any related liability for penalties only if Y has failed to comply with or perform any agreement contained in Section 4(a)(i), 4(a)(iii) or 4(d)).

(e) ***Default Interest; Other Amounts***. Prior to the occurrence or effective designation of an Early Termination Date in respect of the relevant Transaction, a party that defaults in the performance of any payment obligation will, to the extent permitted by law and subject to Section 6(c), be required to pay interest (before as well as after judgment) on the overdue amount to the other party on demand in the same currency as such overdue amount, for the period from (and including) the original due date for payment to (but excluding) the date of actual payment, at the Default Rate. Such interest will be calculated on the basis of daily compounding and the actual number of days elapsed. If, prior to the occurrence or effective designation of an Early Termination Date in respect of the relevant Transaction, a party defaults in the performance of any obligation required to be settled by delivery, it will compensate the other party on demand if and to the extent provided for in the relevant Confirmation or elsewhere in this Agreement.

(ii)

Section 2(d)(ii) covers the situation where the payer makes a payment without withholding tax relying upon tax documentation received from the payee and is unaware of any breach of a Payee Tax Representation by the payee (which is not caused by a Change in Tax Law) and the payer's tax authority then requires him to pay withholding tax in respect of that previous payment. In these circumstances, the payee will indemnify the payer for that withholding tax, any interest on it or any other penalty for failing to provide the payer with necessary tax documentation so that, inter alia, the payer could avoid the withholding tax or pay it at a reduced rate.

Section 2(e)

This means that late payments in the normal course will attract interest at the Default Rate (i.e. 1% over the payee's cost of funds) from, and including the date the payment was due to but excluding the date it was actually paid – the normal practice in the derivatives markets. If an Early Termination Date occurs (Section 6(c)), interest on overdue amounts will accrue as provided in Section 6(d)(ii).

During ISDA Working Group meetings there was no agreement on how to apply the concept of default interest to physically settled transactions. Section 2(e) provides that compensation for late delivery will be determined "as provided in the relevant Confirmation or elsewhere in this Agreement".

However, this matter is extensively treated in Section 9(h) of the 2002 ISDA Master Agreement (see pages 256–67).

3. Representations

Each party represents to the other party (which representations will be deemed to be repeated by each party on each date on which a Transaction is entered into and, in the case of the representations in Section 3(f), at all times until the termination of this Agreement) that:-

(a) ***Basic Representations.***

(i) ***Status***. It is duly organised and validly existing under the laws of the jurisdiction of its organisation or incorporation and, if relevant under such laws, in good standing;

(ii) ***Powers***. It has the power to execute this Agreement and any other documentation relating this Agreement to which it is a party, to deliver this Agreement and any other documentation relating to this Agreement that it is required by this Agreement to deliver and to perform its obligations under this Agreement and any obligations it has under any Credit Support Document to which it is a party and has taken all necessary action to authorise such execution, delivery and performance;

(iii) ***No Violation or Conflict***. Such execution, delivery and performance do not violate or conflict with any law applicable to it, any provision of its constitutional documents, any order or judgment of any court or other agency of government applicable to it or any of its assets or any contractual restriction binding on or affecting it or any of its assets;

(iv) ***Consents***. All governmental and other consents that are required to have been obtained by it with respect to this Agreement or any Credit Support Document to which it is a party have been obtained and are in full force and effect and all conditions of any such consents have been complied with; and

(v) ***Obligations Binding***. Its obligations under this Agreement and any Credit Support Document to which it is a party constitute its legal, valid and binding obligations, enforceable in accordance with their respective terms (subject to applicable bankruptcy, reorganisation, insolvency, moratorium or similar laws affecting creditors' rights generally and subject, as to enforceability, to equitable principles of general application (regardless of whether enforcement is sought in a proceeding in equity or at law)).

Section 3 – Representations

Each party represents various matters listed in this Section to the other. These representations are considered to be repeated each time a new Transaction is undertaken between the parties and the Payee Tax Representations in Section 3(f) are deemed made at all times until the termination of the Agreement. This is because payments need to be made periodically throughout the lives of the Transactions. Many of these representations are commonly seen in loan agreements.

Where parties are very active and enter into hundreds of deals over several years they should take care in agreeing representations which would require constant monitoring over the lives of deals so as to avoid a Misrepresentation Event of Default (under Section 5(a)(iv)) if a representation became untrue.

The basic representations in Section 3(a) are largely self explanatory and are:

- **each party is properly organised and has a valid legal existence in its jurisdiction of incorporation;**
- **each party has the power and is authorised to execute, deliver and perform under the Agreement, related documentation and any Credit Support Document which it is providing itself (e.g an English law ISDA Credit Support Annex). A party's capacity and authority to enter into derivatives transactions are vital to the Agreement's effectiveness (as we shall see in Chapter 5 on legal issues);**
- **such actions do not conflict with a party's legal obligations, constitutional documents or any court or government agency order relating to its assets or any contractual restriction on them;**
- **each party has obtained any necessary government or other consents for the Agreement or any Credit Support Document and ensured that such consents are in full force and effect and fully complied with by the party concerned; and**
- **each party's obligations under the Agreement or any Credit Support Document constitute legal, valid and binding obligations enforceable against it subject to insolvency laws or general equitable legal principles. This is regardless of whether proceedings take place under common law or in equity. However, it is important that the Agreement or any Credit Support Document does not offend the public policy rules of any jurisdiction where you may seek to enforce it. Provided the Agreement is not, for instance, solely used for gambling purposes, this is not likely.**

(b) ***Absence of Certain Events***. No Event of Default or Potential Event of Default or, to its knowledge, Termination Event with respect to it has occurred and is continuing and no such event or circumstance would occur as a result of its entering into or performing its obligations under this Agreement or any Credit Support Document to which it is a party.

(c) ***Absence of Litigation***. There is not pending or, to its knowledge, threatened against it or any of its Affiliates any action, suit or proceeding at law or in equity or before any court, tribunal, governmental body, agency or official or any arbitrator that is likely to affect the legality, validity or enforceability against it of this Agreement or any Credit Support Document to which it is a party or its ability to perform its obligations under this Agreement or such Credit Support Document.

(d) ***Accuracy of Specified Information***. All applicable information that is furnished in writing by or on behalf of it to the other party and is identified for the purpose of this Section 3(d) in the Schedule is, as of the date of the information, true, accurate and complete in every material respect.

(e) ***Payer Tax Representation***. Each representation specified in the Schedule as being made by it for the purpose of this Section 3(e) is accurate and true.

(f) ***Payee Tax Representations***. Each representation specified in the Schedule as being made by it the purpose of this Section 3(f) is accurate and true.

Section 3(b)

This is a useful representation made by each party that no actual or potential close-out event has occurred or persists and none would arise from entering into or performing its obligations under the Agreement or a Credit Support Document.

Section 3(c)

Absence of Litigation deals with actual and threatened litigation against a party and its Affiliates (i.e. other group companies) which is likely to affect the legal enforceability of the Agreement or any Credit Support Document or a party's performance under them. Some market players seek to delete Affiliates by a Schedule amendment as, with a widely spread group like a major bank, it may not know of such litigation affecting its Affiliates in other parts of the world. Others seek to limit the clause to Specified Entities or Credit Support Providers. (These terms are explained in the commentary on Section 5.) In other cases parties amend the provision by stating that the litigation must have a material adverse effect on its ability to perform under the Agreement or upon the Agreement's enforceability.

Please note that Sections 3(a)(ii), (iv), (v) and 3(b) and (c) capture Credit Support Documents entered into by parties to the Agreement.

Section 3(d)

Parties specify in Part 3(b) of the Schedule, the categories of information to which this representation applies. The test is rigorous – the information must be true, accurate and complete in every material respect. In Chapter 8, I discuss this representation in connection with audited accounts (see pages 487–8).

Sections 3(e) and 3(f)

In Sections 3(e) and (f), the parties state that the Payer and Payee Tax Representations they have made are true and accurate. These representations are made in Parts 2(a) and (b) of the Schedule.

4. Agreements

Each party agrees with the other that, so long as either party has or may have any obligation under this Agreement or under any Credit Support Document to which it is a party:-

(a) ***Furnish Specified Information***. It will deliver to the other party or, in certain cases under subparagraph (iii) below, to such government or taxing authority as the other party reasonably directs:-

(i) any forms, documents or certificates relating to taxation specified in the Schedule or any Confirmation;

(ii) any other documents specified in the Schedule or any Confirmation; and

(iii) upon reasonable demand by such other party, any form or document that may be required or reasonably requested in writing in order to allow such other party or its Credit Support Provider to make a payment under this Agreement or any applicable Credit Support Document without any deduction or withholding for or on account of any Tax or with such deduction or withholding at a reduced rate (so long as the completion, execution or submission of such form or document would not materially prejudice the legal or commercial position of the party in receipt of such demand), with any such form or document to be accurate and completed in a manner reasonably satisfactory to such other party and to be executed and to be delivered with any reasonably required certification,

in each case by the date specified in the Schedule or such Confirmation or, if none is specified, as soon as reasonably practicable.

(b) ***Maintain Authorisations***. It will use all reasonable efforts to maintain in full force and effect all consents of any governmental or other authority that are required to be obtained by it with respect to this Agreement or any Credit Support Document to which it is a party and will use all reasonable efforts to obtain any that may become necessary in the future.

(c) ***Comply with Laws***. It will comply in all material respects with all applicable laws and orders to which it may be subject if failure so to comply would materially impair its ability to perform its obligations under this Agreement or any Credit Support Document to which it is a party.

Section 4 – Agreements

Section 4 contains agreements of the parties which survive while they have any obligations under the Agreement or any Credit Support Document.

Section 4(a)

Section 4(a) records the agreement of each party to supply certain specified information. In Section 4(a)(i), they must state in the Schedule or in a Confirmation any tax related forms, documents or certificates which are required to be delivered and the timescales for such delivery. Delivery will normally be to the other party but it can also be to a relevant government or tax authority.

Section 4(a)(ii) enables them to require delivery of financial statements, board resolutions, legal opinions, signatory lists and other appropriate documents for their contractual relationship. The actual documents and any Credit Support Documents are normally specified in Parts 3(b) and/or 4(f) of the Schedule but could also be referred to in a Confirmation.

Section 4(a)(iii) states that one party may be required to send the other party or a government or tax authority certain forms or documents so as to permit the other party or its Credit Support Provider (e.g. a guarantor) to make a payment under an Agreement or Credit Support Document without deduction or withholding for tax or, if necessary, at a lower rate. Under Section 4(a)(iii) of the Agreement, however, a party need not comply with this if doing so would "materially prejudice" its "legal or commercial position". Where a timescale for compliance is not specified in the Schedule or a Confirmation, it must be done as soon as reasonably practicable.

Section 4(b)

The obligation is self-explanatory. Sometimes these authorisations are referred to in Part 3(b) of the Schedule, e.g. licence renewals or exchange control permissions. A party must use all reasonable efforts to comply with this and any ongoing requirements in this respect.

Section 4(c)

The obligation is self-explanatory. The test is if a party's failure to comply with laws would *significantly* impair its ability to perform its obligations under the Agreement or any Credit Support Document. It must comply in all material respects which is a tougher standard than in Section 4(b).

(d) ***Tax Agreement***. It will give notice of any failure of a representation made by it under Section 3(f) to be accurate and true promptly upon learning of such failure.

(e) ***Payment of Stamp Tax***. Subject to Section 11, it will pay any Stamp Tax levied or imposed upon it or in respect of its execution or performance of this Agreement by a jurisdiction in which it is incorporated, organised, managed and controlled, or considered to have its seat, or in which a branch or office through which it is acting for the purpose of this Agreement is located ("Stamp Tax Jurisdiction") and will indemnify the other party against any Stamp Tax levied or imposed upon the other party or in respect of the other party's execution or performance of this Agreement by any such Stamp Tax Jurisdiction which is not also a Stamp Tax Jurisdiction with respect to the other party.

Section 4(d)

A party is obliged to give notice of any failure of a Payee Tax Representation made by it promptly upon becoming aware of it. Where such notice is not given and a payer has to pay a withholding tax, the payee will need to indemnify the payer for the tax, interest and any penalties thereon except where the failure of the Payee Tax Representation is due to a Change in Tax Law which is beyond the payee's control. An example of such a situation would be where a tax authority decided that the nature of a payee's business made it ineligible for tax treaty benefits.

Section 4(e)

Each party agrees to pay Stamp Taxes imposed on it by its home or branch jurisdiction and indemnify the other party against such Stamp Taxes if their jurisdiction is not the same. Section 4(e) is subordinate to the Section 11 remit that a Defaulting Party has, upon demand, to indemnify the Non-defaulting Party against certain Stamp Taxes. The indemnification only applies in a cross-border situation. The provision does not deal with Stamp Taxes levied in connection with Credit Support Documents.

Section 5 – Events of Default and Termination Events

Introduction

Section 5 is very important and contains the Master Agreement's Events of Default and Termination Events. Events of Default are common in loan agreements – Termination Events far less so. Both Events of Default and Termination Events can be triggered by either party or by a condition or event involving a third party, e.g. a Specified Entity.

Section 5(a) covers Events of Default (where only one party is culpable) and there are eight of them. However, before looking at them I want to discuss Specified Entities and Credit Support Providers who feature a lot in this Section.

A Specified Entity is essentially another member or members in a party's group whom you want to join through the Schedule into certain Events of Default and Termination Events. The aim is to draw in those members of a party's group (such as its parent or asset rich fellow subsidiaries) whose relationship is so close to the contracting party that if an Event of Default happened to them it would be very likely to affect the contracting party too. The same reasoning applies to Credit Support Providers.

A Credit Support Provider is a third party providing security or a guarantee for a party's liabilities. It can also be one of the parties to the Agreement providing security for itself (e.g. a corporate providing an all moneys debenture). In the 1987 Agreement, the Credit Support Provider was usually nominated as a Specified Entity for those Events of Default and Termination Events which referred to Specified Entities. In the 1992 Agreement it is in a separate category and there is no need to do this.

The following Events of Default and Termination Events include any Credit Support Provider specified in respect of a party:

- **Credit Support Default;**
- **Misrepresentation;**
- **Default under Specified Transaction;**
- **Cross Default;**
- **Bankruptcy;**
- **Merger Without Assumption;**
- **Illegality;**
- **Credit Event Upon Merger.**

The Credit Support Provider is also mentioned in Section 4(a)(iii) in relation to providing tax forms.

The various Events of Default are now reviewed.

5. Events of Default and Termination Events

(a) *Events of Default*. The occurrence at any time with respect to a party or, if applicable, any Credit Support Provider of such party or any Specified Entity of such party of any of the following events constitutes an event of default (an "Event of Default") with respect to such party:-

(i) ***Failure to Pay or Deliver***. Failure by the party to make, when due, any payment under this Agreement or delivery under Section 2(a)(i) or 2(e) required to be made by it if such failure is not remedied on or before the third Local Business Day after notice of such failure is given to the party;

(ii) ***Breach of Agreement***. Failure by the party to comply with or perform any agreement or obligation (other than an obligation to make any payment under this Agreement or delivery under Section 2(a)(i) or 2(e) or to give notice of a Termination Event or any agreement or obligation under Section 4(a)(i), 4(a)(iii) or 4(d)) to be complied with or performed by the party in accordance with this Agreement if such failure is not remedied on or before the thirtieth day after notice of such failure is given to the party;

Section 5(a)(i)

Section 5(a)(i) covers a party's failure to make any payment or delivery when due under Section 2(a)(i) or 2(e) of the Agreement after a grace period of three Local Business Days following notice. The ISDA Master Agreement drafters chose this length of grace period because they believed it might take longer to terminate an Agreement than a loan agreement, for instance, where the failure to pay grace period is usually shorter. This thinking has changed as we shall see in Chapter 4.

Section 5(a)(ii)

Section 5(a)(ii) covers a failure by either party to comply with any agreement or obligation under the Agreement by the expiry of a 30-day grace period following notice. The following are excluded from this provision:

- **any obligations covered by the Failure to Pay or Deliver Event of Default (which has a shorter grace period of three Local Business Days);**
- **any failure to give notice of a Termination Event. The thinking here is that this failure should not be treated as an Event of Default when the subject of the notice could well be a less serious Termination Event;**
- **any failure to comply with certain tax related agreements or obligations contained in Section 4 of the Agreement (since denial of payment gross up is the penalty).**

Since such events are subject to different treatment elsewhere, it was considered that *per se* they should not give rise to an Event of Default under Section 5(a)(ii). Examples of breaches of agreement could include failure to maintain authorisations as required in Section 4(b) or failure to provide accounting information or a legal opinion within an agreed deadline.

Some parties consider the 30-day grace period to be too long and seek to reduce it in the Schedule to 10–15 days.

(iii) ***Credit Support Default.***

(1) Failure by the party or any Credit Support Provider of such party to comply with or perform any agreement or obligation to be complied with or performed by it in accordance with any Credit Support Document if such failure is continuing after any applicable grace period has elapsed;

(2) the expiration or termination of such Credit Support Document or the failing or ceasing of such Credit Support Document to be in full force and effect for the purpose of this Agreement (in either case other than in accordance with its terms) prior to the satisfaction of all obligations of such party under each Transaction to which such Credit Support Document relates without the written consent of the other party; or

(3) the party or such Credit Support Provider disaffirms, disclaims, repudiates or rejects, in whole or in part, or challenges the validity of, such Credit Support Document;

(iv) ***Misrepresentation.*** A representation (other than a representation under Section 3(e) or (f)) made or repeated or deemed to have been made or repeated by the party or any Credit Support Provider of such party in this Agreement or any Credit Support Document proves to have been incorrect or misleading in any material respect when made or repeated or deemed to have been made or repeated;

Section 5(a)(iii)

The Credit Support Provider first appears here in the Events of Default.

Section 5(a)(iii) first applies to a party if a Credit Support Document is provided by or on behalf of that party and is identified as such with its nature described in Part 4(f) of the Schedule or in the Credit Support Document itself. If the Credit Support Document is a third party guarantee, the name of the guarantor would be specified as a Credit Support Provider in Part 4(g) of the Schedule since this Event of Default also applies to a party's outside Credit Support Provider(s).

An English Law ISDA Credit Support Annex entered into by either party to the Agreement should not be specified in Part 4(f) and (g) of the Schedule because it is a title transfer document under which ownership of the collateral passes to the other party. However, the New York Law ISDA Credit Support Annex and the English Law ISDA Credit Support Deed are usually referred to as Credit Support Documents because they are by nature pledges or security interests. Normally Part 4(f) and (g) describe third party Credit Support Documents and Credit Support Providers.

This Event of Default is triggered if:

- **a party or its Credit Support Provider(s) breaches a Credit Support Document and the breach persists beyond any agreed grace period; or**
- **the Credit Support Document becomes ineffective before discharge of all obligations under related Transactions without the other party's written consent; or**
- **a party or a Credit Support Provider repudiates or disowns its Credit Support Document.**

Section 5(a)(iv)

Section 5(a)(iv) applies to certain representation breaches (but excludes tax representations where gross up would be denied if misrepresentation occurred) made in the Agreement or in a Credit Support Document by a party or a Credit Support Provider which result in the representations made being materially misleading or incorrect. It is important to remember that most representations under the Agreement are deemed to be repeated with each new Transaction.

(v) ***Default under Specified Transaction***. The party, any Credit Support Provider of such party or any applicable Specified Entity of such party (1) defaults under a Specified Transaction and, after giving effect to any applicable notice requirement or grace period, there occurs a liquidation of, an acceleration of obligations under, or an early termination of, that Specified Transaction, (2) defaults, after giving effect to any applicable notice requirement or grace period, in making any payment or delivery due on the last payment, delivery or exchange date of, or any payment on early termination of, a Specified Transaction (or such default continues for at least three Local Business Days if there is no applicable notice requirement or grace period) or (3) disaffirms, disclaims, repudiates or rejects, in whole or in part, a Specified Transaction (or such action is taken by any person or entity appointed or empowered to operate it or act on its behalf);

Section 5(a)(v)

The term Specified Transaction is defined in Section 14 of the Agreement and is one or more of a wide range of OTC derivatives transactions between each party to the Agreement, a party and the other party's Credit Support Provider or Specified Entity or between their respective Specified Entities or Credit Support Providers, but which are not entered into under the Agreement nor governed by it. These might include transactions the parties have concluded under other agreements or under long form confirmations.

Figure 3.2 illustrates this.

FIG. 3.2

Type of Transaction	Between whom
An OTC derivative transaction described in Section 14 but transacted outside the Agreement	(i) Each party to the Agreement; or (ii) One of the parties to the Agreement and the other party's Credit Support Provider or Specified Entity; or (iii) Each party's respective Specified Entities or Credit Support Providers.

The categories of default in this sub-Section are:

- **acceleration or early termination of the Specified Transaction;**
- **payment or delivery default on the final Scheduled Payment Date or with any early termination settlement payment after the lapse of notice of a minimum three Local Business Day grace period;**
- **repudiation of a Specified Transaction by the party itself or third parties such as liquidators or regulators.**

This makes the provision similar to the Cross Default provision discussed below.

In the Schedule, the scope of this Event of Default may be widened or reduced by changing the definition of Specified Transaction to include other products, e.g. repos. Parties can also broaden the scope of the provision to include any third party contracting with one of the parties to this Agreement or their Specified Entities or Credit Support Providers. I will have more to say about this when we look at credit issues in the Schedule in Chapter 6.

Please note there is no Threshold Amount with Default under Specified Transaction.

This Event of Default is very important because it impacts the parties joined to this Agreement if a default occurs in transactions between them outside it. In other words, it has a direct impact on the credit risk of the respective parties to this Agreement on the basis that if they default outside the Agreement they will probably default within it too.

(vi) ***Cross Default***. If "Cross Default" is specified in the Schedule as applying to the party, the occurrence or existence of (1) a default, event of default or other similar condition or event (however described) in respect of such party, any Credit Support Provider of such party or any applicable Specified Entity of such party under one or more agreements or instruments relating to Specified Indebtedness of any of them (individually or collectively) in an aggregate amount of not less than the applicable Threshold Amount (as specified in the Schedule) which has resulted in such Specified Indebtedness becoming, or becoming capable at such time of being declared, due and payable under such agreements or instruments, before it would otherwise have been due and payable or (2) a default by such party, such Credit Support Provider or such Specified Entity (individually or collectively) in making one or more payments on the due date thereof in an aggregate amount of not less than the applicable Threshold Amount under such agreements or instruments (after giving effect to any applicable notice requirement or grace period);

Section 5(a)(vi)

Section 5(a)(vi) is very important. It also applies to Specified Entities and Credit Support Providers. This Event of Default is triggered by:

- **a default or similar event under financial agreements or instruments that has resulted in indebtedness (above a Threshold Amount) becoming capable of being accelerated and terminated early by a Non-defaulting Party; or**
- **a failure to make any payments (above a Threshold Amount) on their due date under such agreements or instruments after notice or the expiry of a grace period.**

A Threshold Amount is a monetary figure above which a Non-defaulting Party may exercise its rights following its counterparty's default elsewhere to terminate all Transactions under the Agreement. It is essentially the credit risk you are prepared to accept on your counterparty before you trigger your close-out rights under this Section 5(a)(vi). Specified Indebtedness essentially means "borrowed money" but it is possible in the Schedule to extend it to other types of indebtedness (e.g. lease purchase obligations, commercial paper, acceptances, factoring or derivative transactions with third parties), or alternatively to narrow it to exclude, for example, banking deposits. I will have more to say about this in Chapter 6, pages 386–7.

Section 5(a)(vi) only applies to a party if stated in Part 1(c) of the Schedule which is also an important reason to get an Agreement signed. If Cross Default applies, a Threshold Amount is nominated in Part 1(c) of the Schedule (either a fixed monetary sum or a small percentage of shareholders' equity are most common). Unless otherwise agreed, this Event of Default will automatically catch the Credit Support Provider of any party subject to Cross Default, but not any Specified Entity unless it is expressly nominated in Part 1(a) of the Schedule. If both Credit Support Providers and Specified Entities are included, it means that if a default occurred under any Specified Indebtedness owed by a contracting party, its Credit Support Provider(s) or Specified Entity(ies) elsewhere then the amounts of each of these defaults could be added together collectively to see if the relevant Threshold Amount under this Agreement had been breached. This applies to both parts of Section 5(a)(vi).

Note that unless the provision is amended in the Schedule, the Threshold Amounts of the two sub-clauses of Section 5(a)(vi) cannot be aggregated (see Chapter 8, page 547). Therefore, on an unamended basis, close-out can only be triggered by a breach of the Threshold Amount in an individual sub-clause i.e. Section 5(a)(vi) (1) or (2).

Sometimes there is a Schedule amendment which excludes Cross Default being triggered through operational or administrative error provided that the party concerned was solvent, had access to sufficient funds when such error occurred and paid up within an agreed grace period. An example of such wording may be found in Chapter 8, page 406.

This provision is very versatile and its scope can be expanded or contracted depending upon how Threshold Amount, Specified Entity, Specified Indebtedness and Credit Support Provider are defined.

(vii) ***Bankruptcy***. The party, any Credit Support Provider of such party or any applicable Specified Entity of such party:-

(1) is dissolved (other than pursuant to a consolidation, amalgamation or merger); (2) becomes insolvent or is unable to pay its debts or fails or admits in writing its inability generally to pay its debts as they become due; (3) makes a general assignment, arrangement or composition with or for the benefit of its creditors; (4) institutes or has instituted against it a proceeding seeking a judgment of insolvency or bankruptcy or any other relief under any bankruptcy or insolvency law or other similar law affecting creditors' rights, or a petition is presented for its winding-up or liquidation, and, in the case of any such proceeding or petition instituted or presented against it, such proceeding or petition (A) results in a judgment of insolvency or bankruptcy or the entry of an order for relief or the making of an order for its winding-up or liquidation or (B) is not dismissed, discharged, stayed or restrained in each case within 30 days of the institution or presentation thereof; (5) has a resolution passed for its winding-up, official management or liquidation (other than pursuant to a consolidation, amalgamation or merger); (6) seeks or becomes subject to the appointment of an administrator, provisional liquidator, conservator, receiver, trustee, custodian or other similar official for it or for all or substantially all its assets; (7) has a secured party take possession of all or substantially all its assets or has a distress, execution, attachment, sequestration or other legal process levied, enforced or sued on or against all or substantially all its assets and such secured party maintains possession, or any such process is not dismissed, discharged, stayed or restrained, in each case within 30 days thereafter; (8) causes or is subject to any event with respect to it which, under the applicable laws of any jurisdiction, has an analogous effect to any of the events specified in clauses (1) to (7) (inclusive); or (9) takes any action in furtherance of, or indicating its consent to, approval of, or acquiescence in, any of the foregoing acts; or

(viii) ***Merger Without Assumption***. The party or any Credit Support Provider of such party consolidates or amalgamates with, or merges with or into, or transfers all or substantially all its assets to, another entity and, at the time of such consolidation, amalgamation, merger or transfer:-

(1) the resulting, surviving or transferee entity fails to assume all the obligations of such party or such Credit Support Provider under this Agreement or any Credit Support Document to which it or its predecessor was a party by operation of law or pursuant to an agreement reasonably satisfactory to the other party to this Agreement; or

(2) the benefits of any Credit Support Document fail to extend (without the consent of the other party) to the performance by such resulting, surviving or transferee entity of its obligations under this Agreement.

Section 5(a)(vii)

Section 5(a)(vii) is very broad. Again, it applies to each party and its Credit Support Provider or a Specified Entity (specified in Part 1(a) of the Schedule). It can be triggered by many bankruptcy events or insolvency proceedings under New York or English law but recognises that market players will also be located in and organised under the laws of other countries.

It is important to note that in an insolvency it is the laws of the insolvent party's jurisdiction of incorporation which prevail over the governing law of the Agreement.

This Event of Default is drafted broadly enough to be triggered by proceedings or events under any insolvency laws likely to affect a particular party. Sometimes Schedule amendments are made to specify certain types of bankruptcy officials, e.g. an examiner in Irish Schedules. It is wise to check that an insolvency regime in an emerging market or exotic country is covered by the categories outlined in this provision. If not, an amendment will need to be made to it in the Schedule. Another Schedule amendment that may need to be made relates to partnerships which might be dissolved when a partner leaves but which are immediately reconstituted by the remaining partners.

Section 5(a)(viii)

Merger Without Assumption applies to parties and their Credit Support Providers but not to their Specified Entities. It covers situations where a party or its Credit Support Provider amalgamates, merges or transfers all or most of its assets to another entity and such entity:

- **fails to assume that party's obligations under the Agreement; or**
- **fails to assume that party's or the Credit Support Provider's obligations under a Credit Support Document.**

In either case, the contractual position is weaker than originally envisaged and gives the non-merging party (who is also the Non-defaulting Party) the right to close out all Transactions under the Agreement.

Merger Without Assumption also arises where the benefits of a Credit Support Document fail to extend post-merger to the transferee's performance obligations under the Agreement (unless the other party consents).

Please note that just because a merger may involve companies in two different legal and tax jurisdictions, this is not relevant for this particular Event of Default but may possibly be for the Tax Event Upon Merger Termination Event (Section 5(b)(iii)) discussed below.

It is possible for a merger, consolidation or asset transfer to trigger Credit Event Upon Merger (see commentary on Section 5(b)(iv) at page 73) as well as Merger Without Assumption. Where this occurs, Section 5(b)(iv) indicates that it will be treated more severely as an Event of Default.

(b) ***Termination Events***. The occurrence at any time with respect to a party or, if applicable, any Credit Support Provider of such party or any Specified Entity of such party of any event specified below constitutes an Illegality if the event is specified in (i) below, a Tax Event if the event is specified in (ii) below or a Tax Event upon Merger if the event is specified in (iii) below, and, if specified to be applicable, a Credit Event Upon Merger if the event is specified pursuant to (iv) below or an Additional Termination Event if the event is specified pursuant to (v) below:-

(i) ***Illegality***. Due to the adoption of, or any change in, any applicable law after the date on which a Transaction is entered into, or due to the promulgation of, or any change in, the interpretation by any court, tribunal or regulatory authority with competent jurisdiction of any applicable law after such date, it becomes unlawful (other than as a result of a breach by the party of Section 4(b)) for such party (which will be the Affected Party):-

(1) to perform any absolute or contingent obligation to make a payment or delivery or to receive a payment or delivery in respect of such Transaction or to comply with any other material provision of this Agreement relating to such Transaction; or

(2) to perform, or for any Credit Support Provider of such party to perform, any contingent or other obligation which the party (or such Credit Support Provider) has under any Credit Support Document relating to such Transaction;

Section 5(b) Termination Events

Termination Events allow a party to close out where the event substantially alters the Transaction economics or the risk profile of its counterparty. Sometimes no one party is sufficiently at fault but the effect of the Termination Event means it is not financially beneficial for the parties to continue the Transaction(s) concerned.

There are four Termination Events listed with the option of a fifth. Please note that with Termination Events, the party at fault is generally called the Affected Party. Under Section 5(b)(i)–(iii), if a Termination Event occurs and close-out follows through designating an Early Termination Date in a notice, only Transactions affected by the Termination Event ("Affected Transactions") are closed out. Under Section 5(b)(iv) and usually under Section 5(b)(v), the Affected Transactions comprise all Transactions because the Termination Event taints the whole contractual relationship and all Transactions need to be terminated.

Section 5(b)(i)

Section 5(b)(i) states that a Termination Event will arise if it becomes unlawful for a party to make or receive a payment or delivery or comply with any material provision of the Agreement or it becomes unlawful for a party or a Credit Support Provider to perform under a Credit Support Document. For the avoidance of doubt, the party impacted by the Illegality (i.e. the one faced with breaking the law in order to perform) will be the Affected Party.

Illegality excludes any breach by a party of the agreement in Section 4(b) to maintain authorisations necessary in connection with the Agreement or any Credit Support Document. Any such breach will be treated as a Breach of Agreement Event of Default and not as an Illegality.

As with the next two Termination Events an effort must be made to try to transfer the Affected Transactions to a third party or to a different Office of the party so as to avoid the Termination Event happening (please see commentary on Section 6(b)).

(ii) ***Tax Event***. Due to (x) any action taken by a taxing authority, or brought in a court of competent jurisdiction, on or after the date on which a Transaction is entered into (regardless of whether such action is taken or brought with respect to a party to this Agreement) or (y) a Change in Tax Law, the party (which will be the Affected Party) will, or there is a substantial likelihood that it will, on the next succeeding Scheduled Payment Date (1) be required to pay to the other party an additional amount in respect of an Indemnifiable Tax under Section 2(d)(i)(4) (except in respect of interest under Section 2(e), 6(d)(ii) or 6(e)) or (2) receive a payment from which an amount is required to be deducted or withheld for or on account of a Tax (except in respect of interest under Section 6(d)(ii) or 6(e)) and no additional amount is required to be paid in respect of such Tax under Section 2(d)(i)(4) (other than by reason of Section 2(d)(i)(4)(A) or (B));

Section 5(b)(ii)

A Tax Event takes place when a Change in Tax Law occurs and results in a party becoming (or very likely to become) burdened by a withholding tax which leads to a payer being required to gross up or a payee receiving a lower payment net of withholding with no gross up. A termination right arises in such cases because neither party is regarded as sufficiently "at fault" for it to be burdened by an unexpected tax charge until the maturity of the Transaction. The party having to gross up or the party receiving less than it expected because the withholding tax is being levied is called the Affected Party and is entitled to call for close out of Affected Transactions.

A Tax Event does not occur if a withholding tax is levied on default interest under Section 2(e) or interest payments upon early termination under Section 6(d)(ii) or (e).

So, if any withholding tax arises because of a Change in Tax Law after the date the parties enter into a Transaction, the party impacted by the withholding tax has a right to terminate the Transaction(s) concerned under Sections 5(b)(ii) and 6(b) of the Agreement. The Section 6 procedure involves trying to transfer the Affected Transactions to a third party or to a different Office to avoid the Tax Event. The termination for the Affected Transactions is made on the basis that there is one Affected Party. This means the non-Affected Party makes the termination calculations.

However, if a change of facts occurs at the start or during the life of the Transaction, this will not give a right to trigger a Tax Event because the party concerned should have done its analysis properly in the first place and should not be able to close out as a result of its own actions if the change of facts happens later in the Transaction's life.

(iii) ***Tax Event Upon Merger***. The party (the "Burdened Party") on the next succeeding Scheduled Payment Date will either (1) be required to pay an additional amount in respect of an Indemnifiable Tax under Section 2(d)(i)(4) (except in respect of interest under Section 2(e), 6(d)(ii) or 6(e)) or (2) receive a payment from which an amount has been deducted or withheld for or on account of any Indemnifiable Tax in respect of which the other party is not required to pay an additional amount (other than by reason of Section 2(d)(i)(4)(A) or (B)), in either case as a result of a party consolidating or amalgamating with, or merging with or into, or transferring all or substantially all its assets to, another entity (which will be the Affected Party) where such action does not constitute an event described in Section 5(a)(viii);

Section 5(b)(iii)

Under Section 5(b)(iii), a Tax Event Upon Merger arises if a withholding tax is levied which results in a merging party having to gross up its payment or a non-merging party receiving any payment due to it net of withholding tax with no gross up. Such a party is called the Burdened Party. Such a transaction could result in the charging of withholding tax, for example, if the acquiror's jurisdiction of incorporation is different from that of the company being acquired. Again, only Affected Transactions are terminated because the trading relationship is fundamentally altered. Please note that the Affected Party is the one engaged in merging.

Certain exceptions apply to this. For instance, a Tax Event Upon Merger cannot occur because of interest payments due under Sections 2(e) or 6(b) or 6(d)(ii), nor will it apply if Transactions are impacted by the Merger Without Assumption Event of Default (Section 5(a)(viii)) because they can be terminated through an Event of Default which is more serious and will close out all Transactions under the Agreement.

If a Tax Event Upon Merger happens, only the Burdened Party can terminate the Affected Transactions and both it and the non-Affected Party must try to find a means to transfer them to a third party or another Office so that this Termination Event disappears. Again any termination payment to be made in respect of Affected Transactions is calculated on the basis of one Affected Party with the non-Affected Party making the termination calculations.

If a payee is not entitled to receive a gross up payment because it has given a false Payee Tax Representation or failed to deliver requested tax documentation, it will not be entitled to call a Tax Event Upon Merger. Please note that a Tax Event and a Tax Event Upon Merger will not apply if it is a Credit Support Provider that unexpectedly needs to gross up.

(iv) ***Credit Event Upon Merger***. If "Credit Event Upon Merger" is specified in the Schedule as applying to the party, such party ("X"), any Credit Support Provider of X or any applicable Specified Entity of X consolidates or amalgamates with, or merges with or into, or transfers all or substantially all its assets to, another entity and such action does not constitute an event described in Section 5(a)(viii) but the creditworthiness of the resulting, surviving or transferee entity is materially weaker than that of X, such Credit Support Provider or such Specified Entity, as the case may be, immediately prior to such action (and, in such event, X or its successor or transferee, as appropriate, will be the Affected Party); or

Section 5(b)(iv)

The rationale for Credit Event Upon Merger is that a party may not have entered into an Agreement in the first place had it known that its counterparty would merge or be taken over and, as a result, become a much worse credit risk. However, parties do not usually invoke Credit Event Upon Merger as a knee jerk reaction but try to evaluate if the new counterparty will be able to perform its obligations under the Agreement or if, for example, credit support will need to be taken.

Section 5(b)(iv) of the Agreement only applies to a party if this is stated in Part 1(d) of the Schedule. It addresses the situation where your counterparty, its Credit Support Provider or any applicable Specified Entity (specified in Part 1(a) of the Schedule) is taken over by, or merges with, another entity and this results in a material reduction in their creditworthiness. A Termination Event will occur under this provision if the Transaction does not result in a Merger Without Assumption Event of Default (Section 5(a)(viii). If this Termination Event occurs, the party who has entered into, or whose Credit Support Provider or Specified Entity has entered into, a merger or takeover transaction is the Affected Party and the other party is entitled to terminate all Transactions under the Agreement. The merger taints all Transactions, not just some of them.

Some market players amend this Termination Event to define "materially weaker" more objectively in terms of, for example, credit rating agency downgrades, a set minimum level of credit ratings or the loss by a merged party of its credit rating.

The basic Credit Event Upon Merger provision describes North American merger practice. In many European Schedules, the definition of Credit Event Upon Merger is expanded to include the purchase of voting shares giving the power to elect a majority of the board of directors of a party or its Credit Support Provider(s) or Specified Entity(ies). We shall review the standard amendment in the Schedule in Chapter 8, pages 448–9. This "European" language has now been adopted in the Credit Event Upon Merger provision in the main text of the 2002 Agreement.

The overriding point here is that the merged entity must be materially financially weaker post-merger.

(v) ***Additional Termination Event***. If any "Additional Termination Event" is specified in the Schedule or any Confirmation as applying, the occurrence of such event (and, in such event, the Affected Party or Affected Parties shall be as specified for such Additional Termination Event in the Schedule or such Confirmation).

(c) ***Event of Default and Illegality***. If an event or circumstance which would otherwise constitute or give rise to an Event of Default also constitutes an Illegality, it will be treated as an Illegality and will not constitute an Event of Default.

Section 5(b)(v)

Section 5(b)(v) of the Agreement has been added so that parties may specify Additional Termination Events in Part 1(h) of the Schedule or any Confirmation and any Affected Party or Affected Parties for such Additional Termination Events.

It is assumed that where an Additional Termination Event arises, all Transactions will be Affected Transactions and the non-Affected Party will be entitled to terminate them. Many Additional Termination Events are credit related (e.g. rating agency downgrades of a party's outstanding long-term debt securities below a minimum rating or the cancellation of a rating by a credit ratings agency) and therefore impact the entire contractual relationship between the parties and not just a particular group of Transactions. A Change of Ownership clause and full prepayment of a loan linked to a swap are other common examples of an Additional Termination Event.

Section 5(c)

Section 5(c) of the Agreement covers the position where an Event of Default can also be classified as an Illegality by providing that in those circumstances it will be treated as an Illegality. This is done to lessen the effect of the event by closing out only the Affected Transaction(s) rather than all Transactions. It protects a party unable to make a necessary payment because to do so would be unlawful but it does not defer the Scheduled Payment Date. Interest would accrue at the Default Rate from and including the Scheduled Payment Date to but excluding the date on which any early termination notice is given for the Illegality if the parties cannot transfer the deal under Section 6(b)(ii) to avoid the Illegality.

Section 6 – Early Termination

Section 6 describes the detailed close-out netting mechanism where an Event of Default or Termination Event occurs.

Close-out netting is vital to the ISDA Master Agreement; so vital that ISDA has commissioned legal opinions from 39 countries to find out if they would recognise close-out netting if a Non-defaulting Party exercised its rights in a default or bankruptcy situation involving one of their nationals. The vast majority of jurisdictions do recognise the effectiveness of close-out netting. A list of these opinions is shown in Annex 4, pages 725–6. In order to minimise the capital allocated to derivatives' counterparty exposure, regulators require written, reasoned, independent legal opinions from major law firms for each jurisdiction where a bank is seeking to net its exposure in respect of Transactions under Agreements with various counterparties in that country. Regulators require these legal opinions to be updated at least once a year.

It is vital for a solvent party to have a clear and effective close-out mechanism so that it can replace the Terminated Transactions it had with an insolvent party as quickly as possible so as to maintain any underlying hedging transactions.

Before entering the tall grass and describing the Section 6 provisions in depth, I should first like to attempt a summary of them.

When an Event of Default occurs, only the Non-defaulting Party can choose an Early Termination Date and close out and net off all Transactions between the parties to reach a single figure payable one way or the other. This payment essentially represents damages for the curtailed Transactions. The Early Termination Date may be designated at any time that the Event of Default persists but it must be designated within 20 days of the termination notice.

Please note that once an Early Termination Date has been designated it can only be cancelled with the consent of both parties. Otherwise there is no turning back. Termination is not the sole remedy of an innocent party as Section 9(d) provides the possibility for other remedies to be pursued (see commentary on page 107).

With a Termination Event (except for Credit Event Upon Merger and probably Additional Termination Events), the parties have to find a way to keep the Affected Transaction alive possibly by transferring it to another office or group company. They have 20–30 days to do this but if they fail, the Affected Transaction or Transactions are closed out. This is done by using payment measures and methods which are chosen in the Schedule.

The payment measures are Market Quotation or Loss which each describe how termination payments are calculated. Market Quotation involves the Non-defaulting Party obtaining close-out quotations from four major dealers (called Reference Market-makers) for the replacement cost of the Terminated

Transactions (i.e. how much it would theoretically cost to step into the Non-defaulting Party's shoes). Under this measure the highest and lowest quotations are disregarded and the arithmetic mean of the two remaining quotations is taken to which are added any net Unpaid Amounts to produce the net termination payment (see commentary on Section 6(e)).

But how does a Reference Market-maker make his calculation?

If, for example, the overall position was profitable for the Non-defaulting Party (i.e. he was "in the money") the quotation would represent how much the Reference Market-maker would have to be paid to take over the Defaulting Party's future payment obligations. The Reference Market-maker would calculate the net present value of these and add a margin to compensate it for theoretically assuming them. He does not really assume them because he is just providing a quotation.

If the overall position was unprofitable (i.e. "out of the money") for the Non-defaulting Party, the Reference Market-maker's quotation would represent what he would potentially need to pay to take over the Defaulting Party's rights to receive future payments. This time the Reference Market-maker would deduct its compensatory margin.

Loss can be used as a fallback measure to Market Quotation where the Non-defaulting Party believes that using Market Quotation may not produce a commercially reasonable result perhaps because there are grounds for believing Market Quotations could be distorted (e.g. many traders requesting termination figures in a major close-out situation – Barings in 1995). In these circumstances dealers are also wary about disclosing the terms for a Defaulting Party whom the other dealer may also have as a counterparty and so may prefer the greater privacy of Loss.

Loss can also be used where a market is thin or not liquid or because that is the norm for that market (e.g. the FX market). It may also be preferable for Transactions settling by physical delivery.

Under Loss, the Non-defaulting Party makes its own good faith calculations as to what its losses and costs are (i.e. if it is "in the money") and the level of its gains if it is "out of the money". The losses and costs are expressed as positive numbers and the gains as negative numbers.

If the Non-defaulting Party is "in the money", its position is impaired because it will not receive any future payments from the Defaulting Party. If it is "out of the money" it will gain because it will not need to make future payments to the Defaulting Party. The Non-defaulting Party can include hedging transaction unwind or breakage costs and funding costs in its calculation of Loss. Section 11 expenses (e.g. legal fees and stamp duties) are excluded.

Loss can include obtaining market quotations (see the last sentence of the Section 14 definition of Loss) which indicates that it is a broader measure than Market Quotation.

Calculations have to be made on the Early Termination Date or on the earliest date as soon as reasonably practicable thereafter. Concerns of some commentators in 1992 that this could lay parties open to attack from liquidators if calculations were not made on the Early Termination Date itself and markets moved quickly thereafter in their favour, have not materialised.

Parties normally adopt one payment measure to apply to all Transactions documented under the Agreement but I have seen Loss stated as applying to foreign exchange and currency option Transactions (the norm in those markets) and Market Quotation as applying to all other products under the same Agreement.

The payment methods are the First Method or the Second Method. The choice is made in Part 1(f) of the Schedule. Where no choice is made, the fallback is the Second Method. The Non-defaulting Party makes the calculations and the payments due are netted off to produce a single figure payable one way or the other.

Under the First Method, if the single net payment is due to the Defaulting Party he does not get it. The Non-defaulting Party keeps it as a windfall. Under the Second Method, the Defaulting Party would receive the payment.

The First Method is often referred to as "limited two-way payments" or a "walk away clause" because the Non-defaulting Party can walk away from its obligations. This represents a punishment for the Defaulting Party. The First Method was the basic approach under the 1987 Agreement.

The Financial Services Authority and other regulators prohibit the use of the First Method where banks are seeking to have derivatives contracts reported on a net basis for capital adequacy and large exposure purposes relating to counterparty risk. Here, the Second Method must be used. In addition, limited two-way payments were not widely accepted outside the swaps market and in several jurisdictions it was doubtful whether they could be enforced especially where caps or options were concerned and the Defaulting Party had fulfilled its obligations by paying the agreed premium.

There is more about the calculation of termination payments in the commentary on Section 6(e), pages 92–9.

Thoroughly confused? Hopefully, Figures 3.3 and 3.4 will help.

Figure 3.3 shows who has the right to terminate under the Section 5 events. Figure 3.4 illustrates the effect of termination on the Transactions involved.

I would also like to discuss Automatic Early Termination.

Under Section 6(a), the Non-defaulting Party has the right to designate an Early Termination Date (for close-out purposes) for all outstanding Transactions upon an Event of Default arising and continuing. Section 6(a) also allows parties to choose in Part 1(e) of the Schedule that "Automatic Early Termination" will apply to a party if certain bankruptcy or insolvency

FIG. 3.3

Early termination: who can terminate

Reason	Who may terminate
Events of Default	
• Bankruptcy	• Non-defaulting Party or Automatic*
• Other	• Non-defaulting Party
Termination Event	
• Illegality	• either party
• Tax Event	• Affected Party
• Tax Event Upon Merger	• Burdened Party
• Credit Event Upon Merger	• non-Affected Party
• Additional Termination Event	• non-Affected Party or either party (if there are two Affected Parties)

* only applies if selected in Schedule

FIG. 3.4

Early termination: effect of termination

Event of Default	• all Transactions terminated
Credit Event Upon Merger	• all Transactions terminated
Additional Termination Event	• all Transactions terminated (presumably)
Other Termination Events	• only Affected Transactions terminated

events occur. If parties fail to make a selection in Part 1(e), Automatic Early Termination will not apply. If Automatic Early Termination applies and certain Section 5(a)(vii) insolvency events occur, an Early Termination Date will arise automatically for all outstanding Transactions.

Automatic Early Termination was the norm for Bankruptcy Events of Default under the 1987 Agreement. It means that with the happening of certain bankruptcy events (e.g. the presentation of a winding-up order), an Early Termination Date is automatically and immediately designated without notice to the Defaulting Party. Quite possibly, the Non-defaulting Party may be unaware of the bankruptcy event and when he finds out, markets may have moved significantly since the deemed Early Termination Date. This could result in hedging transactions having to be replaced at higher cost in the market.

In general, lawyers consider that the drawbacks of Automatic Early Termination outweigh its benefits. However, it is helpful to apply it to counterparties subject to certain insolvency regimes, e.g. Germany, Japan, Belgium, Denmark and Switzerland. It is not necessary in the UK or the USA. This subject is discussed further in Chapters 5 and 8.

To mitigate its effects, you sometimes see clauses in the Schedule (see Chapter 8, pages 451–3) which indemnify the Non-defaulting Party against movements in prices and rates from the Automatic Early Termination date until the Non-defaulting Party becomes aware of the insolvency event. Note that Automatic Early Termination only applies to certain Bankruptcy events and not to other types of Events of Default.

Some market players have been concerned that Automatic Early Termination might not be enforceable because it might cut across automatic stay bankruptcy proceedings. In many jurisdictions this issue has been addressed in Automatic Early Termination's favour but this point should always be checked if it is important for Automatic Early Termination to be fully effective.

The individual sub-Sections of Section 6 are now reviewed.

6. Early Termination

(a) ***Right to Terminate Following Event of Default.*** If at any time an Event of Default with respect to a party (the "Defaulting Party") has occurred and is then continuing, the other party (the "Non-defaulting Party") may, by not more than 20 days notice to the Defaulting Party specifying the relevant Event of Default, designate a day not earlier than the day such notice is effective as an Early Termination Date in respect of all outstanding Transactions. If, however, "Automatic Early Termination" is specified in the Schedule as applying to a party, then an Early Termination Date in respect of all outstanding Transactions will occur immediately upon the occurrence with respect to such party of an Event of Default specified in Section 5(a)(vii)(1), (3), (5), (6) or, to the extent analogous thereto, (8), and as of the time immediately preceding the institution of the relevant proceeding or the presentation of the relevant petition upon the occurrence with respect to such party of an Event of Default specified in Section 5(a)(vii)(4) or, to the extent analogous thereto, (8).

Section 6

Section 6(a)

Where an Event of Default occurs and is continuing, the Non-defaulting Party has the option (but not the obligation) to terminate all outstanding Transactions under the Agreement by giving the Defaulting Party not more than 20 days' notice of its intention to close out all Transactions on a certain date called the Early Termination Date. The notice must describe the Event of Default and the Early Termination Date is normally much sooner than 20 days after the notice is given.

With certain insolvency events (as described in Section 5(a)(vii)) termination may be automatic rather than by notice. These insolvency events are:

- **dissolution (except in the case of a merger, amalgamation or consolidation); or**
- **a general arrangement, assignment or composition with creditors; or**
- **a winding-up resolution is passed (except again in the case of a merger, amalgamation or consolidation); or**
- **the appointment of an administrator or similar insolvency official over all or most of a party's assets.**

In these four cases termination takes place immediately after they happen. However, with the insolvency Event of Default in Section 5(a)(vii)(4) (which is the starting of proceedings or the filing of a winding-up order which either results in a bankruptcy adjudication or is not dismissed within 30 days), the close out is deemed to occur immediately before the proceedings start or the order is presented. The problem here is that the Non-defaulting Party may not be aware of the insolvency event and by the time it is the markets may have moved strongly against it. Chapter 8 examines possible indemnifying amendments designed to protect the Non-defaulting Party in these circumstances (see pages 451–3).

If an Event of Default impacting a party is cured before a termination notice is given, the Non-defaulting Party loses its right to give such a notice because Section 6(d)(i) requires that the Event of Default is "continuing". However, once the notice is given, the Defaulting Party cannot then cure the Event of Default. As soon as the Non-defaulting Party gives notice it must have certainty and be free to enter into replacement Transactions to cover the open position that will arise on the Early Termination Date or unwind existing hedging Transactions without concern that a late performance by the Defaulting Party of its obligations will mean the Non-defaulting Party will have to reverse its actions, possibly at a loss. It is important for the parties to set sensible cure periods for Events of Default if the ones in the Agreement are not suitable for their particular circumstances.

(b) ***Right to Terminate Following Termination Event.***

(i) ***Notice.*** If a Termination Event occurs, an Affected Party will, promptly upon becoming aware of it, notify the other party, specifying the nature of that Termination Event and each Affected Transaction and will also give such other information about that Termination Event as the other party may reasonably require.

(ii) ***Transfer to Avoid Termination Event.*** If either an Illegality under Section 5(b)(i)(1) or a Tax Event occurs and there is only one Affected Party, or if a Tax Event Upon Merger occurs and the Burdened Party is the Affected Party, the Affected Party will, as a condition to its right to designate an Early Termination Date under Section 6(b)(iv), use all reasonable efforts (which will not require such party to incur a loss, excluding immaterial, incidental expenses) to transfer within 20 days after it gives notice under Section 6(b)(i) all its rights and obligations under this Agreement in respect of the Affected Transactions to another of its Offices or Affiliates so that such Termination Event ceases to exist.

If the Affected Party is not able to make such a transfer it will give notice to the other party to that effect within such 20 day period, whereupon the other party may effect such a transfer within 30 days after notice is given under Section 6(b)(i).

Any such transfer by a party under this Section 6(b)(ii) will be subject to and conditional upon the prior written consent of the other party, which consent will not be withheld if such other party's policies in effect at such time would permit it to enter into transactions with the transferee on the terms proposed.

Section 6(b)

Generally speaking, except for Credit Event Upon Merger and some Additional Termination Events, a non-Affected Party will only have the option to terminate individual Transactions affected by some specified event rather than *all* Transactions as under an Event of Default.

The process is as follows:

Notice

Under Section 6(b)(i), if a Termination Event occurs, an Affected Party must promptly inform and provide reasonable information to the other party of the particular Termination Event and each Affected Transaction.

Transfer to avoid Termination Event

However, there is a duty by both parties to try to mitigate a Termination Event on the principle that it is better to continue a Transaction if possible. With Tax Event Upon Merger this duty arises for the Burdened Party where it is also engaging in the merger.

Consequently Section 6(b)(ii) of the Agreement requires an Affected Party impacted by one or more Termination Events first to use all reasonable efforts to transfer all Affected Transactions to another of its Offices or Affiliates (i.e. other group companies) to avoid the Termination Event concerned. The Affected Party is given a period of up to 20 days after notice to do this.

Where the Affected Party cannot make such a transfer, it must within the 20-day notice period notify the non-Affected Party who can try to do so within 30 days from the original notice date. So if the Affected Party tries to transfer and fails on the twentieth day and then notifies the non-Affected Party, the non-Affected Party only has ten days in which to make a transfer.

The prior written consent of the other party is necessary to make this transfer but must not be unreasonably withheld, especially if the non-Affected Party's policies would, in the normal course, allow it to enter into Transactions with the proposed transferee Office or Affiliate of the Affected Party.

(iii) ***Two Affected Parties***. If an Illegality under Section 5(b)(i)(1) or a Tax Event occurs and there are two Affected Parties, each party will use all reasonable efforts to reach agreement within 30 days after notice thereof is given under Section 6(b)(i) on action to avoid that Termination Event.

(iv) ***Right to Terminate***. If:-

(1) a transfer under Section 6(b)(ii) or an agreement under Section 6(b)(iii), as the case may be, has not been effected with respect to all Affected Transactions within 30 days after an Affected Party gives notice under Section 6(b)(i); or

(2) an Illegality under Section 5(b)(i)(2), a Credit Event Upon Merger or an Additional Termination Event occurs, or a Tax Event Upon Merger occurs and the Burdened Party is not the Affected Party,

either party in the case of an Illegality, the Burdened Party in the case of a Tax Event Upon Merger, any Affected Party in the case of a Tax Event or an Additional Termination Event if there is more than one Affected Party, or the party which is not the Affected Party in the case of a Credit Event Upon Merger or an Additional Termination Event if there is only one Affected Party may, by not more than 20 days' notice to the other party and provided that the relevant Termination Event is then continuing, designate a day not earlier than the day such notice is effective as an Early Termination Date in respect of all Affected Transactions.

Two Affected Parties

Where an Illegality under Section 5(b)(i)(1) or Tax Event under Section 5(b)(ii) has occurred and there are two Affected Parties, they must both use all reasonable efforts to agree on action to avoid the relevant Termination Event within 30 days following notice.

Right to Terminate

If the parties are unable to agree to transfer or otherwise avoid the relevant Termination Event, an Early Termination Date may be designated in accordance with Section 6(b)(iv) of the Agreement.

Where a transfer fails to be made by either party in the 30-day period following the original notice in respect of a Termination Event, the Affected Party may choose an Early Termination Date (not earlier than the date the original notice became effective) in respect of all Affected Transactions. With Tax Event Upon Merger the Burdened Party has this right provided that it is not engaging in the merger.

(c) ***Effect of Designation.***

(i) If notice designating an Early Termination Date is given under Section 6(a) or (b), the Early Termination Date will occur on the date so designated, whether or not the relevant Event of Default or Termination Event is then continuing.

(ii) Upon the occurrence or effective designation of an Early Termination Date, no further payments or deliveries under Section 2(a)(i) or 2(e) in respect of the Terminated Transactions will be required to be made, but without prejudice to the other provisions of this Agreement. The amount if any, payable in respect of an Early Termination Date shall be determined pursuant to Section 6(e).

Section 6(c)

Where an Early Termination Date notice is given for an Event of Default or Termination Event, the Early Termination Date will occur on the chosen date whether or not the Event of Default or Termination Event is then continuing.

When an Early Termination Date happens or is chosen, neither party is required to make normal payments or deliveries under Sections 2(a)(i) or 2(e) of the Agreement for Transactions to be terminated. The Agreement itself is not terminated by the giving of an early termination notice; only the parties' obligations to make payments or deliveries terminate. Several provisions (e.g. obligation to gross up payments (Section 2(d)(i)), obligation to make settlement payments under Section 6(e); currency conversion obligations (Section 8); and obligation to pay enforcement expenses (Section 11)) all survive because of Section 9(c) – Survival of Obligations. Payments or deliveries that would have been due on dates after the termination notice takes effect but on or before the Early Termination Date (as well as any obligations that did not become payable or deliverable because of the failure to satisfy all conditions precedent) are included in the definition of Unpaid Amounts (if Market Quotation applies) or Loss (if it applies), as the case may be, and are therefore included in the close-out calculation.

(d) ***Calculations.***

(i) ***Statement.*** On or as soon as reasonably practicable following the occurrence of an Early Termination Date, each party will make the calculations on its part, if any, contemplated by Section 6(e) and will provide to the other party a statement (1) showing, in reasonable detail, such calculations (including all relevant quotations and specifying any amount payable under Section 6(e)) and (2) giving details of the relevant account to which any amount payable to it is to be paid. In the absence of written confirmation from the source of a quotation obtained in determining a Market Quotation, the records of the party obtaining such quotation will be conclusive evidence of the existence and accuracy of such quotation.

(ii) ***Payment Date.*** An amount calculated as being due in respect of any Early Termination Date under Section 6(e) will be payable on the day that notice of the amount payable is effective (in the case of an Early Termination Date which is designated or occurs as a result of an Event of Default) and on the day which is two Local Business Days after the day on which notice of the amount payable is effective (in the case of an Early Termination Date which is designated as a result of a Termination Event). Such amount will be paid together with (to the extent permitted under applicable law) interest thereon (before as well as after judgment) in the Termination Currency, from (and including) the relevant Early Termination Date to (but excluding) the date such amount is paid, at the Applicable Rate. Such interest will be calculated on the basis of daily compounding and the actual number of days elapsed.

Section 6(d)

On, or shortly after, an Early Termination Date, each party, where practicable, is to provide the other with a statement of early termination payment calculations in reasonable detail and advise the account to which any termination payment is to be made. The records of the Non-defaulting Party or both parties where no party is at fault shall be conclusive evidence of Market Quotations received from dealers who do not confirm them in writing.

Early termination payments for Events of Default are payable on the day that the Early Termination Date notice becomes effective. Early termination payments for Termination Events are payable two Local Business Days after the day that the Early Termination Date notice becomes effective. The amount concerned will be paid with accrued interest and in the Termination Currency agreed in Part 1(g) of the Schedule (otherwise the fallback is US$). In calculating net termination payments, the relevant payment measure (i.e. Market Quotation or Loss) and any Unpaid Amounts are converted into a Termination Currency Equivalent by obtaining a market foreign exchange rate from an FX dealer chosen by the Non-defaulting Party.

With Events of Default, interest is payable on an early termination payment from and including the relevant Early Termination Date to but excluding the day on which it is actually paid. A Defaulting Party will pay interest at the Default Rate (i.e. 1% over the payee's cost of funds).

A Non-defaulting Party will pay interest at the Non-default Rate (i.e. the Non-defaulting Party's cost of funds) from and including the Early Termination Date to, but excluding the date (i.e. two Local Business Days following the date) the termination notice is effective. If it fails to pay on time it will be charged at the Default Rate.

With Termination Events (and one Affected Party) the Affected Party will pay interest at the Default Rate from and including the Early Termination Date to but excluding the date (i.e. two Local Business Days following the date) the termination notice is effective.

With Termination Events (and two Affected Parties) interest is paid at the Termination Rate (i.e. the arithmetic mean of each party's cost of funds). Where payment is late interest is charged at the Default Rate. The same rates apply to interest on Unpaid Amounts. However, the interest period is from and including the date such payments are required to be paid to, but excluding the Early Termination Date.

(e) ***Payments on Early Termination.*** If an Early Termination Date occurs. the following provisions shall apply based on the parties' election in the Schedule of a payment measure, either "Market Quotation" or "Loss", and a payment method, either the "First Method" or the "Second Method". If the parties fail to designate a payment measure or payment method in the Schedule, it will be deemed that "Market Quotation" or the "Second Method", as the case may be, shall apply. The amount, if any, payable in respect of an Early Termination Date and determined pursuant to this Section will be subject to any Set-off.

(i) ***Events of Default.*** If the Early Termination Date results from an Event of Default:-

(1) ***First Method and Market Quotation.*** If the First Method and Market Quotation apply, the Defaulting Party will pay to the Non-defaulting Party the excess, if a positive number, of (A) the sum of the Settlement Amount (determined by the Non-defaulting Party) in respect of the Terminated Transactions and the Termination Currency Equivalent of the Unpaid Amounts owing to the Non-defaulting Party over (B) the Termination Currency Equivalent of the Unpaid Amounts owing to the Defaulting Party.

(2) ***First Method and Loss.*** If the First Method and Loss apply, the Defaulting Party will pay to the Non-defaulting Party, if a positive number, the Non-defaulting Party's Loss in respect of this Agreement.

(3) ***Second Method and Market Quotations.*** If the Second Method and Market Quotation apply, an amount will be payable equal to (A) the sum of the Settlement Amount (determined by the Non-defaulting Party) in respect of the Terminated Transactions and the Termination Currency Equivalent of the Unpaid Amounts owing to the Non-defaulting Party less (B) the Termination Currency Equivalent of the Unpaid Amounts owing to the Defaulting Party. If that amount is a positive number, the Defaulting Party will pay it to the Non-defaulting Party; if it is a negative number, the Non-defaulting Party will pay the absolute value of that amount to the Defaulting Party.

(4) ***Second Method and Loss.*** If the Second Method and Loss apply, an amount will be payable equal to the Non-defaulting Party's Loss in respect of this Agreement. If that amount is a positive number, the Defaulting Party will pay it to the Non-defaulting Party; if it is a negative number, the Non-defaulting Party will pay the absolute value of that amount to the Defaulting Party.

Section 6(e)

Section 6(e) provides four ways for the calculation of payments on early termination arising from an Event of Default :

- **First Method and Market Quotation**
- **First Method and Loss**
- **Second Method and Market Quotation**
- **Second Method and Loss.**

Under the Agreement an early termination payment consists of the following three components:

- **payments for the future replacement value of the Terminated Transactions (included in the definition of "Market Quotation");**
- **contractual payment or delivery obligations (i.e. amounts due under Section 2(a)(i)) which were due before the Early Termination Date but not paid ("Unpaid Amounts"); and**
- **payments or deliveries which would have been due before the Early Termination Date if all pre-conditions (such as no Event of Default having taken place) had been satisfied or if the Early Termination Date had not been designated. These are amounts due under Section 2(a)(iii) and are also called "Unpaid Amounts").**

These amounts are covered in the definition of "Loss". Unpaid Amounts are computed separately under the Agreement when calculating termination payments under Market Quotation. With Loss, Unpaid Amounts are part of the Loss calculation (unless Loss is used as a fallback to Market Quotation). Depending on whether Market Quotation or Loss, the First Method or the Second Method, an Event of Default or Termination Event applies (and, if a Termination Event occurs, whether one or two Affected Parties are involved), calculations of early termination payments are made as follows:

(e)(i) Payments arising from an Event of Default

First Method and Market Quotation First the positive and negative values of all Transactions are calculated and added together. The resulting net figure is then added to the Unpaid Amounts due to the Non-defaulting Party. From it are subtracted the Unpaid Amounts due to the Defaulting Party.

If the resultant net amount is a positive number, it is paid by the Defaulting Party to the Non-defaulting Party. Where the net amount is a negative figure the Non-defaulting Party makes no payment to the Defaulting Party. This is known as "limited two-way payments". The Non-defaulting Party makes the necessary calculations in this case.

First Method and Loss If Loss is used and the amount of a Non-defaulting Party's Loss is a positive number, the Defaulting Party pays that sum to the Non-defaulting Party but if it is a negative number, no payment is made. The Non-defaulting Party again makes the necessary calculations.

Second Method and Market Quotation Where the net amount is a positive number, it is paid by the Defaulting Party to the Non-defaulting Party. Where it is a negative number, it is paid by the Non-defaulting Party to the Defaulting Party. This is known as "full two-way payments" and is favoured by regulators. The Non-defaulting Party still makes the necessary calculations.

Second Method and Loss If the amount of a Non-defaulting Party's Loss is a positive number, the Defaulting Party pays that sum to the Non-defaulting Party but if it is a negative number, the Non-defaulting Party pays the absolute value of that amount to the Defaulting Party. The Non-defaulting Party makes the calculations.

An easy way to remember who gets what (particularly under the Second Method) is to view the positive and negative amounts from the Non-defaulting Party's viewpoint. If the close-out amount is positive, the Non-defaulting Party receives it and could be said to view the situation positively. If the close-out amount is negative, the Non-defaulting Party has to pay it over and so views the situation negatively.

Figure 3.5 illustrates the above payments.

FIG. 3.5

Payments arising from an Event of Default

Process for Market Quotation:

1. Calculate and add together the positive and negative values of all Transactions.
2. Add Unpaid Amounts due to the Non-defaulting Party.
3. Subtract Unpaid Amounts due to the Defaulting Party.

Method and Measure	Positive net figure	Action	Negative net figure	Action
First Method and Market Quotation	Yes	Defaulting Party pays Non-defaulting Party	Yes	Non-defaulting Party does not pay Defaulting Party
First Method and Loss	Yes	Defaulting Party pays Non-defaulting Party	Yes	Non-defaulting Party does not pay Defaulting Party
Second Method and Market Quotation	Yes	Defaulting Party pays Non-defaulting Party	Yes	Non-defaulting Party pays Defaulting Party
Second Method and Loss	Yes	Defaulting Party pays Non-defaulting Party	Yes	Non-defaulting Party pays Defaulting Party

1. Note that whichever payment method is chosen, the Defaulting Party will always pay the Non-Defaulting Party where it is "out of the money".
2. Note that, as defined, Loss includes Unpaid Amounts and is a single figure for all Terminated Transactions. When used as a fallback to Market Quotation, Loss excludes Unpaid Amounts.

(ii) ***Termination Events***. If the Early Termination Date results from a Termination Event:-

(1) ***One Affected Party***. If there is one Affected Party, the amount payable will be determined in accordance with Section 6(e)(i)(3), if Market Quotation applies, or Section 6(e)(i)(4), if Loss applies, except that, in either case, references to the Defaulting Party and to the Non-defaulting Party will be deemed to be references to the Affected Party and the party which is not the Affected Party, respectively, and, if Loss applies and fewer than all the Transactions are being terminated, Loss shall be calculated in respect of all Terminated Transactions.

(2) ***Two Affected Parties***. If there are two Affected Parties:-

(A) if Market Quotation applies, each party will determine a Settlement Amount in respect of the Terminated Transactions, and an amount will be payable equal to (i) the sum of (a) one-half of the difference between the Settlement Amount of the party with the higher Settlement Amount ("X") and the Settlement Amount of the party with the lower Settlement Amount ("Y") and (b) the Termination Currency Equivalent of the Unpaid Amounts owing to X less (ii) the Termination Currency Equivalent of the Unpaid Amounts owing to Y; and

(B) if Loss applies, each party will determine its Loss in respect of this Agreement (or, if fewer than all the Transactions are being terminated, in respect of all Terminated Transactions) and an amount will be payable equal to one-half of the difference between the Loss of the party with the higher Loss ("X") and the Loss of the party with the lower Loss ("Y").

If the amount payable is a positive number, Y will pay it to X; if it is a negative number, X will pay the absolute value of that amount to Y.

(e)(ii) Close out arising from a Termination Event

If close out arises from a Termination Event, the net payment figure is calculated as follows:

Market Quotation (One Affected Party) Where the net amount is a positive number it is paid by the Affected Party to the non-Affected Party. Where it is a negative number it is paid by the non-Affected Party to the Affected Party. The non-Affected Party makes the calculations.

Loss (One Affected Party) If the amount of a non-Affected Party's Loss is a positive number, the Affected Party pays that sum to the non-Affected Party, but if it is a negative number, the non-Affected Party pays the absolute value of that amount to the Affected Party. The non-Affected Party again makes the calculations.

Market Quotation (Two Affected Parties) Each Affected Party solicits Market Quotations from Reference Market-makers for all Transactions to be terminated and adds the resultant positive and negative figures together so that two close-out amounts are calculated.

They then split the difference between the higher and lower close-out amounts. This amount is then added to the Unpaid Amounts payable to the party with the higher close-out amount and Unpaid Amounts due to the other party are then subtracted. If the net amount is a positive number, the party with the lower net amount pays that amount to the other party. If the net amount is negative, the party with the higher net amount pays the absolute value of that amount to the other party.

This is referred to as a "mid market" calculation and, as there are two Affected Parties, it will result in a smaller net sum payable.

Loss (Two Affected Parties) Each party calculates its own Loss and splits the difference equally between them. If the amount is positive, the party which calculated the lower Loss will pay the amount to the other party. If it is negative, the party with the higher Loss will pay it to the other party.

The First and Second Method are not used in the termination of Transactions following a Termination Event because they are only used where *all* Transactions are closed out under an Event of Default.

(iii) ***Adjustment for Bankruptcy***. In circumstances where an Early Termination Date occurs because "Automatic Early Termination" applies in respect of a party, the amount determined under this Section 6(e) will be subject to such adjustments as are appropriate and permitted by law to reflect any payments or deliveries made by one party to the other under this Agreement (and retained by such other party) during the period from the relevant Early Termination Date to the date for payment determined under Section 6(d)(ii).

(iv) ***Pre-Estimate***. The parties agree that if Market Quotation applies an amount recoverable under this Section 6(e) is a reasonable pre-estimate of loss and not a penalty. Such amount is payable for the loss of bargain and the loss of protection against future risks and except as otherwise provided in this Agreement neither party will be entitled to recover any additional damages as a consequence of such losses.

(iii) Adjustment for Bankruptcy

Section 6(e)(iii) deals with the situation where the close-out amount will be adjusted where an Early Termination Date is deemed to have occurred because Automatic Early Termination applies. It is designed to protect a Non-defaulting Party who has made payments to an insolvent counterparty and was unaware that Automatic Early Termination had occurred. In such circumstances appropriate adjustments can be made to the close-out amount payable.

(iv) Pre-estimate

This clause states that an amount recovered through an early termination payment (calculated using the Market Quotation measure) reflects a loss of bargain and loss of protection against future risks and is not a penalty. Parties cannot claim additional damages because of such losses. Hence consequential loss claims are prohibited.

7. Transfer

Subject to Section 6(b)(ii), neither this Agreement nor any interest or obligation in or under this Agreement may be transferred (whether by way of security or otherwise) by either party without the prior written consent of the other party, except that:-

(a) a party may make such a transfer of this Agreement pursuant to a consolidation or amalgamation with, or merger with or into, or transfer of all or substantially all its assets to, another entity (but without prejudice to any other right or remedy under this Agreement); and

(b) a party may make such a transfer of all or any part of its interest in any amount payable to it from a Defaulting Party under Section 6(e).

Any purported transfer that is not in compliance with this Section will be void.

Section 7

Section 7 forbids either party to transfer the Agreement or any rights and obligations under it without prior written consent. However, there are three exceptions:

- **if the purpose of a transfer is to avoid an Illegality, Tax Event or Tax Event Upon Merger as per Section 6(b)(ii), consent may not be withheld if a party's current policies would permit it to deal with the proposed transferee on the proposed Transaction terms;**
- **where a transfer of an Agreement arises from a merger or amalgamation type event involving the transfer of all or most of a party's assets to another entity. The words in brackets indicate that other restrictions in the Agreement relating to mergers and similar transactions are in no way prejudiced by this exception, e.g. the Merger Without Assumption Event of Default which will not be extinguished because of Section 7(a));**
- **if a Non-defaulting Party transfers its interest in any close-out amount payable to it from a Defaulting Party under Section 6(e).**

Section 7 also makes clear that granting a security interest in respect of an Agreement constitutes a transfer and is prohibited to ensure that mutuality between the parties is present for the purposes of close-out netting. Any transfers not complying with the Section's terms will be void. It is becoming more common to see amendments to this transfer provision in the Schedule. These vary from general phrasing that consent to a transfer shall not be unreasonably withheld to blanket advance approvals of transfers to unspecified Affiliates upon an agreed notice period. The pros and cons of these amendments are examined in Chapters 6 and 8.

8. Contractual Currency

(a) ***Payment in the Contractual Currency.*** Each payment under this Agreement will be made in the relevant currency specified in this Agreement for that payment (the "Contractual Currency"). To the extent permitted by applicable law, any obligation to make payments under this Agreement in the Contractual Currency will not be discharged or satisfied by any tender in any currency other than the Contractual Currency, except to the extent such tender results in the actual receipt by the party to which payment is owed, acting in a reasonable manner and in good faith in converting the currency so tendered into this Contractual Currency, of the full amount in the Contractual Currency of all amounts payable in respect of this Agreement. If for any reason the amount in the Contractual Currency so received falls short of the amount in the Contractual Currency payable in respect of this Agreement, the party required to make the payment will, to the extent permitted by applicable law, immediately pay such additional amount in the Contractual Currency as may be necessary to compensate for the shortfall. If for any reason the amount in the Contractual Currency so received exceeds the amount in the Contractual Currency payable in respect of this Agreement, the party receiving the payment will refund promptly the amount of such excess.

(b) ***Judgments.*** To the extent permitted by applicable law, if any judgment or order expressed in a currency other than the Contractual Currency is rendered (i) for the payment of any amount owing in respect of this Agreement, (ii) for the payment of any amount relating to any early termination in respect of this Agreement or (iii) in respect of a judgment or order of another court for the payment of any amount described in (i) or (ii) above, the party seeking recovery, after recovery in full of the aggregate amount to which such party is entitled pursuant to the judgment or order, will be entitled to receive immediately from the other party the amount of any shortfall of the Contractual Currency received by such party as a consequence of sums paid in such other currency and will refund promptly to the other party any excess of the Contractual Currency received by such party as a consequence of sums paid in such other currency if such shortfall or such excess arises or results from any variation between the rate of exchange at which the Contractual Currency is converted into the currency of the judgment or order for the purposes of such judgment or order and the rate of exchange at which such party is able, acting in a reasonable manner and in good faith in converting the currency received into the Contractual Currency, to purchase the Contractual Currency with the amount of the currency of the judgment or order actually received by such party. The term "rate of exchange" includes, without limitation, any premiums and costs of exchange payable in connection with the purchase of or conversion into the Contractual Currency.

Section 8

The Contractual Currency and judgment currency provisions here protect a party against foreign exchange losses.

Section 8(a)

Section 8(a) provides that all payments made in the normal course of business (i.e. where no Event of Default or Termination Event has intervened) must be made in the contractual currency agreed by the parties (normally in a Confirmation). Where payments are made in another currency it must be converted into the Contractual Currency and any conversion shortfalls or surpluses must be paid to the party owed them.

Section 8(b)

The same principle applies where this happens to payments under the Agreement due after legal proceedings where a recovering party has the right to convert an alternative currency into the Contractual Currency. Premia and exchange costs incurred in the conversion process are also payable to the recovering party. This is an example of a judgment currency clause and it is necessary because courts in some jurisdictions will only make awards in their local currency which may well be different from the Contractual Currency.

(c) ***Separate Indemnities.*** To the extent permitted by applicable law, these indemnities constitute separate and independent obligations from the other obligations in this Agreement, will be enforceable as separate and independent causes of action, will apply notwithstanding any indulgence granted by the party to which any payment is owed and will not be affected by judgment being obtained or claim or proof being made for any other sums payable in respect of this Agreement.

(d) ***Evidence of Loss.*** For the purpose of this Section 8, it will be sufficient for a party to demonstrate that it would have suffered a loss had an actual exchange or purchase been made.

Section 8(c)

This is rather technical. The provisions in Section 8(a) and (b) are described as separate and independent indemnities which are separately enforceable to avoid the risk that a court might combine a claim based on either indemnity with other claims being pursued for other sums under the Agreement. The indemnities will remain separate notwithstanding any indulgence or concessions granted by a creditor to his debtor or any judgment made or other claim being pursued for other sums payable under the Agreement.

Section 8(d)

Section 8(d) states that it will be enough for a party to show that it would have suffered a loss had an actual exchange or purchase of currency been made.

9. Miscellaneous

(a) ***Entire Agreement.*** This Agreement constitutes the entire agreement and understanding of the parties with respect to its subject matter and supersedes all oral communication and prior writings with respect thereto.

(b) ***Amendments.*** No amendment, modification or waiver in respect of this Agreement will be effective unless in writing (including a writing evidenced by a facsimile transmission) and executed by each of the parties or confirmed by an exchange of telexes or electronic messages on an electronic messaging system.

(c) ***Survival of Obligations.*** Without prejudice to Sections 2(a)(iii) and 6(c)(ii), the obligations of the parties under this Agreement will survive the termination of any Transaction.

(d) ***Remedies Cumulative.*** Except as provided in this Agreement, the rights, powers, remedies and privileges provided in this Agreement are cumulative and not exclusive of any rights, powers, remedies and privileges provided by law.

(e) ***Counterparts and Confirmations.***

(i) This Agreement (and each amendment, modification and waiver in respect of it) may be executed and delivered in counterparts (including by facsimile transmission), each of which will be deemed an original.

(ii) The parties intend that they are legally bound by the terms of each Transaction from the moment they agree to those terms (whether orally or otherwise). A Confirmation shall be entered into as soon as practicable and may be executed and delivered in counterparts (including by facsimile transmission) or be created by an exchange of telexes or by an exchange of electronic messages on an electronic messaging system, which in each case will be sufficient for all purposes to evidence a binding supplement to this Agreement. The parties will specify therein or through another effective means that any such counterpart, telex or electronic message constitutes a Confirmation.

(f) ***No Waiver of Rights.*** A failure or delay in exercising any right, power or privilege in respect of this Agreement will not be presumed to operate as a waiver, and a single or partial exercise of any right, power or privilege will not be presumed to preclude any subsequent or further exercise, of that right, power or privilege or the exercise of any other right, power or privilege.

(g) ***Headings.*** The headings used in this Agreement are for convenience of reference only and are not to affect the construction of or to be taken into consideration in interpreting this Agreement.

Section 9

Section 9(a)

The ISDA Master Agreement is stated as forming the entire agreement between the parties and supersedes all previous oral and written communications.

Section 9(b)

Amendments (communicated by a variety of traditional means) are only effective if in writing and executed by both parties. Alternatively this can take place through the exchange of telexes or electronic messages. This does not include e-mails.

Section 9(c)

This provision is self-explanatory, but note that Transactions subject to early termination are excluded from it. Section 2(a)(iii) and Section 6(c)(ii) respectively introduce conditions precedent and the replacement of normal payment and delivery obligations by a close-out regime. These provisions therefore limit survival of obligations which is why the Agreement wording was drafted this way.

Section 9(d)

It should be remembered that termination is not the sole remedy of a Non-defaulting Party. It also has the options of leaving the Agreement in place or seeking specific performance of its counterparty's obligations where monetary compensation is not sufficient, e.g. where physical delivery of a share or commodity is required.

Section 9(e)

Parties may execute and deliver in counterparts an Agreement, amendment, modification and waiver and transmit the same by fax. Each document will be regarded as an original.

Parties are legally bound by the terms of each Transaction from the moment they agree to them (orally or otherwise). A Confirmation should follow as soon as possible and may be executed in counterparts using traditional or electronic means of communication but not e-mail.

Section 9(f)

Variations of this standard provision are also commonly seen in loan agreements. No precedent is set if a full or partial waiver is exercised in respect of any right, power or privilege under the Agreement.

Section 9(g)

Headings in the Agreement are for convenience only and do not affect its interpretation.

10. Offices; Multibranch Parties

(a) If Section 10(a) is specified in the Schedule as applying, each party that enters into a Transaction through an Office other than its head or home office represents to the other party that, notwithstanding the place of booking office or jurisdiction of incorporation or organisation of such party, the obligations of such party are the same as if it had entered into the Transaction through its head or home office. This representation will be deemed to be repeated by such party on each date on which a Transaction is entered into.

(b) Neither party may change the Office through which it makes and receives payments or deliveries for the purpose of a Transaction without the prior written consent of the other party.

(c) If a party is specified as a Multibranch Party in the Schedule, such Multibranch Party may make and receive payments or deliveries under any Transaction through any Office listed in the Schedule, and the Office through which it makes and receives payments or deliveries with respect to a Transaction will be specified in the relevant Confirmation.

Section 10

Section 10(a)

Parties must choose in Part 4(c) of the Schedule if they want Section 10(a) to apply. Section 10(a) stipulates that both parties may have recourse to each other's Head Office regardless of the credit or political risk of branches through which they are transacting should a default occur under the Agreement.

Parties to an Agreement may regard Transactions entered into through their branches as equivalent to Transactions entered into through their Head Offices. This represents an implied payment or performance guarantee to their counterparty.

This representation, if stipulated in Part 4(c) of the Schedule as applying, relates to all parties and not only Multibranch Parties. The representation is also repeated by a party on each date on which a Transaction is undertaken. The giving of this representation was automatic in the 1987 Agreement but now parties can choose if it will apply. If a Multibranch Party does not want this provision to apply, then it is seeking to shift the political risk of dealing with its overseas branch on to its counterparty. It is therefore vital where this is agreed that the branch is located in a jurisdiction favourable to close-out netting.

Some banks believe their counterparties should bear this risk in the same way they would have to accept it if they dealt with a local bank in the same country.

Section 10(b)

Section 10(b) prevents a party from changing the Office through which it makes and receives payments or deliveries without the other party's written consent beforehand in order to avoid, *inter alia*, possible unfavourable tax consequences for the other party. Booking offices may also be relevant for the payment netting provisions in Section 2(c). Although not stated here, Section 6(b)(ii) probably overrides this as a party cannot unreasonably refuse consent to a transfer to avoid a Section 5(b)(i)–(iii) Termination Event.

Section 10(c)

If a party wants to make and receive payments under different Transactions through different Offices, it should be nominated in Part 4(d) of the Schedule as a Multibranch Party and the addresses of all such Offices should be listed in Part 4(a) of the Schedule. The relevant Office for each Transaction should also be stated in the Confirmation.

11. Expenses

A Defaulting Party will, on demand, indemnify and hold harmless the other party for and against all reasonable out-of-pocket expenses, including legal fees and Stamp Tax, incurred by such other party by reason of the enforcement and protection of its rights under this Agreement or any Credit Support Document to which the Defaulting Party is a party or by reason of the early termination of any Transaction, including, but not limited to, costs of collection.

Section 11

The expenses referred to in this Section are different to those incurred on early termination in Section 6(e)(iv).

This Section requires a Defaulting Party to pay certain reasonable out-of-pocket expenses (including legal fees and stamp duties) incurred by the Non-defaulting Party when enforcing and protecting its rights under an Agreement or any Credit Support Document given by the Defaulting Party. However, the Section does not specifically provide for the payment of expenses arising from the enforcement and protection of rights under any third party Credit Support Document and it is therefore necessary to check that such a Credit Support Document contains an acceptable indemnity for expenses.

Note that the Section 6(e)(iv) prohibition on recovering consequential losses is not intended to prevent recovery of the expenses specified in Section 11.

However, Section 11 legal fees and out-of-pocket expenses are excluded in the definition of Loss in Section 14.

12. Notices

(a) ***Effectiveness.*** Any notice or other communication in respect of this Agreement may be given in any manner set forth below (except that a notice or other communication under Section 5 or 6 may not be given by facsimile transmission or electronic messaging system) to the address or number or in accordance with the electronic messaging system details provided (see the Schedule) and will be deemed effective as indicated:-

(i) if in writing and delivered in person or by courier, on the date it is delivered;

(ii) if sent by telex, on the date the recipient's answerback is received;

(iii) if sent by facsimile transmission, on the date that transmission is received by a responsible employee of the recipient in legible form (it being agreed that the burden of proving receipt will be on the sender and will not be met by a transmission report generated by the sender's facsimile machine);

(iv) if sent by certified or registered mail (airmail, if overseas) or the equivalent (return receipt requested), on the date that mail is delivered or its delivery is attempted; or

(v) if sent by electronic messaging system, on the date that electronic message is received,

unless the date of that delivery (or attempted delivery) or that receipt, as applicable, is not a Local Business Day or that communication is delivered (or attempted) or received, as applicable, after the close of business on a Local Business Day, in which case that communication shall be deemed given and effective on the first following day that is a Local Business Day.

(b) ***Change of Addresses.*** Either party may by notice to the other change the address, telex or facsimile number or electronic messaging system details at which notices or other communications are to be given to it.

Section 12

Section 12 states the means by which any notice or communication in connection with an Agreement may be made, including by fax or electronic messaging systems which does not include e-mail. Notices relating to Section 5 or 6 may not be given by fax or electronic messaging system because an original signature is necessary for them.

Section 12(a)

Section 12(a) defines when receipt is considered to take place with the recipient. As regards a fax (Section 12(a)(iii)), its receipt is only effective on the date a responsible employee receives the fax in legible form. The sender has to prove receipt and a transmission report from a fax machine is not good enough for this purpose. There is no definition of who is a responsible employee and any doubts about this could affect the timing of receipt of the notice. A permitted electronic message is effective on receipt. If the date of delivery or receipt is not a Local Business Day or takes place after close of business on a Local Business Day, then it will only become effective on the next following Local Business Day.

Section 12(b)

Changes to relevant addresses, numbers or electronic messaging details specified in Part 4(a) of the Schedule to the Agreement may be made by either party notifying the other in any of the prescribed forms under sub-section (a) above.

13. Governing Law and Jurisdiction

(a) ***Governing Law***. This Agreement will be governed by and construed in accordance with the law specified in the Schedule.

(b) ***Jurisdiction***. With respect to any suit, action or proceedings relating to this Agreement ("Proceedings"), each party irrevocably:-

(i) submits to the jurisdiction of the English courts, if this Agreement is expressed to be governed by English law, or to the non-exclusive jurisdiction of the courts of the State of New York and the United States District Court located in the Borough of Manhattan in New York City, if this Agreement is expressed to be governed by the laws of the State of New York; and

(ii) waives any objection which it may have at any time to the laying of venue of any Proceedings brought in any such court, waives any claim that such Proceedings have been brought in an inconvenient forum and further waives the right to object, with respect to such Proceedings, that such court does not have any jurisdiction over such party.

Nothing in this Agreement precludes either party from bringing Proceedings in any other jurisdiction (outside, if this Agreement is expressed to be governed by English law, the Contracting States, as defined in Section 1(3) of the Civil Jurisdiction and Judgments Act 1982 or any modification, extension or re-enactment thereof for the time being in force) nor will the bringing of Proceedings in any one or more jurisdictions preclude the bringing of Proceedings in any other jurisdiction.

Section 13

Section 13(a)

Parties to the Agreement choose its governing law in Part 4(h) of the Schedule. The Agreement offers a choice between English law and the laws of the State of New York because it was composed with the requirements of the common law codes of those jurisdictions in mind. Where it is proposed that the governing law is to be other than English law or the laws of the State of New York, this should be the subject of specific legal advice. There are no real exceptions to this because it is vital to ensure that the Agreement (and particularly its close-out netting provisions) are effective under any law other than English or New York law. It is conceivable that two parties might enter into a Local Currency Master Agreement where they are both located in the same jurisdiction and only entering Transactions in their own local currency but this is a comparatively rare occurrence.

Section 13(b)

Section 13(b) provides that the parties submit to the jurisdiction of the English courts if English law is chosen and to the jurisdiction of the courts of the State of New York and the US District Court located in the Borough of Manhattan in New York if New York law is selected. Waivers of objection to venue, inconvenient forum and objection to questioning the court's jurisdiction are also included. The submission to the jurisdiction of the New York courts is non-exclusive which means that actions may be commenced in other courts. The submission to the jurisdiction of the English courts is exclusive as far as courts of the Contracting States of the European Union are concerned and non-exclusive for other courts. This complies with the provisions of the English Civil Jurisdiction and Judgments Act 1982.

(c) ***Service of Process***. Each party irrevocably appoints the Process Agent (if any) specified opposite its name in the Schedule to receive, for it and on its behalf, service of process in any Proceedings. If for any reason any party's Process Agent is unable to act as such, such party will promptly notify the other party and within 30 days appoint a substitute process agent acceptable to the other party. The parties irrevocably consent to service of process given in the manner provided for notices in Section 12. Nothing in this Agreement will affect the right of either party to serve process in any other manner permitted by law.

(d) ***Waiver of Immunities***. Each party irrevocably waives, to the fullest extent permitted by applicable law, with respect to itself and its revenues and assets (irrespective of their use or intended use), all immunity on the grounds of sovereignty or other similar grounds from (i) suit, (ii) jurisdiction of any court, (iii) relief by way of injunction, order for specific performance or for recovery of property, (iv) attachment of its assets (whether before or after judgment) and (v) execution or enforcement of any judgment to which it or its revenues or assets might otherwise be entitled in any Proceedings in the courts of any jurisdiction and irrevocably agrees, to the extent permitted by applicable law, that it will not claim any such immunity in any Proceedings.

Section 13(c)

Process Agents for the receipt of writs or other legal documents, where applicable, are to be specified in Part 4(b) of the Schedule. They are necessary where a Defaulting Party cannot easily be served with the necessary legal papers required to commence legal proceedings in the jurisdiction whose laws govern the Agreement.

Section 13(c) states that each party also consents to service of process in the manner provided for notices in Section 12. However, certain means of providing notice in Section 12 may not be practical for serving process (e.g. telex or electronic messaging systems) and may not be a valid means of serving process in certain countries despite the parties' consent in Section 13(c). Section 13(c) also provides that where a party's Process Agent is unable to act, such party will promptly notify its counterparty and, by mutual agreement, appoint a substitute Process Agent within 30 days. Service of notice by a Process Agent can be very important where failure to serve process in a jurisdiction could result in a foreign judgment not being enforceable in that country.

Section 13(d)

Section 13(d) provides for a waiver of immunities from prosecution by the parties to the greatest extent permitted by applicable law. This provision is also common in loan agreements.

14. Definitions

As used in this Agreement:-

"***Additional Termination Event***" has the meaning specified in Section 5(b).

"***Affected Party***" has the meaning specified in Section 5(b).

"***Affected Transactions***" means (a) with respect to any Termination Event consisting of an Illegality, Tax Event or Tax Event Upon Merger, all Transactions affected by the occurrence of such Termination Event and (b) with respect to any other Termination Event, all Transactions.

"***Affiliate***" means, subject to the Schedule, in relation to any person, any entity controlled, directly or indirectly, by the person, any entity that controls, directly or indirectly, the person or any entity directly or indirectly under common control with the person. For this purpose, "control" of any entity or person means ownership of a majority of the voting power of the entity or person.

"***Applicable Rate***" means:-

(a) in respect of obligations payable or deliverable (or which would have been but for Section 2(a)(iii)) by a Defaulting Party, the Default Rate;

(b) in respect of an obligation to pay an amount under Section 6(e) of either party from and after the date, (determined in accordance with Section 6(d)(ii)) on which that amount is payable, the Default Rate;

(c) in respect of all other obligations payable or deliverable (or which would have been but for Section 2(a)(iii)) by a Non-defaulting Party, the Non-default Rate; and

(d) in all other cases, the Termination Rate.

"***Burdened Party***" has the meaning specified in Section 5(b).

"***Change in Tax Law***" means the enactment, promulgation, execution or ratification of, or any change in or amendment to, any tax law (or in the application or official interpretation of any law) that occurs on or after the date on which the relevant Transaction is entered into.

"***consent***" includes a consent, approval, action, authorisation, exemption, notice, filing, registration or exchange control consent.

"***Credit Event Upon Merger***" has the meaning specified in Section 5(b).

"***Credit Support Document***" means any agreement or instrument that is specified as such in this Agreement.

Section 14 – Definitions

All significant terms in the Agreement are defined, sometimes exhaustively, in Section 14. No doubt with the disapproval of lawyers, but with a big "government health warning" I set out below a simple glossary of most of these Definitions except where they are self-evident.

GLOSSARY OF MOST TERMS IN SECTION 14

Additional Termination Event	An extra Termination Event chosen by the parties, e.g. a change of control event or a credit ratings downgrade event.
Affected Party	The party at fault under a Termination Event.
Affected Transactions	The relevant Transactions affected by a Termination Event.
Affiliate	Essentially any other company or entity in a party's group.
Applicable Rate	The relevant interest rate in a series of penalty rates for late payment or delivery.
Burdened Party	The party afflicted or at fault (if it is the merging party) in the Tax Event Upon Merger Termination Event as the case may be.
Credit Event Upon Merger	A deterioration in the creditworthiness of a party to the Agreement following a merger type event.
Credit Support Document	A document securing a party's obligations under the Agreement provided either by the party itself or a third party (e.g. a guarantor).

"***Credit Support Provider***" has the meaning specified in the Schedule.

"***Default Rate***" means a rate per annum equal to the cost (without proof or evidence of any actual cost) to the relevant payee (as certified by it) if it were to fund or of funding the relevant amount plus 1% per annum.

"***Defaulting Party***" has the meaning specified in Section 6(a).

"***Early Termination Date***" means the date determined in accordance with Section 6(a) or 6(b)(iv).

"***Event of Default***" has the meaning specified in Section 5(a) and, if applicable, in the Schedule.

"***Illegality***" has the meaning specified in Section 5(b).

"***Indemnifiable Tax***" means any Tax other than a Tax that would not be imposed in respect of a payment under this Agreement but for a present or former connection between the jurisdiction of the government or taxation authority imposing such Tax and the recipient of such payment or a person related to such recipient (including, without limitation, a connection arising from such recipient or related person being or having been a citizen or resident of such jurisdiction, or being or having been organised, present or engaged in a trade or business in such jurisdiction, or having or having had a permanent establishment or fixed place of business in such jurisdiction, but excluding a connection arising solely from such recipient or related person having executed, delivered, performed its obligations or received a payment under, or enforced, this Agreement or a Credit Support Document).

"***law***" includes any treaty, law, rule or regulation (as modified, in the case of tax matters, by the practice of any relevant governmental revenue authority) and "***lawful***" and "***unlawful***" will be construed accordingly.

"***Local Business Day***" means, subject to the Schedule, a day on which commercial banks are open for business (including dealings in foreign exchange and foreign currency deposits) (a) in relation to any obligation under Section 2(a)(i), in the place(s) specified in the relevant Confirmation or, if not so specified, as otherwise agreed by the parties in writing or determined pursuant to provisions contained, or incorporated by reference, in this Agreement, (b) in relation to any other payment, in the place where the relevant account is located and, if different, in the principal financial centre, if any, of the currency of such payment, (c) in relation to any notice or other communication, including notice contemplated under Section 5(a)(i), in the city specified in the address for notice provided by the recipient and, in the case of a notice contemplated by Section 2(b), in the place where the relevant new account is to be located and (d) in relation to Section 5(a)(v)(2), in the relevant locations for performance with respect to such Specified Transaction.

Credit Support Provider	The party providing security under a Credit Support Document.
Default Rate	1% over the payee's cost of funds.
Defaulting Party	The party at fault under an Event of Default.
Early Termination Date	The date upon which close-out occurs.
Event of Default	One or more events in Section 5(a) of the Agreement which can trigger close-out of all Transactions with a Defaulting Party under the Agreement.
Illegality	Under Section 5(b)(i) an event which prevents lawful payment or performance under the Agreement or a Credit Support Document.
Indemnifiable Tax	Essentially a cross-border tax against which a party to the Agreement is entitled to be indemnified by the other party. It excludes domestic income, sales and capital taxes.
Local Business Day	A normal business day in the location required for the performance of various obligations under the Agreement.

"***Loss***" means, with respect to this Agreement or one or more Terminated Transactions, as the case may be, and a party, the Termination Currency Equivalent of an amount that party reasonably determines in good faith to be its total losses and costs (or gain, in which case expressed as a negative number) in connection with this Agreement or that Terminated Transaction or group of Terminated Transactions, as the case may be, including any loss of bargain, cost of funding or, at the election of such party but without duplication, loss or cost incurred as a result of its terminating, liquidating, obtaining or reestablishing any hedge or related trading position (or any gain resulting from any of them). Loss includes losses and costs (or gains) in respect of any payment or delivery required to have been made (assuming satisfaction of each applicable condition precedent) on or before the relevant Early Termination Date and not made, except, so as to avoid duplication, if Section 6(e)(i)(1) or (3) or 6(e)(ii)(2)(A) applies. Loss does not include a party's legal fees and out-of-pocket expenses referred to under Section 11. A party will determine its Loss as of the relevant Early Termination Date, or, if that is not reasonably practicable, as of the earliest date thereafter as is reasonably practicable. A party may (but need not) determine its Loss by reference to quotations of relevant rates or prices from one or more leading dealers in the relevant markets.

Loss	A party's good faith determination of its losses and costs (except legal fees and Section 11 expenses) minus its gains in respect of Terminated Transactions.

"***Market Quotation***" means, with respect to one or more Terminated Transactions and a party making the determination, an amount determined on the basis of quotations from Reference Market-makers. Each quotation will be for an amount, if any, that would be paid to such party (expressed as a negative number) or by such party (expressed as a positive number) in consideration of an agreement between such party (taking into account any existing Credit Support Document with respect to the obligations of such party) and the quoting Reference Market-maker to enter into a transaction (the "Replacement Transaction") that would have the effect of preserving for such party the economic equivalent of any payment or delivery (whether the underlying obligation was absolute or contingent and assuming the satisfaction of each applicable condition precedent) by the parties under Section 2(a)(i) in respect of such Terminated Transaction or group of Terminated Transactions that would, but for the occurrence of the relevant Early Termination Date, have been required after that date. For this purpose, Unpaid Amounts in respect of the Terminated Transaction or group of Terminated Transactions are to be excluded but, without limitation, any payment or delivery that would, but for the relevant Early Termination Date, have been required (assuming satisfaction of each applicable condition precedent) after that Early Termination Date is to be included. The Replacement Transaction would be subject to such documentation as such party and the Reference Market-maker may, in good faith, agree. The party making the determination (or its agent) will request each Reference Market-maker to provide its quotation to the extent reasonably practicable as of the same day and time (without regard to different time zones) on or as soon as reasonably practicable after the relevant Early Termination Date. The day and time as of which those quotations are to be obtained will be selected in good faith by the party obliged to make a determination under Section 6(e), and, if each party is so obliged, consultation with the other. If more than three quotations are provided, the Market Quotation will be the arithmetic mean of the quotations, without regard to the quotations having the highest and lowest values. If exactly three such quotations are provided, the Market Quotation will be the quotation remaining after disregarding the highest and lowest quotations. For this purpose, if more than one quotation has the same highest value or lowest value, then one of such quotations shall be disregarded. If fewer than three quotations are provided, it will be deemed that the Market Quotation in respect of such Terminated Transaction or group of Terminated Transactions cannot be determined.

Market Quotation	Replacement value of Terminated Transactions calculated by reference to quotations from Reference Market-makers. Fallback is Loss.

"***Non-default Rate***" means a rate per annum equal to the cost (without proof or evidence of any actual cost) to the Non-defaulting Party (as certified by it) if it were to fund the relevant amount.

"***Non-defaulting Party***" has the meaning specified in Section 6(a).

"***Office***" means a branch or office of a party, which may be such party's head or home office.

"***Potential Event of Default***" means any event which, with the giving of notice or the lapse of time or both, would constitute an Event of Default.

"***Reference Market-makers***" means four leading dealers in the relevant market selected by the party determining a Market Quotation in good faith (a) from among dealers of the highest credit standing which satisfy all the criteria that such party applies generally at the time in deciding whether to offer or to make an extension of credit and (b) to the extent practicable, from among such dealers having an office in the same city.

"***Relevant Jurisdiction***" means, with respect to a party, the jurisdictions (a) in which the party is incorporated, organised, managed and controlled or considered to have its seat, (b) where an Office through which the party is acting for purposes of this Agreement is located, (c) in which the party executes this Agreement and (d) in relation to any payment, from or through which such payment is made.

"***Scheduled Payment Date***" means a date on which a payment or delivery is to be made under Section 2(a)(i) with respect to a Transaction.

"***Set-off***" means set-off, offset, combination of accounts, right of retention or withholding or similar right or requirement to which the payer of an amount under Section 6 is entitled or subject (whether arising under this Agreement, another contract, applicable law or otherwise) that is exercised by, or imposed on, such payer.

Non-default Rate	The Non-defaulting Party's cost of funding.
Non-defaulting Party	The party not at fault in an Event of Default.
Office	A branch or office of a party including its head or home office.
Potential Event of Default	An event which would become an Event of Default if not cured within a grace period or if a default notice was issued in relation to it.
Reference Market-makers	Four leading dealers in the relevant market satisfactory to the party seeking the Market Quotations.
Scheduled Payment Date	The date on which a normal payment or delivery under a Transaction is due.
Set-Off	The right to net other amounts owing by the two parties to the Agreement to each other after calculation of the close-out amount on the Early Termination Date.

"***Settlement Amount***" means, with respect to a party and any Early Termination Date, the sum of:-

(a) the Termination Currency Equivalent of the Market Quotations (whether positive or negative) for each Terminated Transaction or group of Terminated Transactions for which a Market Quotation is determined; and

(b) such party's Loss (whether positive or negative and without reference to any Unpaid Amounts) for each Terminated Transaction or group of Terminated Transactions for which a Market Quotation cannot be determined or would not (in the reasonable belief of the party making the determination) produce a commercially reasonable result.

"***Specified Entity***" has the meaning specified in the Schedule.

"***Specified Indebtedness***" means, subject to the Schedule, any obligation (whether present or future, contingent or otherwise, as principal or surety or otherwise) in respect of borrowed money.

"***Specified Transaction***" means, subject to the Schedule, (a) any transaction (including an agreement with respect thereto) now existing or hereafter entered into between one party to this Agreement (or any Credit Support Provider of such party or any applicable Specified Entity of such party) and the other party to this Agreement (or any Credit Support Provider of such other party or any applicable Specified Entity of such other party) which is a rate swap transaction, basis swap, forward rate transaction, commodity swap, commodity option, equity or equity index swap, equity or equity index option, bond option, interest rate option, foreign exchange transaction, cap transaction, floor transaction, collar transaction, currency swap transaction, cross-currency rate swap transaction, currency option or any other similar transaction (including any option with respect to any of these transactions), (b) any combination of these transactions and (c) any other transaction identified as a Specified Transaction in this Agreement or the relevant confirmation.

"***Stamp Tax***" means any stamp, registration, documentation or similar tax.

"***Tax***" means any present or future tax, levy, impost, duty, charge, assessment or fee of any nature (including interest, penalties and additions thereto) that is imposed by any government or other taxing authority in respect of any payment under this Agreement other than a stamp, registration, documentation or similar tax.

"***Tax Event***" has the meaning specified in Section 5(b).

Settlement Amount	The Non-defaulting Party's or the non-Affected Party's determination of the close-out amount taking into account Market Quotation and Unpaid Amounts or Loss. The net sum to be paid over on the Early Termination Date.
Specified Entity	An entity a party wants to join to certain Section 5 events named in Part 1(a) of the Schedule.
Specified Indebtedness	Borrowed money.
Specified Transaction	One of a list of OTC derivatives Transactions between the two parties to the Agreement or their Specified Entities or Credit Support Providers but which are outside of the Agreement.
Tax Event	The Termination Event in Section 5(b)(ii) which can conditionally trigger termination of Affected Transactions due to adverse changes in tax law or their implementation by tax authorities or courts.

"***Tax Event Upon Merger***" has the meaning specified in Section 5(b).

"***Terminated Transactions***" means with respect to any Early Termination Date (a) if resulting from a Termination Event, all Affected Transactions and (b) if resulting from an Event of Default, all Transactions (in either case) in effect immediately before the effectiveness of the notice designating that Early Termination Date (or, if "Automatic Early Termination" applies, immediately before that Early Termination Date).

"***Termination Currency***" has the meaning specified in the Schedule.

"***Termination Currency Equivalent***" means, in respect of any amount denominated in the Termination Currency, such Termination Currency amount and, in respect of any amount denominated in a currency other than the Termination Currency (the "Other Currency"), the amount in the Termination Currency determined by the party making the relevant determination as being required to purchase such amount of such Other Currency as at the relevant Early Termination Date, or, if the relevant Market Quotation or Loss (as the case may be), is determined as of a later date, that later date, with the Termination Currency at the rate equal to the spot exchange rate of the foreign exchange agent (selected as provided below) for the purchase of such Other Currency with the Termination Currency at or about 11:00 a.m. (in the city in which such foreign exchange agent is located) on such date as would be customary for the determination of such a rate for the purchase of such Other Currency for value on the relevant Early Termination Date or that later date. The foreign exchange agent will, if only one party is obliged to make a determination under Section 6(e), be selected in good faith by that party and otherwise will be agreed by the parties.

"***Termination Event***" means an Illegality, a Tax Event or a Tax Event Upon Merger or, if specified to be applicable, a Credit Event Upon Merger or an Additional Termination Event.

"***Termination Rate***" means a rate per annum equal to the arithmetic mean of the cost (without proof or evidence of any actual cost) to each party (as certified by such party) if it were to fund or of funding such amounts.

Tax Event Upon Merger	The Termination Event in Section 5(b)(iii) which conditionally can trigger termination of Affected Transactions due to adverse changes in tax law or their implementation by tax authorities and which affect one party to the Agreement where its counterparty has merged with a third party.
Terminated Transactions	Transactions terminated or to be terminated on the Early Termination Date.
Termination Currency	The currency (selected in Part 1(g) of the Schedule) into which all Transactions are converted when calculating a final close-out amount on the Early Termination Date.
Termination Currency Equivalent	The equivalent value of the Terminated Transactions in the Termination Currency chosen in Part 1(g) of the Schedule.
Termination Event	The events in Section 5(b) which can trigger close-out.
Termination Rate	In a no fault termination, the arithmetic mean of the funding costs of both parties.

"***Unpaid Amounts***" owing to any party means, with respect to an Early Termination Date, the aggregate of (a) in respect of all Terminated Transactions, the amounts that became payable (or that would have become payable but for Section 2(a)(iii)) to such party under Section 2(a)(i) on or prior to such Early Termination Date and which remain unpaid as at such Early Termination Date and (b) in respect of each Terminated Transaction, for each obligation under Section 2(a)(i) which was (or would have been but for Section 2(a)(iii)) required to be settled by delivery to such party on or prior to such Early Termination Date and which has not been so settled as at such Early Termination Date, an amount equal to the fair market value of that which was (or would have been) required to be delivered as of the originally scheduled date for delivery, in each case together with (to the extent permitted under applicable law) interest, in the currency of such amounts, from (and including) the date such amounts or obligations were or would have been required to have been paid or performed to (but excluding) such Early Termination Date, at the Applicable Rate. Such amounts of interest will be calculated on the basis of daily compounding and the actual number of days elapsed. The fair market value of any obligation referred to in clause (b) above shall be reasonably determined by the party obliged to make the determination under Section 6(e) or, if each party is so obliged, it shall be the average of the Termination Currency Equivalents of the fair market values reasonably determined by both parties.

Unpaid Amounts	Payments or deliveries due to a party on a Scheduled Payment Date which remain unpaid due to an Early Termination Date occurring, plus interest. Unpaid Amounts are used in close-out calculations.

IN WITNESS WHEREOF the parties have executed this document on the respective dates specified below with effect from the date specified on the first page of this document.

By:...	By:...
(Name of Party)	(Name of Party)
Name:	Name:
Title:	Title:
Date:	Date:

Signature Block

The name of each party and the names and titles of signatories must be filled in on the signature page along with the dates of signing by each signatory. The main text of the Master Agreement must be signed. A Schedule can, but need not, be signed.

The pre-printed text of the Master Agreement ends on page 18. A Schedule is always attached and begins on page 19.

The Schedule is where provisions in the ISDA Master Agreement are amended or added through negotiation. We shall examine the Schedule in Chapter 8.

The 2002 ISDA Master Agreement

4

Evolution of the 2002 ISDA Master Agreement

Section by section analysis of the 2002 ISDA Master Agreement

Glossary of most terms in Section 14

Analysis of Schedule

What did not make it into the 2002 Agreement

Likely implementation of the 2002 Agreement

EVOLUTION OF THE 2002 ISDA MASTER AGREEMENT

The 2002 ISDA Master Agreement (the "2002 Agreement") was published by ISDA on 8 January 2003. The review and drafting process which created this document took 12 months. This is less than 50% of the time it took to draft the 1992 Agreement from the 1987 Interest Rate and Currency Exchange Agreement. So it took half the time to create a document which is 50% longer than its predecessor. About 100 of ISDA's 600 member firms took part in the process.

We shall be looking at the main changes later but for those who like statistics comparing the 2002 Agreement with the 1992 Agreement, there were 1,025 changes between the documents. These consist of 618 additions, 353 deletions and 54 transfers of wording.

The genesis of the 2002 ISDA Master Agreement lay in a Strategic Documentation Review which ISDA started conducting in late 1999 and which, as far as the ISDA Master Agreement is concerned, stemmed from three factors:

- **the Agreement was nearly seven years old then;**
- **experiences from the 1997 currency crises in Asia and the 1998 Russian debt default;**
- **the risk management recommendations of the Counterparty Risk Management Policy Group ("G12") report called *Improving Counterparty Risk Management Practices* published in June 1999.**

The real impetus for this Review arose from turmoil in various Asian economies in 1997 and the following events in 1998:

- **the failure of the Hong Kong broker-dealer Peregrine Investments Holdings Limited;**
- **exchange controls imposed by the Malaysian central bank on the ringgit;**
- **the 90 day moratorium imposed by the Russian government in August 1998 on certain foreign payments by Russian residents; and**
- **the crisis at major hedge fund, Long Term Capital Management, in September 1998. A bank consortium stepped in due to fears of systemic risk (i.e. collapse) in the derivatives markets.**

These events stress tested ISDA documentation with varying intensity and led to ISDA's Strategic Documentation Review which also covered the 1991 Definitions and existing credit support documents.

In January 1999, the Counterparty Risk Management Policy Group ("CRMPG") was set up by 12 international and commercial banks to review the events of 1997/98 and to recommend enhancements to counterparty credit and risk management practices. As well as the banks, representatives from the Federal Reserve Bank of New York, The Bond Market Association, The Emerging Markets Traders Association, The Security Industry Association, The Financial Lawyers Group and some ISDA members all participated in the CRMPG.

In June 1999, it published its report – *Improving Counterparty Risk Management Practices.*

The report contained a section on documentation policies and practices especially in troubled markets. It noted that variations in events of default, grace periods, close-out, valuation and notice provisions among the various types of master agreements used in the markets created documentation basis risk because of their inconsistencies. The risk arises where economically similar transactions are documented under different master agreements which may have varying valuation and termination provisions and produce different economic results on close-out.

The G12 Report supported harmonisation of standard form market documentation wherever practicable. This lead to ISDA working on various bridge agreements which would enable non-defaulting parties to terminate all types of market documentation at the same time and to net off all individual termination amounts under these agreements against each other as far as the law permitted. The various ISDA bridge agreements, e.g. the 2001 Cross-Agreement Bridge permit close-out amounts under other agreements to be netted off against the close-out amount under the ISDA Master Agreement to produce a net net figure payable to one party or the other. The revised provisions of Section 5(a)(v) Default under Specified Transaction in the 2002 Agreement also help to achieve this.

The language of the various ISDA Bridges can be incorporated in Part 5 of a Schedule.

In the light of all this, ISDA's Strategic Documentation Review decided to focus on the following four key areas:

- **termination, valuation and close-out issues arising from the 1992 Agreement;**
- **force majeure, impossibility and sovereign risk issues which were not really addressed in the 1992 Agreement;**
- **structural issues and means of extending close-out netting to other products or linking into other master agreements for this purpose primarily through bridge agreements; and**
- **a review of existing credit support documents.**

As a result of this and in connection with the Agreement various groups had drafted a total of 14 Annexes for use with a Protocol by November 2001. However, the project was abandoned then because it was becoming too complex and it was decided to produce a new draft ISDA Master Agreement (the "2002 Agreement") which was first circulated to members on 27 November 2001. This went through several mass meetings and six drafts before being published on 8 January 2003.

Its publication has resulted in the revised ISDA documentation architecture structure which was shown as Figure 2.1 in Chapter 2 page 21.

ISDA recommends the use of the 2002 Agreement for new Agreements and for implementing the 2002 documentation architecture into existing contractual arrangements. This can, of course, be achieved by replacing a 1992 Agreement by a 2002 Agreement. ISDA has also published a bilateral Amendment which replaces Market Quotation and Loss in the Section 6(e) termination arrangements by a single payment measure of Close-out Amount. This Amendment is reproduced as Annex 3 by the kind permission of the International Swaps and Derivatives Association, Inc.

SECTION BY SECTION ANALYSIS OF THE 2002 ISDA MASTER AGREEMENT

The revision of the ISDA Master Agreement has been uneven but the principal changes are in Sections 5, 6, 9, 10, 12 and the Schedule.

I think rather than just picking out the changes it would be more sensible to go through the 2002 Agreement section by section so that we obtain a complete picture of how it hangs together. Therefore, there will be some repetition of points made in Chapter 3 as where the Agreement text has not changed between the two versions neither will the commentary.

The main interpretative document for the 2002 ISDA Master Agreement is the *User's Guide to the 2002 ISDA Master Agreement (the User's Guide)*, which was published in July 2003. It describes:

- **how the ISDA Master Agreement evolved;**
- **gives technical interpretations and reasoning for the provisions; and**
- **mentions areas where agreement was not reached by the Working Group.**

The *User's Guide* has a wealth of information but its language can at times be complex and it is likely that many of its users may not be legal or tax technicians, nor speak English as their first language. The following section by section interpretation of the 2002 Agreement should, I hope, therefore be useful.

ISDA®

International Swap Dealers Association, Inc.

2002 MASTER AGREEMENT

dated as of ....

.... and ....

have entered and/or anticipate entering into one or more transactions (each a "Transaction") that are or will be governed by this Master Agreement, which includes the schedule (the "Schedule"), and the documents and other confirming evidence (each a "Confirmation") exchanged between the parties or otherwise effective for the purpose of confirming or evidencing those Transactions. This 2002 Master Agreement and the Schedule are together referred to as this "Master Agreement".

Preamble

First of all the words "Multicurrency-Cross Border" in the top left hand corner of the Agreement have been deleted because this is now the only version of the Agreement. There is to be no Single Currency-Local Jurisdiction version of the 2002 Agreement.

The 2002 Agreement starts by being expressed as "dated as of". It is customary to date the Agreement and its Schedule as of the date of the first trade between the parties even if the Agreement is not signed until some months later. This is based on US practice where the words "as of" mean "with effect from" a specified date. This is contrary to best English practice where it is normal to date an agreement on the day it is signed. Under English law you cannot create a contract retrospectively through backdating it. If you do, you run the high risk of it being considered a forgery. To avoid misleading any court, the preamble to the signing block on page 28 makes it clear that the "as of" date is merely the effective date. The signing block records the date upon which the Agreement is actually signed.

The two parties then enter their full legal names and can add details of their nature and the jurisdictions where they were incorporated. If cited, this would also be repeated on the first page of the Schedule.

Then there is a statement that the parties have entered or propose to enter into Transactions under the Agreement which includes its Schedule (used to add to or amend the basic Agreement provisions and which is what negotiators negotiate) and any Confirmations exchanged between the parties. This is the basis for the parties' contractual relationship and is important for the single agreement concept as we shall see shortly in Section 1(c).

It is made clear that the Agreement can cover transactions entered into before it was executed.

The reference to "or otherwise effective for the purpose of confirming or evidencing those Transactions" covers both electronic Confirmations which are not so much exchanged between the parties as communicated from one to the other and where only one party issues a Confirmation or other confirming evidence. In that case no exchange occurs at all.

However, it should be borne in mind that Confirmations entered into other than by way of written and signed documents may fall foul of statute of frauds or other legislation in some jurisdictions and this should be checked. These would include Confirmations using FpML mark-up language.

Market practice is not to make changes directly on to the pre-printed Agreement text (although this was sometimes done in the early days of the market) but rather in the Schedule. This avoids the need to search the pre-printed text for changes when reviewing it at a later date.

Principal changes from the 1992 Agreement

- Deletion of Multicurrency-Cross Border because this is the only version of the 2002 Agreement;
- Updating of ISDA's full name;
- Reference to the 2002 Master Agreement;
- Electronic and unilaterally issued Confirmations point;
- Emphasis on the 2002 Master Agreement and its Schedule together constituting this "Master Agreement".

Accordingly, the parties agree as follows:-

1. Interpretation

(a) ***Definitions.*** The terms defined in Section 14 and elsewhere will have the meanings therein specified for the purpose of this Master Agreement.

(b) ***Inconsistency.*** In the event of any inconsistency between the provisions of the Schedule and the other provisions of this Master Agreement, the Schedule will prevail. In the event of any inconsistency between the provisions of any Confirmation and this Master Agreement, such Confirmation will prevail for the purpose of the relevant Transaction.

(c) ***Single Agreement.*** All Transactions are entered into in reliance on the fact that this Master Agreement and all Confirmations form a single agreement between the parties (collectively referred to as this "Agreement"), and the parties would not otherwise enter into any Transactions.

Section 1 – Interpretation

Section 1(a)

Defined terms which appear in Section 14 and elsewhere in the Agreement including its Schedule will have their relevant meanings for the purpose of the Agreement.

Section 1(b)

Where there is any inconsistency between the Agreement text and the Schedule, the Schedule will prevail. Where there is a conflict between a Confirmation and the Master Agreement, the Confirmation will prevail in respect of the relevant Transaction. This gives the Confirmation supremacy in respect of individual deals.

Section 1(c)

The single agreement concept is vitally important and is the basis of close-out netting. Section 1(c) states that all Transactions are entered into relying upon the fact that the Master Agreement and all Confirmations under it form a single agreement between the parties and they would not have entered into these Transactions otherwise.

What this means is that each Confirmation is not treated as a separate agreement between the parties. Therefore, in a close-out situation, the values of all Transactions between the parties are calculated and netted off against each other so as to produce a single figure payable one way or the other. In an insolvency situation this prevents a liquidator cherrypicking, i.e. making payments on those Transactions which are profitable to his insolvent client and refusing to do so on other Transactions which are not profitable to them. A liquidator cannot do this if all the Transactions are collapsed into a single payment due to one party or the other. In other words there is then only one cherry. The single agreement concept reinforces this position.

Principal changes from the 1992 Agreement

- **Section 1(a) – some defined terms are now made in the body of the Agreement text rather than just in Section 14 or the Schedule (e.g. Multiple Transaction Payment Netting or Additional Representation).**
- **Section 1(b) – Deletion of "including the Schedule" after "Master Agreement" in line 3. This is not necessary because of the statement in the last sentence of the preamble.**
- **Section 1(c) – None.**

2. Obligations

(a) ***General Conditions.***

(i) Each party will make each payment or delivery specified in each Confirmation to be made by it, subject to the other provisions of this Agreement.

(ii) Payments under this Agreement will be made on the due date for value on that date in the place of the account specified in the relevant Confirmation or otherwise pursuant to this Agreement, in freely transferable funds and in the manner customary for payments in the required currency. Where settlement is by delivery (that is, other than by payment), such delivery will be made for receipt on the due date in the manner customary for the relevant obligation unless otherwise specified in the relevant Confirmation or elsewhere in this Agreement.

(iii) Each obligation of each party under Section 2(a)(i) is subject to (1) the condition precedent that no Event of Default or Potential Event of Default with respect to the other party has occurred and is continuing, (2) the condition precedent that no Early Termination Date in respect of the relevant Transaction has occurred or been effectively designated and (3) each other condition specified in this Agreement to be a condition precedent for the purpose of this Section 2(a)(iii).

Section 2 – Obligations

Section 2(a)

(a)(i) This is a simple statement that each party will make each payment or delivery required from it under the relevant Confirmation unless other terms of the Agreement (e.g. Early Termination provisions) intervene. The numerous references to "delivery" in the Agreement cover Transactions which are settled by physical delivery (i.e. delivery of a share or commodity instead of cash) which can also be covered by the Agreement. However, the Agreement itself cannot fully document physically settled Transactions which is why Confirmations for them are very detailed. However, the coverage is better than it was in the 1992 Agreement as we shall see.

(a)(ii) This is a general statement to the effect that payments and deliveries will be made promptly, in freely transferable funds and in the customary manner in the place of settlement unless otherwise agreed in a Confirmation or elsewhere in the Agreement.

(a)(iii) This means that normal payments or deliveries under Section 2(a)(i) will stop if an Event of Default or Potential Event of Default (an event which could lead to an Event of Default if it develops) occurs to one of the parties or if an Early Termination Date (when close-out calculations are made) is designated for a Termination Event or if any other condition precedent (e.g. the provision of credit support) in the Agreement is unfulfilled.

Please note that under Section 2(a)(iii)(1) the default could be outside the Agreement, e.g. non-payment of indebtedness under another agreement which might trigger the Cross Default clause in this Agreement.

Section 2(a)(iii)(3) of the Agreement makes clear that if people want to stipulate any condition precedent other than the standard ones in Section 2(a)(iii)(1) and (2) they must clearly add the wording that the relevant condition will be "a condition precedent for the purpose of Section 2(a)(iii)". This might be stated in Part 3(b) of the Schedule or possibly in Part 5 or even in a Confirmation. Effectively, this narrows the scope of the corresponding provision of the 1992 Agreement where no such statement was necessary.

Any payments withheld because of the events in section 2(a)(iii) will be treated as Unpaid Amounts under the Section 6 close-out calculations (see page 235).

(b) ***Change of Account.*** Either party may change its account for receiving a payment or delivery by giving notice to the other party at least five Local Business Days prior to the Scheduled Settlement Date for the payment or delivery to which such change applies unless such other party gives timely notice of a reasonable objection to such change.

Section 2(b)

One party to the Agreement may give the other at least five Local Business Days' notice of a change in its account for payments or deliveries. This notice period is calculated in the Local Business Days of the place where the new account is to be located. The other party may object to this (there is a reasonableness standard) by giving notice to the first party. It might do this if such a change of account is to an overseas Office of the first party and a withholding tax charge might arise. It might also object to an overseas transfer of account if there was a risk of exchange controls being imposed.

Principal changes from the 1992 Agreement

- **None until Section 2(a)(iii)(3).**
- **Section 2(a)(iii)(3) – Narrowing of scope of other conditions precedent which now need to be specified as applying for the purposes of Section 2(a)(iii).**
- **Section 2(b) – Tautological use of new defined term – Scheduled Settlement Date.**

(c) ***Netting of Payments***. If on any date amounts would otherwise be payable:-

(i) in the same currency; and

(ii) in respect of the same Transaction,

by each party to the other, then, on such date, each party's obligation to make payment of any such amount will be automatically satisfied and discharged and, if the aggregate amount that would otherwise have been payable by one party exceeds the aggregate amount that would otherwise have been payable by the other party, replaced by an obligation upon the party by whom the larger aggregate amount would have been payable to pay to the other party the excess of the larger aggregate amount over the smaller aggregate amount.

The parties may elect in respect of two or more Transactions that a net amount and payment obligation will be determined in respect of all amounts payable on the same date in the same currency in respect of such Transactions, regardless of whether such amounts are payable in respect of the same Transaction. The election may be made in the Schedule or a Confirmation by specifying that "Multiple Transaction Payment Netting" applies to the Transactions identified as being subject to the election (in which case clause (ii) above will not apply to such Transactions). If Multiple Transaction Payment Netting is applicable to Transactions, it will apply to those Transactions with effect from the starting date specified in the Schedule or such Confirmation, or if a starting date is not specified in the Schedule or such Confirmation, the starting date otherwise agreed by the parties in writing.This election may be made separately for different groups of Transactions and will apply separately to each pairing of Offices through which the parties make and receive payments or deliveries.

Section 2(c)

Section 2(c) of the Agreement is about payment or settlement netting and aims to reduce settlement risk – sometimes called daylight risk.

The basic ISDA position is that payments can be made net if they are in the same currency, for the same Transaction and payable on the same date. This means that both parties do not have to make payments to each other, but the one who owes the most pays the difference between the two amounts to the other party. This avoids the inconvenience of each party making a gross payment to the other and also reduces settlement risk (i.e. that one party will fail to make its payment after the other party has done so).

The basic payment netting position is therefore single Transaction netting, i.e. same Transaction, same currency and same value date.

Previously in the 1992 Agreement if you did not want this to apply you stated in Part 4(i) of the Schedule that "Sub-paragraph (ii) of Section 2(c) of the Agreement will not apply to all Transactions". This enabled you to payment net more than one of the same type of Transaction (e.g. interest rate swaps) or across different products (e.g. currency swaps and forward foreign exchange transactions) where payments in the same currency on the same day were involved.

Instead of making a negative election to achieve this effect, you can now elect positively for Multiple Transaction Payment Netting to apply in Part 4(i) of the Schedule from a starting date agreed in the Schedule, a Confirmation or a side letter.

It is still possible to apply these payment or delivery netting arrangements to each pairing of the parties' Offices. They cannot be applied multilaterally.

Indeed the provisions are very flexible but you should only really agree to what you can actually do operationally or you could incur operational risk.

The legal drafting is much better and the overall position much clearer than before.

Principal changes from the 1992 Agreement

- **Section now entitled "Netting of Payments" rather than just "Netting".**
- **We are reminded that the net amount calculated in respect of the netting of obligations under two or more Transactions is also a payment obligation.**
- **A positive election can now be made in the Schedule for Multiple Transaction Payment Netting to apply from an agreed starting date.**

(d) ***Deduction or Withholding for Tax.***

(i) ***Gross-Up.*** All payments under this Agreement will be made without any deduction or withholding for or on account of any Tax unless such deduction or withholding is required by applicable law, as modified by the practice of any relevant governmental revenue authority, then in effect. If a party is so required to deduct or withhold, then that party ("X") will:-

(1) promptly notify the other party ("Y") of such requirement;

(2) pay to the relevant authorities the full amount required to be deducted or withheld (including the full amount required to be deducted or withheld from any additional amount paid by X to Y under this Section 2(d)) promptly upon the earlier of determining that such deduction or withholding is required or receiving notice that such amount has been assessed against Y;

(3) promptly forward to Y an official receipt (or a certified copy), or other documentation reasonably acceptable to Y, evidencing such payment to such authorities; and

(4) if such Tax is an Indemnifiable Tax, pay to Y, in addition to the payment to which Y is otherwise entitled under this Agreement, such additional amount as is necessary to ensure that the net amount actually received by Y (free and clear of Indemnifiable Taxes, whether assessed against X or Y) will equal the full amount Y would have received had no such deduction or withholding been required. However, X will not be required to pay any additional amount to Y to the extent that it would not be required to be paid but for:-

Section 2(d)

(i)

This is a complex clause on withholding tax but it becomes clearer if you see X as the payer and Y as the payee or recipient. Please note that under ISDA a withholding tax only applies in cross-border transactions.

The Agreement is an international agreement and where cross-border Transactions occur, tax authorities may impose taxes called withholding taxes on payments made under those Transactions. Where this happens and you were due to receive a payment as payee you would receive less than you expected. Section 2(d) provides an indemnity that a payer has to increase his payment if a withholding tax is charged so that the payee receives what he expected to receive. Generally speaking, the burden of withholding taxes usually falls on the payer.

Withholding taxes can arise in three ways:

- **incorrect initial analysis that no withholding tax applied;**
- **a change in Tax Law or similar legal development;**
- **a change of facts relating to either the payer or payee which occurs after a Transaction is entered.**

This could arise through a change of status or business resulting in the party concerned being no longer eligible for tax treaty benefits. If a withholding tax is levied because of a change of facts, the responsible party will need to pay it or suffer it but will have no right to call a Tax Event Termination Event.

Going through the various points, if a withholding tax is levied on a payer, it must:

- **promptly notify the payee of this;**
- **promptly pay the withholding tax calculated or assessed to the tax authorities;**
- **promptly send the payee satisfactory documentation evidencing the tax payment to the authorities; and**
- **pay the equivalent of the withholding tax together with the net payment to the payee so that it ends up with the amount it originally anticipated.**

(A) the failure by Y to comply with or perform any agreement contained in Section 4(a)(i), 4(a)(iii) or 4(d); or

(B) the failure of a representation made by Y pursuant to Section 3(f) to be accurate and true unless such failure would not have occurred but for (I) any action taken by a taxing authority, or brought in a court of competent jurisdiction, after a Transaction is entered into (regardless of whether such action is taken or brought with respect to a party to this Agreement) or (II) a Change in Tax Law.

However, (A) and (B) (in the text opposite) provide two exceptions to this.

The payee will not receive a payment grossed up for withholding tax where it has failed to provide any tax documentation necessary to the payer or a Payee Tax Representation it has made has become false after a Transaction has been entered into, unless this has happened because of tax authority or court action or a Change in Tax Law.

Let's take an example to illustrate this. Suppose that a US payer has to pay a foreign payee US$1 million under the terms of a Confirmation. Assume further that the US levies withholding tax at 30% on this payment and under the terms of the Agreement the payer has to gross up the payment. The payer's total grossed up payment would be US$1,428,571.

This is calculated as follows:

Confirmation Payment/1–Withholding Tax rate = Grossed up payment US$1,000,000/0.70 (i.e. 100%–30%) = US$1,428,571.

The amount of the gross up payment as a percentage of the Confirmation payment is greater than the 30% withholding tax rate because it also applies to the additional gross up payment the payer is required to make. This is because the obligation to indemnify applies to gross payments.

Similar provisions are common in loan agreements where cross-border payments have to be made.

(ii) ***Liability***. If:-

(1) X is required by any applicable law, as modified by the practice of any relevant governmental revenue authority, to make any deduction or withholding in respect of which X would not be required to pay an additional amount to Y under Section 2(d)(i)(4);
(2) X does not so deduct or withhold; and
(3) a liability resulting from such Tax is assessed directly against X,

then, except to the extent Y has satisfied or then satisfies the liability resulting from such Tax, Y will promptly pay to X the amount of such liability (including any related liability for interest, but including any related liability for penalties only if Y has failed to comply with or perform any agreement contained in Section 4(a)(i), 4(a)(iii) or 4(d)).

(ii)

Section 2(d)(ii) covers the situation where the payer makes a payment without withholding tax relying upon tax documentation received from the payee and is unaware of any breach of a Payee Tax Representation by the payee (which is not caused by a Change in Tax Law) and the payer's tax authority then requires him to pay withholding tax in respect of that previous payment. In these circumstances, the payee will indemnify the payer for that withholding tax, any interest on it or any other penalty for failing to provide the payer with necessary tax documentation so that, *inter alia*, the payer could avoid the withholding tax or pay it at a reduced rate.

Principal changes from the 1992 Agreement

- **In Section 2(d)(i)(4)(B) the failure of a payee tax representation to remain valid (unless this invalidity arises following a tax authority or court decision) now applies only *after* a Transaction is entered into and not also on its trade date.**
- **The old Section 2(e) has been deleted and much more extensive provisions now appear in Section 9(h).**

3. Representations

Each party makes the representations contained in Sections 3(a), 3(b), 3(c), 3(d), 3(e) and 3(f) and, if specified in the Schedule as applying, 3(g) to the other party (which representations will be deemed to be repeated by each party on each date on which a Transaction is entered into and, in the case of the representations in Section 3(f), at all times until the termination of this Agreement). If any "Additional Representation" is specified in the Schedule or any Confirmation as applying, the party or parties specified for such Additional Representation will make, and, if applicable, be deemed to repeat such Additional Representation at the time or times specified for such Additional Representation.

(a) ***Basic Representations.***

(i) ***Status.*** It is duly organised and validly existing under the laws of the jurisdiction of its organisation or incorporation and, if relevant under such laws, in good standing;

(ii) ***Powers.*** It has the power to execute this Agreement and any other documentation relating this Agreement to which it is a party, to deliver this Agreement and any other documentation relating to this Agreement that it is required by this Agreement to deliver and to perform its obligations under this Agreement and any obligations it has under any Credit Support Document to which it is a party and has taken all necessary action to authorise such execution, delivery and performance;

(iii) ***No Violation or Conflict.*** Such execution, delivery and performance do not violate or conflict with any law applicable to it, any provision of its constitutional documents, any order or judgment of any court or other agency of government applicable to it or any of its assets or any contractual restriction binding on or affecting it or any of its assets;

(iv) ***Consents.*** All governmental and other consents that are required to have been obtained by it with respect to this Agreement or any Credit Support Document to which it is a party have been obtained and are in full force and effect and all conditions of any such consents have been complied with; and

(v) ***Obligations Binding.*** Its obligations under this Agreement and any Credit Support Document to which it is a party constitute its legal, valid and binding obligations, enforceable in accordance with their respective terms (subject to applicable bankruptcy, reorganisation, insolvency, moratorium or similar laws affecting creditors' rights generally and subject, as to enforceability, to equitable principles of general application (regardless of whether enforcement is sought in a proceeding in equity or at law)).

Section 3 – Representations

Each party represents various matters listed in this Section to the other. These representations are considered to be repeated each time a new Transaction is undertaken between the parties and the Payee Tax Representations in Section 3(f) are deemed made at all times until the termination of the Agreement. This is because payments need to be made periodically throughout the lives of the Transactions.

There is a new Section 3(g) which is a no agency representation which is activated by a positive choice in Part 4(l) of the Schedule.

In addition there is a framework for Additional Representations to be inserted in Part 4(m) of the Schedule together with their frequency of application.

Many of these representations are commonly seen in loan agreements.

Where parties are very active and enter into hundreds of deals over several years they should take care in agreeing representations which would require constant monitoring over the lives of deals so as to avoid a Misrepresentation Event of Default (under Section 5(a)(iv)) if a representation became untrue.

The basic representations in Section 3(a) are largely self explanatory and are:

- **each party is properly organised and has a valid legal existence in its jurisdiction of incorporation;**
- **each party has the power and is authorised to execute, deliver and perform under the Agreement, related documentation and any Credit Support Document which it is providing itself (e.g. an English law ISDA Credit Support Annex). A party's capacity and authority to enter into derivatives transactions are vital to the Agreement's effectiveness (as we shall see in Chapter 5 on legal issues);**
- **such actions do not conflict with a party's legal obligations, constitutional documents or any court or government agency order relating to its assets or any contractual restriction on them;**
- **each party has obtained any necessary government or other consents for the Agreement or any Credit Support Document and ensured that such consents are in full force and effect and fully complied with by the party concerned; and**
- **each party's obligations under the Agreement or any Credit Support Document constitute legal, valid and binding obligations enforceable against it subject to insolvency laws or general equitable legal principles. This is regardless of whether proceedings take place under common law or in equity. However, it is important that the**

Agreement or any Credit Support Document does not offend the public policy rules of any jurisdiction where you may seek to enforce it. Provided the Agreement is not, for instance, solely used for gambling purposes, this is unlikely.

Principal change from the 1992 Agreement

- Introduction of a framework for Additional Representations and their frequency of application to be inserted in Part 4(m) of the Schedule.

(b) ***Absence of Certain Events.*** No Event of Default or Potential Event of Default or, to its knowledge, Termination Event with respect to it has occurred and is continuing and no such event or circumstance would occur as a result of its entering into or performing its obligations under this Agreement or any Credit Support Document to which it is a party.

(c) ***Absence of Litigation.*** There is not pending or, to its knowledge, threatened against it, any of its Credit Support Providers or any of its applicable Specified Entities any action, suit or proceeding at law or in equity or before any court, tribunal, governmental body, agency or official or any arbitrator that is likely to affect the legality, validity or enforceability against it of this Agreement or any Credit Support Document to which it is a party or its ability to perform its obligations under this Agreement or such Credit Support Document.

(d) ***Accuracy of Specified Information.*** All applicable information that is furnished in writing by or on behalf of it to the other party and is identified for the purpose of this Section 3(d) in the Schedule is, as of the date of the information, true, accurate and complete in every material respect.

Section 3(b)

This is a useful representation made by each party that no actual or potential close-out event has occurred or persists and none would arise from entering into or performing its obligations under the Agreement or a Credit Support Document.

Section 3(c)

Absence of Litigation deals with actual and threatened litigation against a party, its Credit Support Provider(s) or Specified Entities listed in the Schedule which is likely to affect the legal enforceability of the Agreement or any Credit Support Document or a party's performance under them.

The scope of the Absence of Litigation provision has been narrowed from Affiliates (i.e. other group companies) which appeared in the 1992 Agreement and which were frequently deleted by a Schedule amendment because with a widely spread group like a major bank, it might not know of such litigation affecting its Affiliates in other parts of the world.

The representation now covers a party or its Credit Support Provider(s) or Specified Entities listed in Part 4(k) of the Schedule.

The provision is sometimes amended in the Schedule by stating that the litigation must have a material adverse effect upon its ability to perform under the Agreement or upon the Agreement's enforceability.

Please note that Sections 3(a)(ii), (iv), (v) and 3(b) and (c) capture Credit Support Documents entered into by the contracting parties to the Agreement.

Section 3(d)

Parties specify in Part 3(b) of the Schedule, the categories of information to which this representation applies. The test is rigorous – the information must be true, accurate and complete in every material respect. In Chapter 8, I discuss this representation in connection with audited accounts (see pages 487–8).

(e) ***Payer Tax Representation***. Each representation specified in the Schedule as being made by it for the purpose of this Section 3(e) is accurate and true.

(f) ***Payee Tax Representations***. Each representation specified in the Schedule as being made by it the purpose of this Section 3(f) is accurate and true.

(g) ***No Agency***. It is entering into this Agreement, including each Transaction, as principal and not as agent of any person or entity.

Sections 3(e) and 3(f)

In Sections 3(e) and (f), the parties state that the Payer and Payee Tax Representations they have made are true and accurate. These representations are made in Parts 2(a) and (b) of the Schedule.

Section 3(g)

This optional No Agency Representation in Part 3(g) of the Schedule is there to ensure the mutual nature of the parties' rights and obligations under the Agreement (i.e. that they are acting in the same capacity–principal to principal). This is vital for the effectiveness of close-out netting in the vast majority of jurisdictions. If the parties cannot represent they are both acting as principals, then special provisions relating to agency trades would be needed in the Schedule and Confirmations.

Principal changes from the 1992 Agreement

- **Section 3(c) – Absence of litigation narrowed to Credit Support Provider(s) and listed Specified Entities in Part 4(k) of the Schedule.**
- **Section 3(g) – New No Agency representation.**

4. Agreements

Each party agrees with the other that, so long as either party has or may have any obligation under this Agreement or under any Credit Support Document to which it is a party:-

(a) ***Furnish Specified Information.*** It will deliver to the other party or, in certain cases under subparagraph (iii) below, to such government or taxing authority as the other party reasonably directs:-

(i) any forms, documents or certificates relating to taxation specified in the Schedule or any Confirmation;

(ii) any other documents specified in the Schedule or any Confirmation; and

(iii) upon reasonable demand by such other party, any form or document that may be required or reasonably requested in writing in order to allow such other party or its Credit Support Provider to make a payment under this Agreement or any applicable Credit Support Document without any deduction or withholding for or on account of any Tax or with such deduction or withholding at a reduced rate (so long as the completion, execution or submission of such form or document would not materially prejudice the legal or commercial position of the party in receipt of such demand), with any such form or document to be accurate and completed in a manner reasonably satisfactory to such other party and to be executed and to be delivered with any reasonably required certification,

in each case by the date specified in the Schedule or such Confirmation or, if none is specified, as soon as reasonably practicable.

(b) ***Maintain Authorisations.*** It will use all reasonable efforts to maintain in full force and effect all consents of any governmental or other authority that are required to be obtained by it with respect to this Agreement or any Credit Support Document to which it is a party and will use all reasonable efforts to obtain any that may become necessary in the future.

(c) ***Comply with Laws.*** It will comply in all material respects with all applicable laws and orders to which it may be subject if failure so to comply would materially impair its ability to perform its obligations under this Agreement or any Credit Support Document to which it is a party.

Section 4 – Agreements

Section 4 contains agreements of the parties which survive while they have any obligations under the Agreement or any Credit Support Document.

Section 4(a)

Section 4(a) records the agreement of each party to supply certain specified information. In Section 4(a)(i), they must state in the Schedule or in a Confirmation any tax related forms, documents or certificates which are required to be delivered and the timescales for such delivery. Delivery will normally be to the other party but it can also be to a relevant government or tax authority.

Section 4(a)(ii) enables them to require delivery of financial statements, board resolutions, legal opinions, signatory lists and other appropriate documents for their contractual relationship. The actual documents and any Credit Support Documents are normally specified in Parts 3(b) and/or 4(f) of the Schedule but could also be referred to in a Confirmation.

Section 4(a)(iii) states that one party may be required to send the other party or a government or tax authority certain forms or documents so as to permit the other party or its Credit Support Provider (e.g. a guarantor) to make a payment under an Agreement or Credit Support Document without deduction or withholding for tax or, if necessary, at a lower rate. Under Section 4(a)(iii) of the Agreement, however, a party need not comply with this if doing so would "materially prejudice" its "legal or commercial position". Where a timescale for compliance is not specified in the Schedule or a Confirmation, it must be done as soon as reasonably practicable.

Section 4(b)

The obligation is self-explanatory. Sometimes these authorisations are referred to in Part 3(b) of the Schedule, e.g. licence renewals or exchange control permissions. A party must use all reasonable efforts to comply with this and any ongoing requirements in this respect.

Section 4(c)

The test here is if a party's failure to comply with laws would *significantly* impair its ability to perform its obligations under the Agreement or any Credit Support Document. It must comply in all material respects which is a tougher standard than in Section 4(b).

Principal changes from the 1992 Agreement

- **Section 4(c) – Minor change in heading.**

(d) ***Tax Agreement.*** It will give notice of any failure of a representation made by it under Section 3(f) to be accurate and true promptly upon learning of such failure.

(e) ***Payment of Stamp Tax.*** Subject to Section 11, it will pay any Stamp Tax levied or imposed upon it or in respect of its execution or performance of this Agreement by a jurisdiction in which it is incorporated, organised, managed and controlled, or or where an Office through which it is acting for the purpose of this Agreement is located ("Stamp Tax Jurisdiction") and will indemnify the other party against any Stamp Tax levied or imposed upon the other party or in respect of the other party's execution or performance of this Agreement by any such Stamp Tax Jurisdiction which is not also a Stamp Tax Jurisdiction with respect to the other party.

Section 4(d)

A party is obliged to give notice of any failure of a Payee Tax Representation made by it promptly upon becoming aware of it. An example of such a situation would be where a change in the nature of a payee's business made it ineligible for tax treaty benefits.

Where such notice is not given and a payer has to pay a withholding tax, the payee will need to indemnify the payer for the tax, interest and any penalties thereon except where the failure of the Payee Tax Representation is due to a Change in Tax Law or a court or tax authority decision which is beyond the payee's control.

Section 4(e)

Each party agrees to pay Stamp Taxes imposed on it by its home or branch jurisdiction and indemnify the other party against such Stamp Taxes if their jurisdiction is not the same. Section 4(e) is subordinate to the Section 11 remit that a Defaulting Party has, upon demand, to indemnify the Non-defaulting Party against certain Stamp Taxes. The indemnification only applies in a cross-border situation. The provision does not deal with Stamp Taxes levied in connection with Credit Support Documents.

Principal changes from the 1992 Agreement

- **Section 4(e) – Use of defined term "Office" rather than "branch or office" in line 3.**

Section 5 – Events of Default and Termination Events

Introduction

The changes in the first four Sections of the 2002 Agreement have been relatively minor and these Sections have largely survived intact.

However, starting with Section 5, the major changes stemming from the Strategic Documentation Review and the 12-month long composition of the 2002 Agreement start to appear en masse.

Section 5 is very important and contains the Master Agreement's Events of Default and Termination Events. Events of Default are common in loan agreements – Termination Events far less so. Both Events of Default and Termination Events can be triggered by either party or by a condition or event affecting a third party, e.g. a Specified Entry.

Section 5(a) covers Events of Default (where only one party is culpable) and there are eight of them. However, before looking at them, I want to discuss Specified Entities and Credit Support Providers who feature a lot in this Section.

A Specified Entity is essentially another member or members in a party's group whom you want to join through the Schedule into certain Events of Default and Termination Events. The aim is to draw in those members of a party's group (such as its parent or asset rich fellow subsidiaries) whose relationship is so close to the contracting party that if an Event of Default happened to them it would be very likely to affect the contracting party too. The same reasoning applies to Credit Support Providers.

A Credit Support Provider is a third party providing security or a guarantee for a party's liabilities. It can also be one of the parties to the Agreement providing security for itself (e.g. a corporate providing an all moneys debenture).

The following Events of Default and Termination Events include any Credit Support Provider specified in respect of a party:

- **Credit Support Default;**
- **Misrepresentation;**
- **Default under Specified Transaction;**
- **Cross Default;**
- **Bankruptcy;**
- **Merger Without Assumption;**
- **Illegality;**
- **Force Majeure Event; and**
- **Credit Event Upon Merger.**

The Credit Support Provider is also mentioned in Section 4(a)(iii) in relation to providing tax forms.

The various Events of Default are now reviewed.

5. Events of Default and Termination Events

(a) *Events of Default*. The occurrence at any time with respect to a party or, if applicable, any Credit Support Provider of such party or any Specified Entity of such party of any of the following events constitutes (subject to Sections 5(c) and 6(e)(iv) an event of default (an "Event of Default") with respect to such party:-

(i) ***Failure to Pay or Deliver***. Failure by the party to make, when due, any payment under this Agreement or delivery under Section 2(a)(i) or 9(h)(i)(2) or (4) required to be made by it if such failure is not remedied on or before the first Local Business Day in the case of any such payment or the first Local Delivery Date in the case of any such delivery after, in each case, notice of such failure is given to the party;

Events of Default

The Agreement has eight Events of Default which are listed subject to two qualifications in Sections 5(c) and 6(e)(iv). These relate to Events of Default arising in circumstances where Illegality and Force Majeure Event are also present. We will review those provisions later.

Section 5(a)(i)

Section 5(a)(i) covers a party's failure to make any payment or delivery when due under Section 2(a)(i) or 9(h)(i)(2) or (4) – Compensation for defaulted or deferred deliveries – of the Agreement after a grace period of one Local Business Day or one Local Delivery Day following notice. Please note that the notice does not need to state the consequences of not curing the failure within a specific timescale.

Under the 1992 Agreement the grace period for a failure to pay or deliver under Section 5(a)(i) of the Agreement was three Local Business Days following notice. Due to events in the Asian and Russian crises in 1997 and 1998 market players considered this too long to allow a potential default to continue. The grace period has been reduced to one Local Business Day or one Local Delivery Day following notice in the 2002 Agreement.

"Local Delivery Day" is a new term in the 2002 Agreement and covers the position that a day might be a Local Business Day for commercial banks and foreign exchange markets but that delivery of assets such as securities might not be possible on that day perhaps because of settlement system problems outside the delivering party's control. Therefore, the Section 14 definition of Local Delivery Day focuses on whether relevant settlement systems are open for business rather than if commercial banks are.

(ii) ***Breach of Agreement; Repudiation of Agreement.***

(1) Failure by the party to comply with or perform any agreement or obligation (other than an obligation to make any payment under this Agreement or delivery under Section 2(a)(i) or 9(h)(i)(2) or (4) or to give notice of a Termination Event or any agreement or obligation under Section 4(a)(i), 4(a)(iii) or 4(d)) to be complied with or performed by the party in accordance with this Agreement if such failure is not remedied within 30 days after notice of such failure is given to the party; or

(2) the party disaffirms, disclaims, repudiates or rejects, in whole or in part, or challenges the validity of, this Master Agreement, any Confirmation executed or delivered by that party or any Transaction evidenced by such a Confirmation (or such action is taken by any person or entity appointed or empowered to operate it or act on its behalf);

Section 5(a)(ii)

As its title indicates, Breach of Agreement now embraces Repudiation of Agreement too.

Section 5(a)(ii)(1) covers a failure by either party to comply with any agreement or obligation under the Agreement by the expiry of a 30-day grace period following notice. The following are excluded from this provision:

- **any obligations covered by the Failure to Pay or Deliver Event of Default (which has a shorter grace period of one Local Business Day);**
- **any failure to give notice of a Termination Event. The thinking here is that this failure should not be treated as an Event of Default when the subject of the notice could well be a less serious Termination Event;**
- **any failure to comply with certain tax related agreements or obligations contained in Section 4 of the Agreement (since denial of payment gross up is the penalty).**

Since such events are subject to different treatment elsewhere, it was considered that *per se* they should not give rise to an Event of Default under Section 5(a)(ii)(1). Examples of breaches of agreement could include failure to maintain authorisations as required in Section 4(b) or failure to provide accounting information or a legal opinion within an agreed deadline.

Section 5(a)(ii)(2) is a new clause which parallels the repudiation provisions in Section 5(a)(iii) (Credit Support Default) and Section 5(a)(v) (Default Under Specified Transaction) and like them has no grace period.

It means that a party now does not need to wait until its counterparty has actually defaulted on a payment or delivery (or otherwise failed to perform an obligation) where that counterparty has clearly repudiated the Master Agreement, a Confirmation or a Transaction.

Principal changes from the 1992 Agreement

- **Section 5(a)(i) – Reduction of the grace period by two-thirds to one Local Business Day or one Local Delivery Day.**
- **Section 5(a)(ii) – New sub-section (2) concerning repudiation of the Master Agreement, a Confirmation or a Transaction. No grace period allowed.**

(iii) ***Credit Support Default.***

(1) Failure by the party or any Credit Support Provider of such party to comply with or perform any agreement or obligation to be complied with or performed by it in accordance with any Credit Support Document if such failure is continuing after any applicable grace period has elapsed;

(2) the expiration or termination of such Credit Support Document or the failing or ceasing of such Credit Support Document, or any security interest granted by such party or such Credit Support Provider to the other party pursuant to any such Credit Support Document, to be in full force and effect for the purpose of this Agreement (in either case other than in accordance with its terms) prior to the satisfaction of all obligations of such party under each Transaction to which such Credit Support Document relates without the written consent of the other party; or

(3) the party or such Credit Support Provider disaffirms, disclaims, repudiates or rejects, in whole or in part, or challenges the validity of, such Credit Support Document (or such action is taken by any person or entity appointed or empowered to operate it or act on its behalf);

Section 5(a)(iii)

The Credit Support Provider first appears here in the Events of Default.

Section 5(a)(iii) first applies to a party if a Credit Support Document is provided by or on behalf of that party and is identified as such with its nature described in Part 4(f) of the Schedule or in the Credit Support Document itself. If the Credit Support Document is a third party guarantee, the name of the guarantor would be stated as a Credit Support Provider in Part 4(g) of the Schedule since this Event of Default also applies to a party's outside Credit Support Provider(s). Failure of a security interest is also now covered in this Section.

An English Law ISDA Credit Support Annex entered into by either party to the Agreement should not be specified in Part 4(f) and (g) of the Schedule because it is a title transfer document under which ownership of the collateral passes to the other party. However, the New York Law ISDA Credit Support Annex and the English Law ISDA Credit Support Deed are usually referred to as Credit Support Documents because they are by nature pledges or security interests. Normally Part 4(f) and (g) describe third party Credit Support Documents and Credit Support Providers.

This Event of Default is triggered if:

- **a party or its Credit Support Provider(s) breaches a Credit Support Document and the breach survives any agreed grace period; or**
- **the Credit Support Document or any security interest granted by one party to the other under it becomes ineffective before discharge of all obligations under related Transactions without the other party's written consent; or**
- **a party or a Credit Support Provider or a third party entitled to act on their behalf repudiates or disowns or challenges the validity of its Credit Support Document. Such a third party could include a regulator, liquidator or a donee under a power of attorney.**

(iv) ***Misrepresentation***. A representation (other than a representation under Section 3(e) or 3(f)) made or repeated or deemed to have been made or repeated by the party or any Credit Support Provider of such party in this Agreement or any Credit Support Document proves to have been incorrect or misleading in any material respect when made or repeated or deemed to have been made or repeated;

Section 5(a)(iv)

Section 5(a)(iv) applies to certain representation breaches (but excludes tax representations where gross up would be denied if misrepresentation occurred) made in the Agreement or in a Credit Support Document by a party or a Credit Support Provider which result in the representations made being materially misleading or incorrect. It is important to remember that most representations under the Agreement are deemed to be repeated when each new Transaction is undertaken.

Principal changes from the 1992 Agreement

- **Section 5(a)(iii)(2) – Addition of security interests granted by a party or its Credit Support Provider to the other party pursuant to a Credit Support Document. This is meant to highlight that Credit Support Documents are not just confined to third party guarantees but can include security interests such as third party mortgages or an ISDA Credit Support Annex under New York Law or a Credit Support Deed under English Law.**
- **Section 5(a)(iii)(3) – Repudiation now extends to any person appointed or empowered to act on behalf of a party providing direct credit support or its Credit Support Provider, e.g. the donee of a power of attorney, a liquidator or a regulator.**
- **Section 5(a)(iv) – Minor change to a cross reference.**

(v) ***Default under Specified Transaction.*** The party, any Credit Support Provider of such party or any applicable Specified Entity of such party:-

(1) defaults (other than by failing to make a delivery) under a Specified Transaction or any credit support arrangement relating to a Specified Transaction and, after giving effect to any applicable notice requirement or grace period, such default results in a liquidation of, an acceleration of obligations under, or an early termination of, that Specified Transaction;

(2) defaults, after giving effect to any applicable notice requirement or grace period, in making any payment due on the last payment or exchange date of, or any payment on early termination of, a Specified Transaction (or, if there is no applicable notice requirement or grace period such default continues for at least one Local Business Day);

(3) defaults in making any delivery due under (including any delivery due on the last delivery or exchange date of) a Specified Transaction or any credit support arrangement relating to a Specified Transaction and, after giving effect to any applicable notice requirement or grace period, such default results in a liquidation of, an acceleration of obligations under, or an early termination of, all transactions outstanding under the documentation applicable to that Specified Transaction; or

(4) disaffirms, disclaims, repudiates or rejects, in whole or in part, or challenges the validity of, a Specified Transaction or any credit support arrangement relating to a Specified Transaction that is, in either case, confirmed or evidenced by a document or other confirming evidence executed and delivered by that party, Credit Support Provider or Specified Entity (or such action is taken by any person or entity appointed or empowered to operate it or act on its behalf);

Section 5(a)(v)

The term Specified Transaction is defined in Section 14 of the Agreement and is one or more of a wide range of OTC derivatives transactions between each party to the Agreement, a party and the other party's Credit Support Provider or Specified Entity or between their respective Specified Entities or Credit Support Providers, but which are not entered into under the Agreement nor governed by it. These might include transactions the parties have concluded under other agreements or under long form confirmations. Some people regard this provision as a type of limited cross default.

In the 2002 Agreement the definition of Specified Transaction has been extended to cover newer types of derivatives such as credit and weather derivatives as well as forward purchases of securities or commodities, securities lending and repo transactions. It also refers to transactions which are recurrently contracted in the market and future variants of them.

It is worth noting that the definition excludes Transactions under the 2002 Agreement thereby clarifying the original intention of this provision and perhaps partly accounting for the inclusion of repudiation in the Breach of Agreement Event of Default (i.e. Section 5(a)(ii)(2)).

In the 1992 Agreement if no grace period was specified in the Specified Transaction documentation there was a three Local Business Day fallback grace period for any failure to pay or deliver at the maturity of a Specified Transaction. In the 2002 Agreement this fallback grace period is reduced to one Local Business Day for payments and eliminated altogether for deliveries because of the new sub-clause (3).

Please note that Default Under Specified Transaction now extends to any credit support arrangement underpinning a Specified Transaction.

The categories of default in this sub-Section are:

- **acceleration or early termination of the Specified Transaction or any related credit support arrangement underpinning it;**
- **payment default on the final scheduled payment date or with any early termination settlement payment after the lapse of notice of a minimum one Local Business Day grace period;**
- **any delivery default under a Specified Transaction or any related credit support arrangement underpinning it which, following the giving of notice or the expiry of a grace period, results in the liquidation of all transactions under the Specified Transaction documentation;**
- **repudiation of a Specified Transaction by the party itself or third parties such as Specified Entities, Credit Support Providers, liquidators or regulators.**

This makes the provision similar to the Cross Default provision discussed below.

The new sub-clause (3) responds to concerns of market players in including repos or securities lending transactions under the definition of Specified Transaction. Repos, for instance, are subject to different close-out regimes under the PSA/ISMA GMRA 1995 or the TBMA/ISMA GMRA 2000. Repo delivery failures are common in the market and the purpose of the wording in Section 5(a)(v)(3) is to ensure that a mini-close-out (essentially a close-out of Affected Transactions) under a repo master agreement cannot result in a Default Under Specified Transaction here. The way this is accomplished is for the right to terminate to relate to all transactions under the relevant documentation and for that right to be exercised. Under the TBMA/ISMA 2000, there is an option for failure to deliver to be an Event of Default and where this is the case, it would, if exercised, involve the close-out of all transactions governed by the TBMA/ISMA GMRA 2000 and would lead to Default Under Specified Transaction being invoked here.

In the Schedule, the scope of this Event of Default may be widened by including any third party contracting with one of the parties to this Agreement or their Specified Entities or Credit Support Providers.

I will have more to say about this when we look at credit issues in the Schedule in Chapter 6.

Note there is no Threshold Amount with Default under Specified Transaction.

This Event of Default is very important because it impacts the parties joined to this Agreement if a default occurs in transactions between them outside it. In other words, it has a direct impact on the credit risk of the respective parties to this Agreement on the basis that if they default outside the Agreement they will probably default within it too.

Principal changes from the 1992 Agreement

- **Section 5(a)(v)(1) – Delivery defaults excluded. Default extends to any credit support arrangement relating to a Specified Transaction.**
- **Section 5(a)(v)(2) – Grace period for failed final maturity payments or early termination payments for a Specified Transaction reduced to one Local Business Day. Failed deliveries at such times deleted.**
- **Section 5(a)(v)(3) – New clause dealing with delivery defaults under Specified Transactions or related credit support arrangements. Close-out of all Transactions only possible if delivery defaults under Specified Transactions would result in close-out of all Transactions in the documentation governing them.**
- **Section 5(a)(v)(4) – Broadening of repudiation for triggering close-out – a challenge to the validity of a Specified Transaction or a related credit support arrangement by the party itself, a Credit Support Provider, Specified Entity, donee of a power of attorney, liquidator, regulator or similar person.**

(vi) ***Cross Default***. If "Cross Default" is specified in the Schedule as applying to the party, the occurrence or existence of:-

(1) a default, event of default or other similar condition or event (however described) in respect of such party, any Credit Support Provider of such party or any applicable Specified Entity of such party under one or more agreements or instruments relating to Specified Indebtedness of any of them (individually or collectively) where the aggregate principal amount of such agreements or instruments, either alone or together with the amount, if any, referred to in clause (2) below, is not less than the applicable Threshold Amount (as specified in the Schedule) which has resulted in such Specified Indebtedness becoming, or becoming capable at such time of being declared, due and payable under such agreements or instruments before it would otherwise have been due and payable;

or

(2) a default by such party, such Credit Support Provider or such Specified Entity (individually or collectively) in making one or more payments under such agreements or instruments on the due date for payment (after giving effect to any applicable notice requirement or grace period) in an aggregate amount, either alone or together with the amount, if any, referred to in clause (1) above, of not less than the applicable Threshold Amount;

Section 5(a)(vi)

Section 5(a)(vi) is very important. It also applies to Specified Entities and Credit Support Providers. This Event of Default is triggered by:

- **a default or similar event under financial agreements or instruments that has resulted in indebtedness (above a Threshold Amount) becoming capable of being accelerated and terminated by a Non-defaulting Party; or**
- **a failure to make any payments (above a Threshold Amount) on their due date under such agreements or instruments after notice or the expiry of a grace period.**

A Threshold Amount is a monetary figure above which a Non-defaulting Party may exercise its rights, following its counterparty's default elsewhere, to terminate all Transactions under the Agreement. It is essentially the credit risk you are prepared to accept on your counterparty before you trigger your close-out rights under this Section 5(a)(vi). Specified Indebtedness essentially means "borrowed money" but it is possible in the Schedule to extend it to other types of indebtedness (e.g. lease purchase obligations, commercial paper, acceptances, factoring or derivative transactions with third parties) or alternatively to narrow it to exclude, for example, banking deposits. I will have more to say about this in Chapter 6, pages 386–7.

Section 5(a)(vi) only applies to a party if this is stated in Part 1(c) of the Schedule which is also an important reason to get an Agreement signed. If Cross Default applies, a Threshold Amount is nominated in Part 1(c) of the Schedule (either a fixed monetary sum or a small percentage of shareholders' equity is most common). It is advisable to add that the amount includes its equivalent in any other currency, currency unit or combination of them. Unless otherwise agreed, this Event of Default will automatically catch the Credit Support Provider of any party subject to Cross Default but not any Specified Entity unless it is expressly nominated in Part 1(a) of the Schedule. If both Credit Support Providers and Specified Entities are included it means that if a default occurred under any Specified Indebtedness owed by a contracting party, its Credit Support Provider(s) or Specified Entity(ies) elsewhere then the amounts of each of these defaults could be added together collectively to see if the Threshold Amount under the Agreement had been breached.

Now Section 5(a)(vi) of the 1992 Agreement did not provide for this Cross Default provision to be triggered by aggregating amounts under sub-clauses (1) and (2), but the 2002 Agreement does this. In other words, under the 1992 Agreement the Threshold Amount under each sub-clause

was applied separately (unless a Schedule amendment was made). So if the Cross Default clause had a US$ 10 million Threshold Amount and defaults of US$ 7 million each occurred under each of the sub-clauses they could not be aggregated under the 1992 Agreement but they can under the 2002 Agreement because of new wording to that effect. During drafting discussions it emerged that some ISDA members regarded the two limbs of Section 5(a)(vi) as separate and independent tests of Cross Default. Nevertheless most members wanted them aggregated.

Sometimes there is a Schedule amendment which excludes Cross Default being triggered through operational or administrative error provided that the party concerned was solvent, had access to sufficient funds when such error occurred and paid up within an agreed grace period.

Where Cross Default does not apply there is no Threshold Amount either.

This provision is very versatile and its scope can be expanded or contracted depending upon how Threshold Amount, Specified Entity, Specified Indebtedness and Credit Support Provider are defined.

Principal changes from the 1992 Agreement

- **Section 5(a)(vi)(1) – Inclusion of wording to aggregate defaults under the two sub-clauses of Section 5(a)(vi).**
- **Section 5(a)(vi)(2) – Ditto.**

(vii) ***Bankruptcy***. The party, any Credit Support Provider of such party or any applicable Specified Entity of such party:-

(1) is dissolved (other than pursuant to a consolidation, amalgamation or merger); (2) becomes insolvent or is unable to pay its debts or fails or admits in writing its inability generally to pay its debts as they become due; (3) makes a general assignment, arrangement or composition with or for the benefit of its creditors; (4)(A) institutes or has instituted against it, by a regulator, supervisor or any similar official with primary insolvency, rehabilitative or regulatory jurisdiction over it in the jurisdiction of its incorporation or organisation or the jurisdiction of its head or home office, a proceeding seeking a judgment of insolvency or bankruptcy or any other relief under any bankruptcy or insolvency law or other similar law affecting creditors' rights, or a petition is presented for its winding-up or liquidation by it or such regulator, supervisor or similar official, or (B) has instituted against it a proceeding seeking a judgment of insolvency or bankruptcy or any other relief under any bankruptcy or insolvency law or other similar law affecting creditors' rights, or a petition is presented for its winding-up or liquidation, and such proceeding or petition is instituted or presented by a person or entity not described in clause (A) above and either (I) results in a judgment of insolvency or bankruptcy or the entry of an order for relief or the making of an order for its winding-up or liquidation or (II) is not dismissed, discharged, stayed or restrained in each case within 15 days of the institution or presentation thereof; (5) has a resolution passed for its winding-up, official management or liquidation (other than pursuant to a consolidation, amalgamation or merger); (6) seeks or becomes subject to the appointment of an administrator, provisional liquidator, conservator, receiver, trustee, custodian or other similar official for it or for all or substantially all its assets; (7) has a secured party take possession of all or substantially all its assets or has a distress, execution, attachment, sequestration or other legal process levied, enforced or sued on or against all or substantially all its assets and such secured party maintains possession, or any such process is not dismissed, discharged, stayed or restrained, in each case within 15 days thereafter; (8) causes or is subject to any event with respect to it which, under the applicable laws of any jurisdiction, has an analogous effect to any of the events specified in clauses (1) to (7) above (inclusive); or (9) takes any action in furtherance of, or indicating its consent to, approval of, or acquiescence in, any of the foregoing acts; or

Section 5(a)(vii)

Section 5(a)(vii) is very broad. Again, it applies to each party and its Credit Support Provider or a Specified Entity (specified in Part 1(a) of the Schedule). It can be triggered by many bankruptcy events or insolvency proceedings under New York or English law but recognises that market players will also be located in and organised under the laws of other countries.

It is important to note that in an insolvency it is the laws of the insolvent party's jurisdiction of incorporation which prevail over the governing law of the Agreement.

This Event of Default is drafted broadly enough to be triggered by proceedings or events under any insolvency laws likely to affect a particular party. Sometimes Schedule amendments are made to specify certain types of bankruptcy officials, e.g. an examiner in Irish Schedules. It is wise to check that an insolvency regime in an emerging market or exotic country is covered by the categories outlined in this provision. If not, an amendment will need to be made to it in the Schedule. Another Schedule amendment that may need to be made relates to partnerships which might be dissolved when a partner leaves but which are immediately reconstituted by the remaining partners.

In the 1992 Agreement no grace period applies where a party or its Specified Entity or Credit Support Provider starts insolvency proceedings against itself. However, where a third party does this and the proceeding is dismissed within 30 days, no Event of Default occurs.

In the 2002 Agreement proceedings started by an insolvent party or its regulator or its insolvency official are differentiated from those commenced by third parties. Where a regulator or insolvency official starts insolvency proceedings, the Bankruptcy Event of Default occurs immediately as it would if the insolvent party started the proceeding itself. Proceedings started by third parties now have a 15-day waiting period for the petition to be discharged or stayed in contrast to the previous 30-day period which was considered too long by market players in view of the turmoil of the 1997/98 crises. While it is unlikely that a winding up order would be dismissed in this time, it would allow the parties time to talk and ascertain if the filing is vexatious or serious. This change affects Section 5(a)(vii)(4).

In relation to Section 5(a)(vii)(7), in the 1992 Agreement there was a 30-day grace period for the dismissal of execution proceedings by secured creditors. This has now been reduced to 15 days in the 2002 Agreement.

Principal changes from the 1992 Agreement

- **Section 5(a)(vii)(4) – No grace period allowed where the party itself or a regulator or insolvency official instigates formal insolvency proceedings. Grace period is reduced to 15 days where others do so.**
- **Section 5(a)(vii)(7) – Discharge of distress, execution or similar proceedings affecting secured assets reduced to 15 days.**

(viii) ***Merger Without Assumption***. The party or any Credit Support Provider of such party consolidates or amalgamates with, or merges with or into, or transfers all or substantially all its assets to, or reorganises, reincorporates or reconstitutes into or as, another entity and, at the time of such consolidation, amalgamation, merger, transfer, reorganisation, reincorporation or reconstitution:-

(1) the resulting, surviving or transferee entity fails to assume all the obligations of such party or such Credit Support Provider under this Agreement or any Credit Support Document to which it or its predecessor was a party; or

(2) the benefits of any Credit Support Document fail to extend (without the consent of the other party) to the performance by such resulting, surviving or transferee entity of its obligations under this Agreement.

Section 5(a)(viii)

Merger Without Assumption applies to parties and their Credit Support Providers, but not to their Specified Entities. It describes significant changes in corporate identity in different jurisdicitions. It covers situations where a party or its Credit Support Provider amalgamates, merges or transfers all or most of its assets to another entity or reorganises or reconstitutes itself as another entity and that entity:

- **fails to assume that party's obligations under the Agreement; or**
- **fails to assume that party's or the Credit Support Provider's obligations under a Credit Support Document.**

In either case the contractual position is weaker than originally envisaged and gives the non-merging party (who is also the Non-defaulting Party) the right to close out all Transactions under the Agreement.

Merger Without Assumption also arises where the benefits of a Credit Support Document fail to extend post-merger to the transferee's performance obligations under the Agreement (unless the other party consents).

Please note that just because a merger may involve companies in two different legal and tax jurisdictions this is not relevant for this particular Event of Default but may possibly be for the Tax Event Upon Merger Termination Event (see Section 5(b)(iv) below).

It is possible for a merger, consolidation or asset transfer to trigger Credit Event Upon Merger (see commentary on Section 5(b)(v) at page 205) as well as Merger Without Assumption. Where this occurs, Section 5(b)(v) indicates that it will be treated as an Event of Default.

Principal changes from the 1992 Agreement

- **Preamble – Inclusion of reorganisation, reincorporation and reconstitution as methods of corporate transformation.**
- **Section 5(a)(viii)(1) – Deletion of the words "by operation of law or pursuant to an agreement reasonably satisfactory to the other party" after the word "party" in line 3. This was because the assumption of obligations by the other party in these circumstances was deemed to be contrary to the merger exception for transfer under Section 7 where no consent by the other party is needed.**

(b) ***Termination Events***. The occurrence at any time with respect to a party or, if applicable, any Credit Support Provider of such party or any Specified Entity of such party of any event specified below constitutes (subject to Section 5(c)) an Illegality if the event is specified in clause (i) below, a Force Majeure Event if the event is specified in clause (ii) below, a Tax Event if the event is specified in clause (iii) below, a Tax Event Upon Merger if the event is specified in clause (iv) below, and, if specified to be applicable, a Credit Event Upon Merger if the event is specified pursuant to clause (v) below or an Additional Termination Event if the event is specified pursuant to (vi) below:-

(i) ***Illegality***. After giving effect to any applicable provision, disruption fallback or remedy specified in, or pursuant to, the relevant Confirmation or elsewhere in this Agreement, due to an event or circumstance (other than any action taken by a party or, if applicable, any Credit Support Provider of such party) occurring after a Transaction is entered into, it becomes unlawful under any applicable law (including without limitation the laws of any country in which payment, delivery or compliance is required by either party or any Credit Support Provider, as the case may be), on any day, or it would be unlawful if the relevant payment, delivery or compliance were required on that day (in each case, other than as a result of a breach by the party of Section 4(b)):-

(1) for the Office through which such party (which will be the Affected Party) makes and receives payments or deliveries with respect to such Transaction to perform any absolute or contingent obligation to make a payment or delivery in respect of such Transaction, to receive a payment or delivery in respect of such Transaction or to comply with any other material provision of this Agreement relating to such Transaction; or

(2) for such party or any Credit Support Provider of such party (which will be the Affected Party) to perform any absolute or contingent obligation to make a payment or delivery which such party or Credit Support Provider has under any Credit Support Document relating to such Transaction, to receive a payment or delivery under such Credit Support Document or to comply with any other material provision of such Credit Support Document;

Section 5(b) Termination Events

Generally speaking, Termination Events allow a party to close out where the event substantially alters the Transaction economics or the risk profile of its counterparty. Sometimes no one party is sufficiently at fault but the effect of the Termination Event means it is not financially beneficial for the parties to continue the Transaction(s) concerned.

There are now five Termination Events listed with the option of a sixth. Please note that with Termination Events the party at fault is generally called the Affected Party. Under Section 5(b)(i)–(iv) if a Termination Event occurs and close-out follows through designating an Early Termination Date in a notice, only Transactions affected by the Termination Event ("Affected Transactions") are closed out although there is the possibility for all Transactions to be closed out under Force Majeure Event. Under Section 5(b)(v) and usually under Section 5(b)(vi), the Affected Transactions comprise all Transactions because the Termination Event taints the whole contractual relationship and all Transactions need to be terminated.

The key changes with the Termination Events are the revamping of Illegality and the introduction of Force Majeure Event. Before they can be invoked, any Market Disruption Events and Disruption Fallbacks have to be exhausted. Where these do not resolve the problem, the Illegality and Force Majeure Event provisions come into play.

In its amended form Illegality concerns events where it becomes illegal to pay or perform through an Office, under the Agreement or a Credit Support Document.

Force Majeure Event covers all events outside the parties' control (e.g. acts of state, wars, riots, natural disasters etc) which make performance through an Office, under the Agreement or under a Credit Support Document impossible or impracticable.

Either party may terminate Affected Transactions under Illegality and Force Majeure Event.

The features of these two Termination Events have significant knock on effects impacting on the hierarchy of different Events of Default and Termination Events (Section 5(c)), the close-out provisions (Section 6(e)), the interest and compensation provisions of Section 9(h) and the Section 10 multibranch provisions.

The ISDA working group was concerned that the occurrence of an Illegality or Force Majeure Event should not invoke a knee jerk reaction to terminate Transactions when it is possible that challenging circumstances might be promptly resolved. So they introduced Waiting Periods to give a breathing space to see if these problems could be overcome. The Waiting Period for Illegality is three Local Business Days and for Force Majeure Event it is eight Local Business Days.

The different durations reflect different purposes. With Force Majeure Event, the problem is likely to be a short-term catastrophic event like a terrorist attack and it is possible that resumption of trading in the financial markets might only be delayed for a few days. The eight Local Business Day Waiting Period should help keep Transactions alive. The effects of legal changes are, however, likely to be long term (and unlikely to be reversed quickly) and the shorter three Local Business Day Waiting Period for Illegality is designed to allow fact finding to take place and for market solutions to be found rather than unilateral terminations being triggered.

Waiting Periods are also relevant to payments and deliveries because during them these are suspended and a temporary standstill prevails.

However, if the problem cannot be resolved within the Waiting Period, then the right to terminate can be invoked.

In contrast to the position under the 1992 Agreement, there is no longer any obligation on the parties to try and transfer Affected Transactions due to an Illegality to another Office or Affiliate. Instead at the end of the Waiting Period either party can terminate the Affected Transactions on a no fault basis using mid-market values calculated pursuant to Section 6(e)(ii)(3). There is also no transfer obligation with Force Majeure Event either.

Another important innovation is that parties can choose to terminate less than all the Affected Transactions. The rationale for this is that while a party might be content to terminate short-dated FX or option transactions it might prefer to keep alive longer-term structured transactions which involved heavy set up costs. There is, of course, a risk of cherry picking here and so there is a reciprocal right that the other party can terminate all or some of the Affected Transactions the first party chooses not to terminate on the same Early Termination Date.

Illegality like Force Majeure Event but in contrast to other Termination Events is anticipatory in effect, i.e. it may be triggered if it *would* be unlawful to pay, deliver or perform on a particular day even if such payment, delivery or performance was not required on that day. Because of their anticipatory nature, Market Disruption Events (as per the ISDA product Definitions booklets) may not apply themselves at the time a party believes an Illegality or Force Majeure Event has occurred.

Section 5(b)(i)

Section 5(b)(i) states that, after giving effect to any formally agreed disruption fallback or remedy (i.e. permitted in one of the ISDA product Definitions booklets), a Termination Event will arise if it becomes unlawful for a party or its Credit Support Provider to make or receive a payment or delivery through an agreed Office or comply with any material provision of the Agreement or it becomes unlawful for a party or a Credit Support Provider to pay or perform under a Credit Support Document. For the avoidance of doubt, the party impacted by the Illegality (i.e. the one faced with breaking the law in order to perform) will be the Affected Party.

Illegality excludes any breach by a party of the agreement in Section 4(b) to maintain authorisations necessary in connection with the Agreement or any Credit Support Document. Any such breach will be treated as a Breach of Agreement Event of Default and not as an Illegality.

So Illegality still covers events beyond the parties' control which arise from government directives or changes of law. The imposition of exchange controls by a government would be an example. Illegality is deemed to occur on the date on which the event occurred irrespective of whether a payment or delivery was actually due on that day. It is also made clear that an Illegality will still occur if it is unlawful for the Affected Party to make or receive payments and deliveries through the Office where they are habitually transacted but not illegal for it to do so through another of its Offices.

As mentioned before there is no longer any obligation on the parties to try and transfer Affected Transactions due to an Illegality to another Office or Affiliate. This is because, in practice, the market found this very difficult to achieve. Consequently it was considered better to try and terminate the Affected Transactions as soon as possible after the Waiting Period expires.

There is a three Local Business Day Waiting Period for Illegality. During this period all payment and delivery obligations under the Agreement are suspended.

The definition of Waiting Period is in Section 14.

Principal changes from the 1992 Agreement

- **Section 5(b)(i) preamble – Need first to give effect to any agreed disruption fallback as specified in the ISDA product Definitions booklets, for instance, before an Illegality Termination Event can be declared and termination rights invoked.**
- **Section 5(b)(i)(1) – Emphasis on the Illegality arising in the Office through which payments and deliveries are habitually made and received.**
- **Section 5(b)(i)(2) – Language added to clarify and elaborate on the circumstances under which it would be illegal to pay or perform under a Credit Support Document.**

(ii) *Force Majeure Event.* After giving effect to any applicable provision, disruption fallback or remedy specified in, or pursuant to, the relevant Confirmation or elsewhere in this Agreement, by reason of force majeure or act of state occurring after a Transaction is entered into, on any day:-

(1) the Office through which such party (which will be the Affected Party) makes and receives payments or deliveries with respect to such Transaction is prevented from performing any absolute or contingent obligation to make a payment or delivery in respect of such Transaction, from receiving a payment or delivery in respect of such Transaction or from complying with any other material provision of this Agreement relating to such Transaction (or would be so prevented if such payment, delivery or compliance were required on that day), or it becomes impossible or impracticable for such Office so to perform, receive or comply (or it would be impossible or impracticable for such Office so to perform, receive or comply if such payment, delivery or compliance were required on that day); or

(2) such party or any Credit Support Provider of such party (which will be the Affected Party) is prevented from performing any absolute or contingent obligation to make a payment or delivery which such party or Credit Support Provider has under any Credit Support Document relating to such Transaction, from receiving a payment or delivery under such Credit Support Document or from complying with any other material provision of such Credit Support Document (or would be so prevented if such payment, delivery or compliance were required on that day), or it becomes impossible or impracticable for such party or Credit Support Provider so to perform, receive or comply (or it would be impossible or impracticable for such party or Credit Support Provider so to perform, receive or comply if such payment, delivery or compliance were required on that day),

so long as the force majeure or act of state is beyond the control of such Office, such party or such Credit Support Provider, as appropriate, and such Office, party or Credit Support Provider could not, after using all reasonable efforts (which will not require such party or Credit Support Provider to incur a loss, other than immaterial, incidental expenses), overcome such prevention, impossibility or impracticability;

Section 5(b)(ii)

Force Majeure Event is triggered if, after giving effect to any agreed disruption fallback (e.g. as permitted by the various ISDA product Definitions booklets) or other remedy, it becomes impossible or impracticable due to an event such as a war, riot, labour disruption, natural disaster or act of state (i.e. invasion by a foreign power), for example, for:-

(1) **the Affected Party's Office to make or receive payments or deliveries in respect of a Transaction or to comply with any material provision of the Agreement in relation to that Transaction if such performance or compliance was required on that very day; or**

(2) **the party or its Credit Support Provider to pay or deliver under its Credit Support Document in relation to a Transaction or to comply with any material Credit Support Document provision again if such performance or compliance was required on that very day.**

The pre-conditions for this are that the force majeure or act of state are beyond the control of the Office concerned or the Affected Party or its Credit Support Provider and that none of them after using reasonable efforts and minimal expense could overcome the impossibility or impracticality.

The occurrence of the Force Majeure Event is deemed to happen on the day it actually occurred whether or not a payment or delivery was due on that day.

Principal change from the 1992 Agreement

- **Completely new provision.**

(iii) ***Tax Event***. Due to (1) any action taken by a taxing authority, or brought in a court of competent jurisdiction, after a Transaction is entered into (regardless of whether such action is taken or brought with respect to a party to this Agreement) or (2) a Change in Tax Law, the party (which will be the Affected Party) will, or there is a substantial likelihood that it will, on the next succeeding Scheduled Settlement Date (A) be required to pay to the other party an additional amount in respect of an Indemnifiable Tax under Section 2(d)(i)(4) (except in respect of interest under Section 9(h)) or (B) receive a payment from which an amount is required to be deducted or withheld for or on account of a Tax (except in respect of interest under Section 9(h)) and no additional amount is required to be paid in respect of such Tax under Section 2(d)(i)(4) (other than by reason of Section 2(d)(i)(4)(A) or (B));

Section 5(b)(iii)

A Tax Event takes place when a Change in Tax Law occurs and results in a party becoming (or very likely to become) burdened by a withholding tax which leads to a payer being required to gross up or a payee receiving a lower payment net of withholding with no gross up. A termination right arises in these cases because neither party is regarded as sufficiently "at fault" for it to be burdened by an unexpected tax charge until the maturity of the Transaction. The party having to gross up or the party receiving less than it expected because the withholding tax is being levied is called the Affected Party and is entitled to call for close out of Affected Transactions.

A Tax Event does not occur if a withholding tax is levied on default interest under Section 9(h).

So, if any withholding tax arises because of a Change in Tax Law after the date the parties enter into a Transaction, the party impacted by the withholding tax has a right to terminate the Transaction(s) concerned under Sections 5(b)(iii) and 6(b) of the Agreement. The Section 6 procedure involves trying to transfer the Affected Transactions to a third party or a different Office within 20–30 days of the notice to avoid the Tax Event. The termination for the Affected Transactions is made on the basis that there is one Affected Party. This means the non-Affected Party makes the termination calculations.

However, please note that an Affected Party cannot unilaterally terminate an Affected Transaction before the 30 days following notice have expired. Hence an Affected Party may be unable to do anything about payments due within this 30 day period, i.e. he may have to gross up for them or receive his payment net.

If a change of facts occurs at the start or during the life of the Transaction this will not give a right to trigger a Tax Event because the party concerned should have done its analysis properly in the first place and should not be able to close out as a result of its own actions if the change of facts happens later in the Transaction's life.

Principal changes from the 1992 Agreement

- **The court or tax authority decision (which leads to a Tax Event being declared by the Affected Party) must now arise after the date a Transaction is entered into and *not* as before "on or after" that date.**
- **A new definition – "Scheduled Settlement Date" is used instead of Scheduled Payment Date.**

(iv) ***Tax Event Upon Merger***. The party (the "Burdened Party") on the next succeeding Scheduled Settlement Date will either (1) be required to pay an additional amount in respect of an Indemnifiable Tax under Section 2(d)(i)(4) (except in respect of interest under Section 9(h)) or (2) receive a payment from which an amount has been deducted or withheld for or on account of any Tax in respect of which the other party is not required to pay an additional amount (other than by reason of Section 2(d)(i)(4)(A) or (B)), in either case as a result of a party consolidating or amalgamating with, or merging with or into, or transferring all or substantially all its assets (or any substantial part of the assets comprising the business conducted by it as of the date of this Master Agreement) to, or reorganising, reincorporating or reconstituting into or as, another entity (which will be the Affected Party) where such action does not constitute a Merger Without Assumption;

Section 5(b)(iv)

Under Section 5(b)(iv), a Tax Event Upon Merger arises if a withholding tax is levied which results in a merging party (the "Affected Party") having to gross up its payment or a non-merging party receiving any payment due to it net of such withholding tax with no gross up. Such a party is called the Burdened Party. Such a transaction could result in the charging of withholding tax, for example, if the acquiror's jurisdiction of incorporation is different from that of the company being acquired. Again, only Affected Transactions are terminated because the trading relationship is fundamentally altered.

Certain exceptions apply to this. For instance, a Tax Event Upon Merger cannot occur because of interest payments due under Section 9(h) nor will it apply if Transactions are impacted by the Merger Without Assumption Event of Default (Section 5(a)(viii)) because they can be terminated through an Event of Default which is more serious and will terminate all Transactions.

If a Tax Event Upon Merger happens, the Burdened Party can terminate the Affected Transactions immediately upon giving notice if it is not the Affected Party (i.e. the party who is merging). Otherwise it must try and transfer the Affected Transaction(s) to another of its Offices or Affiliates within 20 days of giving notice failing which the other party must try to do so for the balance of the period up to 30 days after the original notice. If he fails, the Affected Party can go ahead and terminate the Affected Transaction(s). Where the Burdened Party is also the Affected Party it will be unable upon the occurrence of a Tax Event Upon Merger unilaterally to terminate the Affected Transaction(s) until after 30 days from when it first gives notice to the other party. During that 30-day period it could be exposed to having to pay a gross up or receive its payments net of withholding tax. There is nothing it can do about it.

Any termination payment to be made in respect of Affected Transactions is calculated on the basis of one Affected Party with the non-Affected Party making the termination calculations.

If a payee is not entitled to receive a gross up payment because it has given a false Payee Tax Representation or failed to deliver requested tax documentation, it will not be entitled to call a Tax Event Upon Merger. Please note, that a Tax Event and a Tax Event Upon Merger will not apply if it is a Credit Support Provider that unexpectedly needs to gross up.

Principal changes from the 1992 Agreement

- **The new definition – Scheduled Settlement Date – is used instead of Scheduled Payment Date.**
- **A Tax Event Upon Merger can now arise where a party receives a net payment because of any Tax and not just an Indemnifiable Tax suffering a withholding.**
- **Extension of "merger" events to a substantial portion of a party's business assets as at the date of the Agreement and to reorganisation, reincorporation or reconstitution into or as another entity.**

(v) ***Credit Event Upon Merger***. If "Credit Event Upon Merger" is specified in the Schedule as applying to the party, a Designated Event (as defined below) occurs with respect to such party, any Credit Support Provider of such party or any applicable Specified Entity of such party (in each case, "X") and such Designated Event does not constitute a Merger Without Assumption, and the creditworthiness of X or, if applicable, the successor, surviving or transferee entity of X, after taking into account any applicable Credit Support Document, is materially weaker immediately after the occurrence of such Designated Event than that of X immediately prior to the occurrence of such Designated Event (and, in any such event, such party or its successor, surviving or transferee entity, as appropriate, will be the Affected Party). A "Designated Event" with respect to X means that:-

(1) X consolidates or amalgamates with, or merges with or into, or transfers all or substantially all its assets (or any substantial part of the assets comprising the business conducted by X as of the date of this Master Agreement) to, or reorganises, reincorporates or reconstitutes into or as, another entity;

(2) any person, related group of persons or entity acquires directly or indirectly the beneficial ownership of (A) equity securities having the power to elect a majority of the board of directors (or its equivalent) of X or (B) any other ownership interest enabling it to exercise control of X; or

(3) X effects any substantial change in its capital structure by means of the issuance, incurrence or guarantee of debt or the issuance of (A) preferred stock or other securities convertible into or exchangeable for debt or preferred stock or (B) in the case of entities other than corporations, any other form of ownership interest; or

Section 5(b)(v)

The rationale for Credit Event Upon Merger is that a party may not have entered into an Agreement in the first place had it known that its counterparty would merge or be taken over and, as a result, become a much worse credit risk. However, parties do not usually invoke Credit Event Upon Merger as a knee jerk reaction but try to evaluate if the new counterparty will be able to perform its obligations under the Agreement or if, for example, credit support will need to be taken.

Section 5(b)(v) of the Agreement only applies to a party if this is stated in Part 1(d) of the Schedule. It addresses the situation where your counterparty, its Credit Support Provider or any applicable Specified Entity (specified in Part 1(a) of the Schedule) is taken over by, or merges with, another entity and this results in a material reduction in their creditworthiness even after taking into account any Credit Support Document. A Termination Event will occur under this provision if the Transaction does not result in a Merger Without Assumption Event of Default (Section 5(a)(viii)). If this Termination Event occurs, the party who has entered into or whose Credit Support Provider or Specified Entity has entered into a merger or takeover transaction is the Affected Party and the other party is entitled to terminate all Transactions under the Agreement. The merger taints all Transactions, not just some of them.

The basic Credit Event Upon Merger provision in the 1992 Agreement described North American merger practice where the surviving entity is not the same as the original party to the Agreement. Over the years in many European Schedules this provision has been expanded through the term Designated Event to include the purchase of voting shares giving the power to elect a majority of the board of directors or any other interest enabling the purchaser to control the original party (which might not be a limited company).

In addition changes to the original party's capital structure (e.g. following a leveraged buy-out) through the issue of bonds, preference shares or convertible securities is also covered provided that this results in a deterioration of the other party's creditworthiness.

The Designated Event concept appears in this Section 5(a)(v) and covers a wide range of change of central events viz: mergers, asset transfers, reorganisations, reincorporations and reconstitutions. Also direct or indirect changes in: beneficial ownership of equity securities with the power to elect a board majority or any other controlling ownership interest. Finally, any major change in a party's capital or indebtedness structure.

The overriding point is that the merged entity must be much weaker financially after the merger.

In the 1992 Agreement the materially weaker assessment of creditworthiness was made immediately before the Transaction. Now it is made immediately after.

Finally, the 2002 Agreement also covers the situation where the surviving party is the same entity that originally entered into the Agreement.

(vi) ***Additional Termination Event***. If any "Additional Termination Event" is specified in the Schedule or any Confirmation as applying, the occurrence of such event (and, in such event, the Affected Party or Affected Parties will be as specified for such Additional Termination Event in the Schedule or such Confirmation).

Section 5(b)(vi)

Section 5(b)(vi) of the Agreement has been added so that parties may specify Additional Termination Events in Part 1(g) of the Schedule or any Confirmation and any Affected Party or Affected Parties for such Additional Termination Events.

It is assumed that where an Additional Termination Event arises, all Transactions will be Affected Transactions and the non-Affected Party will be entitled to terminate them. Many Additional Termination Events are credit related (e.g. rating agency downgrades of a party's outstanding long-term debt securities below a minimum rating or the cancellation of a rating by a credit ratings agency) and therefore impact the entire contractual relationship between the parties and not just a particular group of Transactions. A Change of Ownership clause and full prepayment of a loan linked to a swap are other common examples of an Additional Termination Event.

Principal changes from the 1992 Agreement

- **Designated Event referred to and detailed in 5(b)(v)(1)–(3) covering European style merger practice now.**
- **Analysis of "materially weaker" in 5(b)(v) now takes account of any Credit Support Document held.**
- **Minor change of "shall" to "will" in line 3 of 5(b)(vi).**

(c) ***Hierarchy of Events.***

(i) An event or circumstance that constitutes or gives rise to an Illegality or a Force Majeure Event will not, for so long as that is the case, also constitute or give rise to an Event of Default under Section 5(a)(i), 5(a)(ii)(1) or 5(a)(iii)(1) insofar as such event or circumstance relates to the failure to make any payment or delivery or a failure to comply with any other material provision of this Agreement or a Credit Support Document, as the case may be.

(ii) Except in circumstances contemplated by clause (i) above, if an event or circumstance which would otherwise constitute or give rise to an Illegality or a Force Majeure Event also constitutes an Event of Default or any other Termination Event, it will be treated as an Event of Default or such other Termination Event, as the case may be, and will not constitute or give rise to an Illegality or a Force Majeure Event.

(iii) If an event or circumstance which would otherwise constitute or give rise to a Force Majeure Event also constitutes an Illegality, it will be treated as an Illegality, except as described in clause (ii) above, and not a Force Majeure Event.

Section 5(c)

(i)

The 2002 version of this provision is more sophisticated than its predecessor with the arrival of Force Majeure Event on the scene. The nub of this is that where an Illegality or Force Majeure Event arises, for so long as it persists it will not give rise to a Failure to Pay or Deliver, Breach of Agreement or Credit Support Default Event of Default where this relates to a failure to pay, deliver or perform under any material provision of the Agreement or a Credit Support Document. Therefore, Illegality and Force Majeure Event override an Event of Default in these circumstances but not otherwise.

(ii)

Barring this, where an Illegality or Force Majeure Event also constitutes an Event of Default or other Termination Event, it will be treated more severely as the latter because that would allow earlier close-out. So, for example, if a Bankruptcy Event of Default exists at the same time as an Illegality in respect of the same counterparty, the Non-defaulting Party can close out on that basis in respect of all Transactions and on its own side of the market without the delay of a Waiting Period. This provision arose from the 1998 Russian debt crisis where a Bankruptcy Event of Default and an Illegality were considered to have occurred and people were not in favour of treating the situation as an Illegality.

(iii)

A similar principle applies here. Where an event arises which could constitute either an Illegality or a Force Majeure Event, it will constitute an Illegality because it has a shorter three Local Business Day Waiting Period.

Principal change from the 1992 Agreement

- **Totally new provision.**

(d) ***Deferral of Payments and Deliveries During Waiting Period.*** If an Illegality or a Force Majeure Event has occurred and is continuing with respect to a Transaction, each payment or delivery which would otherwise be required to be made under that Transaction will be deferred to, and will not be due until:-

(i) the first Local Business Day or, in the case of a delivery, the first Local Delivery Day (or the first day that would have been a Local Business Day or Local Delivery Day, as appropriate, but for the occurrence of the event or circumstance constituting or giving rise to that Illegality of Force Majeure Event) following the end of any applicable Waiting Period in respect of the Illegality or Force Majeure Event, as the case may be; or

(ii) if earlier, the date on which the event or circumstance constituting or giving rise to that Illegality of Force Majeure Event ceases to exist or, if such date is not a Local Business Day or, in the case of a delivery, a Local Delivery Day, the first following day that is a Local Business Day or Local Delivery Day, as appropriate.

Section 5(d)

This new provision concerns postponement of payments or deliveries while an Illegality or Force Majeure Event persists. The provision states that they will not be due until:

(i) **the first Local Business Day or first Local Delivery Day after the end of the appropriate Waiting Period for an Illegality or Force Majeure Event; or**

(ii) **if the event ceases before the end of a Waiting Period on that very day or if that is not a Local Business Day or Local Delivery Day, the next following Local Business Day or Local Delivery Day.**

Principal change from the 1992 Agreement

- **Totally new provision.**

(e) ***Inability of Head or Home Office to Perform Obligations of Branch.*** If (i) an Illegality or a Force Majeure Event occurs under Section 5(b)(i)(1) or 5(b)(ii)(1) and the relevant Office is not the Affected Party's head or home office, (ii) Section 10(a) applies, (iii) the other party seeks performance of the relevant obligation or compliance with the relevant provision by the Affected Party's head or home office and (iv) the Affected Party's head or home office fails so to perform or comply due to the occurrence of an event or circumstance which would, if that head or home office were the Office through which the Affected Party makes and receives payments and deliveries with respect to the relevant Transaction, constitute or give rise to an Illegality or a Force Majeure Event, and such failure would otherwise constitute an Event of Default under Section 5(a)(i) or 5(a)(iii)(1) with respect to such party, then, for so long as the relevant event or circumstance continues to exist with respect to both the Office referred to in Section 5(b)(i)(1) or 5(b)(ii)(1), as the case may be, and the Affected Party's head or home office, such failure will not constitute an Event of Default under Section 5(a)(i) or 5(a)(iii)(1).

Section 5(e)

This convoluted provision concerns both the inability of a branch to pay or perform following an Illegality or a Force Majeure Event and the same thing happening to its head or home office at the time the Non-affected Party invokes its recourse against that head or home office because Section 10(a) of the Agreement applies.

In those circumstances while the Illegality or Force Majeure Event persists for both Offices, the failure to pay or perform will not constitute an Event of Default under Section 5(a)(i) – Failure to Pay or Deliver or 5(a)(iii)(1) – Credit Support Default in respect of either of them.

Principal change from the 1992 Agreement

- **Totally new provision.**

Section 6 – Early Termination

Section 6 describes the detailed close-out netting mechanism where an Event of Default or Termination Event occurs.

Close-out netting is vital to the ISDA Master Agreement; so vital that ISDA has commissioned legal opinions from 36 countries to find out if they would recognise close-out netting under the 2002 Agreement if a Non-defaulting Party exercised its rights in a default or bankruptcy situation involving one of their nationals. The vast majority of jurisdictions do recognise the effectiveness of close-out netting. A list of these opinions is shown in Annex 4, page 726. In order to minimise the capital allocated to derivatives' counterparty exposure, regulators require written, reasoned, independent legal opinions from major law firms for each jurisdiction where a bank is seeking to net its exposure in respect of Transactions under Agreements with various counterparties in that country. Regulators require these legal opinions to be updated at least once a year.

It is vital for a solvent or non-defaulting party to have a clear and effective close-out mechanism so that it can replace the Terminated Transactions it had with an insolvent party or defaulting as quickly as possible so as to maintain any underlying hedging transactions.

Before entering the tall grass and describing the Section 6 provisions in depth, I should first like to attempt a summary of them.

When an Event of Default occurs, only the Non-defaulting Party can choose an Early Termination Date and close out and net off all Transactions between the parties to reach a single figure payable one way or the other. This payment essentially represents damages for the curtailed Transactions. The Early Termination Date may be designated at any time that the Event of Default persists but it must be designated within 20 days of the termination notice.

Please note that once an Early Termination Date has been designated it can only be cancelled with the consent of both parties. Otherwise there is no turning back. Termination is not the sole remedy of an innocent party as Section 9(d) provides the possibility for other remedies to be pursued (see commentary on page 253).

With a Termination Event (except for Illegality, Force Majeure Event, Credit Event Upon Merger and probably Additional Termination Events) the parties have to find a way to keep an Affected Transaction alive possibly by transferring it to another office or group company. They have 20–30 days to do this but if they fail, the Affected Transaction or Transactions are closed out.

There are a number of major changes to the close-out provisions in Section 6 of the 2002 Agreement. These were grounded on lessons learned from various crises and court cases in the late 1990s.

Most important of all is that Market Quotation and Loss are both replaced by Close-out Amount.

Close-out Amount is a valuation measure formulated by a number of leading market players who wanted to move away from what they saw as the rather rigid procedures of Market Quotation but wanted to combine this with greater objectivity and transparency than the Loss measure had. We shall review the components of Close-out Amount later.

Some of the problems with obtaining Market Quotations were considered to be:

- **failure of a major market name leading to difficulties in obtaining quotations from major dealers trying to manage their own portfolios in the turmoil;**
- **due to this it might be difficult to obtain the required number of quotations at least in a timely fashion;**
- **in market turmoil the quotations might be unreliable and might be widely divergent.**

The Close-out Amount methodology, as we shall see, is more flexible but is still weighted in favour of third party information and therefore transparency. The whole process is controlled by principles of commercial reasonableness.

In addition the First Method has been abolished largely because it was not regarded favourably by regulators and was little used in the market. The Second Method therefore always applies and no choice has to be made of it now in the Schedule.

I would also like to say a few words about Automatic Early Termination. This may be useful where the Non-defaulting Party can exercise its rights outside the insolvency proceedings or where it is favourably received by a liquidator because it provides certainty and objectivity with its timing.

Under Section 6(a), the Non-defaulting Party has the right to designate an Early Termination Date (for close-out purposes) for all outstanding Transactions upon an Event of Default arising and continuing. Section 6(a) also allows parties to choose in Part 1(e) of the Schedule that "Automatic Early Termination" will apply to a party if certain bankruptcy or insolvency events occur. If they fail to make a selection in Part 1(e), Automatic Early Termination will not apply. If Automatic Early Termination applies and certain Section 5(a)(vii) insolvency events occur, an Early Termination Date will arise automatically for all outstanding Transactions without notice to the Non-defaulting Party who may be unaware of the bankruptcy event and, when he finds out, markets may have moved significantly since the deemed Early Termination Date. In addition this could result in hedging transactions having to be replaced at higher cost in the market. Often the Non-defaulting Party seeks an indemnity for this in the Schedule.

In general, lawyers consider the drawbacks of Automatic Early Termination to outweigh its benefits. However, it is helpful to apply it to counterparties subject to certain insolvency regimes, e.g. Germany, Japan, Belgium, Denmark and Switzerland. It is not necessary in the UK or the US.

Please note that Automatic Early Termination only applies to certain insolvency events and not to other types of Events of Default.

The individual sub-Sections of Section 6 are now reviewed.

6. Early Termination; Close-Out Netting

(a) ***Right to Terminate Following Event of Default.*** If at any time an Event of Default with respect to a party (the "Defaulting Party") has occurred and is then continuing, the other party (the "Non-defaulting Party") may, by not more than 20 days notice to the Defaulting Party specifying the relevant Event of Default, designate a day not earlier than the day such notice is effective as an Early Termination Date in respect of all outstanding Transactions. If, however, "Automatic Early Termination" is specified in the Schedule as applying to a party, then an Early Termination Date in respect of all outstanding Transactions will occur immediately upon the occurrence with respect to such party of an Event of Default specified in Section 5(a)(vii)(1), (3), (5), (6) or, to the extent analogous thereto, (8), and as of the time immediately preceding the institution of the relevant proceeding or the presentation of the relevant petition upon the occurrence with respect to such party of an Event of Default specified in Section 5(a)(vii)(4) or, to the extent analogous thereto, (8).

Section 6

Section 6(a)

Where an Event of Default occurs and is continuing, the Non-defaulting Party has the option (but not the obligation) to terminate all outstanding Transactions under the Agreement by giving the Defaulting Party not more than 20 days' notice of its intention to close out all Transactions on a certain date called the Early Termination Date. The notice must describe the Event of Default and the Early Termination Date is normally much sooner than 20 days after the notice is given.

With certain insolvency events (those described in Section 5(a)(vii)(1), (3), (5) and (6)) termination may be automatic rather than by notice. These insolvency events are:

- **dissolution (except in the case of a merger, amalgamation or consolidation); or**
- **a general arrangement, assignment or composition with creditors; or**
- **a winding-up resolution is passed (except again in the case of a merger, amalgamation or consolidation); or**
- **the appointment of an administrator or similar insolvency official over all or most of a party's assets.**

In these four cases termination takes place immediately after they happen. However, with the insolvency Event of Default in Section 5(a)(vii)(4) (which is the starting of proceedings or the filing of a winding-up order by a party or by its regulator or liquidator which either results in a bankruptcy adjudication or is not dismissed within 15 days) then the close-out is deemed to occur immediately before the proceedings start or the order is presented. The problem here is that the Non-defaulting Party may not be aware of the insolvency event and by the time they are the markets may have moved strongly against them. Chapter 8 examines possible indemnifying amendments designed to protect the Non-defaulting Party in these circumstances (see pages 451–3).

If an Event of Default impacting a party is cured before a termination notice is given, the Non-defaulting Party loses its right to give such a notice because Section 6(d)(i) requires that the Event of Default is "continuing". However, once the notice is given, the Defaulting Party cannot then cure the Event of Default. As soon as the Non-defaulting Party gives notice it must have certainty and be free to enter into a replacement Transaction to cover the open position that will arise on the Early Termination Date or unwind an existing hedging Transaction without concern that a late performance by the Defaulting Party of its obligations will mean the Non-defaulting Party will have to reverse its actions, possibly at a loss. It is important for the parties to set sensible cure periods for Events of Default if the ones in the Agreement are not suitable for their particular circumstances.

Principal change from the 1992 Agreement

- **The words "Close-Out Netting" are added in the heading.**

(b) ***Right to Terminate Following Termination Event.***

(i) ***Notice.*** If a Termination Event other than a Force Majeure Event occurs, an Affected Party will, promptly upon becoming aware of it, notify the other party, specifying the nature of that Termination Event and each Affected Transaction, and will also give the other party such other information about that Termination Event as the other party may reasonably require. If a Force Majeure Event occurs, each party will, promptly upon becoming aware of it, use all reasonable efforts to notify the other party, specifying the nature of that Force Majeure Event, and will also give the other party such other information about that Force Majeure Event as the other party may reasonably require.

(ii) ***Transfer to Avoid Termination Event.*** If a Tax Event occurs and there is only one Affected Party, or if a Tax Event Upon Merger occurs and the Burdened Party is the Affected Party, the Affected Party will, as a condition to its right to designate an Early Termination Date under Section 6(b)(iv), use all reasonable efforts (which will not require such party to incur a loss, other than immaterial, incidental expenses) to transfer within 20 days after it gives notice under Section 6(b)(i) all its rights and obligations under this Agreement in respect of the Affected Transactions to another of its Offices or Affiliates so that such Termination Event ceases to exist.

If the Affected Party is not able to make such a transfer it will give notice to the other party to that effect within such 20 day period, whereupon the other party may effect such a transfer within 30 days after the notice is given under Section 6(b)(i).

Any such transfer by a party under this Section 6(b)(ii) will be subject to and conditional upon the prior written consent of the other party, which consent will not be withheld if such other party's policies in effect at such time would permit it to enter into transactions with the transferee on the terms proposed.

(iii) ***Two Affected Parties.*** If a Tax Event occurs and there are two Affected Parties, each party will use all reasonable efforts to reach agreement within 30 days after notice of such occurrence is given under Section 6(b)(i) to avoid that Termination Event.

Section 6(b)

(i) Where a non Force Majeure Event Termination Event occurs, the Affected Party will promptly notify the other party of it and its nature and each Affected Transaction and any other information the Affected Party may require. However, where a Force Majeure Event occurs each party has a duty to use all reasonable efforts to notify the other party of the nature of the Force Majeure Event and supply the other party with such other information as it may need. Only "reasonable efforts" are required because of the nature of the event (e.g. a natural disaster may make notification impossible to achieve).

(ii) This sub-section deals with transfers to avoid certain Termination Events on the principle that it is better to continue a Transaction where a "no fault" Termination Event occurs than to close it out. Please note, however, that it is no longer required to try and transfer a Transaction afflicted by an Illegality because the market hitherto found this difficult to achieve in practice.

If a Tax Event or Tax Event Upon Merger happens, the Affected Party has the right to choose an Early Termination Date but must use all reasonable efforts to try to transfer all rights and obligations in respect of Affected Transactions to another of its Offices or Affiliates within 20 days of giving its notice to the Non-affected Party under Section 6(b)(i). The aim is to extinguish the Termination Event. The Affected Party is not required to incur a loss but is expected to pay minor expenses to achieve this.

Where the Affected Party cannot make such a transfer, it must within the 20-day notice period notify the non-Affected Party who can try to do so within 30 days from the original notice date. So if the Affected Party tries to transfer and fails on the twentieth day and then notifies the non-Affected Party, the non-Affected Party only has ten days in which to make a transfer.

The prior written consent of the other party is necessary to make this transfer but must not be unreasonably withheld especially if the non-Affected Party's policies would, in the normal course, allow it to enter into Transactions with the proposed transferee Office or Affiliate of the Affected Party.

(iii) Where a Tax Event under Section 5(b)(iii) has occurred and there are two Affected Parties, they must both use all reasonable efforts to agree on action to avoid the relevant Termination Event within 30 days following notice.

Principal changes from the 1992 Agreement

- **Section 6(b)(i) – Force Majeure Event is excluded from the first sentence of this notice provision but is the subject of a new second sentence.**
- **Section 6(b)(ii) – There is no longer any obligation to seek to transfer a Transaction affected by an Illegality to another Office or Affiliate.**
- **Section 6(b)(iii) – Illegality no longer applies to this provision.**

(iv) *Right to Terminate.*

(1) If:-

(A) a transfer under Section 6(b)(ii) or an agreement under Section 6(b)(iii), as the case may be, has not been effected with respect to all Affected Transactions within 30 days after an Affected Party gives notice under Section 6(b)(i); or

(B) a Credit Event Upon Merger or an Additional Termination Event occurs, or a Tax Event Upon Merger occurs and the Burdened Party is not the Affected Party,

the Burdened Party in the case of a Tax Event Upon Merger, any Affected Party in the case of a Tax Event or an Additional Termination Event if there are two Affected Parties, or the Non-affected Party in the case of a Credit Event Upon Merger or an Additional Termination Event if there is only one Affected Party may, if the relevant Termination Event is then continuing, by not more than 20 days notice to the other party, designate a day not earlier than the day such notice is effective as an Early Termination Date in respect of all Affected Transactions.

(iv)(1)
If the parties are unable to agree, transfer or otherwise avoid the relevant Termination Event within 30 days of the giving of the notice, an Early Termination Date may be designated in accordance with Section 6(b)(iv) of the Agreement.

Here this is extended to Credit Event Upon Merger or an Additional Termination Event or Tax Event Upon Merger where the Burdened Party is the Non-affected Party (i.e. the party not engaged in the merger).

There then follow some rules as to which party has the right to terminate an Affected Transaction. These are:

- **the Burdened Party (i.e. the Non-affected Party) with a Tax Event Upon Merger;**
- **any Affected Party with a Tax Event;**
- **either Affected Party with an Additional Termination Event (provided there are two Affected Parties);**
- **the Non-affected Party with a Credit Event Upon Merger;**
- **the Non-affected Party with an Additional Termination Event if there is one Affected Party.**

Provided the Termination Event is still continuing, the terminator can issue a notice to the other party giving not more than 20 days' notice (and usually a lot less) choosing an Early Termination Date (not earlier than the date the original notice became effective) in respect of all Affected Transactions.

(2) If at any time an Illegality or a Force Majeure Event has occurred and is then continuing and any applicable Waiting Period has expired:-

(A) Subject to clause (B) below, either party may, by not more than 20 days notice to the other party, designate (I) a day not earlier than the day on which such notice becomes effective as an Early Termination Date in respect of all Affected Transactions or (II) by specifying in that notice the Affected Transactions in respect of which it is designating the relevant day as an Early Termination Date, a day not earlier than two Local Business Days following the day on which such notice becomes effective as an Early Termination Date in respect of less than all Affected Transactions. Upon receipt of a notice designating an Early Termination Date in respect of less than all Affected Transactions, the other party may, by notice to the designating party, if such notice is effective on or before the day so designated, designate that same day as an Early Termination Date in respect of any or all other Affected Transactions.

(B) An Affected Party (if the Illegality or Force Majeure Event relates to performance by such party or any Credit Support Provider of such party of an obligation to make any payment or delivery under, or to compliance with any other material provision of, the relevant Credit Support Document) will only have the right to designate an Early Termination Date under Section 6(b)(iv)(2)(A) as a result of an Illegality under Section 5(b)(i)(2) or a Force Majeure Event under Section 5(b)(ii)(2) following the prior designation by the other party of an Early Termination Date, pursuant to Section 6(b)(iv)(2)(A), in respect of less than all Affected Transactions.

(iv)(2)

Where an Illegality or Force Majeure Event has happened and persists and any Waiting Period has expired the following termination rights arise:

(A) Either party may by no more than 20 days' notice to the other choose an Early Termination Date not earlier than the date the notice becomes effective to terminate all or some Affected Transactions. This approach provides some flexibility where it is not in the parties' best interests for all Affected Transactions to be terminated. Where the terminator chooses to close out less than all Affected Transactions, settlement would take place not earlier than two Local Business Days after the date the notice becomes effective in order to give the other party time to decide whether it wants to close out other Affected Transactions. There is, of course, a danger of cherry picking here which is why when this arises the other party may issue a counternotice specifying the same Early Termination Date in respect of any or all other Affected Transactions.

(B) This is the corresponding right where the Illegality or Force Majeure Event impacts a party's or its Credit Support Provider's rights to pay, deliver or perform under material provisions under the Credit Support Document. It provides that because the Non-affected Party is impacted by the Affected Party's Credit Support Provider being unable to perform under its Credit Support Document, it initially has the right to terminate Transactions in this situation. Only where it exercises this right in respect of less than all Affected Transactions can the Affected Party give notice to terminate some or all of the remaining Affected Transactions. The rationale for this process is that ISDA members did not believe that an Affected Party who could not make a required delivery of collateral should have unilateral rights to terminate Affected Transactions.

Principal changes from the 1992 Agreement

- Section 6(b)(iv)(1)(B) is new and replaces Section 6(b)(iv)(2) in the 1992 Agreement.
- Section 6(b)(iv)(2) is virtually entirely new especially with the concept of partial termination of Affected Transactions.

(c) ***Effect of Designation.***

(i) If notice designating an Early Termination Date is given under Section 6(a) or (b), the Early Termination Date will occur on the date so designated, whether or not the relevant Event of Default or Termination Event is then continuing.

(ii) Upon the occurrence or effective designation of an Early Termination Date, no further payments or deliveries under Section 2(a)(i) or 9(h)(i) in respect of the Terminated Transactions will be required to be made, but without prejudice to the other provisions of this Agreement. The amount, if any, payable in respect of an Early Termination Date will be determined pursuant to Sections 6(e) and 9(h)(ii).

Section 6(c)

Where an Early Termination Date notice is given for an Event of Default or Termination Event, the Early Termination Date will occur on the chosen date whether or not the Event of Default or Termination Event is then continuing.

When an Early Termination Date happens or is chosen, neither party is any longer required to make normal payments or deliveries under Sections 2(a)(i) or 9(h)(i) of the Agreement for Transactions to be terminated. The Agreement itself is not terminated by the giving of an early termination notice; only the parties' obligations to make payments or deliveries terminate. Please note that several provisions, e.g. obligation to gross up payments (Section 2(d)(i)), obligation to make settlement payments under Section 6(e); currency conversion obligations (Section 8); and obligation to pay enforcement expenses (Section 11) all survive because of Section 9(d) – Survival of Obligations. Payments or deliveries that would have been due on dates after the termination notice takes effect but on or before the Early Termination Date (as well as any obligations that did not become payable or deliverable because of the failure to satisfy all conditions precedent) are included in the definition of Unpaid Amounts and are therefore included in the Early Termination Amount, a new shorthand term describing the total settlement amount payable under Section 6(e).

Principal change from the 1992 Agreement

- **Minor changes principally to Section numbers.**

(d) ***Calculations; Payment Date.***

(i) ***Statement.*** On or as soon as reasonably practicable following the occurrence of an Early Termination Date, each party will make the calculations on its part, if any, contemplated by Section 6(e) and will provide to the other party a statement (1) showing, in reasonable detail, such calculations (including any quotations, market data or information from internal sources used in making such calculations), (2) specifying (except where there are two Affected Parties) any Early Termination Amount payable and (3) giving details of the relevant account to which any amount payable to it is to be paid. In the absence of written confirmation from the source of a quotation or market data obtained in determining a Close-out Amount, the records of the party obtaining such quotation or market data will be conclusive evidence of the existence and accuracy of such quotation or market data.

(ii) ***Payment Date.*** An Early Termination Amount due in respect of any Early Termination Date will, together with any amount of interest payable pursuant to Section 9(h)(ii)(2), be payable (1) on the day on which notice of the amount payable is effective in the case of an Early Termination Date which is designated or occurs as a result of an Event of Default and (2) on the day which is two Local Business Days after the day on which notice of the amount payable is effective (or, if there are two Affected Parties, after the day on which the statement provided pursuant to clause (i) above by the second party to provide such a statement is effective) in the case of an Early Termination Date which is designated as a result of a Termination Event.

Section 6(d)

(i) On or shortly after an Early Termination Date, each party, where practicable, is to provide the other with a statement of early termination payment calculations in reasonable detail and advise the account to which any termination payment is to be made. Such a statement will not only show details of any quotations but also specify market data or information from internal sources used in making the calculations. This is the first sign of the broader scope of Close-out Amount. The records of the Non-defaulting Party or both parties where no party is at fault shall be conclusive evidence of quotations received from dealers who do not confirm them in writing or of market data used. The statement will not specify a net close-out amount payable if there are two Affected Parties because both of them will make their own calculations and the difference will be split.

(ii) Early termination payments for Events of Default are payable on the day that the Early Termination Date notice becomes effective. Early termination payments for Termination Events are payable two Local Business Days after the day that the Early Termination Date notice becomes effective. The amount concerned will be paid with accrued interest calculated pursuant to Section 9(h)(ii)(2) in the Termination Currency agreed in Part 1(f) of the Schedule. In calculating the Early Termination Amount, Close-out Amount and any Unpaid Amounts are converted into a Termination Currency Equivalent by obtaining a market foreign exchange rate from an FX dealer chosen by the Non-defaulting Party.

If there are two Affected Parties, the agreed split Early Termination Amount is payable two Local Business Days after the second party's statement becomes effective.

Principal changes from the 1992 Agreement

Section 6(d)(i)

- **Addition of the words "Payment Date" to sub-section heading.**
- **First mention of wider scope of Close-out Amount to include market data and information from internal sources.**
- **Differentiation made in respect of Early Termination Amounts calculable in respect of two Affected Parties.**

Section 6(d)(ii)

- **Any interest due on Early Termination Amounts is now calculated according to Section 9(h)(ii)(2).**
- **It is clarified that where there are two Affected Parties the split Early Termination Amount is payable two Local Business Days after the second party's statement becomes effective.**

(e) ***Payments on Early Termination.*** If an Early Termination Date occurs, the amount, if any, payable in respect of that Early Termination Date (the "Early Termination Amount") will be determined pursuant to this Section 6(e) and will be subject to Section 6(f).

Introduction to Section 6(e)

As mentioned in the introduction to this Section 6, substantial changes have been made to the calculation of early termination payments. Elements of the payment measures of Market Quotation and Loss have been subsumed into the new single payment measure of Close-out Amount which also has various additional features.

During discussions in 2002, ISDA members decided that a single payment measure of Close-out Amount was preferable to the choices of Market Quotation and Loss in the 1992 Agreement. They were influenced by the following factors:-

- **difficulties in obtaining four quotations from Reference Market-makers in market crises in 1997 and 1998 as required by the Market Quotation measure;**
- **even where four quotations were obtained they could diverge widely in an illiquid market;**
- **market players considering Loss was not transparent or objective enough.**

The First Method has been discarded completely largely because it was frowned upon by regulators. The Second Method now applies in all cases but is not referred to by name at all and, of course, there is no election in Part 1(f) of the Schedule any more.

The Section 14 definition of Close-out Amount is about a page long.

Close-out Amount is a Determining Party's calculations of replacement losses, costs or gains in respect of Terminated Transactions in order for the Determining Party to obtain the economic equivalent of the material terms (i.e direct payment flows and pricing related factors) of the Terminated Transactions or any option rights attaching to them. Normal (i.e. Section 2(a)(i)) payments and deliveries due after the Early Termination Date (assuming all Section 2(a)(iii) conditions precedent are met) are taken into account in the calculation of Close-out Amount on a net present value basis.

The Determining Party who could be the Non-defaulting Party, the Non-affected Party or two Affected Parties or their agents must act in good faith and use commercially reasonable procedures in obtaining a commercially reasonable result. This is always a key principle for the Determining Party in calculating the Close-out Amount. Close-out Amount can be separately calculated for an individual Terminated Transaction or group of them provided that this is done for all Transactions to be terminated. Close-out Amounts will be calculated as of the Early Termination Date or if this is not commercially reasonable as of the next commercially reasonable date.

Unpaid Amount and Section 11 expenses are excluded from the calculation of Close-out Amount and are dealt with separately after the Close-out Amount has been calculated.

The Determining Party can consider any relevant information, without limitation, in calculating a Close-out Amount. The definition, however, suggests the following:

(i) **firm or indicative quotations from third parties for replacement transactions (i.e. other dealers) which take into account the Determining Party's creditworthiness and any credit support documentation between them when the quotation is requested; there is no requirement as with Market Quotation for four quotations to be obtained nor for an arithmetic average to be calculated.**

(ii) **relevant market data, e.g. rates, prices, yield curves, volatilities supplied by third parties in the relevant market; or**

(iii) **the same information in (i) and (ii) available to the Determining Party or its Affiliates from its own internal sources provided it is of the same type which it uses in valuing similar transactions in the normal course of its business.**

The Determining Party will use these inputs for calculating Close-out Amount unless it reasonably believes in good faith that such quotations or market data are not readily obtainable or, if used, would not produce a commercially reasonable result. However, where market conditions cause quotations or market data to produce a commercially unreasonable result, then the Determining Party need not spend more time trying to obtain such information from third parties.

The Determining Party may include costs of funding in all cases provided they are not already included in the information or quotations.

Quotation and information providers may include dealers, end-users, brokers, information vendors and providers. This is broader than just Reference Market-makers as with the old Market Quotation measure.

Provided no duplication occurs, the Determining Party can add on hedging unwind costs in connection with the Terminated Transactions to the Close-out Amount or it can deduct any hedging gains. This may be more relevant with structured transactions such as credit or equity derivatives which are being terminated.

The final provision of the definition again stresses the need to use commercially reasonable procedures. These are the need for the Determining Party to use third party or internal data in valuing Terminated Transactions in the same way as it would with similar transactions with unrelated third parties. Its approach must be consistent.

However, it is acknowledged that commercially reasonable different valuation methods may be appropriate to Terminated Transactions depending upon their type, size, complexity or number.

(i) ***Events of Default***. If the Early Termination Date results from an Event of Default, the Early Termination Amount will be an amount equal to (1) the sum of (A) the Termination Currency Equivalent of the Close-out Amount or Close-out Amounts (whether positive or negative) determined by the Non-defaulting Party for each Terminated Transaction or group of Terminated Transactions, as the case may be, and (B) the Termination Currency Equivalent of the Unpaid Amounts owing to the Non-defaulting Party less (2) the Termination Currency Equivalent of the Unpaid Amounts owing to the Defaulting Party. If the Early Termination Amount is a positive number, the Defaulting Party will pay it to the Non-defaulting Party; if it is a negative number, the Non-defaulting Party will pay the absolute value of the Early Termination Amount to the Defaulting Party.

Section 6(e)(i)

The broad scope of this definition is applied as follows:

Early Termination Amounts are calculated in accordance with Section 6(e) and are subject to set off in accordance with the set off clause now included in the Agreement's main text as Section 6(f).

All Transactions are closed out under an Event of Default.

Under the Agreement an Early Termination Amount consists of the following three components:

- **payments for the future replacement value of Terminated Transactions calculated by the Determining Party in reaching the Close-out Amount;**
- **contractual payment or delivery obligations (i.e. amounts due under Section 2(a)(i) which were due before the Early Termination Date but not paid ("Unpaid Amounts");**
- **payments or deliveries which would have been due before the Early Termination Date if all pre-conditions (such as no Event of Default having taken place) had been satisfied or if the Early Termination Date had not been designated. There are amounts due under Section 2(a)(iii) and are also called "Unpaid Amounts".**

As a portfolio of Terminated Transactions may be in different currencies they are converted into a single base currency (the Termination Currency Equivalent) which is chosen in Part 1(f) of the Schedule. The fallbacks are US dollars if no choice is made and the Agreement is governed by New York law and the Euro if the Agreement is governed by English law.

So in Section 6(e)(i) where an Early Termination Date is called for an Event of Default, the Early Termination Amount will be:

- **the net Termination Currency Equivalent of the Close-out Amount calculated by the Non-defaulting Party for all Terminated Transactions; plus**
- **the Termination Currency Equivalent of the Unpaid Amounts owing to the Non-defaulting Party; minus**
- **the Termination Currency Equivalent of the Unpaid Amounts owing to the Defaulting Party.**

If the net early termination figure is a positive number, the Defaulting Party pays it to the Non-defaulting Party. If it is a negative figure, the Non-defaulting Party pays it to the Defaulting Party.

An easy way to remember who gets what is to view the positive and negative amounts from the Non-defaulting Party's viewpoint. If the Early Termination Amount is positive the Non-defaulting Party receives it and could be said to view the situation positively. If the Early Termination Amount is negative, the Non-defaulting Party has to pay it over and so views the situation negatively.

Principal change from the 1992 Agreement

- **Significant wide-ranging changes to accommodate the new single payment measure of Close-out Amount particularly the deletion of all references to Market Quotation, Loss, First Method and Second Method.**

(ii) ***Termination Events***. If the Early Termination Date results from a Termination Event:-

(1) ***One Affected Party***. Subject to clause (3) below, if there is one Affected Party, the Early Termination Amount will be determined in accordance with Section 6(e)(i), except that references to the Defaulting Party and to the Non-defaulting Party will be deemed to be references to the Affected Party and to the Non-affected Party, respectively.

(2) ***Two Affected Parties***. Subject to clause (3) below, if there are two Affected Parties, each party will determine an amount equal to the Termination Currency Equivalent of the sum of the Close-out Amount or Close-out Amounts (whether positive or negative) for each Terminated Transaction or group of Terminated Transactions, as the case may be, and the Early Termination Amount will be an amount equal to (A) the sum of (I) one-half of the difference between the higher amount so determined (by party "X") and the lower amount so determined (by party "Y") and (II) the Termination Currency Equivalent of the Unpaid Amounts owing to X less (B) the Termination Currency Equivalent of the Unpaid Amounts owing to Y. If the Early Termination Amount is a positive number, Y will pay it to X; if it is a negative number, X will pay the absolute value of the Early Termination Amount to Y.

Section 6(e)(ii)

(1) If there is a Termination Event with one Affected Party, the Early Termination Amount will be calculated as per Section 6(e)(i). However, in these circumstances the Defaulting Party is called the Affected Party and the Non-defaulting Party is called the Non-affected Party.

(2) Where there are two Affected Parties involved in a "no fault" Termination Event other than Illegality or Force Majeure Event, each Affected Party will calculate the net Termination Currency Equivalent of the Close-out Amount for Affected Transactions and split the difference. To this will be added and deducted the Termination Currency Equivalents of the Unpaid Amounts owed to each of them.

If the net Early Termination Amount (the "net amount") is a positive number, the party which has calculated the lower Close-out Amount pays the net amount to the other party. If it is a negative figure, the party which has calculated the higher Close-out Amount, will pay the absolute value of that amount to the other party.

This is referred to as a "mid market" calculation and, as there are two Affected Parties, it will result in a smaller net amount payable.

Principal changes from the 1992 Agreement

- **Section 6(e)(ii)(1) and (2) – Principally revamping following the scrapping of Market Quotation and Loss and the use of the new term, Early Termination Amount.**

(3) ***Mid-Market Events.*** If that Termination Event is an Illegality or a Force Majeure Event, then the Early Termination Amount will be determined in accordance with clause (1) or (2) above, as appropriate, except that, for the purpose of determining a Close-out Amount or Close-out Amounts, the Determining Party will:-

(A) if obtaining quotations from one or more third parties (or from any of the Determining Party's Affiliates), ask each third party or Affiliate (I) not to take account of the current credit- worthiness of the Determining Party or any existing Credit Support Document and (II) to provide mid-market quotations; and

(B) in any other case, use mid-market values without regard to the creditworthiness of the Determining Party.

Section 6(e)(ii)(3)

(3) This is a new sub-clause and concerns Illegality and Force Majeure Event.

(A) Early Termination Amount calculations are performed under (1) or (2) above as appropriate except that in calculating a Close-out Amount, the Determining Party will request that a quoting third party or Affiliate will disregard the Determining Party's current creditworthiness or any Credit Support Document and provide mid-market quotations. This is because the Illegality or Force Majeure Event is outside the Determining Party's control and its creditworthiness is not a relevant factor in obtaining the quotations. This approach emphasises the "no fault" nature of these Termination Events and ISDA members considered it unfair to value the Transaction on only one party's side of the market or to average the calculations of two Affected Parties.

(B) Where internal or other market data is being used to value Terminated Transactions in these circumstances, mid-market values are to be used by the Determining Party and its creditworthiness is to be ignored.

Principal change from the 1992 Agreement

- **Totally new provision.**

(iii) ***Adjustment for Bankruptcy***. In circumstances where an Early Termination Date occurs because Automatic Early Termination applies in respect of a party, the Early Termination Amount will be subject to such adjustments as are appropriate and permitted by applicable law to reflect any payments or deliveries made by one party to the other under this Agreement (and retained by such other party) during the period from the relevant Early Termination Date to the date for payment determined under Section 6(d)(ii).

(iv) ***Adjustment for Illegality or Force Majeure Event***. The failure by a party or any Credit Support Provider of such party to pay, when due, any Early Termination Amount will not constitute an Event of Default under Section 5(a)(i) or 5(a)(iii)(1) if such failure is due to the occurrence of an event or circumstance which would, if it occurred with respect to payment, delivery or compliance related to a Transaction, constitute or give rise to an Illegality or a Force Majeure Event. Such amount will (1) accrue interest and otherwise be treated as an Unpaid Amount owing to the other party if subsequently an Early Termination Date results from an Event of Default, a Credit Event Upon Merger or an Additional Termination Event in respect of which all outstanding Transactions are Affected Transactions and (2) otherwise accrue interest in accordance with Section 9(h)(ii)(2).

(v) ***Pre-Estimate***. The parties agree that an amount recoverable under this Section 6(e) is a reasonable pre-estimate of loss and not a penalty. Such amount is payable for the loss of bargain and the loss of protection against future risks, and, except as otherwise provided in this Agreement, neither party will be entitled to recover any additional damages as a consequence of the termination of the Terminated Transactions.

Section 6(e)(iii)

Section 6(e)(iii) deals with the situation where the Early Termination Amount will be adjusted where an Early Termination Date is deemed to have occurred because Automatic Early Termination applies. It is designed to protect a Non-defaulting Party who has made payments to an insolvent counterparty and was unaware that Automatic Early Termination had occurred. In such circumstances, appropriate adjustments can be made to the Early Termination Amount.

Section 6(e)(iv)

This is a new provision and concerns the non-payment of an Early Termination Amount by the party or Credit Support Provider due to pay it where this arises because an Illegality or Force Majeure Event has intervened. Where this happens the non-payment will not be treated as an Event of Default (i.e. Failure to Pay or Deliver or Credit Support Default). However, interest will accrue on this sum and if later an Early Termination Date arises from an Event of Default, Credit Event Upon Merger or an Additional Termination Event tainting all Transactions which are then terminated, the sum will be treated as an Unpaid Amount. Otherwise interest will accrue as per Section 9(h)(ii)(2).

Section 6(e)(v)

This clause states that an amount recovered through an early termination payment reflects a loss of bargain and loss of protection against future risks and is not a penalty. Parties cannot claim additional damages because of such losses. Hence consequential loss claims are prohibited.

Principal changes from the 1992 Agreement

Section 6(e)(iii)

Small changes for new terminology.

Section 6(e)(iv)

Totally new provision.

Section 6(e)(v)

Deletion of reference to Market Quotation and clarification that the prohibition of consequential losses applies to the termination of Terminated Transactions.

(f) ***Set-Off.*** Any Early Termination Amount payable to one party (the "Payee") by the other party (the "Payer"), in circumstances where there is a Defaulting Party or where there is one Affected Party in the case where either a Credit Event Upon Merger has occurred or any other Termination Event in respect of which all outstanding Transactions are Affected Transactions has occurred, will, at the option of the Non-defaulting Party or the Non-affected Party, as the case may be ("X") (and without prior notice to the Defaulting Party or the Affected Party, as the case may be), be reduced by its set-off against any other amounts ("Other Amounts") payable by the Payee to the Payer (whether or not arising under this Agreement, matured or contingent and irrespective of the currency, place of payment or place of booking of the obligation). To the extent that any Other Amounts are so set off, those Other Amounts will be discharged promptly and in all respects. X will give notice to the other party of any set-off effected under this Section 6(f).

For this purpose, either the Early Termination Amount or the Other Amounts (or the relevant portion of such amounts) may be converted by X into the currency in which the other is denominated at the rate of exchange at which such party would be able, in good faith and using commercially reasonable procedures, to purchase the relevant amount of such currency.

If an obligation is unascertained, X may in good faith estimate that obligation and set off in respect of the estimate, subject to the relevant party accounting to the other when the obligation is ascertained.

Nothing in this Section 6(f) will be effective to create a charge or other security interest. This Section 6(f) will be without prejudice and in addition to any right of set-off, offset, combination of accounts, lien, right of retention or withholding or similar right or requirement to which any party is at any time otherwise entitled or subject (whether by operation of law, contract or otherwise).

Section 6(f)

Because of a lack of consensus, the 1992 Agreement did not contain a set off clause in its main text but invariably one was included in Part 5 of the Schedule and many people selected the set off clause wording which appeared on page 56 of the *User's Guide to the 1992 ISDA Master Agreements.* The Section 6(f) set off clause here is based upon that one.

The set off is limited to the two parties to the Agreement. There is no extension to the Non-defaulting Party's Affiliates in this text although they can be added by a Schedule amendment if the parties are convinced that this would be legally robust in the jurisdictions concerned.

The set off can be triggered where an Event of Default, Credit Event Upon Merger or any Termination Event affecting all Transactions has been declared. Set off can be against any obligations of the Defaulting Party or the Affected Party held by the other party and in the same name and right (i.e. capacity). A deposit account would be a typical example. Set off can be useful where a Non-defaulting Party has to pay an Early Termination Amount to an insolvent Defaulting Party and does not have any realistic hopes of receiving any payments due to it by the Defaulting Party under other agreements.

The set off can take place without prior notice and is wide-ranging. It can involve currency conversion provided this is conducted in a commercially reasonable manner.

Unascertained obligations can be estimated and set off but there has to be a final settlement when the value of the obligation is subsequently crystallised.

The set off is stated not to constitute any kind of security interest and is a separate legal right to a list of other rights contained in the final sentence.

Under English law a mandatory right of set off arises under Rule 4.90 of the 1986 Insolvency Rules but this set off clause extends beyond this as described above.

It is vital to establish mutuality when invoking set off rights. If the "No Agency" representation is chosen to apply to both parties this is a strong reinforcement of mutuality for this purpose.

Principal changes from the 1992 Agreement

- **Totally new provision in the main text but a close variant of this wording has been included in Schedules for many years.**

7. Transfer

Subject to Section 6(b)(ii) and to the extent permitted by applicable law, neither this Agreement nor any interest or obligation in or under this Agreement may be transferred (whether by way of security or otherwise) by either party without the prior written consent of the other party, except that:-

(a) a party may make such a transfer of this Agreement pursuant to a consolidation or amalgamation with, or merger with or into, or transfer of all or substantially all its assets to, another entity (but without prejudice to any other right or remedy under this Agreement); and

(b) a party may make such a transfer of all or any part of its interest in any Early Termination Amount payable to it by a Defaulting Party, together with any amounts payable on or with respect to that interest and any other rights associated with that interest pursuant to Sections 8, 9(h) and 11.

Any purported transfer that is not in compliance with this Section 7 will be void.

Section 7

Section 7 forbids either party to transfer the Agreement or any rights and obligations under it without prior written consent. However, there are three exceptions to this:

- **If the purpose of a transfer is to avoid a Tax Event or Tax Event Upon Merger as per Section 6(b)(ii) consent may not be withheld if a party's current policies would permit it to deal with the proposed transferee on the proposed Transaction terms.**
- **Where a transfer of an Agreement arises from a merger or the transfer of all or most of a party's assets to another entity. The words in brackets indicate that other restrictions in the Agreement relating to mergers and similar transactions are in no way prejudiced by this exception, e.g. the Merger Without Assumption Event of Default which will not be extinguished because of Section 7(a)).**
- **If a Non-defaulting Party transfers its interest in any Early Termination Amount payable to it from a Defaulting Party under Section 6(e). This now includes any interest, foreign exchange conversion costs and Section 11 expenses.**

Section 7 also makes clear that granting a security interest in respect of an Agreement constitutes a transfer for the purposes of Section 7 and is prohibited in order to ensure that mutuality between the parties is present for the purposes of close-out netting.

Any transfers not complying with the Section's terms will be void.

It is becoming more common to see amendments to this transfer provision in the Schedule. These vary from general phrasing that consent to a transfer shall not be unreasonably withheld to blanket advance approvals of transfers to unspecified Affiliates with or without an agreed notice period. The pros and cons of these amendments are examined in Chapters 6 and 8.

Principal changes from the 1992 Agreement

- **Inclusion of the words "to the extent permitted by applicable law" added in line 1 of the preamble.**
- **In Section 7(b) interest, foreign exchange conversion costs and Section 11 expenses may be added on to the Early Termination Amount which a Non-defaulting Party desires to transfer.**

8. Contractual Currency

(a) ***Payment in the Contractual Currency.*** Each payment under this Agreement will be made in the relevant currency specified in this Agreement for that payment (the "Contractual Currency"). To the extent permitted by applicable law, any obligation to make payments under this Agreement in the Contractual Currency will not be discharged or satisfied by any tender in any currency other than the Contractual Currency, except to the extent such tender results in the actual receipt by the party to which payment is owed, acting in good faith and using commercially reasonable procedures in converting the currency so tendered into this Contractual Currency, of the full amount in the Contractual Currency of all amounts payable in respect of this Agreement. If for any reason the amount in the Contractual Currency so received falls short of the amount in the Contractual Currency payable in respect of this Agreement, the party required to make the payment will, to the extent permitted by applicable law, immediately pay such additional amount in the Contractual Currency as may be necessary to compensate for the shortfall. If for any reason the amount in the Contractual Currency so received exceeds the amount in the Contractual Currency payable in respect of this Agreement, the party receiving the payment will refund promptly the amount of such excess.

(b) ***Judgments.*** To the extent permitted by applicable law, if any judgment or order expressed in a currency other than the Contractual Currency is rendered (i) for the payment of any amount owing in respect of this Agreement, (ii) for the payment of any amount relating to any early termination in respect of this Agreement or (iii) in respect of a judgment or order of another court for the payment of any amount described in clause (i) or (ii) above, the party seeking recovery, after recovery in full of the aggregate amount to which such party is entitled pursuant to the judgment or order, will be entitled to receive immediately from the other party the amount of any shortfall of the Contractual Currency received by such party as a consequence of sums paid in such other currency and will refund promptly to the other party any excess of the Contractual Currency received by such party as a consequence of sums paid in such other currency if such shortfall or such excess arises or results from any variation between the rate of exchange at which the Contractual Currency is converted into the currency of the judgment or order for the purpose of such judgment or order and the rate of exchange at which such party is able, acting in good faith and using commercially procedures in converting the currency received into the Contractual Currency, to purchase the Contractual Currency with the amount of the currency of the judgment or order actually received by such party.

Section 8

The Contractual Currency and judgment currency provisions here protect a party against foreign exchange losses.

Section 8(a)

Section 8(a) provides that all payments made in the normal course of business (i.e. where no Event of Default or Termination Event has intervened) must be made in the contractual currency agreed by the parties (normally in a Confirmation). Payments will not be discharged in a non-contractual currency unless the payee can convert it into the Contractual Currency. Where payments are made in another currency it must be converted into the Contractual Currency and any conversion shortfalls or surpluses must be paid to the party owed them. The party making the currency conversion calculations must act in good faith and use commercially reasonable procedures.

Section 8(b)

The same principle applies where this happens to payments under the Agreement due after legal proceedings where a recovering party has the right to convert an alternative currency into the Contractual Currency.

This is an example of a judgment currency clause and is necessary because courts in some jurisdictions will only make awards in their local currency which may well be different to the Contractual Currency.

Principal changes from the 1992 Agreement

- **In both clauses currency conversion must be performed in good faith and using commercially reasonable procedures – the same standard required from a Determining Party in selecting the inputs for the calculation of Close-out Amount.**
- **In Section 8(b) the last sentence defining "rate of exchange" has been deleted. This is now a separate definition in Section 14.**

(c) ***Separate Indemnities***. To the extent permitted by applicable law, the indemnities in this Section 8 constitute separate and independent obligations from the other obligations in this Agreement, will be enforceable as separate and independent causes of action, will apply notwithstanding any indulgence granted by the party to which any payment is owed and will not be affected by judgment being obtained or claim or proof being made for any other sums payable in respect of this Agreement.

(d) ***Evidence of Loss***. For the purpose of this Section 8, it will be sufficient for a party to demonstrate that it would have suffered a loss had an actual exchange or purchase been made.

Section 8(c)

This is rather technical. The provisions in Section 8(a) and (b) are described as separate and independent indemnities which are separately enforceable to avoid the risk that a court might combine a claim based on either indemnity with other claims being pursued for other sums under the Agreement. The indemnities will remain separate notwithstanding any indulgence or concessions granted by a creditor to his debtor or any judgment made or other claim being pursued for other sums payable under the Agreement

Section 8(d)

Section 8(d) states that it will be enough for a party to show that it would have suffered a loss had an actual exchange or purchase of currency been made.

Principal changes from the 1992 Agreement

- **Section 8(c) – Minor clarifying wording.**
- **Section 8(d) – None.**

9. Miscellaneous

(a) ***Entire Agreement.*** This Agreement constitutes the entire agreement and understanding of the parties with respect to its subject matter. Each of the parties acknowledges that in entering into this Agreement it has not relied on any oral or written representation, warranty or other assurance (except as provided for or referred to in this Agreement) and waives all rights and remedies which might otherwise be available to it in respect thereof, except that nothing in this Agreement will limit or exclude any liability of a party for fraud.

(b) ***Amendments.*** An amendment, modification or waiver in respect of this Agreement will only be effective if in writing (including a writing evidenced by a facsimile transmission) and executed by each of the parties or confirmed by an exchange of telexes or by an exchange of electronic messages on an electronic messaging system.

(c) ***Survival of Obligations.*** Without prejudice to Sections 2(a)(iii) and 6(c)(ii), the obligations of the parties under this Agreement will survive the termination of any Transaction.

(d) ***Remedies Cumulative.*** Except as provided in this Agreement, the rights, powers, remedies and privileges provided in this Agreement are cumulative and not exclusive of any rights, powers, remedies and privileges provided by law.

(e) ***Counterparts and Confirmations.***

(i) This Agreement (and each amendment, modification and waiver in respect of it) may be executed and delivered in counterparts (including by facsimile transmission and by electronic messaging system), each of which will be deemed an original.

(ii) The parties intend that they are legally bound by the terms of each Transaction from the moment they agree to those terms (whether orally or otherwise). A Confirmation will be entered into as soon as practicable and may be executed and delivered in counterparts (including by facsimile transmission) or be created by an exchange of telexes, by an exchange of electronic messages on an electronic messaging system or by an exchange of e-mails, which in each case will be sufficient for all purposes to evidence a binding supplement to this Agreement. The parties will specify therein or through another effective means that any such counterpart, telex, electronic message or e-mail constitutes a Confirmation.

(f) ***No Waiver of Rights.*** A failure or delay in exercising any right, power or privilege in respect of this Agreement will not be presumed to operate as a waiver, and a single or partial exercise of any right, power or privilege will not be presumed to preclude any subsequent or further exercise, of that right, power or privilege or the exercise of any other right, power or privilege.

(g) ***Headings.*** The headings used in this Agreement are for convenience of reference only and are not to affect the construction of or to be taken into consideration in interpreting this Agreement.

Section 9

Section 9(a)

The Agreement is stated as forming the entire agreement between the parties. Each party acknowledges that it has not relied upon oral or written representations from the other (unless already present in the Agreement) and waives all rights it could otherwise invoke. However, nothing in the Agreement excludes a party from liability for fraud.

Section 9(b)

Amendments (communicated by a variety of traditional means) are only effective if in writing and executed by both parties. Alternatively this can take place through the exchange of telexes or electronic messages. This does not include e-mails.

Section 9(c)

This provision is self-explanatory but please note that Transactions subject to early termination are excluded from it. Section 2(a)(iii) and Section 6(c)(ii) respectively introduce conditions precedent and the replacement of normal payment and delivery obligations by a close-out regime. These provisions therefore limit survival of obligations which is why the Agreement wording was drafted this way.

Section 9(d)

This provision is also self-explanatory. It should be remembered that termination is not the sole remedy of a Non-defaulting Party. It also has the options of leaving the Agreement in place or seeking specific performance of its counterparty's obligations where monetary compensation is not sufficient, e.g. where physical delivery of a share or commodity is required.

Section 9(e)

- Parties may execute and deliver in counterparts an Agreement, amendment, modification and waiver and transmit the same by fax or electronic messaging system but not e-mail. Each document will be regarded as an original.
- Parties are legally bound by the terms of each Transaction from the moment they agree to them (orally or otherwise). A Confirmation must be entered into as soon as possible and may be executed in counterparts

using traditional or electronic means of communication. Deals may now be confirmed by an exchange of e-mails but you would need to check that this is not prohibited by any statute of frauds or other legal regulation in a particular jurisdiction.

Section 9(f)

Variations of this standard provision are also commonly seen in loan agreements. No precedent is set if a full or partial waiver is exercised in respect of any right, power or privilege under the Agreement.

Section 9(g)

Headings in the Agreement are for convenience only and are not to affect its interpretation.

Principal changes from the 1992 Agreement

- **Section 9(a) – Addition of acknowledgment that neither party has relied on any oral or written representation, warranty or other assurance except as provided in the Agreement. Neither party can exclude liability from fraud from the Agreement.**
- **Section 9(b) – Minor changes.**
- **Section 9(e)(i) – Addition of electronic messaging systems for executing and delivering the 2002 Agreement or any amendments.**
- **Section 9(e)(ii) – Confirmations may now be executed by an exchange of e-mails.**

(h) ***Interest and Compensation***

(i) ***Prior to Early Termination***. Prior to the occurrence or effective designation of an Early Termination Date in respect of the relevant Transaction:-

Section 9(h)

Section 9(h) is new and brings together and expands on penalties for late payment or delivery which were previously largely in Sections 2(e) and 6(d)(ii) of the 1992 Agreement. It is far more detailed on interest or compensation for late deliveries and adds provisions dealing with certain consequences of an Illegality or Force Majeure Event.

Section 2(e) of the 1992 Agreement stated that compensation for defaulted deliveries depended upon what was in the relevant Confirmation or elsewhere in the Agreement (i.e. in its Schedule). The 2002 Agreement goes further by providing that where the Confirmation or the Agreement is silent on this point, the Defaulting Party must pay interest on the fair market value of the undelivered assets at the Default Rate. The fair market value of the asset will be calculated by the deliveree as of the original date for delivery, in good faith and using commercially reasonable procedures.

Section 9(h) also deals with interest and compensation both before and after an Early Termination Date.

A payment or delivery may not be made for a number of reasons:

- **a party may default in making it;**
- **a payment may be withheld because of an unfulfilled condition precedent in Section 2(a)(iii);**
- **a payment is not made because an Illegality or Force Majeure Event Waiting Period applies; or**
- **a payment is not made because although a Waiting Period has expired the parties choose not to terminate Affected Transactions.**

Section 9(h)(i)(1)–(4) deals with interest and compensation for defaulted and deferred payments and deliveries before an Early Termination Date is designated. In other words, in the normal course of business.

(1) *Interest on Defaulted Payments.* If a party defaults in the performance of any payment obligation, it will, to the extent permitted by applicable law and subject to Section 6(c), pay interest (before as well as after judgment) on the overdue amount to the other party on demand in the same currency as the overdue amount, for the period from (and including) the original due date for payment to (but excluding) the date of actual payment (and excluding any period in respect of which interest or compensation in respect of the overdue amount is due pursuant to clause (3)(B) or (C) below), at the Default Rate.

(2) *Compensation for Defaulted Deliveries.* If a party defaults in the performance of any obligation required to be settled by delivery, it will on demand (A) compensate the other party to the extent provided for in the relevant Confirmation or elsewhere in this Agreement and (B) unless otherwise provided in the relevant Confirmation or elsewhere in this Agreement, to the extent permitted by applicable law and subject to Section 6(c), pay to the other party interest (before as well as after judgment) on an amount equal to the fair market value of that which was required to be delivered in the same currency as that amount, for the period from (and including) the originally scheduled date for delivery to (but excluding) the date of actual delivery (and excluding any period in respect of which interest or compensation in respect of that amount is due pursuant to clause (4) below), at the Default Rate. The fair market value of any obligation referred to above will be determined as of the originally scheduled date for delivery, in good faith and using commercially reasonable procedures, by the party that was entitled to take delivery.

Section 9(h)(i)(1)

If a party defaults on a payment it will, on demand, pay interest on the overdue amount at the Default Rate (1% over the payee's cost of funds) from and including the date it was originally due to and excluding the date it is actually paid which is the normal overdue interest calculation period in the derivatives markets. Any period during which payments or deliveries are suspended due to an Illegality or Force Majeure Event are excluded from this calculation. This interest shall be paid in the same currency as the overdue amount.

Section 9(h)(i)(2)

Where a party defaults on the delivery of an obligation it will first, upon demand, pay compensation to the other party as detailed in the Confirmation and then if required by the Confirmation or the Agreement or allowed by law, pay interest to the other party at the Default Rate from and including the original date for scheduled delivery to and excluding the date of actual delivery. Interest will be calculated by the deliveree in the same currency on the fair market value of the assets to be delivered to the Non-defaulting Party in good faith and using commercially reasonable procedures.

Principal change from the 1992 Agreement

- **Totally new provisions.**

(3) *Interest on Deferred Payments.* If:-

(A) a party does not pay any amount that, but for Section 2(a)(iii), would have been payable, it will, to the extent permitted by applicable law and subject to Section 6(c) and clauses (B) and (C) below, pay interest (before as well as after judgment) on that amount to the other party on demand (after such amount becomes payable) in the same currency as that amount, for the period from (and including) the date the amount would, but for Section 2(a)(iii), have been payable to (but excluding) the date the amount actually becomes payable, at the Applicable Deferral Rate;

(B) a payment is deferred pursuant to Section 5(d), the party which would otherwise have been required to make that payment will, to the extent permitted by applicable law, subject to Section 6(c) and for so long as no Event of Default or Potential Event of Default with respect to that party has occurred and is continuing, pay interest (before as well as after judgment) on the amount of the deferred payment to the other party on demand (after such amount becomes payable) in the same currency as the deferred payment, for the period from (and including) the date the amount would, but for Section 5(d), have been payable to (but excluding) the earlier of the date the payment is no longer deferred pursuant to Section 5(d) and the date during the deferral period upon which an Event of Default or Potential Event of Default with respect to that party occurs, at the Applicable Deferral Rate; or

(C) a party fails to make any payment due to the occurrence of an Illegality or a Force Majeure Event (after giving effect to any deferral period contemplated by clause (B) above), it will, to the extent permitted by applicable law, subject to Section 6(c) and for so long as the event or circumstance giving rise to that Illegality or Force Majeure Event continues and no Event of Default or Potential Event of Default with respect to that party has occurred and is continuing, pay interest (before as well as after judgment) on the overdue amount to the other party on demand in the same currency as the overdue amount, for the period from (and including) the date the party fails to make the payment due to the occurrence of the relevant Illegality or Force Majeure Event (or, if later, the date the payment is no longer deferred pursuant to Section 5(d)) to (but excluding) the earlier of the date the event or circumstance giving rise to that Illegality or Force Majeure Event ceases to exist and the date during the period upon which an Event of Default or Potential Event of Default with respect to that party occurs (and excluding any period in respect of which interest or compensation in respect of the overdue amount is due pursuant to clause (B) above), at the Applicable Deferral Rate.

Section 9(h)(i)(3)

(A) This sub-section concerns interest on deferred payments which arise because a Section 2(a)(iii) event, i.e. an Event of Default or Potential Event of Default has occurred and continues; an Early Termination Date has arisen or a condition precedent is unfulfilled. Such an event has the effect of deferring normal payments. Interest will accrue on this deferred payment in the same currency from and including the date it should have been paid (but for the Section 2(a)(iii) event) to but excluding the date upon which it actually becomes payable. Interest is charged at the Applicable Deferral Rate which is this case is an interbank overnight deposit rate offered by a major bank and chosen in good faith by the payer.

(B) If a payment is deferred because of an Illegality or Force Majeure Event Waiting Period and provided no Event of Default (actual or potential) has occurred, the payer will pay interest on the deferred payment in the same currency from and including the date when the payment was originally due to but excluding the earlier of:

- the date the payment is no longer deferred because the Illegality or Force Majeure Event has gone away; or
- the date during the deferred period when an Event of Default (actual or potential) arises in respect of the payer.

Again interest is charged at an interbank overnight deposit rate offered by a major bank but this time to prime banks and chosen in good faith by the payer. However, in this instance the payer needs to consult with the payee if this is practicable.

(C) Here a payer fails to make a payment due to an Illegality or Force Majeure Event following a Waiting Period and the Illegality or Force Majeure Event persists but the payer is not impacted by an actual or potential Event of Default (perhaps because the narrow window of the Section 5(a)(i) grace period has not expired or notice has not been given for some reason). Here the payer will be obliged to pay interest in the same currency from and including the date the payment should have been made (but for the Illegality or Force Majeure Event) or, if later, the date the Waiting Period ends to but excluding the earlier of the date these Termination Events cease to exist or the date an actual or potential Event of Default occurs to the payer.

A deduction is made for any period which overlaps with the one in clause (B) above.

This time the interest rate is calculated as the arithmetic mean of the payee's cost of funds and the interbank overnight deposit rate offered by a major bank and chosen in good faith by the payer.

Principal change from the 1992 Agreement

- **Totally new provisions.**

(4) *Compensation for Deferred Deliveries.* If:-

(A) a party does not perform any obligation that, but for Section 2(a)(iii), would have been required to be settled by delivery;

(B) a delivery is deferred pursuant to Section 5(d); or

(C) a party fails to make a delivery due to the occurrence of an Illegality or a Force Majeure Event at a time when any applicable Waiting Period has expired,

the party required (or that would otherwise have been required) to make the delivery will, to the extent permitted by applicable law and subject to Section 6(c), compensate and pay interest to the other party on demand (after, in the case of clauses (A) and (B) above, such delivery is required) if and to the extent provided for in the relevant Confirmation or elsewhere in this Agreement.

Section 9(h)(i)(4)

This sub-section concerns compensation for deferred deliveries arising because:

- **a party does not make a delivery due to a Section 2(a)(iii) event; or**
- **a delivery is deferred because an Illegality or Force Majeure Event has occurred and a Waiting Period exists; or**
- **a party does not make a delivery because an Illegality or Force Majeure Event persists after the Waiting Period has expired.**

In these circumstances, the party that should have delivered the asset will compensate and pay interest to the other party on demand to the extent specified in the Confirmation or elsewhere in the Agreement. This is typical of the woollier compensation arrangements for deliveries and the reliance placed in these circumstances on the Confirmation.

Principal change from the 1992 Agreement

- **Totally new provision.**

(ii) ***Early Termination***. Upon the occurrence or effective designation of an Early Termination Date in respect of a Transaction:-

(1) *Unpaid Amounts.* For the purpose of determining an Unpaid Amount in respect of the relevant Transaction, and to the extent permitted by applicable law, interest will accrue on the amount of any payment obligation or the amount equal to the fair market value of any obligation required to be settled by delivery included in such determination in the same currency as that amount, for the period from (and including) the date the relevant obligation was (or would have been but for Section 2(a)(iii) or 5(d)) required to have been performed to (but excluding) the relevant Early Termination Date, at the Applicable Close-out Rate.

Section 9(h)(ii)(1)

Up to now we have been concerned with interest and compensation before an Early Termination Date is designated but when this happens Section 9(h)(ii) kicks in.

Section 9(h)(ii)(1) concerns Unpaid Amounts where interest will accrue on any payments or deliveries constituting the Unpaid Amounts in the same currency from and including the date the obligation should have been performed (but for Section 2(a)(iii) or 5(d)) to but excluding the Early Termination Date. Interest is payable at the Applicable Close-out Rate. This is defined in relation to Unpaid Amounts as:

- **the Default Rate (1% over the payee's cost of funds) where a Defaulting Party is involved; or**
- **at the Non-default Rate (i.e. an interbank overnight deposit rate offered to the Non-defaulting Party by a major bank selected in good faith by them) if a Non-defaulting Party should have made the payment or delivery; or**
- **where an Illegality or Force Majeure Event has occurred and there is no Defaulting Party and a Waiting Period is continuing at the Applicable Deferral Rate. This is a rate certified by the payer to be offered by a major bank to other prime banks in the interbank overnight deposit market. The bank is selected by the payer in good faith and in consultation with the payee, if possible; or**
- **with all other Termination Events, the Applicable Deferral Rate will apply in its form of the arithmetic mean of the payee's cost of funds and the interbank overnight deposit rate offered by a major bank chosen in good faith by the payer.**

(2) *Interest on Early Termination Amounts.* If an Early Termination Amount is due in respect of such Early Termination Date, that amount will, to the extent permitted by applicable law, be paid together with interest (before as well as after judgment) on that amount in the Termination Currency, for the period from (and including) such Early Termination Date to (but excluding) the date the amount is paid, at the Applicable Close-out Rate.

(iii) ***Interest Calculation.*** Any interest pursuant to this Section 9(h) will be calculated on the basis of daily compounding and the actual number of days elapsed.

Section 9(h)(ii)(2)

Where an Early Termination Amount is late in being paid interest will accrue on it in the Termination Currency from and including the Early Termination Date to but excluding the date it is actually paid. Interest will be charged at the Applicable Close-out Rate which is defined in this context as follows:

- **The Default Rate (i.e. 1% over the payer's cost of funds) if the Early Termination Amount is owed by the Defaulting Party;**
- **the Non-default Rate (i.e. an interbank overnight deposit rate offered to the Non-defaulting Party by a major bank selected in good faith by them) if it is owed by a Non-defaulting Party; and**
- **the Applicable Deferral Rate in all other cases. This would be the arithmetic mean of the payee's cost of funds and the interbank overnight deposit rate offered by a major bank chosen in good faith by the payer.**

The following rules apply from and including the Early Termination Date to but excluding the date on which the Early Termination Amount is due to be paid under the timetable in Section 6(d)(ii):

- **If a party fails to pay the Early Termination Amount due to the occurrence or continuation of an Illegality or Force Majeure Event, the Applicable Deferral Rate will apply provided that non-payment is due to the continuance of that event. This again will be the arithmetic mean of the payee's cost of funds and the interbank overnight deposit rate offered by a major bank and chosen in good faith by the payer.**
- **Ignoring any Illegality or Force Majeure Event, if the Early Termination Amount is due from a Defaulting Party, the Default Rate will apply.**
- **Again ignoring any Illegality or Force Majeure Event, if an Early Termination Amount is due from a Non-defaulting Party, the Non-default Rate will apply; and**
- **in all other cases the Termination Rate will apply. This means the arithmetic mean of each party's self certified cost of funding.**

Section 9(h)(iii)

It is made clear that any interest chargeable under Section 9(h) will be calculated on a daily compounded basis for the actual number of days the payment due is unpaid.

Principal change from the 1992 Agreement

- Totally new provisions.

10. Offices; Multibranch Parties

(a) If Section 10(a) is specified in the Schedule as applying, each party that enters into a Transaction through an Office other than its head or home office represents to and agrees with the other party that, notwithstanding the place of booking or its jurisdiction of incorporation or organisation, its obligations are the same in terms of recourse against it as if it had entered into the Transaction through its head or home office, except that a party will not have recourse to the head or home office of the other party in respect of any payment or delivery deferred pursuant to Section 5(d) for so long as the payment or delivery is so deferred. This representation and agreement will be deemed to be repeated by each party on each date on which the parties enter into a Transaction.

(b) If a party is specified as a Multibranch Party in the Schedule, such party may, subject to clause (c) below, enter into a Transaction through, book a Transaction in and make and receive payments and deliveries with respect to a Transaction through any Office listed in respect of that party in the Schedule (but not any other Office unless otherwise agreed by the parties in writing).

(c) The Office through which a party enters into a Transaction will be the Office specified for that party in the relevant Confirmation or as otherwise agreed by the parties in writing, and, if an Office for that party is not specified in the Confirmation or otherwise agreed by the parties in writing, its head or home office. Unless the parties otherwise agree in writing, the Office through which a party enters into a Transaction will also be the Office in which it books the Transaction and the Office through which it makes and receives payments and deliveries with respect to the Transaction. Subject to Section 6(b)(ii), neither party may change the Office in which it books the Transaction or the Office through which it makes and receives payments or deliveries with respect to a Transaction without the prior written consent of the other party.

Section 10

Section 10(a)

Parties must choose in Part 4(c) of the Schedule if they want Section 10(a) to apply. Section 10(a) stipulates that both parties may have recourse to each other's Head Office regardless of the credit or political risk of branches through which they are transacting should a default occur under the Agreement.

Parties to the Agreement now agree that Transactions entered into by their branches are equivalent to Transactions entered into by their Head Offices. This represents an implied payment or performance guarantee to their counterparty.

This representation is separate from the representation concerning Multibranch Parties in Section 10(b). The representation is also repeated by a party on each date on which a Transaction is undertaken. However, there is one exception. Where during an Illegality or Force Majeure Event Waiting Period, a branch's payment or delivery obligations are suspended, the other party has no recourse to that branch's home or head office.

If a Multibranch Party does not want this provision to apply then it is seeking to shift the political risk of dealing with its overseas branch on to its counterparty. It is therefore vital where this is agreed that the branch is located in a jurisdiction favourable to close-out netting.

Sections 10(b) and (c) have been revamped.

Section 10(b)

If a party is a Multibranch Party under the Schedule, it can enter into and book Transactions and make payments and deliveries under the Agreement through any of the Offices listed in the Schedule but not any other Office unless the parties agree to this in writing.

Section 10(c)

The relevant Office for each Transaction will be stated in the Confirmation or as otherwise agreed in writing by the parties. Otherwise if no Office is specified it will be deemed to be that party's home or head office. Unless they agree otherwise, the Office through which the parties book a Transaction will also be the one through which they make payments or deliveries in respect of it.

Section 10(c) prevents a party from changing the Office through which it makes and receives payments or deliveries without the other party's written consent beforehand in order to avoid, inter alia, possible unfavourable tax consequences for the other party. Section 6(b)(ii) overrides this as a party cannot unreasonably refuse consent to a transfer to avoid a Section 5(b)(iii) or (iv) Termination Event.

Principal changes from the 1992 Agreement

- Section 10(a) – Clarifying wording that each party agrees that where they deal with a counterparty branch they have recourse to its head or home office except where a payment is deferred because of Illegality or Force Majeure Event.
- Section 10(b) – Instead of the general prohibition on changing Offices for payments or deliveries unless the other party gives its written consent, now payments or deliveries can be made through any of their Offices listed in the Schedule but through no other Office without written consent.
- Section 10(c) – Basically a new provision but some wording has been transferred from Section 10(b) in the 1992 Agreement.

11. Expenses

A Defaulting Party will, on demand, indemnify and hold harmless the other party for and against all reasonable out-of-pocket expenses, including legal, execution fees and Stamp Tax, incurred by such other party by reason of the enforcement and protection of its rights under this Agreement or any Credit Support Document to which the Defaulting Party is a party or by reason of the early termination of any Transaction, including, but not limited to, costs of collection.

Section 11

The expenses referred to in this Section are different to those incurred on early termination in Section 6(e)(v).

This Section requires a Defaulting Party to pay certain reasonable out-of-pocket expenses (including legal and execution fees and stamp duties) incurred by the Non-defaulting Party in enforcing and protecting its rights under an Agreement or any Credit Support Document given by the Defaulting Party. However, the Section still does not specifically provide for the payment of expenses arising from the enforcement and protection of rights under any third party Credit Support Document and it is therefore necessary to check that such a Credit Support Document contains an acceptable indemnity for expenses.

Please note that the Section 6(e)(v) prohibition on recovering consequential losses is not intended to prevent recovery of the expenses specified in Section 11.

However, legal fees and out-of-pocket expenses are excluded from the definition of Close-out Amount in Section 14.

Principal change from the 1992 Agreement

- **Reference to execution fees now being covered.**

12. Notices

(a) ***Effectiveness.*** Any notice or other communication in respect of this Agreement may be given in any manner described below (except that a notice or other communication under Section 5 or 6 may not be given by electronic messaging system or e-mail) to the address or number or in accordance with the electronic messaging system or e-mail details provided (see the Schedule) and will be deemed effective as indicated:-

(i) if in writing and delivered in person or by courier, on the date it is delivered;

(ii) if sent by telex, on the date the recipient's answerback is received;

(iii) if sent by facsimile transmission, on the date it is received by a responsible employee of the recipient in legible form (it being agreed that the burden of proving receipt will be on the sender and will not be met by a transmission report generated by the sender's facsimile machine);

(iv) if sent by certified or registered mail (airmail, if overseas) or the equivalent (return receipt requested), on the date it is delivered or its delivery is attempted;

(v) if sent by electronic messaging system, on the date it is received; or

(vi) if sent by e-mail, on the date it is delivered,

unless the date of that delivery (or attempted delivery) or that receipt, as applicable, is not a Local Business Day or that communication is delivered (or attempted) or received, as applicable, after the close of business on a Local Business Day, in which case that communication will be deemed given and effective on the first following day that is a Local Business Day.

(b) ***Change of Details.*** Either party may by notice to the other change the address, telex or facsimile number or electronic messaging system or e-mail details at which notices or other communications are to be given to it.

Section 12

Section 12 states the means by which any notice or communication in connection with an Agreement may be made. The Section 14 definition of "electronic messages" excludes e-mails but includes documents in mark-up languages such as FpML. Notices relating to Section 5 or 6 may not be given by electronic messaging system or e-mail. The prohibition on the use of faxes for giving Section 5 or 6 notices has been lifted.

Section 12(a)

Section 12(a) defines when receipt is considered to take place with the recipient. As regards a fax (Section 12(a)(iii)) its receipt is only effective on the date a responsible employee receives the fax in legible form. The sender has to prove receipt and a transmission report from a fax machine is not good enough for this purpose. There is no definition of who a responsible employee is and any doubts about this could affect the timing of receipt of the notice. A permitted electronic message is effective on receipt and for e-mail it is effective on the date on which it is delivered. However, if the date of delivery or receipt is not a Local Business Day or takes place after close of business on a Local Business Day then it will only become effective on the next following Local Business Day.

Section 12(b)

Changes to relevant addresses, numbers, electronic messaging details or e-mail addresses specified in Part 4(a) of the Schedule to the Agreement may be made by either party notifying the other in any of the prescribed forms under clause (a).

Principal changes from the 1992 Agreement

- **Section 12(a) – Prohibition on faxes being used for Section 5 or 6 notices lifted but they may still not be given by electronic messaging systems and e-mail is now added to this prohibition. E-mail added as a permissible means for giving other notices in Section 12(a)(vi).**
- **Section 12(b) – Minor change in heading – the word "Details" replaces "Addresses" and notices under Section 12(b) may also be given by e-mail.**

13. Governing Law and Jurisdiction

(a) ***Governing Law***. This Agreement will be governed by and construed in accordance with the law specified in the Schedule.

(b) ***Jurisdiction***. With respect to any suit, action or proceedings relating to any dispute arising out of or in connection with this Agreement ("Proceedings"), each party irrevocably:-

(i) submits:-

(1) if this Agreement is expressed to be governed by English law, to (A) the non-exclusive jurisdiction of the English courts if the Proceedings do not involve a Convention Court and (B) the exclusive jurisdiction of the English courts if the Proceedings do involve a Convention Court; or

(2) if this Agreement is expressed to be governed by the laws of the State of New York, to the non-exclusive jurisdiction of the courts of the State of New York and the United States District Court located in the Borough of Manhattan in New York City;

(ii) waives any objection which it may have at any time to the laying of venue of any Proceedings brought in any such court, waives any claim that such Proceedings have been brought in an inconvenient forum and further waives the right to object, with respect to such Proceedings, that such court does not have any jurisdiction over such party; and

(iii) agrees, to the extent permitted by applicable law, that the bringing of Proceedings in any one or more jurisdictions will not preclude the bringing of Proceedings in any other jurisdiction.

Section 13

Section 13(a)

Parties to the Agreement choose its governing law in Part 4(h) of the Schedule. The Agreement offers a choice between English law and the laws of the State of New York because it was composed with the requirements of the common law codes of those jurisdictions in mind. Where it is proposed that the governing law is to be other than English law or the laws of the State of New York, this should be the subject of specific legal advice so as to minimise conflicts of law. There are no real exceptions to this because it is vital to ensure that the Agreement (and particularly its close-out netting provisions) is effective under any law other than English or New York law.

Section 13(b)

As far as the jurisdiction of the English courts are concerned, there is a change here arising from the EU's Regulation on Jurisdiction and Recognition of Enforcement of Judgments in Civil and Commercial Matters (the "Brussels Regulation") which came into force in all 15 EU states except Denmark on 1 March 2002. The Brussels Regulation applies to all legal proceedings started after 1 March 2002 even if they involve an ISDA Master Agreement executed before that date.

Consequently, because of the implementation of the Brussels Regulation there are now three jurisdiction regimes running in parallel which regulate jurisdiction between European countries. These are:

- **the Brussels Regulation governing jurisdiction issues between all Brussels Convention states except Denmark;**
- **the 1968 Brussels Convention governing jurisdiction issues between Denmark and all other Brussels Convention states; and**
- **the 1988 Lugano Convention governing jurisdiction issues between the EFTA countries and the Brussels Convention states.**

The Brussels Regulation needed an amendment made to the definition of Contracting State in s 1(3) of the English Civil Jurisdiction and Judgments Act 1982 which is referred to in Section 13 of the 1992 Agreement.

The most significant amendment as regards the ISDA Master Agreement is that non-exclusive jurisdiction clauses are now expressly allowed by Article 23 of the Brussels Regulation.

The change in the opening wording of Section 13(b) is to make it clear that the jurisdiction clause covers *all* claims concerning the Agreement including claims for tort.

A Convention Court is one which is bound to apply Article 17 of the 1968 Brussels Convention or Article 17 of the 1988 Lugano Convention to its proceedings.

Accordingly, except in cases where the rival choice of court would be that of Denmark, Iceland, Norway, Poland or Switzerland which are Convention Courts, submission to the English courts is now non-exclusive. However, where a Convention Court is the rival court, the jurisdiction of the English courts will be exclusive.

Where New York law is chosen, the jurisdiction of the courts of the State of New York and the US District Court located in the Borough of Manhattan in New York will apply. The submission to the jurisdiction of the New York courts is non-exclusive which means that actions may be commenced in other courts.

Waivers of objection to venue, inconvenient forum and objection to questioning the court's jurisdiction are also included.

Principal changes from the 1992 Agreement

Section 13(a) – None.
Section 13(b):

- **Additional of the words "any dispute arising out of or in connection with" in preamble so that all actions are covered.**
- **It is made clear that jurisdiction of the English courts will be non-exclusive where a non-Convention Court is involved but will be exclusive where a Convention Court is concerned.**
- **Rearrangement of wording in Section 13(b)(i)(2).**
- **Deletion of reference to the Civil Jurisdiction and Judgments Act 1982 following it being superseded by the Brussels Regulation.**

(c) ***Service of Process***. Each party irrevocably appoints the Process Agent (if any) specified opposite its name in the Schedule to receive, for it and on its behalf, service of process in any Proceedings. If for any reason any party's Process Agent is unable to act as such, such party will promptly notify the other party and within 30 days appoint a substitute process agent acceptable to the other party. The parties irrevocably consent to service of process given in the manner provided for notices in Section 12(a)(i), 12(a)(iii) or 12(a)(iv). Nothing in this Agreement will affect the right of either party to serve process in any other manner permitted by applicable law.

(d) ***Waiver of Immunities***. Each party irrevocably waives, to the extent permitted by applicable law, with respect to itself and its revenues and assets (irrespective of their use or intended use), all immunity on the grounds of sovereignty or other similar grounds from (i) suit, (ii) jurisdiction of any court, (iii) relief by way of injunction or order for specific performance or recovery of property, (iv) attachment of its assets (whether before or after judgment) and (v) execution or enforcement of any judgment to which it or its revenues or assets might otherwise be entitled in any Proceedings in the courts of any jurisdiction and irrevocably agrees, to the extent permitted by applicable law, that it will not claim any such immunity in any Proceedings.

Section 13(c)

Process Agents for the receipt of writs or other legal documents, where applicable, are nominated in Part 4(b) of the Schedule. They are necessary because the Agreement is under English or New York law and it is a requirement that process be served in those jurisdictions where a Defaulting Party is not incorporated in them and cannot easily be served with the necessary legal papers required to commence legal proceedings in them.

Section 13(c) states that each party also consents to service of process in the manner provided for notices in Section 12. However, certain means of providing notice in Section 12 may not be practical for serving process (e.g. telex or electronic messaging system) and may not be a valid means of serving process in certain countries despite the parties' consent in Section 13(c). In fact the parties now agree to notice only being served by hand delivered mail, airmail, fax or registered or certified mail. Section 13(c) also provides that where a party's Process Agent is unable to act, it will promptly notify its counterparty and by mutual agreement appoint a substitute Process Agent within 30 days. Service of notice by a Process Agent can be very important where failure to serve process in a jurisdiction could result in a foreign judgment not being enforced in that country.

Where a foreign counterparty does not appoint an English Process Agent, an English counterparty will have to obtain separate permission from the court to serve process in these circumstances. This is even the case where a serving party complies with the methods for service set out in Section 12. If the party simply relies on these methods to serve the foreign counterparty direct, this will not constitute valid service. This is why it is important for an English contracting party to insist that a foreign counterparty appoints an English Process Agent.

Section 13(d)

Section 13(d) provides for a waiver of immunities from prosecution by the parties to the extent permitted by applicable law. This provision is also common in loan agreements.

Principal changes from the 1992 Agreement

- **Section 13(c) – Service of process only to be notified by hand delivered mail, fax or registered or certified mail.**
- **Section 13(d) – Deletion of "fullest" in line 1 before "extent".**

14. Definitions

As used in this Agreement:-

"***Additional Representation***" has the meaning specified in Section 3.

"***Additional Termination Event***" has the meaning specified in Section 5(b).

"***Affected Party***" has the meaning specified in Section 5(b).

"***Affected Transactions***" means (a) with respect to any Termination Event consisting of an Illegality, Force Majeure Event, Tax Event or Tax Event Upon Merger, all Transactions affected by the occurrence of such Termination Event (which, in the case of an Illegality under Section 5(b)(i)(2) or a Force Majeure Event under Section 5(b)(ii)(2), means all Transactions unless the relevant Credit Support Document references only certain Transactions, in which case those Transactions and, if the relevant Credit Support Document constitutes a Confirmation for a Transaction, that Transaction) and (b) with respect to any other Termination Event, all Transactions.

"***Affiliate***" means, subject to the Schedule, in relation to any person, any entity controlled, directly or indirectly, by the person, any entity that controls, directly or indirectly, the person or any entity directly or indirectly under common control with the person. For this purpose, "control" of any entity or person means ownership of a majority of the voting power of the entity or person.

"***Agreement***" has the meaning specified in Section 1(c).

Section 14 – Definitions

All significant terms in the Agreement are defined, sometimes exhaustively, in Section 14. No doubt with the disapproval of lawyers but with a big "government health warning" I set out below a simple glossary of most of these Definitions except where they are self-evident.

GLOSSARY OF MOST TERMS IN SECTION 14

Additional Representation	An extra representation which can be stated in Part 4(m) of the Schedule or in a Confirmation. ISDA's non-reliance language can be chosen as an additional representation in Part 4(m) of the Schedule.
Additional Termination Event	An extra Termination Event chosen by the parties, e.g. a change of control event or a credit ratings downgrade event.
Affected Party	The party at fault under a Termination Event.
Affected Transactions	The relevant Transactions affected by a Termination Event.
Affiliate	Essentially any other company or entity in a party's group.

"Applicable Close-out Rate" means:-

(a) in respect of the determination of an Unpaid Amount:-

(i) in respect of obligations payable or deliverable (or which would have been but for Section 2(a)(iii)) by a Defaulting Party, the Default Rate;

(ii) in respect of obligations payable or deliverable (or which would have been but for Section 2(a)(iii)) by a Non-defaulting Party, the Non-default Rate;

(iii) in respect of obligations deferred pursuant to Section 5(d), if there is no Defaulting Party and for so long as the deferral period continues, the Applicable Deferral Rate; and

(iv) in all other cases following the occurrence of a Termination Event (except where interest accrues pursuant to clause (iii) above), the Applicable Deferral Rate; and

(b) in respect of an Early Termination Amount:-

(i) for the period from (and including) the relevant Early Termination Date to (but excluding) the date (determined in accordance with Section 6(d)(ii)) on which that amount is payable:-

(1) if the Early Termination Amount is payable by a Defaulting Party, the Default Rate;

(2) if the Early Termination Amount is payable by a Non-defaulting Party, the Non-default Rate; and

(3) in all other cases, the Applicable Deferral Rate; and

(ii) for the period from (and including) the date (determined in accordance with Section 6(d)(ii)) on which that amount is payable to (but excluding) the date of actual payment:-

(1) if a party fails to pay the Early Termination Amount due to the occurrence of an event or circumstance which would, if it occurred with respect to a payment or delivery under a Transaction, constitute or give rise to an Illegality or a Force Majeure Event, and for so long as the Early Termination Amount remains unpaid due to the continuing existence of such event or circumstance, the Applicable Deferral Rate;

(2) if the Early Termination Amount is payable by a Defaulting Party (but excluding any period in respect of which clause (1) above applies), the Default Rate;

(3) if the Early Termination Amount is payable by a Non-defaulting Party (but excluding any period in respect of which clause (1) above applies), the Non-default Rate; and

(4) in all other cases, the Termination Rate.

Applicable Close-out Rate	One of a series of penalty interest rates arising in specific circumstances relating to Unpaid Amounts and Early Termination Amounts.

"Applicable Deferral Rate" means:-

(a) for the purpose of Section 9(h)(i)(3)(A), the rate certified by the relevant payer to be a rate offered to the payer by a major bank in a relevant interbank market for overnight deposits in the applicable currency, such bank to be selected in good faith by the payer for the purpose of obtaining a representative rate that will reasonably reflect conditions prevailing at the time in that relevant market;

(b) for purposes of Section 9(h)(i)(3)(B) and clause (a)(iii) of the definition of Applicable Close-out Rate, the rate certified by the relevant payer to be a rate offered to prime banks by a major bank in a relevant interbank market for overnight deposits in the applicable currency, such bank to be selected in good faith by the payer after consultation with the other party, if practicable, for the purpose of obtaining a representative rate that will reasonably reflect conditions prevailing at the time in that relevant market; and

(c) for purposes of Section 9(h)(i)(3)(C) and clauses (a)(iv), (b)(i)(3) and (b)(ii)(1) of the definition of Applicable Close-out Rate, a rate equal to the arithmetic mean of the rate determined pursuant to clause (a) above and a rate per annum equal to the cost (without proof or evidence of any actual cost) to the relevant payee (as certified by it) if it were to fund or of funding the relevant amount.

"Automatic Early Termination" has the meaning specified in Section 6(a).

"Burdened Party" has the meaning specified in Section 5(b)(iv).

"Change in Tax Law" means the enactment, promulgation, execution or ratification of, or any change in or amendment to, any law (or in the application or official interpretation of any law) that occurs after the parties enter into the relevant Transaction.

Applicable Deferral Rate	One of a series of penalty interest rates applicable to specific circumstances arising from defaulted or deferred payments or deliveries.
Automatic Early Termination	Automatic close-out arising from certain Bankruptcy events.
Burdened Party	The party afflicted or at fault (if it is the merging party) in the Tax Event Upon Merger Termination Event, as the case may be.

"Close-out Amount" means, with respect to each Terminated Transaction or each group of Terminated Transactions and a Determining Party, the amount of the losses or costs of the Determining Party that are or would be incurred under then prevailing circumstances (expressed as a positive number) or gains of the Determining Party that are or would be realised under then prevailing circumstances (expressed as a negative number) in replacing, or in providing for the Determining Party the economic equivalent of, (a) the material terms of that Terminated Transaction or group of Terminated Transactions, including the payments and deliveries by the parties under Section 2(a)(i) in respect of that Terminated Transaction or group of Terminated Transactions that would, but for the occurrence of the relevant Early Termination Date, have been required after that date (assuming satisfaction of the conditions precedent in Section 2(a)(iii)) and (b) the option rights of the parties in respect of that Terminated Transaction or group of Terminated Transactions.

Any Close-out Amount will be determined by the Determining Party (or its agent), which will act in good faith and use commercially reasonable procedures in order to produce a commercially reasonable result. The Determining Party may determine a Close-out Amount for any group of Terminated Transactions or any individual Terminated Transaction but, in the aggregate, for not less than all Terminated Transactions. Each Close-out Amount will be determined as of the Early Termination Date or, if that would not be commercially reasonable, as of the date or dates following the Early Termination Date as would be commercially reasonable.

Unpaid Amounts in respect of a Terminated Transaction or group of Terminated Transactions and legal fees and out-of-pocket expenses referred to in Section 11 are to be excluded in all determinations of Close-out Amounts.

In determining a Close-out Amount, the Determining Party may consider any relevant information, including, without limitation, one or more of the following types of information:-

(i) quotations (either firm or indicative) for replacement transactions supplied by one or more third parties that may take into account the creditworthiness of the Determining Party at the time the quotation is provided and the terms of any relevant documentation, including credit support documentation, between the Determining Party and the third party providing the quotation;

(ii) information consisting of relevant market data in the relevant market supplied by one or more third parties including, without limitation, relevant rates, prices, yields, yield curves, volatilities, spreads, correlations or other relevant market data in the relevant market; or

(iii) information of the types described in clause (i) or (ii) above from internal sources (including any of the Determining Party's Affiliates) if that

Close-out Amount	The replacement cost for Terminated Transactions potentially calculable from a wide variety of valuation inputs, both arm's length and internal.

information is of the same type used by the Determining Party in the regular course of its business for the valuation of similar transactions.

The Determining Party will consider, taking into account the standards and procedures described in this definition, quotations pursuant to clause (i) above or relevant market data pursuant to clause (ii) above unless the Determining Party reasonably believes in good faith that such quotations or relevant market data are not readily available or would produce a result that would not satisfy those standards. When considering information described in clause (i), (ii) or (iii) above, the Determining Party may include costs of funding, to the extent costs of funding are not and would not be a component of the other information being utilised. Third parties supplying quotations pursuant to clause (i) above or market data pursuant to clause (ii) above may include, without limitation, dealers in the relevant markets, end-users of the relevant product, information vendors, brokers and other sources of market information.

Without duplication of amounts calculated based on information described in clause (i), (ii) or (iii) above, or other relevant information, and when it is commercially reasonable to do so, the Determining Party may in addition consider in calculating a Close-out Amount any loss or cost incurred in connection with its terminating, liquidating or re-establishing any hedge related to a Terminated Transaction or group of Terminated Transactions (or any gain resulting from any of them).

Commercially reasonable procedures used in determining a Close-out Amount may include the following:-

(1) application to relevant market data from third parties pursuant to clause (ii) above or information from internal sources pursuant to clause (iii) above of pricing or other valuation models that are, at the time of the determination of the Close-out Amount, used by the Determining Party in the regular course of its business in pricing or valuing transactions between the Determining Party and unrelated third parties that are similar to the Terminated Transaction or group of Terminated Transactions; and

(2) application of different valuation methods to Terminated Transactions or groups of Terminated Transactions depending on the type, complexity, size or number of the Terminated Transactions or group of Terminated Transactions.

"Confirmation" has the meaning specified in the preamble.

"consent" includes a consent, approval, action, authorisation, exemption, notice, filing, registration or exchange control consent.

"Contractual Currency" has the meaning specified in Section 8(a).

"Convention Court" means any court which is bound to apply to the Proceedings either Article 17 of the 1968 Brussels Convention on Jurisdiction and the Enforcement of Judgments in Civil and Commercial Matters or Article 17 of the 1988 Lugano Convention on Jurisdiction and the Enforcement of Judgments in Civil and Commercial Matters.

"Credit Event Upon Merger" has the meaning specified in Section 5(b).

"Credit Support Document" means any agreement or instrument that is specified as such in this Agreement.

"Credit Support Provider" has the meaning specified in the Schedule.

"Cross-Default" means the event specified in Section 5(a)(vi).

"Default Rate" means a rate per annum equal to the cost (without proof or evidence of any actual cost) to the relevant payee (as certified by it) if it were to fund or of funding the relevant amount plus 1% per annum.

"Defaulting Party" has the meaning specified in Section 6(a).

"Designated Event" has the meaning specified in Section 5(b)(v).

"Determining Party" means the party determining a Close-out Amount.

"Early Termination Amount" has the meaning specified in Section 6(e).

Convention Court	An English court will apply exclusive jurisdiction where the rival court is in Denmark, Iceland, Norway, Poland or Switzerland.
Credit Event Upon Merger	A deterioration in the creditworthiness of a party to the Agreement following a merger type event.
Credit Support Document	A document securing a party's obligations under the Agreement provided either by the party itself or a third party (e.g. a guarantor).
Credit Support Provider	The party providing security under a Credit Support Document.
Default Rate	1% over the payee's cost of funds.
Defaulting Party	The party at fault under an Event of Default.
Determining Party	The party calculating a Close-out Amount.
Early Termination Amount	The net settlement payment due to one party or the other when Transactions are terminated. It will comprise the Close-out Amount and any net Unpaid Amounts.

"Early Termination Date" means the date determined in accordance with Section 6(a) or 6(b)(iv).

"electronic messages" does not include e-mails but does include documents expressed in markup languages, and ***"electronic messaging system"*** will be construed accordingly.

"English law" means the law of England and Wales, and ***"English"*** will be construed accordingly.

"Event of Default" has the meaning specified in Section 5(a) and, if applicable, in the Schedule.

"Force Majeure Event" has the meaning specified in Section 5(b).

"General Business Day" means a day on which commercial banks are open for general business (including dealings in foreign exchange and foreign currency deposits).

"Illegality" has the meaning specified in Section 5(b).

"Indemnifiable Tax" means any Tax other than a Tax that would not be imposed in respect of a payment under this Agreement but for a present or former connection between the jurisdiction of the government or taxation authority imposing such Tax and the recipient of such payment or a person related to such recipient (including, without limitation, a connection arising from such recipient or related person being or having been a citizen or resident of such jurisdiction, or being or having been organised, present or engaged in a trade or business in such jurisdiction, or having or having had a permanent establishment or fixed place of business in such jurisdiction, but excluding a connection arising solely from such recipient or related person having executed, delivered, performed its obligations or received a payment under, or enforced, this Agreement or a Credit Support Document).

"law" includes any treaty, law, rule or regulation (as modified, in the case of tax matters, by the practice of any relevant governmental revenue authority), and ***"unlawful"*** will be construed accordingly.

Early Termination Date	The date upon which close-out occurs.
Event of Default	One or more events in Section 5(a) of the Agreement which can trigger close-out of all Transactions by a Non-defaulting Party under the Agreement.
Force Majeure Event	An event which makes it impossible or impracticable for a party to perform its obligations through an Office, under the Agreement or a Credit Support Document.
General Business Day	A day on which commercial banks are open for general business including foreign exchange trading.
Illegality	Under Section 5(b)(i) an event which prevents lawful payment or performance through an Office, under the Agreement or a Credit Support Document.
Indemnifiable Tax	Essentially a cross border tax against which a party to the Agreement is entitled to be indemnified by the other party. It excludes domestic income, sales and capital taxes.

"Local Business Day" means (a) in relation to any obligation under Section 2(a)(i), a General Business Day in the place or places specified in the relevant Confirmation and a day on which a relevant settlement system is open or operating as specified in the relevant Confirmation or, if a place or a settlement system is not so specified, as otherwise agreed by the parties in writing or determined pursuant to provisions contained, or incorporated by reference, in this Agreement, (b) for the purpose of determining when a Waiting Period expires, a General Business Day in the place where the event or circumstance that constitutes or gives rise to the Illegality or Force Majeure Event, as the case may be, occurs, (c) in relation to any other payment, a General Business Day in the place where the relevant account is located and, if different, in the principal financial centre, if any, of the currency of such payment and, if that currency does not have a single recognised principal financial centre, a day on which the settlement system necessary to accomplish such payment is open, (d) in relation to any notice or other communication, including notice contemplated under Section 5(a)(i), a General Business Day (or a day that would have been a General Business Day but for the occurrence of an event or circumstance which would, if it occurred with respect to payment, delivery or compliance related to a Transaction, constitute or give rise to an Illegality or a Force Majeure Event) in the place specified in the address for notice provided by the recipient and, in the case of a notice contemplated by Section 2(b), in the place where the relevant new account is to be located and (e) in relation to Section 5(a)(v)(2), a General Business Day in the relevant locations for performance with respect to such Specified Transaction.

"Local Delivery Day" means, for purposes of Sections 5(a)(i) and 5(d), a day on which settlement systems necessary to accomplish the relevant delivery are generally open for business so that the delivery is capable of being accomplished in accordance with customary market practice, in the place specified in the relevant Confirmation or, if not so specified, in a location as determined in accordance with customary market practice for the relevant delivery.

"Master Agreement" has the meaning specified in the preamble.

"Merger Without Assumption" means the event specified in Section 5(a)(viii).

"Multiple Transaction Payment Netting" has the meaning specified in Section 2(c).

Local Business Day	A day when commercial banks are open for general business and when settlement systems are also open and operational so that obligations under OTC derivatives transactions can be performed.
Local Delivery Day	A day on which settlement systems are open so that deliveries and be made or received according to custom in the market(s) specified in a Confirmation.

"Non-affected Party" means, so long as there is only one Affected Party, the other party.

"Non-default Rate" means the rate certified by the Non-defaulting Party to be a rate offered to the Non-defaulting Party by a major bank in a relevant interbank market for overnight deposits in the applicable currency, such bank to be selected in good faith by the Non-defaulting Party for the purpose of obtaining a representative rate that will reasonably reflect conditions prevailing at the time in that relevant market.

"Non-defaulting Party" has the meaning specified in Section 6(a).

"Office" means a branch or office of a party, which may be such party's head or home office.

"Other Amounts" has the meaning specified in Section 6(f).

"Payee" has the meaning specified in Section 6(f).

"Payer" has the meaning specified in Section 6(f).

Non-affected Party	The party not at fault in a Termination Event.
Non-default Rate	The market interest rate for an interbank overnight deposit offered by a major bank selected in good faith by the Non-defaulting Party.
Non-defaulting Party	The party not at fault in an Event of Default.
Office	A branch or office of a party including its head or home office.

"Potential Event of Default" means any event which, with the giving of notice or the lapse of time or both, would constitute an Event of Default.

"Proceedings" has the meaning specified in Section 13(b).

"Process Agent" has the meaning specified in the Schedule.

"rate of exchange" includes, without limitation, any premiums and costs of exchange payable in connection with the purchase of or conversion into the Contractual Currency.

"Relevant Jurisdiction" means, with respect to a party, the jurisdictions (a) in which the party is incorporated, organised, managed and controlled or considered to have its seat, (b) where an Office through which the party is acting for purposes of this Agreement is located, (c) in which the party executes this Agreement and (d) in relation to any payment, from or through which such payment is made.

"Schedule" has the meaning specified in the preamble.

"Scheduled Settlement Date" means a date on which a payment or delivery is to be made under Section 2(a)(i) with respect to a Transaction.

"Specified Entity" has the meaning specified in the Schedule.

"Specified Indebtedness" means, subject to the Schedule, any obligation (whether present or future, contingent or otherwise, as principal or surety or otherwise) in respect of borrowed money.

Potential Event of Default	An event which would become an Event of Default if not cured within a grace period or if a default notice is issued in relation to it.
Scheduled Settlement Date	The date on which a normal payment or delivery under a Transaction is due.
Specified Entity	An entity a party wants to join to the Section 5 events named in Part 1(a) of the Schedule.
Specified Indebtedness	Borrowed money.

"Specified Transaction" means, subject to the Schedule, (a) any transaction (including an agreement with respect to any such transaction) now existing or hereafter entered into between one party to this Agreement (or any Credit Support Provider of such party or any applicable Specified Entity of such party) and the other party to this Agreement (or any Credit Support Provider of such other party or any applicable Specified Entity of such other party) which is not a Transaction under this Agreement but (i) which is a rate swap transaction, swap option, basis swap, forward rate transaction, commodity swap, commodity option, equity or equity index swap, equity or equity index option, bond option, interest rate option, foreign exchange transaction, cap transaction, floor transaction, collar transaction, currency swap transaction, cross-currency rate swap transaction, currency option, credit protection transaction, credit swap, credit default swap, credit default option, total return swap, credit spread transaction, repurchase transaction, reverse repurchase transaction, buy/sell-back transaction, securities lending transaction, weather index transaction or forward purchase or sale of a security, commodity or other financial instrument or interest (including any option with respect to any of these transactions) or (ii) which is a type of transaction that is similar to any transaction referred to in clause (i) above that is currently, or in the future becomes, recurrently entered into in the financial markets (including terms and conditions incorporated by reference in such agreement) and which is a forward, swap, future, option or other derivative on one or more rates, currencies, commodities, equity securities or other equity instruments, debt securities or other debt instruments, economic indices or measures of economic risk or value, or other benchmarks against which payments or deliveries are to be made, (b) any combination of these transactions and (c) any other transaction identified as a Specified Transaction in this Agreement or the relevant confirmation.

Specified Transaction	One of a list of OTC derivatives Transactions between the two parties to the Agreement or their Specified Entities or Credit Support Providers but which are outside of the Agreement.

"Stamp Tax" means any stamp, registration, documentation or similar tax.

"Stamp Tax Jurisdiction" has the meaning specified in Section 4(e).

"Tax" means any present or future tax, levy, impost, duty, charge, assessment or fee of any nature (including interest, penalties and additions thereto) that is imposed by any government or other taxing authority in respect of any payment under this Agreement other than a stamp, registration, documentation or similar tax.

"Tax Event" has the meaning specified in Section 5(b).

"Tax Event Upon Merger" has the meaning specified in Section 5(b).

"Terminated Transactions" means, with respect to any Early Termination Date, (a) if resulting from an Illegality or a Force Majeure Event, all Affected Transactions specified in the notice given pursuant to Section 6(b)(iv), (b) if resulting from any other Termination Event, all Affected Transactions and (c) if resulting from an Event of Default, all Transactions in effect either immediately before the effectiveness of the notice designating that Early Termination Date or, if Automatic Early Termination applies, immediately before that Early Termination Date.

"Termination Currency" means (a) if a Termination Currency is specified in the Schedule and that currency is freely available, that currency, and (b) otherwise, euro if this Agreement is expressed to be governed by English law or United States Dollars if this Agreement is expressed to be governed by the laws of the State of New York.

"Termination Currency Equivalent" means, in respect of any amount denominated in the Termination Currency, such Termination Currency amount and, in respect of any amount denominated in a currency other than the Termination Currency (the "Other Currency"), the amount in the Termination Currency determined by the party making the relevant determination as being required to purchase such amount of such Other Currency as at the relevant Early Termination Date, or, if the relevant Close-out Amount is determined as of a later date, that later date, with the Termination Currency at the rate equal to the spot exchange rate of the foreign exchange agent (selected as provided below) for the purchase of such Other Currency with the Termination Currency at or about 11:00 a.m. (in the city in which such foreign exchange agent is located) on such date as would be customary for the determination of such a rate for the purchase of such Other Currency for value on the relevant Early Termination Date or that later date. The foreign exchange agent will, if only one party is obliged to make a determination under Section 6(e), be selected in good faith by that party and otherwise will be agreed by the parties.

"Termination Event" means an Illegality, a Force Majeure Event, a Tax Event, a Tax Event Upon Merger or, if specified to be applicable, a Credit Event Upon Merger or an Additional Termination Event.

Tax Event	The Termination Event in Section 5(b)(iii) which can conditionally trigger termination of Affected Transactions due to adverse changes in tax law or their implementation by tax authorities or courts.
Tax Event Upon Merger	The Termination Event in Section 5(b)(iv) which can conditionally trigger termination of Affected Transactions due to adverse changes in tax law or their implementation by tax authorities and which affect one party to the Agreement where it or its counterparty has merged with a third party.
Terminated Transactions	Transactions terminated or to be terminated on the Early Termination Date.
Termination Currency	The currency (selected in Part 1(f) of the Schedule) into which all Transactions are converted when calculating a final close-out amount on the Early Termination Date.
Termination Currency Equivalent	The equivalent value of the Terminated Transactions in the Termination Currency chosen in Part 1(f) of the Schedule.
Termination Event	The events in Section 5(b) which can trigger close-out.

"Termination Rate" means a rate per annum equal to the arithmetic mean of the cost (without proof or evidence of any actual cost) to each party (as certified by such party) if it were to fund or of funding such amounts.

"Threshold Amount" means the amount, if any, specified as such in the Schedule.

"Transaction" has the meaning specified in the preamble.

Termination Rate	In a no fault termination, the arithmetic mean of the self certified funding costs of both parties.
Threshold Amount	The monetary or money equivalent trigger for a Non-defaulting Party to exercise its close-out rights under the Agreement's Cross Default provision.

"Unpaid Amounts" owing to any party means, with respect to an Early Termination Date, the aggregate of (a) in respect of all Terminated Transactions, the amounts that became payable (or that would have become payable but for Section 2(a)(iii) or due but for Section 5(d)) to such party under Section 2(a)(i) or 2(d)(i)(4) on or prior to such Early Termination Date and which remain unpaid as at such Early Termination Date, (b) in respect of each Terminated Transaction, for each obligation under Section 2(a)(i) which was (or would have been but for Section 2(a)(iii) or 5(d)) required to be settled by delivery to such party on or prior to such Early Termination Date and which has not been so settled as at such Early Termination Date, an amount equal to the fair market value of that which was (or would have been) required to be delivered and (c) if the Early Termination Date results from an Event of Default, a Credit Event Upon Merger or an Additional Termination Event in respect of which all outstanding Transactions are Affected Transactions, any Early Termination Amount due prior to such Early Termination Date and which remains unpaid as of such Early Termination Date, in each case together with any amount of interest accrued or other compensation in respect of that obligation or deferred obligation, as the case may be, pursuant to Section 9(h)(ii)(1) or (2), as appropriate. The fair market value of any obligation referred to in clause (b) above will be determined as of the originally scheduled date for delivery, in good faith and using commercially reasonable procedures, by the party obliged to make the determination under Section 6(e) or, if each party is so obliged, it will be the average of the Termination Currency Equivalents of the fair market values so determined by both parties.

"Waiting Period" means:-

(a) in respect of an event or circumstance under Section 5(b)(i), other than in the case of Section 5(b)(i)(2) where the relevant payment, delivery or compliance is actually required on the relevant day (in which case no Waiting Period will apply), a period of three Local Business Days (or days that would have been Local Business Days but for the occurrence of that event or circumstance) following the occurrence of that event or circumstance; and

(b) in respect of an event or circumstance under Section 5(b)(ii), other than in the case of Section 5(b)(ii)(2) where the relevant payment, delivery or compliance is actually required on the relevant day (in which case no Waiting Period will apply), a period of eight Local Business Days (or days that would have been Local Business Days but for the occurrence of that event or circumstance) following the occurrence of that event or circumstance.

Unpaid Amounts	A payment or delivery due to a party on a Scheduled Settlement Date which remains unpaid due to an Early Termination Date occurring, plus interest. Unpaid Amounts form part of Early Termination Amounts.
Waiting Period	Generally three Local Business Days for an Illegality and eight Local Business Days for a Force Majeure Event

IN WITNESS WHEREOF the parties have executed this document on the respective dates specified below with effect from the date specified on the first page of this document.

By:...	By:...
(Name of Party)	(Name of Party)
Name:	Name:
Title:	Title:
Date:	Date:

Signature Block

The name of each party and the names and titles of signatories must be filled in on the signature page along with the dates of signing by each signatory. The main text of the Master Agreement must be signed. A Schedule can, but need not, be signed although the Schedule to the 2002 Agreement offers this.

The pre-printed text of the Master Agreement ends on page 28. A Schedule is always attached and begins on page 29.

The Schedule is where provisions in the ISDA Master Agreement are amended or added to through negotiation.

We shall examine Schedules in general in Chapters 8 and 9. However, there now follows the 2002 ISDA Master Agreement Schedule with commentary on new items and major changes.

ISDA®

International Swaps and Derivatives Association, Inc.

SCHEDULE

to the

2002 MASTER AGREEMENT

dated as of ....

between .... and ....

("Party A")	("Party B")
[established as a [COUNTERPARTY TYPE]]	[established as a [COUNTERPARTY TYPE]]
[with company number [NUMBER]]	[with company number [NUMBER]]
[under the laws of [JURISDICTION]]	[under the laws of [JURISDICTION]]
[acting through its [BRANCH]]*	[acting through its [BRANCH]]*

Part 1. **Termination Provisions.**

(a) ***"Specified Entity"*** means in relation to Party A for the purpose of:-

Section 5(a)(v), ...

Section 5(a)(vi), ...

Section 5(a)(vii), ...

Section 5(b)(v), ...

and in relation to Party B for the purpose of:-

Section 5(a)(v), ...

Section 5(a)(vi), ...

Section 5(a)(vii), ...

Section 5(b)(v), ...

---

* Include if applicable.

ANALYSIS OF SCHEDULE

Commentary

Fortunately the Schedule is similar in structure to the Schedule in the 1992 Agreement.

Under the heading there is an opportunity to add descriptive detail as to the nature of the counterparties and their jurisdictions which is often useful to know.

In Part 1(a) Credit Event Upon Merger has been renumbered as Section 5(b)(v).

(b) ***"Specified Transaction"*** [will have the meaning specified in Section 14 of this Agreement.][means

....

....

....]*

(c) The ***"Cross-Default"*** provisions of Section 5(a)(vi)

[will][will not]* apply to Party A

[will][will not]* apply to Party B

[***"Specified Indebtedness"*** [will have the meaning specified in Section 14 of this Agreement.][means ....

....]*

"Threshold Amount" means..

....]**

(d) The ***"Credit Event Upon Merger"*** provisions of Section 5(b)(v)

[will][will not]* apply to Party A

[will][will not]* apply to Party B

(e) The ***"Automatic Early Termination"*** provision of Section 6(a)

[will][will not]* apply to Party A

[will][will not]* apply to Party B

---

* Delete as applicable.

** Include if Cross-Default will apply to either Party A or Party B.

Commentary

For commentary on Part 1(b)–(e) please see Chapter 8 pages 427–54.

(f) ***"Termination Currency"*** [will have the meaning specified in Section 14 of this Agreement.][means.......................................

....]*

(g) ***Additional Termination Event*** [will][will not]* apply. [The following will constitute an Additional Termination Event:-

....

....

For the purpose of the foregoing Termination Event, the Affected Party or Affected Parties will be:-

....

....]***

Part 2. **Tax Representations.******

(a) ***Payer Representations.*** For the purpose of Section 3(e) of this Agreement[, Party A and Party B do not make any representations.][:-

[[(i)] [Party A] [and] [Party B] [each] make[s] the following representation:-

It is not required by any applicable law, as modified by the practice of any relevant governmental revenue authority, of any Relevant Jurisdiction to make any deduction or withholding for or on account of any Tax from any payment (other than interest under Section 9(h) of this Agreement) to be made by it to the other party under this Agreement. In making this representation, it may rely on (i) the accuracy of any representations made by the other party pursuant to Section 3(f) of this

---

* Delete as applicable.

*** Include if Additional Termination Event will apply.

**** N.B.: the following representations may need modification if either party is a Multibranch Party.

Commentary

Please note that payment measures and methods are no longer selected in Part 1(f) of the Schedule because Close-out Amount and the Second Method now always apply.

Hence Termination Currency and Additional Termination Event move up one item to Part 1(f) and (g) respectively. For commentary on them please see Chapter 8 pages 461–7.

For commentary on 2(a) please see Chapter 8 pages 473.

Agreement, (ii) the satisfaction of the agreement contained in Section 4(a)(i) or 4(a)(iii) of this Agreement and the accuracy and effectiveness of any document provided by the other party pursuant to Section 4(a)(i) or 4(a)(iii) of this Agreement and (iii) the satisfaction of the agreement of the other party contained in Section 4(d) of this Agreement, except that it will not be a breach of this representation where reliance is placed on clause (ii) above and the other party does not deliver a form or document under Section 4(a)(iii) by reason of material prejudice to its legal or commercial position.]*

[[(ii)] [Party A] [and] [Party B] [each] make[s] the following representation[s]:-

....

....

....]]*

(b) ***Payee Representations***. For the purpose of Section 3(f) of this Agreement[, Party A and Party B do not make any representations.][:-

[[(i)] [Party A] [and] [Party B] [each] make[s] the following representation:-

It is fully eligible for the benefits of the "Business Profits" or "Industrial and Commercial Profits" provision, as the case may be, the "interest" provision or the "Other Income" provision, if any, of the Specified Treaty with respect to any payment described in such provisions and received or to be received by it in connection with this Agreement and no such payment is attributable to a trade or business carried on by it through a permanent establishment in the Specified Jurisdiction.

"Specified Treaty" means with respect to Party A ....

"Specified Jurisdiction" means with respect to Party A ....

"Specified Treaty" means with respect to Party B ....

"Specified Jurisdiction" means with respect to Party B ....]*

* Delete as applicable.

Commentary

For commentary on Part 2(b)(i) and (ii) please see Chapter 8 pages 468–79. Likewise for commentary on Part 3(a) please see Chapter 8 pages 481–3.

[[(ii)] [Party A] [and] [Party B] [each] make[s] the following representation:-

Each payment received or to be received by it in connection with this Agreement will be effectively connected with its conduct of a trade or business in the Specified Jurisdiction.

"Specified Jurisdiction" means with respect to Party A ....

"Specified Jurisdiction" means with respect to Party B ....]*

[[(iii)] [Party A] [and] [Party B] [each] make[s] the following representation:-

It is a "U.S. person" (as that term is used in section 1.1441-4 (a)(3)(ii) of United States Treasury Regulations) for United States federal income tax purposes.]*

[[(iv)] [Party A] [and] [Party B] [each] make[s] the following representation:-

It is a "non-U.S. branch of a foreign person" (as that term is used in section 1.1441-4(a)(3)(ii) of United States Treasury Regulations) for United States federal income tax purposes.]*

[[(v)] [Party A] [and] [Party B] [each] make[s] the following representation:-

With respect to payments made to an address outside the United States or made by a transfer of funds to an account outside the United States, it is a "non-U.S. branch of a foreign person" (as that term is used in section 1.1441-4(a)(3)(ii) of United States Treasury Regulations) for United States federal income tax purposes.]*

[[(vi)] [Party A] [and] [Party B] [each] make[s] the following representation:-

---

* Delete as applicable.

Commentary

Part 2(b)(iii)–(vii) is new and Christian Johnson has provided the following commentary on these provisions.

It is a "foreign person" (as that term is used in section 1.6041-4 (a)(4) of United States Treasury Regulations) for United States federal income tax purposes.]*

[[(vii)] [Party A] [and] [Party B] [each] make[s] the following representation[s]:-

....

....

....]]*

Part 3. **Agreement to Deliver Documents.**

For the purpose of Sections 4(a)(i) and 4(a)(ii) of this Agreement, each party agrees to deliver the following documents, as applicable:-

(a) Tax forms, documents or certificates to be delivered are[: none][:-

Party required to deliver document	**Form/Document/ Certificate**	**Date by which to be delivered**
....	....	....
....	....	....
....	....	....
....	....	....
....	....	...................................]*

* Delete as applicable.

US payee tax representations

The United States made significant changes to the rules governing withholding and reporting to the Internal Revenue Service ("IRS") in 2001. The new rules significantly reduce the possibility that withholding will be required on derivative payments made to non-US taxpayers. However, the rules imposed new reporting obligations on payments made by US parties to non-US taxpayers that constitute income effectively connected with that non-US taxpayer's US trade or business. To deal with these tax issues, US parties request that non-US taxpayers make certain payee tax representations to them and deliver certain tax forms. These new representations are set out in Part 2(b)(iii)–(vi) of the Schedule and are designed to reduce or eliminate any reporting or withholding tax obligations. Which one of these representations should be given will depend upon the US payee's tax status.

Although the possibility that a US party would be required to withhold US taxes on payments to a non-US taxpayer has significantly decreased, the penalties for failing to do so are severe. First, if a US party does not withhold properly when required to do so, it may be personally liable for those taxes to the IRS. Under the ISDA Master Agreement, it may also be required to gross up the payment to the non-US taxpayer. In other words, it would be required to make the same total payment to the non-US taxpayer but would still be required to pay the withholding tax to the IRS.

Under the new US tax regulations, the IRS also requires a US party to report payments made to non-US taxpayers that constitute effectively connected income ("ECI") with a US trade or business for such person. Failure to properly report could subject the US party to penalties.

US tax withholding concerns

The United States currently imposes a withholding tax equal to 30% on cross-border payments made by a US party to a non-US taxpayer. The withholding tax is imposed on interest and dividends and on other types of income referred to as "fixed or determinable annual or periodical gains". As a practical matter, however, there are many exceptions to the withholding rules.

There was significant concern that OTC derivative payments made by a US party to a non-US taxpayer would constitute "fixed or determinable annual or periodical gains", and thus be subject to withholding. US Treasury regulations, however, have clarified that no withholding is required on payments made on a notional principal contract although they may be subject to IRS reporting requirements. This is the case whether or not the payments are effectively connected with a payee's US trade or business. The definition of a notional principal contract is defined in a manner similar to the definition of a "Specified Transaction" in the ISDA Master Agreement. The definition includes swaps, caps, floors, collars and similar transactions.

The concern over possible withholding for payments made under notional principal contracts has essentially been eliminated. However, there are still two concerns. First, there may still be withholding on payments characterised as interest. Second, as OTC derivative transactions become more sophisticated, parties may enter into transactions that do not clearly fall under the definition of a notional principal contract. Failure to qualify as a notional principal contract would reintroduce many of the old legal uncertainties.

Interest generally must be paid on overdue or late payments under the ISDA Master Agreement and on cash collateral under the ISDA Credit Support Annex. (These types of interest payments, however, are typically not subject to the gross up requirement.) Some enterprising counterparties are also developing transactions that are in substance a lending transaction in which one party makes a large up-front payment to the other.

Interest payments made to a non-US taxpayer under the ISDA Master Agreement will generally not be subject to withholding. First, a tax treaty between the US and the jurisdiction of the non-US taxpayer may reduce or eliminate any withholding on interest payments. Second, if the interest payments made to a non-US taxpayer are considered to be effectively connected to the US business of the such non-US taxpayer, it would also not be subject to withholding as discussed below. Finally, interest payments made under the ISDA Master Agreement generally will qualify for the portfolio interest exception under US law, exempting the interest from withholding.

The portfolio interest exception is intended to eliminate withholding on interest payments made to non-US taxpayers. The exception requires that the financial instrument be in registered form (thus identifying the recipient of the interest payment). If a document is in registered form, the non-US taxpayer's identity is known at the time of the payment. The ISDA Master Agreement is generally considered to meet the registered form requirements.

The portfolio interest exception exists because the US wants to encourage foreign taxpayers to lend into the US and not discourage them by imposing withholding tax. The IRS, however, is concerned that if there is no withholding, a US taxpayer might try to disguise itself as a foreign taxpayer (and thus avoid any tax liability) by receiving the payments outside the US. The registered form requirements generally minimise that risk by clearly identifying the payee.

There are two exceptions in which the portfolio interest exception does not apply. It does not apply if the non-US taxpayer is a 10% or greater shareholder of the US party paying the interest. It also does not apply if the foreign payee is bank that has actually made a disguised loan to the US payer in the ordinary course of its trade or business. The US party can eliminate any risk of these two events occurring by requiring that the non-US taxpayer represent that it is not a 10% shareholder or a bank making a loan if the US payer is concerned about these two factors.

Tax representations

Parties organised in different foreign jurisdictions generally require each other to make a payer tax representation that no taxes need be withheld on payments made under the ISDA Master Agreement. The party making the payer representation may rely on payee tax representations made to it in order to make its payer representation. The payer is not obliged to gross-up its derivative payments for any required tax withholding if the payee's representations prove to be false.

A US party will also request that the non-US taxpayer deliver certain IRS tax forms that parallel the requested payee tax representations. These forms provide important protection from personal liability to the IRS in the event that the US party should have withheld but did not. The tax forms are evidence that the US party had done the necessary due diligence to determine if it was required to withhold.

Some non-US taxpayers may argue that providing the forms should be sufficient and they do not need to make payee tax representations. Their argument is that a US party is protected from having to gross-up not only if a foreign payee makes a false representation but also if the non-US taxpayer fails to deliver an agreed upon US tax form. A US party, however, should still require the payee tax representations.

The ISDA Master Agreement relieves the US payer of the obligation to withhold if the payee tax representation is not true in the future. There is no similar protection, however, with respect to the delivery of a tax form. Generally, the form is only required to be delivered at the execution of the ISDA Master Agreement. The tax form may no longer be true or accurate, however, if a non-US taxpayer's situation changes. Although the tax form would protect the US party from liability with the IRS for failure to withhold, it would not alleviate the US payer's gross-up obligation.

Treaty representation

Requiring a non-US taxpayer to represent that it is entitled to the benefits of the relevant tax treaty between the US and a foreign jurisdiction has always been a standard practice in this area. The relevant treaty for US purposes is the US tax treaty with the country of residence for the non-US taxpayer. It is irrelevant for US tax purposes if the non-US taxpayer's branch that is receiving the payment is not located in that jurisdiction. Although important, the standard treaty representation only requires the non-US taxpayer to represent that it is eligible for treaty benefits not that the treaty exempts payments under the ISDA Master Agreement from withholding. This is a subtle but important distinction.

The treaty representation is important to minimise any withholding risk with respect to interest payments. Many US tax treaties provide for a zero withholding rate with respect to cross-border interest payments. The tax treaties with countries such as Germany, France, the Netherlands, Switzerland and the UK have a zero withholding rate for interest payments.

The treaty representation may even be helpful if a transaction is not considered to be a notional principal contract. The payment may not be subject to withholding if the payment under the non-qualifying transaction could be characterised as "business profits" or "industrial and commercial profits".

A US party should request that the non-US taxpayer deliver a Form W-8BEN if it requests the treaty representation. The form requires the non-US taxpayer to declare that it is eligible for treaty benefits. The form is provided only to the US payer and not to the IRS even though the form is executed under penalties of perjury.

Effectively connected income representation

The US party will request that a non-US taxpayer that enters into transactions through its US trade or business to represent that each payment it receives through that business will be effectively connected income. Under US law, no withholding is required for payments that are effectively connected with a non-US taxpayer's US trade or business. Instead, the non-US taxpayer is required to file a US tax return with respect to its US effectively connected income. Effectively connected income would include not only interest payments but also payments made under a notional principal contract. The US party will also request that the non-US taxpayer deliver a Form W-8ECI to certify that such payments are effectively connected income.

The US party must report the effectively connected income of the non-US taxpayer to the IRS using form 1042-S. Such reporting helps the IRS to ensure that the non-US taxpayer reports all of its effectively connected income on the tax return that it files with the IRS. The US party is subject to penalties in the event that it does not report the non-US taxpayer's effectively connected income to the IRS.

A US party may not know whether the payments that it makes to the non-US taxpayer are effectively connected with the non-US taxpayer's US trade or business. Because the IRS will match the amounts reported to it against the amounts that the non-US taxpayer reports to the IRS on its US tax return, it is in the interest of the foreign payee that the correct amount is reported. In order to determine the proper amount, the US party often requests that the non-US taxpayer designate which payments made to it are effectively connected.

There is no requirement to report if the payments are not effectively connected. A US party may be reluctant not to report, however, because of the penalties associated with non-compliance unless it is sure that there is no effectively connected income. A US party, however, is relieved of a reporting obligation if the non-US taxpayer will represent that it is a "non-US branch of a foreign person". The payee tax representation in Part 2(b)(iv) of the Schedule is an example of such a representation.

Although there is no safe harbour, the same result could be achieved by having the non-US taxpayer represent that no payments made to it constitute effectively connected income for it.

ISDA has provided three sample payee tax representatives relating to reporting effectively connected income in Part 2(b)(iii)–(v):

- **Part 2(b)(iii) is for US persons;**
- **Part 2(b)(iv) is for foreign persons who cannot act through a US branch; and**
- **Part 2(b)(v) is for foreign persons who are multibranch parties and can act through a US branch.**

However, a foreign payee will be unable to make the Part 2(b)(v) representation where payments under Transactions are made to an address or account outside the US in respect of Transactions where it is acting out of its US branch.

In addition, a payer cannot rely on a Part 2(b)(iv) or (v) payee representation to avoid IRS Form 1042-S reporting where it knows or suspects that the payment is in fact effectively connected with the conduct of a trade or business in the US.

IRS Form 1099

Notional principal contract payments must be reported on IRS From 1099 unless the payee is a corporation or can claim another exemption. A payer could rely on an IRS Form W-9 with an employer identification number from a payee and a statement that the payee is a domestic corporation to avoid reporting on IRS Form 1099. Payments also need not to be reported if the payee represents it is a foreign person in the Schedule. Therefore, foreign payees making the representation in Part 2(b)(iv) or (v) to avoid IRS Form 1042 will also avoid IRS Form 1099 reporting. Other foreign payees may make the sample representation in Part 2(b)(vi) to avoid IRS Form 1099 reporting.

The payer will request the following payee tax representations depending upon the nature of the payee:

	If payee is	Payer will want
(1)	US person	Part 2(b)(iii)
(2)	A non-US person with no US office	Part 2(b)(iv)
(3)	A non-US person with a US office	Part 2(b)(v)
(4)	None of the above	Part 2(b)(vi)

Effect

- **If the payee provides the Part 2(b)(iii) representation, the payer will not need to report payments on IRS Form 1042-S. However, the payer may need to report on IRS Form 1099, unless the payee is a corporation or otherwise exempt. If the IRS decides that the payer needs to report, backup withholding will also be needed if the payee does not provide an IRS tax payer identification number to the payer.**
- **If the payee gives the Part 2(b)(iv) representation, the payer generally will not need to report payments on either IRS Form 1042-S or IRS Form 1099.**
- **If the payee makes the Part 2(b)(v) representation the payer will not need to report payments on IRS Form 1099. Moreover, the payer will not need to report on IRS Form 1042-S payments to an address or bank account outside the US because the payee will have represented that it is a non-US branch of a foreign person in respect of such**

payments. A non-US party which enters into swaps through both its US and non-US branches under a multibranch Schedule but directs all payments to be made to an account outside the US could not make this representation.

- If a payee makes this the Part 2(b)(vi) representation, the payer will not need to report any payments on IRS Form 1099 but may need to do so on IRS Form 1042-S.

(b) Other documents to be delivered are[: none][:-

Party required to deliver document	Form/ Document/ Certificate	Date by which to be delivered	Covered by Section 3(d) Representation
....	....	....	[Yes][No]
....	....	....	[Yes][No]
....	....	....	[Yes][No]
....	....	....	[Yes][No]
....	....	....	[Yes][No]]*

Part 4. **Miscellaneous.**

(a) ***Addresses for Notices***. For the purpose of Section 12(a) of this Agreement:-

Address for notices or communications to Party A:-

Address: ....

Attention: ....

Telex No.: .... Answerback: ....

Facsimile No.: .... Telephone No.: ....

E-mail: ....

Electronic Messaging System Details: ....

Specific Instructions: ....

Address for notices or communications to Party B:-

Address: ....

Attention: ....

Telex No.: .... Answerback: ....

Facsimile No.: .... Telephone No.: ....

E-mail: ....

Electronic Messaging System Details: ....

Specific Instructions: ....

* Delete as applicable.

Commentary

For commentary on Part 3(b) please refer to Chapter 8 pages 485–8.

In Part 4(a) there is the opportunity to include e-mail address details and also specific instructions if needed. These would be used if certain notices, e.g in respect of Section 5 or 6 needed to be directed to a certain person or department or in a certain form.

(b) ***Process Agent.*** For the purpose of Section 13(c) of this Agreement:–

Party A appoints as its Process Agent: [not applicable] [...]*

Party B appoints as its Process Agent: [not applicable] [...]*

(c) ***Offices.*** The provisions of Section 10(a) [will][will not]* apply to this Agreement.

(d) ***Multibranch Party.*** For the purpose of Section 10(b) of this Agreement:-

Party A [is not a Multibranch Party.][is a Multibranch Party and may enter into a Transaction through any of the following Offices:-

....

....]*

Party B [is not a Multibranch Party.][is a Multibranch Party and may enter into a Transaction through any of the following Offices:-

....

....]*

* Delete as applicable.

Commentary

For commentary on Part 4(b) and (c) please refer to Chapter 8 pages 493–9.

Part 4(d) now emphasises that a Multibranch Party can now enter into a Transaction through any listed Office. It can also make payments or deliveries in respect of that Transaction through any of them but no others (see commentary on Section 10(b) on page 269).

[(e)] ***Calculation Agent***. The Calculation Agent is ...., unless otherwise specified in a Confirmation in relation to the relevant Transaction.]**

[(f)] ***Credit Support Document***. Details of any Credit Support Document:– [none][.. ....]*

[(g)] ***Credit Support Provider.*** Credit Support Provider means in relation to Party A, [none][.. ....]*

Credit Support Provider means in relation to Party B, [none] [... ....]*

[(h)] ***Governing Law.*** This Agreement will be governed by and construed in accordance with [English law][the laws of the State of New York (without reference to choice of law doctrine)]*.

[(i)] ***Netting of Payments.*** "Multiple Transaction Payment Netting" [will not apply for the purpose of Section 2(c) of this Agreement.][will apply for the purpose of Section 2(c) of this Agreement to [all Transactions][the following Transactions or groups of Transactions:–

....

....]

(in each case starting from [the date of this Agreement][..........])]*

[(j)] ***"Affiliate"*** [will have the meaning specified in Section 14 of this Agreement.][means ....]*

* Delete as applicable.

** Include if applicable.

Commentary

For commentary on Part 4(e)–(h) please refer to Chapter 8 pages 503–11.

In Part 4(i) which relates to netting for payments, there is now the opportunity to make a positive choice for Multiple Transaction Payment Netting to apply and from when.

For commentary on Part 4(j) please see Chapter 8 page 517.

[(k)] ***Absence of Litigation***. For the purpose of Section 3(c):-

"Specified Entity" means in relation to Party A, ...

"Specified Entity" means in relation to Party B, ...

[(l)] ***No Agency***. The provisions of Section 3(g) [will][will not]* apply to this Agreement.

[(m)] ***Additional Representation*** [will][will not]* apply. [For the purpose of Section 3 of this Agreement, the following will constitute an Additional Representation:-

* Delete as applicable.

Commentary

In Part 4(k) you can name particular Specified Entities whom you wish to join to the Absence of Litigation representation in Section 3(b).

Part 4(l) gives you the chance to choose whether the No Agency representation in Section 3(g) will apply.

In Part 4(m) it is possible to add a series of Additional Representations and to state if they are to apply. The example given shows ISDA's standard non-reliance representation (see also page 338).

[[(i)] ***Relationship Between Parties***. Each party will be deemed to represent to the other party on the date on which it enters into a Transaction that (absent a written agreement between the parties that expressly imposes affirmative obligations to the contrary for that Transaction):–

[(1)] *Non-Reliance*. It is acting for its own account, and it has made its own independent decisions to enter into that Transaction and as to whether that Transaction is appropriate or proper for it based upon its own judgment and upon advice from such advisers as it has deemed necessary. It is not relying on any communication (written or oral) of the other party as investment advice or as a recommendation to enter into that Transaction, it being understood that information and explanations related to the terms and conditions of a Transaction will not be considered investment advice or a recommendation to enter into that Transaction. No communication (written or oral) received from the other party will be deemed to be an assurance or guarantee as to the expected results of that Transaction.

[(2)] *Assessment and Understanding*. It is capable of assessing the merits of and understanding (on its own behalf or through independent professional advice), and understands and accepts, the terms, conditions and risks of that Transaction. It is also capable of assuming, and assumes, the risks of that Transaction.

[(3)] *Status of Parties*. The other party is not acting as a fiduciary for or an adviser to it in respect of that Transaction.]]*

[[(n)] ***Recording of Conversations***. Each party (i) consents to the recording of telephone conversations between the trading, marketing and other relevant personnel of the parties in connection with this Agreement or any potential Transaction, (ii) agrees to obtain any necessary consent of, and give any necessary notice of such recording to, its relevant personnel and (iii) agrees, to the extent permitted by applicable law, that recordings may be submitted in evidence in any Proceedings.]**

---

* Delete as applicable.

** Include if applicable.

Commentary

Finally in Part 4(n) you can include an optional Recording of Conversations provision which is likely to be included in the vast majority of cases.

Part 5. **Other Provisions.**

....	....
(Name of Party)	(Name of Party)
By:	By: ....
Name:	Name:
Title:	Title:
Date:	Date:

Commentary

For commentary on Part 5 provisions please see Chapter 8 pages 519–45.

ISDA did consider during the drafting of the Schedule whether to include standard provisions for FX and Currency Option Transactions in Part 6 of the Schedule. Ultimately no work was done on this.

ISDA offers parties a signing block for the Schedule. This is optional but is a widespread practice in the market.

WHAT DID NOT MAKE IT INTO THE 2002 AGREEMENT

During the discussions on the six drafts of the 2002 Agreement there was inevitably much to-ing and fro-ing on numerous points. The following were the main issues which did not make the final version for a variety of reasons:

- **Section 2(a)(ii) – Attempts to define "freely transferable" funds were eventually dropped. A final sub-clause on conferring beneficial ownership of a delivered asset to the recipient was scrapped due to different laws on this issue in different countries.**
- **Section 2(a)(iii) – Reference to Force Majeure Event and Illegality and Additional Termination Events were dropped as were efforts to try and establish a time limit for a Non-defaulting Party to initiate termination of Transactions rather than merely suspending its own payment or delivery obligations indefinitely.**
- **Fully paid Transaction wording (see page 572) as a new Section 2(a)(iv) was not adopted.**
- **In Section 3(a) an apparent authority representation was discarded.**
- **A separate Section 3(d) representation for financial information with a "true and fair" standard was not progressed.**
- **Separate Section 5(a)(v) and 5(a)(vi) Threshold Amounts for derivative and non-derivative transactions and for transactions between close to home parties (e.g. a party, its Credit Support Provider or its Specified Entity) and with unconnected third parties were not adopted.**
- **In Section 9 it was decided that execution and delivery of Confirmations via the internet or world wide web was a step too far at present.**
- **Dispute resolution, severability language and escrow provisions were not added to the main Agreement text.**
- **No standardised Part 6 of the Schedule (FX Transactions and Currency Options) was formulated.**
- **No mechanism to terminate an Agreement which had become redundant was included.**

Perhaps some of these will make the 2012(!) Agreement.

LIKELY IMPLEMENTATION OF THE 2002 AGREEMENT

So how is the 2002 Agreement likely to be implemented in practice?

First let us look back. When the 1992 Agreement was published in January 1993 with its *User's Guide* it took about two years on average for most of the market to make it their ISDA Agreement of choice for use with new counterparties. Renegotiation and upgrading from the 1987 Interest Rate and Currency Exchange Agreement to the 1992 Agreement took until about 1998 in some cases. Either Appendix B of the *User's Guide* was used or a suitable short provision was included in the amended and restated 1992 Agreement.

There is no compulsion to change to the 2002 Agreement.

In the first instance, ISDA has obtained for its members 36 legal opinions on the close-out netting arrangements under the new Agreement. This is to enable the Agreement to be used in order for banks to be able to obtain regulatory capital savings on their trading books which they can already do with the 1992 Agreement.

ISDA considers that most North American banks will move over to the new Agreement quickly but that Europe and Japan will do so more slowly and possibly may use the new ISDA Amendment Agreement it published in March 2003 which would incorporate the new Section 6 early termination arrangements into a 1992 Agreement.

In Europe we are also likely to see Amendment Agreements incorporating the new Illegality and Force Majeure Event provisions.

In my opinion many European banks will start considering use of the 2002 Agreement with new counterparties later this year but it may be two to three years before its use is widespread.

Legal issues relating to the ISDA Master Agreement from the European and US perspectives

5

EUROPEAN PERSPECTIVE BY SIMON J. LEIFER

Gaming/wagering

Capacity and UK Local Authority litigation

Credit derivatives

Derivatives and building societies, pension funds and hedge funds

Authority

Suitability

Financial Services and Markets Act 2000

Enforceability of close-out netting and set off

Cross-border netting on insolvency

ISDA collective legal opinions

Automatic Early Termination

Credit Support

Third party rights

US PERSPECTIVE BY CHRISTIAN A. JOHNSON

Enforcement of New York choice of law

US bankruptcy and banking insolvency law

Non-New York head office of a US counterparty

The Commodity Exchange Act (1974) and the Commodity Futures Modernization Act (2000)

Gaming and bucket-shop laws

EUROPEAN PERSPECTIVE BY SIMON J. LEIFER

An ISDA Master Agreement is a form of agreement which has been developed to cover certain types of derivative contracts. It was primarily developed by the financial markets for documenting interest rate and currency swaps and has evolved as a globally used market standard agreement. As the name of the Agreement itself suggests, it seeks to act as a master agreement that captures all transactions entered into under it. The document is lengthy and complex in parts but one of its main aims is to consolidate all relevant transactions as one contract. The rationale for this is simply that in the event of a termination under the Agreement, all the constituent transactions can themselves be terminated and a calculation performed to arrive at one net sum owed by one party to the other. This characteristic has the advantage that it can prevent a liquidator accepting or rejecting individual contracts to its advantage – a process known as "cherry picking".

However, the negotiation of an ISDA Master Agreement involves more than just the physical signing of a document. As a matter of English law there are some important considerations which, if overlooked, can have potentially disastrous consequences. The key issues to be considered include gaming/wagering, capacity and authority. These issues are now explored as follows:

GAMING/WAGERING

The Gaming Act of 1845 (as extended by the Gaming Act 1892) provides that all gaming contracts are void and therefore unenforceable. The question that has arisen in respect of derivative contracts is whether such contracts are gaming contracts.

This has been a matter of debate for lawyers and the courts and is an issue which should always be considered where derivative contracts are concerned. A degree of clarification has been achieved by s 63 of the Financial Services Act 1986 which was enacted to give protection to the financial markets. It provides that where at least one of the parties enters into a wagering contract by way of business and provided such contract constitutes an investment then the contract will be valid. Part 12 of Schedule 1 of the Financial Services Act sets out the types of contracts covered by the Act. It is recognised that these include swaps, cash-settled futures and options (although loans are specifically not included in this definition).

It can therefore be said that provided there is a *bona fide* transaction falling within the scope of s 63, there is no risk that the English courts will declare such a transaction void or unenforceable.

In many developed legal jurisdictions, the issue of gaming/wagering has been largely resolved. Less mature legal systems, however, may take a different view of derivative transactions although they may be recognised as enforceable contracts where they are entered into for specific hedging purposes. Specialist advice may be necessary.

CAPACITY AND UK LOCAL AUTHORITY LITIGATION

What is capacity? This is a reference to the legal ability of an individual or an entity such as a company to enter into a legally binding contract. In the case of the Agreement this will generally mean derivative contracts.

If an entity is acting outside of its powers or authority, it is said to be acting *ultra vires*. Capacity may be viewed differently in other jurisdictions and it is therefore important to seek advice in the jurisdiction in which the other party to the Agreement is located.

It is vital to establish that the party with whom you wish to sign an Agreement has the necessary capacity to enter into such an agreement and any transactions under it. If no such capacity exists then your counterparty may be acting *ultra vires* by entering into transactions under an Agreement and any such transactions would be invalid. The consequence of this problem has been starkly highlighted by the experiences of many banks who entered into interest rate swap transactions with UK local authorities in the 1980s.

When dealing with a company, whether English or otherwise, its constitutional documents will usually play an important part in determining whether it has the requisite capacity as will any specific board resolutions.

When dealing with an English company there is a degree of protection offered by the Companies Acts. Section 35 of the Companies Act 1985 states:

> **The validity of an act done by a company should not be called into question on the ground of lack of capacity by reason of anything in the company's memorandum.**

The Companies Act 1989 added a new s 35A to the 1985 Act. Section 35A(1) provides:

> **In favour of a person dealing with a company in good faith, the power of the board of directors to bind the company, or authorise others to do so, shall be deemed to be free of any limitation under the company's constitution.**

The effect of these provisions is further explained in s 35A(2):

(b) **a person shall not be regarded as acting in bad faith by reason only of his knowing that an act is beyond the powers of the directors under the company's constitution; and**

(c) **a person shall be deemed to have acted in good faith unless the contrary is proved.**

Section 35(B) goes on to provide some further clarification by stating that when dealing with a company, there is no duty to enquire as to the capacity of the company or the authority of the directors. However, it is not entirely clear whether the Companies Act gives the same protection where a board of directors has delegated its power to a sub-committee for the purposes of authorising the entry into Agreements and transactions.

It is nevertheless good practice when contemplating a derivative transaction with an English corporate, to check its Memorandum of Association for any explicit powers to transact in derivatives. If these powers do not exist in the Memorandum then caution should be exercised and serious consideration be given to requiring the company to amend its Memorandum. However, this may not be a practical issue and other evidence may be available to give comfort that derivative transactions are within the company's capacity. It is also good practice to obtain a board resolution from the company giving specific authorisation for derivative transactions and authorising certain specified individuals as being able to enter into derivative transactions on the company's behalf.

Local authorities

As briefly mentioned above, the consequences of making an error as to capacity have been demonstrated by the experiences of many banks who entered into interest rate swap transactions with UK local authorities in the 1980s. Many local authorities used these transactions for the purposes of managing their interest rate risk on their loans. This, to many onlookers, seemed to be a very sensible use of derivatives.

However, not all local authorities used derivatives in quite the same way and in particular Hammersmith and Fulham London Borough Council entered into more interest rate swap transactions than all the other local authorities put together. The other distinguishing feature about Hammersmith and Fulham was that the sum of the notional amounts of all its derivative transactions was more than ten times the size of its borrowings. It could hardly be said to be hedging its interest rate risk and was essentially speculating.

The landmark case of *Hazell* v *Hammersmith and Fulham LBC* [1992] AC 1 ended in a House of Lords decision which held that interest rate swaps were not only outside the capacity of Hammersmith and Fulham but were also beyond the powers of all local authorities under the provisions of the Local Government Acts (1963 and 1972). The total losses to the numerous banks who had entered into interest rate swaps with local authorities was estimated at around £500 million. These losses take account of the fact that, in entering into interest rate swaps, banks would in many cases have entered into corresponding contracts in the swaps market to hedge their positions. Consequently, when the contracts with local authorities were declared invalid, the banks suddenly found themselves stuck with these corresponding hedging contracts which cost them substantial sums of money to terminate.

Much case law followed during the 1990s. This centred mainly on the rights of the banks and those of some local authorities, to recover payments which they had made under these invalid contracts. These claims for restitution were based on the premise that a party should not be entitled to unjust enrichment. In other words, if the net effect of an invalid contract between two parties was that one of the parties would end up better off than it was before, then that benefit should be returned to the other party.

As an object lesson in determining whether another party has the requisite authority to enter into a derivative contract, the example of the local authorities is somewhat anomalous. The reason is simply that much legal advice was sought by the banks to determine this issue and there was much positive advice which led them to believe that they could enter into these contracts with local authorities without fear of this particular issue. History has decided otherwise and it has been a salutary lesson. Whether it will be heeded in the future is another matter.

It is interesting to note that of the 200 plus writs for restitution that were issued mainly by banks in the English High Court, the great majority of these were settled at an early stage. It is probably true to comment that, without exception, these early settlements were less favourable than for those banks that held on and pursued their actions against the local authorities. These latter banks which included most notably Kleinwort Benson Ltd, Guinness Mahon & Co Ltd, Morgan Grenfell & Co Ltd and Westdeutsche Landesbank Girozentrale were more successful in forcing larger settlements from the local authorities once the courts had fixed their interpretation of the applicable law.

Insurance companies

The basic rule concerning insurance companies is set out in s 16 of the Insurance Companies Act 1982. This provides that an insurance company:

> **shall not carry on any activities in the United Kingdom or elsewhere otherwise than in connection with or for the purpose of its insurance business.**

The business of an insurance company may range from the provision of household insurance cover to pensions. The insurance company may depend on the investment of its premium income or payments by policyholders to meet future claims or to pay pension annuities. As a result of its investments it may be exposed to interest rate movements and, in such circumstances, derivatives may be a very sensible and proper way of hedging that exposure and would therefore meet the test under the Act.

However, if an insurance company enters into a derivative transaction which does not meet this test, then the Act will be breached (see Credit Derivatives, below). The effect of such a breach is not entirely clear as the Act does not state whether such a transaction would be void and therefore unenforceable. However, the common sense approach is to assume that if the courts were faced with speculative transactions by an insurance company then they would be likely to determine that the transactions are unenforceable.

CREDIT DERIVATIVES

A credit derivative is a form of derivative transaction in which the payout is linked to the occurrence of certain credit events. It has been widely used since its invention enabling market participants such as banks to reduce their counterparty risk. A good example of this is where a bank has lent money to a corporate customer under the terms of a bilateral loan. The bank may decide that it wants to reduce its loan exposure to the particular company and will enter into a credit derivative whereby in return for a payment, a counterparty will agree to take delivery of a loan if the company defaults and in return will pay the full amount of the loan to the bank. This method of credit protection is regarded by some as a reinvention of traditional methods of credit protection (e.g. participations) which have been commonly used in the banking industry for a long time.

However, the advent of the credit derivative has raised the question as to whether this is not just insurance by another name. This raises the interesting point that if it is insurance, then anyone entering into such a transaction may be committing a criminal offence unless they are authorised to carry out insurance business by a regulator.

Sections 2 and 14 of the Insurance Companies Act 1982 specify in what circumstances insurance business can be carried out. However, s 2(4) of the Act also provides that it is not an offence for others to carry on certain classes of insurance business if that business takes place "solely in the course of carrying on, and for the purposes of, banking business". The Act does not define what is meant by this and it has been open to interpretation. One such interpretation is that it is not enough just to be a bank – there must be sufficient demonstration that there is banking *business* in order for the exception in the Insurance Companies Act to apply.

However, two legal opinions obtained separately by The Financial Law Panel* and ISDA concluded that the insurance issue was unlikely to be a problem to the development of the credit derivatives market and to date this has proved to be the case in practice.

Subject to the above, it does appear that a bank with a demonstrable banking business may be able to claim the benefit of s 2(4) as a defence to a claim that a credit derivative contract was unauthorised insurance business. However, there is at this time no definitive case law on this issue and therefore the merits of entering into a credit derivative transaction must be carefully examined in the light of the contracting parties and the nature of the contract.

It is interesting to note that in its latest report on the size of the credit derivatives market by the British Bankers' Association there is strong interest from insurance companies as protection sellers and they are now rivalling banks in this respect (33% market share against 39% for banks) and could overtake them by 2004.

DERIVATIVES AND BUILDING SOCIETIES, PENSION FUNDS AND HEDGE FUNDS

Building societies

Although these may be considered to be a dying breed of institution, it is still very important to understand the legal position when it comes to entering into derivative transactions with building societies. With the coming into force of the Financial Services and Markets Act 2000 ("FSMA") at midnight on 30 November 2001, the Financial Services Authority ("FSA") succeeded the Building Societies Commission as the prudential supervisor for societies.

A substantial part of the Building Societies Act 1986 (as amended 1997) is still in force. However, nearly all of those sections relating to prudential supervision have been repealed. The FSA Handbook of rules and guidance contains an Interim Prudential sourcebook for building societies which can be found at http://www.fsa.gov.uk/handbook/ipru_bs.pdf. The Sourcebook also contains guidance for building societies when entering into credit derivative transactions.

In relation to the 1986 Act, Section 23(1) states that a building society may:

* The Financial Law Panel was established to identify areas of uncertainty in the law affecting financial markets in England and Wales and to seek to remove them or limit their scope. It ceased to operate with effect from 31 March 2002.

> **enter into contracts of a prescribed description for the purposes of reducing the risk of loss arising from changes in interest rates, currency exchange rates or other factors of a prescribed description which affect its business.**

A number of other requirements must be met to avoid falling foul of the *ultra vires* rule. The memorandum of the building society in question must state that it has the ability to enter into derivative transactions of the type envisaged. The society should also adopt the provisions of s 23 as amended by the 1997 Act (see below). The society must comply with the FSA Interim Prudential sourcebook by stating which of five approaches it has adopted towards its hedging – Administered, Matched, Extended, Comprehensive and Trading. Trading is the most sophisticated approach.

The Building Societies Act 1997 defines more clearly the types of derivative transactions that building societies may enter into. These are set out in s 9(A) of the 1997 Act and include transactions:

> **entered into for the purpose of limiting the extent to which the society, or a connected undertaking of a building society, will be affected by changes in any of the following factors, namely –**
>
> (a) **interest rates;**
>
> (b) **exchange rates;**
>
> (c) **any index of retail prices;**
>
> (d) **any index of residential property prices; and**
>
> (e) **any index of the prices of securities.**

Building societies have the power to enter into derivatives in the form of certain instruments defined in Schedule 1 of the Financial Services Act 1986. These are:

- **instruments entitling to shares or securities;**
- **options;**
- **futures; and**
- **contracts for differences.**

The 1997 Act and the FSMA have helped to reduce the uncertainty by defining more precisely what contracts are within the powers of building societies. However, the overriding issue when dealing with building societies is that transactions must be for the reduction of risk and must fit within the statutory limits.

Pension funds

When dealing in derivatives with pension funds, different considerations arise as to whether the fund is permitted to enter into these types of transactions. A pension fund is different from a corporate entity in that it will be constituted as a trust. There are no shareholders, only beneficiaries under the terms of the trust. Day-to-day management is in the hands of the fund's trustees and they, in turn, will usually delegate authority to an investment manager who will take all necessary investment decisions and enter into transactions on the fund's behalf. In reality, a contract with a fund will be entered into with the trustees, albeit that it is physically transacted by the investment manager.

Trust assets are available to meet trust obligations provided that the trustees enter into any transactions or investments within the terms of the trust. The starting point for determining the terms of a trust will be the relevant trust deed, although some terms may be imposed either as a result of case law or in the absence of provision in the trust deed. Trustees' duties are set out in the Trustee Investment Act 1961.

Trustees act in their personal capacity and will be indemnified by the fund against any liabilities incurred by them on its behalf. However, if the trustees act outside of their powers or do not satisfy their fiduciary duties to the fund then they may be personally liable and would not be able to claim any indemnity from the fund. It can therefore be very difficult to establish the precise position.

It has become increasingly common to require the investment manager to provide certain representations and warranties in respect of the fund for which it acts. These will usually include (among others) representations and warranties that:

- **the fund/trustees have the necessary capacity to enter into the proposed types of derivative transactions;**
- **any transactions entered into will be in accordance with the terms of the trust;**
- **the investment manager will at all times have sufficient assets of the fund under its control to meet the fund's obligations; and**
- **the investment manager is duly authorised to act on behalf of the fund/trustees.**

The object of these types of representations and warranties is to expand the potential avenues of legal redress in the event that the trustees of a pension fund or the investment manager act outside of the terms of the trust. In such circumstances, the trust itself might disclaim liability for any derivative transactions.

Hedge funds

Hedge funds are usually companies established in tax havens for the purpose of providing investment opportunities to investors. Because they are often located offshore, they are less regulated than investment companies incorporated in jurisdictions such as England and the US.

Care should be taken when dealing with hedge funds to ensure that any intended transactions are within the scope of the fund's objectives and therefore, within its capacity. A hedge fund's Memorandum and Articles of Association or equivalent constitutional documents should be examined for evidence of such capacity. These should also be read in conjunction with a hedge fund's prospectus. Particular attention should be paid to any investment restrictions. In addition, a hedge fund may be split into sub-funds which each have their own investment limits. Regardless of the above, proper, relevant, legal advice should be sought as a matter of course where foreign jurisdictions are concerned.

AUTHORITY

Signing authority

When it comes to signing the Agreement it is all too easy to forget the importance of ensuring that the persons who sign on behalf of a counterparty are authorised to do so. Checks should be made to ensure that suitable documentation is received evidencing the authority of the signatories as well as specimen signatures. This may take the form of a signature book, board resolution or perhaps an incumbency certificate. The latter is a certificate issued by the counterparty exhibiting a specimen signature of the signatory and usually signed by the company secretary or similar official, attesting to the veracity of the specimen.

SUITABILITY

Suitability describes an area of potential liability which could arise from misselling of derivatives. The case of *Bankers Trust International Plc* v *PT Dharmala Sakti Sejahtera* [1996] CLC 581 (an Indonesian company) in which judgment was given in 1995 highlighted this very issue. The case is viewed as important as it examined the issue of a bank's duty of care as a seller of derivative contracts. It established that there could certainly be circumstances in which a bank could breach such a duty and suitability is very much an issue which they and other like sellers of derivatives need to consider.

Dharmala were the defendants in the action which was brought by Bankers Trust in the Commercial Court in London. Bankers Trust sued for payment of monies arising from two swap transactions which had gone disastrously wrong for the defendants. Dharmala counterclaimed on a number of different grounds, all of which failed.

The facts of the case concerned certain swap contracts which were entered into by Bankers Trust and Dharmala. There had been a number of meetings between the parties and it was the content of these meetings and other pre-contract discussions and negotiations which formed the basis of a counterclaim by Dharmala. Dharmala counterclaimed that before entering into the transactions, Bankers Trust made various misrepresentations about the nature and effect of the contracts. Dharmala also claimed that Bankers Trust breached a duty of care to explain fully and properly the operation, terms, meaning and effect of the swaps and the potential consequences to Dharmala of accepting them.

In its pleadings, Dharmala argued that Bankers Trust had failed to:

- **establish Dharmala's skill and knowledge in derivatives;**
- **give any warnings to Dharmala as to the inherent risks in each swap;**
- **illustrate the financial consequences of each swap transaction by reference to a range of possible circumstances;**
- **establish Dharmala's requirements and in particular the principal amount of its exposure to movements in US$ interest rates;**
- **advise Dharmala of other possible means apart from swaps for achieving Dharmala's objectives;**
- **consider or advise Dharmala as to the desirability of achieving its objectives by a range of different products or transactions other than by way of the proposed swaps;**
- **advise Dharmala to seek independent legal advice; and**
- **satisfy itself that Dharmala had understood the meaning and potential consequences of the swaps.**

The court did not accept that misrepresentation had occurred. On the issue of suitability the court found that Dharmala was a sophisticated counterparty and that it had been made clear to it by Bankers Trust that it should satisfy itself as to the inherent risks of the proposed transactions.

The lesson of this case above all others is the importance of knowing your counterparty in the context of that counterparty's own knowledge and experience in relation to the derivative products marketed to it. This "knowing your counterparty" is a cornerstone of the UK regulatory regime and is an important requirement for any organisation when determining the question of suitability of a derivative product in relation to its proposed counterparty.

Other cases where the issue has arisen in recent years were *Bankers Trust Company* v *The Procter & Gamble Company* (1995), *Bankers Trust Company* v *Gibsons Greetings Inc* (1995) and *County of Orange et al* v *Merrill Lynch & Co.* (1995). These cases led to the development of "non-reliance" language including ISDA's own "Relationship between Parties" provision commonly seen in ISDA Master Agreement Schedules today.

FINANCIAL SERVICES AND MARKETS ACT 2000

The Financial Services Authority ("FSA") is the independent non-governmental body responsible for regulation of all financial services in the UK. It was created under the provisions of the Financial Services and Markets Act 2000 ("FSMA") which came fully into force at midnight on 30 November 2001 (a date known as N2).

Pending the occurrence of N2, the FSA published a code (*The London Code of Conduct*) applicable to principals and brokers trading in the wholesale markets, i.e. products which were not regulated by the rules of a recognised investment exchange. This was an interim code which was in many respects identical to the code of the same name which it replaced and which had previously been published by the Bank of England.

With the occurrence of N2, the types of products and users to which the *London Code of Conduct* previously applied have been largely replaced by the provisions of the FSA's Handbook of rules and guidance and in particular the *Inter-Professional Conduct* chapter. However not all products and users covered by the FSA's *London Code of Conduct* are captured by the FSA Handbook. Those products not covered are foreign exchange (spot and forward*) and money markets and bullion markets wholesale deposits. These are now dealt with by *The Non-Investment Products Code* published by the Bank of England in November 2001. The Inter-Professional Conduct chapter can be found in the FSA Handbook on its website at www.fsa.gov.uk and The Non-Investment Products Code can be found on the Bank of England's website at www.bankofengland.co.uk/markets/nips.htm.

The importance of the FSA Handbook is to set out expected practice in the UK financial markets in certain relevant products. Breaches of the rules

* Forward foreign exchange transactions which are subject to margin requirements may fall under the FSA Handbook where they are deemed to constitute investment business. For further information on this see footnotes 2 and 3 on page 4 of the The Non-Investment Products Code.

and guidance contained in the Handbook can result in the FSA reviewing the fitness and propriety of individuals or institutions for future dealings in financial services in the UK. The FSA can also bring criminal or civil proceedings against those whom it considers to be in breach. For further information see the FSA website as above.

ENFORCEABILITY OF CLOSE-OUT NETTING AND SET OFF

One of the principal aims of the Agreement is to reduce risk by way of close-out netting. This means that if there is an early termination of transactions under an Agreement, the sums due in respect of those transactions are aggregated to produce a net sum payable by one party to the other.

The added benefits of netting, aside from risk reduction, are that it:

- **may enable a party to transact more business in relation to the size of its capital; and/or**
- **will entail a lower cost to that party because less capital is required by regulators to be allocated against any netted transactions.**

Parties governed by regulatory bodies will almost invariably have to allocate capital against their transaction exposures. Regulators are usually prepared to lower capital requirements where it can be demonstrated to their satisfaction that exposure across a number of transactions can be netted. The requirement is normally that the transactions in issue are governed by a single master agreement and that there is a clean legal opinion covering among other matters, the issue of close-out netting.

Regulators may also lay down size requirements known as "Large Exposures" in respect of transactions with particular counterparties. Again, netting can be advantageous in reducing the exposure and enabling a transaction or transactions to take place without breaching any "Large Exposure" limits.

The question of whether close-out netting is effective is one which most often arises in the context of insolvency. The reason for this is that on insolvency, the courts and liquidators may have powers to override contractual provisions. The concern is that a liquidator could "cherry pick", i.e. accept those contracts which are favourable to the insolvent party and reject those contracts which are not. A non-defaulting party could find itself in the unfortunate position that although the sum of all transactions with an insolvent defaulting counterparty may be profitable, once the liquidator has stripped out the trades which are profitable or "in the money" for it, the net effect is that the non-defaulting party has to perform the non-profitable contracts and stand in line as an unsecured creditor in respect of the profitable ones.

In England and Wales, the position is that close-out netting is effective on insolvency. There are also mandatory rules of set-off on insolvency (Rule 4.90 of the Insolvency Rules 1986) which have the same economic effect as the contractual netting provisions of the Agreement.

Rule 4.90(1) applies:

> **where, before the company goes into liquidation there have been mutual credits, mutual debts or other mutual dealings between the company and any creditor of the company proving or claiming to prove for a debt in the liquidation.**

Rule 4.90(2) then continues:

> **An account shall be taken of what is due from each party to the other in respect of the mutual dealings and the sums due from one party shall be set off against the sums due from the other.**

The economic effect of Rule 4.90 is that a net sum is payable by one party to the other. If it is owed by the insolvent party then it will rank as an unsecured debt and rank equally with all other unsecured debt in respect of the right to receive payment from the insolvent estate after payment of debts with greater priority, e.g. debts secured by a charge.

Parties to an Agreement will therefore enjoy the benefit of netting which acts to reduce their exposure to each other at any given time. It also benefits the solvent party on the other's insolvency by eliminating the risk of "cherry picking" by a liquidator.

Where an Agreement is entered into between counterparties where either one or both are domiciled other than in England, it is important to check the local insolvency laws. In some countries close-out netting simply does not work because the insolvency legislation will override and may even set aside certain transactions entered into within a certain period of time, commonly called a "suspect period" before the commencement/formal recognition of insolvency. In England and Wales these are six months and 24 months (the latter for connected parties) but the timescales vary in other jurisdictions.

CROSS-BORDER NETTING ON INSOLVENCY

Multibranch close-out netting documented under an Agreement is designed to remove the uncertainty which might otherwise arise on the insolvency of a counterparty. However, some jurisdictions may not recognise the netting provisions and this can have particular implications for bank branches on the insolvency of a bank. It can upset the contractual arrangement and the calculation of what is due to whom on close-out.

The concern is that a branch in a jurisdiction which does not recognise close-out netting could taint the effectiveness of the Agreement as a whole – rather like one rotten apple in a barrel of good ones. In 1995, ISDA took legal advice which confirmed that this was not an issue for the jurisdictions of England, France, Germany, Japan, Singapore and Switzerland. This matter is also regularly addressed whenever ISDA obtains new or full updated opinions. When other jurisdictions are being considered for the purposes of multi-branch netting, this issue should be considered to decide whether any particular branches should not be specified in the Agreement as multibranch offices. This would mean that the particular branch would be excluded from the Agreement and any issue of "tainting" would be avoided.

Within the EU there has been some important new legislation which is designed to simplify cross-border insolvency within the EU and which, if used correctly, will simplify and reinforce netting on insolvency when using netting agreements such as the ISDA Master Agreement.

On 31 May 2002, the EU Insolvency Regulation came into force in respect of all EU Member States with the exception of Denmark. The Regulation is intended to lay down a common set of rules to determine which insolvency laws will apply in respect of an insolvency in the EU. The Regulation applies to individuals, partnerships and corporates but does not apply to insurers, banks or investment undertakings which hold funds or securities for third parties or collective investment undertakings. Provision in respect of insurers is the subject of the EU Winding Up Directive for Insurance Undertakings which EU Member States had to implement by 20 April 2003. In respect of credit institutions, the EU Winding Up Directive for Credit Institutions must be implemented by EU Member States by 5 May 2004.

The main provision of the legislation is that insolvency proceedings will be subject to the law of the EU country where the debtor has the centre of its main interests. This will usually be, although not necessarily, the country where it is domiciled. Secondary proceedings can also be implemented in one or more other EU countries but must be limited to assets located in those countries.

There are also certain exceptions to the application of the legislation and these include *rights in rem* (property rights), set off, employment contracts, reservation of title and rights and obligations of parties to a payment or settlement system or a financial market which is governed by the Settlement Finality Directive 1998.

The significance of the new legislation for the ISDA Master Agreement and other forms of netting agreements is that it includes provisions which state that the opening of insolvency proceedings will not affect the right of creditors to demand the set off of their claims against the claims of the debtor where such set off is permitted by the law applicable to the insolvent party's claim. In other words this seems to provide that if the governing law of the contract recognises set off then it does not matter that the law governing the insolvency is equivocal or even contrary. Furthermore, Article 25 of the Winding Up Directive for Credit Institutions provides that netting agreements will be governed solely by the governing law of the netting agreement. This piece of legislation should therefore clearly be of great benefit in clarifying and simplifying the insolvency process within the EU and more particularly in simplifying the netting analysis on insolvency necessary on each occasion that an ISDA Master Agreement is negotiated.

However, time will be needed for cases to come before the courts to enable them to interpret and apply the new legislation and rule on any inconsistencies and other problematic issues. Nevertheless, the legislation is an important new development within the EU and requires attention and analysis.

ISDA COLLECTIVE LEGAL OPINIONS

By June 2003, The International Swaps & Derivatives Association, Inc had commissioned 39 netting legal opinions in many jurisdictions in respect of the 1992 Agreement and 36 opinions in respect of the new 2002 Agreement with the aim of providing its members with a library of legal opinions. These are separately listed in Annex 4, see pages 725–6. The opinions can be of great help in providing a clearer understanding of the approach taken by legal systems in different jurisdictions on the issues of close-out netting and insolvency as well as other matters related to the use of an Agreement.

The opinions are only available to ISDA members. They aim both to provide members with the necessary information to determine if derivative transactions are enforceable in any particular country and also the effectiveness of close-out netting on insolvency in that country. However, the opinions are not necessarily definitive and an opinion should be carefully reviewed to see whether it provides the right legal answers. It may be necessary to seek supplemental opinions to clarify certain issues especially when dealing with counterparties stated as falling outside the scope of these opinions. It is important to study the annual updates of these opinions which ISDA obtains for its members.

AUTOMATIC EARLY TERMINATION

Part 1(e) of the Schedule to the ISDA Master Agreement contains an election which parties must make in respect of the termination of transactions because of the Bankruptcy Event of Default.

If a party chooses termination by notice on the insolvency of its counterparty then this may have advantages but may also have disadvantages. It means that the solvent party can precisely time the termination of transactions as well as any related hedging transactions thus avoiding any unmatched positions. However, the downside is that in some jurisdictions the netting benefit may be threatened because the delay may give a liquidator an opportunity to "cherry pick" transactions.

If Automatic Early Termination is chosen, this will ensure that termination takes place at the earliest possible opportunity. This will defeat a "cherry-picking" liquidator in those jurisdictions where close-out netting is valid but it does mean that the timing of the termination on insolvency is outside the solvent party's control. It could mean in theory that a non-defaulting party is unaware of the termination of a transaction and that by the time it becomes aware and is able to hedge out the position it may have incurred a loss as a result of market movements.

There is no right choice when it comes to the issue of automatic or non-automatic termination. The decision may be influenced by insolvency implications in some jurisdictions or pure counterparty preference in others.

CREDIT SUPPORT

Collateral can be taken in connection with an ISDA Master Agreement by using one of the credit support documents in the ISDA stable. Collateral taken in support of derivatives transactions is typically cash in US$, Euros or £ Sterling or government securities of G10 countries.

The English Law ISDA Credit Support Annex provides for any collateral placed by one party with another to pass by way of outright transfer of title. This means that the title to the collateral transfers to the party to whom it is given and does not give rise to any registrable security interests. It has the advantage that the collateral can then be used by the collateral receiver for whatever purposes it may require, e.g. using it to give as its own collateral in respect of another transaction or selling it. When it comes to returning the collateral the receiving party's obligation is only to redeliver equivalent cash or securities, i.e. not the actual collateral transferred to it.

The English Law ISDA Credit Support Deed provides for any collateral placed by one party with another to be subject to a security interest. This means that the collateral receiver has legal rights over the collateral but no rights of ownership. The collateral receiver cannot use the collateral as it might have done had the collateral been transferred under an ISDA Credit Support Annex.

Security interests may require registration at Companies House where the collateral provider is a company registered in England and Wales. If registration is necessary, failure to register within 21 days will render the security interest void (Companies Act 1985, s 395).

The outright transfer method as contained in the ISDA Credit Support Annex does raise issues of recharacterisation risk. This simply means that although collateral is expressed to be passed by outright transfer of title from one party to the other, it may be argued that the effect of the document is to create a security interest that may then require registration. It is generally accepted that the ISDA Credit Support Annex works as a title transfer document under English law, but it is an issue which needs to be considered in relation to taking collateral in other jurisdictions.

Practice has shown that the English Law ISDA Credit Support Annex is the document of choice in England when taking collateral in connection with a derivative transaction documented under an Agreement. The ISDA Credit Support Deed does have a use in particular circumstances where it is important that the collateral is held and retained by the collateral receiver to be returned in exactly the same form at the end of the transaction. However, the *ISDA 2000 Collateral Survey* showed that it was only used in 1% of cases where collateral was taken from counterparties. The ISDA Margin Survey 2003 indicates usage at 0.7%.

This whole subject of collateral and the ISDA Credit Support documentation is covered extensively in another book in this series, *Mastering Collateral Management and Documentation* by Paul C. Harding and Christian A. Johnson.

THIRD PARTY RIGHTS

The Contracts (Rights of Third Parties) Act 1999 reformed an area of English law known as privity of contract. Prior to the Act coming into force a person could only enforce a contract if they were party to it. The new law permits third parties to enforce contracts that benefit them, and which were entered into on or after 11 May 2000, as long as they are identified in the contract by name, as a class or by a particular description. There are certain exceptions set out in the Act and it is possible to exclude the effect of the Act altogether to ensure that privity of contract will apply.

In the context of the Agreement, it is perhaps hard to foresee any particular situations where the Act could present difficulties. However, the Act should be borne in mind and it may be prudent always to include a provision in the Agreement excluding its provisions. This will then prevent any possibility of future problems. Such a provision is now regularly included in the following form:

> **Third Party Rights. Nothing in this Agreement is intended to confer on any person any right to enforce any term which that person would not have but for the Contracts (Rights of Third Parties) Act 1999.**

The above section of Chapter 5 contains a broad outline of UK legal issues in relation to derivatives and the Agreement. It is always advisable to consult an experienced derivatives lawyer or law firm on specific legal issues relating to individual transactions.

The views, thoughts and opinions expressed in this chapter are those of the author in his individual capacity and should not in any way be attributed to Dresdner Kleinwort Wasserstein, or to Simon Leifer as a representative, officer or employee of Dresdner Kleinwort Wasserstein.

US PERSPECTIVE BY CHRISTIAN A. JOHNSON*

As a practical matter, the enforcement of one's rights under the ISDA Master Agreement will be substantively similar whether New York or English law is selected by the parties. However, there are important regulatory and insolvency regimes under US, Federal and New York law that either do not exist under English law or take a different form. When negotiating an ISDA Master Agreement on behalf of a party it is important to understand and appreciate those differences.

ENFORCEMENT OF NEW YORK CHOICE OF LAW

US parties often will insist that New York law be applied to govern the ISDA Master Agreement. Indeed the Agreement was written on the basis of the common law codes of the State of New York and England. Non-US parties often question whether such a choice of law would be respected by the courts of the State of New York or the United States District Court located in the Borough of Manhattan in New York City ("New York Courts"). This is an especially important question if the non-US party has no contacts with New York or is not incorporated or organised under New York law. There appears to be little doubt, however, that a New York Court would enforce the selection of New York law and would grant jurisdiction to the parties in the event of any litigation.

New York Courts are required by the laws of the State of New York to enforce the choice of New York law. The aggregate amount of obligations arising out of the contract, however, cannot be less than US$250,000 (N.Y. General Obligation Law, §5–1401(1)). Although the issue has not been litigated, it is generally understood that the notional amount of any transaction

* For an additional discussion of the effect of US law on OTC derivatives, see *Mastering Collateral Management: a Practical Guide to the ISDA Credit Support Documents* by Paul C. Harding and Christian A. Johnson (Financial Times/Prentice Hall, November 2002) and *Over-the-Counter Derivatives Documentation: A Practical Guide for Executives* (Browne Publishing, 2000) by Christian A. Johnson.

entered into must exceed US$250,000 as opposed to the net mark-to-market amount. In any case a transaction in litigation would probably have a net mark-to-market amount in excess of US$250,000 anyway.

New York Courts are also required by the laws of the State of New York to enforce New York as the forum for litigation "for which a choice of New York has been made" (NY General Obligation Law, §5–1402(1)). The aggregate amount of obligations arising out of the contract, however, cannot be less than US$1 million. Again, although the issue has not been litigated, it is generally understood that the notional amount of any transaction entered into must exceed US$1 million as opposed to the net mark-to-market amount. Again, any transaction in litigation would probably have a net mark-to-market amount in excess of US$1 million anyway.

US BANKRUPTCY AND BANKING INSOLVENCY LAW

A principal concern for a party is whether, upon the bankruptcy or insolvency of its counterparty, the solvent party will still be able to enforce it rights under the ISDA Master Agreement. Such party's rights will depend upon the bankruptcy or insolvency rules that apply to the insolvent party. Most corporate parties organised under state law in the US are subject to the US Bankruptcy Code. Debtors that are financial institutions and that take federally insured deposits, such as banks and savings institutions, are not subject to the insolvency rules in the US Bankruptcy Code. Instead, they are subject to insolvency rules found in the Federal Deposit Insurance Act ("FDIA").

In addition to these two types of parties, there are others that are also not subject to these rules. For example, insurance companies are subject to the insurance laws of the state under which they are organised. Quasi-government entities such as Federal Home Loan Banks have their own insolvency rules. Municipalities and other government subdivisions also have their own insolvency regime. A discussion of these rules is beyond the scope of this chapter.

US Bankruptcy Code

The US Bankruptcy Code has special rules dealing with a bankrupt debtor (the party that has filed for its own bankruptcy) that has entered into a "swap agreement" with a "swap participant". A swap participant is defined under the US Bankruptcy Code as "an entity that, at the time before the filing of the petition, has an outstanding swap agreement with the debtor" (11 USC, §101(53C)). A swap agreement is broadly defined in a manner similar to the definition of a "Specified Transaction" in the ISDA Master Agreement. It includes the majority of OTC derivative transactions and any master agreement governing these transactions (11 USC, §101(53B)).

Definition of Swap Agreement

A principal concern for the solvent party is whether the definition of a swap agreement includes the many types of new and exotic OTC derivative transactions that are being developed. If the definition of the subject transaction does not fall under the definition of a swap agreement under the US Bankruptcy Code, it will not be entitled to the special protections and rules governing swap agreements. For example, some parties have questioned whether the definition of a swap agreement under the US Bankruptcy Code would include certain equity derivatives and credit derivatives. Although the general market considers that these transactions should be included in the definition of a swap agreement, there is little authority. Current legislation before the US Congress significantly broadens the definition of a swap agreement to eliminate these ambiguities.

The automatic stay

When a debtor files for bankruptcy under the US Bankruptcy Code, the law imposes an automatic stay under Section 362 of the Code. The stay ordinarily prevents the creditor of a bankrupt debtor from exercising the majority of its legal rights and remedies under the relevant contract. Generally, the automatic stay remains in effect until the case is dismissed, completed, or the judge grants relief, unless a specific exemption from the automatic stay applies.

For example, assuming there was no relevant exemption, upon the filing of a bankruptcy petition, a swap participant would normally be automatically stayed from exercising any of the self-help remedies found in the ISDA Master Agreement (and any Credit Support Document) against its bankrupt counterparty. Without a specific exemption, the solvent party would be prevented from liquidating collateral or exercising its right to set off amounts it owes the bankrupt counterparty under the ISDA Master Agreement against amounts the bankrupt counterparty owes it under any other swap agreements.

Creditors were concerned about the delays that would be caused by the application of the automatic stay. A stay would be problematic because the amount owed to the swap participant under the ISDA Master Agreement could fluctuate as markets move, resulting in additional losses. Creditors were also concerned that the value of the collateral could deteriorate before it was permitted to foreclose or liquidate it.

Congress, however, enacted Section 362(b)(17) of the Code to provide a specific exemption from the automatic stay for swap agreements. The exemption permits a swap participant to set off any amounts that the bankrupt counterparty owes to it under any other swap agreements against any amounts that the swap participant owes the bankrupt counterparty under the ISDA Master Agreement. The exemption also permits a swap participant immediately to liquidate any collateral or margin held to secure the bankrupt counterparty's obligation under a swap agreement.

Termination

There was also concern that a party could not terminate the ISDA Master Agreement without the bankruptcy court's permission even though the Agreement provides that a party may terminate it upon the bankruptcy or insolvency of its counterparty. The US Bankruptcy Code, however, now permits a swap participant to exercise its rights under the ISDA Master Agreement to terminate it and any underlying Transactions upon the bankruptcy of its counterparty (11 USC, §560).

Parties were also concerned about a problem referred to as "cherry picking" by the trustee of the bankrupt counterparty. Cherry picking occurs when a bankruptcy trustee can terminate individual transactions for which the bankrupt party was out-of-the-money (i.e. had payment obligations to the solvent party) and keep those transactions for which the bankrupt party was in-the-money (i.e. was entitled to payments from the solvent party).

Congress resolved the cherry-picking concern by permitting the solvent party to terminate the ISDA Master Agreement and all of the underlying transactions upon the bankruptcy of its counterparty. Section 560 of the US Bankruptcy Code also allows close-out netting. Close-out netting permits the solvent party to net together any amounts payable under all the transactions to be terminated under the ISDA Master Agreement.

Preference payments and avoiding power

A bankruptcy trustee has the power to reclaim or unwind property transfers made to a creditor prior to the bankruptcy in certain situations, commonly referred to as a trustee's avoiding power. The avoiding power permits a trustee to reclaim preference payments made to a creditor up to 90 days prior to the filing of a bankruptcy petition (and up to one year in the case of transfers to insiders) (11 USC, §547(b)). Swap participants were concerned that this avoiding power was disruptive of a party's netting rights and collateral arrangements under the ISDA Master Agreement.

Congress resolved this by enacting Section 546(g) which generally exempts transfers made under a swap agreement from a trustee's avoiding powers, particularly with respect to preference payments. Section 548(d)(2) also provides that a trustee cannot avoid a "fraudulent transfer" under a swap agreement because such transfer is always deemed to be made "for value to the extent of such payment".

US banking insolvency law

As mentioned above, financial institutions are generally not subject to the US Bankruptcy Code. Instead they are subject to various banking law insolvency statutes such as the Federal Deposit Insurance Act, the National Bank Act or the New York Banking Law. Generally, if the party accepts insured deposits it will be subject to the FDIA.

Parties had many of the same concerns about US banking law as they did about the US Bankruptcy Code. Congress, however, has generally resolved these concerns by amending the various banking law statutes in a manner similar to the US Bankruptcy Code.

Generally, US banking law provides similar exemptions and provisions that favour the solvent counterparty with respect to "swap agreements". A "swap agreement" is defined in a manner similar to provisions in the US Bankruptcy Code. Again, this is akin to the definition of a Specified Transaction in the ISDA Master Agreement and catches the majority of typical OTC derivatives and any master agreement governing those transactions (12 USC, §1821(e)(8)(D)(iv)).

Termination

Similar to the US Bankruptcy Code, the solvent party will generally have the right to terminate the ISDA Master Agreement upon the appointment of a receiver (and under certain circumstances upon the appointment of a conservator). Upon a permitted termination of the ISDA Master Agreement, the solvent party will also have the right to exercise close-out netting rights (12 USC, §1821(e)(8)(a)).

Under US banking law, the solvent party is generally precluded from terminating the ISDA Master Agreement and underlying transactions solely because of the financial institution's insolvency. The FDIA, however, provides that a swap agreement can be terminated under certain circumstances depending upon whether the Federal Deposit Insurance Corporation ("FDIC") is appointed as a receiver or a conservator of the insolvent financial institution.

The solvent counterparty of an insolvent financial institution can terminate the swap agreement upon the appointment of the FDIC as a receiver one day after such appointment (12 USC, §1821(e)(8)(D)(vii)). As a receiver, the FDIC has the power to liquidate (but not operate) the financial institution and wind up its affairs.

In contrast, if the FDIC is appointed as conservator of the insolvent financial institution, the solvent party will not have the right to terminate the ISDA Master Agreement because of the insolvency of the financial institution. The FDIC, as conservator, has the right to operate the financial institution as a going concern. The FDIC essentially steps into the shoes of the insolvent institution. To terminate the ISDA Master Agreement upon appointment of the FDIC as a conservator, an Event of Default (other than an insolvency) or a Termination Event would have to occur.

Upon a permitted termination of the ISDA Master Agreement, the FDIA must recognise the close-out netting rights under the agreement. This permits the solvent party to net any amounts that it owes the insolvent financial institution under the agreement with any amounts owing to the solvent party (12 USC, §1821(e)(8)(A)(iii)).

Under general insolvency rules, the FDIC has the right to transfer or repudiate the contracts of an insolvent financial institution. This could result in the FDIC cherry picking by selectively terminating or transferring the disadvantageous contracts and maintaining the advantageous ones. The FDIA, however, provides that if the FDIC is going to transfer any swap agreements, it must transfer all the swap agreements of a creditor to the same party if it is going to transfer any (12 USC, §1821(e)(3)(C)). The FDIC also may not selectively repudiate or terminate any individual transaction or contract under an ISDA Master Agreement that the insolvent financial institution had with its counterparty; rather it must terminate the Agreement and any underlying transactions all at once if it intends to terminate any individual transaction (12 USC, §1821(e)(8)(D)(vii)).

Solvent parties have also worried in the past that the FDIC may try to avoid certain payments made before the insolvency of the financial institution as a preferential payment. Such payments, however, may not be avoided unless "the transferee had actual intent to hinder, delay, or defraud such institution" (12 USC, §1821(e)(8)(c)). This should protect the vast majority of payments made in the normal course of business under the ISDA Master Agreement.

It is possible that the New York Banking Law may apply to the insolvency of a financial institution. Its rules generally parallel those described above under FDIA. Generally, however, an insolvency that would involve the New York Banking Law would also involve FDIC and the FDIA rules. Although it is possible that the New York Banking Law may apply alone, it is more likely that this would occur with a New York branch of a non-US bank that does not have deposits insured by the FDIC, a situation beyond the scope of this discussion.

Pending legislation to the US Bankruptcy Code and FDIA

Although the majority of the concerns regarding US bankruptcy and banking insolvency issues were resolved in the early 1990s, participants have wanted these provisions to be strengthened and clarified especially as the OTC derivatives market has grown and become more complex. The US Senate and the US House of Representatives have responded by each passing bills to resolve these issues. The provisions regarding OTC derivatives in the two bills are in most respects identical.

Unfortunately, due to concerns over consumer bankruptcy protection provisions in the two bills, the House and Senate have been unable to reconcile the two bills for final passage into law. Once the controversial consumer bankruptcy provisions are resolved, it is likely that these OTC derivatives provisions will be passed into law. So far this has taken five years. The following is a brief summary of several of the most important provisions that will be added to the bankruptcy and insolvency statutes.

Participants in the OTC derivatives market have been concerned that the current definitions of "swap agreement" found in the US Bankruptcy Code and in FDIA were too narrow. In particular, there have been concerns that certain equity derivatives and credit derivatives would not fall under the phrase "any other similar agreement" found in the definition of swap agreement. If the transactions did not fall under the definition of swap agreement, these transactions would be ineligible for the special treatment described in the relevant statutes.

The pending legislation eliminates any uncertainty by expressly including "an equity index or equity swap, option, future, or forward agreement" in the definition of swap agreement. In addition, the definition is also expanded by adding "a total return, credit spread or credit swap, option, future, or forward agreement".

The pending legislation also broadens the concept of "any other similar agreement" language in the current statute. The provision provides broad criteria that help clarify the types of other transactions that Congress intended to be covered by the provisions that may not yet have been developed.

The pending legislation clarifies that the existence of a non-qualifying transaction under the same swap agreement does not disqualify the other qualifying transactions from the statute's benefits. Finally, the legislation clarifies that any credit enhancement such as a guarantee that is related to a swap agreement is shielded from a trustee's powers.

Increasingly, parties that enter into not only OTC derivatives with each other but also other types of transactions such as repurchase agreements, are entering into cross-product master agreements (often referred to as "master master agreements"). Under these cross-product master agreements, upon a default under one of the underlying master agreements (such as an ISDA Master Agreement or a Master Repurchase Agreement), the non-defaulting party would be able to terminate all of the underlying master agreements and net the termination payment amounts all together.

There has been some concern that the different insolvency statutes would not permit such close-out netting. The pending legislation amends both the Bankruptcy Code and FDIA in order to ensure that such cross-product netting is enforced provided that all of the underlying master agreements qualify as qualified financial contracts under FDIA.

In addition to these major changes, the pending legislation also (i) expands the protections from the automatic stay under the Code; (ii) denies enforcement to "walkaway" clauses (i.e. First Method) under the FDIA; (iii) codifies that the FDIC may not engage in selective repudiation; and (iv) clarifies the Bankruptcy Code with respect to timing of the calculation of damages.

FDICIA

In addition to the statutory provisions favouring creditors in both FDIA and the US Bankruptcy Code, the US Congress has enacted additional statutory provisions as part of the Federal Deposit Insurance Corporation Improvement Act of 1991 ("FDICIA") to enforce close-out netting. Under FDICIA, netting rights are enforced regardless of whether they would be enforced under the US Bankruptcy Code or the FDIA provided that both parties are "financial institutions" as defined in FDICIA. In addition, under current law, the ISDA Master Agreement would have to be governed by Federal law or by state law (such as the laws of the State of New York).

The definition of financial institution includes not only financial institutions that accept federally insured deposits but also "a broker or dealer, a depository financial institution, a futures commission merchant, or any other financial institution as determined by the Board of Governors of the Federal Reserve System" (12 USC, §4402(9)). Under Federal Reserve Board regulations, a financial institution also includes substantial parties that meet quantitative and qualitative tests that generally describe the characteristics of a dealer in the derivatives area. The financial institution, however, does not need to be chartered or organised under US Federal or state law in order to benefit from FDICIA.

The qualitative test requires that a party "engage in financial contracts as a counterparty on both sides in one or more financial markets". The quantitative test measures the volume of a party's activity in the derivatives markets. If a party has entered into financial contracts totaling at least US$1 billion in outstanding notional principal amount, it will meet the quantitative test. It will also satisfy the test if it can demonstrate that it has financial contracts with gross mark-to-market positions of at least US$100 million. Financial contracts include securities contracts, commodity contracts, forward contracts, repurchase agreements, swap agreements, and any similar agreement as defined in the FDIA (12 USC, §1821(e)(8)(D)(i)).

Pending legislation

As part of the pending legislation described above, there are several additional amendments proposed to strengthen further the enforcement of netting between financial institutions under the FDICIA. First, the pending legislation makes FDICIA applicable to bilateral netting contracts governed by non-US law (e.g. English law). Previously only bilateral netting contracts governed by US law were eligible for the protections. Second, the definition of financial institutions was expanded to include uninsured national and state member banks and foreign banks (expressly rather than possibly indirectly through Regulation EE). Third, the pending legislation clarifies that FDICIA does not override the FDIC's power to transfer a swap agreement or permit a party to terminate the swap agreement during the time period provided to the FDIC to repudiate or transfer a swap agreement when the FDIC is appointed as a receiver or conservator.

NON-NEW YORK HEAD OFFICE OF A US COUNTERPARTY

Non-US parties are often concerned about dealing with the non-NewYork head office of a US counterparty. There are several large US dealers with their head offices located outside of New York and there are even a few large foreign banks with US branch offices located outside of New York. Non-US parties are concerned about whether the close-out netting provisions found in the ISDA Master Agreement will be enforced in the event of an insolvency of these US dealers.

Initially, non-US parties should remember that FDICIA (as discussed above) will always enforce close-out netting between "financial institutions" under the ISDA Master Agreement provided that the Agreement is governed by US Federal or state law. Even if the ISDA Master Agreement is not governed by US Federal or state law, there is, as mentioned above, legislation before Congress that would broaden FDICIA to include Agreements governed by non-US law such as English law. In addition, as discussed above, the financial institutions themselves do not need to be chartered under US Federal or state law to qualify as a financial institution; they only need to meet the quantitative and qualitative definitions described above in order to benefit from FDICIA.

There should be little concern about a US dealer that is a national bank, even if its home office is outside of New York. A national bank is organised under the laws of the US and is regulated by the Office of the Comptroller of the Currency. The netting protections found in the FDIA will ensure that close-out netting will be enforced.

There should also be little concern about a US dealer that is an insured depository institution (i.e. the bank accepts deposits insured by the Federal Deposit Insurance Corporation). The netting protections found in the FDICIA will ensure that close-out netting provisions will be enforced for an insured depository institution.

There are two situations that may be more problematic. The first is a state-chartered bank that is not an insured depository institution or that is not chartered under New York state law. The second is a foreign bank that has a

US branch located outside of New York. The first concern is that such institutions would not be subject to the netting protection provisions of either the FDIA or the US Bankruptcy Code. Most state banking laws (other than those of New York) do not have express provisions that protect netting for a state-chartered bank or for a US branch of a foreign bank. Because of this, there may be some concern that a state banking authority may engage in ringfencing in the event that the bank or branch became insolvent.

However, this may be less problematic than it appears. First, assuming that both parties are financial institutions and the ISDA is governed by New York law, they would still be subject to the netting protection provisions of FDICIA. As explained above, even if the ISDA Master Agreement is not governed by US Federal or state law, there is currently legislation pending before Congress that will expand FDICIA's reach by including ISDA Master Agreements governed by non-US law.

Second, there is no authority that a state banking authority would engage in ring fencing in the event of such an insolvency. This is still an issue that many state banking authorities (unlike New York's) have never had to address.

Finally, I am unaware of any OTC derivatives dealer that is a state chartered bank that is not an insured depository or is not chartered under New York state law. There are also few, if any, US branches of foreign banks that are not licensed in New York and many of these probably have some kind of an office or branch in New York that they could utilise for these particular trading relationships.

THE COMMODITY EXCHANGE ACT (1974) AND THE COMMODITY FUTURES MODERNIZATION ACT (2000)

Since the inception of the OTC derivatives market, participants have been concerned that OTC derivatives may be subject to the Commodity Exchange Act (the "CEA") (see 7 USC, §§1 et al). This would subject OTC derivatives activity to regulation by the Commodity Futures Trading Commission ("CFTC") just as the CFTC regulates the organised derivative exchanges and the derivatives traded on them such as the Chicago Board of Trade and the Chicago Mercantile Exchange.

Because all transactions subject to the CEA are required to be traded through a "contract market" such as the Chicago Board of Trade, failure to do this could result in the transactions being classified as illegal, off-exchange futures transactions. This could subject the parties to various fines and penalties and result in a finding that the OTC derivative transactions are void or unenforceable.

The vast majority of these concerns were eliminated by passage of the Commodity Futures Modernization Act of 2000 (the "CFMA"). Any legal uncertainty in this area has been put to rest by the statutory changes made to the Commodity Exchange Act.

The CFMA essentially eliminated the possibility that a contract entered into under an ISDA Master Agreement would be considered to be an illegal off-exchange futures contract and therefore void and unenforceable. The CFMA also excluded from the reach of the CFTC several classes of swap agreements that were entered into by "eligible contract participants". The definition of an eligible contract participants is broader than the definition of "eligible swap participants" under the CFTC Regulations.

The full reach of the CFMA will be addressed initially. Because there are still limited circumstances in which the CFMA may not provide the necessary protections but earlier exemptions provided by the CFTC may, it is also worth briefly reviewing the 1989 Policy Statement Concerning Swap Transactions issued by the CFTC and the CFTC Regulations issued in 1994 (17 CFR Part 35). These limited situations typically include when a party is entering into commodities derivatives that reference agricultural commodities and when a participant may not be considered to be an eligible contract participant but may still qualify under the 1989 Policy Statement or CFTC Regulations.

The Commodity Futures Modernization Act of 2000

The changes made by the CFMA were extremely important. Not only did the CFMA generally expand the exclusions available from the CEA and the jurisdiction of the CFTC but such changes were also statutory as opposed to being a CFTC pronouncement or a regulation promulgated by the CFTC that could be either reversed by the CFTC itself or invalidated by the courts.

The most important change made by the CFMA was to eliminate the possibility that a contract entered into between "eligible contract participants" would be considered to be an illegal off-exchange futures contract and therefore void and unenforceable:

> **No agreement, contract, or transaction between eligible contract participants . . . shall be void, voidable, or unenforceable, and no such party shall be entitled to rescind, or recover any payment made with respect to, such an agreement, contract, transaction, or instrument under this section . . . based solely on the failure of the agreement, contract, transaction, or instrument to comply with the terms or conditions of an exemption or exclusion from any provision of [the Commodity Exchange Act] or regulations of the [CFTC]. [7 USC, §25].**

The definition of an "eligible contract participant" is very similar to (and also broader than) the definition of an "eligible swap participant under the CFTC

Regulations. To be an "eligible contract participant", the party must (i) be a certain designated type of financial entity (typically based on how it is regulated or (ii) meet certain financial tests (7 USC, §1a(12).

The following entities are designated as eligible contract participants:

- **a bank or trust company;**
- **a savings association;**
- **a credit union;**
- **an insurance company;**
- **certain kinds of investment companies;**
- **certain commodity pools;**
- **broker-dealers;**
- **futures commission merchants; and**
- **floor brokers or floor traders. In addition, certain employee benefit plans and any government entity are also eligible contract participants.**

If a party is not one of the designated financial entities, it can still qualify as an eligible contract participant by meeting certain financial tests. A corporation, partnership, proprietorship, organisation, trust or other entity is an eligible contract participant if:

- **it has total assets exceeding US$10 million;**
- **it has its obligations guaranteed by an entity that is a designated financial entity described above;**
- **it has a net worth exceeding US$1 million and enters into an agreement, contract or transaction in connection with the conduct of the entity's business; or**
- **it has a net worth exceeding US$1 million and enters into an agreement, contract or transaction to manage the risk associated with an asset or liability owned or incurred in the conduct of the entity's business.**

In addition, an individual can also be an eligible contract participant if it has (i) total assets in an amount in excess of US$10 million; or (ii) has assets in excess of US$5 million and enters into the agreement, contract or transaction in order to manage the risk associated with an asset owned or liability incurred by the individual.

The CFMA expressly excludes several classes of swap agreements from the reach of the Commodity Exchange Act and the Commodity Futures Trading Commission that were entered into by eligible contract participants. The first exclusion is for Transactions involving "excluded commodities" between eligible contract participants.

Excluded commodities are defined to include the following:

(i) an interest rate, exchange rate, currency, security, security index, credit risk or measure, debt or equity instrument, index or measure of inflation, or other macroeconomic index or measure;

(ii) any other rate, differential, index, or measure of economic or commercial risk, return, or value that is

(I) not based in substantial part on the value of a narrow group of commodities not described in clause (i); or

(II) based solely on one or more commodities that have no cash market;

(iii) any economic or commercial index based on prices, rates, values, or levels that are not within the control of any party to the relevant contract, agreement, or transaction; or

(iv) an occurrence, extent of an occurrence, or contingency (other than a change in the price, rate, value, or level of a commodity not described in clause (i)) that is

(I) beyond the control of the parties to the relevant contract, agreement, or transaction; and

(II) associated with a financial, commercial or economic consequence.

[7 USC, §1a(13).]

Transactions based on excluded commodities include interest rate, currency, credit, equity and weather derivatives and transactions involving commodities that have no cash market. This provision excludes what is referred to as "agricultural commodities" such as wheat or timber. Evidently, agricultural commodities were excluded from the definition because of concern that these transactions might be subject to market manipulation. There appeared to be a belief that although the CFMA may not provide sufficient regulatory protections for transactions involving agricultural commodities, the 1989 Policy Statement and CFTC Regulations do.

The second group of transactions eligible for exclusion are transactions based on "exempt commodities". These are transactions not based on either agricultural commodities (for the reasons discussed directly above) or excluded commodities and are generally understood to be transactions based on chemicals, metals or energy products (7 USC, 1a(14)). The exclusion for transactions based on exempt commodities is more limited in that these transactions are still subject to the anti-fraud and anti-manipulation jurisdiction of the CFTC.

The CFMA also provides an exemption for transactions based on either excluded or exempt commodities that are traded over an electronic trading facility. A "trading facility" is defined as:

a person or group of persons that constitutes, maintains, or provides a physical or electronic facility or system in which multiple participants have the ability to execute or trade agreements, contracts, or transactions by accepting bids and offers made by other participants that are open to multiple participants in the facility or system.

[7 USC, §1a(33).]

An electronic trading facility is a trading facility that operates essentially by "means of an electronic or telecommunications network" (7 USC, §1a(10)).

Because of the CFMA, the representations that should now be required in the ISDA Master Agreement with respect to exemptions from the Commodity Exchange Act are much simpler than those representations required under the 1989 Statement or the Regulations promulgated by the CFTC.

It is now market practice that a party only require that the other party represent that it is an "eligible contract participant":

It is an "eligible contract participant" as defined in the Commodity Futures Modernization Act of 2000.

Although parties could conceivably request a party to represent that the transactions are based on excluded or exempt commodities, these definitions are so broad that there is typically little risk of not meeting them. In addition, because the risk of a transaction between eligible contract participants being declared void or unenforceable is now so small, any representation beyond a party being an eligible contract participant is considered to be unnecessary except in unusual circumstances.

1989 Policy Statement

Prior to the passage of the CFMA, Congress and the CFTC resolved concerns about the application of the CEA by effectively exempting most OTC derivatives from the CEA and from the jurisdiction of the CFTC. The CFTC first accomplished this by issuing in 1989 a "Policy Statement Concerning Swap Transactions" ("1989 Policy Statement") (54 Fed. Reg. 30694-01 (1989)). The CFTC stated that it would "take no action to preclude the effectuation of or to regulate such [swap] transactions". In other words, the CFTC would not exercise its jurisdiction over OTC derivatives provided that the transactions met several "safe harbor criteria". This policy statement was later expanded to include collar transactions (CFTC-OETC Interpretive Letter No. 90-1 (18 January 1990)). The CFTC also ruled that it would not apply its regulatory framework to "swaps settled in cash (with foreign currencies considered to be cash)" if the swap satisfied several safe harbour criteria. These criteria related to an OTC derivative not resembling the more common exchange-traded transactions.

Although the Policy Statement was helpful, participants were concerned that legal uncertainty still existed in the area because the 1989 Policy Statement could be withdrawn. It was also unclear whether the CFTC even had the authority to surrender jurisdiction over OTC derivatives by issuing the 1989 Policy Statement. Because of this, Congress provided the CFTC with authority to exempt "swap agreements" from the requirements of the CEA.

CFTC Regulations – 17 CFR Part 35

After receiving authority from Congress to exempt certain types of transactions from its jurisdiction, the CFTC promptly promulgated Regulations (17 CFR Part 35). The Regulations provided that a swap agreement was exempt from the provisions of the CEA provided that the parties and the relevant transactions met certain requirements. The CFTC definition of swap agreement closely resembled the definition for swap agreement found in the US Bankruptcy Code, banking insolvency law and the definition of Specified Transaction in the ISDA Master Agreement.

Based upon these Regulations, parties asked their counterparties to make several different representations to determine if their counterparty qualified for the exemption. As a general rule, the statutory changes made in the CFMA now provide the statutory exclusions and protections from the CEA that were originally dealt with in the CFTC Regulations. The CFTC Regulations, however, are still valid and were not revoked by the CFMA. In rare and specialised circumstances, the CFTC Regulations may even provide some protections that are not present in the CFMA.

In order to determine if there was an exemption from the CEA based upon the CFTC Regulations, parties often requested the following representations, which, because the CFMA now generally provides statutory protections, will only be discussed briefly.

The first representation concerns whether the parties have entered into a "swap agreement". A swap agreement is defined similarly to the way it is defined under the US Bankruptcy Code and banking insolvency laws.

The next representation concerns whether the party is an eligible "swap participant". To be an eligible swap participant, the party must (i) be a particular kind of dealer or financial institution or (ii) meet certain financial tests. In addition, "a natural person with total assets exceeding US$10,000,000" is also an eligible swap participant.

The parties also requested a representation that the transaction was not one of a fungible class of agreements that are standardised as to their material economic terms. This was requested in order to distinguish between an OTC derivative and an exchange-traded transaction which has a standardised contract and economic terms. The only customised term of an exchange-traded transaction is its price as opposed to an OTC derivative in which all terms are open for negotiation between the parties.

Another representation requested that each party represented that the creditworthiness of the other party was a material consideration in entering into or determining the terms of this Agreement including pricing, cost or credit enhancement terms. This again was requested in order to distinguish the OTC derivatives transaction from an exchange traded derivative.

In addition to the representations related to the CFTC Regulation, parties have continued to require the line of business representation requested before the CFTC Regulations. The line of business representation does not come from, nor is it required to be made, under the CFTC Regulations found in 7 CFR Part 35. Instead, the representation comes from the fourth criteria delineated by the CFTC in its 1989 Policy Statement for a swap agreement to qualify under its safe harbour exemption from CFTC Regulation.

Examples of these representations can be found in Chapter 9 at page 640.

Parties represented that the swap agreement was entered into in conjunction with their line of business to hedge "exchange rate, interest rate, or other price exposure". The CFTC Policy Statement made clear, however, that financial intermediation services performed by the dealer would also meet this requirement. The thrust of this representation appears to be to limit the CFTC exemption under the 1989 Policy Statement to transactions entered into for the purpose of hedging business and market risks. This representation should be easy to make for end users entering into OTC derivative transactions to hedge their business and market risks.

GAMING AND BUCKET-SHOP LAWS

Historically, there has been concern that contracts for OTC derivative transactions may not be enforceable because they violated the state laws governing gaming regulation and bucket-shops. Parties were first anxious that because OTC derivatives could possibly be characterised as a zero sum game based upon whether a particular index or price moves in one direction or another, they might violate a state's gaming or gambling laws. Parties were also concerned that a state's "bucket-shop" rules governing sham transactions involving commodities and securities might also be applicable. The Commodities Futures Modernization Act of 2000, however, has virtually eliminated any possibility that these rules could be applicable (except for general antifraud provisions).

The above section of Chapter 5 contains a broad outline of US legal issues in relation to derivatives and the Agreement. It is always advisable to consult an experienced derivatives lawyer or law firm on specific legal issues relating to individual transactions.

Credit issues relating to the ISDA Master Agreement

6

Downgrade from Cross Default to cross acceleration

Threshold Amount

Credit Event Upon Merger

Addition of Specified Entities

Specified Indebtedness

Set off

Transfers

Political risk

Other credit issues

Pre-signing trade policies

Categories of risk in the Agreement

Using the ISDA Master Agreement to enhance credit protection

The "vanilla ISDA"

The ISDA Master Agreement and its Schedule has a number of credit-related issues that can be proposed by the parties and which are frequently referred to credit officers. The main ones are:

DOWNGRADE FROM CROSS DEFAULT TO CROSS ACCELERATION

Corporates often seek to downgrade Cross Default to cross acceleration. This has important implications.

Under Cross Default a Non-defaulting Party to an Agreement has an automatic right to terminate all Transactions under it where it is aware that its counterparty has defaulted under third party agreements or instruments elsewhere and such default exceeds the Threshold Amount in its own Agreement with its counterparty.

With cross acceleration, the innocent third party actually has to start proceedings against the defaulting counterparty before you can trigger your transaction termination rights under your Agreement with that same defaulting counterparty. The downgrading therefore affects the timing of your right to terminate. It is no longer automatic but deferred.

If the third party is your counterparty's main relationship bank it may take some time to review its position and may then propose a compromise which does not suit you.

Bank credit departments regularly face consideration of this issue and there is no scientific answer. Analysts have to do their best to envisage the likelihood of a third party bank or group of creditors taking immediate default proceedings against an important but stricken corporate. If the bank is the main relationship bank it might be to its advantage (to give it more time to think) to have cross acceleration apply but only if this is the case with all the corporate's Agreements with other banks which may be an unlikely situation.

I believe such downgrade requests should only be considered favourably if specific foreseeable circumstances justify them (i.e. it is already in a loan agreement you have with your counterparty and it would be consistent to have it here too) or if your counterparty gives written confirmation that cross acceleration applies to all its agreements and will do so in the future. This is because if even one counterparty has Cross Default it would be in pole position to trigger its termination rights.

The way to identify if a party is seeking to negotiate cross acceleration is to look out for the following amendment in Part 1 or 5 of the Schedule:

> **In line 7 of Section 5(a)(vi) the words ", or becoming capable at such time of being declared," are deleted.**

Where cross acceleration is agreed, it is normal for it to apply to both parties.

THRESHOLD AMOUNT

The appropriate level of a Threshold Amount for Cross Default purposes should be considered by the credit function. Sometimes this is done by internal or external credit ratings. A monetary figure is often applied across the board, e.g. US$ 10 million or a small percentage of a party's shareholders' equity (e.g. 3%). Of course, the monetary equivalent of this will vary over the years. Sometimes the 3% level is applied uncritically and it is important to find out what it represents in real money. I can recall an occasion where a small bank proposed a Threshold Amount of £10 million for itself. Prima facie, this seemed reasonable (it was a bank after all!) but, referring to its audited accounts, I found it represented 20% of its shareholders' funds and so was excessive. This shows that even proposals for what seem relatively low Threshold Amounts need to be critically assessed.

Banks will usually propose low Threshold Amounts for corporates, even zero in particularly risky cases. Sometimes if the corporate is lowly capitalised but is guaranteed by a substantial parent, it may be possible to link the Threshold Amount to a percentage of the parent's shareholders' funds.

You can also look at the Threshold Amount as the monetary exposure you are comfortable in allowing to your counterparty before you invoke your termination rights under the Cross Default provision.

A bank will always regard a corporate as more likely to default than itself.

It is important for each party to an Agreement to have a standard policy for Threshold Amounts.

CREDIT EVENT UPON MERGER

Occasionally you may be asked to consider Credit Event Upon Merger applying to you but not your counterparty. Usually this can be rejected and occasionally negotiated for it not to apply either way. I think the imbalance is only acceptable if your counterparty is a sovereign state, because it is very unlikely to merge with another state. It would also be appropriate if your counterparty was a natural person, i.e. an individual.

Sometimes the rather vague term "materially weaker" is objectively linked to formal long-term credit ratings (e.g. from Moody's or Standard & Poor's). A list of these ratings appears in Annex 7, page 734. The level at which these ratings are pitched will need to be critically considered (i.e. they must not have to fall too many notches before you can invoke your termination rights). Falls of two or three notches are commonly seen in such provisions. It is proper for a credit or risk function to consider this matter.

ADDITION OF SPECIFIED ENTITIES

In Part 1(a) of the Schedule to the Agreement it is possible to add other group companies as Specified Entities to Section 5(a)(v) (Default under Specified Transaction), Section 5(a)(vi) (Cross Default), Section 5(a)(vii) (Bankruptcy) and Section 5(b)(iv) (Credit Event Upon Merger). Sometimes these Specified Entities are named (they may be asset rich subsidiaries of the counterparty) and sometimes a general term "Affiliates" is used – this essentially means any other group company. Specified Entities can be proposed to apply to all the above sub-Sections or just to Section 5(a)(v) which is probably the least desirable as there is no Threshold Amount with Default under Specified Transaction.

If, for instance, a corporate counterparty agrees to add its Affiliates as Specified Entities for all these sub-Sections it means that if there is a default under any of these sub-Sections in a separate agreement between the bank and any of the corporate's Affiliates, then the Non-defaulting Party (probably the bank) has the option to close out all Transactions under its Agreement with the corporate itself even though it is not in default under that Agreement.

While it is true that the legal effectiveness of Specified Entities (i.e. joining other parties to an Agreement of which they may not be aware and which they do not sign) is untested in the courts, corporates will try very hard to disapply the Specified Entity provisions if possible. They would fear the extreme case where a near dormant subsidiary with one old swap transaction defaults under an Agreement leading an inflexible bank to close out all its other agreements with the corporate's group, none of which are in default themselves.

Few banks offer their Affiliates as Specified Entities because the majority of their assets are in the bank itself. Substantial companies are often able to negotiate the disapplication of Specified Entities. Smaller ones may be able to limit Specified Entities to material Affiliates only (e.g. those which account for, say, 15–20% of consolidated pre-tax profits or assets). Credit Support Providers are automatically included in most Events of Default and Termination Events and do not need to be named as Specified Entities. Whether Specified Entities are needed or acceptable should be considered by the credit function particularly in cases where the bank's counterparty is a corporate holding company whose main assets are investments in operating subsidiaries.

SPECIFIED INDEBTEDNESS

Specified Indebtedness basically means "borrowed money" but three variations from this standard definition regularly feature in Schedules and are worthy of credit attention:

Expansion of definition to other types of borrowing

Banks sometimes seek to expand this definition for corporates and non-banks to embrace other types of indebtedness, e.g. bonds, commercial paper, acceptance credits, factoring, leasing, hire purchase etc. which they may use. The list can be very extensive and should be carefully considered where it is to apply mutually. Specified Indebtedness links in with the Cross Default provision and if you or your counterparty defaults under an Agreement with a third party, any money outstanding under the above instruments will count as part of the Threshold Amount (the monetary figure above which a Non-defaulting Party can terminate all Transactions under its Agreement with you).

Inclusion of derivatives transactions in the definition of Specified Indebtedness

The Section 14 definition of Specified Transaction is essentially one or more of a list of derivatives transactions between the two parties to the Agreement and refers to transactions they may have together under other agreements. Sometimes this is amended to one party to the Agreement and any other party which considerably broadens the definition. With this amendment made, a financial institution may then import either the Section 14 Specified Transaction definition list of derivatives transactions into Specified Indebtedness wholesale or just add the revised Specified Transaction definition. The effect of this change is that Specified Indebtedness would now extend to all borrowings and derivatives transactions.

It is important to note that while borrowings are expressed in outstanding balance terms, derivatives are linked to notional amounts. While 100% of an overdraft balance is at risk, for instance, only 1–2% of the notional amount is at risk with a plain vanilla interest rate swap. As Specified Indebtedness links into Cross Default and Threshold Amount it is important that the mark-to-market or replacement value of the swap and not the notional amount is used in a close-out situation to calculate if the Threshold Amount has been breached. For instance, the Threshold Amount in an Agreement might be US$ 10 million. If your counterparty defaulted elsewhere and the only exposure you had against them was a US$ 20 million interest rate swap, then the Threshold Amount would be breached on an unamended (i.e. notional) basis and the Transaction could be terminated. However, if the real risk were only 1–2% of the US$ 20 million notional amount (i.e. US$ 200,000–400,000) then the Threshold Amount would not be breached if a replacement value amendment were made. Examples of this may be found in Chapter 8, page 441.

Watch out for the importation of derivatives transactions into the Specified Indebtedness definition and bear in mind that repos and securities lending are also included in the revised definition of Specified Transaction in the 2002 Agreement.

Exclusion of banking deposits from Specified Indebtedness

Banks will commonly seek to exclude customers' bank deposits from the Specified Indebtedness definition. A bank may argue that its deposit business (against which, in the UK, regulators require it to provide reserves and operate a compensation scheme) is separate from its trading businesses and ought to be excluded. Technically, of course, these deposits are money borrowed by the bank from its customers.

Whether this exclusion is acceptable is a policy matter. Many will agree to this exclusion while others consider that if a bank defaulted on repaying customer deposits it would be in a very serious state indeed and its counterparty would want to close out its transactions under the Agreement. How practical this would be is debatable but the counterparty would have the right to do so. The problem is that including customer deposits (which would be huge for a major bank) would potentially breach any reasonable Threshold Amount level. If this is a sticking point a compromise is usually reached where:

- **non-repayment is caused by *force majeure* or government action;**
- **there has been no decline in the bank's creditworthiness and it would have been able to repay its deposits if permitted;**
- **it undertakes to repay any requesting depositor within three Local Business Days of the lifting of any deposit repayment prohibition;**
- **a combination of two or more of the above.**

Again the credit function should opine on this and ideally supply a policy.

SET OFF

A set off clause is normally included in Part 5 of the Schedule. When the ISDA Working Party was composing the 1992 Agreement they could not agree on the wording of a set off clause, so it did not appear in the main text of the 1992 Agreement. However, there is now a set off clause in Section 6(f) of the 2002 Agreement.

The set off clause is useful in a default situation. Imagine you are a bank and your counterparty defaults. You net off all the Transactions and reach a single figure that they owe you. If you have a set off clause you can look around the horizon and see if they have any other assets you can attach, e.g. a deposit account in their own name. If you can, you can set it off against the amount they owe you and reduce it further. This is vital if they are insolvent.

Sometimes parties want to add other companies (i.e. Affiliates) in the Non-defaulting Party's group to the set off clause and this may cause negotiation because it extends a Non-defaulting Party's set off rights against a Defaulting Party. A set off clause is a standard feature in a Schedule and if someone refuses to have one it can lead to a serious breakdown in negotiations.

The effect of this, except in an insolvency situation, is to throw the parties purely upon the Agreement's close-out mechanism and disbar a Non-defaulting Party still owed money from setting this off against any credit balances it may hold from the Defaulting Party. ISDA recommended the inclusion of a set off provision in the Agreement Schedule and any requests for its exclusion should be very carefully considered by the credit function. This is even more the case now that it is in the main text of the 2002 ISDA Master Agreement.

It may, however, be permissible with special purpose vehicle loans involving a syndicate or club of banks where any set off benefits would be allocated by a facility agent between the banks and unilateral set off by a syndicate or club bank would be prohibited by the loan agreement terms.

TRANSFERS

Section 7 of the Agreement requires one party to consent in writing to the other party's request to transfer its rights and obligations under the Agreement. This does not apply in a full merger situation.

Sometimes banks or corporates request the unfettered right to transfer rights and obligations under the Agreement to any Affiliate without prior written consent. Generally speaking, I would not give blanket advance clearance to such transfers because I prefer to consider them in the light of all prevailing circumstances at the time they are made. However, parties may decide to concede on this if certain safeguards are in place, e.g.:

- **a parent guarantee for the transferee or at least as good an external credit rating as the transferor;**
- **no withholding taxes are imposed post transfer;**
- **the transfer will not make payments under or performance of the Agreement unlawful;**
- **no costs will be incurred by the non-transferring party;**

- **no Event of Default or Termination Event will occur because of the transfer;**
- **the transfer is for the whole of a party's interests and obligations under the Agreement and not part only;**
- **the transfer provisions are mutual.**

Again this is an area which the credit function should review and ideally make a policy.

POLITICAL RISK

Section 10(a) states that the parties to an Agreement may regard Transactions entered into through their branches as equivalent to Transactions entered into through their Head Offices. This represents an implied payment or performance guarantee. In Section 10(a) of the 2002 Agreement each party now agrees as well as represents that if it enters into a Transaction through a branch, its counterparty can regard this as tantamount to entering into that Transaction with the first party's head office.

If a counterparty does not want Section 10(a) to apply to the Agreement it means it wants to shift the political risk of its branch on to the other party. This may not matter if the branches are all in mainstream financial centres, but I think this is a matter for the credit function and the Legal Department if the disapplication would involve exotic locations or jurisdictions unfavourable to close-out netting and where transactions may already be outstanding.

The credit effect of disapplying Section 10(a) is that the parties would have to evaluate each other's branches as they would a local bank in the jurisdiction concerned.

OTHER CREDIT ISSUES

These would include change of ownership provisions, credit rating downgrades and payment frequency imbalances under swaps where this is a regular pattern of dealing between the parties. This could arise where there is a greater infrequency of payments made by your counterparty under a series of swaps than by you, e.g. they pay every six months and you pay every three months. If this happens in every swap the counterparty risk should be revisited by the credit function. In most cases, any concessions granted by the credit function would be two way or reciprocal.

PRE-SIGNING TRADE POLICIES

Parties are most interested in signing Agreements when they are required as a pre-condition of trading. After the deal is done, enthusiasm for ISDA negotiation wanes dramatically. Consequently, many banks have policies on which types of entities (including minimum credit rating levels) have to sign Agreements before trading. These may include corporates, building societies, insurance companies and hedge funds, for instance. I think it appropriate for a credit function to be involved in such policy formation.

It might now be useful to summarise the types of risk associated with Sections of both the 1992 and 2002 versions of the ISDA Master Agreement.

CATEGORIES OF RISK IN THE AGREEMENT

Legal Risk

Section 1(b):	Inconsistency
Section 1(c):	Single Agreement
Section 3:	Representations
Section 4(b) and (c):	Agreements
Section 5(a):	Events of Default (including insolvency risk)
Section 5(b):	Termination Events (i.e. jurisdictional risk)
Section 7:	Transfer
Section 8(c):	Contractual Currency
Section 9(d):	Remedies Cumulative
Section 13:	Governing Law and Jurisdiction.

Counterparty Risk

Section 5:	Events of Default and Termination Events
Section 11:	Expenses.

Market Risk

Section 6:	Early termination especially with Automatic Early Termination.

Documentation Risk

Section 4(a):	Agreements.

Payment/Settlement Risk

Section 2: Obligations.

Political Risk

Section 10: Offices; Multibranch Parties.

All these risks can recur in the Schedule where the parties make specific choices on what provisions are to apply in their Agreement.

USING THE ISDA MASTER AGREEMENT TO ENHANCE CREDIT PROTECTION

There are a number of ways you can try to improve your position under an Agreement and some of these regularly appear at the earliest stages of negotiation. Some of them we have just also studied.

Examples are:

- **join your counterparty's Affiliates or nominated companies as Specified Entities to the four Section 5 events quoted in Part 1(a) of the Schedule. This basically means that if they defaulted in any of those ways in another agreement you could close out your Transactions with your counterparty under your Agreement;**
- **negotiate a low Threshold Amount for your counterparty's Cross Default;**
- **take collateral;**
- **in long-dated transactions, have an optional early termination provision or break clause midway through the term (e.g. after five years of a ten-year deal) but be careful about terminating any matched hedging arrangements and incurring breakage costs;**
- **reduce your exposure by assigning some Transactions for a fee. This involves finding another counterparty to take on your obligations under a Transaction;**
- **cross refer to covenants or Events of Default in an existing loan facility agreement with your counterparty to ensure Cross Default into the Agreement if a loan facility breach occurs;**
- **with investment manager or hedge fund counterparties set a minimum net asset value covenant for the underlying fund;**

- **if you can, use adequate assurance provisions with weak counterparties. These are invoked where you have reasonable doubts about whether they will be able to make their payment on the next Scheduled Payment Date and the weaker party fails to give adequate assurances within a time limit. This can give rise to an Additional Termination Event or allow the stronger party to defer its payment to the next following Payment Date at an interest cost. This is an unpopular provision and does not enhance the commercial relationship with a weaker counterparty.**

The Agreement already offers strong protection. Deployment of some of the above measures reinforces these benefits. The problem is, that in many cases, counterparties will try to negotiate reciprocity.

THE "VANILLA ISDA"

What happens if a deal is done and your Agreement is not signed

The trade Confirmation normally states parties must use their best endeavours to enter into an Agreement if one is not in place already.

Total deadlock in negotiations is rare but where it arises and it is likely to be prolonged, an early block is put on further trading and the residual limit. At that point the parties would normally sign an Agreement incorporating areas where they can agree and not trade further. Deadlock areas can be cross acceleration, set off and Threshold Amount.

Then the more flexible party can wait for the deals to mature or try to assign them or terminate them if a Section 5 event occurs.

However, there is, of course, a more normal documentation risk during the period between a deal being transacted and an Agreement being signed. Following the signing of a Confirmation, lawyers believe that a "vanilla ISDA" exists until an Agreement is signed. The Confirmation is usually stated to be subject to the terms of an ISDA Master Agreement without a Schedule (i.e. unamended). However, without the Schedule the parties cannot make their own choices for:

- **Specified Entities**
- **Threshold Amount**
- **Cross Default and Credit Event Upon Merger to apply**
- **Automatic Early Termination**
- **Payment measures and methods with respect to the 1992 Agreement only**
- **Termination Currency**

- Additional Termination Events
- Tax Representations
- Documents to be delivered
- Notices
- Process Agent
- Multibranch Parties
- Credit support
- Scope of payment netting
- Set off with respect to the 1992 Agreement only
- Non-reliance
- No agency
- Specified Entities for Absence of Litigation representation (2002 Agreement only)
- Consent to recording.

Some, but not all of these might be covered in a Confirmation but this would make the Confirmation unwieldy and difficult to negotiate. If no choices are made at all certain fallbacks automatically kick in, e.g. Market Quotation, Second Method and US$ as the Termination Currency under the 1992 Agreement.

It is therefore important to execute an Agreement as quickly as possible for four good reasons:

- it is easy to do further transactions (credit lines permitting) if an Agreement is already in place;
- many products can be covered under the terms of the same Agreement;
- the close-out mechanism under the Agreement is proven;
- the single agreement concept prevents liquidators "cherry picking".

The importance of the right documentation for product and branch cover purposes

It is no good having signed but defective ISDA documentation. This normally happens in two ways.

A bank may only have a 1987 Agreement in place with a particular counterparty (e.g. another bank). The 1987 Agreement in itself only covers interest rate and currency swaps. If dealers trade a cap it would not be covered by the 1987 Agreement. To remedy this you could either enter into a 1989 Addendum (which would be an enormously old fashioned thing to do) or a 1992 or 2002 Agreement which automatically covers caps. This is the better solution.

The 1987 Agreement has largely been replaced by the 1992 Agreement, but not in all cases. I know one bank which sought to document credit derivatives under a 1987 Agreement it had with another bank. They have now negotiated a 1992 Agreement.

It is possible that an existing Agreement only covers your counterparty's overseas Head Office. Your dealer trades a swap with their London branch. An Amendment Agreement or the negotiation of a multibranch Agreement would be necessary to cover the new trade.

If nothing is done, the parties are left with the Confirmation, rights under any signed 1987 Agreement between them or the "vanilla ISDA" if no ISDA has been signed between them. As always, it is better to get things right and not incur credit and documentation risk.

Operational issues 7

Confirmations

Payments

Deliveries

Close-out

Administrative matters

Chapter 1 briefly described some of the functions of an Operations Department but let us now review the elements of the 1992 and 2002 Agreements impacted by operational issues.

CONFIRMATIONS

The Confirmation makes its first appearance in the preamble on page 1 of both Agreements where it is described, with the Schedule, as included in the relevant Agreement.

In Section 1(b), the Confirmation has supremacy over the relevant Agreement where there is any conflict or inconsistency involving specific Transactions. It is therefore vital that the terms of the Confirmation are correctly drafted because they will prevail, unless otherwise agreed in the Schedule (which is rare) in respect of individual Transactions.

In Section 1(c), the Confirmations are one of the elements forming the single agreement designed to stop liquidators cherry picking.

In Section 2(a)(i), parties are obliged to make each payment or delivery specified in the Confirmation. This is expanded upon in Section 2(a)(ii) which states that payments will be made promptly on their due date in the recipient's jurisdiction as specified in the Confirmation. As regards deliveries, these will be made on the due date in the customary manner unless the Confirmation specifies otherwise. The Confirmation is very much tailored to the requirements of the particular deal.

In Part 2(c) payment netting across more than one Transaction in the same currency and for the same value date may be chosen in the Confirmation although it is more likely the election will be made in Part 4(i) of the Schedule.

In the preamble to Section 3 in the 2002 Agreement it is possible for Additional Representations to be specified in a Confirmation as an alternative to Part 4(m) of the Schedule.

Section 4(a)(i) and (ii) state that tax or other required documentation may be specified in a Confirmation although it is more usual to do this in Part 3 of the Schedule.

In the new Section 5(a)(ii)(2) which concerns Repudiation of Agreement if a party repudiates a Confirmation this constitutes an Event of Default without any grace period.

In Section 5(b)(i) and (ii) the calling of an Illegality or Force Majeure Event Termination Event will follow giving effect to any disruption fallback or remedy allowed in an ISDA Definitions booklet or in a Confirmation.

In Section 8 the Contractual Currency in which payments will be made under the Agreement will be part of the economic terms of the Confirmation.

Section 9(e)(ii) states that a Confirmation will be entered into as soon as possible after the oral telephone contract for the deal. A Confirmation can be a single document signed by both parties or two identical documents (called counterparts) signed by each party and which they would normally fax to each other. Together they constitute a fully signed Confirmation. The use of telexes or electronic messaging systems can also create a legally binding Confirmation and with the 2002 Agreement e-mail can also be used to confirm Transactions.

In Section 9(h)(i)(2) of the 2002 Agreement compensation for defaulted deliveries will be calculated in accordance with the Confirmation terms. The same applies to deferred deliveries under Section 9(h)(i)(4).

Section 10(c) deals with a multibranch situation where there is a requirement that payments through a party's Offices (branches) need to be specified in the Confirmation. Where this is not done the fallback in the 2002 Agreement (but not in the 1992 Agreement) will be that payment will be made through the party's head or home office.

The Confirmation will state who is Calculation Agent but this can also, or alternatively, be specified in Part 4(e) of the Schedule.

PAYMENTS

Clearly payments and deliveries are very important under both the Confirmation and the Agreement itself.

Section 2(a)(i) and (ii) have already been referred to in connection with Confirmations. Section 2(a)(iii) states that normal payments or deliveries could be abandoned under the Agreement if the Non-defaulting Party so chooses if:

- **an Event of Default or a Potential Event of Default (which would become an Event of Default if notice is given by the Non-defaulting Party) occurs or continues; or**
- **an Early Termination Date for close out of one, some or all Transactions has been designated by the Non-defaulting Party; or**
- **some other condition precedent in the Agreement (e.g. provision of credit support or a legal opinion) is unfulfilled.**

If the Non-defaulting Party decides to act on any of these events all payments and deliveries are suspended and the parties move into a close-out situation under Section 6(c).

In Section 2(b) a party may give five Local Business Days' notice to change its account for receiving payments or deliveries provided the other party does not reasonably object.

Payment or settlement netting first appears in Section 2(c). It is designed to reduce settlement risk by avoiding the need for gross payments to flow in opposite directions under the same Transaction between the two parties in the same currency and on the same value date. That obligation is replaced by another under which payments are offset or netted against each other and the party owing the most pays the difference to the other.

The basic position in Section 2(c) is single Transaction netting where payments or deliveries are netted in respect of the same Transaction, value date and currency. These conditions need not apply if parties so choose in Part 4(i) of the Schedule. That would allow payments under more than one Transaction of the same type (e.g. interest rate swaps) to be netted or even for payments due in the same currency and on the same value dates but for different products to be netted.

It is vital that parties only commit to what they can actually do operationally.

There has been a tendency in Part 4(i) of the Schedule for parties to agree to multiple Transaction or cross-product netting whether or not they have systems to cope with this. They do this in the hope that one day they will develop such systems and will not need to amend the Schedule. Clearly the sophistication of parties' systems develops at different speeds and it would be embarrassing if one party developed a state of the art payment netting system and then called the other's bluff by insisting on cross-product netting because of a commitment given in Part 4(i) of the Schedule.

Many banks have adopted a more critical approach to their payment netting capabilities by agreeing to multiple Transaction or cross-product netting with particular products but stating that this will not apply to other categories such as FX Transactions or Currency Options.

The choice of the scope of payment netting can therefore impact upon certain groups of Transactions or in respect of the parties' individual pairs of Offices.

There is less scope for netting in respect of deliveries of physical stocks or commodities which is why I have focused on payment netting. However, it is possible on some occasions.

The position with payments afflicted by withholding tax as described in Section 2(d) has already been discussed at pages 41–5.

Section 2(e) in the 1992 Agreement deals with the question of default interest which is incurred following late payments of amounts due. Default interest is payable at the Default Rate (i.e. 1% over the Non-defaulting Party's cost of funds) from and including the date the payment was actually due to but excluding the date it is actually made. This is in respect of payments made in the normal course, i.e. in the absence of any Early Termination Date having been designated.

The compensation mechanism for late deliveries needs to be specified in the Confirmation for the deal concerned.

In the 2002 Agreement interest or compensation for late payments or deliveries is extensively treated in Section 9(h), a sub-section which accounts for about 7% of the Agreement's main text.

Payments or deliveries are also suspended during Waiting Periods for Illegality or Force Majeure Event (see Section 5(d) of the 2002 Agreement).

DELIVERIES

It is worth stressing that while the 1992 Agreement provides a detailed description of payment obligations it is more "woolly" on delivery obligations which are normally fleshed out in Confirmations for physically settled Transactions. For instance, it is important that the Confirmation has provisions for interest and/or damages for late delivery of securities or commodities (which the Non-defaulting Party may have pre-sold to a third party). As mentioned above, Section 9(h) of the 2002 Agreement now covers this comprehensively.

Matters relevant to physical deliveries which are not really covered by the 1992 Agreement itself include:

- **delivery versus payment or what happens if this is not possible;**
- **treatment of partial deliveries;**
- **compensation for delivery failures (but see Section 9(h) of the 2002 Agreement);**
- **relevant grace periods (the 2002 Agreement provides for a one Local Delivery Day grace period);**
- **market disruption events;**
- **disruption fallbacks;**
- **failures in settlement systems;**
- **redefinition of Local Business Day in terms of exchange trading days (partially done in the 2002 Agreement in respect of days when settlement systems are open for business within the definition of Local Delivery Day);**
- **who bears registration and settlement costs;**
- **automatic exercise with physically settled options;**
- **representation as to delivery being made with good title;**
- **possible inclusion of Impossibility clause (Force Majeure Event in the 2002 Agreement);**
- **use of Loss as payment measure (generally regarded as better for physical delivery);**
- **consideration of tax issues relating to physical delivery of assets.**

Of course, some of these matters can be included in special additional Parts to the Agreement Schedule, e.g. a Part 7 on metals or other commodity products.

These matters are usually either expanded upon in Confirmations themselves or, more often, are dealt with by way of choices in Confirmations which refer to very detailed provisions in the relevant product Definitions based upon market practice.

CLOSE-OUT

This area has undergone substantial alteration in the 2002 Agreement (see Chapter 4 pages 215–17).

With close-out situations in Section 6 of the 1992 Agreement it would be normal for dealers to obtain Market Quotations and calculate the replacement value of Transactions to be terminated or to determine the amounts due under Loss. The same would apply with the calculation of Close-out Amount by a Determining Party under the 2002 Agreement.

However, an Operations section would normally be involved in checking the calculations. The Legal Department would usually compose and send a notice specifying the nature of the Event of Default and claiming the relevant termination payment from a Defaulting Party or advising such party of any net amount due to it. The Operations section would need to monitor receipt of such payment from the Defaulting Party or make any necessary close-out net payment to them after taking account of any possible set off against any of the Defaulting Party's other assets or liabilities recorded in the Non-defaulting Party's books.

The Operations section and the Legal Department would also work closely together to monitor the effects of any Illegality or Force Majeure Event which led to a suspension of payments or deliveries during a Waiting Period under the 2002 Agreement. The Operations Department and the dealers would gauge if they wanted to close out further Affected Transactions in these circumstances if the Affected Party chose only to close out some of them.

Section 8 of the Agreement would also involve an Operations section. In the normal course they would need to ensure that payments are received in the Contractual Currency. Where any other currency is involved they would make any necessary currency conversion and claim any shortfall or pay over any surplus arising from the conversion.

While it is possible that a Non-defaulting Party's Operations section might be involved in the invoicing and collection of Section 11 expenses arising from the enforcement or protection of its rights under the Agreement or any Credit Support Document given by the Defaulting Party, this would more likely be done by the Legal Department.

ADMINISTRATIVE MATTERS

These include:

- recording change of account details (Section 2(b));
- calculating default interest or compensation for late deliveries (Section 2(e) of the 1992 Agreement or Section 9(h) of the 2002 Agreement);
- paying relevant Stamp Tax (Section 4(e));
- giving notice under the Agreement including in relation to such matters as address changes and other changes to static data (Section 12). It is likely that the Legal Department will give any notices required in connection with Sections 5 and 6 of the Agreement.

Negotiation of an ISDA Master Agreement Schedule

8

Sample Schedule

Variants and implications of each provision

Other provisions commonly seen in the market and their implications

Part 6 – FX Transactions and Currency Options

ISDA Master Agreement Schedules come in all shapes and sizes. Many banks compose a general Schedule and base variants for specific entities (e.g. corporates, building societies, pension fund trustees and hedge funds) upon it.

Starting with such a general purpose Schedule, the purpose of this chapter is to comment on the items covered in the Schedule – to play Devil's Advocate to some extent and to point out variants and their implications. Clearly, I cannot show every single variant ever devised but I hope to cover a good cross-section of what has been seen in the European market over the past few years. As in the previous version of this book this chapter will focus upon the 1992 ISDA Master Agreement as so few 2002 Agreement Schedules exist at present.

Let's start with a sample Schedule between an imaginary German bank and an English company.

SAMPLE SCHEDULE

SCHEDULE
to the
ISDA Master Agreement

dated as of [ ]

between:

X Bank AG ("Party A")

and

Rollerblade plc ("Party B")

Part I Termination provisions

(a) ***"Specified Entity"*** means in relation to Party A for the purpose of:

Section 5(a)(v), none

Section 5(a)(vi), none

Section 5(a)(vii), none

Section 5(b)(iv), none

and in relation to Party B for the purpose of:

Section 5(a)(v), Any Affiliate.

Section 5(a)(vi), Any Affiliate.

Section 5(a)(vii), Any Affiliate.

Section 5(b)(iv), Any Affiliate.

(b) *"Specified Transaction"* will have the meaning specified in Section 14 of this Agreement.

(c) The ***"Cross Default"*** provisions of Section 5(a)(vi) will apply to Party A and will apply to Party B except that the following provision shall be inserted at the end of Section 5(a)(vi):

"*provided, however*, that an Event of Default shall not occur under either (1) or (2) above if the default, Event of Default or other similar event or condition referred to in (1) or the failure to pay referred to in (2) is a failure to pay caused by an error or omission of an administrative or operational nature and funds were available to such party to enable it to make the relevant payment when due and such payment is in fact made on or before the third Local Business Day following receipt of written notice from the other party of such failure to pay".

If such provisions apply:

"Specified Indebtedness" shall mean any obligation (whether present or future, contingent or otherwise, as principal or surety or otherwise) in respect of borrowed money other than indebtedness in respect of deposits received in the ordinary course of business.

"Threshold Amount" means for Party A and Party B and any relevant Specified Entity (if any) an amount equal to 3% of that party's shareholders' equity as specified in that party's latest published audited accounts, or its equivalent in any other currency.

(d) The ***"Credit Event Upon Merger"*** provisions of Section 5(b)(iv) will apply to Party A and will apply to Party B, amended as follows:

"Credit Event Upon Merger" shall mean that a Designated Event (as defined below) occurs with respect to a party ("X"), and such Designated Event does not constitute an event described in Section 5(a)(viii) but the creditworthiness of X or, if applicable, the successor, surviving or transferee entity of X, (which in either case will be the Affected Party) is materially weaker than that of X, immediately prior to such event. For purposes hereof, a Designated Event means that after the execution date hereof:

(i) X consolidates, amalgamates with or merges with or into, or transfers all or substantially all its assets to, or receives all or substantially all the assets or obligations of, another entity; or
(ii) any person or entity acquires directly or indirectly the beneficial ownership of equity securities having the power to elect a majority of the board of directors of X or otherwise acquires directly or indirectly the power to control the policy-making decisions of X; or
(iii) X enters into an agreement providing for any of the foregoing.

For purposes hereof, X or the successor, surviving or transferee entity, as appropriate, will be the Affected Party.

Moreover, for the purposes of Section 5(b)(iv) "materially weaker" shall mean the following:

> If either Party A or Party B fails to maintain a long term, unsecured and unsubordinated debt rating of at least BBB – as determined by Standard & Poor's Ratings Group, a division of the McGraw-Hill Companies or Baa3 as determined by Moody's Investors Service Inc.

(e) The ***"Automatic Early Termination"*** provision of Section 6(a) will not apply to Party A and Party B; provided, however, that where there is an Event of Default under Section 5(a)(vii)(1), (3), (4), (5), (6) or to the extent analogous thereto, (8), and the Defaulting Party is governed by a system of law that would not otherwise permit termination to take place, then the Automatic Early Termination provisions of Section 6(a) will apply.

(f) ***Payments on Early Termination.*** For the purpose of Section 6(e) of this Agreement:

  (i) Market Quotation will apply.

  (ii) The Second Method will apply.

(g) ***"Termination Currency"*** means the currency selected by the Non-defaulting Party or the non-Affected Party, as the case may be, or, in circumstances where there are two Affected Parties, as agreed by Party A and Party B. However, the Termination Currency shall be one of the currencies in which payments in respect of Transactions are required to be made by the Confirmations. If the currency selected is not freely available, or, where there are two Affected Parties, and Party A and Party B cannot agree on a Termination Currency, the Termination Currency shall be United States Dollars.

(h) ***Additional Termination Event*** will apply and the following shall constitute an Additional Termination Event:

> ***Change of Ownership.*** Rollerblade Corporation Inc either directly or indirectly ceases to own directly or indirectly 51 per cent of the issued share capital of Party B carrying voting rights in ordinary circumstances in a general meeting of shareholders or a comparable meeting of Party B or otherwise directly or indirectly ceases to control the board of directors of Party B and/or Party B ceases to be a fully consolidated subsidiary of Rollerblade Corporation Inc.

For the purposes of the foregoing Termination Event, Party B shall be the Affected Party.

Part 2 Tax Representations

(a) ***Payer Representations.*** For the purpose of Section 3(e) of this Agreement, Party A will make the following representation and Party B will make the following representation:

It is not required by any applicable law, as modified by the practice of any relevant governmental revenue authority of any Relevant Jurisdiction to make any deduction or withholding for or on account of any Tax from any payment (other than interest under Section 2(e), 6(d)(ii) or 6(e) of this Agreement) to be made by it to the other party under this Agreement. In making this representation, it may rely on (i) the accuracy of any representations made by the other party pursuant to Section 3(f) of this Agreement, (ii) the satisfaction of the agreement contained in Section 4(a)(i) or 4(a)(iii) of this Agreement and the accuracy and effectiveness of any document provided by the other party pursuant to Section 4(a)(i) or 4(a)(iii) of this Agreement and (iii) the satisfaction of the agreement of the other party contained in Section 4(d) of this Agreement provided that it shall not be a breach of this representation where reliance is placed on clause (ii) and the other party does not deliver a form or document under Section 4(a)(iii) by reason of material prejudice to its legal or commercial position.

(b) ***Payee Representations.*** For the purpose of Section 3(f) of this Agreement, neither Party A nor Party B makes any Payee Tax Representations.

Part 3 Agreement to Deliver Documents

For the purpose of Sections 4(a)(i) and (ii) of this Agreement, each party agrees to deliver the following documents:

(a) Tax forms, documents or certificates to be delivered are:

None.

(b) Other documents to be delivered are:

	Party required to deliver document	**Document**	**Date by which to be delivered**	**Covered by Section 3(d) representation**
(i)	Party A and Party B	Certified evidence of the authority, incumbency and specimen signature of each person executing any document on its behalf in connection with this Agreement.	Upon execution of this Agreement and upon request.	Yes
(ii)	Party A and Party B	A copy of its most recent Annual Report containing consolidated financial statements, prepared in accordance with accounting principles that are generally accepted for institutions of its type in the jurisdiction of its organisation and certified by independent public accountants.	Upon request.	No
(iii)	Party B	Evidence of its capacity and ability to enter into this Agreement and any Transaction hereunder.	Upon execution of this Agreement and upon request.	Yes

Part 4 Miscellaneous

(a) ***Addresses for notices.*** For the purpose of Section 12(a) of this Agreement:

Addresses for notices or communications to Party A

For all purposes of this Agreement:

X Bank AG, Frankfurt Head Office

Address: Complete relevant details
Attention: Complete relevant details
Telex: Complete relevant details Answerback: Complete details
Facsimile: Complete relevant details
Telephone: Complete relevant details
Electronic Messaging System Details: Complete relevant details

X Bank AG, London Branch

Address: Complete relevant details
Attention: Complete relevant details
Telex: Complete relevant details Answerback: Complete details
Facsimile: Complete relevant details
Telephone: Complete relevant details
Electronic Messaging System Details: Complete relevant details

Address for notices or communications to Party B:

Address: Complete relevant details
Attention: Complete relevant details
Telex: Complete relevant details Answerback: Complete details
Facsimile: Complete relevant details
Telephone: Complete relevant details
Electronic Messaging System Details: Complete relevant details

(b) ***Process Agent.*** For the purpose of Section 13(c) of this Agreement:

Party A appoints as its Process Agent:
X Bank AG, London Branch
[*Insert London address*]

Attention: General Manager

Party B appoints as its Process Agent:

Not applicable.

(c) ***Offices.*** The provisions of Section 10(a) will apply to this Agreement.

(d) ***Multibranch Party.*** For the purpose of Section 10(c) of this Agreement:

Party A is a Multibranch Party and may act through the following Offices:

Frankfurt and London.

Party B is not a Multibranch Party.

(e) ***Calculation Agent.*** The Calculation Agent is Party A, unless otherwise specified in a Confirmation in relation to the relevant Transaction.

(f) ***Credit Support Document.*** Details of any Credit Support Document.

None.

(g) ***Credit Support Provider.***

Credit Support Provider means in relation to Party A: Not applicable.

Credit Support Provider means in relation to Party B: Not applicable.

(h) ***Governing Law.*** This Agreement will be governed by and construed in accordance with English law.

(i) ***Netting of Payments.*** Subparagraph (ii) of Section 2(c) of this Agreement will not apply to any Transactions or group of Transactions.

(j) ***"Affiliate"*** will have the meaning specified in Section 14 of this Agreement.

Part 5 Other Provisions

(a) *No Agency*. Section 3(a) of this Agreement is hereby amended by the deletion of "and" at the end of sub-clause (iv), the substitution of a semi-colon for the full-stop at the end of sub-clause (v) and the addition of the following at the end thereof:

"and (vi) *No Agency*. Each party represents to the other that it is entering into this Agreement, any Credit Support Document to which it is a party, each Transaction and any other documentation relating to this Agreement or any Transaction as principal and not as agent of any person."

(b) (f) Section 6 of this Agreement is amended by the addition of the following new Section 6(f):

"(f) *Set-off* Any amount (the 'Early Termination Amount') payable to one party (the Payee) by the other party (the Payer) under Section 6(e), in circumstances where there is a Defaulting Party or one Affected Party in the case where a Termination Event under Section 5(b)(iv) has occurred, will, at the option of the party ('X') other than the Defaulting Party or the Affected Party (and without prior notice to the Defaulting Party or the Affected Party), be reduced by its set-off against any amount(s) (the 'Other Agreement Amount') payable (whether at such time or in the future or upon the occurrence of a contingency) by the Payee to the Payer (irrespective of the currency, place of payment or booking office of the obligation) under any other agreement(s) between the Payee and the Payer or instrument(s) or undertaking(s) issued or executed by one party to, or in favour of, the other party (and the Other Agreement Amount will be discharged promptly and in all respects to the extent it is so set-off). X will give notice to the other party of any set-off effected under this Section 6(f).

For this purpose, either the Early Termination Amount or the Other Agreement Amount (or the relevant portion of such amounts) may be converted by X into the currency in which the other is denominated at the rate of exchange at which such party would be able, acting in a reasonable manner and in good faith, to purchase the relevant amount of such currency.

If an obligation is unascertained, X may in good faith estimate that obligation and set-off in respect of the estimate, subject to the relevant party accounting to the other when the obligation is ascertained.

Nothing in this Section 6(f) shall be effective to create a charge or other security interest. This Section 6(f) shall be without prejudice and in addition to any right of set-off, combination of accounts, lien or other right to which any party is at any time otherwise entitled (whether by operation of law, contract or otherwise)."

(c) ***Definitions.*** "Indemnifiable Tax" add after "or a Credit Support Document)":

"Notwithstanding the foregoing, 'Indemnifiable Tax' also means any Tax imposed in respect of a payment under this Agreement by reason of a Change in Tax Law by a government or taxing authority of a Relevant Jurisdiction of the party making such payment, unless the other party is incorporated, organised, managed and controlled or considered to have its seat in such jurisdiction, or is acting for purposes of this Agreement through a branch or office located in such jurisdiction."

(d) ***Transfer.*** Section 7 of this Agreement shall be amended by inserting the following phrase "which consent shall not be unreasonably withheld" in the third line thereof after the word "party" and before the word "except".

(e) ***Consent to recording.*** Each party (i) consents to the recording of the telephone conversations of trading, marketing and other relevant personnel of the parties in connection with this Agreement or any potential Transaction and (ii) agrees that any such recording may be submitted in evidence to any court or in any proceedings with respect to this Agreement or any Transaction thereunder.

(f) ***Relationship between parties.*** Each party will be deemed to represent to the other party on the date on which it enters into a Transaction that (absent a written agreement between the parties that expressly imposes affirmative obligations to the contrary for that Transaction):

(a) ***Non-Reliance.*** It is acting for its own account, and it has made its own independent decisions to enter into that Transaction and as to whether that Transaction is appropriate or proper for it based upon its own judgment and upon advice from such advisers as it has deemed necessary. It is not relying on any communication (written or oral) of the other party as investment advice or as a recommendation to enter into that Transaction; it being understood that information and explanations related to the terms and conditions of a Transaction shall not be considered investment advice or a recommendation to enter into that Transaction. No communication (written or oral) received from the other party shall be deemed to be an assurance or guarantee as to the expected results of that Transaction.

(b) ***Assessment and Understanding.*** It is capable of assessing the merits of and understanding (on its own behalf or through independent professional advice), and understands and accepts the terms, conditions and risks of that Transaction. It is also capable of assuming, and assumes, the risks of that Transaction.

(c) ***Status of Parties.*** The other party is not acting as a fiduciary or an adviser to it in respect of that Transaction.

[(g) ***Incorporation of ISDA EMU Protocol.*** The parties agree that the definitions and provisions contained in Annexes 1 to 5 and Section 6 of the EMU Protocol published by the International Swaps and Derivatives Association, Inc. on 6 May 1998 are incorporated into and apply to this Agreement. References in those definitions and provisions to any "ISDA Master Agreement" will be deemed to be references to this Agreement.]

(h) *Scope of Agreement.* Notwithstanding anything contained in the Agreement to the contrary, if the parties enter or have entered into any Specified Transaction, such Specified Transaction shall be subject to, governed by and construed in accordance with the terms of the Agreement unless the Confirmation relating thereto shall specifically state to the contrary. Each such Specified Transaction shall be a Transaction for the purposes of this Agreement. In the event of any inconsistency between the terms of such Specified Transaction and the terms of this Agreement, the terms of that Specified Transaction shall prevail.

(i) ***Contracts (Rights of Third Parties)* Act 1999.** A person who is not a party to this Agreement shall have no right under the Contracts (Rights of Third Parties) Act 1999 to enforce any of its terms.

Part 6 – FX Transactions and Currency Options

(a) **Incorporation and Amendment of 1998 FX and Currency Option Definitions**

(i) *Incorporation of 1998 FX and Currency Option Definitions*

The 1998 FX and Currency Option Definitions (the "1998 Definitions"), published by the International Swaps and Derivatives Association, Inc., the Emerging Markets Traders Association and The Foreign Exchange Committee, are hereby incorporated by reference with respect to any "Currency Option Transactions" and "FX Transactions" as defined by the 1998 Definitions, except as otherwise specifically provided herein or in the Confirmation.

(ii) *Amendment of 1998 FX and Currency Option Definitions.* The following amendments are made to the 1998 Definitions:

(1) Section 2.1 of the 1998 Definitions is amended by adding the following as Section 2.1(b):

(b) **Currency Obligation.** "Currency Obligation" means the undertaking of a party hereunder to receive or deliver an amount of currency, including a netted Currency Obligation, and including any Currency Obligation previously entered into by the parties.

(2) The following provision is hereby added to Article 3.4:

(c) **Remedies in Event of Non-Payment.** If a Premium is not received on the Premium Payment Date, the Seller may elect: (i) to accept a late payment of such Premium; (ii) to give written notice of such non-payment and, if such payment shall not be received within two (2) Local Business Days of such notice, treat the related Currency Option Transaction as void; or (iii) to give written notice of such non-payment and, if such payment shall not be received within two (2) Local Business Days of such notice, treat such non-payment as an Event of Default under Section 5(a)(i). If the Seller elects to act under clause (i) of the preceding sentence, the Buyer shall pay interest on such Premium in the same currency as such Premium from the day such Premium was due until the day paid at the Default Rate; if the Seller elects to act under clause (ii) of the preceding sentence, the Buyer shall pay all out-of-pocket costs and actual damages incurred in connection with such unpaid or late Premium in the same currency as such Premium at the then prevailing market rate and any other costs or expenses incurred by the Seller in covering its obligations (including, without limitation, a delta hedge) with respect to such Currency Option Transaction.

(3) Section 3.6(a) is hereby amended by deleting in its entirety the final sentence thereof and adding in its place the following:

"A Currency Option Transaction may be exercised in whole or in part. If a Currency Option Transaction is exercised in part, the unexercised portion shall not be extinguished thereby but shall remain a Currency Option Transaction to the extent of such unexercised portion until the earlier of: (i) the expiration of the Currency Option Transaction; or (ii) an exercise of the Currency Option Transaction that leaves no remaining unexercised portion thereof."

(b) **Confirmations.** Any confirmation in respect of any FX Transaction or Currency Option Transaction into which the parties may enter, or may have entered into prior to the date hereof, that fails by its terms expressly to exclude the application of this Agreement shall (to the extent not otherwise provided for in this Agreement) (i) constitute a "Confirmation" as referred to in this Agreement even where not so specified in such confirmation and (ii) supplement, form a part of, and be subject to this Agreement, and all provisions in this Agreement will govern such Confirmation except as modified therein. Without limitation of the foregoing, where an FX Transaction or Currency Option Transaction is confirmed by means of exchange of electronic messages on an electronic messaging system or by means of facsimile or telex (whether manually or automatically generated) or other document or confirming evidence exchanged between the parties confirming such Transaction, such messages, facsimile transmission, document or evidence shall constitute a Confirmation for the purposes of this Agreement even where not so specified therein. FX Transactions and Currency Option Transactions shall be promptly confirmed by the parties by Confirmations exchanged by mail, telex, facsimile or other electronic means. Unless either party objects to the terms of an FX Transaction or Currency Option Transaction contained in any Confirmation within three (3) Local Business Days of receipt thereof, the terms of such Confirmation shall be deemed correct and accepted absent manifest error, unless a corrected Confirmation is sent by a party within such three Local Business Day period, in which case the party receiving such corrected Confirmation shall have two (2) Local Business Days after receipt thereof to object to the terms contained in such corrected Confirmation.

(c) **Netting and Related Provisions.** Section 2(c) shall not apply to FX Transactions or Currency Option Transactions. In lieu thereof, the following shall apply:

(i) *Netting. Offset and Discharge with Respect to Currency Options.* The following provisions shall apply to Currency Option Transactions:

(1) If, on any date, and unless otherwise mutually agreed by the parties Premium would otherwise be payable hereunder in the same currency between a pair of Offices of the parties, then, on such date, each party's obligation to make payment of any such Premium will be automatically satisfied and discharged and, if the aggregate Premium(s) that would otherwise have been payable by such Office of one party exceeds the aggregate Premium(s) that would otherwise have been payable by such Office of the other party, be replaced by an obligation upon the party by whom the larger aggregate Premium(s) would have been payable to pay the other party the excess of the larger aggregate Premium(s) over the smaller aggregate Premium(s).

(2) If, on any date, and unless otherwise mutually agreed by the parties, amounts other than Premium payments would otherwise be payable hereunder in the same currency between a pair of Offices of the parties, then, on such date, each party's obligation to make payment of any such amount will be automatically satisfied and discharged and, if the aggregate amount that would otherwise have been payable by such Office of one party exceeds the aggregate amount that would otherwise have been payable by such

Office of the other party, be replaced by an obligation upon the party by whom the larger aggregate amount would have been payable to pay the other party the excess of the larger aggregate amount over the smaller aggregate amount.

(3) Unless otherwise agreed, any Call or any Put written by a party will automatically be terminated and discharged, in whole or in part, as applicable, against a Call or a Put, respectively, written by the other party, such termination and discharge to occur automatically upon the payment in full of the last Premium payable in respect of such Currency Option Transactions; provided that such termination and discharge may only occur in respect of Currency Option Transactions:

(A) each being with respect to the same Put Currency and the same Call Currency;

(B) each having the same Expiration Date and Expiration Time, and with respect to Bermuda Style Options, each having the same Specified Exercise Dates;

(C) each being of the same style, i.e. both being American Style Options or both being European Style Options or both being Bermuda Style Options;

(D) each having the same Strike Price;

(E) neither of which shall have been exercised by delivery of a Notice of Exercise;

(F) which are entered into by the same Offices of the parties; and

(G) which are otherwise identical in terms that are material for the purposes of offset and discharge;

and, upon the occurrence of such termination and discharge, neither party shall have any further obligation to the other party in respect of the relevant Currency Option Transactions or, as the case may be, parts thereof so terminated and discharged. In the case of a partial termination and discharge (i.e. where the relevant Currency Option Transactions are for different amounts of the Currency Pair), the remaining portion of the Currency Option Transaction which is partially discharged and terminated shall continue to be a Currency Option Transaction for all purposes of this Agreement.

(ii) *Netting, Discharge and Termination of FX Transactions.* The following provisions shall apply to FX Transactions:

(1) Unless otherwise agreed by the parties hereto, whenever an FX Transaction is entered into between a pair of Netting Offices of the parties which creates a Currency Obligation in the same currency and for the same Settlement Date as an existing Currency Obligation between such Netting Offices, such Currency Obligations shall automatically and without further action be netted, individually cancelled and simultaneously replaced through novation by a new Currency Obligation determined as follows: (A) if the cancelled Currency Obligations evidence an undertaking by the same party to deliver the underlying currency, the new Currency Obligation shall equal the aggregate of the cancelled Currency Obligations, and (B) if the cancelled Currency Obligations evidence an undertaking by each party to deliver the underlying currency, the amount of the underlying currency to be delivered by each party under the cancelled Currency Obligations shall be compared, and the new Currency Obligation shall equal the amount by which the Currency Obligation of the party having the greater obligation with respect to such currency exceeds the Currency Obligation of the party having the lesser obligation with respect to such currency. Such new Currency Obligation shall be considered a "Currency Obligation" under this Agreement.

(2) The provisions of Part 6(c)(ii)(1) above shall apply notwithstanding that either party (A) may fail to send out a Confirmation, (B) may not on its books treat the Currency Obligations as cancelled and simultaneously replaced by a new Currency Obligation as provided herein, or (C) may send out a Confirmation that incorrectly states any term of a Currency Obligation.

(3) If on any Settlement Date, and unless otherwise mutually agreed by the parties, Currency Obligations (which are not subject to the provisions of Part 6(c)(ii)(1) hereof) for the delivery of the same currency shall exist between a pair of Netting Offices of the parties, then on such Settlement Date, each party's Currency Obligation to deliver that currency will be automatically satisfied and discharged and, if the aggregate amount that would otherwise have been delivered by such Netting Office of one party exceeds the aggregate amount that would otherwise have been

delivered by such Netting Office of the other party, replaced by a Currency Obligation upon the party by whom the larger aggregate amount would have been deliverable to deliver to the other party the excess of the larger aggregate amount over the smaller aggregate amount and if the aggregate amounts are equal no delivery of that Currency Obligation shall be made.

(4) For the purposes of this Part 6(d), "Netting Offices" means (i) with respect to Party A, Frankfurt and London; and (ii) with respect to Party B, London. The Netting Offices with respect to a party may be modified from time to time pursuant to notice given in accordance with the terms of Section 12.

(d) **Definitions.** Section 14 is hereby amended as follows:

The definition of "Terminated Transactions" shall be deemed to include Currency Obligations.

Let us now review the various Parts of the Schedule, comment on the provisions and show common variants drawing out their implications where necessary.

SCHEDULE
to the
ISDA Master Agreement

dated as of [ ]

between:

X Bank AG ("Party A")

and

Rollerblade plc ("Party B")

VARIANTS AND IMPLICATIONS OF EACH PROVISION

First of all the Schedule is dated as of the same date as the Agreement. This is normally the date of the first trade outstanding between the parties. Where the Agreement is an update or restatement of a previous Agreement and there are many trades between the parties, for the sake of convenience, they often choose to date the restated Agreement as of the same date as the original one.

The full legal names of Party A and Party B are then set out.

Occasionally you may have joint counterparties as in this example:-

X Bank AG

("Party A")

and

Tuna Fisheries LP and Piscatorial Processing LLC

(collectively "Party B")

This is, however, rare.

Part 1 Termination Provisions

(a) "*Specified Entity*" means in relation to Party A for the purpose of:

Section 5(a)(v), none

Section 5(a)(vi), none

Section 5(a)(vii), none

Section 5(b)(iv), none

and in relation to Party B for the purpose of:

Section 5(a)(v), Any Affiliate.

Section 5(a)(vi), Any Affiliate.

Section 5(a)(vii), Any Affiliate.

Section 5(b)(iv), Any Affiliate.

Part 1(a) Specified Entity

Specified Entities are nominated third parties or generic groups which one or both of the parties to an Agreement want to join in to Section 5(a)(v)–(vii) and Section 5(b)(iv) so that in its basic form any Default Under Specified Transaction, Cross Default, Bankruptcy and Credit Event Upon Merger under another agreement between that Specified Entity and one of the parties to this Agreement would give the party not at fault the right to close out all Transactions under this Agreement. Please note that Credit Support Providers are automatically joined to these provisions in the 1992 Agreement and do not need to be separately specified.

The aim of the Specified Entity provision is to draw in those entities whose fortunes are closely correlated to those of the contracting party itself, e.g. its parent or asset rich fellow subsidiaries. A bank might feel insecure about its counterparty's ability to perform under the Agreement if any of its Affiliates were impacted, for instance, by an Event of Default under another agreement.

X Bank AG does not offer any Specified Entities because most of the assets of its group will be in the bank itself and there is no point in it opening itself to the risk of close-out under this Agreement through the default of a lesser subsidiary in another agreement with Rollerblade plc or one of its Specified Entities.

Therefore banks and many other substantial financial institutions will not seek to tie their Specified Entities into these provisions. However, with corporates, a bank will often try to make a named group company or the corporate's Affiliates in general Specified Entities to these Section 5 events. A strong corporate can fight this off because the generic term Affiliates means effectively any group company and the corporate would not want a weak subsidiary triggering close-out of its Agreement with the bank.

With medium-sized corporates compromises are often reached where Affiliates are defined as any group company accounting for more than 10% of consolidated assets or pre-tax profits. Here is an example of the wording for such a provision:

> **"Affiliate" means, notwithstanding the meaning in Section 14 of this Agreement, for the purposes of Section 5(a)(v), (vi) and (vii) and Section 5(b)(iv) only, those Affiliates of Party B whose total assets as shown in the latest audited balance sheet of such party amount in value to at least ten per cent of the consolidated assets of the group of which such party is a member.**

It is not obligatory for Section 5(a)(v) – (vii) and Section 5(b)(iv) to have Specified Entities applying to them. It is not uncommon for parties just to apply Specified Entities to Section 5(a)(v) – Default Under Specified Transaction.

This is because parties to derivatives transactions may think that this type of default is the most likely to occur. An example of such wording is:

> **"Specified Entity" means "Affiliates" in relation to Party A and Party B for the purposes of Section 5(a)(v).**

However, Section 5(a)(v) lacks a Threshold Amount.

Alternatively, the parties could just state "Applicable" against the list of Specified Entity provisions where they want them to apply.

Where a counterparty never gives its Affiliates as Specified Entities, they should confirm this in writing and possibly even represent it in a clause such as:

> **Party B represents to Party A at all times until the termination of this Agreement and all Transactions hereunder that Party B will not enter into an ISDA Master Agreement with any party under which it will offer or nominate any of its Affiliates as a Specified Entity for the purposes of Section 5(a)(v), Section 5(a)(vi), Section 5(a)(vii) or Section 5(b)(iv). If at any time this representation proves to be incorrect or misleading Party B agrees that it will enter into an agreement amending the terms of this Agreement so that Party A's position under this Agreement is no less favourable with regard to the inclusion of Affiliates as a Specified Entity than that of the relevant third party with whom Party B has entered into an Agreement containing the aforesaid provision(s).**

Here, the counterparty undertakes to put the bank in the same position if it gives its Affiliates as Specified Entities in an ISDA Master Agreement with another counterparty.

(b) "*Specified Transaction*" will have the meaning specified in Section 14 of this Agreement.

Part 1(b) Specified Transaction

The Section 14 definition of Specified Transaction is:

> **"Specified Transaction" means, subject to the Schedule, (a) any transaction (including an agreement with respect thereto) now existing or hereafter entered into between one party to this Agreement (or any Credit Support Provider of such party or any applicable Specified Entity of such party) and the other party to this Agreement (or any Credit Support Provider of such other party or any applicable Specified Entity of such other party) which is a rate swap transaction, basis swap, forward rate transaction, commodity swap, commodity option, equity or equity index swap, equity or equity index option, bond option, interest rate option, foreign exchange transaction, cap transaction, floor transaction, collar transaction, currency swap transaction, cross-currency rate swap transaction, currency option or any other similar transaction (including any option with respect to any of these transactions), (b) any combination of these transactions and (c) any other transaction identified as a Specified Transaction in this Agreement or the relevant confirmation.**

In its unamended form, Specified Transaction means any OTC derivative transaction existing in another agreement between the parties to this Agreement or their Affiliates or Specified Entities. The definition can be broadened by amending words in line 4 which would mean that a default under any third party agreement involving either party to this Agreement could trigger a default under this Agreement. An example of such wording is:

> ***Specified Transaction.*** **Instead of the definition in Section 14 of this Agreement "Specified Transaction" shall be amended as follows:**
>
> **the words "and any other entity" shall be substituted for the words "and the other party to this Agreement (or any Credit Support Provider of such other party or any applicable Specified Entity of such other party)" where they appear in the definition of Specified Transaction.**

In addition other products such as repos could be added to the definition:

> ***"Specified Transaction"*** **will have the meaning specified in Section 14 of this Agreement. For purposes of clause (c) of such definition, Specified Transaction includes any securities lending agreement, securities options, margin loans, short sales, repurchase agreement, reverse repurchase agreement and forward securities contract, and any other similar transaction now existing or hereafter entered into between Party A (or any Affiliate of Party A) and Party B (or any Affiliate of Party B).**

Where they are added they tend to be resisted by the counterparty because repo settlement systems are prone to failure and a counterparty will want a carve-out for operational error so that an Event of Default is not triggered. This particular problem is dealt with in the revised Section 5(a)(v) of the 2002 Agreement.

Credit derivatives might be added too if this is major business between the two parties to the Agreement:

> **"Specified Transaction" will have the meaning specified in Section 14 of this Agreement with the addition of the words "credit swap, credit default swap, credit default option, total return swap, credit spread transaction, repurchase transaction, reverse repurchase transaction, buy/sell-back transaction" after the word "currency option" in the eighth line.**

Sometimes a new sub-section (3) is added to Section 5(a)(v) concerning the repudiation of a Specified Transaction as in this example:

> **or (3) repudiates or rejects a Specified Transaction (or such action is taken by any person or entity appointed or empowered to operate it or act on its behalf.**

This additional provision is now included in Section 5(a)(v)(3) of the 2002 Agreement in slightly expanded wording.

Whether any of this is a good thing is a matter of policy for the parties concerned. Personally, I am not in favour of broadening the Specified Transaction definition to third parties except where the counterparty is deemed very risky. To have an arsenal of additional exit clauses beyond the normal ones in ordinary circumstances begs the question of whether the parties should be doing business together in the first place.

(c) The "***Cross Default***" provisions of Section 5(a)(vi) will apply to Party A and will apply to Party B except that the following provision shall be inserted at the end of Section 5(a)(vi):

"provided, however, that an Event of Default shall not occur under either (1) or (2) above if the default, Event of Default or other similar event or condition referred to in (1) or the failure to pay referred to in (2) is a failure to pay caused by an error or omission of an administrative or operational nature and funds were available to such party to enable it to make the relevant payment when due and such payment is in fact made on or before the third Local Business Day following receipt of written notice from the other party of such failure to pay".

Part 1(c) Cross Default

Cross Default is common in many other financial agreements (including loan agreements) beyond the ISDA Master Agreement. The basic ISDA provision catches contractual term and payment defaults in relation to borrowed money in agreements between either of the parties to this Agreement or their Specified Entities or Credit Support Providers with any other third party. Such a default must exceed a defined Threshold Amount (which can be an absolute monetary figure or some other measure such as a small percentage of shareholders' equity, i.e. share capital plus distributable reserves).

One common amendment is for the parties to agree to cross acceleration. This is achieved by the following amendment in Part 1 or Part 5 of the Schedule:

The following words are deleted from line 7 of Section 5(a)(vi):

,or becoming capable at such time of being declared,

This changes who is in the driving seat. Assume your counterparty is the Defaulting Party. With Cross Default a Non-defaulting Party's awareness of or the existence of a default under a third party agreement by the Defaulting Party which is above your Agreement's Threshold Amount is enough to trigger close-out under your Agreement with your counterparty. However, with cross acceleration the party defaulted against in the third party agreement actually has to accelerate the indebtedness and take proceedings to terminate their agreement with your defaulting counterparty before you can do so under yours. In other words your close-out rights are no longer automatic but deferred and you are dependent upon third party action. This would prevent you from striking a deal with your defaulting counterparty, e.g. they give you collateral for you not terminating Transactions under the Agreement.

This process is called a "downgrading" from Cross Default to cross acceleration because by accepting it parties are relinquishing their rights to take immediate action where they become aware of a Cross Default situation which exceeds the agreed Threshold Amount in their Agreement. Credit departments often have to decide whether or not to accept cross acceleration. There is no real scientific test to apply in their decision making process. However, I would say that it is only really justifiable if your counterparty applies it uniformly across all its Agreements (they may do if they are substantial multi-banked companies, for instance) and you have written confirmation from them or their legal advisers of this. Even so you would not want to apply it with very weak counterparties. Here is an example of such wording:

> **Representation of Party B in relation to cross acceleration. Party B represents to Party A at all times from the date hereof until the termination of this Agreement and all Transactions hereunder that Party B has only entered into Agreements where Section 5(a)(vi) thereof is amended in the same manner as herein so that cross acceleration will apply to each party. If at any time this representation proves to be incorrect or misleading and Party B does enter into an ISDA Master Agreement with any party under which Section 5(a)(vi) "Cross Default" will apply to either party without amendment, then Party B agrees that it will enter into an agreement amending the terms of this Agreement so that Party A's position under this Agreement is no less favourable with regard to the application of Cross Default than that of the relevant third party with whom Party B has entered into an Agreement containing the aforesaid provision.**

Accepting cross acceleration with a multi-banked counterparty where you are not the lead bank could involve you in a work out situation where the wishes of the lead bank or majority banks could outweigh your own preferences.

Some banks which rigidly stick by Threshold Amounts measured by a percentage of shareholders' funds for Cross Default purposes may accept a monetary Threshold Amount if cross acceleration applies. This is because they believe they will never default themselves or if they do they will default in an aggregate amount well beyond the Threshold Amount and so any action against them would probably be stayed until a creditor group met and agreed a course of action. In such circumstances, all the bank's agreements would be in jeopardy and a number of interest groups would be jockeying for position and seeking not to make matters worse.

In my opinion, it is surprising that cross acceleration is often conceded without a struggle and with no tangible negotiation benefit from the other side. I think that provided there is no intrinsic objection to cross acceleration *per se* it could be used more as a bargaining counter in negotiations.

Where a swap hedges a loan and the loan agreement contains cross acceleration it is normal to mirror this in the Agreement.

In Agreement negotiations you sometimes see sovereign counterparties seeking to disapply Cross Default to themselves but apply it to their counterparties. There is no real justification for this as history has proved that countries are not immune from default. If this becomes an issue it may occasionally be possible to negotiate that Cross Default does not apply either way. Where Cross Default does not apply, Threshold Amount is also not applicable.

The Cross Default provision often has language, commonly called "carve-out" language, excluding payment delays caused by operational and administrative error with a three Local Business Day cure period after notice. Our Schedule example is quite common. This carve-out is often accepted in the market. The only occasion on which it might be resisted is where your counterparty had a history of late payments under Confirmations before the Agreement is signed.

The most detailed version of this provision I have seen is as follows:

> **(c) The *"Cross Default"* provisions of Section 5(a)(vi) of this Agreement (as amended in Part 5(*) of this Schedule) will apply to Party A and Party B but shall exclude any default that results solely from wire transfer difficulties or an error or omission of an administrative or operational nature, provided that (i) sufficient funds were available for such party to fulfil its obligations hereunder on the relevant date, (ii) no other Event of Default was or is subsisting at the time, (iii) such default does not subsist for more than three Local Business Days and (iv) no creditor under any agreement or instrument for Specified Indebtedness has become entitled to declare an Event of Default hereunder or as a consequence of such default.**

Some German banks like to include the following language to amend the Cross Default provision:

> **The Cross Default provisions of Section 5(a)(vi) will apply to both parties subject to amendment by adding at the end thereof the following words:**
>
> **and in either case the other party determines in good faith that it has reasonable grounds to conclude that the performance by the Defaulting Party of its financial obligations hereunder is endangered.**

Similar wording may also be found in the European Master Agreement issued by the European Banking Federation in October 1999. The purpose is to add a little extra materiality (beyond the Threshold Amount) to the Cross Default provision. Not only must there be a technical default but there must also be a good faith determination that the Defaulting Party is in danger of not fulfilling its obligations, i.e. he is in serious trouble.

Where Transactions under the Agreement are specifically to hedge loans, you sometimes see an additional sub-section to Section 5(a)(vi) relating to the termination of a lender's commitments:

> **Section 5(a)(vi) will be amended to include the following Section 5(a)(vi)(3):**

> **"or (3) a default or event of default in respect of such party, such Credit Support Provider or such Specified Entity (individually or collectively) which has resulted in termination of the commitment of any person or entity under any agreement to lend or advance or make available funds to such party (or any such Credit Support Provider or Specified Entity) in respect of an aggregate amount of not less than the Threshold Amount under such agreements or instruments."**

Occasionally where Cross Default is not to apply to any agreement between the parties you might see the following:

> **Party B warrants and undertakes to Party A that it has not entered and will not enter into any agreements for either raising debt or concluding interest rate currency swap transactions which contain a provision that the counterparty or Party B may terminate such agreement in the circumstances set out in Section 5(a)(vi) of this Agreement or in circumstances similar to those set out in Section 5(a)(vi) of this Agreement.**

Finally, another amendment occasionally seen relates to a party wanting to delete the words "or collectively" in line 5 of the Cross Default provision. This should be resisted because it means that each individual agreement must default in an amount above the Threshold Amount rather than be aggregated together. The effect could obviously be to delay close-out under the Agreement if, for instance, you had three individual agreement defaults of £24 million each with a £25 million Threshold Amount applying to the Agreement. This might sound extreme but it could arise from the deletion of these two words.

If such provisions apply:

"***Specified Indebtedness***" shall mean any obligation (whether present or future, contingent or otherwise, as principal or surety or otherwise) in respect of borrowed money other than indebtedness in respect of deposits received in the ordinary course of business.

Specified Indebtedness

Specified Indebtedness basically means borrowed money but quite often the definition is reduced or extended in scope by negotiators.

Banks might seek to reduce it by excluding deposits from it received in the ordinary course of business (which are after all borrowings from customers). The pros and cons of this approach were outlined in Chapter 6, page 387.

Where a counterparty is unhappy with a bank's exclusion of its deposit base it may be possible to negotiate a compromise. This may include situations where a government-inspired payment moratorium arises and does not last more than a few days. In the 1980s Scandinavia experienced a number of banking strikes (some lasting several weeks) and Scandinavian counterparties occasionally still ask for exclusion of banking deposits from Specified Indebtedness for this reason.

Set out below are examples of compromise wording I have seen in the market. In all cases the banks represent that they had the necessary funds to repay deposits if they had been permitted.

> ***"Specified Indebtedness"*** **means, instead of the definition thereof in Section 14 of this Agreement, any indebtedness or obligation for borrowed money, other than indebtedness in respect of deposits received, the repayment of which:**
>
> **(i) is not delayed for more than two (2) Local Business Days after written notice of non-payment or demand for payment has been given; or**
>
> **(ii) is prevented or hindered and is in good faith beyond control by reason of force majeure or act of state or of the making of such payment being Unlawful or impossible provided that such repayment is not prevented or hindered for a period not exceeding ten (10) Local Business Days.**
>
> **In this context 'Unlawful' shall, without limitation, include where the making of such payment would result in the payer or any person through whom such payment is or would be made being in breach of any statute, regulation, order or other instrument having force of law or any request or requirement of any actual bank or monetary authority in any relevant jurisdiction.**

OR

> ***"Specified Indebtedness"*** **means any obligation (whether present or future, contingent or otherwise) in respect of borrowed money, other than indebtedness in relation to bank deposits received in the ordinary course of business which the relevant party is prevented from repaying**

due to governmental action prohibiting or restricting the repayment of such deposits, provided that

(i) such action is not a direct or indirect consequence of, or related to, any act or omission on the part of, or is as a result of the decline in creditworthiness of such party; and

(ii) if any depositor requests the repayment of any such deposit, such deposit is repaid within three (3) Local Business Days after the relevant governmental action prohibiting or restricting the repayment of such deposit has ended.

OR

"Specified Indebtedness" will have the meaning specified in Section 14 of this Agreement except that indebtedness in respect of deposits received and not repaid due to government action or intervention shall not constitute Specified Indebtedness, provided that such government action or intervention is not due to the bankruptcy, insolvency or severe decline in creditworthiness of the party affected by this government action or intervention.

Please note there is no time limit here.

OR

"Specified Indebtedness". **Add at the end of the definition "provided, however, with respect to either party, Specified Indebtedness shall not include deposits received in the ordinary course of such party's business, the repayment of which is being disputed in good faith or contested by government action."**

In a potential civil action scenario you might see the following:

Section 5(a)(vi) is amended by the addition of the words "provided that for the purposes of this Section 5(a)(vi), no party, Credit Support Provider or Specified Entity shall be deemed to be in default in respect of Specified Indebtedness if it shall be contesting in good faith by appropriate means its liability to make payment thereunder and has been advised by independent legal advisers of recognised standing that it is reasonable for it to do so;" at the end thereof.

Occasionally you see Specified Indebtedness clauses including interest on borrowed money:

"Specified Indebtedness" **means any obligations (whether present or future, contingent or otherwise as principal or surety or otherwise) in respect of borrowed money including interest on any such obligation.**

Specified Indebtedness can be extended to draw in other types of financial instruments, e.g. commercial paper, derivatives and even repos. An example of a particularly wide-ranging provision is as follows:

> ***"Specified Indebtedness"*** **shall mean any obligation (whether present or future, contingent or otherwise, as principal or surety or otherwise) (a) in respect of borrowed money (which, for the avoidance of doubt shall include, without limitation, bonds, notes, commercial paper or similar instruments issued or guaranteed by the relevant party), and (b) any amount due and payable in respect of any Specified Transaction (except that, for this purpose only, the words "and any other entity" shall be substituted for the words "and the other party to this Agreement (or any Credit Support Provider of such other party or any applicable Specified Entity of such other party)" where they appear in the definition of Specified Transaction), and any repo transaction, any reverse repo transaction and any stock loan transaction.**

Sometimes repos are negotiated out of the definition because they are regarded as "secured transactions" with their own close-out regime under the PSA/ISMA Global Master Repurchase Agreement or the TBMA/ISMA Global Master Repurchase Agreement.

From time to time the definition of Specified Indebtedness involves the payment or repayment of money generally and excludes intra-group indebtedness as in the following:

> ***"Specified Indebtedness"*** **means any obligation (whether present or future, secured or unsecured, as principal or surety or otherwise) for the payment or repayment of money borrowed or raised, by whatever means (including letters of credit, bankers' acceptances or documentary credits or any guarantee given in respect of borrowed money) but excluding any obligations owed by a party or Credit Support Provider or Specified Entity to that party to any Affiliate of that party or Credit Support Provider for that party or Specified Entity of that party.**

A variation on this is:

> ***"Specified Indebtedness"*** **means any obligation (whether present or future, actual or contingent, secured or unsecured, as principal or surety or otherwise) in respect of borrowed money, but shall exclude (a) intra-Group indebtedness, (b) any obligation owed to trade creditors in respect of the purchase of goods in the ordinary course of business and (c) any obligation, liability for payment of which is being contested in good faith, provided the company's auditors verify that the amount in dispute is fully provided against.**

With hedging transactions for special purpose projects, Specified Indebtedness might exclude debt repayable from project revenues as in the following instance:

> ***"Specified Indebtedness"* will have the meaning specified in Section 14 of this Agreement except that in the case of Party B it shall exclude any indebtedness incurred under or in respect of financing of any asset or project in respect of which the payment of that indebtedness is to be made from the revenues arising out of that asset or project with recourse to those revenues and any other assets (whether of Party B or any other member of Party B's group) used in connection with, or forming the subject matter of, that asset or project but without recourse (or with such limited recourse as Party A may agree with Party B from time to time) to any other assets of Party B or any other member of Party B's group.**

Parties sometimes want to include derivatives directly in the definition of Specified Indebtedness:

> ***"Specified Indebtedness"* means any obligation (whether present or future, contingent or otherwise, as principal or surety or otherwise) in respect of borrowed money or any Derivative Transaction other than any Specified Transaction.**

"Derivative Transaction" is then or later described as:

> **The following definition shall appear in Section 14 after the definition of "Defaulting Party":**

Definitions

> **"Derivative Transaction" means:**
> **(i) any transaction (including an agreement with respect thereto) which is a rate swap transaction, basis swap, forward rate transaction, commodity swap, commodity option, equity or equity index swap, equity or equity index option, bond option, interest rate option, foreign exchange transaction, cap transaction, floor transaction, collar transaction, currency swap transaction, cross-currency rate swap transaction, currency option or any other similar transaction (including any option with respect to any of these transactions); and**
> **(ii) any combination of these transactions.**

The inclusion of derivatives calls for special care. The scope of Specified Indebtedness comes into play in the Cross Default provision with the Threshold Amount and the more types of financial instruments which fall within its definition, the more chance there will be that the Cross Default clause could be triggered. As mentioned at page 386, this is particularly risky in the case of derivatives measured purely by their notional amount rather than their replacement value. This hazard can be avoided by the use of wording along the following lines which focuses on the replacement value of derivatives in calculating Specified Indebtedness for Threshold Amount purposes:

After a definition of Specified Indebtedness which can include derivatives transactions the following is added:

For purposes of Section 5(a)(vi) of this Agreement, any reference in Section 5(a)(vi)(1) to Specified Indebtedness becoming or becoming capable of being declared due and payable before it would otherwise have been due and payable shall, in the case of a Derivative Transaction, be deemed to be a reference to such Derivative Transaction being or becoming capable of being, liquidated or terminated before it otherwise would have been terminated, and any reference in Section 5(a)(vi)(1) to any amount of Specified Indebtedness shall, in the case of a Derivative Transaction, be deemed to mean the amount which becomes, or would become, payable as a result of the liquidation or termination of such Derivative Transaction.

OR

For the purpose of Section 5(a)(vi)(1):

(a) any reference to Specified Indebtedness becoming, or becoming capable of being declared, due and payable shall, in the case of Specified Indebtedness which is a Specified Transaction, be deemed to be a reference to Specified Indebtedness being, or becoming capable of being, terminated by the other party to such Specified Transaction; and

(b) in determining the amount to be included in "Threshold Amount" with respect to Specified Indebtedness which is a Specified Transaction, the mark-to-market value of such Specified Transaction shall be used or, if it is not available, the Non-defaulting Party shall determine the mark-to-market value of such Specified Transaction in good faith on the basis of the information available to it.

OR

***Derivative Transactions.* For the purposes of Section 5(a)(vi)(1), any reference to Specified Indebtedness becoming due and payable shall, in the case of Specified Indebtedness which is a Derivative Transaction, be deemed to be an amount becoming due and payable under such Derivative Transaction as a result of such Derivative Transaction and any relevant master agreement being terminated as a result of an Event of Default.**

Sometimes banks consider that the bare "borrowed money" definition of Specified Indebtedness is insufficient to describe the financial instruments through which their corporate counterparties can raise money. In those circumstances the following type of wording might be seen (probably in Part 5 of the Schedule):

The definition of "Specified Indebtedness" shall mean for Party B:

any obligation (whether present or future, contingent or otherwise, as principal or surety or otherwise) in respect of:

(i) any moneys borrowed or raised (excluding deposits received in the ordinary course of business);
(ii) any commercial paper programme, debenture, bond, note, loan stock or similar instrument;
(iii) amounts raised under any acceptance credit, bill of exchange discounting or note purchase facility;
(iv) any lease or hire purchase agreement entered into primarily as a method of raising finance;
(v) any part of the purchase price for any assets or services, payment of which is agreed to be or has been deferred but excluding amounts owing for assets purchased or services obtained on trade credit terms in the ordinary course of business;
(vi) amounts raised under any other transaction which, in accordance with principles and practices generally accepted and adopted in the country of incorporation of Party B have the commercial effect of a borrowing; and
(vii) any guarantee, indemnity or instrument of suretyship, howsoever described.

As to whether it is a good idea to extend the definition of Specified Indebtedness depends on the circumstances and the risks you think you run. For sovereign counterparties you might well need to redefine Specified Indebtedness to include, for instance, all the sovereign's external indebtedness.

You might well not allow the banking deposit exclusion or permit it with modifications if you thought that this was a key indicator of pending insolvency. It is likely that if a bank defaulted in its deposit base it would do so in a big way (well beyond any reasonable Threshold Amount) and while you may trigger close-out under the Agreement, how would you collect the net amount owed to you quickly?

Some might consider that national bank deposit insurance schemes for personal customers (100% of the first £2,000 and 90% of the next £33,000 resulting in a maximum payment of £31,700 in the UK) obviate the need to include banking deposits in the definition. Others might just want to import derivatives into the Specified Indebtedness definition and extend the Specified Transaction definition to third parties in case counterparties have offered this to another institution and they want to have the same level of protection.

"Threshold Amount" means for Party A and Party B and any relevant Specified Entity (if any) an amount equal to 3% of that party's shareholders' equity as specified in that party's latest published audited accounts, or its equivalent in any other currency.

Threshold Amount

The Threshold Amount is the money or money equivalent limit of Specified Indebtedness (however defined) below which you cannot trigger your close-out rights under the Agreement's Cross Default clause. Threshold Amounts are commonly a fixed sum such as US$ 10 million or a small percentage of shareholders' equity (which may be defined in a number of ways). The most common percentage in this respect is 3%. Where applicable, the Threshold Amount will apply collectively to Specified Indebtedness defaults of a party, its Credit Support Provider and/or its Specified Entities.

Threshold Amounts should be critically reviewed but apart from corporates rarely are. In Chapter 6, (page 384) I mentioned the story of the small unguaranteed bank which wanted a Threshold Amount of £10 million which, in fact, at the time represented 20% of its shareholders' equity.

Where Cross Default does not apply Threshold Amount will also not apply.

Banks usually assign Threshold Amounts of zero to particularly risky counterparties. Threshold Amounts are often linked to external or internal long-term unsecured debt credit ratings. It is rare for this to appear in tables in the Agreement because most counterparties require some certainty in the level of Threshold Amount they have agreed to accept. It is interesting that, by contrast, Thresholds (i.e. the amount of unsecured exposure parties allow each other) in ISDA Credit Support Annexes often make use of credit rating tables.

With guaranteed or collateralised counterparties the Threshold Amount might be directly linked to a large fixed amount or a percentage of the Credit Support Provider's shareholders' equity or there may be separate Threshold Amounts for the counterparty and its Credit Support Provider. It is also possible for different Threshold Amounts to be quoted for each of subparagraphs (1) and (2) of Section 5(a)(vi).

Finally it sometimes happens that the two parties to the Agreement may have completely opposing policies on Threshold Amounts – one favouring a fixed monetary sum and the other a percentage of shareholders' funds. When I was confronted by one of these situations, the following provision was agreed as a compromise:

> **"Threshold Amount" means US$10,000,000 or the equivalent thereof in any other currency and Party A, in its reasonable discretion, determines that Party B will be unable to perform its obligations hereunder or under any Transaction.**

Party A was the bank wanting a fixed percentage of shareholders' equity. It conceded on that but linked the US$10 million Threshold Amount to its reasonable opinion of a serious decline in Party B's fortunes.

Corporates will need to ensure that the Threshold Amount they agree here is not lower than the cross default thresholds in their loan agreements. If they are, a default under another agreement could cross default into both its ISDA Master Agreement(s) and its loan agreements.

(d) *The "Credit Event Upon Merger"* provisions of Section 5(b)(iv) will apply to Party A and will apply to Party B, amended as follows:

"Credit Event Upon Merger" shall mean that a Designated Event (as defined below) occurs with respect to a party ("X"), and such Designated Event does not constitute an event described in Section 5(a)(viii) but the creditworthiness of X or, if applicable, the successor, surviving or transferee entity of X, (which in either case will be the Affected Party) is materially weaker than that of X, immediately prior to such event. For purposes hereof, a Designated Event means that after the execution date hereof:

(i) X consolidates, amalgamates with or merges with or into, or transfers all or substantially all its assets to, or receives all or substantially all the assets or obligations of, another entity; or

(ii) any person or entity acquires directly or indirectly the beneficial ownership of equity securities having the power to elect a majority of the board of directors of X or otherwise acquires directly or indirectly the power to control the policy-making decisions of X; or

(iii) X enters into an agreement providing for any of the foregoing.

For purposes hereof, X or the successor, surviving or transferee entity, as appropriate, will be the Affected Party.

Moreover, for the purposes of Section 5(b)(iv) "materially weaker" shall mean the following:

If either Party A or Party B fails to maintain a long term, unsecured and unsubordinated debt rating of at least BBB- as determined by Standard & Poor's Ratings Group, a division of the McGraw-Hill Companies or Baa3 as determined by Moody's Investors Service Inc.

Part 1(d) Credit Event Upon Merger

The Credit Event Upon Merger provision is a Termination Event which will close out all Transactions under the Agreement if triggered. It will never apply to a sovereign counterparty (although in the early 1970s Libya and Tunisia spoke of merging).

The rationale behind Credit Event Upon Merger is that a contracting party should be allowed to terminate the Agreement with its counterparty where that counterparty has been taken over by or merges with another party and as a result becomes a much worse credit risk than it was before. This could happen where the resulting merged entity carries much more debt (because of merger financing arrangements) than the original one and so could be considered a riskier counterparty than the original pre-merger one.

In the provision the words "materially weaker" appear and in order to make Credit Event Upon Merger less of a subjective judgment, linkage to external credit ratings is often used as in our example and in the following wording:

(d) The "Credit Event Upon Merger" provisions of Section 5(b)(iv) will apply to Party A and will apply to Party B, provided however, that "Credit Event upon Merger" shall not have its meaning as defined in Section 5(b)(iv), but it shall mean that:

(i) such party, Credit Support Provider or Specified Entity, as the case may be, ("X") consolidates or amalgamates with, or acquires the majority of the shares in, or merges into, or transfers all or substantially all its assets to, another entity ("Y") or Y consolidates or amalgamates with, or acquires the majority of the shares in, or merges into, or transfers all or substantially all its assets to X; and

(ii) such action does not constitute an event described in Section 5(a)(viii); and

(iii) (a) in the event X, immediately prior to such action, was rated by Standard and Poor's Ratings Group, a division of The McGraw-Hill Companies ("S&P") and/or Moody's Investors Service, Inc. ("Moody's") or any successor organisation and (i) S&P and/or Moody's rates the long term, unsecured, unsubordinated debt obligations of the resulting, surviving or transferee entity immediately after such action at least three modifiers (a modifier being 1, 2, or 3 for Moody's; plus, neutral or minus for S&P) lower than that of the long term, unsecured, unsubordinated debt obligations of X immediately prior to such action or such

rating is below investment grade, being BBB- for S&P and Baa3 for Moody's, or (ii) the resulting, surviving or transferee entity ceases to be rated by S&P and/or Moody's immediately after such action, or

(b) in the event X, immediately prior to such action, was not rated by S&P and/or Moody's, the creditworthiness of the resulting, surviving or transferee entity is, in the reasonable opinion of the Party which is not X, materially weaker than that of X immediately prior to such action.

For purposes hereof, X or the resulting, surviving or transferee entity, as appropriate, will be the Affected Party.

Where no ratings apply, I have also seen the following provision relating to internal credit rating policies deciding if a Credit Event Upon Merger Termination Event has occurred:

...in the event that there are no S&P or Moody's ratings the Policies (as defined below) in effect at the time, of the party which is not the Affected Party, would lead such non-Affected Party solely as a result of a change in the nature, character, identity or condition of the Affected Party from its state (as a party to this Agreement) prior to such consolidation, amalgamation, merger or transfer, to decline to make an extension of credit to, or enter into a Transaction with, the resulting, surviving or transferee entity. "Policies" for the purpose of this definition means:

(x) (i) internal credit limits applicable to individual entities; or

(ii) other limits on doing business with entities domiciled or doing business in certain jurisdictions or engaging in certain activities; or

(y) internal restrictions on doing business with entities with whom the party which is not the Affected Party has had prior adverse business relations.

In addition, the basic ISDA wording in the 1992 Agreement tends to describe North American merger practice. In European Agreements the wording in our example is frequently used to describe typical situations where control of a counterparty passes and its operating decisions can be controlled in ways different from a pure merger. Similar wording is now in Section 5(b)(v) of the 2002 Agreement.

Sometimes language concerning indebtedness is added such as the following:

(iii) X effects any substantial change in its capital structure by means of the issuance or incurrence of debt or preferred stock or securities convertible into or exchangeable for, debt or preferred stock....

This should be resisted if it is mutual because for a bank it is too intrusive and would restrict its ability to change its capital structure in this context and may even impact on any syndicated loans it had raised if it could be shown that this made it financially weaker following a merger. I remain convinced that it should be resisted by banks even though it is now part of Section 5(b)(v) of the 2002 Agreement.

Finally, there may be an exclusion from the scope of Designated Event where a Credit Support Provider unconditionally continues its guarantee or the merger is with an Affiliate as in the following example:

However, these subsections (i) and (ii) shall not apply to either party if (1) the obligations of the relevant party under any transaction benefiting from a guarantee continue to be unconditionally guaranteed by its Credit Support Provider and (2) such person or entity consolidating, amalgamating with or merging with or into or transferring or receiving assets to or from such party or acquiring such beneficial ownership or power to control is an Affiliate of such party.

(e) ***The "Automatic Early Termination"*** provision of Section 6(a) will not apply to Party A and Party B; provided, however, that where there is an Event of Default under Section 5(a)(vii)(1), (3), (4), (5), (6) or to the extent analogous thereto, (8), and the Defaulting Party is governed by a system of law that would not otherwise permit termination to take place, then the Automatic Early Termination provisions of Section 6(a) will apply.

Part 1(e) Automatic Early Termination

Automatic Early Termination, if chosen to apply, only impacts on Bankruptcy Events of Default, in particular Section 5(a)(vii)(1) (dissolution), (3) (composition with creditors), (5) (winding-up resolution passed), (6) (appointment of administrator) or (8) (analogous circumstances to the above).

The effect of Automatic Early Termination is for all Transactions under the Agreement to be deemed terminated as of a date *immediately before* a winding-up order was presented against the Defaulting Party in respect of Section 5(a)(vii)(4) and *immediately at the time* bankruptcy proceedings were instituted against the Defaulting Party in all other cases. Therefore the Non-defaulting Party can exercise its rights outside the insolvency proceedings and use the Section 6 close-out mechanism.

The problem is that the Non-defaulting Party may have been unaware of this and by the time it becomes aware markets may have moved adversely against it because the deemed Early Termination Date will be at or just before bankruptcy proceedings were started.

In these circumstances, a Non-defaulting Party often seeks to negotiate two-way indemnity language such as the following in order to mitigate the situation:

The following shall be added at the end of Section 6(e)(iii):

", provided that in addition to, and notwithstanding anything to the contrary in Section 6(e)(iii), if an Early Termination Date is deemed to have occurred under Section 6(a) as a result of an Automatic Early Termination, the Defaulting Party shall indemnify the Non-defaulting Party on demand against all expense, loss, cost, damages or liability ('Indemnified Costs') that the Non-defaulting Party may sustain or incur in respect of each Transaction as a result of a movement in interest rates, currency exchange rates or market quotations between the Early Termination Date and the date (the 'Determination Date') upon which the Non-defaulting Party first becomes aware that the Early Termination Date has been deemed to have occurred under Section 6(a). The Non-defaulting Party shall endeavour to mitigate its Indemnified Costs, if any, and shall submit to the Defaulting Party a written statement of such Indemnified Costs.

If the Non-defaulting Party shall determine that it would gain or benefit from the movement in interest rates, currency exchange rates or market quotations between the Early Termination Date and the Determination Date, the amount of such gain or benefit shall be deducted from the amount payable by the Defaulting Party pursuant to Section 6(e)(i)(3).

(*NOTE* THE REFERENCE WILL BE TO SECTION 6(e)(i)(4) IF LOSS IS THE CHOSEN PAYMENT MEASURE.)

> **The Determination Date shall be a date not later than the date upon which creditors of the Defaulting Party generally become aware or are notified by the Defaulting Party of the occurrence of the Event of Default leading to the deemed Early Termination Date".**

Whether an insolvent Defaulting Party would actually be able to honour such an indemnity is a moot point as also whether it would be seen as a preference or unfair advantage against other creditors. This is untested in the courts.

Other examples I have seen in the market are:

> **(e) Automatic Early Termination. The "Automatic Early Termination" provision of Section 6(a) will apply to Party A and Party B.**
>
> **If an Early Termination Date is deemed to have occurred under Section 6(a) as a result of Automatic Early Termination, the Defaulting Party shall fully indemnify the Non-defaulting Party on demand against all expense, loss, damage or liability that the Non-defaulting Party may incur in respect of each Transaction as a consequence of movements of interest rates, currency exchange rates or market quotations between the Early Termination Date and the date upon which the Non-defaulting Party first becomes aware that the Early Termination Date is deemed to have occurred under Section 6(a), the latter date being no later than that upon which creditors generally of the Defaulting Party receive notice of the occurrence of the relevant Event of Default. The Non-defaulting Party may for this purpose convert any expense, loss, damage or liability into the Termination Currency.**

OR

> **(e) The *Automatic Early Termination* provisions of Section 6(a) of this Agreement will apply to Party A and Party B.**
>
> **The "Automatic Early Termination" provisions of Section 6(a) will apply; provided (1) that each party (the "Defaulting Party") hereby agrees to indemnify and hold harmless the other party hereto (the "Non-defaulting Party") from all losses and costs ("Indemnity Costs") arising from the fact that the Non-defaulting Party did not terminate, liquidate, acquire, establish or re-establish any hedge or related trading position in respect of the Transactions upon the occurrence of a Bankruptcy Event (as hereinafter defined) until such time as the Non-defaulting Party learns of such event and is satisfied, in its sole discretion, that termination resulting from such event is legally valid, (ii) that the Defaulting Party hereby agrees that the Non-defaulting Party shall be able to set off the Indemnity Costs against any amount it owes, and (iii) that the Non-defaulting Party hereby agrees to use its**

> **best efforts to mitigate its losses, if any, and to submit to the Defaulting Party a written statement of its Indemnity Costs (and the basis for calculating such Indemnity Costs in reasonable detail) which statement shall, in the absence of manifest error, be presumed correct.**
> **"Bankruptcy Event" shall include, for the purpose of Section 6(a) of the Agreement and Part 1(e) of the Schedule an event set forth in Section 5(a)(vii)(1), (3), (4), (5), (6), or the extent analogous thereto, (8) of the Agreement.**

OR

> **In circumstances where an Early Termination Date occurs because "Automatic Early Termination" applies in respect of a party, the amount determined under Section 6(e) will be subject to such adjustments as are necessary to reflect any movements in relevant rates or prices during the period from the date as of which Loss is determined to the date as of which Loss would have been determined had the Early Termination Date been the date upon which the Non-defaulting Party first became aware of the occurrence of the Automatic Early Termination.**

Generally speaking, Automatic Early Termination is a matter of choice. However, in some jurisdictions notice of termination is deemed to be less effective or even prejudicial to a Non-defaulting Party's position in its counterparty's insolvency. In those jurisdictions if Automatic Early Termination is not selected, outstanding Transactions would remain open, close-out netting would not operate and a liquidator would have scope to cherry pick. Therefore lawyers recommend it is necessary in those jurisdictions. From my study of the ISDA collective legal opinions these jurisdictions are in October 2003:

Countries where Automatic Early Termination needs to apply

FIG. 8.1

Belgium
Denmark
Germany
Japan
Netherlands Antilles
South Africa (for certain commodity swaps and options)
Switzerland

I have heard that Automatic Early Termination is also advisable with counterparties incorporated in:

- **Czech Republic**
- **Hungary**
- **Poland**
- **Romania**
- **Russia**
- **Slovenia.**

However, I have no direct experience of this and this should be checked in lawyers in relevant circumstances.

ISDA obtains annual updates of the netting opinions it commissions and these should be studied for any changes in Automatic Early Termination application. In order to cover a situation where it is not clear whether Automatic Early termination should apply or not a "half way house" type of clause may be proposed as in the wording in our sample Schedule.

In many jurisdictions there is no benefit in preferring Automatic Early Termination over normal termination by notice. In those circumstances because of the market movement problem it is best, in my opinion, for Automatic Early Termination not to apply.

(f) ***Payments on Early Termination.*** For the purpose of Section 6(e) of this Agreement:

(i) Market Quotation will apply.

(ii) The Second Method will apply.

Part 1(f) Payments on Early Termination

The payment measures and methods for close-out purposes are selected in Part 1(f) of the Schedule. A frequent choice is Market Quotation and the Second Method as here.

Market Quotation involves a series of four arm's length quotations from market dealers for the replacement value of Transactions to be terminated. Where there are insufficient Market Quotations available for this (e.g. exotic Transactions in an illiquid market) Loss can be used as a fallback.

Loss is the Non-defaulting or non-Affected Party's good faith determination of its losses and costs (minus its gains) in respect of potentially replacing Terminated Transactions. The use of Loss is a matter of preference. It is a long established payment measure in the foreign exchange market. However, because it is inevitably more subjective than Market Quotation I think that potentially it is more likely to be challenged by a liquidator because the valuations are not at arm's length.

As shown in Figure 3.5 on page 95, under the Second Method if the net close-out amount is due to the Defaulting Party, it is paid out to them. Under the First Method it is not – it is a windfall for the Non-defaulting Party. This is unacceptable to regulators who insist upon the Second Method for banks if they want derivatives contracts to be netted for regulatory capital purposes.

However, one occasionally sees the First Method proposed particularly by sovereign entities who consider they would never have to pay over a net close-out amount to a Defaulting Party. Such an approach would be vigorously rejected by a bank for regulatory capital reasons.

Sometimes conditionality language is inserted to the effect that a Non-defaulting Party's payment of the net close-out amount to a Defaulting Party is conditional upon all Transactions being terminated in accordance with Section 6(c) (an unqualified opinion of counsel may be sought for this although I have never heard of any counsel giving an unqualified opinion!) and all obligations of the Defaulting Party and the Non-defaulting Party and their respective Affiliates having been fully and finally performed. An example of such language is:

> **The Second Method will apply and, notwithstanding the provisions of Section 6 (e) (i) (3) and (4), as applicable, if the amount referred to therein is a positive number, the Defaulting Party will pay such amount to the Non-defaulting Party, and if the amount referred to therein is a negative number, the Non-defaulting Party shall have no obligation to pay any amount thereunder to the Defaulting Party unless and until the conditions set forth in (A) and (B) below have been satisfied at which time there shall arise an obligation of the Non-defaulting Party to pay to the Defaulting Party an amount equal to the absolute value of such negative number less any and all amounts which the Defaulting Party may be obligated to pay under Section 11:**

(A) the Non-defaulting Party shall have received confirmation satisfactory to it in its sole discretion (which may include an unqualified opinion of its counsel) that (x) all Transactions are terminated in accordance with Section 6(c) and (y) each Specified Transaction shall have terminated pursuant to its specified termination date or through the exercise by a party of a right to terminate and all amounts due under each Specified Transaction shall have been fully and finally paid; and

(B) all obligations (contingent or absolute, matured or unmatured) of the Defaulting Party and any Affiliate of the Defaulting Party to make any payment to the Non-defaulting Party or any Affiliate of the Non-defaulting Party shall have been fully and finally performed.

The approach can be extended to the Credit Event Upon Merger Termination Event through reference to the Affected Party and the non-Affected Party. In my opinion the provision should be resisted as it dilutes the effectiveness of the Second Method.

Page 59 of the 1992 ISDA *User's Guide* includes sample conditionality language but this has been largely superseded since 1993 by regulators' disfavour towards "walkaway" or "limited two-way payments" clauses.

(g) *"Termination Currency"* means the currency selected by the Non-defaulting Party or the non-Affected Party, as the case may be, or, in circumstances where there are two Affected Parties, as agreed by Party A and Party B. However, the Termination Currency shall be one of the currencies in which payments in respect of Transactions are required to be made by the Confirmations. If the currency selected is not freely available, or, where there are two Affected Parties, and Party A and Party B cannot agree on a Termination Currency, the Termination Currency shall be United States Dollars.

Part 1(g) Termination Currency

Termination Currency is simply the currency into which all Transactions are converted on close-out. Sometimes it is just stated baldly as US Dollars, Euro or Sterling depending upon the domiciles or preferences of the parties. Sometimes it is stated as having to be one of the currencies in which Transactions are denominated as in the sample provision opposite.

The provisions can be slightly more elaborate:

> **Termination Currency means the currency selected by the Non-defaulting Party or the non-Affected Party or in the circumstance where there are two Affected Parties, agreed by Party A and Party B: and failing such agreement the Termination Currency shall be United States Dollars. However, the Termination Currency selected by the Non-defaulting Party or the non-Affected Party (i) shall be one of the currencies in which payment in respect of any Terminated Transaction is required to be made, except, in case of termination pursuant to Section 5(a)(vii) in which case it shall be the currency of the jurisdiction of incorporation of the Defaulting Party and (ii) shall be freely transferable into all other currencies in which payments are to be made in respect of any Terminated Transaction.**

However, in general, this provision is not one which is much argued over by negotiators. Please note that if no Termination Currency is specified, the ISDA fallback is US Dollars in the 1992 Agreement.

(h) ***Additional Termination Event*** will apply and the following shall constitute an Additional Termination Event:-

Change of Ownership. X Corporation Inc either directly or indirectly ceases to own directly or indirectly 51 per cent of the issued share capital of Party B carrying voting rights in ordinary circumstances in a general meeting of shareholders or a comparable meeting of Party B or otherwise directly or indirectly ceases to control the board of directors of Party B; and/or Party B ceases to be a fully consolidated subsidiary of X Corporation Inc.

For the purposes of the foregoing Termination Event, Party B shall be the Affected Party.

Part 1(h) Additional Termination Event

Additional Termination Events come in all shapes and sizes and frequently depend upon the type of counterparties involved. Additional Termination Events will always identify who is the Affected Party.

Types of Additional Termination Events include:

- **Change of control**
- **Ratings downgrade**
- **Optional early termination of Transactions**
- **Non-renewal of licences or suspension by a regulatory authority**
- **Death or resignation of key men**
- **Breach of key agreements**
- **Sovereign Event**
- **Branch closure.**

Change of control

A typical example of a change of ownership or control provision is shown opposite.

Sometimes there is provision for a negotiation period before a termination right is triggered as in the following example:

> **The following shall constitute an Additional Termination Event in relation to Party B: [name of parent company] ceases to own directly or indirectly 100% of Party B, provided however that if a change of ownership occurs, then Party B shall give notice within 10 Local Business Days thereof to Party A ("Change of Ownership Notice") and the parties shall use all reasonable endeavours to agree on mutually acceptable credit support to be provided by Party B to Party A. If no such agreement can be reached within 15 Local Business Days of the receipt of the Change of Ownership Notice, a Termination Event shall be deemed to have then occurred.**

Ratings downgrade

A typical example is:

> *Downgrade*
>
> **(i) S&P or Moody's or both rate the long-term, unsecured, unsubordinated debt obligations of Party A or Party B at least three modifiers (a modifier being 1, 2, or 3 for Moody's; plus, neutral or minus for S&P) lower than the highest rating which had previously applied (from the date of this Agreement) to the long-term unsecured, unsubordinated debt obligations of Party A or Party B; or**

> **(ii) such long-term unsecured, unsubordinated rating of Party A or Party B is downgraded below investment grade, being BBB- for S&P and Baa3 for Moody's; or**
>
> **(iii) Party A or Party B ceases to be rated by both of S&P and Moody's.**
>
> **For the purposes of the foregoing Termination Event, the Affected Party shall be the party that was downgraded or ceased to be rated.**

This is a useful provision covering as it does a situation where a long-term credit rating falls by three modifiers or plunges below investment grade or is cancelled altogether. It is also possible to negotiate for this to be applied one way rather than mutually.

Optional early termination of Transactions

Optional early termination or "break" clauses have become more common as a measure to terminate Transactions where there are potential concerns over creditworthiness. An example follows:

> **Provided that no Early Termination Date has occurred or been designated in accordance with the terms of this Agreement, either party (the "Terminating Party") may, by at least ten Local Business Days' prior written and telephonic notice to the other party (the "Other Party") before 11:00 a.m. London time on that date, terminate any Transaction hereunder with an original maturity at inception in excess of five years, such termination to be effective on the fifth anniversary and any subsequent annual anniversary (if applicable) of the Trade Date of the relevant Transaction (or, if such anniversary is not a Local Business Day, the next succeeding Local Business Day) (the "Alternate Termination Date").**
>
> **In that event, the Terminating Party shall be the sole Affected Party and the Other Party shall calculate the payment due in respect of such early termination in accordance with Section 6(e)(ii)(1) of the Agreement on the basis that the Alternate Termination Date results from a Termination Event, that the relevant Transaction is the sole Terminated Transaction and that the parties had specified Market Quotation.**
>
> **The party which owes a payment on termination of the relevant Transaction to the Other Party shall make such payment to the other party within two Local Business Days of the later of (1) the relevant Alternate Termination Date or (2) notification from the other party as to the amount owed. Upon such payment having been made, the obligations of both parties to make any further payments contemplated by Section 2(a)(i) of the Agreement with respect to the relevant Transaction will terminate.**

As mentioned in Chapter 2, pages 23–4 the problem with this type of provision is that there could be costs in unwinding any mirror transactions hedging them. This problem would be exacerbated by the following provision where objections might also arise from the proposal that both parties shall be Affected Parties:

The following shall constitute an Additional Termination Event:-

Party B's Option to Terminate. **Party B has the right at any time and at its sole discretion to terminate any Transaction by giving to Party A two (2) Local Business Days' prior written notice. For purposes hereof, each such terminated Transaction shall constitute an Affected Transaction under the Agreement. Such termination shall not affect the validity or enforceability of Transactions which are not terminated pursuant to this Termination Event. For the purpose of the foregoing Termination Event the Affected Parties shall be Party A and Party B.**

Non-renewal of licences or suspension by a regulatory authority

This type of provision would be an Additional Termination Event in Schedules for funds under management. An example is:

Additional Termination Event will apply as follows:

If X Management Company ceases to be regulated by the Financial Services Authority or the US Securities and Exchange Commission (the "Regulators") or any successor of them or has its licence or authorisation withdrawn by one or both of the Regulators then this shall constitute an Additional Termination Event with the fund(s) concerned as the Affected Party(ies).

OR

Counterparty has lost its licence necessary to conduct banking business in [*name of country*] for any reason whatsoever after the date on which such Transaction is entered into. The occurrence of this event shall be deemed to constitute an Illegality under Section 5(b)(i) with the Affected Party being Counterparty for the purpose of the application of Sections 6 and 14.

Death or resignation of keymen

Again this is an Additional Termination Event you might find with Schedules for funds under management, e.g.:

> **All of [*name key individuals*] cease to perform the function of investment advisers to Party B by reason of death, incapacity or on account of vacating their current positions. In these circumstances an Additional Termination Event will be deemed to have arisen and Party B shall be the Affected Party.**

If there is just one key individual and his group has some negotiating clout you might get the following:

> ***Key Individuals*. It shall be an Additional Termination Event with Party B as the Affected Party if [*name of key person*] is no longer active in the management of the assets of Party B; provided that, in such event, if Party A elects to exercise its right to terminate, then notwithstanding anything in this Agreement to the contrary, Party A may not designate an Early Termination Date in respect of such Additional Termination Event sooner than sixty (60) calendar days following the date of notice to Party B of such designation; and each of the parties will exercise commercially reasonable efforts to wind down, settle and liquidate all open Transactions between them on mutually agreeable terms prior to the Early Termination Date.**

Breach of key agreements

Where contracts are vital to a deal, project or relationship, it is normal for a breach of key agreement provision to be included as an Additional Termination Event. Here is an example:

> **It shall be an Additional Termination Event with respect to Party B who will be the Affected Party if the [*name of Agreement*] between Party B and [*name other party or parties*] dated [*insert date*] is terminated, cancelled, voided, breached or amended in a manner which affects Party B's ability to perform its obligations under the Agreement.**

Sometimes it is proposed that both parties should be Affected Parties if neither of them was sufficiently at fault when the Additional Termination Event arose. In the normal course of events, whichever party triggers the provision is the sole Affected Party which means that the other party can choose the close-out date and make the termination payment calculations. Any alternative proposal needs to be carefully considered in the prevailing circumstances to see if it is justifiable.

Sovereign Event

With ring fencing of branches becoming more popular in order to shift political risk on to a counterparty, Sovereign Event language is starting to appear as an Additional Termination Event as in the following example:

Sovereign Event. A party is not able to discharge its obligations with respect to a Transaction through the relevant specified Office as a result of any law (other than bankruptcy, insolvency or similar laws), order or other act or threat of any authority (de jure or de facto) at the location of such specified Office.

In such circumstances, such party will be the Affected Party.

Branch closure

With banks cutting back their branch networks you sometimes see Additional Termination Events such as the following:

Branch Closure Event.

If Party B closes its branch in [*name of city and country*] and loses its licence to conduct foreign exchange transactions in [*name of country*] and, in connection therewith any Transaction becomes unlawful for Party A under any applicable law, regulation or governmental directive or interpretation, then Party B will negotiate with Party A in good faith with a view towards transferring the relevant Transaction to another party in [*name of same country*] or terminating the relevant Transaction on a fair and reasonable basis to both parties. Failure in agreement of the parties upon transferring the relevant Transaction shall constitute a Termination Event with Party B being the Affected Party and such event shall be treated as an Illegality.

Not all Additional Termination Events are tightly drawn and some can be too subjective as in the following example:

The following shall constitute an Additional Termination Event:-

Any event or series of events whether connected or not and whether or not within the control of Party B occurs (including without limitation, any material adverse change in Party B's business, assets or financial condition), which in Party A's opinion may adversely affect Party B's ability or willingness to perform any of its obligations under this Agreement or under any one or more Transaction(s).

For the purpose of the foregoing Termination Event, the Affected Party shall be Party B.

Part 2 Tax Representations

Chapters 3 and 4 discussed what happens when withholding tax is levied upon payments under the Agreement. Before studying the Agreement's tax representations it might be useful to give some background on why they may be necessary.

Please note that the following information must, of necessity, be a brief analysis and must not be relied upon in the context of structuring any transaction for tax purposes. In those and other circumstances specialist tax advice must be obtained.

When the swaps markets started in the early 1980s there was a great deal of uncertainty (especially in the US) about whether a payer's tax authority would levy a withholding tax on its cross-border OTC derivatives payments. To counter this uncertainty, ISDA developed tax provisions in the Agreement and its Schedule. Over the years many of these concerns have evaporated but under the Agreement's terms parties are still obliged to check if such payments could be subject to withholding tax and to take remedial action. Withholding tax provisions were not necessary in the Local Currency–Single Jurisdiction Master Agreement and were not included. In the Agreement's cross-border version they are extensive and they serve to:

- **confirm no withholding tax is likely to arise**
- **indemnify an innocent payee if it does**
- **offer an exit to the problem by allowing termination of Transactions on various conditions.**

Likelihood of withholding tax arising

The parties need to do detailed legal and tax analysis at the start of their relationship to ensure that no withholding tax on payments is likely to be levied in any of the jurisdictions through which they propose to trade. A payer will normally seek comfort on this point by obtaining tax documentation confirming this from the payee or ensuring that the payee is covered by an exemption from withholding tax in the double tax treaty between their two countries by asking the payee for a Payee Tax Representation to this effect in Part 2(b) of the Schedule. This will enable the payer to make its standard Payer Tax Representation in Part 2(a) of the Schedule. Where each party wants to deal through several Offices (i.e. on a Multibranch basis) the analytical principles are the same but are made more complex by the need for a payer to consider if a withholding tax could be levied through each combination of its own and the payee's Offices.

It is worth noting that under US tax law withholding tax is not levied on payments under many notional principal contracts (1992 *User's Guide*, page 46 footnote).

Indemnification of payee

Under the gross up mechanism of Section 2(d)(i)(4) of the Agreement the onus is basically on the payer to gross up its payment to the payee if the payer's tax authority decides to levy a withholding tax on its payment to the payee.

Tax authorities call this type of tax an Indemnifiable Tax, i.e. because the tax arises from payments under a cross-border Transaction and the payee is indemnified by the payer for its imposition. If it was not, the payee would receive its payment with the withholding tax deducted and hence would receive less than it expected. This would arise where the Tax was not classified as an Indemnifiable Tax or where the payee had a connection (e.g. an office there) with the tax jurisdiction concerned.

The cross-border nature of the tax and the fact that the payer is dealing with a foreign payee are the key features here. Withholding tax does not arise where the parties to the Agreement are both incorporated in the same tax jurisdiction and even if it did it would not be classified as an Indemnifiable Tax under the Agreement and be subject to gross up. In those circumstances the payee would have to bear it.

However, the basic concept is that notwithstanding a withholding tax charge on the payer, the payee should be protected and entitled to receive the amount he expected from the payer and which is specified in the Confirmation. However, there are two exceptions to this where:

- **the payee has made a payee tax representation which proves to be untrue at the outset or later on (except where this arises from a Change in Tax Law or a binding decision from a court or tax authority); or**
- **the payee fails to provide requested tax documentation to eliminate or reduce the payer's withholding tax charge.**

The reason for these exceptions is that a payer would quite rightly be reluctant to take on the potential gross up obligation and transact with the payee if it could not rely strongly upon the payee's tax representations or the tax documentation it supplied. The increased cost of doing business might well be uneconomic for the payer. It would also be unfair for it to be penalised for the payee's shortcomings here.

In brief, where a Change in Tax Law results in a withholding tax on payments being levied, then the payer has to gross up but has the right to terminate under the Tax Event Termination Event (Section 5(b)(ii)). Where the payee makes an incorrect tax representation upon which the payer has relied (and no Change in Tax Law has intervened) the payee receives its payments with withholding tax deducted, i.e. net.

Payee Tax Representations apply continuously under the Agreement (see the preamble to Section 3).

Where there is a change of facts about a payer or payee (e.g. the termination of a payer's status as a financial trader which is beneficial in the UK for exemption of certain payments from withholding tax) or the termination of a payee's status as a tax resident of a treaty country, then a withholding tax requirement might arise if a Payee Tax Representation is breached or the payee fails to provide a requested tax form. Where a change of facts affects the payer, he will have to gross up unless again the payee fails to provide a requested tax form. Generally speaking the party responsible suffers in these circumstances.

Termination of Affected Transactions

Either the payer (if it has to gross up) or the payee (if it receives its payment after deduction of withholding tax) can terminate Affected Transactions by invoking the Tax Event or Tax Event Upon Merger Termination Events (as appropriate) but only if there has been a Change in Tax Law or a binding decision issued by a court or tax authority. Termination because of a Change in Tax Law is done on a "no fault" basis, i.e. two Affected Parties.

In addition, if a payee refuses to deliver a tax form under Section 4(a)(iii) because it "would materially prejudice its legal or commercial position" the payer would still have to gross up but would also be able to close out under the Tax Event Termination Event if it requested that a tax form be provided under Section 4(a)(i). If it fails to do this it will not be able to invoke a Tax Event Termination Event. Section 4(a)(i) has no "material prejudice" exception.

The tax analysis on pp. 39–54 of the 1992 *User's Guide* is very useful but like all tax analysis needs to be read slowly and patiently.

Figure 8.2 shows when gross up needs to be made under the Agreement.

When gross up needs to be made under the Agreement

FIG 8.2

Circumstances	*Who suffers?*	*Why?*	*Close-out possible?*
Payer's tax jurisdiction levies withholding tax	Payer grosses up.	Required under Section 2(d)(i).	Yes
Payer makes incorrect tax representation	Payer grosses up.	Fair. Payer cannot breach its own tax rep in these circumstances.	No
Change in Tax Law or binding court or tax authority decision affects payee	Payer grosses up.	Required under Section 2(d)(i).	Yes
Payee's tax reps become untrue but not due to a Change in Tax Law etc	Payee receives net.	Unfair to Payer to gross up.	No
Payee fails to provide requested tax documentation.	Payee receives net.	Unfair for Payer to gross up.	No
Tax authoriy requires Payer to gross up previous payments to Payee because Payee's Tax Refs have become untrue (but not due to Change in Tax Law)	Payee indemnifies Payer	Section 2(d)(ii)	No
Payer fails to request necessary tax form	Payer	Fair	No in view of p. 50 of the *User's Guide*
Change of facts affects a party	Responsible party	Section 4(d)	No
Payee refuses to provide tax documentation because it would materially predjudice its legal or commercial position (Section 4(a)(iii))	Payer	Required under *User's Guide* p. 49	Yes
Tax not Indemnifiable	Payee	*User's Guide* p. 39	No

Part 2. Tax Representations.

(a) ***Payer Representations***. For the purpose of Section 3(e) of this Agreement, Party A will make the following representation and Party B will make the following representation:

It is not required by any applicable law, as modified by the practice of any relevant governmental revenue authority of any Relevant Jurisdiction to make any deduction or withholding for or on account of any Tax from any payment (other than interest under Section 2(e), 6(d)(ii) or 6(e) of this Agreement) to be made by it to the other party under this Agreement. In making this representation, it may rely on (i) the accuracy of any representations made by the other party pursuant to Section 3(f) of this Agreement, (ii) the satisfaction of the agreement contained in Section 4(a)(i) or 4(a)(iii) of this Agreement and the accuracy and effectiveness of any document provided by the other party pursuant to Section 4(a)(i) or 4(a)(iii) of this Agreement and (iii) the satisfaction of the agreement of the other party contained in Section 4(d) of this Agreement provided that it shall not be a breach of this representation where reliance is placed on clause (ii) and the other party does not deliver a form or document under Section 4(a)(iii) by reason of material prejudice to its legal or commercial position.

Part 2(a) Payer Tax Representations

Generally speaking, transacting parties deal with each other on the basis that no withholding tax will be levied by a Relevant Jurisdiction on Transaction payments. They therefore each make the Payer Tax Representation opposite.

The term "Relevant Jurisdiction" means:

- **the payer's home jurisdiction**
- **the jurisdiction where its transacting Office is based**
- **the jurisdiction where it executed the Agreement**
- **the jurisdiction from which it makes payments under the Transactions.**

However, it is still possible for another jurisdiction to impose a tax on the payer's payment and the fact that a non-Relevant Jurisdiction did so will not preclude the tax from being an Indemnifiable Tax. However, few parties are likely to extend their tax analysis this far.

Most tax jurisdictions do not charge withholding taxes on payments for the types of Transactions covered by the Agreement. Where they do, the payer must ensure that it can gain relief by the payee making a representation or providing tax documentation granting exemption under the double tax treaty between their two countries. The payee is only excused from its obligation to deliver tax forms to the payer if it is truthfully able to assert that providing them would materially prejudice its commercial position. The payer still has a gross up obligation in these circumstances but can call a Tax Event to terminate the Affected Transaction(s).

The Payer Tax Representation excludes default interest payments under Section 2(e) or interest on early termination payments under Sections 6(d)(ii) or 6(e). In other words, the parties do not represent that there will be no withholding tax on interest payable in these circumstances under the Agreement. This shifts any such withholding tax on interest payable on to the payer. However, to get this into perspective any withholding tax on interest payable would be much lower than such a tax levied upon a Transaction payment.

The Payer Tax Representation in Part 2(a) is in the market standard wording and is always included. If by any chance a cross-border counterparty does not propose to include it (which is very rare – I have seen one example in 12 years) this should be carefully investigated. Even if this does happen, both parties are still subject to Section 2(d)(i).

(b) ***Payee Representations.*** For the purpose of Section 3(f) of this Agreement, neither Party A nor Party B makes any Payee Tax Representations.

Part 2(b) Payee Tax Representations

As there are a large number of double tax treaties in existence whose Income and Interest provisions give protection against the imposition of withholding taxes, parties frequently make no Payee Tax Representations in Part 2(b) of the Schedule.

However, where they need to do so the following representation is the one normally included in Schedules:

(b) ***Payee Representations.* For the purpose of Section 3(f) of this Agreement, Party A and Party B make the representations specified below, if any:**

(i) The following representation will apply to Party A and will apply to Party B:

It is fully eligible for the benefits of the "Business Profits" or "Industrial and Commercial Profits" provision, as the case may be, the "Interest" provision or the "Other Income" provision (if any) of the Specified Treaty with respect to any payment described in such provisions and received or to be received by it in connection with this Agreement and no such payment is attributable to a trade or business carried on by it through a permanent establishment in the Specified Jurisdiction.

If such representation applies, then:

***"Specified Treaty"* means with respect to Party A ....**

***"Specified Jurisdiction"* means with respect to Party A.........................**

***"Specified Treaty"* means with respect to Party B.................................**

***"Specified Jurisdiction"* means with respect to Party B.........................**

Payee Tax Representations are made continuously while any Transactions exist under the Agreement. Where a Payee Tax Representation becomes untrue there is an obligation under Section 4(d) of the Agreement to disclose this.

Please note that the standard treaty representation does not mean that payments under a particular derivatives transaction will be eligible for withholding tax at zero or a reduced rate. Rather the payee is only representing that it is eligible for the treaty benefits.

Imagine that the payer is X Bank AG incorporated in Germany who is also Party A and the payee is Rollerblade plc incorporated in the UK which is Party B. The Specified Treaty in each case will be the double taxation treaty between Germany and the UK. The Specified Jurisdiction is the jurisdiction which could impose the withholding tax and for Party A is the UK and for Party B, Germany.

In addition, the payee represents that it is not acting through a permanent establishment in the Specified Jurisdiction which could potentially levy a withholding tax because most tax treaties do not protect income arising from a permanent establishment.

When dealing with US counterparties, the following is a common Payee Tax Representation:

(ii) The following representation will apply to Party A and will apply to Party B:

Each payment received or to be received by it in connection with this Agreement will be effectively connected with its conduct of a trade or business in the Specified Jurisdiction.

If such representation applies, then:

***"Specified Jurisdiction"* means with respect to Party A..........................**

***"Specified Jurisdiction"* means with respect to Party B..........................**

Here, a US payer is asking a foreign payee to represent that each payment it receives will be effectively connected with its trade or business in the US. Such a representation is normally required from the US branches, agencies or offices of non-US parties. This is important because in the US, no withholding tax is required for payments effectively connected with the foreign payee's US business because the foreign payee will pay US income tax on profits arising from such business.

The UK Finance Act 1994 contained legislation which introduced new tax rules for interest rate contracts and options and currency rate contracts and options for accounting periods commencing after 22 March 1995. The legislation also introduced various anti-avoidance measures. The Finance Act 2002 has succeeded this legislation (especially Paragraph 31 of Schedule 26) for accounting periods starting on or after 1 October 2002 and references to this new legislation are now being seen in the market.

The effect of the first part of the 1994 legislation has been to make the following very common UK payee tax representation totally redundant:

It is entering into each Transaction in the ordinary course of its trade as, and is, either (1) a recognised U.K. bank or (2) a recognised U.K. swaps dealer (in either case (1) or (2), for purposes of the United Kingdom Inland Revenue extra statutory concession C17 on interest and currency swaps dated March 14, 1989), and (B) it will bring into account payments made and received in respect of each Transaction in computing its income for United Kingdom tax purposes.

The second part of the legislation required a non-resident company to make one or more Payee Tax Representations to a UK tax resident unless:

- **the UK tax resident is a bank, building society or financial trader entering into the interest rate or currency contract as principal for its UK trade; or**
- **the non-resident company is acting as principal and has entered into the transaction for the purposes of a trade carried on by it in the UK; or**
- **the non-resident company is resident in a jurisdiction which has a tax treaty with the UK containing an "interest" article.**

An ordinary UK corporate cannot benefit from these exemptions and quite commonly they will seek one of the following Payee Tax Representations from a foreign bank counterparty in order for the payment to be eligible for tax relief as a business expense:

> **(b) Payee Representations. For the purpose of Section 3(f) of this Agreement, Party A makes the representation specified below:**
>
> **UK Finance Act 2002. Party A represents, warrants and undertakes to Party B (which representation, warranty and undertaking will be deemed to be repeated at all times until the termination of this Agreement) that, in relation to each Transaction, it is not acting as agent or nominee for any other person or persons and that:**
>
> **(A) it is and will be throughout the course of the relevant Transaction resident in the United Kingdom for United Kingdom tax purposes; or**
>
> **(B) it is and will be throughout the course of the relevant Transaction resident in a jurisdiction that has a double taxation convention or treaty with the United Kingdom under which provision, whether for relief or otherwise, in relation to Interest (as defined in the relevant convention or treaty) is made; or**
>
> **(C) it has entered into the relevant Transaction solely for the purposes of a trade or part of a trade carried on by it in the United Kingdom through a branch or agent and will continue so to treat the relevant Transaction throughout the course of the relevant Transaction.**

Normally only one of these is given and it is vital for negotiators to check with their Tax Departments which one may be offered.

Sometimes a counterparty might try to seek an indemnity for this:

> **Indemnity as to UK Finance Act**
>
> **Without prejudice to any other rights, powers and remedies which Party A may have, Party B (*e.g. a bank*) agrees with Party A to indemnify and keep indemnified Party A on an after-tax basis from and against any cost, expense, damage, loss or liability (including, for the avoidance of doubt,**

any tax liability) which Party A may incur or suffer to the extent that Party A would not have incurred or suffered such cost, expense, damage, loss or liability had Party B complied with its representations, warranties and undertakings as set out in paragraph (*) of Part * of this Agreement.

This should be resisted, in my opinion.

Occasionally, you may find the following:

(b) *Payee Tax Representations.* For the purpose of Section 3(f) of this Agreement, Party A represents that it will bring into account payments made and received in respect of each Transaction in computing its income for United Kingdom tax purposes.

Again whether this can be given will depend upon the facts of the case.

Finally, new US tax legislation which took effect from 1 January 2001 has introduced new tax reporting forms (which are referred to on pages 325–9 and in the commentary on Part 3(a) of the Schedule on pages 481–3) and has resulted in US counterparties seeking the following Payee Tax Representations from non-US counterparties as appropriate:

The following representation will/will not apply to Party A and will/will not* apply to Party B:

[[(iii)] [Party A] [and] [Party B] [each] make[s] the following representation:–

It is a "U.S. person" (as that term is used in section 1.1441-4(a)(3)(ii) of United States Treasury Regulations) for United States federal income tax purposes.]*

[[(iv)] [Party A] [and] [Party B] [each] make[s] the following representation:–

It is a "non-U.S. branch of a foreign person" (as that term is used in section 1.1441-4(a)(3)(ii) of United States Treasury Regulations) for United States federal income tax purposes.]*

[[(v)] [Party A] [and] [Party B] [each] make[s] the following representation:–

With respect to payments made to an address outside the United States or made by a transfer of funds to an account outside the United States, it is a "non-U.S. branch of a foreign person" (as that term is used in section 1.1441-4(a)(3)(ii) of United States Treasury Regulations) for United States federal income tax purposes.]*

[[(vi)] [Party A] [and] [Party B] [each] make[s] the following representation:–

It is a "foreign person" (as that term is used in section 1.6041-4(a)(4) of United States Treasury Regulations) for United States federal income tax purposes.]*

***Delete as appropriate.**

In all cases, clearance from your Tax Department is needed for giving any Payee Tax Representations, especially new ones.

Part 3. Agreement to Deliver Documents

For the purpose of Sections 4(a)(i) and (ii) of this Agreement, each party agrees to deliver the following documents:

(a) Tax forms, documents or certificates to be delivered are:

None.

Part 3(a) Agreement to Deliver Documents

Part 3(a) relating to tax forms, documents and certificates to be delivered is not often filled in at all because a general undertaking to provide such documentation may be found in Section 4(a)(iii). Sometimes the following short form wording appears:

> **Each party shall, as soon as practicable after demand, deliver to the other party any form or document reasonably requested by the other party, including without limitation any form or document required to enable such other party to make payments hereunder without withholding for or on account of Taxes or with such withholding at a reduced rate.**

This largely repeats some of the wording of Section 4(a)(iii) and is often deleted during negotiations. However, if a counterparty insists on having it then there is no harm in including it.

If confidentiality is particularly important, the parties may add the following wording to stress this:

> **Any forms, documents or certificates required to be delivered by a party pursuant to Section 4(a)(i) or (iii) which contain any information or material which the party providing the form determines in its sole discretion to be confidential, such party may in lieu of delivering such form, document or certificate to the other party, arrange for its delivery directly to the relevant governmental or taxing authority under such terms and conditions as are satisfactory to the other party in order to protect the confidentiality of the material contained therein.**

Some US counterparties like to have the provision of certain tax forms specified – forms ordinarily required to certify non-resident status or withholding tax exemptions. The following is an example of such wording:

> **For the purpose of Sections 4(a)(i) and (iii) of this Agreement, each party agrees to deliver the following documents, as applicable:**
>
> **(a) Tax forms, documents or certificates to be delivered are:**
>
> **(i) If Party A is acting through a branch in [*insert name of country other than the US*] or any other branch outside the United States, Party A agrees to complete accurately and in a manner reasonably satisfactory to Party B, and to execute and deliver to Party B, a US Internal Revenue Service Form W-8BEN, or any successor Form, (1) promptly upon reasonable demand by Party B, and (2) promptly upon learning that any such Form previously provided by Party A has (or is about to) become obsolete or incorrect.**

> **(ii) If Party A is acting through a branch in the United States, Party A agrees to complete, accurately and in a manner reasonably satisfactory to Party B, and to execute and deliver to Party B, a U.S. Internal Revenue Service Form W8-ECI, or any successor Form, (1) promptly upon reasonable demand by Party B, and (2) promptly upon learning that any such Form previously provided by Party A has (or is about to) become obsolete or incorrect.**

US payers ask non-US payees to complete Form W-8BEN to confirm that they are eligible for double tax treaty benefits which would enable the US payer to avoid withholding tax or pay it at a reduced rate.

Form W8-ECI does the same thing where the foreign payee is doing business through its US branch. The form states that the income being paid is "effectively connected" with the payee's US trade or business. This means its income from the payment by the US payer will be subject to US income tax and no US withholding tax charge arises.

(b) Other documents to be delivered are:

	Party required to deliver document	Document	Date by which to be delivered	Covered by Section 3(d) representation
(i)	Party A and Party B	Certified evidence of the authority, incumbency and specimen signature of each person executing any document on its behalf in connection with this Agreement.	Upon execution of this Agreement and upon request.	Yes
(ii)	Party A and Party B	A copy of its most recent Annual Report containing consolidated financial statements, prepared in accordance with accounting principles that are generally accepted for institutions of its type in the jurisdiction of its organisation and certified by independent public accountants.	Upon request.	No
(iii)	Party B	Evidence of its capacity and ability to enter into this Agreement and any Transaction hereunder.	Upon execution of this Agreement and upon request.	Yes

Part 3(b)

Part 3(b) concerns the delivery of other non-tax related documentation. This normally includes:

- **signing authorities of the parties – sometimes in the form of an incumbency certificate.**
- **A copy of each party's Annual Report and Accounts either deliverable within a certain timescale (where non-delivery could create a potential Breach of Agreement Event of Default) or upon request. Parties should be careful not to agree a deadline for delivery if they do not have the systems in place to ensure this happens.**
- **Evidence of a party's capacity to enter into derivatives Transactions, e.g. a copy of its Memorandum and Articles of Association or by-laws or relevant Board Resolutions. Banks do not provide such evidence themselves because they regard derivatives trading as an ordinary business activity and, moreover, regulators authorise them to enter into such Transactions. Where a party is incorporated in England or Wales, counterparties may rely upon s 35 of the Companies Act 1985 against any claim that the English or Welsh party was acting outside its powers.**

Other documentation required might include:

(iv)	[Party B	Certified evidence of the authority, incumbency and specimen signature of each person executing the Credit Support Document.	Upon execution of this Agreement.	Yes]
(v)	[Party B	The Credit Support Document referred to in Part 4(f) of this Schedule.	Upon execution of this Agreement.	Yes]
(vi)	[Party B	An opinion of counsel of the Credit Support Provider of Party B in form and substance satisfactory to Party A.	Upon execution of this Agreement.	No]
(vii)	[Party B	A letter or other certified document from Party B's Process Agent stating its agreement to act as Process Agent to Party B.	Upon execution of this Agreement.	Yes]

(iv) Signing authority for any Credit Support Provider would be included in Part 3(b).

(v) Mention might be made of a Credit Support Document here although this is also specified in Part 4(f) of the Schedule. However, Letters of Comfort, for instance, which are not Credit Support Documents might also be included here but that depends upon the policy of the negotiating institution.

(vi) A legal opinion as to a party's capacity to enter into derivatives Transactions and the enforceability of close-out netting in its jurisdiction may be required. This is particularly so if the counterparty is of an unusual type (e.g. a supranational body like the European Bank of Reconstruction and Development) or domiciled in an exotic location (e.g. Labuan) or in an emerging economy in Eastern Europe. With reputable, trusted counterparties, an in-house legal opinion may be acceptable.

(vii) Process Agent acceptance letters where one of the parties is not incorporated in England or Wales (English Law) or in New York (New York Law Agreement). Here is an example of such a letter:

Letter typed on Process Agent's letterhead

[Date]

Z Bank PLC
[rest of address]

Dear Sirs

Re: Exotica S.p.A.

We, the undersigned, hereby accept our appointment to receive on behalf of Exotica S.p.A. service of process issued out of the courts of England in respect of any legal action or proceedings arising out of or in connection with the ISDA Master Agreement dated as of [ ] between Z Bank PLC and Exotica S.p.A.

Yours faithfully
for and on behalf of Humdrum Services Limited

Andrew Buccaneer
Director

The market is a little divided on the need for such a letter but, on balance, they are becoming more common and avoid any future argument that a Process Agent had not been informed about its appointment. In English law Agreements Process Agents are typically UK branches of banks, UK subsidiaries of corporates or legal firms or their service offshoots.

There are many other types of documentation for different types of entities which could be requested in the relevant circumstances:

- **a copy of relevant enabling laws for sovereigns;**
- **extracts from a Commercial Register (e.g. for authorities of named personnel to bind a party to the Agreement);**
- **Certificates of Incorporation;**
- **Investment Management Agreements and monthly certificates of net asset values in relation to funds under management;**
- **copies of Trust Deeds in respect of trustees acting for a party;**
- **constituting documents describing the powers of charities, universities, building societies etc.**

The list is long but the key thing is to make sure you have examined every document conferring capacity and authority on your counterparty you can think of or can reasonably obtain. Failure to provide an agreed document more than 30 days after a notice requiring it has been given will constitute an Event of Default under Section 5(a)(ii).

Most of the documents provided will be subject to the Section 3(d) representation that the information provided is true, accurate and complete in every material respect at the time it is supplied. There are normally two exceptions to this:

- **legal opinions – particularly those provided by a barrister; and**
- **audited accounts.**

With respect to the second point you sometimes see the Section 3(d) representation marked as "Yes" rather than "No". In my opinion this is not a good idea because an auditor will only normally certify that audited accounts reflect a "true and fair view". This is far weaker than "true, accurate and complete in every material respect". It seems to me unwise that a party should represent and warrant more about its audited accounts than its expert auditor is prepared to do. It could be said that parties should make a positive representation here to show that they stand behind their accounts. However, I think they show this by signing them.

Where a party refuses to budge on this it is possible to try the following redefinition of terms for audited accounts:

(*)	Party A and Party B	A copy of its most recent Annual Report containing consolidated financial statements, prepared in accordance with accounting principles that are generally accepted for institutions of its type in the jurisdiction of its organisation and certified by independent public accountants.	Upon request.	Yes but the phrase "true, accurate and complete" in Section 3(d) shall be deleted and the words "true and fair" inserted in lieu thereof.

Alternatively, a Part 5 amendment can be made as follows:

> "*Accuracy of Specified Information*" Section 3(d) is hereby amended by adding in the third line thereof after the word "respect" and before the full stop the words 'or, in the case of audited or unaudited financial statements, a fair presentation of the financial condition of the relevant person'.

OR

> Add at the end of the last line of Section 3(d), after "material respect": "except that, with respect to any financial information furnished by or on behalf of a party for that party to the other party, such financial information fairly presents the financial condition and the results of the operations of the party as at the dates at which the financial information is stated to apply."

OR

> Financial Statements
>
> To the extent that any representation is given pursuant to Section 3(d) in relation to the Annual Financial Statements referred to in Part 3(b) then the Section 3(d) representation shall be amended by the deletion of the phrase "is, as of the date of the information, true, accurate and complete in every material respect" and the insertion instead of the phrase "gives a true and fair view of the financial position of the relevant party in relation to the financial period for which the information has been prepared".

Part 4

(a) Addresses for Notices. For the purpose of Section 12(a) of this Agreement:

Addresses for notices or communications to Party A

For all purposes of this Agreement:

X Bank AG, Frankfurt Head Office

Address:	Complete relevant details
Attention:	Complete relevant details
Telex:	Complete relevant details Answerback: Complete details
Facsimile:	Complete relevant details
Telephone:	Complete relevant details

Electronic Messaging System Details: Complete relevant details

X Bank AG, London Branch

Address:	Complete relevant details
Attention:	Complete relevant details
Telex:	Complete relevant details Answerback: Complete details
Facsimile:	Complete relevant details
Telephone:	Complete relevant details

Electronic Messaging System Details: Complete relevant details

Address for notices or communications to Party B:

Address:	Complete relevant details
Attention:	Complete relevant details
Telex:	Complete relevant details Answerback: Complete details
Facsimile	Complete relevant details
Telephone:	Complete relevant details

Electronic Messaging System Details: Complete relevant details

Part 4 Miscellaneous

Part 4 covers numerous important matters.

In Part 4(a) the parties set out their contact details for notices (mostly for administrative purposes). Often wording is included directing any notices under Sections 5 and 6 of the Agreement (concerning termination and close-out) to a party's Legal Department. Where a party lists several branches through which trades may be transacted, this is the first indication that it is a Multibranch Party.

(b) ***Process Agent.*** For the purpose of Section 13(c) of this Agreement:

Party A appoints as its Process Agent:

X Bank AG, London Branch
[Insert London address]
Attention: General Manager

Party B appoints as its Process Agent:

Not applicable.

Part 4(b)

Part 4(b) gives details of any Process Agent appointed to receive writs or termination notices or other such legal documentation. A Process Agent will usually need to be appointed if a party is not incorporated in England (under an English Law Agreement) or New York (under a New York Law Agreement). With a foreign bank this is usually respectively its London or New York Office. Some parties argue that this is not necessary because the branch is part of the bank as a whole but, in practice, the branch is usually specified as Process Agent. Please note that because of the preponderance of state laws in the US a counterparty incorporated say in Illinois will still need to specify a New York Process Agent for termination rights to be fully protected under an Agreement governed by New York law.

A party does not need to specify a Process Agent where it is itself incorporated in England (under an English law Agreement) or in New York (under a New York law Agreement). In those cases it will insert Not Applicable against its designation in Part 4(b).

It is possible that some small continental entities for example in Portugal or Italy may not have a presence in London or New York and may seek to avoid appointing a Process Agent. For instance, counterparties in Ireland or France may argue that their geographical proximity to England makes this unnecessary. I disagree with this because the only certain way for termination rights to be protected under an English law Agreement is for the foreign counterparty to appoint an England-based Process Agent.

The Law Debenture Corporation PLC and English law firms provide Process Agent services at relatively modest cost (£500–£2,000 p.a. depending on level of service required). However, if an ISDA country legal opinion specifically states that there is no need for a Process Agent to be appointed in England or New York this need not be done but the annual updates to the opinion would need to be scrutinised to ensure this continued to be so.

There are not many Process Agent clauses but I have seen the following:

> **Party B hereby agrees that if Party A considers it necessary to appoint an agent for the service of legal proceedings and justifies it in writing, Party B shall forthwith appoint such agent on behalf of Party B with an office in the City of London. If Party B fails to appoint such an agent within five Local Business Days of such request by Party A, without justified reason, then Party A shall be entitled to appoint such an agent on behalf of Party B, in the name of Party B, and at the expense of Party B. Party A shall notify Party B forthwith of the appointment of any such agent.**

OR

Party B appoints no Process Agent. Party B represents that, if, in case of any dispute arising out of or in connection with this Agreement, Party A so requests (which request may be made by telephone or in writing), it shall promptly appoint an agent for the service of legal proceedings on its behalf with an office in the City of London, United Kingdom. All costs in relation to the absence of a Process Agent for Party B, at any stage of the proceedings, shall be attributable to and payable by Party B.

OR

If a party becomes organised outside the United States of America, then promptly upon written demand such party shall irrevocably appoint an agent for service of process in the United States of America reasonably satisfactory to the other party and provide the other party with a copy of such written acceptance of such appointment.

(c) *Offices.* The provisions of Section 10(a) will apply to this Agreement.

Part 4(c)

Section 10(a) of the Agreement provides that if a party enters into a Transaction through one of its branches, its obligations are the same as if it had entered into the Transaction through its Head Office. If this provision is made applicable through Part 4(c) each party is representing that its head or home office is responsible for its obligations where it cannot honour them and effectively provides an implied payment guarantee for Transactions entered into through branches.

However, some banks seek to disapply the provision which indicates that they are not willing to take on the political risk of some of their branches, normally those in more exotic locations. If exchange controls were imposed in such jurisdictions they would not wish to have counterparties approaching their Head Office for payment. Whether this disapplication of Section 10(a) is acceptable to counterparties is a matter of policy and may, in any case, be factored into the pricing of the deal. There may be legal problems over the effectiveness of close-out netting or enforceability of judgments in an exotic jurisdiction. Moreover, the "bad branch" tainting problem could arise as outlined in Chapter 5, pages 359–60.

Occasionally, a party will propose the disapplication of Section 10(a) through Part 4(c) of the Schedule although the Agreement at this stage only covers mainstream branches of both parties. I think this should be resisted in these circumstances because it is potentially giving a blanket advance clearance for such disapplication for the future.

Sometimes market players propose wide-ranging ring fencing language in Part 5 of the Schedule such as this example concerning payments when a Sovereign Event occurs:

Sovereign Event

(i) If due to a moratorium, act of state, governmental regulation (whether temporary or permanent) or analogous occurrence or due to a disruption in the local market for currency Transactions from such or related cause (a "Sovereign Event"), the making or receiving of payments in respect of Transactions entered into by any Office of Party A or Party B is wholly or partially restricted or prohibited, the relevant Office of Party A and/or Party B shall immediately cease to have any obligation to make or receive such payment or delivery until such time as such restriction or prohibition is wholly removed or is wholly inoperative, or the parties agree to enter into a new contractually binding agreement in writing with regard to the making of payments under such Transactions in the context of any relevant sovereign restructuring or rescheduling;

(ii) Party A and Party B agree that the place of performance of any payment obligation in respect of a Transaction shall be the relevant Office of Party A and Party B effecting such Transaction and other than in respect of the Offices listed in (iv) below no other office of Party A or Party B shall be liable or be required to make any payment or delivery in respect of a Transaction which is affected by a Sovereign Event;

(iii) Notwithstanding any provisions to the contrary in this Agreement or any Agreement between the parties constituted by a Confirmation incorporating the printed terms of the Agreement, Section 10(a) of the Agreement shall not apply in respect of Transactions between Party A and Party B save in respect of Offices specified in (iv) below;

(iv) For the purpose of Paragraph (ii) of this clause the following Offices apply to Party A [state names] and to Party B [state names].

(v) For the avoidance of doubt it is agreed that the foregoing provisions of this [state clause number] do not affect any obligations of each party in the event of the insolvency or bankruptcy of the relevant local Office independently of the occurrence of such Sovereign Event and further it is agreed that either party is entitled to terminate the Agreement if an Event of Default has occurred wholly independently of any occurrence constituting a "Sovereign Event".

This deals with payments from branches in jurisdictions where such payments are subject to the conditions of a general sovereign restructuring or rescheduling.

The effect of this is to disapply Section 10(a) for all trades with branches not specified as Multibranch Parties in Part 4(d) of the Schedule where a Sovereign Event (as defined) occurs. It prevents a counterparty trying to enter into deals with a bank branch anywhere in the world and relying upon Section 10(a). This provision extends the disapplication to a Sovereign Event or at least clarifies the circumstances where this could happen depending upon your point of view. While this might be acceptable to some parties, others (especially corporates) will argue that a bank should be able to control the branches through which it deals.

Another variation of this involves the creation of a Section 10(d) through a new Part 5 provision.

First Part 4(c) of the Schedule is amended as follows:

The provisions of Section 10(a) of the Agreement will apply, subject to the provisions of Section 10(d) of the Schedule:

Section 10 of the Agreement is modified by inserting a new sub-Section (d) at the end of such Section:

> (d) Obligations of a party with respect to a Transaction shall not be payable or collectible at an office or branch of such party other than the office or branch specified in the Confirmation with respect to that Transaction (the "Specified Office") if such party is not able to discharge such obligations through the Specified Office as a result of an Illegality or Impossibility. Under these circumstances, neither party to the Agreement shall have any right of action for any loss, damage or other consequence of any such action or threat of action against any office or branch of the other party outside of the jurisdiction in which the Specified Office is located.

and then the following provision is included in Part 5 of the Schedule:

> Section 6(d)(ii) of the Agreement is hereby amended by adding the following proviso at the end of the first sentence: "; provided, however, that if any amount calculated as being due in respect of an Early Termination Date which is designated as a result of an Illegality or an Impossibility cannot be paid on such day by the Office specified in the Confirmation(s) relating to the Terminated Transaction(s) as a result of such event, then such amount will be payable by such Office on the day which is two Local Business Days after the day which the Illegality and/or Impossibility, as the case may be, no longer exists or, if earlier, on the date on which an Event of Default with respect to the Affected Party occurs".

The effect is to ring fence the political risk of a party's branches.

A more shorthand version of this is:

> The provisions of Section 10(a) of this Agreement will apply to this Agreement provided that payments and deliveries by each Party will be made through the Office referred to in the relevant Confirmation and the obligation to make a payment or delivery will be subject to applicable laws, orders and regulations relating to such Office in the jurisdiction in which the Office is located.

A more mealy-mouthed version is:

> The provisions of Section 10(a) will not apply to this Agreement. However, the parties represent to each other that in the event that they enter into a Transaction through an office other than their head or home office, that notwithstanding the place of booking office or jurisdiction of incorporation of the party, the obligations of the party are the obligations of Party A or Party B, as the case may be, but different legal rules might apply where a claim for performance of a payment or delivery obligation is made in a place other than its head or home office. This representation will be deemed to be repeated by each party on each date on which a Transaction is entered into.

(d) ***Multibranch Party.*** For the purpose of Section 10(c) of this Agreement:

Party A is a Multibranch Party and may act through the following Offices:

Frankfurt and London.

Party B is not a Multibranch Party.

Part 4(d)

In Part 4(d) parties specify the identity of those branches through which they wish to enter into OTC derivatives transactions under the Agreement. Both parties will consider these branches from the point of view of close-out netting in the jurisdictions where they are located. They will also consider any withholding tax implications.

Corporates will not normally be Multibranch Parties.

Sometimes a list of Offices are given followed by a catch-all phrase such as "or such other branches as may be specified in a Confirmation".

While this may seem prima facie a good idea so as to avoid having to enter into an Amendment Agreement when new branches are added, it should not be left to traders to decide whether to deal with a counterparty's branch. Legal and tax analyses need to be done as well as the impact of any general disapplication of Section 10(a) through Part 4(c) of the Schedule.

(e) ***Calculation Agent.*** The Calculation Agent is Party A, unless otherwise specified in a Confirmation in relation to the relevant Transaction.

Part 4(e)

The term Calculation Agent is not defined in the ISDA Master Agreement but may be found in the *2000 ISDA Definitions* or in the various product specific Definitions. The Calculation Agent is called to act in good faith and in a commercially reasonable manner. Its typical duties are determining floating rates or prices, calculating payments to be made, verifying if a Market Disruption Event has occurred and resolving disputes.

Normally, a bank will insist that it is Calculation Agent where the Agreement is with a corporate and this is sensible because it is likely to have more sophisticated systems than most corporates. The larger bank will usually be Calculation Agent in an Agreement between two banks.

Where two major banks are involved they slug out this point or agree to be joint Calculation Agents. This is usually no big deal because parties will always check the Calculation Agent's figures and dispute any major discrepancies.

Sometimes, parties agree that one of them shall be Calculation Agent but that this will change if it performs its duties negligently or suffers an Event of Default. Then the other party will become the Calculation Agent or appoint an independent third party. Examples of such wording are as follows:

> ***Calculation Agent.*** **Any failure by a party to perform properly any obligation assumed by it to act as Calculation Agent for the purposes of any Transaction shall not constitute an Event of Default but shall entitle the other party to nominate itself or a third party reasonably selected by such other party as Calculation Agent and upon such nomination, such other party or third party shall be Calculation Agent for the purposes of the relevant Transaction accordingly.**

OR

> **Calculation Agent**
>
> **Failure of the party required to act as Calculation Agent to perform, on a timely basis, any of its responsibilities as Calculation Agent shall not relieve the parties of their respective payment obligations under this Agreement and such failure shall not be considered an event which would permit the termination of this Agreement or any Transaction.**
>
> **If the party required to act as Calculation Agent has not remedied its failure to perform its responsibilities as Calculation Agent within 60 days of notice of such failure having been given to such party by the other party, then that other party shall perform those responsibilities of the Calculation Agent which have not been performed.**

OR

Unless otherwise specified in a Confirmation in relation to the relevant Transaction, Party A is the Calculation Agent, with all calculations and determinations hereunder being subject to the review of Party B. Party A and Party B agree to use their best efforts to resolve expeditiously any disagreements concerning such calculations and determinations. If Party A and Party B cannot agree on such calculation or determination they agree to appoint expeditiously and jointly an independent dealer in the instruments or other obligations, the subject of the particular Transaction, to make such calculation or determination, with the calculation or determination made by such independent dealer to be binding and conclusive absent manifest error.

OR

The Calculation Agent is Party A, unless otherwise specified in a Confirmation in relation to the relevant Transaction, provided, however, that all calculations and determinations made by the Calculation Agent are subject to review and concurrence by Party B. If Party A and Party B disagree with respect to any calculation or determination, Party A and Party B each will appoint an independent Reference Market-maker, and such two Reference Market-makers jointly will appoint a third Reference Market-maker. Such three Reference Market-makers jointly will make such calculation or determination (acting as experts and not as arbitrators), whose calculation or determination will be binding and conclusive absent manifest error. In addition, if at any time a Potential Event of Default, Event of Default, or Termination Event occurs with respect to Party A, Party B will act as the Calculation Agent or will appoint a third party to act as Calculation Agent.

OR even more elaborate:

Co-calculation Agents

Party A and Party B shall be Co-calculation Agents with all calculations and determinations hereunder by each Co-calculation Agent being subject to the review and agreement of Party A and Party B (an "Agreed Calculation" and an "Agreed Determination", respectively), each using its reasonable efforts to resolve expeditiously any disagreements concerning such calculations and determinations. If Party A and Party B cannot reach an Agreed Calculation or an Agreed Determination, then they agree to appoint promptly and jointly three independent leading dealers in the relevant market each to make the relevant calculation or determination, in which case the Agreed Calculation shall be the

arithmetic mean of three calculations by the appointed dealers and the Agreed Determination shall be the determination agreed upon by at least two of the three dealers; provided, however, if fewer than three dealers provide a calculation or determination then Party A and Party B agree to appoint promptly and jointly such number of additional dealers such that Party A and Party B shall receive three calculations or determinations. The Agreed Calculation or Agreed Determination reached by such dealers will be conclusive and binding absent manifest error. In cases where one party erroneously disputes the other party's calculations it shall bear reasonable costs arising from obtaining prices from three leading independent dealers.

If this went on much further it would become Pythonesque!

Sometimes you see attempts to avoid liability such as the following:

In the absence of gross negligence or wilful misconduct by Party A in the execution of its duties as Calculation Agent, Party A shall have no liability for, or arising from, errors or omissions in the execution of such duties (other than for (a) amounts received by Party A as a result of any such error or omission and that would not otherwise have been payable to it and (b) amounts not paid by Party A as a result of any such error or omission and that would otherwise have been payable by it). Amounts determined by the Calculation Agent shall, absent manifest error, be binding upon the parties.

Given that the Calculation Agent should act in good faith and in a commercially reasonable manner this type of provision should be rejected because of the low standards it sets.

(f) *Credit Support Document.* Details of any Credit Support Document:

None.

Part 4(f)

This is where the nature of any Credit Support Document is specified. This would usually be an unconditional and irrevocable third party guarantee or it could be a letter of credit from a bank. ISDA discourages inclusion of the ISDA Credit Support Annex (English Law) here because it is a title transfer document (i.e. ownership of the collateral passes to the other party called the transferee) rather than a security interest document (where the ownership of the collateral remains with the pledgor who grants the pledgee a proprietary interest in it). However, the English Law ISDA Credit Support Deed and the ISDA Credit Support Annex (New York Law) are security interest documents and would normally be specified as Credit Support Documents.

A Letter of Credit (from a bank) for instance or a mortgage of property would be described as a Credit Support Document but a Letter of Comfort would not as it is only a moral obligation. The provision of a Letter of Comfort could be referred to in Part 3(b) of the Schedule if desired.

(g) *Credit Support Provider.*

Credit Support Provider means in relation to Party A: Not applicable.

Credit Support Provider means in relation to Party B: Not applicable.

Part 4(g)

The name of the Credit Support Provider is specified in Part 4(g) of the Schedule. The only point to make here is the obvious one that care should be taken to ensure that the Credit Support Provider's full and precise legal name is given.

(h) *Governing Law.* This Agreement will be governed by and construed in accordance with English law.

Part 4(h)

The Agreement was composed under the common law systems of England and the State of New York and its provisions are deemed fully effective under those governing laws. The drafters of the Agreement sought to make it as neutral as possible between the choices of these two governing laws. Requests for different governing laws (and I have seen Hong Kong, Italy, Ireland, Japan and Ontario proposed) should be resisted unless a legal opinion is obtained which clearly shows the impact of the relevant other law upon the Agreement's core provisions and that impact is not considered material. Requests for other governing laws usually arise when dealing with sovereigns who may be prohibited by statute from entering into Agreements subject to any other governing law than their own.

Where a New York law governed Agreement is concerned, the normal wording of Part 4(h) is:

> ***Governing Law.*** **This Agreement will be governed by and construed in accordance with the laws of the State of New York (without reference to choice of law doctrine).**

The words in brackets clarify that New York law will apply here even if the parties are incorporated in another US state.

Under New York law a contract must have a value of US$250,000 or more before the parties can choose New York law to govern it. This is not usually a problem with the Agreement.

Sometimes you see a more protective clause:

> **This Agreement will be governed by and construed in accordance with the laws of the State of New York, excluding, to the greatest extent a New York court would permit, any rule of law that would cause the application of the laws of any jurisdiction other than the State of New York.**

(i) *Netting of Payments.* Subparagraph (ii) of Section 2(c) of this Agreement will not apply to any Transactions or group of Transactions.

Part 4(i)

This provision chooses the scope of payment netting to be applied to the Agreement, e.g.: payments can be netted:

- **only in respect of the same Transaction, in the same currency and due on the same date ("single Transaction netting"); or**
- **for more than one transaction of the same type, in the same currency and due on the same date ("multiple Transaction netting"); or**
- **for one or more Transactions of different types, in the same currency and due on the same date ("cross-product netting").**

Furthermore, such netting may be limited to a particular pair of Offices of the parties concerned and it could also apply to physical deliveries, where practical, under the Agreement.

However, the cardinal rule is not to agree to do anything which you cannot do operationally.

Parties' payment netting capabilities progress at different speeds and to sign up to a position you cannot currently automate in the hope that you can in the future, could make you a hostage to fortune. Market players do this in order to avoid the need to amend the Agreement but it is a perilous approach and could result in embarrassment. Others believe the full scope of payment netting would enable them, for instance, to cross-product net all Transactions manually if their systems were insufficient and they were concerned about their counterparty's creditworthiness. However, this is easier said than done with a large portfolio where netting might also make it difficult to track if the correct payments had been made.

The basic wording for single Transaction netting is:

> *Netting of Payments.* **Subparagraph (ii) of Section 2(c) of this Agreement will apply to all Transactions.**

So when Subparagraph (ii) of Section 2(c) will apply to the Agreement you know you have single Transaction netting applying. When you see it will not apply, as in our example opposite, you know that multiple Transaction netting and/or cross product netting will apply.

Most banks automate single Transaction netting. Where a party demands more than this various compromise wording is possible:

> *Netting of Payments.* **Subparagraph (ii) of Section 2(c) of this Agreement will apply to any of the Transactions starting from the date of this Agreement. However, Party B undertakes to advise Party A in writing when it is operationally capable of netting payments in respect of more than one Transaction of the same type or between Transactions of different types.**

OR

> *Netting of Payments.* **(i) Subparagraph (ii) of Section 2(c) of this Agreement will apply to all Transactions; however, (ii) at such time as Party B can operationally make net payment across Transactions and gives written notice to Party A, then Subparagraph (ii) of Section 2(c) of this Agreement will not apply to all Transactions. Party B agrees to notify Party A when it operationally has the capability to net payments across all Transactions.**

OR

> *Netting of Payments.* **(i) Subparagraph (ii) of Section 2(c) will apply to amounts payable with respect to all Transactions from the date of this Agreement: provided, however, that if at any time both parties become capable of effecting payment netting across Transactions and give notice to the other that subparagraph (ii) of Section 2(c) shall not apply, then, from the date of such notice, subparagraph (ii) of Section 2(c) will not apply to any amount payable with respect to any Transactions.**

It is also possible to apply single Transaction netting in respect of one specified group of Transactions and multiple Transaction netting to the rest as in the following example:

> *Netting of Payments.* **Subparagraph (ii) of Section 2(c) of this Agreement will not apply to the following Transactions or groups of Transactions (in each case starting from the date of this Agreement: all Transactions except FX Transactions and Currency Options).**

OR

> *Netting of Payments.* **The first paragraph of Section 2(c) will apply as set out in this Agreement. However, the parties may elect in respect of two or more Transactions that a net amount shall be payable on one or more specified Scheduled Payment Dates in respect of such Transactions. Subparagraph (ii) of Section 2(c) of this Agreement will not apply to the payments due on each Scheduled Payment Date in respect of the Transactions for which the parties shall have made such an election.**

OR a vaguer alternative which could cause disputes:

> *Netting of Payments.* **Subparagraph (ii) of Section 2(c) of this Agreement will apply to all Transactions. However, the parties agree that will net across as many Transactions as practicable wherever the parties can administratively do so.**

Sometimes one sees the following wording:

> *Netting of Payments.* **(i) Subparagraph (ii) of Section 2(c) will apply to all Transactions under this Agreement unless otherwise specified in a Confirmation in relation to the relevant Transaction.**

I think this is a bad idea because potentially it could result in a junior Confirmations clerk signing off on an operational issue of which he may know nothing. I would always decline this particular amendment. Of course, if payment netting was ever an issue in a court case in the UK it would always be a question of what the parties actually did (under the "substance over form" principles) rather than what is recorded in the Agreement.

(j) *"Affiliate"* will have the meaning specified in Section 14 of this Agreement.

Part 4(j)

Normally "Affiliate" is defined as per Section 14 but I have seen a major bancassurance group exclude its insurance subsidiaries as Affiliates as follows:

> **"Affiliate" shall have the meaning specified in Section 14 of this Agreement, provided that with respect to Party A the term "Affiliate" shall not include any entity engaged in insurance activities.**

Sometimes parties seek to apply a materiality test to their Affiliates for Specified Entity purposes as in the following example:

> **"Affiliate" will have the meaning specified in Section 14 of this Agreement save that for the purposes of defining Specified Entity in respect to Party B an Affiliate shall only include those Affiliates the turnover of which as shown in the latest audited accounts of Party B amount to more than 5 per cent of the consolidated total turnover of the group of which Party B is a member as recorded in the latest consolidated accounts for that group.**

More frequently one sees a declaration that neither party should be deemed to have any Affiliates for purposes of Section 3(c) of the Agreement, i.e. Absence of Litigation. This modification of the definition of "Affiliates" is usually applied mutually.

Part 5. Other Provisions.

Part 5 Other Provisions

Part 5 contains a series of Other Provisions many of which are very important. Unlike the other Parts of the Schedule, provisions in Part 5 are in no particular order. Indeed, where a Schedule has been added to over the years the order often looks haphazard.

Negotiators should consider which of a host of Part 5 provisions are really necessary for them to have to protect their position so as to reduce negotiation time and documentation risk while an Agreement is unsigned.

I propose to deal with provisions in the order in which they appear in X Bank AG's Schedule and then to discuss other types of provision you may see and give examples. It is true to say that it is in Part 5 that an Agreement is most customised to a particular type of entity, e.g. a building society, insurance company or hedge fund. For while these types of entities may have tailored Additional Termination Events in Part 1 and/or specific documentation required from them in Part 3(b), it is in Part 5 that detailed provisions in relation to them may appear.

Let us now look at the various Part 5 provisions in the X Bank AG Schedule.

(a) *No Agency.* Section 3(a) of this Agreement is hereby amended by the deletion of "and" at the end of sub-clause (iv), the substitution of a semi-colon for the full-stop at the end of sub-clause (v) and the addition of the following at the end thereof:

"and (vi) No Agency. It is entering into this Agreement, any Credit Support Document to which it is a party, each Transaction and any other documentation relating to this Agreement or any Transaction as principal and not as agent of any person."

No Agency

This is a very common addition to the Section 3 representations although some people claim that it is covered in the non-reliance (Relationship between Parties) provision in the words "it is acting for its own account...". Be that as it may, it is normal for a separate no agency representation to be included in Part 5. It can now be chosen to apply as Section 3(g) of the 2002 Agreement in Part 4 (1) of its Schedule.

Another common Section 3 representation you may encounter concerns title transfer rights:

> ***Ownership*. With respect to any physically-settled Transactions, it will at the time of delivery be the legal and beneficial owner free of liens or other encumbrances of any securities or commodities it delivers to the other party.**

However, this should now be revised to:

> ***Ownership*. With respect to any physically-settled Transactions, it will deliver any securities, commodities or other property to the other party with full title guarantee.**

The need to amend this provision arises from a change in UK statute law in The Law of Property (Miscellaneous Provisions) Act 1994 to the effect that a legal and beneficial owner cannot give a full covenant for title to the property in question unless, from July 1995, the words "full title guarantee" are used instead of "legal and beneficial owner".

Numerous additional representations could be added. These usually relate to the nature of the parties to the Agreement, e.g. an insurance company might be required to represent that Transactions under the Agreement are solely to hedge its insurance business.

(b) (f) Section 6 of this Agreement is amended by the addition of the following new Section 6(f):

(f) **Set-off.** Any amount (the "Early Termination Amount") payable to one party (the Payee) by the other party (the Payer) under Section 6(e), in circumstances where there is a Defaulting Party or one Affected Party in the case where a Termination Event under Section 5(b)(iv) has occurred, will, at the option of the party ("X") other than the Defaulting Party or the Affected Party (and without prior notice to the Defaulting Party or the Affected Party), be reduced by its set-off against any amount(s) (the "Other Agreement Amount") payable (whether at such time or in the future or upon the occurrence of a contingency) by the Payee to the Payer (irrespective of the currency, place of payment or booking office of the obligation) under any other agreement(s) between the Payee and the Payer or instrument(s) or undertaking(s) issued or executed by one party to, or in favour of, the other party (and the Other Agreement Amount will be discharged promptly and in all respects to the extent it is so set-off). X will give notice to the other party of any set-off effected under this Section 6(f).

For this purpose, either the Early Termination Amount or the Other Agreement Amount (or the relevant portion of such amounts) may be converted by X into the currency in which the other is denominated at the rate of exchange at which such party would be able, acting in a reasonable manner and in good faith, to purchase the relevant amount of such currency.

If an obligation is unascertained, X may in good faith estimate that obligation and set off in respect of the estimate, subject to the relevant party accounting to the other when the obligation is ascertained.

Nothing in this Section 6(f) shall be effective to create a charge or other security interest. This Section 6(f) shall be without prejudice and in addition to any right of set-off, combination of accounts, lien or other right to which any party is at any time otherwise entitled (whether by operation of law, contract or otherwise).

Set-Off

Set-off has always been regarded as important and allows the cancelling out of debts owed between two parties by offsetting one against the other.

However, the drafters of the 1992 Agreement could not agree on the wording of a set-off clause for inclusion in the body of the text so it was decided that each party should propose its own set-off wording. A similar set-off clause to the one opposite now appears in Section 6(f) of the 2002 Agreement.

A Non-defaulting Party who agrees to the Second Method in Part 1(f) of the Schedule will normally wish to include a set-off clause to avoid having to pay a full termination payment to an insolvent counterparty who owes it money under other agreements.

ISDA made its own suggestion which is found in the 1992 *User's Guide*, p. 56 and is quoted in X Bank AG's Schedule opposite. Only the Non-defaulting Party or non-Affected Party can invoke set-off after close-out and will only do so if the net close-out figure shows that the Defaulting Party still owes it money. It will seek to reduce this liability by checking if it has other assets of the Defaulting Party under its control, e.g. deposit account balances in the Defaulting Party's own name and not held as a trustee or fiduciary for third parties.

Rule 4.90 of the Insolvency Rules (1986) confers a statutory right of set-off but this set-off clause extends it to other Events of Default and to Credit Event upon Merger (where all Transactions would be closed out). It could also be extended to Section 5(b)(v) events, i.e. Additional Termination Events where it is likely that all Transactions would be closed out.

Occasionally parties may try to bring other Termination Events into the ambit of the set-off clause. This seems illogical to me where perhaps only one Transaction is affected by an Illegality or Tax Event and all other Transactions are unaffected. I would resist such an amendment.

A more common amendment under English law Agreement set-off clauses is to extend the set-off to include the Non-defaulting Party's Affiliates. So the set-off would be between the Defaulting Party and the Non-defaulting Party and the Defaulting Party and the Non-defaulting Party's Affiliates. This obviously widens the scope of the set-off provision and may capture, for instance, the Defaulting Party's deposit balances held with the Non-defaulting Party's banking subsidiaries.

This scope of set-off is the best position under English law at present. Occasionally a party may suggest that set-off also be extended to a Defaulting Party's Affiliates. This does not work under English law and is in any case undesirable as the fault is with the Defaulting Party and not with its Affiliates *per se*. An example of a set-off clause which extends to a Non-defaulting Party's Affiliates is as follows:

Set-off. Section 6 of this Agreement shall be amended by the insertion of the following additional provision:

(f) Any amount payable to one party by the other party under Section 6(e), in circumstances where there is a Defaulting Party or one Affected Party in the case where a Termination Event under Section 5(b)(iv) has occurred, will be made without set-off or counter claim except that at the option of the party ("X") other than the Defaulting Party or the Affected Party (and without prior notice to the Defaulting Party or the Affected Party), X may, without prior notice to any person, set-off any sum or obligation (whether or not arising under this Agreement, whether matured or unmatured and irrespective of the currency, place of payment or booking office of the sum or obligation) owed by the Defaulting Party or Affected Party (in either case, "Y") to X or any Affiliate of X against any sum or obligation (whether or not arising under this Agreement, whether matured or unmatured and irrespective of the currency, place of payment or booking office of the sum or obligation) owed by X or any Affiliate of X to Y. X will give notice to the other party of any set-off effected under this Section 6(f).

For this purpose any relevant sum or obligation may be converted by X into the currency in which another is denominated at the rate of exchange at which such party would be able, acting in a reasonable manner and in good faith, to purchase the relevant amount of such currency.

If an obligation is unascertained, X may in good faith estimate that obligation and set-off in respect of the estimate, subject to the relevant party accounting to the other when the obligation is ascertained.

Nothing in this Section 6(f) shall be effective to create a charge or other security interest. This Section 6(f) shall be without prejudice and in addition to any right of set-off, combination of accounts, lien or other right to which any party is at any time otherwise entitled (whether by operation of law, contract or otherwise).

I recall that one European bank refused point blank to sign an Agreement (which was governed by English law) unless the Defaulting Party's Affiliates were also included. The policy of the bank I worked for was to extend set-off only to a Non-defaulting Party's Affiliates. Deadlock looked inevitable until the unusual expedient was proposed of including both set-off clauses in the Agreement on the basis that if there were ever any court proceedings a judge would strike out one of them.

Sometimes the inclusion of Affiliates is resisted because there may be concerns that the expansion of the set-off clause may not be enforceable because the Affiliates are not parties to the Agreement.

Where the relationship covers both trading and lending, set-off may be less important because in a syndicated loan the participating banks will usually share any set-off benefits among them. However, if a participating bank does set off what it owes to the Defaulting Party under the Agreement against the principal and interest owed to it by the Defaulting Party, then it may well have to share the benefit of the set-off with the other syndicate lenders.

A neat short form version of a set-off clause is the following:

> ***Set-off*. In the event that the Non-defaulting Party is required to pay any amount under Section 6(e)(i)(3) of this Agreement to the Defaulting Party, then the Non-defaulting Party shall be irrevocably authorised, without prior notice to the Defaulting Party, at any time without restriction:-**
>
> **(i) to set off the whole or any part of any sum owing from the Defaulting Party to the Non-defaulting Party under this Agreement against any and all of such amount owing to the Defaulting Party from the Non-defaulting Party under this Agreement; and/or**
>
> **(ii) for the purposes of any such set-off, to convert the whole or any part of any sum in a currency other than the Termination Currency, at the expense of the Defaulting Party, into the Termination Currency Equivalent of such amount at (or as nearly practicable to) the time of such set-off.**
>
> **Nothing herein shall be effective to create a charge or other security interest. In addition, the right of set-off detailed herein shall be without prejudice, and in addition, to any right of set-off, combination of accounts, lien or other right to which any party is, at any time, otherwise entitled (whether by operation of law, contract or otherwise).**

If a party declines to include a set-off clause this should be challenged as ISDA recommends the use of a set-off clause and it is now market standard. If the party still insists, the matter should be referred to your Credit and maybe Legal Department. By agreeing to their position you are limiting your close-out rights purely to the early termination mechanism of Section 6 of the Agreement.

(c) ***Definitions.*** "Indemnifiable Tax" add after "or a Credit Support Document)": Notwithstanding the foregoing, "Indemnifiable Tax" also means any Tax imposed in respect of a payment under this Agreement by reason of a Change in Tax Law by a government or taxing authority of a Relevant Jurisdiction of the party making such payment, unless the other party is incorporated, organised, managed and controlled or considered to have its seat in such jurisdiction, or is acting for purposes of this Agreement through a branch or office located in such jurisdiction.

Indemnifiable Tax

This addition to the definition of Indemnifiable Tax is a favourite provision of German banks.

You may recall that in the commentary on Part 2 at page 469, I referred to an Indemnifiable Tax as one where the tax arises from payments under a cross-border Transaction and the payee is entitled to be indemnified by the payer for its imposition. If not, the payee would receive its payment with the withholding tax deducted and hence would receive less than it expected.

The cross-border nature of the tax and the fact that the payer chose to deal with a foreign payee are the key features here. Withholding tax does not arise where the parties to the Agreement are both incorporated in the same tax jurisdiction and even if it did it would not be classified as an Indemnifiable Tax and be subject to gross up under the Agreement. In those circumstances the payee would have to bear it.

The addition to the definition slightly increases the payer's liability to withholding tax due to a Change in Tax Law in its tax jurisdiction provided that the payee or the Office through which it is acting is not a tax resident of the same jurisdiction (in which case any resulting tax would not be an Indemnifiable Tax). The expanded definition may be useful to those payees who want to transfer to the payer the burden of a withholding tax imposed by a jurisdiction to which they are both connected (i.e. the payer because it is tax resident there and the payee because it voluntarily through its Office there enters into a Transaction with the payer).

This is all rather technical and usually if a negotiator resists its inclusion, the other side tends to delete it. They may do this where a party will not accept the risk of having to gross up its payments due to a change in its own country's tax laws.

(d) *Transfer.* Section 7 of this Agreement shall be amended by inserting the following phrase "which consent shall not be unreasonably withheld" in the third line thereof after the word "party" and before the word "except".

Transfer

Transfer provisions have been discussed at pages 388–9 in Chapter 6 on credit issues as a subject requiring credit approval where significant amendments are proposed to the Section 7 standard wording.

A common amendment made is for consent not to be unreasonably withheld as can be seen in our example opposite. The problem here is that the words "unreasonably withheld" could be subjectively interpreted although many parties accept this and live with it.

Transfer clauses can be somewhat one-sided as in the following:

Transfer and Restructuring. **Notwithstanding any provisions of this Agreement to the contrary, the parties hereby agree that:**

(i) consent by Party B shall not be required in connection with the transfer by Party A of all its interests and obligations under any Transaction entered into pursuant to this Agreement to any Affiliate of Party A, and of any further such transfer by any such Affiliate (the "Transferring Affiliate") to any other Affiliate of Party A, so long as (y) as a result of any such transfer Party B would not be required to make or receive any payment from which any Tax (including any Indemnifiable Tax) is required to be withheld or deducted; and (z) the Transaction is at the time of such transfer the legal, valid and binding obligation of the Affiliate or Transferring Affiliate;

(ii) if, as a matter of law, Party B's consent is required for the purposes of perfecting any transfer contemplated in (i) above by Party A, Party B shall give its consent to the transfer;

(iii) in the event of any transfer contemplated in (i) above by Party A, Party B will execute upon the demand of Party A the necessary documentation prepared by Party A;

(iv) consent by Party B shall not be required in the event Party A requires a restructuring of any Transaction that will ensure the same economic effect for Party B by subdividing such Transaction into two or more parts (each a Transaction); and

(v) Party B will execute such revised documentation as Party A shall require to evidence any restructuring contemplated in (iv) above.

Such a clause unilaterally in favour of one party should be resisted as it takes no account of the other party's situation particularly in respect of costs nor does it give them a chance to consider the circumstances surrounding the transfer because there is no prior notice period. In addition it commits the other party to potential further transfers. Far better is a mutual provision along the lines of the following:

Transfer. Section 7 is replaced in its entirety by the following:

"Subject to Section 6(b)(ii), neither this Agreement nor any interest or obligation in or under this Agreement may be transferred (whether by way of security or otherwise) by either party without the prior written consent of the other party, which consent will not be arbitrarily withheld or delayed, except that:

(a) a party may make such a transfer of this Agreement pursuant to a consolidation or amalgamation with, or merger into, or transfer of all or substantially all its assets to or reorganisation, incorporation, reincorporation, or reconstruction into or as, another entity (but without prejudice to any other right or remedy under this Agreement);

(b) a party may make such a transfer of all or any part of its interest in any amount payable to it from a Defaulting Party under Section 6(e); and

(c) in addition to, and not in lieu of, the preceding transfer rights, (1) in the case of Party A, it may, without recourse, transfer this Agreement (in whole and not in part only) to any of its Affiliates provided that [*name of Party A's parent*] (or another entity with a credit rating at least equal to that of [*name of Party A's parent*] must guarantee such transferred obligations of the transferee pursuant to a guarantee in substantially, the form of the guarantee of [*name of Party A's parent*] specified in this Agreement, or such transferee must have a credit rating at least equal to that of [*name of Party A's parent*] and (2) in the case of Party B, it may, without recourse, transfer this Agreement (in whole and in not in part only) to either [*name of Party B's parent*] or a wholly owned subsidiary of [name of Party B's parent] *provided, however*, in the case of either (1) or (2) above:

    (i) *No Gross-up:* The non-transferring party will not, as a result of such transfer, be required to pay to the transferee an amount in respect of an Indemnifiable Tax under Section 2(d)(i)(4) (except in respect of interest under Section 2(e), 6(d)(ii), or 6(e)) greater than the amount which the non-transferring party would have been required to pay to the transferor in the absence of such transfer;

    (ii) *No Withholding:* The transferee will not receive a payment from which an amount has been withheld or deducted, on account of a Tax under Section 2(d)(i) (except in respect of interest under Section 2(e), 6(d)(ii), or 6(e)), in excess of that which transferor would have been required to so withhold or deduct in the absence of such transfer, unless the transferee would be required to make additional payments pursuant to Section 2(d)(i)(4) corresponding to such withholding or deduction;

(iii) *Not Unlawful:* It does not become unlawful for either party to perform any obligation under this Agreement as a result of such transfer; and

(iv) *No Event of Default:* an Event of Default does not occur as a result of such transfer.

With respect to the results described in Clauses (i) and (ii) above, the transferor will cause the transferee to make, and the non-transferring party will make, such reasonable Payer Tax Representations and Payee Tax Representations as may be mutually agreed upon by the transferee and the non-transferring party in order to permit such parties to determine that such results will not occur upon or after the transfer."

Any transfer of all or any part of the obligations of either party made in compliance with this Section 7 will constitute an acceptance and assumption of such obligations by the transferee, a novation of the transferee in place of the transferor with respect to such obligations (and any related interests so transferred), and a release and discharge by the non-transferring party of the transferor from, and an agreement by the non-transferring party not to make any claim for payment, liability, or otherwise against the transferor with respect to such obligations from and after the effective date of the transfer.

This provision provides for:

- mutual transfer rights
- affiliates of each party to be guaranteed by the parent unless the transferee has at least equally as good a credit rating as the parent
- indemnification from withholding taxes
- requirement for appropriate tax representations to be made by each side
- no Event of Default or Termination Event having occurred
- novation of obligations when achieved.

This is fairly comprehensive but, in my opinion, it is debatable whether it is ever desirable to give conditional blanket advance approval to transfers. It is better to consider all the circumstances at the time they are made. In practice this often happens as most transfers are made via Novation Agreements.

Some might say that the above provisions are useful where parties need to act quickly but I think that is exactly when their counterparties need to know the precise circumstances surrounding the transfer.

(e) ***Consent to Recording.*** Each party (i) consents to the recording of the telephone conversations of trading, marketing and other relevant personnel of the parties in connection with this Agreement or any potential Transaction and (ii) agrees that any such recording may be submitted in evidence to any court or in any proceedings with respect to this Agreement or any Transaction thereunder.

Consent to Recording

Market practice is to trade over the telephone. While Consent to Recording provisions are very common, this provision was not included in the main text of the 1992 Agreement (it appears as an option in Part 4(n) of the 2002 ISDA Master Agreement Schedule) because of perceived different legal approaches in various jurisdictions. However, the 1992 *User's Guide*, p. 66 contains the following example:

> **Each party (i) consents to the recording of the telephone conversations of trading and marketing personnel of the parties and their Affiliates in connection with this Agreement or any potential Transaction and (ii) agrees to obtain any necessary consent of, and give notice of such recording to, such personnel of it and its Affiliates.**

Other examples are:

> ***Consent to Recording.*** **Each party:**
>
> (a) **consents to the recording of all telephone conversations in connection with this Agreement or any potential Transaction with or without the use of an automatic tone warning device;**
>
> (b) **agrees to obtain any necessary consent of, and give notice of such recording to, its affected personnel; and**
>
> (c) **agrees that recordings may be submitted in evidence in any proceedings relating to this Agreement.**

OR

> ***Telephonic Recording.*** **The parties agree, subject to any consent required by applicable law, that each may electronically record all telephonic conversations between them and that any such tape recordings may be submitted in evidence in any Proceedings relating to this Agreement. In the event of any dispute between the parties as to the terms of a Transaction governed by this Agreement or the obligations thereby created prior to the execution of a Confirmation for such Transaction, the parties may use electronic recordings between the persons who entered into such Transaction as the preferred evidence of the terms of such Transaction.**

The need to obtain employees' consent to recording varies country by country. For instance it is needed in Germany.

The taping of telephone conversations is recommended in the FSA's *Conduct of Business Rules* (2001).

Sometimes you see wording proposed where the tapes are to be provided to the other party upon request in order to defend a legal action or resolve a dispute. This should be resisted for a number of reasons. First, the tapes may no longer exist as many institutions only keep tapes for three to six months before re-using them. Second, the other dealer should have its own tapes anyway and third, tapes contain many conversations between different dealers. It would be a multiple breach of confidentiality to provide an unedited tape to a counterparty and to provide an edited one could invite accusations of manipulation. So this is potentially a "no win" situation and such requests should be resisted.

(f) ***Relationship Between Parties.*** Each party will be deemed to represent to the other party on the date on which it enters into a Transaction that (absent a written agreement between the parties that expressly imposes affirmative obligations to the contrary for that Transaction):

(a) ***Non-Reliance.*** It is acting for its own account, and it has made its own independent decisions to enter into that Transaction and as to whether that Transaction is appropriate or proper for it based upon its own judgment and upon advice from such advisers as it has deemed necessary. It is not relying on any communication (written or oral) of the other party as investment advice or as a recommendation to enter into that Transaction: it being understood that information and explanations related to the terms and conditions of a Transaction shall not be considered investment advice or a recommendation to enter into that Transaction. No communication (written or oral) received from the other party shall be deemed to be an assurance or guarantee as to the expected results of that Transaction.

(b) ***Assessment and Understanding.*** It is capable of assessing the merits of and understanding (on its own behalf or through independent professional advice), and understands and accepts, the terms, conditions and risks of that Transaction. It is also capable of assuming, and assumes, the risks of that Transaction.

(c) ***Status of Parties.*** The other party is not acting as a fiduciary or an adviser to it in respect of that Transaction.

Non-reliance provisions

Non-reliance provisions arose in derivatives documentation from a series of lawsuits in the US in 1993–1995 involving Bankers Trust and each of Gibson's Greetings (a greetings card company) and Procter & Gamble and Merrill Lynch & Co., Inc and Orange County. Simon Leifer referred to these cases in Chapter 5, page 357.

As a result in 1995/96 ISDA drafted its Relationship between Parties provision which is an ongoing tripartite representation that:

- **each party has made its own independent decision to enter into the Transaction concerned and is not relying on the other party;**
- **each party is capable of understanding and accepts any risks pertaining to the Transaction; and**
- **neither party is acting in a fiduciary (e.g. agent or trustee) or advisory capacity to the other.**

Clearly these tripartite representations cannot be given where one party is clearly relying on the advice of the other in entering into the Transaction.

There are other forms of non-reliance representations many of which predate the ISDA standard and some of which are over a page long. While these may be acceptable in their own right, many people prefer to use the ISDA standard. Sometimes parties add or take away from the ISDA standard wording and so it is important to check that you have the full standard wording if that is what you want. The wording opposite is the standard wording.

Some market players, e.g. major banks do not see the point in having these representations in Agreements between them because, by their very nature, they are capable of assessing the risk of a Transaction and are extremely unlikely to be advising another bank. Nevertheless, more often than not a non-reliance provision of some sort appears in their Agreements.

[(g) ***Incorporation of ISDA EMU Protocol.*** The parties agree that the definitions and provisions contained in Annexes 1 to 5 and Section 6 of the EMU Protocol published by the International Swaps and Derivatives Association, Inc. on 6 May 1998 are incorporated into and apply to this Agreement. References in those definitions and provisions to any "ISDA Master Agreement" will be deemed to be references to this Agreement.]

Incorporation of Protocol terms

In May 1998, ISDA published a Protocol offering parties the chance to accept several general provisions (Annexes 1–5 and Section 6) in relation to European Monetary Union (Phase 2 of which occurred for 11 Member States on 1 January 1999). The use of the Protocol saved the need for the market to put numerous amendment agreements in place because by signing the Protocol and indicating the number of Annexes adopted by each party all Agreements between the parties were deemed to be amended to the extent the Annexes were adopted. Most of the 1,132 parties who signed up to the Protocol adopted all the Annexes.

In December 2000, ISDA completed a similar exercise for Greek counterparties (Greece joined the "Eurozone" on 1 January 2001) and 138 parties signed the "Greek Protocol".

This was followed by a Euro Protocol in late September 2001.

As regards the "EMU Protocol", it still appears in Schedules today although many lawyers consider it unnecessary because many of the operative provisions of the EMU Protocol became redundant after 1 January 1999. However, the Protocol terms still apply to legacy Transactions (in EU national, i.e. original currencies) entered into before 1 January 1999. It can, however, be omitted where a new Agreement is being negotiated and there are no Transactions outstanding between the parties.

A recent variation has been the inclusion of the EMU Protocol (Greece) and the 2001 Euro Protocol in the general EMU Protocol provision as follows:

ISDA EMU Protocol

Annexes 1 to 5 and, for the purpose of construing such Annexes, Section 6 (Definitions) of the ISDA EMU Protocol published on 6th May 1998 by ISDA (the "EMU Protocol"), Annexes 1 to 5 and, for the purpose of construing such Annexes, Section 6 (Definitions) of the ISDA EMU Protocol (Greece) published on 10th October 2000 by ISDA (the "EMU Protocol (Greece)") and Annexes 1 to 4 of the 2001 Euro Protocol published by ISDA on 24th September 2001 shall be incorporated by reference into this Agreement. The term "the parties" as used in the Annexes of the EMU Protocol and the EMU Protocol (Greece) shall be construed as referring to Party A and Party B. References in those definitions and provisions to any "ISDA Master Agreement" will be deemed to be references to this Agreement.

If the United Kingdom entered into European monetary union there would doubtless be a special ISDA EMU Protocol for it.

(h) *Scope of Agreement*

Notwithstanding anything contained in the Agreement to the contrary, if the parties enter or have entered into any Specified Transaction, such Specified Transaction shall be subject to, governed by and construed in accordance with the terms of the Agreement unless the Confirmation relating thereto shall specifically state to the contrary. Each such Specified Transaction shall be a Transaction for the purposes of this Agreement. In the event of any inconsistency between the terms of such Specified Transaction and the terms of this Agreement, the terms of that Specified Transaction shall prevail.

Scope of Agreement

Over the past few years scope of agreement clauses have become more common. They are often called "sweep in" clauses because they seek to sweep into the Agreement OTC derivatives Transactions between the two parties (i.e. Specified Transactions) which are outside it. Only where the Confirmation explicitly states that the transaction is not subject to the Agreement (a very unlikely occurrence) or that it is subject only to its governing terms (e.g. BBAIRS) and none other (again unlikely) will the Scope of Agreement provision not apply.

Some lawyers doubt the legal effectiveness of Scope of Agreement provisions but this is as yet untested in the courts.

Here are some examples:

It is agreed between the parties that all Transactions between Party A and Party B prior to the date of this Agreement which are currently outstanding are deemed to be entered into pursuant to this Agreement and are governed by its laws.

OR

Upon the effectiveness of this Agreement, unless otherwise agreed to in writing by the parties to this Agreement with respect to specific Specified Transactions, all Specified Transactions then outstanding between Offices of the parties listed in Part 4(d) of the Schedule shall be subject to the terms hereof.

OR

Other Agreements: Integration

(i) Notwithstanding any inconsistent or contrary provision of this Agreement, the following will be applicable. Any existing Master Agreement, Interest Rate and Currency Exchange Agreement, Interest Rate Swap Agreement, Swap Agreement, International Foreign Exchange Master Agreement, International Foreign Exchange and Options Master Agreement, International Currency Options Market Master Agreement, and other agreements similar to any of the foregoing (including confirmations and other confirming evidences thereunder or pursuant thereto) into which the parties have entered are superseded and replaced by this Agreement. Any transaction into which the parties may enter and in respect of which the confirmation or other confirming evidence refers to or incorporates any of the above described agreements will be governed by this Agreement in all circumstances except where the

parties expressly agree that this provision will not apply. Each such transaction will be deemed to be a Transaction, and each such confirmation or other confirming evidence will be deemed to be a Confirmation for purposes of this Agreement.

(ii) This Agreement, this Schedule, any Credit Support Document, all Confirmations, and the above described agreements and confirmations and other confirming evidences thereunder or pursuant thereto collectively constitute the entire agreement and understanding of the parties with respect to the subject matter hereof and thereof, and supersede all oral communications and prior writings with respect hereto and thereto.

(iii) Notwithstanding anything to the contrary contained in this Agreement, if the parties enter into any Specified Transaction, such Specified Transaction will be subject to, governed by, and construed in accordance with the terms of, this Agreement unless the Confirmation relating thereto expressly states to the contrary. Each such Specified Transaction will be a Transaction for purposes of this Agreement.

(j) *Contracts (Rights of Third Parties)* Act 1999

A person who is not a party to this Agreement shall have no right under the Contracts (Rights of Third Parties) Act 1999 to enforce any of its terms.

Contracts (Rights of Third Parties) Act 1999

This is now a common provision in Schedules to English law governed Agreements and relates to protecting privity of contract and preventing a third party interfering with the rights of the two parties to the Agreement. Simon Leifer described the background to this provision in Chapter 5 at page 363.

A possible, slightly expanded version of the wording is as follows:

> **(g) *Contracts (Rights of Third Parties) Act 1999.* A person who is not a party to this Agreement has no right under the Contracts (Rights of Third Parties) Act 1999 to enforce any term of this Agreement but this does not affect any right or remedy of a third party which exists or is available apart from that Act.**

OTHER PROVISIONS COMMONLY SEEN IN THE MARKET AND THEIR IMPLICATIONS

Now that we have reviewed the X Bank AG Schedule (up to Part 5) it would also be useful to highlight some other provisions which are commonly found in Part 5 of the Schedule but which did not make it into the X Bank AG Schedule. Inevitably, this will not cover every provision ever seen in Part 5 (which would be an encyclopaedic if not impossible task) but I hope it covers a broad cross section.

I propose to cover these provisions under the following categories:

- **credit related provisions**
- **legal provisions**
- **tax provisions**
- **administrative provisions**
- **other provisions.**

Some provisions fit more easily into these categories than others.

Credit related provisions

Downgrade from Cross Default to cross acceleration

The pros and cons of this amendment were discussed in Chapter 6, page 383. The amendment itself is short and when used is usually placed in Part 5 of the Schedule as follows:

> "***Cross Default.*** **'The following words are deleted from line 7 of Section 5(a)(vi):**
>
> **,or becoming capable at such time of being declared,'.**"

Combined threshold

In a commentary produced by Allen & Overy's Derivatives Product Group in August 1992 on the 1992 ISDA Master Agreement it was pointed out (on p. 7) that the drafters of the 1992 Agreement had not taken the opportunity to sort out an anomaly occurring in the 1987 Agreement in relation to Cross Default. The Threshold Amount applies separately to each sub-Section of Section 5(a)(vi) and so, for example, if a £10 million Threshold Amount applied, you might have a £7 million default in an accelerated third party agreement under Section 5(a)(vi)(1) and a £4 million default under Section 5(a)(vi)(2) in amounts due but unpaid but as these were separate figures neither would, in themselves, trigger the £10 million Threshold Amount. To overcome this problem, Combined Threshold Amount language is used, the most common of which is as follows:

> **If an event has occurred under Section 5(a)(vi)(1) and Section 5(a)(vi)(2), which would constitute an Event of Default but for the fact that neither the aggregate amount calculated in respect of Section 5(a)(vi)(1) nor the aggregate amount calculated in respect of Section 5(a)(vi)(2) exceeds the Threshold Amount, then the aggregate amount arising under Section 5(a)(vi)(1) plus the aggregate amount arising under Section 5(a)(vi)(2) shall be combined so as to produce a "Combined Aggregate Amount". If this Combined Aggregate Amount exceeds the applicable Threshold Amount, then it shall be a Cross Default.**

This situation has been remedied in the 2002 Agreement text for Cross Default and aggregation is now clearly stated.

Material Adverse Change

Material Adverse Change clauses are common in loan agreements but are sometimes proposed in Agreement Schedules typically where Party B is a small corporate.

> ***No Material Adverse Change.*** **Party B represents and warrants to Party A (which representation and warranty will be deemed to be repeated at all times until the termination of this Agreement) that there has been no material adverse change in its financial condition since the last day of the one year period covered by its most recently prepared year end financial statement that is likely to affect its ability to perform its obligations under this Agreement.**

OR

> *Additional Event of Default.* **With respect to Party *, it shall constitute an Event of Default under this Agreement if a material adverse change in its business, operations, assets or financial or other condition shall have occurred and is continuing.**

This is a severe representation because it is continuous. More often the representation only applies at the time each Transaction is undertaken.

If the parties are more equal or if they are both very large there is no justification for giving this representation and warranty partly because it would be difficult to check if it were true.

Material Adverse Change shares the same problem of definition as Heaven. Nobody knows what it means exactly but everyone will know it when they see it.

Notices of Events of Default or Termination Events

Sometimes you may see a provision which entails a continuous obligation on a party to give notice of an Event of Default or Termination Event:

> *Additional Agreements.* **Each party agrees, upon learning of the occurrence of any event or commencement of any condition that constitutes (or that with the giving of notice or passage of time or both would constitute) an Event of Default or Termination Event with respect to such party, promptly to give the other party notice of such event or condition (or, in lieu of giving notice of such event or condition in the case of an event or condition that with the giving of notice or passage of time or both would constitute an Event of Default or Termination Event with respect to the party, to cause such event or condition to cease to exist before becoming an Event of Default or Termination Event).**

Adequate Assurances

Adequate Assurance provisions are unpopular because they cast doubt upon a counterparty's ability to perform under the Agreement as in the following example:

> *Adequate Assurances*
>
> **The failure by a party to this Agreement (the "First Party") to give adequate assurances of its ability to perform any of its obligations under this Agreement within two (2) Local Business Days of a written request to do so when the other party (the "Second Party") has reasonable grounds for insecurity shall be an Additional Termination Event. The**

First Party shall be the Affected Party in respect of this Additional Termination Event.

During the pendency of a reasonable request by the Second Party to the First Party for adequate assurances of the First Party's ability to perform its obligations under the Agreement, the Second Party may, at its election and without penalty, suspend its obligations under the Agreement.

Although an adequate assurances provision can provide protection against events which do not in themselves constitute an Event of Default or Termination Event, it is usually resisted in the market.

Incorporation of the terms of a loan agreement

On many occasions derivatives (e.g. interest rate swaps and caps) are used to hedge the risk of adverse movements in interest rates on loans. There are numerous examples of this in management buy-out transactions where entering into an interest rate swap and an ISDA Master Agreement is a pre-condition of the loan. With project finance loans, currency risk is also hedged by currency swaps or options.

With loans, a number of possible amendments can be made in the ISDA Schedule:

- **details of Events of Default and performance covenants can be imported verbatim into the Schedule and co-exist with the terms of the Agreement. This is rarely done nowadays.**
- **Events of Default and performance covenants in the loan agreement can be incorporated by cross-reference in the Agreement so that a material default under the loan will trigger close-out under the Agreement. Sometimes some or all of the Section 5 events in the Agreement are suspended while the loan exists and similar provisions in the loan prevail during its life. This is done so that any termination discussions are made, for instance, by Majority Banks (usually 66 2/3% by value of the loan outstanding) rather than unilaterally by a bank under an ISDA Master Agreement with a borrower.**

If the loan is repaid or pre-paid during the life of the swap either the Agreement's Section 5 events are revived (see Chapter 9 page 629) or more rarely the repaid loan's Events of Default and performance covenants will continue to apply to the Agreement.

An example of an Incorporation of terms clause is as follows:

Incorporation by Reference of Covenants. **Party B covenants and agrees that, from and after the date hereof and thereafter until all obligations of Party B hereunder are paid in full and this Agreement is terminated, it shall duly keep, perform and observe each and every covenant set forth in the Loan Agreement (as defined below). All of such covenants,**

> together with related definitions and ancillary provisions, are hereby incorporated into this Agreement by reference, mutatis mutandis, as if such terms were set forth in this Agreement in full, without regard to any termination of such Loan Agreement, without regard to any expiration of any commitment thereunder and without regard to the final payment in full of any obligations of Party B or any other person or entity thereunder, provided that no such covenant set forth above shall be incorporated herein by reference if such incorporation, by itself, would be a breach of the Loan Agreement. If an event is the subject of both a covenant incorporated herein by reference and another covenant set forth in this Agreement, Party B shall comply with the covenant which imposes on it the stricter requirement. To the extent that any covenant incorporated herein by reference is inconsistent with the other terms of this Agreement, Party A shall not be deemed to have waived any rights hereunder by virtue of such inconsistency. If the Loan Agreement terminates, any commitment thereunder expires or any obligations of Party B thereunder are paid in full and any covenant incorporated herein by reference requires Party B to obtain the consent of any agent, lender or lenders, then, for the purpose of this Agreement, Party B shall be required to obtain the consent of Party A.
>
> Any failure of Party B to comply with this provision shall constitute an Event of Default with respect to Party B under this Agreement.
>
> For the purpose of the foregoing, "Loan Agreement" means [*describe*]

I shall have more to say about the inter-relation of Loan Agreements and ISDA Master Agreements in Chapter 9, at pages 627–33 and Gary Walker in his book, *Mastering Finance Linked Swaps* also published in this series treats the subject extensively.

Negative pledge

Negative pledges are common in unsecured loan agreements but are less common in ISDA Master Agreements. They are undertakings by a party not to give security interests in support of its obligations to other counterparties. In other words, they are a pledge not to pledge. They arise particularly where a counterparty's indebtedness is all unsecured or it has no borrowings. An example of such wording is:

> *Negative Pledge*. Each of Party B and its Affiliates undertakes from and after the date of this Agreement and as long as an obligation under this Agreement is outstanding not to sell, except in the ordinary course of its business, assign, transfer, charge nor create or permit to subsist any

Encumbrances over any of its assets or revenues and any breach of the agreements by Party B pursuant to this sub-paragraph shall constitute an Event of Default under this Agreement. "Encumbrance" means any mortgage charge pledge lien assignment hypothecation security interest title retention, preferential right or trust arrangement or other security arrangement or agreement or any right conferring a priority of payment.

They can be more elaborate:

Party * undertakes that it shall

not create, permit or suffer to exist any Encumbrance over all or any of its assets except for:

(i) liens arising by operation of law in the ordinary course of business and securing obligations not more than 90 days overdue;

(ii) a banker's lien or right of set-off or combination of accounts arising by operation of law or practice over property or money deposited with a banker in the ordinary course of its business (including but not limited to a transaction banking set-off arrangement);

(iii) arrangements constituted by retention of title in connection with the acquisition of goods provided the goods are acquired in the ordinary course of business on the normal commercial terms of the vendor;

(iv) an Encumbrance over any asset of a company acquired after the date of this Agreement where the Encumbrance was in existence at the date of acquisition and was not created in contemplation of acquisition and which is discharged within 12 months after acquisition;

(v) an Encumbrance created by way of cross charge in favour of a co-venturer or an operator over joint venture assets, as security only for its obligations to such co-venturer or operator in respect of the relevant joint venture and where recourse is limited to the assets of such joint venture;

(vi) Encumbrances arising by operation of statute in favour of any government body including, without limitation, for any nonpayment of taxes (provided such taxes are not overdue by more than 30 days unless subject to an objection or appeal lodged in good faith);

(vii) an Encumbrance over assets of a Project Finance Subsidiary established for the development of a specific project as security only for the Project Finance Subsidiary's borrowings for the acquisition and development of a new project;

(viii) any other approved Encumbrance.

Negative pledges will prevent a party entering into a New York Law ISDA Credit Support Annex or an English Law ISDA Credit Support Deed. They may prevent a party entering into an English Law ISDA Credit Support Annex if the negative pledge is broad enough to catch a set off arrangement.

Pari passu provision

Pari passu provisions are also common in loan agreements. A typical example is:

> ***Pari-passu.*** **Party * undertakes that its obligations hereunder constitute direct, unconditional, unsecured, unsubordinated and general obligations and that such obligations will rank at least pari passu with all other present and future outstanding unsecured obligations issued, created and assumed by Party * save to the extent that such obligations are preferred by laws governing creditor's rights in case of liquidation or insolvency of Party *.**

Or the provision can be mutual as follows:

> ***Pari Passu.*** **All payment and delivery obligations of each party under this Agreement will rank at least pari passu in all respects with all of that party's other unsecured and unsubordinated obligations (except for those which are mandatorily preferred by the operation of law). This representation and warranty shall be deemed to be given as at the date of this Agreement and shall be deemed to be repeated on the date of each Transaction.**

Clearly, the negative pledge and *pari passu* provisions can only be given if they are true and it is important that a small corporate clearly understands their nature. Indeed, even among experienced derivatives professionals there are instances of uncertainty of what a negative pledge actually is!

Collateral security provisions

Collateral security provisions used to be quite common in Agreements with small or medium-sized corporates before the ISDA Credit Support Annexes were published but are worth mentioning for those situations where a counterparty is unfamiliar with or does not wish to enter into an ISDA Credit Support Annex.

Collateral security provisions are used where there is an established banking relationship with a corporate whose obligations to the bank are secured by guarantees and/or charges over tangible assets. Their purpose is to extend the benefit of such guarantees and charges to the corporate's derivatives liabilities. If the bank's guarantee or charge forms are "all moneys" forms then this is essentially already done but some banks like to have a collateral security provision for the avoidance of doubt. For it was not unknown when a corporate defaulted for different parts of the same bank (which were also different profit centres) to fight over who had the right to the liquidated assets of the stricken corporate. Each section in the bank wanted to minimise its losses and sometimes the bank's overall interests were eclipsed in the scramble.

Although rare, an example of such wording (where Party B is the bank) is:

> ***Collateral Security*. Party [A] hereby acknowledges and agrees that any and all obligations it owes to Party [B] under this Agreement shall be fully secured, without the need for any further acknowledgement by either Party [A] or Party [B], by any mortgage, charge, pledge, lien, letter of hypothecation, letter of Set-off or other interest over any cash, securities or other property or any interest therein or any guarantee given to secure any of Party [A's] obligations whether given pursuant to this Agreement or any other agreement, whether existing as at the date of this Agreement or given in the future, given by Party [A] in favour of Party [B] whether solely or jointly with others (the "Security"), and Party [A] further hereby acknowledges and agrees that Party [B] may, in accordance with its terms, enforce the Security and apply the Security in reduction of any and all moneys owing and any other obligations owing by Party [A] to Party [B] under this Agreement.**
>
> **To the extent that any agreement or document granting the Security does not expressly include the obligations of Party [A] to Party [B] under this Agreement, Party (A] and Party [B] hereby confirm and agree that it is their intention that any and all of Party [A's] obligations to Party [B] under this Agreement shall be secured by the Security and that the Security shall not be discharged unless and until Party [A] shall have no obligations (actual or contingent, matured or unmatured) to Party [B] under this Agreement and Party [A], hereby covenants and agrees that it will promptly upon request of Party [B] do any and all acts and will execute and deliver any and all documents reasonably required by Party [B] in order to include the obligations of Party [A] to Party [B] under this Agreement within the Security upon terms reasonably satisfactory to Party [B].**

ISDA Credit Support Annexes are used with liquid collateral, e.g. cash and G10 government securities. The typical security or collateral taken by banks from corporates is a mixture of cash, debtors, stocks and property, some of which is less liquid and in those situations a collateral security provision extending the availability of the security to derivatives exposure is a useful protection. However, to avoid the risk that a liquidator could challenge this in an insolvency or the debtor company or its subsidiaries could challenge it in a termination situation triggered by some other event, I think it advisable for Board Resolutions to be taken from all charging or guaranteeing companies acknowledging the extension of the existing security given to the bank to their derivatives obligations. Such a resolution would be referred to as a documentation requirement in Part 3(b) of the Schedule.

Escrow

An escrow provision is often included where there are concerns over time zone differences in currency settlements, counterparty creditworthiness or political risk.

One of the risks of derivatives trading occurs because of time zone differences. For example, if a bank in Tokyo agrees a big Yen/Sterling currency trade with one in London, on settlement the London bank's Yen payment will reach the Tokyo bank during Japanese business hours (they are eight hours ahead of the UK), but the Japanese bank's sterling payment cannot be transferred to the London bank until the British clearing organisation opens hours later. If the Japanese bank should go bust after it has received a huge payment from London but before it has made its payment, the British bank could suffer crippling losses and may endanger other banks not connected with the trade. This is called "Herstatt risk" after a German bank which failed in 1974 with US$ 620 million of partially completed trades. While banks and their regulators have promoted improvement of the settlement process since then and approved netting of payments, Herstatt risk has not been entirely eliminated from the markets.

The use of an escrow account should ensure that a payment received into the account will not be released until the counterparty's payment has also been received. The first depositing party is entitled to overnight interest where this is relevant.

Escrow provisions often stipulate that escrow agents should have a minimum level of net assets or a minimum short- or long-term formal credit rating, e.g. A1/P1 or A3/A-. This is to minimise the risk that the escrow agent would default during the period the escrow arrangements are in place. If that happened it would defeat their purpose.

It is also regularly stated that the escrow agent must not be affiliated in any way with either party. The reason for this is that an affiliated escrow agent might just "bend the rules" under pressure from a counterparty who was also its parent. In addition, such a requirement distances the fortunes of the escrow agent from those of the counterparty. The party that wants to set up escrow arrangements must pay the costs which can be high. Escrow arrangements are rarely invoked but this does not stop them appearing regularly in Schedules.

A typical example of an escrow provision containing the above elements is as follows:

> ***Escrow Payments.*** **If (whether by reason of the time difference between the cities in which payments are to be made or otherwise), it is not possible for simultaneous payments to be made on any date on which both parties are required to make payments hereunder, either party may at its option and in its sole discretion notify the other party that payments on that date are to be made in escrow. In this case deposit of the payment due earlier on that date shall be made by 2.00 p.m. (local time at the place for the earlier payment) on that date with an escrow agent selected by the notifying party, provided this escrow agent is independent of either party and has a long term credit rating of at least A3 (Moody's) or A- (S&P) as the case may be, accompanied by irrevocable payment instructions (i) to release the deposited payment to the intended recipient upon receipt by the escrow agent of the required deposit of the corresponding payment from the other party on the same date accompanied by irrevocable payment instructions to the same effect or (ii) if the required deposit of the corresponding payment is not made on that same date, to return the payment deposited to the party that paid it into escrow.**
>
> **The party that elects to have payments made in escrow shall pay all costs of the escrow arrangements and shall procure that the intended recipient of the deposited amount shall be entitled to the interest on the deposited payment (offered by the escrow agent at 11.00 a.m. local time for that day for overnight deposits in the relevant currency in the office where the deposited payment is held) if that payment is not released by 5.00 p.m. local time on the date it is deposited, for any reason other than the intended recipient's failure to make the escrow deposit it is required to make hereunder in time.**

Bankruptcy amendment

Sometimes bankruptcy petitions are made vexatiously or frivolously by creditors and are opposed in good faith. Here is an example of such a provision which also offers a third party guarantee while the dispute lasts:

Additional amendments

(i) The following sentence is added at the end of Section 5(a)(vii):–

"On the occurrence of any of the events mentioned under Section 5(a)(vii)(4) or Section 5(a)(vii)(7) here above in relation to Party B (that is an involuntary case or proceeding commenced against Party B which remains undismissed or unstayed for 30 consecutive days) then if, during the period of 30 consecutive days set out therein, the Defaulting Party (a) in good faith contests such involuntary case or proceeding; and (b) procures that a third party acceptable to Party A provides a guarantee or other security in a form and content acceptable to Party A guaranteeing or otherwise securing all of Party B's obligations and liabilities under this Agreement; then Party A will allow Party B a further period of 60 consecutive days in which to dismiss or stay any such case or proceeding provided always that any such court does not at any time during the further period of 60 days enter a decree or order granting the relief sought in any such case or proceeding, in which case Party A may declare an Event of Default."

"Legal" provisions

Bankruptcy

A common addition to UK Schedules is the following amendment to Section 5(a)(vii)(3):

> **"Bankruptcy" Section 5(a)(vii)(3) of the Agreement is hereby amended by the substitution of the following thereof**
>
> **"(3) sends a notice convening a meeting to propose a voluntary arrangement of creditors, or any class thereof, or makes a general assignment, arrangement or composition with or for the benefit of its creditors or any class thereof."**

This enables a Bankruptcy Event of Default to be called when a notice is given to call such a meeting. In England and Wales (unless short notice is permitted) notice must be given at least 21 days in advance of such a meeting. The amendment short circuits that and enables the Non-defaulting Party to accelerate its close-out rights. Because of this it is sometimes resisted.

Illegality

The preamble to Section 5(b)(i) of the Agreement reads as follows:

> (i) ***Illegality*. Due to the adoption of, or any change in, any applicable law after the date on which a Transaction is entered into, or due to the promulgation of, or any change in, the interpretation by any court, tribunal or regulatory authority with competent jurisdiction of any applicable law after such date, it becomes unlawful (other than as a result of a breach by the party of Section 4(b)) for such party (which will be the Affected Party):-**

It then goes on to refer to payment, delivery or performance failures under the Agreement or a Credit Support Document. The following provision is sometimes seen to cover not being able to perform because of government directives rather than laws:

> **"*Illegality*". The "Illegality" provisions Section 5(b)(i) shall be expanded to include the obligation of a party to comply with any directive, direction or similar order issued or given by any government agency or authority with competent jurisdiction (whether or not having the force of law) which prohibits its performance under this Agreement, and in that event such party will be the Affected Party for the purpose of that Section.**

Impossibility

Drafters of the 1992 Agreement argued long and hard whether to include an Impossibility or force majeure provision but could not agree on this. However, page 65 of the *User's Guide* proposed the following wording for use if the parties agreed:

> ***Impossibility*. Due to the occurrence of a natural or man-made disaster, armed conflict, act of terrorism, riot, labour disruption or any other circumstance beyond its control after the date on which a Transaction is entered into, it becomes impossible (other than as a result of its own misconduct) for such a party (which will be the Affected Party):**
>
> (1) **to perform any absolute or contingent obligation, to make a payment or delivery or to receive a payment or delivery in respect of such Transaction or to comply with any other material provision of this Agreement relating to such Transaction; or**
>
> (2) **to perform, or for any Credit Support Provider of such party to perform any contingent or other obligation which the party (or such Credit Support Provider) has under any Credit Support Document relating to such Transaction.**

Additional wording is normally added to round it off as follows:

For the purpose of the foregoing Termination Event both parties shall be Affected Parties.

Sometimes a time limit is incorporated in the Impossibility language.

Impossibility is an Additional Termination Event and if it is included various amendments (listed in the 1992 *User's Guide*) need to be made to other Sections in the Agreement.

The new 2002 Agreement contains substantial and far reaching Force Majeure Event provisions as we saw in Chapter 4.

Affected Parties in Termination Events

Sometimes a party wants no fault termination for the Section 5(b)(i) and Section 5(b)(ii) Termination Events (Illegality and Tax Event respectively). This would involve both parties calculating the early termination payment and splitting the difference. Where this is desired the following provision might be used:

Affected Parties in Termination Events.

For the purposes of Section 6(e) of this Agreement both parties shall be deemed to be Affected Parties in connection with the Termination Events described in Sections 5(b)(i) and 5(b)(ii) so that payments on Early Termination shall be calculated as provided in Section 6(e)(ii)(2).

You need to decide if it is a good thing to give this away in advance of the relevant circumstances arising. I tend to resist it because I believe that the rights given by the Agreement should not be diluted without good reason.

Joint and several liability

Occasionally you come across Schedules where two or more parties are collectively Party A or Party B.

For instance the Agreement might be between:

X Bank AG ("Party A") and Horseshoe Hotels 1 Limited, Horseshoe Hotels 2 Limited and Horseshoe Hotels 3 Limited (collectively "Party B")

Usually the collective party is under common ownership or is a joint venture:

Joint and Several. **Section 9 of this Agreement is amended by adding the following paragraph after paragraph (g):**

"(h) *Joint and Several.* The obligations and liabilities under this Agreement of each of the persons collectively referred to as "Party B" are joint and several. Unless the context otherwise requires every reference to "Party B" will be taken to refer to any one or more (including all) such persons respectively. Further:

(a) if any such person should enter into a Transaction with Party A, all persons referred to as "Party B" will be bound by the Transaction in accordance with its terms and the terms of this Agreement, regardless of whether all, some or only one such person signs or issues the Confirmation; and

(b) for this purpose, each person comprising Party B irrevocably appoints and authorises every other person comprising Party B (jointly and severally) to enter into Transactions on its behalf and do all things reasonably necessary to evidence their terms (including signing or issuing Confirmations)."

This situation can also arise with Agreements involving law firms:

Joint and Several Liability

With reference to Party B only, all the individuals named in Part * of this Schedule as partners of the firm of [name of law firm] shall each be jointly and severally liable to Party A for each of the obligations and liabilities to be undertaken and/or assumed by Party B in terms of this Agreement, including without limitation any Specified Transactions entered into between Party A and Party B. Further, each of the individuals (partners) makes all representations and warranties under this Agreement on a joint and several basis.

Severability

A severability provision is quite commonly seen in European Schedules and a typical example is:

Severability. In the event any one or more of the provisions contained in this Agreement should be held invalid, illegal or unenforceable in any respect, the validity, legality and enforceability of the remaining provisions contained herein shall not in any way be affected or impaired thereby. The parties shall endeavour, in good faith negotiations, to replace the invalid, illegal or unenforceable provision with valid legal or enforceable provisions, the economic effect of which comes as close as reasonably possible to that of the invalid, illegal or unenforceable provisions.

The idea is that this provision allows an afflicted Agreement to continue in effect even if it needs to be amended to remedy the situation.

Occasionally, one sees wording disapplying the severability provision where it involves core provisions of the Agreement as in the following:

> ***Severability.*** **If any term, provision, covenant or condition of this Agreement or the application thereof to any party or circumstance, shall be held to be invalid or unenforceable (in whole or in part) for any reason, the remaining terms, provisions, covenants and conditions hereof shall continue in full force and effect as if this Agreement had been executed with the invalid or unenforceable portion eliminated so long as this Agreement as so modified continues to express, without material change, the original intentions of the parties as to the subject matter of this Agreement and the deletion of such portion of this Agreement will not substantially impair the respective benefits or expectations of the parties to this Agreement; provided, however, that this severability provision shall not be applicable if any provision of Section 2, 5, 6, or 13 (or any definition or provision in Section 14 to the extent it relates to or is used in or in connection with any such Section) shall be so held to be invalid or unenforceable.**

A few years ago some lawyers thought that including such a clause might undermine the single agreement concept of the Agreement but the market no longer regards this as a problem.

However, you sometimes see clarifying wording on this as at the end of the following example:

> ***Severability.*** **If any term, provision, covenant or condition of this Agreement or the application thereof to any party or circumstance, shall be held to be invalid or unenforceable (in whole or in part) for any reason, the remaining terms, provisions, covenants and conditions hereof shall continue in full force and effect as if this Agreement had been executed with the invalid or unenforceable portion eliminated so long as this Agreement as so modified continues to express, without material change, the original intentions of the parties as to the subject matter of this Agreement and the deletion of such portion of this Agreement will not substantially impair the respective benefits or expectations of the parties to this Agreement. *It shall in particular be understood that this severability clause shall not affect the "single agreement" concept of Section 1(c) of this Agreement.*** (my emphasis)

Financial Services and Markets Act 2002

As Simon Leifer pointed out in Chapter 5 at pages 357–8, regulation of financial services has undergone a "sea change" with the implementation of the above Act. This has started to spawn representations such as the following:

> **Financial Services and Markets Act 2000**
>
> **Party A represents, warrants and undertakes to Party B (which representation, warranty and undertaking will be deemed to be repeated at all times until the termination of this Agreement), that to the extent that it acts through its London branch, it is an "authorised person" within the meaning of the Financial Services and Markets Act 2000.**

Netting

A provision occasionally seen relates to Terminated Transactions not capable of being netted on close-out under section 6(e) viz:

> ***Netting.*** **In the event that any Terminated Transaction cannot be aggregated and netted against all other Terminated Transactions under Section 6(e) of the Agreement, such excluded Terminated Transactions shall be aggregated and netted amongst themselves to the fullest extent permitted by law.**

This would cover the position where a type of Transaction could be included under the Agreement but the laws of a party's country of incorporation would not allow the Transactions concerned to be netted under it upon close-out.

It would be as well to check that this provision is acceptable in the counterparty's local jurisdiction because it might possibly invalidate the core provisions of Section 6 of the Agreement in their country.

Tax related provisions

Generally speaking, parties make few if any amendments to the tax provisions in the Agreement (outside of the Part 2 tax representations) except where this is important, for instance, in project finance deals and even then not often. However, some major UK corporates like, for instance, to supplement Section 2(d)(i)(4) and amend Section 5(b)(ii) and I have seen the following:

> ***Tax Credit.*** **Where one of the parties to this Agreement ("X") pays an additional amount in accordance with Section 2(d)(i)(4) above, the other party ("Y") undertakes as follows:**

(i) to the extent that Y obtains Tax credit, allowance, set-off or repayment from the tax authorities of any jurisdiction relating to any deduction or withholding giving rise to such payment, it shall pay to X on the next Scheduled Payment Date after receipt of the same by Y so much of the cash benefit (as calculated below) that it has received as will leave Y in substantially the same (but in any event no worse) position as Y would have been in if no such deduction or withholding had been required;

(ii) the "cash benefit" shall, in the case of credit, allowance or set-off, be the additional amount of Tax which would have been payable by Y in the jurisdiction referred to in (i) above but for the obtaining by it of the said Tax credit, allowance or set-off and, in the case of a repayment, shall be the amount of the repayment and shall be taken to be received, in the case of a Tax credit, allowance or set-off, on the date when the additional amount of Tax would have been payable and, in the case of a repayment, on the date when the repayment is made; and

(iii) it will use all reasonable endeavours to obtain any Tax credit, allowance, set-off or repayment as soon as is reasonably practicable, provided that it shall be the sole judge of the amount of any such Tax credit, allowance, set-off or repayment and of the date on which the same is received and shall not be obliged to disclose to X any information regarding its affairs or tax computations nor to arrange its affairs for the convenience of X.

OR

The following shall be inserted as an additional subsection (iii) of Section 2(d) of the Agreement:

If X is required by any applicable law, as modified by the practice of any relevant government revenue authority, to make a deduction or withholding on any payment under this agreement, and X makes payment of that deduction or withholding in accordance with the terms of clause 2(d)(i)(2), and X is required to make a payment to Y in accordance with the terms of clause 2(d)(i)(4), and Y is entitled to reclaim that deduction or withholding paid by X to the relevant authorities, or is entitled to a tax credit in respect of the payment, Y will, if it is able to identify such tax credit as being applicable to such payment of that deduction or withholding, use all reasonable endeavours to obtain from the relevant authority the repayment or tax credit provided that it shall be the sole judge (but acting in good faith) of the amount of any such tax credit or repayment and of the date on which the same is received and shall not be obliged to disclose to X any information regarding its tax affairs or tax computations and shall have absolute

discretion as to the time and the order and the manner in which it realises or utilises any tax credit and shall not be obliged to arrange its business or its tax affairs in any particular way in order to be eligible for any tax credit or repayment. If Y has obtained, utilised and retained the repayment or tax credit relief, it will pay an amount to X which Y determines (acting in good faith) which will leave it (after that payment) in the same after-tax position as it would have been in had X not been required to make the payment to Y in accordance with the terms of clause 2(d)(i)(4).

OR

> *Refunds*
>
> If the Counterparty has paid an Additional Amount under Section 2(d)(i) or paid any amount pursuant to Section 2(d)(ii) and the Company subsequently receives any refund of any amount deducted or withheld in respect thereof from any revenue authority it shall promptly pay the amount refunded over to the Counterparty, together with any interest received thereon.

Section 5(b)(ii):

> Section 5(b)(ii) is amended in the following respects:
>
> (i) by inserting "(A)" immediately before the words "Due to" at the start of the clause; and,
>
> (ii) by inserting the following at the end of the clause:
>
> and (B) due to a Change in Tax Law, Party *(which will be the Affected Party) will, or there is a substantial likelihood that it will, be unable to claim relief as a deduction against its taxable income for the full amount of each payment that it makes in connection with any Transaction;

This amendment extends the scope of the Tax Event to a Change in Tax Law refusing tax relief as a business expense to payments made under the Agreement.

Sometimes an additional clause may be added to the Tax Event Termination Event viz:

> Tax Event
>
> Add the following paragraph (3) to Section 5(b)(ii):
>
> (3) be denied relief for a payment to be made on the next succeeding Scheduled Payment Date either as a trading or non-trading debit in computing the profits of the Affected Party or otherwise which would, had the relief been available, have had the result of reducing the taxable income or increasing the allowable loss of the Affected Party and such denial results from a Change in Tax Law or practice or withdrawal of any concession adopted by any taxing authority.

A common amendment seen in connection with Section 5(b)(ii)(2) is as follows:

Section 5(b)(ii)(2) is amended by the addition of the following at the end thereof:

provided, however, that the parties acknowledge that the proposal of laws, regulations or guidelines shall not, prior to the actual adoption or enactment thereof, constitute a Termination Event hereunder.

This clarifies the situation, for instance, between the announcement of Budget proposals and their eventual enactment.

A short amendment sometimes seen is:

Tax Event. **Section 5(b)(ii) of this Agreement shall be amended by deleting in the fourth line thereof, the phrase ", or there is a substantial likelihood that it will,...".**

It makes Tax Event apply only when court or tax authority action is actually taken which results in a withholding tax being levied on the Affected Party rather than a substantial likelihood that it will be taken. It aims to remove uncertainty in the application of the Tax Event Termination Event.

A variation on this is:

Tax Event

In Section 5(b)(ii) line 4 will be inserted after "substantial likelihood" "... in the written opinion of legal counsel of recognised standing (which shall include in-house counsel).

Finally, guarantees provided by many foreign Credit Support Providers often lack a withholding tax indemnity. An example of one is as follows:

Taxes. **All payments due under the Agreement or this Guarantee will be made without any deduction or withholding for or on account of any Tax (as defined in the Agreement) unless such deduction or withholding is required by any applicable law, as modified by the practice of any relevant governmental revenue authority, then in effect. In the event that the Guarantor is required by any applicable law to make any deduction or withholding for or on account of any Tax from any payment to be made by it under this Guarantee or in respect of the Agreement, then it shall:**

(a) promptly notify Counterparty of such requirement;

(b) pay to the relevant authorities the full amount required to be deducted or withheld (including the full amount required to be deducted or withheld from any additional amount required to be paid pursuant to this Section *) promptly upon the earlier of

determining that such deduction or withholding is required or receiving notice that such amount has been assessed against Counterparty;

(c) promptly forward to Counterparty an official receipt (or certified copy), or other documentation reasonably satisfactory to Counterparty, evidencing such payment to such authorities; and

(d) if such Tax is an Indemnifiable Tax (as defined in the Agreement), pay to Counterparty together with such payment to which Counterparty is otherwise entitled such additional amounts as may be necessary in order that the net amount actually received by Counterparty (free and clear of such Indemnifiable Taxes) will be equal to the full amount Counterparty otherwise would have received had no such deduction or withholding been required.

Administrative provisions

ISDA Definitions

It is quite common to include reference to the ISDA Definitions in the Schedule although some market players insist that they should only be referred to in Confirmations so as to avoid any inconsistencies and the need to amend the Agreement when a new set of Definitions is published. In July 2000, the *ISDA 2000 Definitions* were published by ISDA and consolidated the *1991 Definitions*, the *1998 Supplement* and part of the *1998 Euro Definitions.* Most institutions have now adopted them.

ISDA Definitions provisions usually deal with the problem of conflict or inconsistency where there is:

- **any inconsistency between the general or product specific ISDA Definitions, the product specific Definitions will prevail.**

Here is an example of part of such a provision:

In the event of any inconsistency between the 2000 Definitions and the 1996 Equity Definitions, the Equity Definitions shall prevail with respect to an Equity Option Transaction or an Equity Swap Transaction.

- **a conflict between the relevant ISDA Definitions and the Confirmation for a specific Transaction, the Confirmation will prevail;**
- **a conflict between the relevant ISDA Definitions and the Schedule, the Schedule will prevail.**

The same applies to any conflict between the relevant Definitions and the rest of the Agreement.

Sometimes a pecking order is given as follows:

> ***Inconsistency.* In the event of any inconsistency between any of the following documents, the relevant document first listed shall govern: (i) a Confirmation, (ii) this Schedule, (iii) the Definitions incorporated by reference into a Transaction, and (iv) the pre-printed form of the Agreement.**

Sometimes you see the wording that the ISDA Definitions "as modified from time to time" will apply to the Agreement. This is included in order to avoid amending the Schedule each time new relevant Definitions are published. However, it effectively commits the parties to accepting these new Definitions in advance without any examination of their terms. With important Definitions such as the *2000 Definitions* market players took a significant time to absorb them. Therefore, amendments approving such Definitions in advance should be resisted.

Adherence to market customs and practice

Occasionally the following harmless provision is proposed:

> ***Interbank customs and practices.* Transactions shall be subject to the customs and practices observed generally in transactions in the interbank over the counter derivatives markets, except to the extent inconsistent with the express terms of this Agreement and the Confirmation specifying the terms of the Transaction.**

Entering into transactions

Sometimes parties want to spell out in detail their rights in entering into Transactions and Confirmations as there is no room to put this in a Confirmation especially if short electronic Confirmations are used. Here is a detailed example:

> ***Entering into Transactions.* Transactions will usually be entered into through oral agreements over the telephone by authorised representatives of the parties hereto; such oral agreements shall be binding also in cases where the parties will not exchange Confirmations as provided for in this Agreement. Any request for correction of error in a Confirmation shall be made by the party receiving such Confirmation (the "Recipient") promptly upon receipt thereof. If such an objection is not received by the other party by the close of business in the place of the Office through which it is acting for the purpose of the relevant Transaction on the third**

> Local Business Day in such place after the Confirmation has been sent by telex or fax with the correct answerback or transmitting protocol, as the case may be, received at the end thereof, the Recipient may not subsequently object and the terms of the Transaction will be as set out in the Confirmation, absent manifest error.
>
> Where a party does object to the terms of a Confirmation before the close of business on the third Local Business Day after receipt of the Confirmation from the other party such party shall inform the other party of the nature of its objection and if the other party accepts the objection and amends the Confirmation, the objecting party shall have three Local Business Days to consider the amended Confirmation. If no further objection is received by the other party by the close of business in the place of the office through which it is acting for the purpose of the relevant Transaction on the third Local Business Day in such place after the amendment has been sent by telex or fax with the correct answerback or transmitting protocol, as the case may be, received at the end thereof, the Recipient may not subsequently object and the terms of the Transaction will be as set out in the Confirmation, absent manifest error.
>
> Each party is entitled to request signed counterparts of a Confirmation. However, the failure of either party to send or to sign a Confirmation shall not affect the validity or the binding effect of the Transaction entered into by oral agreements.
>
> To the extent the provisions of this Agreement dealing with the exchange of Confirmations and Section 9(b) of this Agreement are inconsistent with this paragraph the provisions of this paragraph shall prevail.

A more limited version is:

> The parties hereto agree that with respect to each Transaction hereunder a legally binding agreement shall exist from the moment that the parties hereto agree the essential terms of such Transaction which the parties anticipate will occur by telephone.

Electronic confirmations

Acceptance of Confirmations in electronic format is commonly seen in Schedules. A typical example is:

> *Electronic Confirmations.* Where a Transaction is confirmed by means of an electronic messaging system that the parties have elected to use to confirm such Transaction such confirmation will constitute a "Confirmation" as referred to in this Agreement.

Restatement language

Where a 1987 Agreement is being upgraded to a 1992 Agreement or now more commonly an old 1992 Agreement is being upgraded to a modern one, it is normal for restatement language such as the following to appear in the Schedule:

> ***Restatement.*** **This Agreement amends and restates [*name of previous Agreement*] dated as of [*insert date*] between Party A and Party B (the "Previous Agreement") together with the Confirmations (as defined in the Previous Agreement) relating thereto. All Confirmations relating to the Previous Agreement shall be deemed part of this Agreement and all references to the Agreement in all Confirmations to the Previous Agreement (howsoever described) shall be deemed references to this Agreement. All terms in the Confirmations shall be defined in accordance with this Agreement *mutatis mutandis.***

OR

> Prior Agreement
>
> **This Agreement restates and amends in its entirety the Interest Rate and Currency Exchange Agreement/ISDA Master Agreement dated as of [*insert date*] between Party A and Party B (the "Prior Agreement"). Upon execution of this Agreement, (a) this Agreement shall govern the rights and obligations of the parties hereto in connection with all Transactions (howsoever defined) entered into under the Prior Agreement, (b) the Prior Agreement shall be deemed to be superseded and of no further force or effect and (c) each confirmation which constituted a supplement to the Prior Agreement shall be deemed a Confirmation subject to this Agreement and each swap transaction evidenced by such confirmation shall be governed hereby. To the extent that any such confirmation amended the terms of the Prior Agreement with respect to the particular swap transaction evidenced by such confirmation and to the extent that this Agreement contains terms identical with or parallel to those so amended, this Agreement shall be deemed amended to the same substantive effect with respect to that particular swap transaction.**

A few years ago some lawyers were recommending the use of Appendix B to the *User's Guide* for this purpose and this actually remains my preference but market practice now is to include briefer amendment and restatement language like the above in the Schedule itself.

Change of account

Two common amendments are seen in connection with Section 2(b) – Change of Account.

The first is a simple statement that the new account will be in the same tax jurisdiction as the old one:

> ***Change of Account.*** **Section 2(b) shall be deleted and replaced by the following:**
>
> **Either party may change its account for receiving payment or delivery but only to another bank in the same currency and taxing jurisdiction as specified for the relevant payment in the Transaction by giving notice to the other party at least five Local Business Days prior to the due date for payment for which such change applies unless such other party gives timely notice of a reasonable objection to such change.**

The second amendment stipulates that if the new account is in a different tax jurisdiction it will have no adverse tax consequences for the other party. An example is:

> ***Change of Account.*** **Section 2(b) of this Agreement is hereby amended by the insertion of the following at the end thereof after the word "change":**
>
> **...provided that if such account shall not be in the same tax jurisdiction having the same power to tax as the original account, the party not changing its account shall not be obliged to pay any greater amounts and shall not receive less as a result of such change than would have been the case if such change had not taken place.**

Transactions settling by delivery

As mentioned before, the Agreement is stronger on detailing payment obligations than delivery obligations although this has greatly improved in the 2002 Agreement. However, some or all of the following provisions might be included if it was considered desirable to highlight delivery obligations in the Schedule.

Transactions settling by delivery

The parties may enter into Transactions hereunder under which one or both parties agrees to settle by delivery rather than payment of cash. Accordingly the following further amendments to the Agreement are agreed:

(a) *General Conditions*

(i) Section 2(a)(i) is amended to read as follows:

Each party will make each payment or delivery or adequate arrangements to accept each payment or delivery, specified in each Confirmation to be made by or to it, subject to the other provisions of this Agreement.

(ii) Section 2(a)(ii) is amended by the deletion of its final sentence and the substitution of the following:

Where settlement is by delivery (that is, other than by payment), such delivery will be made for receipt on the due date in the place specified in the relevant Confirmation or otherwise pursuant to this Agreement in the manner customary for the relevant obligation, and the parties agree that any such Transaction shall not be cash settled unless otherwise agreed to by the parties.

(iii) Section 2(b) is amended to read as follows:

Change of Account. Either party may change its account for receiving a payment or place for receiving a delivery by giving notice to the other party at least five Local Business Days prior to the scheduled date for the payment, and at least seven Local Business Days prior to the scheduled date for the delivery to which such change applies unless such other party gives timely notice of reasonable objection to such change.

(b) Default Interest: Other Amounts. The last sentence of Section 2(e) is amended to read as follows:

If prior to the occurrence or effective designation of an Early Termination Date in respect of the relevant Transaction, a party defaults in the performance of any obligation required to be settled by delivery, it will, to the extent permitted by law and subject to Section 6(c), compensate the other party on demand for any costs, losses or expenses reasonably incurred by the other party in connection with such delivery default (including, but not limited to, any costs of funding and/or, if applicable, borrowing any corresponding shares, securities or other instruments). A certificate signed by the deliveree setting out such costs, losses or expenses in reasonable detail shall be conclusive evidence that they have been incurred.

(c) Additional Agreement

Section 4 (Agreements) is amended by the addition at the end thereof as new Section 4(f) of the following additional agreement:

(f) *Transfer of Ownership*. Where it is required to deliver securities or commodities under this Agreement it will at the time of each such delivery convey full title guarantee to such securities or commodities, free from all liens, charges, equities, rights of pre-emption or other security interests or encumbrances whatsoever and it will have at that time the right to transfer those securities or commodities on the terms of this Agreement.

(d) Events of Default

(i) Section 5(a)(i) (Failure to Pay or Deliver) is amended to read as follows:

(i) *Failure to Pay or Deliver*. Failure by the party to make, when due, any payment under this Agreement or delivery under Section 2(a)(i) or 2(e) required to be made by it if such failure is not remedied on or before the third Local Business Day after notice of such failure is given to the party, unless its failure to make delivery results from a failure of the other party to make adequate arrangements to accept delivery if such failure is not remedied on demand after notice of such failure is given to the other party.

(ii) Section 5(a)(ii) (Breach of Agreement) is amended solely as it applies to Section 4(f), by deleting the words "...if such failure is not remedied on or before the thirtieth day after such notice is given to the party".

As mentioned before, coverage of deliveries is much better in the main text of the 2002 Agreement.

Other provisions

Fully paid Transactions

The following provision is quite common:

> ***Fully Paid Transactions.* The condition precedent in Section 2(a)(iii)(1) does not apply to a payment and delivery owing by a party if the other party shall have satisfied in full all its payment or delivery obligations under Section 2(a)(i) of this Agreement and shall at the relevant time have no future payment or delivery obligations, whether absolute or contingent, under Section 2(a)(i).**

This clause covers a situation where a Buyer takes out a cap or option, for example, and pays a single up front premium to a Seller. At that stage the Buyer has a risk that the Seller will not perform its obligations under the cap or option if the strike price is reached. The Seller has no risk on the Buyer because it has received the Buyer's premium up front. Now imagine that the Buyer goes into default under another agreement. The Buyer would not want the Seller to invoke Cross Default and not honour its obligations when the cap or option is the only Transaction under this Agreement. This is the purpose of this provision which is discussed in the 1992 *User's Guide*, p. 7.

Another common version of it is:

> ***Payments on Early Termination.* Notwithstanding the provisions of Sections 5 and 6 of this Agreement, if at any time one of the parties to the Agreement ("X") shall have satisfied in full all of its obligations under Section 2(a) of this Agreement and shall, at the same time, have no future payment obligations whether future or contingent, under such Section and unless the other party ("Y") is required pursuant to appropriate proceedings to return to X or otherwise returns to X on demand from X any portion of such payment, (a) the occurrence of any event described in Section 5(a) of this Agreement with respect to X or any Specified Entity or Credit Support Provider of X shall not constitute an Event of Default or Potential Event of Default with respect to X and (b) Y shall be entitled to designate an Early Termination Date under Section 6 of the Agreement only as a result of the occurrence of a Termination Event (i) under Section 5(b)(i) or 5(b)(ii) of the Agreement or (ii) under Section 5(b)(iii) of this Agreement with Y as the Burdened Party.**

Some collateral practitioners seek to delete this provision where they have it in existing Schedules when they enter into an English Law ISDA Credit Support Annex with a counterparty. This is because there are contingent payment and delivery obligations under the margin call, margin return and substitution provisions of the Credit Support Annex.

Bridge language

In the mid-1990s ISDA developed bridge language for BBAIRS (British Bankers' Association Interest Rate Swap) transactions and FRABBA (Forward Rate Agreement British Bankers' Association) transactions. Both BBAIRS and FRABBA were market terms published in booklet form by the British Bankers' Association in 1985. To make relevant transactions subject to BBAIRS and FRABBA terms could be stated in a shorthand way in Confirmations without needing to spell out all these terms much as a Confirmation governed by ISDA Definitions would cross-refer to those Definitions.

BBAIRS transactions are usually limited to interest rate swaps with a maturity of two years or less unless the parties otherwise agree. They were popular with Japanese banks and others wanting a minimum of documentation. BBAIRS and FRABBA terms can be stated as applying in one sentence on a SWIFT Confirmation.

A potential problem arose in 1995 with the Barings administration. Because the BBAIRS and FRABBA Terms were published in 1985, the concept of administration as an insolvency event was unknown to them. Administration only became a formal feature of the insolvency landscape in England and Wales with the enactment of the Insolvency Act 1986. Hence in 1995 there was some doubt whether BBAIRS- or FRABBA-governed transactions could be closed out due to an administration insolvency event. However, the pace of events with the rapid purchase of Barings by ING did not permit this to be tested in the courts.

The presence of ISDA bridge language for FRABBA and BBAIRS transactions is quite common. However, it is unnecessary where no such trades exist between the parties. In addition some parties prefer to rely on the Scope of Agreement sweep in language rather than spell out the full ISDA FRABBA and BBAIRS language which is as follows:

> ***FRABBA Transactions.* Any forward rate agreement into which thc parties have entered and in respect of which the confirmation or other confirming evidence refers to or incorporates the British Bankers' Association London Interbank Forward Rate Agreements Recommended Terms and Conditions (1985 edition) ("FRABBA Terms") will be governed by this Agreement. Any forward rate agreement into which the parties may enter and in respect of which the confirmation or other confirming evidence refers to or incorporates the FRABBA Terms will be governed by this Agreement in all circumstances except when the parties expressly agree that this provision will not apply. Each such transaction will be deemed to be a Transaction and each such confirmation or other confirming evidence will be deemed to constitute a Confirmation for purposes of this Agreement. Sections B, C and E**

and clauses 1, 4, 5 and 6 of Section D of the FRABBA Terms are hereby incorporated by reference in this Agreement. Those Sections are applicable only to transactions to which this provision relates and will prevail in the event of any inconsistency with any other provision of this Agreement. In the event of any other inconsistency between the FRABBA Terms and this Agreement, this Agreement will govern. Clauses 2, 3, 7, 8, 9 and 10 of Section D of the FRABBA Terms are not applicable to any transaction to which this provision relates.

BBAIRS Transactions. Any interest rate or currency swap transaction into which the parties have entered and in respect of which the confirmation or other confirming evidence refers to or incorporates the British Bankers' Association London Interbank Interest Rate Swaps Recommended Terms and Conditions (1985 edition) ("BBAIRS Terms") will be governed by this Agreement. Any interest rate or currency swap transaction into which the parties may enter and in respect of which the confirmation or other confirming evidence refers to or incorporates the BBAIRS Terms will be governed by this Agreement in all circumstances except where the parties expressly agree that this provision will not apply. Each such transaction will be deemed to be a Transaction and each such confirmation or other confirming evidence will be deemed to constitute a Confirmation for purposes of this Agreement. Sections D (except Section D.5), E (except Section E.5) and F (except Section F.5) of the BBAIRS Terms are hereby incorporated by reference in this Agreement. Those Sections are applicable only to transactions to which this provision relates and will prevail in the event of any inconsistency with any other provision of this Agreement. In the event of any other inconsistency between the BBAIRS Terms and this Agreement, this Agreement will govern. Section G of the BBAIRS Terms is not applicable to any transaction to which this provision relates.

It is possible to combine the two provisions into one as follows:

BBAIRS and FRABBA Bridge. Any interest rate transaction, currency swap transaction or forward rate agreement into which the parties have entered and in respect of which the confirmation or other confirming evidence refers to or incorporates the British Bankers' Association London Interbank Interest Rate Swaps Recommended Terms and Conditions (1985 edition)("BBAIRS Terms") or the British Bankers' Association London Interbank Forward Rate Agreements Recommended Terms and Conditions (1985 edition) ("FRABBA Terms") will be governed by this Agreement. Any interest rate transaction, currency swap transaction or forward rate agreement into which the parties may enter and in respect of which the confirmation or other confirming evidence refers to or incorporates the BBAIRS Terms or the FRABBA Terms will be governed by this Agreement in all circumstances except when the parties expressly agree that this provision will not apply.

Each such transaction will be deemed to be a Transaction and each such confirmation or other confirming evidence will be deemed to constitute a Confirmation for purposes of this Agreement.

Sections D (except Section D.5), E (except Section E.5) and F (except Section F.5) of the BBAIRS Terms and Sections B, C and E and clauses 1, 4, 5 and 6 of Section D of the FRABBA Terms are hereby incorporated by reference in this Agreement. Those Sections are applicable only to transactions to which the above paragraph relates (with the BBAIRS Terms being applicable to interest rate and currency swap transactions and the FRABBA Terms being applicable to forward rate agreements) and will prevail in the event of any inconsistency with any other provision of this Agreement. In the event of any other inconsistency between the BBAIRS Terms or the FRABBA Terms and this Agreement, this Agreement will govern. Section G of the BBAIRS Terms is not, and Clauses 2, 3, 7, 8 and 10 of Section D of the FRABBA Terms are not, applicable to any transaction to which the above paragraph relates.

Negative interest rates

In 1995, ISDA issued wording for a provision covering the situation where interest rates on a swap fell below zero or more likely the negative spread to be deducted from interest rate caused the "net" rate to fall below zero. This was and still is a concern particularly with Japanese interest rates where at the time of writing the three month Yen LIBOR rate is minus 3.125 b.p. A spread of minus 20 b.p. would result in a net rate of minus 23.125 b.p. This would bring the negative interest rate clause into play. The wording of the provision normally seen (there were alternative versions in ISDA's circular of 15 November 1995) was as follows:

Negative interest rates

(a) Floating Amounts. "Swap Transaction" means, for the purposes of this provision concerning Negative Interest Rates, a rate exchange or swap transaction including transactions involving a single currency or two or more currencies. Party A and Party B agree that, if with respect to a Calculation Period for a Swap Transaction either party is obligated to pay a Floating Amount that is a negative number (either due to a quoted negative Floating Rate or by operation of a Spread that is subtracted from the Floating Rate), the Floating Amount with respect to that party for that Calculation Period will be deemed to be zero, and the other party will pay to that party the absolute value of the negative Floating Amount as calculated, in addition to any amounts otherwise owed by the other party for that Calculation Period with respect to that Swap Transaction, on the Payment Date that the Floating Amount would have been due if it had been a positive number. Any amounts paid by the other party with respect to the absolute value of a negative Floating Amount will be paid to such account as the receiving party may designate (unless such other party gives timely notice of a reasonable objection to such designation) in the currency in which that Floating Amount would have been paid if it had been a positive number (and without regard to the currency in which the other party is otherwise obligated to make payments).

(b) Compounding. Party A and Party B agree that, if with respect to one or more Compounding Periods for a Swap Transaction where "Compounding" or "Flat Compounding" is specified to be applicable the Compounding Period Amount, the Basic Compounding Period Amount or the Additional Compounding Period Amount is a negative number (either due to a quoted negative Floating Rate or by operation of a Spread that is subtracted from the Floating Rate), then the Floating Amount for the Calculation Period in which that Compounding Period or those Compounding Periods occur will be either the sum of all the Compounding Period Amounts or the sum of all the Basic Compounding Period Amounts and all the Additional Compounding Period Amounts in that Calculation Period (whether positive or negative). If such sum is positive, then the Floating Rate Payer with respect to the Floating Amount so calculated will pay that Floating Amount to the other party. If such sum is negative, the Floating Amount with respect to the party that would be obligated to pay that Floating Amount will be deemed to be zero, and the other party will pay to that party the absolute value of the negative Floating Amount as calculated, such payment to be made in accordance with (a) above.

However, these provisions are now incorporated in Article 6 Section 6.4 page 12 of the *ISDA 2000 Definitions* and so do not need to be included in Schedules provided that the *ISDA 2000 Definitions* apply in Confirmations.

Labour Disputes

In the 1980s lengthy bank strikes were common in Scandinavia and Schedule language was developed to prevent this being deemed to be an Event of Default but making it rather an Additional Termination Event after an agreed period of time had passed with no resolution of the strike. Here is a detailed example of such a provision:

> Labour Disputes:
>
> (i) A party ("Party X") shall not be deemed to be in breach of this Agreement or otherwise liable to the other party ("Party Y"), and no Event of Default shall be deemed to occur with respect to Party X, as a result of any delay in performance or any non-performance by Party X of any obligations under this Agreement (and the time for performance shall be extended accordingly) if and to the extent that the delay or non-performance is due to lock-outs, strikes or other disputes, in each case directly or indirectly affecting or instigated by Party X or its workforce.
>
> (ii) If Party X cannot receive payment from Party Y or Party Y cannot make payment to Party X due to an event described in sub-clause (i) above (a "labour dispute event"), then Party Y shall not be deemed to be in breach of this Agreement or otherwise liable to Party X, and no Event of Default shall be deemed to occur with respect to Party Y as result of any delay in performance or any non-performance of any obligations under this Agreement resulting therefrom (and the time for performance shall be extended accordingly).
>
> (iii) Party X shall promptly notify Party Y of the nature and extent of the circumstances giving rise to a labour dispute event.
>
> (iv) If, in accordance with this paragraph any payment hereunder is postponed following a labour dispute event interest shall accrue on the relevant amount(s) from the Scheduled Payment Date(s) to the date of actual payment at a rate per annum equal to the cost to the party due to receive payment (as certified by it) if it were to fund or of funding such relevant amount(s).
>
> (v) If the labour dispute event in question prevails for a continuous period in excess of three months such event shall be an Additional Termination Event and each party shall be an Affected Party.

Termination of Agreement

When no Transactions are outstanding under an Agreement and trading is unlikely to resume or the Agreement is redundant, there is no actual mechanism to terminate the Agreement in these circumstances.

What normally happens is that the parties agree by letter or a short Termination Agreement to terminate the Agreement. Sometimes this matter is also referred to in the Schedule as follows:

> *Termination.* **If no Transactions (or any present or future payment obligations, contingent or otherwise, thereunder) are outstanding under this Agreement, either party may terminate this Agreement upon written notice to the other party.**

Finale

Finally, there is the type of provision which really adds nothing and which I call the "Friday afternoon" clause. Here are two examples:

> *Time of the Essence*
>
> **The parties agree that time is of the essence in this Agreement and any Transaction hereunder.**

AND

> *No obligation.* **Neither party to this Agreement shall be required to enter into any Transaction with the other.**

Both are short but neither is really worth saying. Indeed the latter cuts across the whole purpose of negotiating an ISDA Master Agreement.

Let us now review the provisions of Part 6 of X Bank AG's Schedule.

Part 6

In recent years it has become common for a Part 6 dealing with FX Transactions and Currency Options to be added to the Schedule. It was not in the original 1992 Agreement templates. The length of this varies from a few lines to several pages as in our example here. Traditionally foreign exchange and currency options have been traded under their own market terms but the multiproduct nature of the ISDA Master Agreement and its proven close-out netting mechanism has led to their inclusion under it.

(a) Incorporation and Amendment of 1998 FX and Currency Option Definitions

(i) *Incorporation of 1998 FX and Currency Option Definitions*

The 1998 FX and Currency Option Definitions (the "1998 Definitions"), published by the International Swaps and Derivatives Association, Inc., the Emerging Markets Traders Association and The Foreign Exchange Committee, are hereby incorporated by reference with respect to any "Currency Option Transactions" and "FX Transactions" as defined by the 1998 Definitions, except as otherwise specifically provided herein or in the Confirmation.

PART 6 – FX TRANSACTIONS AND CURRENCY OPTIONS

Incorporation and Amendment of 1998 FX and Currency Options Definitions

In 1998, the former *1992 FX and Currency Option Definitions* were substantially revised and extended by a committee involving ISDA, the Emerging Markets Traders Association and the Foreign Exchange Committee. It is normal to state early in Part 6 that the *1998 FX and Currency Option Definitions* will apply to any FX and Currency Option Transactions under the Agreement. Sometimes wording is added concerning conflicts and/or inconsistencies as follows:

In the event of any inconsistency between the provisions of the ISDA 2000 Definitions and the FX and Currency Option Definitions, the FX and Currency Option Definitions (as amended in this Schedule) will prevail. In the event of any inconsistency between the provisions of this Schedule and the FX and Currency Option Definitions, this Schedule will prevail. In the event of any inconsistency between the provisions of this Schedule and the printed Agreement of which it forms a part, this Schedule will prevail. In the event of any inconsistency between the provisions of any Confirmation and this Schedule, such Confirmation will prevail for the purposes of the relevant Transaction.

Sometimes parties want to distinguish between inconsistencies in other provisions in a Confirmation and the Definitions by adding the following:

In the event of any inconsistency between any of the other provisions of a Confirmation and the Definitions, such other provisions will prevail.

Although not a major point, the FX and Currency Option Definitions are deemed to be incorporated in the Confirmation and so, strictly speaking, it does not make sense to differentiate between the Confirmation and the Definitions but rather between the Definitions and the other provisions in the Confirmation.

Occasionally you might see an elaborate order of priority as in the following:

The definitions and provision contained in the *1998 FX and Currency Option Definitions* (the "FX Definitions") as published by the International Swaps and Derivatives Association, Inc., are incorporated by reference into, and made part of, this Part 6 and any Confirmation of a Currency Option or FX Transaction.

In the event of any inconsistencies, the parts of this Agreement shall rank as follows and the relevant term in the highest ranking document shall prevail:

(i) the Confirmation;

(ii) this Part 6 of this Schedule;

(iii) the remainder of this Schedule;

(iv) the printed form of Agreement;

(v) the FX Definitions; and

(vi) the 2000 Definitions.

(ii) *Amendment of 1998 FX and Currency Option Definitions.* The following amendments are made to the 1998 Definitions:

(1) Section 2.1 of the 1998 Definitions is amended by adding the following as Section 2.1(b):

(b) **Currency Obligation.** "Currency Obligation" means the undertaking of a party hereunder to receive or deliver an amount of currency, including a netted Currency Obligation, and including any Currency Obligation previously entered into by the parties.

Amendment of Section 2.1

This is one of various amendments usually made to the FX and Currency Option Definitions in Part 6.

(ii)(a)(1) The definition of Currency Obligation is not in the 1998 Definitions. It is used to describe any obligation to receive or deliver currency including currency obligations in the same currency which have been netted against each other or currency obligations previously entered into between the parties outside the Agreement although a Part 5 Scope of Agreement provision worded as in the example on page 540 would also catch Currency Obligations as would Part 6(b) below.

(2) The following provision is hereby added to Article 3.4:

(c) **Remedies in Event of Non-Payment.** If a Premium is not received on the Premium Payment Date, the Seller may elect: (i) to accept a late payment of such Premium; (ii) to give written notice of such non-payment and, if such payment shall not be received within two (2) Local Business Days of such notice, treat the related Currency Option Transaction as void; or (iii) to give written notice of such non-payment and, if such payment shall not be received within two (2) Local Business Days of such notice, treat such non-payment as an Event of Default under Section 5(a)(i). If the Seller elects to act under clause (i) of the preceding sentence, the Buyer shall pay interest on such Premium in the same currency as such Premium from the day such Premium was due until the day paid at the Default Rate; if the Seller elects to act under clause (ii) of the preceding sentence, the Buyer shall pay all out-of-pocket costs and actual damages incurred in connection with such unpaid or late Premium in the same currency as such Premium at the then prevailing market rate and any other costs or expenses incurred by the Seller in covering its obligations (including, without limitation, a delta hedge) with respect to such Currency Option Transaction.

Addition to Article 3.4

(ii)(a)(2) The provision for remedies for non-payment of premia for currency options is a common Part 6 addition. It originated in the International Currency Option Market Master Agreement issued by the British Bankers' Association in 1993 and gives discretion to the option Seller on how to act if the Buyer fails to pay his premium on time. The provision shown is very common although sometimes the last sentence will refer to any hedge rather than a delta hedge.

A few market players believe that the non-payment of premia for options should be treated in the same manner as any other non-payment under the Agreement, i.e. an Event of Default under Section 5(a)(i) if not cured within three Local Business Days of notice being given. However, this is a minority view.

(3) Section 3.6(a) is hereby amended by deleting in its entirety the final sentence thereof and adding in its place the following:

"A Currency Option Transaction may be exercised in whole or in part. If a Currency Option Transaction is exercised in part, the unexercised portion shall not be extinguished thereby but shall remain a Currency Option Transaction to the extent of such unexercised portion until the earlier of: (i) the expiration of the Currency Option Transaction; or (ii) an exercise of the Currency Option Transaction that leaves no remaining unexercised portion thereof."

Amendment to Section 3.6

(ii)(a)(3) Another common Part 6 amendment is an expansion of Section 3.6.(a) of the 1998 Definitions to cover the partial exercise of currency options. As drafted, the 1998 Definitions only cover 100% exercise unless this is varied by a Confirmation.

(b) **Confirmations.** Any confirmation in respect of any FX Transaction or Currency Option Transaction into which the parties may enter, or may have entered into prior to the date hereof, that fails by its terms to expressly exclude the application of this Agreement shall (to the extent not otherwise provided for in this Agreement) (i) constitute a "Confirmation" as referred to in this Agreement even where not so specified in such confirmation and (ii) supplement, form a part of, and be subject to this Agreement, and all provisions in this Agreement will govern such Confirmation except as modified therein. Without limitation of the foregoing, where an FX Transaction or Currency Option Transaction is confirmed by means of exchange of electronic messages on an electronic messaging system or by means of facsimile or telex (whether manually or automatically generated) or other document or confirming evidence exchanged between the parties confirming such Transaction, such messages, facsimile transmission, document or evidence shall constitute a Confirmation for the purposes of this Agreement even where not so specified therein. FX Transactions and Currency Option Transactions shall be promptly confirmed by the parties by Confirmations exchanged by mail, telex, facsimile or other electronic means. Unless either party objects to the terms of an FX Transaction or Currency Option Transaction contained in any Confirmation within three (3) Local Business Days of receipt thereof, the terms of such Confirmation shall be deemed correct and accepted absent manifest error, unless a corrected Confirmation is sent by a party within such three day period, in which case the party receiving such corrected Confirmation shall have two (2) Local Business Days after receipt thereof to object to the terms contained in such corrected Confirmation.

Part 6(b)

(b) This provision sweeps in FX and currency option Transactions documented under non-ISDA confirmations. Such confirmations are transformed into Confirmations under the Agreement provided that this is not excluded (unlikely) under the terms of the original confirmations. The provision also sweeps in all media through which a Confirmation may be transmitted including Confirmations generated electronically.

It is important for Transactions to be confirmed promptly. This provision includes deemed acceptance of a Confirmation after three Local Business Days (except for obvious error) unless the counterparty objects within that period and a corrected version is sent whereupon the recipient has two Local Business Days to object to the Confirmation's terms. While there is doubt whether deemed acceptance is effective under English law, provisions like these are common in the market.

An alternative provision is as follows:

Any transaction:

(i) outstanding between the parties at the date this Agreement comes into force; or (ii) entered into by the parties at or after the date this Agreement comes into force; which is an FX Transaction or a Currency Option Transaction as defined in the FX and Currency Option Definitions will be a Transaction for the purposes of this Agreement.

The Agreement is amended by the insertion of an additional Section 9(e)(iii), reading in its entirety as follows:

"(iii) Where an FX Transaction or Currency Option Transaction is confirmed by means of an electronic messaging system or other document or other confirming evidence exchanged between the parties confirming such Transaction;

(A) such electronic message, document or evidence will constitute a Confirmation for the purposes of this Agreement even where not so specified therein; and

(B) the definitions and provisions contained in the FX and Currency Option Definitions will be incorporated into the Confirmation.

In the event of any inconsistency between any of the other provisions of a Confirmation and the Definitions, such other provisions will govern."

(c) **Netting and Related Provisions.** Section 2(c) shall not apply to FX Transactions or Currency Option Transactions. In lieu thereof, the following shall apply:

(i) ***Netting. Offset and Discharge with Respect to Currency Options.*** The following provisions shall apply to Currency Option Transactions:

(1) If, on any date, and unless otherwise mutually agreed by the parties Premium would otherwise be payable hereunder in the same currency between a pair of Offices of the parties, then, on such date, each party's obligation to make payment of any such Premium will be automatically satisfied and discharged and, if the aggregate Premium(s) that would otherwise have been payable by such Office of one party exceeds the aggregate Premium(s) that would otherwise have been payable by such Office of the other party, be replaced by an obligation upon the party by whom the larger aggregate Premium(s) would have been payable to pay the other party the excess of the larger aggregate Premium(s) over the smaller aggregate Premium(s).

(2) If, on any date, and unless otherwise mutually agreed by the parties, amounts other than Premium payments would otherwise be payable hereunder in the same currency between a pair of Offices of the parties, then, on such date, each party's obligation to make payment of any such amount will be automatically satisfied and discharged and, if the aggregate amount that would otherwise have been payable by such Office of one party exceeds the aggregate amount that would otherwise have been payable by such Office of the other party, be replaced by an obligation upon the party by whom the larger aggregate amount would have been payable to pay the other party the excess of the larger aggregate amount over the smaller aggregate amount.

(3) Unless otherwise agreed, any Call or any Put written by a party will automatically be terminated and discharged, in whole or in part, as applicable, against a Call or a Put, respectively, written by the other party, such termination and discharge to occur automatically upon the payment in full of the last Premium payable in respect of such Currency Option Transactions; provided that such termination and discharge may only occur in respect of Currency Option Transactions:

(A) each being with respect to the same Put Currency and the same Call Currency;

(B) each having the same Expiration Date and Expiration Time, and with respect to Bermuda Style Options, each having the same Specified Exercise Dates;

Part 6(c)

(c) It is not unusual for netting, offset and discharge provisions for currency options to be introduced and modified in Part 6 of the Schedule.

(c)(i)(1) This is a fairly common premium payment netting provision between a pair of Offices (one on each side) trading currency options.

Many banks do not have automatic systems capability to net premium payments and generally do not accept this provision unless they believe they will have such systems in the near future.

(c)(i)(2) The same applies to other payments in the same currency which do not relate to premia.

(c)(i)(3) The Seller of a call option gives the Buyer the right to buy an agreed amount of currency at an agreed rate (called an exercise or strike price). The Seller of a put option gives the Buyer the right to sell an agreed amount of currency at an agreed rate. Where the Buyer and Seller are the same parties and each is trading different currency options with the other (either as Buyers or Sellers in each individual case) it is possible for such options to be offset against each other subject to certain conditions:

- **they must be in the same currency;**
- **they must expire at the same time on the same date. (Bermuda style options have a number of Exercise Dates and these must be identical if they are to be offset against each other);**

(C) each being of the same style, i.e. both being American Style Options or both being European Style Options or both being Bermuda Style Options;

(D) each having the same Strike Price;

(E) neither of which shall have been exercised by delivery of a Notice of Exercise;

(F) which are entered into by the same Offices of the parties; and

(G) which are otherwise identical in terms that are material for the purposes of offset and discharge;

and, upon the occurrence of such termination and discharge, neither party shall have any further obligation to the other party in respect of the relevant Currency Option Transactions or, as the case may be, parts thereof so terminated and discharged. In the case of a partial termination and discharge (i.e. where the relevant Currency Option Transactions are for different amounts of the Currency Pair), the remaining portion of the Currency Option Transaction which is partially discharged and terminated shall continue to be a Currency Option Transaction for all purposes of this Agreement.

- **they must be of the same option type (e.g. American-exerciseable at any time during the option period; European-exerciseable only on the last day of the option period; Bermuda-exerciseable upon certain specified dates during the option period). American options have more expensive premia than the others because they offer greater flexibility for exercise;**
- **they must each have the same Strike Price (this can be difficult to match up);**
- **no Notice of Exercise must have been given before the proposed offset;**
- **they must be entered into through an agreed pair of the parties' Offices; and**
- **they must be identical in all other material terms.**

When offset in this manner such currency options are deemed terminated or discharged unless only a partial termination or discharge occurs (i.e. the off-setting Transactions are for different currency amounts). In that case the remaining portion of the currency option Transaction will continue. This wording is based upon that found in Section 6 of the International Currency Option Master Agreement ("ICOM") published by the British Bankers' Association in 1993.

(ii) *Netting. Discharge and Termination of FX Transactions.* The following provisions shall apply to FX Transactions:

(1) Unless otherwise agreed by the parties hereto, whenever an FX Transaction is entered into between a pair of Netting Offices of the parties which creates a Currency Obligation in the same currency and for the same Settlement Date as an existing Currency Obligation between such Netting Offices, such Currency Obligations shall automatically and without further action be netted, individually cancelled and simultaneously replaced through novation by a new Currency Obligation determined as follows: (A) if the cancelled Currency Obligations evidence an undertaking by the same party to deliver the underlying currency, the new Currency Obligation shall equal the aggregate of the cancelled Currency Obligations, and (B) if the cancelled Currency Obligations evidence an undertaking by each party to deliver the underlying currency, the amount of the underlying currency to be delivered by each party under the cancelled Currency Obligations shall be compared, and the new Currency Obligation shall equal the amount by which the Currency Obligation of the party having the greater obligation with respect to such currency exceeds the Currency Obligation of the party having the lesser obligation with respect to such currency. Such new Currency Obligation shall be considered a "Currency Obligation" under this Agreement.

Part 6(c)(ii)

This provision concerns currency novation netting, i.e. the creation of a new Currency Obligation from the netting of two FX Transactions in the same currency separately entered into at different times by the same pair of Netting Offices of each party. In this process the original FX Transactions are terminated. Where a currency delivery obligation is one way, the new Currency Obligation will equal the amount of the cancelled one. Where both parties have delivery obligations, thc new Currency Obligation will equal the difference between the two Currency Obligations to be cancelled. Many market players do not have the systems capability to novation net FX Transactions. Again you need to consider if it is operationally sensible to commit to this provision.

(2) The provisions of Part 6(c)(ii)(1) above shall apply notwithstanding that either party (A) may fail to send out a Confirmation, (B) may not on its books treat the Currency Obligations as cancelled and simultaneously replaced by a new Currency Obligation as provided herein, or (C) may send out a Confirmation that incorrectly states any term of a Currency Obligation.

(3) If on any Settlement Date, and unless otherwise mutually agreed by the parties, Currency Obligations (which are not subject to the provisions of Part 6(c)(ii)(1) hereof) for the delivery of the same currency shall exist between a pair of Netting Offices of the parties, then on such Settlement Date, each party's Currency Obligation to deliver that currency will be automatically satisfied and discharged and, if the aggregate amount that would otherwise have been delivered by such Netting Office of one party exceeds the aggregate amount that would otherwise have been delivered by such Netting Office of the other party, replaced by a Currency Obligation upon the party by whom the larger aggregate amount would have been deliverable to deliver to the other party the excess of the larger aggregate amount over the smaller aggregate amount and if the aggregate amounts are equal no delivery of that Currency Obligation shall be made.

(4) For the purposes of this Part 6(d), "Netting Offices" means (i) with respect to Party A, Frankfurt and London; and (ii) with respect to Party B, London. The Netting Offices with respect to a party may be modified from time to time pursuant to notice given in accordance with the terms of Section 12.

Part 6(c)(ii)(2)–(4)

Part 6(c)(ii)(2) allows FX novation netting to take place without much formality. Such novation netting will not be invalidated if either party fails to send out a Confirmation or its accounting records fail to show the novation netting or even if it sends out a Confirmation which incorrectly records any term of a Currency Obligation (undesirable though this may be).

Part 6(c)(ii)(3) takes things one stage further. It covers the payment netting of novation netted Currency Obligations which have not been novation netted under Part 6(c)(ii)(1) above. Again one needs to have the operational capacity to do this and few currently have.

Part 6(c)(ii)(4) usually states each party's Netting Offices and may be subject to future amendment.

(d) **Definitions.** Section 14 is hereby amended as follows:

The definition of "Terminated Transactions" shall be deemed to include Currency Obligations.

Part 6(d)

Definitions

This amendment brings Currency Obligations into the scope of the definition of Terminated Transactions.

Other matters

In the past and still occasionally you might have seen the following provision relating to "swept-in" FX and Currency Option Transactions:

> **Other FX Transactions. Where close-out and liquidation occurs in accordance with Section 6 of the Agreement, the Non-defaulting Party shall also be entitled to close out and liquidate, to the fullest extent permitted by applicable law, any other foreign exchange transactions and currency options entered into between the parties which are then outstanding in accordance with the provisions of Section 6 of the Agreement, as if each such foreign exchange transaction were an FX Transaction and each such currency option were a Currency Option Transaction.**

An additional provision one sometimes sees is a statement that Loss will apply to FX and Currency Option Transactions. This may be despite Part 1(f) of the Schedule specifying Market Quotation. Typical wording of such a provision would be:

> **For purposes of Section 6(e) of the Agreement in respect of Currency Obligations and Currency Option Transactions, the Second Method and Loss will apply.**

Loss is the standard payment measure in the foreign exchange and currency option markets.

Another more obscure way of putting this is:

> ***Payments on Early Termination.*** **Notwithstanding anything to the contrary in the Agreement, for purposes of Section 6(d) and 6(e) of the Agreement, the Settlement Amount with respect to any FX Transactions or Currency Option Transactions shall be determined by clause (b) of the definition of such term.**

It is becoming more common to insert an Inconvertibility or Non-Transferability clause where more exotic currencies are traded under the Agreement:

> ***Inconvertibility and Non-Transferability.*** **If, as determined by either party in good faith and a commercially reasonable manner, an event (a "Disruption Event") occurs and is continuing on any Business Day of any Transaction in the jurisdiction (the "Event Currency Jurisdiction")**

of any one currency for payment specified in such Transaction (the "Event Currency") that has the effect of preventing or delaying either party from:

(i) converting the Event Currency into U.S. Dollars or any other currency which is the subject of such Transaction (the "Non-Event Currency") through customary legal channels;

(ii) converting the Event Currency into the Non-Event Currency at a rate at least as favourable as the rate for domestic institutions located in the Event Currency Jurisdiction;

(iii) delivering the Non-Event Currency from accounts inside the Event Currency Jurisdiction to accounts outside the Event Currency Jurisdiction, or

(iv) delivering the Event Currency between accounts inside the Event Currency Jurisdiction or to a party that is a non-resident of the Event Currency Jurisdiction, then the parties may, by mutual agreement:

(A) extend the settlement date of such contract to a mutually agreed future date for settlement, or

(B) require the payment, exchange or settlement of such Transactions in US$ in an amount mutually agreed in good faith between the parties. Payments of any corresponding amounts due in the Non-Event Currency shall be made on the date such US$ are paid.

If, with respect to such Transaction, a Disruption Event would otherwise constitute an Illegality, Impossibility or other similar event, then such event or circumstance will be treated as a Disruption Event and will be deemed not to constitute an Illegality, Impossibility or other similar event as the case may be, for purposes of such Transaction and this Agreement.

Sometimes FX Transactions and currency options might have been subject to another agreement or netting contract before being swept into the Agreement. For the avoidance of doubt, some parties might like to include wording like the following:

The parties hereto agree that as of the date hereof, the International Foreign Exchange Master Agreement ("IFEMA") between them dated [*insert date*] (the "Prior Agreement") is hereby terminated and replaced by this ISDA Master Agreement. All FX Transactions and Currency Options entered into between the offices specified by the parties in Part 4(d) of this Schedule which are also Designated Offices and all Confirmations executed in respect of such FX Transactions and Currency Options pursuant to the Prior Agreement shall be deemed to be executed pursuant to and shall be governed by and subject in all respects to the terms and conditions of this Agreement whether or not such confirmation specifies that it is a "Confirmation".

OR in shorter form:

Foreign Exchange Contract Netting Agreement

This Agreement supersedes and cancels the terms of all Foreign Exchange contract(s) and/or netting agreement(s) ("the Prior Agreement(s)") entered into between the parties. Such Prior Agreement(s) shall cease to have effect as of the date of this Agreement but without prejudice to any rights and liabilities which may have arisen under the Prior Agreement(s) prior to the date hereof and which have not been replaced by this Agreement.

Finally, it is common to include a provision on payment instructions in Part 6, e.g.:

Payment instructions. All payments to be made hereunder in respect of FX Transactions and Currency Option Transactions shall be made in accordance with standing payment instructions provided by the parties (or as otherwise specified in a Confirmation). Any such instructions from a party must be received no later than two Local Business Days prior to the Value Date or Premium Payment Date (as the case may be) for such Transaction and otherwise be in conformity with standard interdealer market practice regarding foreign currency delivery.

9

Special provisions for special entities and those sought by US counterparties

Building societies

Investment funds

Hedge funds

Pension funds

Insurance companies

Sovereign entities

Special purpose vehicles for loans

Individuals

US Schedule provisions

Having dealt with many of the normal provisions found in Part 5, it might be useful to outline some specialist provisions which may be found in Schedules for the following entities:

- **building societies;**
- **investment funds;**
- **hedge funds;**
- **pension funds;**
- **insurance companies;**
- **sovereign entities;**
- **special purpose vehicles for loans;**
- **individuals.**

Because of the many possible provisions which could appear in Schedules for such entities, it is, of course, only possible to show a representative selection. Clearly the nature and scope of Schedule provisions needed in each situation for such entities will have to be considered in each individual case. The examples given here must not be regarded as comprehensive but for illustrative purposes only.

At the end of the chapter I have included a section on provisions sought by US counterparties in their Schedules with an explanation as to why they are needed. Input and suggestions for this section have been kindly provided by Christian Johnson, Associate Professor at the Loyola University Law School in Chicago. He has also written part of Chapter 5 on US legal issues and in Chapter 4 provided input on the new US Payee Tax Representations in Part 2(b) of the Schedule to the 2002 Agreement.

As regards the special provisions needed by the entities referred to above they tend to be mostly additions to Parts 1, 3 and 5 of the Schedule.

BUILDING SOCIETIES

Input for this section has been kindly provided by Mia Franks of Bradford & Bingley plc.

At the time of writing, there are 65 building societies in the UK and their activities are regulated by the Financial Services Authority (previously the Building Societies Commission). As Simon Leifer pointed out in Chapter 5, pages 352–3 the relevant legislation is the Building Societies Act 1986 as amended by the Building Societies Act 1997.

Part 1

(c) Threshold Amount

Where a monetary figure (e.g. £10 million) is not chosen it is important to remember that a percentage Threshold Amount should refer to a building society's capital and reserves and not its shareholders' equity or similar term. Sometimes, this is extended to include shareholders' equity and reserves in anticipation that the building society might convert to a limited company.

(d) Credit Event Upon Merger

A building society will usually exclude a Permitted Reorganisation (see below for definition) from the Credit Event Upon Merger provision. Whether this should be accepted is debatable as such a merger could result in a poorer credit rating. Perhaps, a rating downgrade below investment grade should still be considered as a Credit Event upon Merger.

Part 3

(b) Documents to be delivered

Items that might be required from a building society (Party B below) apart from the usual signing authority and audited accounts could include:

Party B	A certified copy of the Memorandum and Rules of the Society.	On execution and delivery of the Agreement.	Yes
Party B	A resolution of the board of directors of the Society authorising the execution of this Agreement and any ancillary documentation together with a letter signed by the Society's Secretary stating those persons authorised to commit the Society verbally to any Transaction.*	On execution and delivery of the Agreement.	Yes
Party B	Evidence of any restrictions imposed by the Financial Services Authority upon the ability of Party B to enter into any Transactions under this Agreement.	As soon as practicable after any such restrictions are imposed.	Yes

*With larger building societies, the Board will give a general authorisation to hedge rather than pass individual resolutions in respect of each ISDA Master Agreement.

In these circumstances, reliance is placed on the Section 3 representations and the following requested:

> **Such proof as the other party may reasonably request of the names, true signatures and authority of the persons signing this Agreement and any other document referred to herein to which it is a party.**

Part 5

Additional representations

The important thing about building societies is that they are authorised by the Financial Services Authority only to use derivatives for hedging purposes. This power is found in Section 23(1) of the Building Societies Act 1986 (the "1986 Act"), as amended by Section 9A of The Building Societies Act 1997 (the "1997 Act") and sanctions the use of derivative instruments for hedging purposes. However, the definition of derivative investments in Section 9A(9) includes options and futures and it is not always easy to discern their purpose in hedging changes in interest or exchange rates or movements in price indices.

The FSA, in recognition of the fact that different building societies had different resources and hedging needs, categorised different societies into five broad types – *administered, matched, extended, comprehensive and trading* (with *trading* being the most sophisticated). Prior to the 1997 Act, it was important to know into which category the society fell as that dictated its ability to use different instruments. However, as the 1997 Act introduced protection from *ultra vires* acts in Paragraphs 16(1), 17(1) and 18(1) of Schedule 1 similar to that found in Section 35 of the Companies Act 1985 for limited companies, the above categorisation has lost most of its relevance for counterparties of societies though not for the society itself who can only hedge according to its classification.

Combining this with the proviso to s 9(A)(1) of the 1997 Act renders the making of any representations by building societies unnecessary according to some lawyers.

Nonetheless the following representations are still commonly seen:

> **(i) In addition to its representations under Section 3, Party B represents to Party A (which representations will be deemed to be repeated by Party B on each date on which a Transaction is entered into) that for so long as Party B is a building society:**
>
> **(A) it has adopted without restriction the powers to effect contracts of a "prescribed description" conferred by Section 9A of the Building Societies Act 1997 or any statutory modification or re-enactment thereof (the "Act") and such power remains valid and subsisting;**

(B) it has adopted the ["Administered"], ["Matched"], ["Extended"], ["Comprehensive"] ["Trading"] Approach (as described in the Prudential Note 1998/4 issued by the Building Societies Commission);

(C) each Transaction will be entered into by Party B for the purpose of reducing the risk of loss arising from changes in interest rates, currency rates or other factors (as such term is used in the Act) which affect its business.

Permitted reorganisation

Because there have been a large number of mergers between UK building societies in recent years and a smaller number of conversions of major building societies to public limited companies it is common for Permitted Reorganisation language to appear in Part 5 of Building Society Schedules. It is important to remember that each transfer or conversion needs the approval of the Financial Services Authority who vets each application very carefully. The Building Societies (Transfer of Business) Regulations 1998 (SI 1998 No 212) provides that contracts entered into with a building society will be transferred to the new company, under operation of law, when that society converts. The regulations state that the successor company will be construed as if it were the same person in law as the transferring society once the vesting date has occurred.

However, it is still usual to see Permitted Reorganisation wording as follows:

In Section 14 after the definition of "Office", add the following:

***"Permitted Reorganisation"* means:**

(A) an amalgamation of Party B with one or more building societies pursuant to Section 93 of the Building Societies Act 1986 or any statutory modification or re-enactment thereof (such Act, as so modified or re-enacted being the "Act"); or

(B) a transfer of all or substantially all of Party B's engagements to another building society, or of all or substantially all of another building society's engagements to Party B, pursuant to Section 94 of the Act; or

(C) a transfer of the whole of the business of Party B to a commercial company pursuant to Section 97 of the Act.

This definition covers a merger, asset transfer or conversion situation. Certain consequential changes are usually made as follows in relation to Credit Event Upon Merger, Bankruptcy and Transfer:

Permitted Reorganisation:

(i) In Section 5(b)(iv) of the Agreement, after the words "immediately prior to such action" in line 6, add the words "provided that (for the avoidance of doubt) a Permitted Reorganisation by Party B shall not constitute a "Credit Event Upon Merger".

(ii) In Section 5(a)(vii):

(A) after the words "amalgamation or merger", in lines 3 and 14, add the words "or other than for the purposes of a Permitted Reorganisation";

(B) after the words "any of the foregoing acts" in line 24, add the words "other than, in the case of clause (1) or (5) above or, to the extent it relates to those clauses, clause (9), for the purposes of a Permitted Reorganisation".

(iii) The following shall be inserted at the end of Section 7 of this Agreement:

"If Party B effects a Permitted Reorganisation, its successor shall automatically be substituted in place of Party B as a party to this Agreement without the prior approval of Party A."

The reason for (iii) is that a building society will regard the approval of its counterparty as superfluous because a statute – *The Building Societies (Transfer of Business) Regulations 1998 (SI 1998 No 212)* comes into play.

INVESTMENT FUNDS

With a group of funds, one or more Investment Managers invest on behalf of each fund in accordance with the terms of the Investment Management Agreement(s) between them. It is vital to establish their authority to commit the fund. Where the fund is offering an investment opportunity to the general public, it must issue a prospectus or Offering Memorandum where its authority may also be stated. Such funds will be regulated by an appointed regulator, e.g. the Financial Services Authority in the UK. An agency letter making representations and warranties is also evidence of authority (see below).

Special features of investment fund Schedules are as follows:

Number of investment funds in group

Where there are many funds in a group it would be wasteful to enter into an Agreement with each one essentially duplicating the terms of each other Agreement. In these circumstances it may be feasible to list the individual Funds in an Annex.

A useful preamble to the Schedule in these circumstances is:

PREAMBLE

Party A will maintain segregated accounts for each Fund listed in Annex A hereto and accordingly this Agreement shall take effect as a separate agreement between Party A and each Fund in respect of Transactions entered into between them. For the avoidance of doubt, the obligations of each Fund shall be several and not joint in respect of any Transactions they enter into with Party A. In particular, without limitation, Section 1(c) shall take effect so that a single agreement shall be formed by the Agreement and all Confirmations issued by Party A to each individual Fund and the provisions of Section 5 and 6 shall apply separately in relation to each Fund so that an Event of Default in respect of one Fund shall not be treated as an Event of Default in respect of any other Fund.

OR

This Agreement is entered into severally and not jointly by Party A in its capacity as the Management Company of each Fund listed in Annex A hereto. Party A recognises and agrees that, for purposes of this Agreement, each Fund's obligations are separate and distinct from those of each other Fund. Each reference in this Agreement to Party A shall be a reference to Party A as the Management Company for a given Fund, individually and not jointly with any other Fund. Notwithstanding anything in this Agreement to the contrary, each of the parties agrees that, for all purposes, Transactions entered into between the parties where Party A has entered into such Transactions on behalf of any given Fund (as specified in the relevant Confirmation) shall be treated as if they had been entered into under a separate Master Agreement to Transactions entered into by Party A on behalf of each other Fund. Party A acknowledges and agrees that each representation made to Party B under this Agreement shall be deemed to be made by each Fund and by Party A taken in its own independent capacity.

Part I

(c) Threshold Amount

Where a monetary figure (e.g. £10 million) is not chosen it is important to remember that a percentage Threshold Amount should refer to an investment fund's net asset value and not its shareholders' equity or similar term.

(h) Additional Termination Event

Normally these would include the Investment Manager ceasing to act and the Investment Manager ceasing to be regulated by a leading regulator as in the following examples:

(i) **If [name of Investment Manager] ceases to act as investment manager to any Fund this shall constitute an Additional Termination Event with the Fund concerned as the Affected Party.**

(ii) **If [name of Investment Manager] ceases to be regulated by the Financial Services Authority or the U.S. Securities and Exchange Commission or any successor of them then this shall constitute an Additional Termination Event with each Fund concerned as an Affected Party.**

It can also include in the case of a single fund a minimum net asset value level or a reduction in net asset value in a rolling period, e.g.:

Minimum Net Asset Value. The Net Asset Value of Party B at any time is less than £500,000,000.

Decline of Net Asset Value. The Net Asset Value of Party B at the end of any calendar quarter is less than 75% of the Net Asset Value of Party B at the end of the immediately preceding calendar quarter.

In the last example, the Fund's Net Asset Value would have to fall more than 25% in a calendar quarter for the Additional Termination Event to be triggered.

Here is an example of a more detailed provision:

(h) Additional Termination Events will apply.

The following shall constitute Additional Termination Events with respect to Party B:

(1) **If during any calendar month Party B's Net Asset Value declines by 15% or more when compared to the Net Asset Value of Party B for the immediately preceding calendar month; or**

(2) **If during any three (3) calendar month period the Net Asset Value of Party B declines by 25% or more when compared to the**

Net Asset Value of Party B from the calendar month immediately preceding such three (3) calendar month period; or

(3) If during any twelve (12) month calendar period the Net Asset Value of Party B declines by 40% or more when compared to the Net Asset Value of Party B from the calendar month immediately preceding such 12 month calendar period.

(4) If at any time (a) the Net Asset Value of Party B declines by 50% or more when compared to the Net Asset Value of Party B from the immediately preceding calendar year end, or (b) the Net Asset Value of Party B declines to or below $75,000,000.00 whichever of (a) or (b) is the lesser.

Part 3

(b) Documents to be delivered

Items that might be required from an investment fund (which is Party B below) apart from the usual signing authority and audited accounts could include:

Party B	A certified copy of the Investment Management Agreement between Party B and [*name of Investment Manager*] dated as of [*date*]	On execution and delivery of the Agreement.	Yes
Party B	A certified copy of the constituting documents of Party B.	On execution and delivery of the Agreement.	Yes
Party B	An agency letter from the Investment Manager in form and substance satisfactory to Party A certifying, *inter alia*, that the Investment Manager has full authority to act on behalf of Party B.	On execution and delivery of the Agreement.	Yes
Party B	A copy of the monthly report on the performance and Net Asset Value of Party B.	Within 21 days of the end of the preceding calendar month.	Yes

Part 5

Definition of Net Asset Value

This often appears in Part 5 and may be along the following lines:

> **For the purposes of this Agreement, "Net Asset Value" shall mean the total assets of Party B minus its total liabilities as stated in the monthly report on Fund performance and Net Asset Values referred to in Part 3(b) of the Schedule.**

Additional Undertaking

A typical inclusion might be:

> **Party B agrees to notify Party A as soon as reasonably practicable of any material default by it of any of its obligations under any other agreement or transaction or of any other matter which might prejudice its ability to meet its obligations under this Agreement or any Transaction or any other agreement or transaction.**

An agency letter is entered into between the Investment Manager and Party A. The text of such a letter might be as follows:

ON INVESTMENT MANAGER LETTERHEAD

[Date]

X Bank AG
[address]

Dear Sirs

ISDA Master Agreement (the "Agreement") dated as of [Date] between X Bank AG and the Genghis Khan Investment Fund (the "Principal")

As a condition precedent to, and in consideration of, your agreeing to deal with us on an agency basis rather than a principal basis under the Agreement, we represent to you certain matters and undertake certain obligations relating to the Principal in connection with the Transactions contemplated under the Agreement which we have entered or will enter into with you on their behalf or which you have entered or will enter into directly with the Principal. We understand, in these circumstances, you will be relying on these representations and undertakings in agreeing to deal with us under the Agreement and each and every Transaction thereunder.

(1) You are advised that we are acting as Investment Manager and continue to act for the Principal.

(2) We represent and warrant that on execution of every Transaction under the Agreement:

(a) there will be sufficient assets of the Principal to meet its obligations to you.

(b) we shall only execute a Transaction under the Agreement through or with you if there are sufficient assets of the Principal in our possession or under our control to perform its obligations under the Agreement. If, at any time until the termination of the Agreement there is a material reduction in the aggregate value of the assets belonging to the Principal we shall notify you as soon as reasonably practicable.

(c) on execution of every Transaction under the Agreement:

(i) the Principal has the full legal capacity and power to enter into and to perform its obligations under the Agreement and all Transactions contemplated thereby;

(ii) we have full authority to enter into the relevant Transaction on behalf of and to bind the Principal and its assets;

(iii) any authorisation required for the Principal to enter into a Transaction under the Agreement has been or, by the time it is entered into, will have been, obtained;

(iv) the Agreement and the Transactions thereunder constitute legal, valid, binding and enforceable obligations of the Principal, and

(v) there are no laws or regulations of the residence or place of incorporation of the Principal which (A) would be violated or breached by you or (B) would subject you to any regulation, qualification or filing requirement, as a result of such Transaction or the performance by you or the Principal in connection therewith;

(d) the Principal is an ordinary business investor within the meaning of the rules of the Investment Management Regulatory Organisation Limited (or any successor body thereto);

(e) we reasonably believe that the Principal will not default on its payment or delivery obligations to you.

(3) In the event of a default by the Principal of any of its obligations under the Agreement we undertake to notify you forthwith of such default.

(4) We undertake to notify you as soon as reasonably practicable of any material default by the Principal of any of its obligations under any other agreement or transaction that we become aware of or if we become aware of any other matter that might prejudice the Principal's ability to meet its obligations to you under the Agreement.

(5) We undertake to notify you as soon as reasonably practicable in the event that we become aware that any of the above representations and warranties being or becoming untrue or incorrect in any material respect on any date.

(6) We undertake to notify you immediately upon the insolvency of the Principal and/or any intention to wind down the Principal or to transfer the Principal's assets into another fund.

(7) If our agency on behalf of the Principal is terminated, we remain authorised to settle the Transactions under the Agreement.

(8) This letter constitutes a written agreement that you may continue to regard us as your direct customer and hold us alone responsible for all matters involving the placing of orders with you (including, but not limited to, orders for options, futures, contracts for differences and other forms of derivative transactions) and for the acceptance or refusal of all offerings to us which we undertake on the Principal's behalf. Any dispute on such matters will be between you and us alone and you will not recognise any participation by the Principal directly or indirectly in such

disputes. You will, therefore, expect the Principal to honour any instructions given by us to you in this respect.

Only insofar as settlement itself is concerned shall you regard the Principal as your indirect customer.

(9) We have made checks on the identity of the Principal and we have taken steps to comply with the Money Laundering Regulations 1993 (or any successor regulations or comparable regulations in other jurisdictions) as they will apply with respect to the Principal. Based on information made available to us, after making all reasonable inquiries, we consider that all Transactions executed under the Agreement by the Principal are legitimate and that all monies and assets applied to such transactions are as a result of the Principal's bona fide activities and, in particular, that the Principal is not using the Agreement, the Transactions contemplated thereby or their account with us to launder money.

This letter will be governed by and construed in accordance with the laws of England.

For and on behalf of
Vigilant Investment Management Limited

By: ....

Name: ....

Title:

Signed for and on behalf of
X Bank AG

By:	By: ....
Name:	Name: ....
Title:	Title:
Date:	Date:

Note that you would probably be *very* lucky to get all of this.

Alternatively, you sometimes find just a simple statement as follows in Part 5 of the Schedule:

> **This Agreement will be deemed to govern the relationship between Party A and Party B. Each Transaction made pursuant to this Agreement shall be entered into by the Fund Manager solely in its capacity as agent for Party B as identified in the Confirmation relating to such Transaction.**

HEDGE FUNDS

The basic difference between hedge funds and other funds is that they are less regulated. They are often based in tax havens and adopt higher risk investment strategies. They also have investment managers but they are usually part of the same group.

Because of the higher risk, banks will only transact with hedge funds on a collateralised basis so ISDA Credit Support Annexes under either English or New York law will form part of the Agreement. Many of the provisions mentioned for investment funds also apply to hedge funds although the agency or representation letter from the Investment Manager is typically only about a page long or not given at all. Other typical provisions follow.

Part 1

(c) Specified indebtedness

As hedge funds obtain much of their funding through repos, banks often propose that Specified Indebtedness be extended to cover repos and stocklending. Hedge funds tend to resist this because failures to deliver are quite common with repos and they fear Cross Default could be triggered through operational or administrative error. A carve-out of such error can be the compromise. Hedge funds also like to downgrade Cross Default to cross acceleration to reduce the risk of their counterparties acting precipately and unilaterally if trouble arises.

(h) Additional Termination Event

Hedge funds are often promoted by one key individual, e.g. George Soros, so there may be a keyman Additional Termination Event added to a hedge fund Schedule as follows:

> ***Key Individuals.*** **[Name of key person] dies, is declared incompetent due to a physical, mental or emotional condition or otherwise is no longer active in the management of the assets of Party B; [provided that, in such event, if Party A elects to exercise its right to terminate, then**

notwithstanding anything in this Agreement to the contrary, Party A may not designate an Early Termination Date in respect of such Additional Termination Event sooner than sixty (60) calendar days following the date of notice to Party B of such designation; and each of the parties will exercise commercially reasonable efforts to wind down, settle and liquidate all open Transactions between them on mutually agreeable terms prior to the Early Termination Date].

Part 3

(b) Documents to be delivered

In addition to the documents listed for investment funds above, a legal opinion on the hedge fund's capacity to enter into derivatives transactions will undoubtedly be required.

Other matters are as per investment funds, mutatis mutandis.

PENSION FUNDS

The key document with pension funds is the Trust Deed which details the trustees' powers to manage the fund or contract out its management. In the UK, s 34 of the Pensions Act 1995 gives trustees a general power to invest on behalf of a pension fund but nothing is said about hedging. It is important to scrutinise the Trust Deed for such a power. The Agreement would be entered into with the Trustees of the Fund acting on behalf of the Fund.

Bespoke features for a pension fund Schedule would be:

Part 1

(c) Threshold Amount

For a pension fund counterparty, this would need to be a fixed monetary amount.

(d) Credit Event Upon Merger

The trustees might argue that this should not apply to them.

(h) Additional Termination Event

If particular trustees were regarded as key, there might be an Additional Termination Event if they died or became incapacitated. Similarly any move by the trustees to wind up the pension fund or a materially adverse change in pensions legislation might also inspire customised Additional Termination Events.

Part 3

(b) Documents to be delivered

As well as the usual items, the following would also be required from the pension fund trustees:

Party B	A certified copy of the Trust Deed dated as of [*date*] and other constituting documentation for the Trust.	On execution and delivery of the Agreement.	Yes
Party B	A legal opinion in form and substance satisfactory to Party B on the Trust's capacity and authority to enter into Transactions under the Agreement.	On execution and delivery of the Agreement.	Yes
Party B	Resolutions of the Trustees approving Transactions under the Agreement.	On execution and delivery of the Agreement and each time a Transaction is entered into under the Agreement.	Yes

Part 5

Additional Representations

The following may be appropriate:

Additional Representation of Party B. Party B additionally represents to Party A further to Section 3 of the Agreement (which additional representations will be deemed to be repeated by Party B on each date on which a Transaction is entered into):

(i) that it has taken all necessary actions required by its constitutional documents and by all applicable laws and regulations to authorise the execution, delivery and performance of the Agreement;

(ii) that all approvals, authorisations, permissions or consents required by any applicable laws, regulations or supervisory authority to enable Party B to enter into the Agreement have been duly obtained; and

(iii) that Party B entering into the Agreement does not breach any limitation, of whatsoever nature, contained in any applicable law or regulation or imposed by any regulatory authority.

(iv) that the Agreement has been entered into and each Transaction will be entered into by Party B with consideration given to the overall context of the investment portfolio of the pension fund managed by Party B in respect of [*name of fund/plan*] without undue risk of loss or impairment and with a reasonable expectation of a fair return or appreciation given the nature of the Agreement or the Transaction, as the case may be.

There may also be a Part 5 provision limiting a pension fund trustee's liability as in the following example:

Trustee capacity and liability

(a) Party B is entering into this Agreement, and will enter into any Transaction, solely in its capacity as the trustee of [*Scheme Name*] and not in any other capacity. No action taken by, or matter affecting Party B in any capacity other than as such trustee shall be relevant for the purposes of Section 5 of this Agreement.

(b) Party B shall have no liability under this Agreement or any Transaction except to the extent that such liability can be satisfied out of the assets of [*Scheme Name*] available for such purpose and without infringement of the Applicable Regulations or of the Trust Deed or Scheme Particulars governing the [*Scheme Name*]. Party B reserves the right under the Applicable Regulations to require the reversal of any transaction initiated or purportedly initiated by the Agent of [*Scheme Name*] which, in Party B's opinion infringes the Applicable Regulations or the Trust Deed or Scheme Particulars governing the [*Scheme Name*].

(c) Notwithstanding anything to the contrary set out in this Agreement Party A acknowledges that the assets of [*Scheme Name*] belong exclusively to [*Scheme Name*] and will be segregated from all other accounts and shall not be used to discharge directly or indirectly the liabilities of, or claims against, any other account.

INSURANCE COMPANIES

In the UK, insurance companies are either limited companies incorporated under the Companies Acts or mutual organisations established under their own

Acts of Parliament. Legal due diligence needs to establish that mutual insurance entities have the authority and capacity to enter into derivatives transactions.

The Schedule requirements for insurance companies are basically the same as for any other type of company except that for a mutual a fixed monetary Threshold Amount in Part 1(c) would probably apply although this could be linked to a percentage of their capital and reserves. In Part 3(b) the mutual's constituting documents and incorporating Act of Parliament would be requested, but in Part 5 the following Additional Representations and Events of Default might be asked for:

Additional Representations of Party B

Party B additionally represents to Party A further to Section 3 of this Agreement (which additional representations will be deemed to be repeated by Party B on each date on which a Transaction is entered into) that:

(a) Party B is duly authorised by the Financial Services Authority ("FSA") to carry on the class or classes of insurance business carried on by it in the United Kingdom under the Insurance Companies Act 1982 (which shall include any amendment thereto or re-enactment thereof) and under the Financial Services Act 1986 (which shall include any amendment thereto or re-enactment thereof).

(b) Transactions constitute and are intended by Party B to constitute activities in connection with, or for the purposes of its insurance business in accordance with section 16 of the Insurance Companies Act 1982 and section 22 of the Financial Services Act 1986.

(c) Transactions constitute, and are intended by Party B to constitute, activities concerning investment of the assets representing the fund or funds maintained by Party B in relation to its long-term insurance business pursuant to the Insurance Companies Act 1982.

(d) None of the powers of intervention conferred on the FSA by the Insurance Companies Act 1982 or otherwise have been exercised or have become exercisable in connection with Party B in a manner which might affect the validity of this Agreement or the ability of Party B to perform any or all of its obligations under this Agreement.

(e) There are no grounds for the exercise of the powers described in (d) above.

(f) All activities carried on by Party B are in accordance with all laws, regulations and other rules applicable to it and any guidance issued by the FSA and there are no existing guidelines or directives or similar instructions of any nature whatsoever from the FSA prohibiting or in any way limiting Party B's ability properly to enter into and execute Transactions.

(g) There are no existing guidelines or directives or similar instructions of any nature whatsoever from the FSA or any of its predecessors or any other statutory body or organisation prohibiting or in any way limiting Party B's ability properly to enter into and execute Transactions.

(h) Party B only represents that all Transactions will be "approved derivatives contracts" within the meaning of regulation 55 of the Insurance Companies Regulations 1994.

I have seen the following representations given by an Irish assurance company:

Further representations of Party B. Party B represents that (i) this Agreement and each Transaction is being entered into for the purposes of its insurance business as defined in the European Communities (Life Assurance) Framework Regulations 1994 and (ii) it is an insurance company authorised pursuant to the European Communities (Life Assurance) Framework Regulations 1994 or any statutory modification or re-enactment thereof.

Additional Events of Default

Section 5 is amended to include the occurrence at any time of any of the following events in respect to Party B only:

(a) *Withdrawal or Suspension or Authorisation.* Withdrawal or suspension (pursuant to Section 11, 12A or 13 of the Insurance Companies Act 1982 or any subsequent amendment thereof) of Party B's authorisation to carry on insurance business in whole or in part.

(b) Any of the powers conferred on the FSA by Sections 38 to 45 of the Insurance Companies Act 1982 or any subsequent amendment thereof become exercisable or are exercised in relation to Party B or any Specified Entity.

SOVEREIGN ENTITIES

Sovereign entities are governments or government agencies. Schedules involving them require the following changes.

Part 1

The heading on Page 1 of the Agreement, the first page of the Schedule and the signing block should refer to the name of the Sovereign and state if it is acting through one of its agencies, e.g. the Ministry of Finance. We will assume the Sovereign is Party B.

A change will be necessary in the definition of "Specified Indebtedness" to read as follows:

"Specified Indebtedness" shall mean (i) in respect of Party B, any External Indebtedness.

The Threshold Amount for Party B needs to be a fixed monetary sum.

"Credit Event Upon Merger" will not apply to Party B.

There may be Additional Termination Events to cover any discontinuance of a government agency (by statute or otherwise) unless the government itself takes over the former agency's obligations or if any government guarantee is revoked.

Part 3

The Annual Report for Party B will need to be that of its central bank. Other documentation requirements could be as follows:

Party required to deliver document	Form/Document/Certificate	Date by which to be delivered	Covered by Section 3(d) Representation
Party B	[Insert description of relevant authorising statute and regulations in relation to Transactions and signatory], (the "Enabling Laws"), accompanied by an English translation if not originally in English, certified as of the delivery date as being a true, complete and correct copy thereof by the [ ]	[Execution of the Agreement]	Yes.
Party B	Each amendment, supplement or variation to the Enabling Laws material to this Agreement, certified as of the delivery date as being a true, complete and correct copy thereof by [ ]	Promptly on its effectiveness but in any event at least one Local Business Day prior to the first Transaction following its effectiveness	Yes.

Part 5

Consider a submission to arbitration (ICC or UNCITRAL) if Party B is a sovereign which refuses to accept the judgments of English courts (e.g. Russia).

Other matters

( ) Amendment to Representation. Section 3(a)(i) of the Agreement is hereby amended in its entirety to read as follows:

(i) Status. It is, with respect to Party A, duly organised and validly existing under the laws of the jurisdiction of its organisation or incorporation and, if relevant under such laws, in good standing and it is, with respect to Party B, a member in good standing of the International Monetary Fund (the "IMF") and is fully eligible so to utilise the resources of the IMF;

( ) Additional Party B Undertakings. There shall be added a new-subsection (f) to Section 4 of the Agreement as follows:

(f) Additional Party B Undertaking. Solely with respect to Party B, Party B agrees to notify Party A prior to [insert department or entity through which Sovereign is acting] for any reason ceasing to be authorised to bind Party B under this Agreement and in respect of Transactions;

( ) Events of Default: Clauses (1), (2), (3), (4) and (5) and, to the extent relating to the foregoing, (8) and (9) of Section 5(a)(vii) and Section 5(a)(viii) shall not apply to Party B and there shall be added a new subsection (ix) to Section 5(a) of the Agreement as follows:

(ix) Solely with respect to Party B:

(A) Party B [or any Governmental Authority] (1) disaffirms, disclaims, repudiates or rejects, in whole or in part, or challenges the validity of, or is or admits that it is unable to pay, External Indebtedness in an aggregate amount of not less than the Threshold Amount, or (2) declares or imposes a moratorium, standstill, waiver, or deferral, whether de facto or de jure, with respect to External Indebtedness in an aggregate amount of not less than the Threshold Amount.

(B) Party B ceases to be a member in good standing of the IMF or ceases to be fully eligible to utilise the resources of the IMF;

(*) There shall be added new Definitions to Section 14 of the Agreement as follows:

"Domestic Currency" means the lawful currency of Party B and any successor currency provided that in no event shall Domestic Currency include any successor currency if such successor currency is the lawful currency of any of Canada, Federal Republic of Germany, Japan, Republic of France, Republic of Italy, United Kingdom, or the United States of America or the euro (or any successor currency to any such currency).

"External Indebtedness" means any obligation of Party B [or any Governmental Authority] (whether present or future, contingent or otherwise, as principal or surety or otherwise) in respect of borrowed money other than an obligation that:

(a) is payable in Domestic Currency;

(b) is governed by the laws of Party B; and

(c) in the determination of Party A, was, at the time the relevant obligation was issued (or reissued, as the case may be) or incurred, intended to be offered for sale primarily in the domestic market of Party B.

"Governmental Authority" means any state or political sub-division of Party B, or any agency, instrumentality, ministry, department or other authority (including, without limiting the foregoing, the central bank) thereof, whether autonomous or not.

Based on due diligence with respect to the sovereign, it is worth checking if there are other provisions necessary or advisable (e.g. representations, documents to be delivered, covenants or Events of Default).

It is likely that the sovereign may want Section 13(d) Waiver of Immunities not to apply to it.

SPECIAL PURPOSE VEHICLES FOR LOANS

Nowadays it is a pre-condition of many syndicated or club loans to corporates specially formed to undertake projects (commonly called special purpose vehicles) that hedging is taken out in the form of interest rate caps or swaps or currency swaps to protect against adverse movements in interest or foreign exchange rates.

These loans typically involve a long Loan or Facility Agreement (150 pages plus would be typical), an Intercreditor Agreement (governing the rights and relationship of the various banks providing the loan) and the Security Documents (which charge the collateral to the banks for the loan and which are referred to as Credit Support Documents in Part 4(f) of the Schedule).

The Facility Agreement will be the main document and will describe, *inter alia*, the hedging arrangements required. The hedging and, by extension, the ISDA Master Agreement is subordinate to the requirements of the Facility Agreement. This can be seen in the following provisions:

> **Facility Agreement and Intercreditor Agreement.**
>
> **Each of the parties acknowledges the existence of the terms of the Intercreditor Agreement dated the [*insert date*] and the Facilities Agreement dated [*insert date*] and acknowledges that in the event of any inconsistency between the terms of this Agreement and the Intercreditor and Facilities Agreement, the terms of the Intercreditor and Facilities Agreements shall prevail.**

OR

> **Both Party A and Party B acknowledge, as at the date hereof, the existence of the Senior Credit Agreement and the Finance Documents (as defined in the Senior Credit Agreement) and further acknowledge that their respective rights under this Agreement are subject to the terms and conditions of the Senior Credit Agreement and the Finance Documents.**

It is common to link the Agreement to a loan facility which it hedges by referring to the Facility Agreement in a preamble to Part 1 of the Schedule as follows:

> **This Agreement is entered into in connection with the £50,000,000 Facilities Agreement dated 17 October 2002 (as amended pursuant to an Amendment Agreement entered into on or around 7 January 2003) defined below as the "Facilities Agreement" and any Transaction entered into under this Agreement constitutes a "Hedging Agreement" for the purposes of this Agreement. Capitalised terms used but not defined in this Agreement shall have the meanings given to them in the Facilities Agreement.**

As far as the ISDA Master Agreement is concerned, the two major amendments required in Schedules for special purpose vehicles are:

- The application of Events of Default
- How to deal with loan pre-payments and their effect upon Transactions and the Agreement.

The application of Events of Default

This usually involves suspension of the Agreement Events of Default (except for Section 5(a)(i) – Failure to Pay or Deliver) and incorporation of the Facility Agreement Events of Default in their place. Assuming no Event of Default intervenes, this arrangement lasts until the Facility Agreement is terminated through the repayment of all loans. If any swaps are still outstanding they continue under the Agreement and its Events of Default are reinstated in full.

Here is an example of such wording:

Default under Facility: Until the Facility is repaid in full, the Events of Default specified in Section 5(a)(ii) to (viii) will not apply with respect to Party B and its Credit Support Provider and, in substitution thereof, the giving of a notice by the Agent under the Facility Agreement to the Borrower pursuant to Clause [*insert reference to Event of Default clause in the Facility Agreement*] of the Facility Agreement in respect of the events listed in Schedule [*] thereof shall constitute an Event of Default in relation to Party B under this Agreement. In respect of the period from the full repayment of the Facility the foregoing provisions of this Part 5[*] shall cease to apply and Section 5(a)(ii) to (viii) of this Agreement shall be reinstated and apply in respect of Party B with full force and effect [and for these purposes the Threshold Amount in relation to Party B shall be zero].

Another commonly seen version of this is:

Events of Default. Sections 5(a)(i) to (viii) inclusive, shall be deleted in their entirety in respect of Party B and two Events of Default applicable to Party B shall be inserted as Section 5(a)(ix) and Section 5(a)(x):

"5(a)(ix) It shall be an Event of Default in respect of Party B if Party B fails to make, when due, any payment under this Agreement or any delivery under Section 2(a)(i) or 2(e) required to be made by it if, in either case, such failure is not remedied on or before the tenth Local Business Day after notice of such failure is given to Party B in writing by Party A.

5(a)(x) It shall be an Event of Default if the Agent (as defined in the Senior Credit Agreement) has exercised its remedies under Clause [*insert number*] of the Senior Credit Agreement, as the case may be, owing to an acceleration under Clause [*insert number*] (Events of Default) of the Senior Credit Agreement."

Sometimes an Additional Event of Default is added as in the following example:

Additional Event of Default. Section 5(a) of the Agreement is hereby amended by adding the following:

"(ix) It shall be an Additional Event of Default under the Agreement in the event of (1) the occurrence of any of the Default events specified in clause [*insert number*] of the Facilities Agreement dated [*insert date*]; and (2) the Agent pursuant to clause [*insert number*] of the said Facilities Agreement:

(i) cancels any unutilised amount of the Facilities and any obligation of the Senior Lenders to make any Advance or provide any Facility; and/or

(ii) declares the Facilities to be immediately due and payable; and/or

(iii) declares the Facilities to be due and payable on demand; and/or

(iv) suspends the right of the Borrowers to make any utilisation of the Working Capital Facility; and/or (v) declares that the Security Documents (or any of them) have become enforceable; and/or

(vi) calls for collateral cash cover from the Borrowers and/or any of them in respect of a contingent liability assumed by the Senior Lenders under the Facilities; and/or

(vii) requires the Borrowers and/or any of them to charge by way of first fixed charge any cash collateral cover called for to secure to the Senior Lenders the repayment of any sums which the Senior Lenders are, or may become, liable to pay in connection with the Facilities.

In some Agreements typically involving offshore special purpose vehicles there is a NO bankruptcy petition provision to the effect that you cannot issue a bankruptcy petition until 366 days after any Loan has been repaid. This is a requirement of ratings agencies to underline the bankruptcy remote nature of the special purpose vehicle. An example of such wording is:

No Bankruptcy Petition. Party A agrees that, prior to the date which is at least one year and one day after all Related Indebtedness has been paid in full, it will not institute against, or join any other person or entity in instituting against, Party B any petition or proceeding referred to in Section 5(a)(vii)(4) of this Agreement, provided that nothing herein shall preclude, or be deemed to estop, Party A from taking any

action in any case or proceeding voluntarily filed or commenced by or on behalf of Party B or in any involuntary case or proceeding after it has commenced.

Loan pre-payments

An example of pre-payment wording is:

Optional Reduction: Each party may reduce all or part of the Notional Amount of any Transaction, subject to the following terms and conditions:

(i) that reduction occurs contemporaneously with a repayment of an amount outstanding under the Facility Agreement which cannot be redrawn thereunder or a cancellation of the Term Loan Commitments (as defined in the Facility Agreement) and which repayment or cancellation is not reflected in an agreed reduction in the Notional Amount in the Confirmation for the relevant Transaction;

(ii) that reduction is in a Notional Amount not more than that repayment or cancellation;

(iii) that repayment or cancellation is in excess of £1,000,000;

(iv) that party gives to the other party at least ten Local Business Days' prior written notice specifying its election to reduce all or part of the Notional Amount of a Transaction (the "Relevant Transaction") on a specified date (the "Optional Reduction Date"); and

(v) the amount payable in respect of that reduction will be calculated in accordance with Sections 6(d) and (e) of this Agreement, *mutatis mutandis*, as though the Optional Reduction Date were an Early Termination Date, the Relevant Transaction (or, as the case may be, a Transaction identical to the Relevant Transaction save that its Notional Amount shall be deemed to be the amount of the reduction) were a Terminated Transaction, a Termination Event had occurred and Party B was the Affected Party.

In other words, if the loan is reduced the notional amount of the swap is correspondingly reduced. Where full pre-payment is envisaged a provision terminating any outstanding swaps at that time may also be included. Sometimes this type of provision can be expressed as an Additional Termination Event:

(h) Additional Termination Event will apply and the following will constitute Additional Termination Event:-

(i) The prepayment in full of any advance made under the Facility Agreement, in which event Party A will be the Affected Party and the date on which such prepayment is made will be the relevant Early Termination Date.

(ii) In the event of a prepayment of part only of any advance made under the Facility Agreement, then to the extent (if any) that after such prepayment the aggregate Notional Amount(s) under outstanding Transactions would otherwise exceed the aggregate amount of advances outstanding under the Facility Agreement after such prepayment (the amount of such excess being hereafter referred as the "Excess Amount"):-

(A) Party A or Party B, as the case may be, will be obliged to make a payment to the other party determined as though an Additional Termination Event had occurred in respect of the outstanding Transaction(s) and in respect of which Party A will be the Affected Party provided that for this purpose the relevant Notional Amount of such Affected Transaction(s) shall be deemed to be an amount equal to the Excess Amount; and

(B) such Affected Transaction(s) will be amended with effect from the date on which such prepayment is made, such date being the relevant Early Termination Date; and

with effect from the Early Termination Date, the Notional Amount of the Affected Transaction(s) will be reduced by the Excess Amount

You might want to include some Additional Termination Events such as:

The following shall constitute an Additional Termination Event:

If the Total Term Loan Outstandings (as defined in the Facility Agreement) are prepaid in full in accordance with Clause [*] of the Facility Agreement.

For the purposes of the foregoing Additional Termination Event, the Affected Party shall be Party B.

If the loan is pre-paid, you may well want to terminate the swap(s).

AND/OR

The following will constitute an Additional Termination Event:

Notice is given pursuant to clause [*] of the Facility Agreement to cancel a Facility in whole or in part.

Other provisions included in special purpose vehicle Schedules are Definitions of:

- **Facility Agreement**
- **Intercreditor Agreement and**
- **Security Documents.**

An Intercreditor Agreement might be described as follows:

> **Intercreditor Agreement: Party A (as a Hedging Counterparty for the purposes of the Intercreditor Agreement) acknowledges that its rights under this Agreement (and its ability to exercise the same) are subject to the provisions of the Intercreditor Agreement relating to Hedging Counterparties (as defined in the Intercreditor Agreement).**

OTHER MATTERS

Recourse against assets

It is typical in Agreements involving special purpose vehicles for there to be provisions covering limited recourse against outside assets owned by a special purpose vehicle's group:

> *Non-recourse.* **Notwithstanding anything to the contrary contained in this Agreement or any schedule, addendum, confirmation or other document issued or delivered in connection with any Transaction entered into under this Agreement, any amounts owed or liability incurred by Party B in respect of any Transaction entered into under this Agreement may be satisfied wholly from the assets of Party B.**

Transfers

Another issue relates to transfers. Before the loan is repaid it is normal to prohibit transfers of interests and obligations under the Agreement as in the following example:

> **Transfer**
>
> (i) **In respect of the period prior to Senior Debt Discharge Section 7 shall be deleted and the following shall be inserted in its place:**
>
> **"Subject to Section 6(b)(ii), prior to the Senior Debt Discharge, neither this Agreement nor any interest or obligation in or under this Agreement may be transferred (whether by way of security or otherwise save in respect of any transfer under the Security**

Documents (as defined in the Facility Agreement)) by either party without the prior written consent of the Agent (as defined in the Facility Agreement). Any purported Transfer that is not in compliance with this Section will be void."

(ii) In respect of the period subsequent to the Senior Debt Discharge the amendments to Section 7 specified in the foregoing Part 5 (*insert reference to previous sub-clause*) shall cease to apply and Section 7 shall be reinstated with full force and effect in its original form.

A related issue is transfer of security interests and with special purpose vehicles it is normal for interests under the Agreement to be transferred by way of security to the Security Agent:

Security Interest

Notwithstanding Section 7, Party A hereby agrees and consents to the assignment by way of security by Party B of its interests under this Agreement (without prejudice to, and after giving effect to, any contractual netting or set-off provision contained in this Agreement) to the Security Agent. Each of the parties hereby confirms and agrees that the Security Agent shall not be liable for any of the obligations of Party B hereunder.

Scope of Agreement

A Scope of Agreement clause is often included stating that only liabilities under the Facility Agreement are hedged under the Agreement:

Scope of Agreement. **This Agreement shall only apply to interest rate swap transactions entered into between Party A and Party B to hedge interest rate exposure under the Facility Agreement.**

OR

Scope of Agreement. **Each of the parties acknowledge and agrees that no Transaction may be entered into under this Agreement other than for the purpose of hedging the liabilities of Party B under the Facilities Agreement.**

This whole subject is treated in much greater detail in Gary Walker's *Mastering Finance Linked Swaps* also published in this series.

Arbitration

If the special purpose vehicle is incorporated in Russia, Eastern Europe or in another emerging country certain additional factors should be borne in mind.

In Part 3(b) of the Schedule among the documents required should be a legal opinion on the special purpose vehicle's capacity to enter into derivatives transactions. A current excerpt from the Commercial Register should also be requested. You might also want to see any foreign exchange permission given by the central bank or Ministry of Finance for the Transaction.

The legal opinion should deal not only with enforceability but also confirm the:

- **withholding tax position**
- **counterparty's payment obligations rank pari passu**
- **recognition of the choice of law for the counterparty's jurisdiction**
- **recognition of foreign judgments in the counterparty's jurisdiction.**

You will want to have an additional representation to the effect that Party B will notify Party A of any changes to the relevant entries relating to Party B in the Commercial Register.

Some countries do not recognise or enforce judgments given in foreign courts but do accept international arbitration proceedings because they are one of the 120 plus countries who have signed the 1958 New York Convention on the Recognition and Enforcement of Foreign Arbitral Awards. If this is relevant in the jurisdiction of the special purpose vehicle, you would want an arbitration clause as follows:

> ***Governing Law and Jurisdiction.*** **Section 13(b) of this Agreement shall be amended to read such as the following:**
>
> **(b) Arbitration Rules. Any dispute, controversy or claim arising out of or relating to this Agreement or any Transaction, or the breach, termination or invalidity thereof, shall be settled by arbitration in accordance with the UNCITRAL Arbitration Rules as at present in force and:**
>
> **(i) The appointing authority shall be the London Court of International Arbitration;**
>
> **(ii) The number of arbitrators shall be one;**
>
> **(iii) The place of arbitration shall be London;**
>
> **(iv) The language to be used in the arbitral proceedings shall be English; and**
>
> **(v) The parties will abide by any resulting arbitral award arising from these proceedings.**

INDIVIDUALS

ISDA Master Agreements involving individuals are comparatively rare but might arise where a sole trader takes out a medium term business loan which a bank requires to be hedged by an interest rate swap.

The following matters might require particular attention:

Preamble

There might be a preamble before Part 1 of the Schedule confirming that the Agreement relates to a loan facility letter as in the following example:

> **This Agreement is entered into in connnection with the facility letter referred to in Part 5(*) of this Schedule as the "Facility Letter" and any Transaction entered into under this Agreement is entered into by Party B for the sole purpose of hedging interest rate risk arising from moneys borrowed under the Facility Letter.**

Part 1

- **Another individual or a company might be nominated as a Specified Entity for all but Section 5(b)(iv) where they were regarded as crucial to the creditworthiness of the individual counterparty.**
- **Only a monetary Threshold Amount would apply to an individual.**
- **Credit Event Upon Merger will not apply to the individual. There may be reference in Part 1 to Merger Without Assumption and Tax Event Upon Merger also not applying to the individual.**
- **The death or insanity of the individual might also constitute an Additional Termination Event with them being the Affected Party.**

Compliance departments will wish to send out Terms of Business and Derivatives Warning Notices to individuals outlining the risks they could run in entering into derivatives transactions.

US SCHEDULE PROVISIONS

United States counterparties regularly ask for a number of provisions to be included when negotiating Schedules which can perplex non-US negotiators when first encountered. The purpose of this section is to clarify why US counterparties want these provisions and to try to dispel some of the "fear of the unknown".

Some of the more common provisions are as follows:

Waiver of Jury Trial

Short form

> **Each party hereby irrevocably waives any and all right to trial by jury with respect to any legal proceedings arising out of or relating to this Agreement or any Transaction contemplated hereunder.**

OR

> **Each party hereby irrevocably waives any and all right to trial by jury in any suit, action or proceeding arising out of or relating to this Agreement or any Transaction and acknowledges that this waiver is a material inducement to the other Party's entering into this Agreement.**

OR

> ***Waiver of Jury Trial.*** **To the extent permitted by applicable law, each party irrevocably waives any and all right to trial by jury in any legal proceeding in connection with this Agreement, any Credit Support Document to which it is a party, or any Transaction.**

Longer form

> **Each of Party A and Party B, respectively, hereby waives, to the fullest extent permitted by applicable law any right it may have to a trial by jury in respect of any suit, action or proceeding relating to this Agreement or any Credit Support Document. Each of Party A and Party B (i) certifies that no representative, agent or attorney of the other party and/or the Credit Support Provider has represented, expressly or otherwise, that such other party would not, in the event of such suit, action or proceeding, seek to enforce the foregoing waiver and (ii) acknowledges that it and the other party have been induced to enter into this Agreement and provide for any Credit Support Document, as applicable, by among other things, the mutual waivers and certifications in this section.**

Market Practice

The short forms are generally used. Although there is nothing improper about the longer forms, they are relatively uncommon.

Explanation

Unlike in English law, the right to trial by jury is guaranteed by the constitution of the State of New York for civil as well as criminal trials. The New York constitution, however, provides that "a jury trial may be waived by the parties in all civil cases". Many large financial institutions have policies that require that its customers and counterparties agree to waive their right to a jury trial before they will do business with them.

Large financial institutions insist on waiver of jury trial provisions because they believe that juries are not appropriate for deciding legal disputes with their customers or counterparties. They believe that a judge will have a better grasp of the sophisticated arguments involved in derivatives litigation than a jury. Secondly, they consider that a judge will apply the relevant law, however sympathetic he might feel towards the plaintiff. A jury might be tempted to downgrade legal precedents in order to reach the verdict they think is just. They believe that a judge is less likely to award multi-million dollar damages than a jury against what it may see as "fat cat institutions".

Even if an Agreement is governed by English law, a US financial institution may still insist on a waiver of jury trial provision. The US institution might be concerned that even if English law governs, litigation may still occur in the US or in another jurisdiction where a court may grant a jury trial. A waiver of jury trial provision would limit that risk.

Regulation EE

Short form

It is a "financial institution" within the meaning of the Federal Deposit Insurance Corporation Improvement Act of 1991 (as supplemented by Regulation EE of the Federal Reserve Board).

OR

It engages, will engage and holds itself out as engaging in "financial contracts" as defined in Regulation EE of the Federal Reserve Board as a counterparty on both sides of one or more financial markets (as defined in the regulation) and it fulfils at least one of the quantitative tests contained in such regulation.

Longer form

Each party represents and warrants to the other Party that it is a financial institution under the provisions of Title IV of the Federal Deposit Insurance Corporation Improvement Act of 1991 ("FDICIA") and the Parties agree that this Agreement shall be a netting contract, as defined in FDICIA, and each receipt or payment or delivery obligation hereunder shall be a covered contractual payment obligation, respectively, as defined in and subject to FDICIA.

Market Practice

Market practice among dealers is only to request the first short-form provision above. There is little doubt that the ISDA Master Agreement would constitute a netting contract under FDICIA and this clause would therefore appear to be superfluous. If there is any question whether a party would meet the Regulation EE tests, the representations will become much more detailed.

Explanation

The US Congress enacted the Federal Deposit Insurance Corporation Improvement Act of 1991 ("FDICIA") to ensure that close-out netting provisions found in Agreements between "financial institutions" were enforced regardless of any other statutory limitations including stays and court orders. The representation is only relevant, however, if the Agreements are governed by New York law or by the laws of the US. Please also see the discussion at pages 371–2. The definition of financial institutions in FDICIA goes well beyond banks and savings associations. Indeed, Congress authorised the Federal Reserve Board to issue regulations that would expand the definition of a financial institution under FDICIA. The Federal Reserve Board did this with Regulation EE which extended the definition of "financial institutions" to "a broker or dealer, a depository financial institution, a futures commission merchant or any other financial institution as determined by the Board of Governors of the Federal Reserve System".

Dealers try to verify which of their counterparties qualifies as a financial institution under Regulation EE to determine the capital weighting of their credit risk. Under Regulation EE, a party will be considered a financial institution for purposes of FDICIA if it meets both a qualitative and a quantitative test.

The qualitative test requires that a party "engage in financial contracts as a counterparty on both sides in one or more financial markets". The test is used to identify entities that have trading activities and characteristics more similar to a dealer than to a typical end user that only hedges its business and market risks on one side of the market.

The quantitative test measures a party's level of activity in the financial markets. A party meets the test if it has entered into financial contracts totaling at least US$ 1 billion in outstanding notional principal amount. Alternatively, it will meet the test if it can establish that it has financial contracts with gross mark-to-market positions of at least US$ 100 million. Financial contracts include securities contracts, commodity contracts, forward contracts, repurchase agreements, swap agreements, and any similar agreement as defined in another piece of US legislation – the Federal Deposit Insurance Act ("FDIA").

The above representation is typically required by dealers to determine if the other party meets the definition of a financial institution. It is important to remember, however, that FDICIA only applies if both parties are financial institutions under it.

Eligible Swap Participant and related pre-CFMA representations

It is an "eligible swap participant" as defined in Section 35.1. (b) of the Regulations of the Commodity Futures Trading Commission.

The Agreement and each Transaction constitutes a "swap agreement" within the meaning of 17 C.F.R. §35.1(b)(1).

It is an "eligible swap participant" within the meaning of 17 C.F.R. §35.1(b)(2).

Neither this agreement nor any Transaction is one of a fungible class of agreements that are standardised as to their material economic terms within the meaning of 17 C.F.R. §35.2.

The creditworthiness of the other party was a material consideration in entering into or determining the terms of this Agreement, including pricing, cost, or credit enhancement terms of the Agreement.

It has entered into this Agreement (including any Transactions evidenced hereby) in conjunction with its line of business (including financial intermediation services) or the financing of its business.

Market Practice

These representations are now largely obsolete and have now been replaced by the "eligible contract participant" representation (see page 377). US dealers and large corporations no longer request the eligible swap participant representation or the other representations related to it except for situations when the transaction does not qualify as either an excluded commodity or an exempt commodity under the CFMA (see pages 375–6). A party may still request these older representations for commodity OTC derivative transactions involving agricultural commodities such as wheat corn and other similar products. Although the CFMA is now the principal statutory authority in this area, the 1989 CFTC Policy Statement and the CFTC Regulations (found in 17 C.F.R. Part 35) are still valid and can provide important protections when entering into transactions involving agricultural commodities.

Instead, parties typically only request that a party represent that it is an "eligible contract participant". However, it is useful to understand the background behind the evolution of the various representations that deal with issues created by the interaction of OTC derivatives and the Commodity Exchange Act. Please see additional explanatory information at pages 374–6.

Eligible Contract Participant and Related Representations under the CFMA

Short form

It is an "eligible contract participant" within the meaning of the Commodity Exchange Act (as amended by the Commodity Futures Modernization Act of 2000)

Long form

(a) With respect to the Commodity Exchange Act, each party represents to the other party on and as of the date hereof and on each date on which a Transaction is entered into among them that:

(i) such party is an "eligible contract participant" as defined in the U.S. Commodity Exchange Act, as amended (the "CEA");

(ii) neither this Agreement nor any Transaction has been executed or traded on a "trading facility" as such term is defined in the CEA;

(iii) the terms of this Agreement and each Transaction have been subject to individual negotiation; and

(b) with respect to any Transaction that is a commodity option, each party when it is the offeree represents that (i) it is a producer, processor, commercial user or a merchant handling the commodity; and (ii) it is entering into such Transaction solely for purposes relating to its business as such.

Market Practice

Any issues involving OTC derivatives and the Commodity Exchange Act can be almost always be dealt with by using the Short Form of representation. The Long Form is only required when parties begin trading OTC derivatives through trading facilities which for the vast majority of parties would not be happening. A party proposing a long form of representation in the area should be able to explain why the particular types of transactions need those representations.

The full legal background to the CFMA and its predecessor statute and regulations are detailed in Chapter 5 pages 373–9.

The US Bankruptcy Code

Each of Party A and Party B hereby acknowledges and agrees that this Agreement and each Transaction hereunder or thereunder is intended to be a "swap agreement" as that term is defined in the U.S. Bankruptcy Code (as amended from time to time) and that the rights granted to each party under Section 6 of the Agreement include a contractual right to terminate a "swap agreement" and to offset and net out termination values and payment in conjunction therewith.

OR

Without limiting the applicability if any, of any other provision of the U.S. Bankruptcy Code as amended (the "Bankruptcy Code") (including without limitation Sections 362, 546, 556 and 560 thereof and the applicable definitions in Section 101 thereof), the parties acknowledge and agree that all Transactions entered into hereunder will constitute "forward contracts" or "swap agreements" as defined in Section 101 of the Bankruptcy Code or "commodity contracts" as defined in Section 761 of the Bankruptcy Code, that the rights of the parties under Section 6 of this Agreement will constitute contractual rights to liquidate Transactions, that any margin or collateral provided under any margin, collateral, security, pledge, or similar agreement related hereto will constitute a "margin payment" as defined in Section 101 of the Bankruptcy Code, and that the parties are entities entitled to the rights under, and protections afforded by, Sections 362, 546, 556, and 560 of the Bankruptcy Code.

Market Practice

This representation should only be requested of parties that are subject to the US Bankruptcy Code. The party represents how a US bankruptcy court would characterise those particular definitions upon the insolvency of the party subject to the Code. Most corporations organised under US law are subject to the US Bankruptcy Code. However, it does not apply to a financial institution with federally insured deposits, broker dealers, insurance companies, quasi-government agencies and entities organized in non-US jurisdictions.

Explanation

The US Bankruptcy Code provides significant protection to solvent parties that that have entered into derivatives with counterparties that become bankrupt and are governed by the US Bankruptcy Code. These statutes provide detailed definitions as to which agreements and transactions benefit from these provisions. If the parties' agreement is subject to the US Bankruptcy

Code such creditors can terminate the Agreement, foreclose on collateral or exercise set off rights against amounts under other swap agreements without being subject to the automatic stay and other restrictions imposed on creditors in a bankruptcy proceeding.

In a bankruptcy or insolvency of its counterparty, the solvent party may be concerned that the counterparty/debtor might try and argue that its agreement with the solvent party was not eligible to benefit from the preferential provisions found in the US Bankruptcy Code subjecting the solvent party to the same restrictions as other creditors.

Even if the counterparty/debtor itself did not make this argument in the bankruptcy court, other creditors might do so to limit the solvent party's ability to terminate the Agreement or exercise its other remedies. By requiring the representation, the solvent party and the counterparty have indicated how the Agreement should be characterised for bankruptcy law purposes.

US Banking Insolvency Law

Each party represents and intends that each Transaction entered into under this Agreement is, and shall constitute, a "qualified financial contract" as that term is defined in Section 212 of the Financial Institutions Reform, Recovery and Enforcement Act of 1989, as the same may be amended, modified or supplemented from time to time.

OR

In the case of Party A, Party A intends and acknowledges that this Agreement, including all Transactions hereunder, shall constitute a "qualified financial contract" and a "swap agreement" as those terms are defined in 12 U.S.C. 1821(e)(8)(D) as in effect on the date of this Agreement.

Market Practice

This representation should only be requested of parties that are financial institutions subject to US banking insolvency law. The party represents how a US regulator acting as a receiver or conservator would characterise those particular definitions upon the insolvency of the party subject to the insolvency rules.

Explanation

US banking insolvency law provides significant protection to solvent parties that have entered into derivatives with counterparties that become insolvent and are governed by US banking insolvency law. These statutes provide detailed definitions as to which agreements and transactions benefit from these provisions. If the parties' agreement is subject to the US banking insolvency law, such creditors can terminate the Agreement, foreclose on collateral or exercise set off rights without being subject to the restrictions imposed on creditors in a banking insolvency proceeding.

In the insolvency of its counterparty, the solvent party may be concerned that the financial institution might try and argue that its agreement with the solvent party was not eligible to the preferential provisions found in US banking insolvency law, subjecting the solvent party to the same restrictions as other creditors.

Even if the insolvent financial institution itself did not make this argument to the receiver or conservator, other creditors might do so to limit the solvent party's ability to terminate the Agreement or exercise its other remedies. By requiring the representation, the solvent party and the counterparty have indicated how the Agreement should be characterised for banking insolvency law purposes.

Enforcing Agreement Against the FDIC

Short form

If it is a bank subject to the requirements of 12 U.S.C. § 1823(e), its execution, delivery and performance of this Agreement (including the Credit Support Annex and each Confirmation) have been approved by its board of directors or its loan committee, such approval is reflected in the minutes of said board of directors or loan committee, and this Agreement (including the Credit Support Annex and each Confirmation) will be maintained as one of its official records continuously from the time of its execution (or in the case of any Confirmation, continuously until such time as the relevant Transaction matures and the obligations therefor are satisfied in full).

OR

Party B (if a FDIC insured depository institution) represents that an officer of the level of vice president or higher is executing this Agreement on behalf of Party B.

Long form

If Party B is an insured depository institution under the U.S. Federal Deposit Insurance Act as amended (the "FDI Act"), Party B represents to Party A as follows:

(i) the necessary action to authorise referred to in the representation in Section 3(a)(ii) includes all authorisations required under the FDI

Act and under any agreement, writ, decree or order entered into with its supervisory authorities;

(ii) at all times during the term of this Agreement and any Credit Support Document to which it is a party, it will continuously include and maintain as part of its official written books and records this Agreement, this Schedule, any Credit Support Document to which it is a party, and all other exhibits, supplements, annexes, and attachments hereto and documents incorporated by reference herein, all Confirmations and evidence of all necessary authorisations; and

(iii) This Agreement, any Credit Support Document to which it is a party, each Confirmation, and any other documentation relating to this Agreement to which it is a party or that it is required to deliver will be executed and delivered by a duly appointed or elected and authorised officer of it of the level of vice president or higher.

Market Practice

The first representation above generally reflects what the market requires. Because of the safe harbour language (see discussion below), many parties ask that their FDIC insured counterparties represent that the document was executed by an authorised officer at or above the level of a *vice president.* While the safe harbour provides more certainty, FDIC insured depositories will resist the language that focuses on a vice president signing the Agreement. This is because many of these institutions authorise individuals (who are not vice presidents) in their documentation unit to sign ISDA Master Agreements and Confirmations. The vice president language is not literally required because the FDIC's policy statement on the issue itself only requires as a threshold matter that "The depository institution, by corporate action, was authorised under applicable non-insolvency law to enter into the QFC (i.e qualified financial contract)".

Explanation

In dealing with US parties that are subject to the Federal Deposit Insurance Act (such as banks that hold insured deposits), foreign counterparties should be aware that there are certain additional requirements that must be met other than those with respect to a non-bank counterparties.

Generally, to establish a claim with respect to the ISDA Master Agreement or a Transaction thereunder that would be enforceable against the Federal Deposit Insurance Corporation (the "FDIC"), the ISDA Master Agreement and Transactions must be (i) in writing, (ii) executed contemporaneously with the transaction, (iii) approved by the bank's board of directors, and (iv) an official record of the bank (12 U.S.C. §1823(e)).

It would appear easy to fail any of these requirements in considering how OTC derivative documentation often is negotiated. However, the FDIC has provided several safe harbours for OTC derivative documentation to meet these requirements. For example, a Confirmation will generally be considered to meet the writing requirement. In addition, a party may rely on corporate resolutions provided by the bank to meet the board of directors' approval requirement or by a written representation from an officer of the level of vice president or higher, as to the depository institution's authority. Finally, the non-bank party may meet the official record requirement by providing copies of its own records documenting the transactions (FDIC, Statement of Policy on Qualified Financial Contracts, 1989, found at http://www.fdic.gov/regulations/laws/rules/5000-1100.html).

As discussed above, most contention between the parties centres around whether a vice president is required to execute the documents. A counterparty can deal with this issue in several ways. As explained above, it can insist that all documents are executed by a vice president of its counterparty. As explained above, many insured financial depositories are not operationally set up to do that. Second, it can request a secretary's certificate that certifies the relevant board resolution (this is something that every insured financial depository should be able to give). Third, it can simply rely on the representations provided in the ISDA Master Agreement or on an express representation like the first one above that all necessary corporate approvals have been obtained. Even if not executed by a vice president, such representations should satisfy the statute.

Securities Act representations

Although equity derivatives are an extremely important element in the OTC derivative area, it is an area of great complexity coupled with large potential civil and criminal penalties for violation of US securities laws. It is important when entering into equity derivatives and when making representations involving US securities laws, that experienced legal counsel be utilised.

Security-based Swap Agreements.

It is an "eligible contract participant" within the meaning of the Commodity Exchange Act (as amended by the Commodity Futures Modernization Act of 2000) and the material terms of each Transaction must be subject to individual negotiation.

Explanation

The Commodity Futures Modernization Act (the "CFMA") has recently helped create legal certainty in the area. The CFMA provides that the definition of a security for purposes of the Securities Act and the Securities Exchange Act does not include "security-based swap agreements". This provides that a security-based swap agreement is exempt from registration under US securities laws. To qualify for the exemption, the parties must qualify as eligible contract participants under the CFMA, the material economic terms of the transaction must be subject to individual negotiation and the transaction must be of the type set forth in the CFMA for security-based swap agreements. Although security-based swap agreements are exempt from registration, they are still subject to various provisions of US securities laws that prohibit fraud, manipulation and insider trading.

Securities Registration

Explanation

In the event that an equity or security-linked derivative transaction does not meet the security-based swap agreement exemption in the CFMA, the parties may still attempt to rely on other exemptions from registration or express restrictions on a party's behaviour to avoid liability under US securities laws.

Possible Representations

Parties often request of each other to make representations when entering into equity or security linked derivatives that focus on several different issues:

- **the derivative has not been registered under US securities law;**
- **the derivative will not necessarily be registered in the future;**
- **the derivative will only be transferred in accordance with applicable securities law;**
- **the parties may settle their obligations to each other without needing to comply with registration requirements;**
- **the transaction will not violate any legal or contractual restrictions on the transfer of any security;**
- **the party is not entering into the transaction with an intention to distribute securities except in compliance with US securities laws.**

Here is an example:

> ***Securities Act Representations.*** **Each party represents to the other party (which representations will be deemed to be repeated by each party on each date on which a Transaction is entered into) that:**

(i) It is a "qualified institutional buyer" as defined in Rule 144A under the US Securities Act of 1933, as amended (the "Securities Act") or an "accredited investor" as defined under the Securities Act; and

(ii) it acknowledges that certain Transactions under the Agreement may involve the purchase or sale of "securities" as defined in the Securities Act and understands that any such purchase or sale of securities will not be registered under the Securities Act and that any such securities may not be re-offered, resold, pledged or otherwise transferred except (1) pursuant to an effective registration statement under the Securities Act or pursuant to an exemption from the registration requirements of the Securities Act and (2) in accordance with any applicable securities laws of any state of the United States.

Rule 144A became effective on 30 April 1990. It concerns the resale of securities which are not registered as required by Section 5 of the Securities Act (1933). It allows dealers to resell securities purchased from issuers provided the resale is to "qualified institutional buyers" in the US.

"Qualified institutional buyers" are basically large US institutions who act on their own account or on behalf of other qualified institutional buyers and own and invest on a discretionary basis at least US$ 100 million in the securities of issuers unaffiliated to them. Securities firms qualify if they have assets of US$ 10 million or more.

No Pension Plan Assets

No Pension Plan Assets. **Party A represents to Party B that, with respect to each source of funds to be used by it to enter into Transactions (the "Source"), the Source is not the assets of: (i) any "plan" (as such term is defined in Section 4975 of the US Internal Revenue Code of 1986 as amended (the "Code")) subject to Section 4975 of the Code: (ii) any "employee benefit plan" (as such term is defined in Section 3(3) of the US Employee Retirement Income Security Act of 1974 as amended ("ERISA")) subject to Title I of ERISA; or (iii) otherwise any "plan assets" within the meaning of U.S. Department of Labor Regulation Section 2510.3–101.29 CFR Section 2510–3–101.**

Market Practice

This representation is mostly typically requested from entities such as a hedge fund that may have pension plans or similar arrangements directly or directly as investors. Large publicly held corporations typically would not be required to make these types of representations.

Explanation

The US has stringent rules that protect employee benefit plans, pension plans and similar types of arrangements (a "Plan"), as well as certain entities in which Plans invest, from being taken advantage of by parties that have an interest or certain relationships with the Plan (a "Related Party"). The principle behind this is that a Related Party may have an opportunity to engage in proprietary trading or similar types of behaviour because of the special relationship it has with the Plan, e.g. serving as an investment adviser. These laws define a Related Party very broadly, for example, an entity may be considered to be a Related Party merely because of its affiliation with another entity.

In certain circumstances, the law permits a Plan to avoid certain transactions with a Related Party. Parties are concerned that if its counterparty is considered to be a Plan, the Plan may be able to avoid its obligations under the ISDA Master Agreement if the other party is considered to be a Related Party. Because it may be difficult to determine if it is a Related Party, a party will request that its counterparty represent that it is not a Plan.

Generally, a counterparty will know whether it is organised as a Plan for the purposes of US law. It is more difficult to determine if the counterparty is holding what are referred to as "plan assets", which may result in the counterparty being treated in the same manner as a Plan for purposes of the law. An entity is sometimes considered to hold plan assets if Plans have made an equity investment in the entity. If the percentage equity ownership of an entity by different Plans exceeds a certain percentage (most commonly 25%), the entity itself may be treated as holding plan assets (unless the entity is an operating company or satisfies certain conditions). In particular the assets of investment funds may inadvertently become plan assets if too many Plans have invested in them.

Uniform Commercial Code

> ***Uniform Commercial Code.* The parties agree that, to the maximum extent possible under the applicable law, no provision of Article 2 of the Uniform Commercial Code (as in effect from time to time in the State of New York) (the "UCC") that is inconsistent with any provision of this Agreement shall apply to this Agreement and that the provisions of Section 2–609 of the UCC and any equivalent rights at common law shall not apply to this Agreement.**

Market Practice

The market generally does not consider this issue to be a concern any longer. Because it was mentioned in older material however, it continues to be requested.

Explanation

UCC Section 2–609 permits a party which has "reasonable grounds for insecurity" about the performance of its counterparty to require written "adequate assurance of due performance" and can suspend performance of its own obligations until it is given. This can be excluded as in the above provision which means that the common law would apply in its place.

Other Areas

US legislation has been very active recently. As well as the CFMA, there is also before Congress a new Bankruptcy Reform Act 2001 which amends the US Bankruptcy Code, FDIA, FDICIA and the Securities Investor Protection Act (1970). This may result in further representations in due course!

New developments 10

ISDA Amendment: Close-out Amount

ISDA Credit Support Annex Amendments

2002 Master Agreement Protocol

Electronic negotiation of the ISDA Master Agreement

ISDA AMENDMENT: CLOSE-OUT AMOUNT

In March 2003, ISDA issued an Amendment to the 1992 Agreement.

The Amendment focuses on replacing Market Quotation and Loss with the 2002 Agreement's new single payment measure, Close-out Amount.

It also makes other consequential amendments, e.g. dropping references to the First Method, updating Section 6(e) – Payments on Early Termination and including the full definition of Close-out Amount.

The aim is for contracting parties to have the benefit of the Close-out Amount payment measure without having to replace their 1992 Agreement in full.

The Amendment is reproduced in Annex 3 by kind permission of the International Swaps and Derivatives Association, Inc.

ISDA CREDIT SUPPORT ANNEX AMENDMENTS

In May 2003, ISDA issued two bilateral Amendments in respect of its Credit Support Annexes under English and New York law.

These Amendments can be used by contracting parties with 1992 Agreements (which have already been amended to include Close-out Amount) to amend their Credit Support Annex too by including Close-out Amount and deleting references to Market Quotation or Loss. Furthermore, parties entering into a 2002 Agreement can use the provisions in their Amendments as a starting point for updating their Credit Support Annex.

The Amendment to the English Law Credit Support Annex amends Paragraph 4(a)(4)(i)(B) which is part of the Dispute Resolution provision; revises Paragraph 6 (Default) in full and redefines the term "Exposure" in Paragraph 10.

The Amendment to the New York Law Credit Support Annex just amends the Dispute Resolution provision and the definition of Exposure.

These Amendments are available on ISDA's website www.isda.org under Publications.

2002 MASTER AGREEMENT PROTOCOL

On 15 July 2003, ISDA published its 2002 Master Agreement Protocol.

The Protocol offers market players an efficient multilateral method to amend 13 ISDA Definitions booklets and 5 credit support documents to reflect the new terminology and provisions of the 2002 Agreement. Essentially it updates these pre 2002 documents which were not written with the 2002 Agreement in mind and which contain non 2002 Agreement concepts such as Market Quotation and Loss.

The Protocol is open to ISDA members and non-members who do not need to enter into a 2002 Agreement to adhere to the Protocol. Annex choices made in the adherence letter take effect whenever the parties execute a 2002 Agreement in the future even if this is after the Protocol closes for adherence on 1 March 2004 (unless ISDA extends it for a further three months).

ELECTRONIC NEGOTIATION OF THE ISDA MASTER AGREEMENT

Software companies continue to work on the electronic negotiation of the ISDA Master Agreement via the internet from any desktop PC. This is an interesting development which has already been applied to Confirmations by different companies. Theoretically, this should be possible at least with "vanilla" Agreements where it is important to put them in place to reduce credit and legal risk. With more customised Schedules this initiative is probably less useful. I do not believe that any software company has yet fully cracked this challenge.

Much negotiation already takes place via e-mail. In the past it used to be said that the negotiation market was a telephone market and negotiators never actually met. Many now do at ISDA conferences etc. but in other cases personal acquaintance has been supplanted by e-mail. Electronic negotiation systems may well be useful for database purposes but I, for one, would hate to see negotiation being downgraded to ticks and clicks.

Annexes

Reproduction of 1992 ISDA Master Agreement

Reproduction of 2002 ISDA Master Agreement

Amendment: Close-out Amount

ISDA legal netting opinion lists for the 1992 and 2002 Agreements

Checklist for New York law Guarantee

Checklist for English law Guarantee

List of long-term credit ratings from three major credit ratings agencies

Sample Board Resolution for UK company

List of useful websites

ANNEXES

I have provided these nine Annexes in the hope that they might provide useful reference material.

Annex 1

A facsimile of the 1992 ISDA Master Agreement and its Schedule (reproduced with the kind permission of the International Swaps and Derivatives Association, Inc).

Annex 2

A facsimile of the 2002 ISDA Master Agreement and its Schedule (reproduced with the kind permission of the International Swaps and Derivatives Association, Inc).

Annex 3

A facsimile of the Amendment: Close-out Amount (reproduced with the kind permission of the International Swaps and Derivatives Association, Inc).

Annex 4

A list of the 39 jurisdictions where ISDA has obtained netting opinions in respect of the 1992 Agreement as at October 2003 and a list of 36 jurisdictions where ISDA has obtained netting opinions in respect of the 2002 Agreement also as at October 2003.

Annex 5

Checklist for the constituents of a New York law governed guarantee.

Annex 6

Checklist for the constituents of an English law governed guarantee.

Annex 7

List of credit ratings from three major credit ratings agencies.

Annex 8

Sample Board resolution for UK corporates.

Annex 9

Useful website addresses.

In relation to Annexes 5 and 6, from my experience, it appears that many banks do not have a formal means of evaluating the contents of a guarantee for derivatives obligations. Sometimes, negotiators just read them through and form an impression as to whether they are OK. These checklists provide a more scientific means of reviewing the constituents of a guarantee to see what may be missing. It is best to base such a checklist on your house standard guarantee and check what is missing or surpassed. Annexes 5 and 6 are merely illustrative. It will not be feasible normally to negotiate all the provisions in each Checklist. You need to identify what is important to you which is why it is important to work from your own house guarantee. In addition there is no strict international divide between Annexes 5 and 6 because provisions listed may appear in either of them.

I have included Annex 7 because it might be useful to have a list of credit ratings in one place.

Negotiators (and that includes me) may find themselves scrabbling around trying to find a sample Board Resolution for a UK company to enter into an Agreement. To avoid this or receiving an inadequate resolution from a company I include a sample Board Resolution for reference in Annex 8.

Annex 9 lists some useful websites in one place.

ANNEX 1 REPRODUCTION OF 1992 ISDA MASTER AGREEMENT

(Multicurrency—Cross Border)

ISDA.®

International Swap Dealers Association, Inc.

MASTER AGREEMENT

dated as of ....

.... and ....

have entered and/or anticipate entering into one or more transactions (each a "Transaction") that are or will be governed by this Master Agreement, which includes the schedule (the "Schedule"), and the documents and other confirming evidence (each a "Confirmation") exchanged between the parties confirming those Transactions.

Accordingly, the parties agree as follows:—

1. Interpretation

(a) ***Definitions.*** The terms defined in Section 14 and in the Schedule will have the meanings therein specified for the purpose of this Master Agreement.

(b) ***Inconsistency.*** In the event of any inconsistency between the provisions of the Schedule and the other provisions of this Master Agreement, the Schedule will prevail. In the event of any inconsistency between the provisions of any Confirmation and this Master Agreement (including the Schedule), such Confirmation will prevail for the purpose of the relevant Transaction.

(c) ***Single Agreement.*** All Transactions are entered into in reliance on the fact that this Master Agreement and all Confirmations form a single agreement between the parties (collectively referred to as this "Agreement"), and the parties would not otherwise enter into any Transactions.

2. Obligations

(a) ***General Conditions.***

(i) Each party will make each payment or delivery specified in each Confirmation to be made by it, subject to the other provisions of this Agreement.

(ii) Payments under this Agreement will be made on the due date for value on that date in the place of the account specified in the relevant Confirmation or otherwise pursuant to this Agreement, in freely transferable funds and in the manner customary for payments in the required currency. Where settlement is by delivery (that is, other than by payment), such delivery will be made for receipt on the due date in the manner customary for the relevant obligation unless otherwise specified in the relevant Confirmation or elsewhere in this Agreement.

(iii) Each obligation of each party under Section 2(a)(i) is subject to (1) the condition precedent that no Event of Default or Potential Event of Default with respect to the other party has occurred and is continuing, (2) the condition precedent that no Early Termination Date in respect of the relevant Transaction has occurred or been effectively designated and (3) each other applicable condition precedent specified in this Agreement.

(b) ***Change of Account.*** Either party may change its account for receiving a payment or delivery by giving notice to the other party at least five Local Business Days prior to the scheduled date for the payment or delivery to which such change applies unless such other party gives timely notice of a reasonable objection to such change.

(c) ***Netting.*** If on any date amounts would otherwise be payable:—

(i) in the same currency; and

(ii) in respect of the same Transaction,

by each party to the other, then, on such date, each party's obligation to make payment of any such amount will be automatically satisfied and discharged and, if the aggregate amount that would otherwise have been payable by one party exceeds the aggregate amount that would otherwise have been payable by the other party, replaced by an obligation upon the party by whom the larger aggregate amount would have been payable to pay to the other party the excess of the larger aggregate amount over the smaller aggregate amount.

The parties may elect in respect of two or more Transactions that a net amount will be determined in respect of all amounts payable on the same date in the same currency in respect of such Transactions, regardless of whether such amounts are payable in respect of the same Transaction. The election may be made in the Schedule or a Confirmation by specifying that subparagraph (ii) above will not apply to the Transactions identified as being subject to the election, together with the starting date (in which case subparagraph (ii) above will not, or will cease to, apply to such Transactions from such date). This election may be made separately for different groups of Transactions and will apply separately to each pairing of Offices through which the parties make and receive payments or deliveries.

(d) ***Deduction or Withholding for Tax.***

(i) ***Gross-Up.*** All payments under this Agreement will be made without any deduction or withholding for or on account of any Tax unless such deduction or withholding is required by any applicable law, as modified by the practice of any relevant governmental revenue authority, then in effect. If a party is so required to deduct or withhold, then that party ("X") will:—

(1) promptly notify the other party ("Y") of such requirement;

(2) pay to the relevant authorities the full amount required to be deducted or withheld (including the full amount required to be deducted or withheld from any additional amount paid by X to Y under this Section 2(d)) promptly upon the earlier of determining that such deduction or withholding is required or receiving notice that such amount has been assessed against Y;

(3) promptly forward to Y an official receipt (or a certified copy), or other documentation reasonably acceptable to Y, evidencing such payment to such authorities; and

(4) if such Tax is an Indemnifiable Tax, pay to Y, in addition to the payment to which Y is otherwise entitled under this Agreement, such additional amount as is necessary to ensure that the net amount actually received by Y (free and clear of Indemnifiable Taxes, whether assessed against X or Y) will equal the full amount Y would have received had no such deduction or withholding been required. However, X will not be required to pay any additional amount to Y to the extent that it would not be required to be paid but for:—

(A) the failure by Y to comply with or perform any agreement contained in Section 4(a)(i), 4(a)(iii) or 4(d); or

(B) the failure of a representation made by Y pursuant to Section 3(f) to be accurate and true unless such failure would not have occurred but for (I) any action taken by a taxing authority, or brought in a court of competent jurisdiction, on or after the date on which a Transaction is entered into (regardless of whether such action is taken or brought with respect to a party to this Agreement) or (II) a Change in Tax Law.

(ii) ***Liability.*** If:—

(1) X is required by any applicable law, as modified by the practice of any relevant governmental revenue authority, to make any deduction or withholding in respect of which X would not be required to pay an additional amount to Y under Section 2(d)(i)(4);

(2) X does not so deduct or withhold; and

(3) a liability resulting from such Tax is assessed directly against X,

then, except to the extent Y has satisfied or then satisfies the liability resulting from such Tax, Y will promptly pay to X the amount of such liability (including any related liability for interest, but including any related liability for penalties only if Y has failed to comply with or perform any agreement contained in Section 4(a)(i), 4(a)(iii) or 4(d)).

(e) ***Default Interest; Other Amounts.*** Prior to the occurrence or effective designation of an Early Termination Date in respect of the relevant Transaction, a party that defaults in the performance of any payment obligation will, to the extent permitted by law and subject to Section 6(c), be required to pay interest (before as well as after judgment) on the overdue amount to the other party on demand in the same currency as such overdue amount, for the period from (and including) the original due date for payment to (but excluding) the date of actual payment, at the Default Rate. Such interest will be calculated on the basis of daily compounding and the actual number of days elapsed. If, prior to the occurrence or effective designation of an Early Termination Date in respect of the relevant Transaction, a party defaults in the performance of any obligation required to be settled by delivery, it will compensate the other party on demand if and to the extent provided for in the relevant Confirmation or elsewhere in this Agreement.

3. Representations

Each party represents to the other party (which representations will be deemed to be repeated by each party on each date on which a Transaction is entered into and, in the case of the representations in Section 3(f), at all times until the termination of this Agreement) that:—

(a) ***Basic Representations.***

(i) ***Status.*** It is duly organised and validly existing under the laws of the jurisdiction of its organisation or incorporation and, if relevant under such laws, in good standing;

(ii) ***Powers.*** It has the power to execute this Agreement and any other documentation relating to this Agreement to which it is a party, to deliver this Agreement and any other documentation relating to this Agreement that it is required by this Agreement to deliver and to perform its obligations under this Agreement and any obligations it has under any Credit Support Document to which it is a party and has taken all necessary action to authorise such execution, delivery and performance;

(iii) ***No Violation or Conflict.*** Such execution, delivery and performance do not violate or conflict with any law applicable to it, any provision of its constitutional documents, any order or judgment of any court or other agency of government applicable to it or any of its assets or any contractual restriction binding on or affecting it or any of its assets;

(iv) ***Consents.*** All governmental and other consents that are required to have been obtained by it with respect to this Agreement or any Credit Support Document to which it is a party have been obtained and are in full force and effect and all conditions of any such consents have been complied with; and

(v) ***Obligations Binding.*** Its obligations under this Agreement and any Credit Support Document to which it is a party constitute its legal, valid and binding obligations, enforceable in accordance with their respective terms (subject to applicable bankruptcy, reorganisation, insolvency, moratorium or similar laws affecting creditors' rights generally and subject, as to enforceability, to equitable principles of general application (regardless of whether enforcement is sought in a proceeding in equity or at law)).

(b) ***Absence of Certain Events.*** No Event of Default or Potential Event of Default or, to its knowledge, Termination Event with respect to it has occurred and is continuing and no such event or circumstance would occur as a result of its entering into or performing its obligations under this Agreement or any Credit Support Document to which it is a party.

(c) ***Absence of Litigation.*** There is not pending or, to its knowledge, threatened against it or any of its Affiliates any action, suit or proceeding at law or in equity or before any court, tribunal, governmental body, agency or official or any arbitrator that is likely to affect the legality, validity or enforceability against it of this Agreement or any Credit Support Document to which it is a party or its ability to perform its obligations under this Agreement or such Credit Support Document.

(d) ***Accuracy of Specified Information.*** All applicable information that is furnished in writing by or on behalf of it to the other party and is identified for the purpose of this Section 3(d) in the Schedule is, as of the date of the information, true, accurate and complete in every material respect.

(e) ***Payer Tax Representation.*** Each representation specified in the Schedule as being made by it for the purpose of this Section 3(e) is accurate and true.

(f) ***Payee Tax Representations.*** Each representation specified in the Schedule as being made by it for the purpose of this Section 3(f) is accurate and true.

4. Agreements

Each party agrees with the other that, so long as either party has or may have any obligation under this Agreement or under any Credit Support Document to which it is a party:—

(a) ***Furnish Specified Information.*** It will deliver to the other party or, in certain cases under subparagraph (iii) below, to such government or taxing authority as the other party reasonably directs:—

(i) any forms, documents or certificates relating to taxation specified in the Schedule or any Confirmation;

(ii) any other documents specified in the Schedule or any Confirmation; and

(iii) upon reasonable demand by such other party, any form or document that may be required or reasonably requested in writing in order to allow such other party or its Credit Support Provider to make a payment under this Agreement or any applicable Credit Support Document without any deduction or withholding for or on account of any Tax or with such deduction or withholding at a reduced rate (so long as the completion, execution or submission of such form or document would not materially prejudice the legal or commercial position of the party in receipt of such demand), with any such form or document to be accurate and completed in a manner reasonably satisfactory to such other party and to be executed and to be delivered with any reasonably required certification,

in each case by the date specified in the Schedule or such Confirmation or, if none is specified, as soon as reasonably practicable.

(b) ***Maintain Authorisations.*** It will use all reasonable efforts to maintain in full force and effect all consents of any governmental or other authority that are required to be obtained by it with respect to this Agreement or any Credit Support Document to which it is a party and will use all reasonable efforts to obtain any that may become necessary in the future.

(c) ***Comply with Laws.*** It will comply in all material respects with all applicable laws and orders to which it may be subject if failure so to comply would materially impair its ability to perform its obligations under this Agreement or any Credit Support Document to which it is a party.

(d) ***Tax Agreement.*** It will give notice of any failure of a representation made by it under Section 3(f) to be accurate and true promptly upon learning of such failure.

(e) ***Payment of Stamp Tax.*** Subject to Section 11, it will pay any Stamp Tax levied or imposed upon it or in respect of its execution or performance of this Agreement by a jurisdiction in which it is incorporated, organised, managed and controlled, or considered to have its seat, or in which a branch or office through which it is acting for the purpose of this Agreement is located ("Stamp Tax Jurisdiction") and will indemnify the other party against any Stamp Tax levied or imposed upon the other party or in respect of the other party's execution or performance of this Agreement by any such Stamp Tax Jurisdiction which is not also a Stamp Tax Jurisdiction with respect to the other party.

5. Events of Default and Termination Events

(a) ***Events of Default.*** The occurrence at any time with respect to a party or, if applicable, any Credit Support Provider of such party or any Specified Entity of such party of any of the following events constitutes an event of default (an "Event of Default") with respect to such party:—

(i) ***Failure to Pay or Deliver.*** Failure by the party to make, when due, any payment under this Agreement or delivery under Section 2(a)(i) or 2(e) required to be made by it if such failure is not remedied on or before the third Local Business Day after notice of such failure is given to the party;

(ii) ***Breach of Agreement.*** Failure by the party to comply with or perform any agreement or obligation (other than an obligation to make any payment under this Agreement or delivery under Section 2(a)(i) or 2(e) or to give notice of a Termination Event or any agreement or obligation under Section 4(a)(i), 4(a)(iii) or 4(d)) to be complied with or performed by the party in accordance with this Agreement if such failure is not remedied on or before the thirtieth day after notice of such failure is given to the party;

(iii) ***Credit Support Default.***

(1) Failure by the party or any Credit Support Provider of such party to comply with or perform any agreement or obligation to be complied with or performed by it in accordance with any Credit Support Document if such failure is continuing after any applicable grace period has elapsed;

(2) the expiration or termination of such Credit Support Document or the failing or ceasing of such Credit Support Document to be in full force and effect for the purpose of this Agreement (in either case other than in accordance with its terms) prior to the satisfaction of all obligations of such party under each Transaction to which such Credit Support Document relates without the written consent of the other party; or

(3) the party or such Credit Support Provider disaffirms, disclaims, repudiates or rejects, in whole or in part, or challenges the validity of, such Credit Support Document;

(iv) ***Misrepresentation.*** A representation (other than a representation under Section 3(e) or (f)) made or repeated or deemed to have been made or repeated by the party or any Credit Support Provider of such party in this Agreement or any Credit Support Document proves to have been incorrect or misleading in any material respect when made or repeated or deemed to have been made or repeated;

(v) ***Default under Specified Transaction.*** The party, any Credit Support Provider of such party or any applicable Specified Entity of such party (1) defaults under a Specified Transaction and, after giving effect to any applicable notice requirement or grace period, there occurs a liquidation of, an acceleration of obligations under, or an early termination of, that Specified Transaction, (2) defaults, after giving effect to any applicable notice requirement or grace period, in making any payment or delivery due on the last payment, delivery or exchange date of, or any payment on early termination of, a Specified Transaction (or such default continues for at least three Local Business Days if there is no applicable notice requirement or grace period) or (3) disaffirms, disclaims, repudiates or rejects, in whole or in part, a Specified Transaction (or such action is taken by any person or entity appointed or empowered to operate it or act on its behalf);

(vi) ***Cross Default.*** If "Cross Default" is specified in the Schedule as applying to the party, the occurrence or existence of (1) a default, event of default or other similar condition or event (however described) in respect of such party, any Credit Support Provider of such party or any applicable Specified Entity of such party under one or more agreements or instruments relating to Specified Indebtedness of any of them (individually or collectively) in an aggregate amount of not less than the applicable Threshold Amount (as specified in the Schedule) which has resulted in such Specified Indebtedness becoming, or becoming capable at such time of being declared, due and payable under such agreements or instruments, before it would otherwise have been due and payable or (2) a default by such party, such Credit Support Provider or such Specified Entity (individually or collectively) in making one or more payments on the due date thereof in an aggregate amount of not less than the applicable Threshold Amount under such agreements or instruments (after giving effect to any applicable notice requirement or grace period);

(vii) ***Bankruptcy***. The party, any Credit Support Provider of such party or any applicable Specified Entity of such party:—

(1) is dissolved (other than pursuant to a consolidation, amalgamation or merger); (2) becomes insolvent or is unable to pay its debts or fails or admits in writing its inability generally to pay its debts as they become due; (3) makes a general assignment, arrangement or composition with or for the benefit of its creditors; (4) institutes or has instituted against it a proceeding seeking a judgment of insolvency or bankruptcy or any other relief under any bankruptcy or insolvency law or other similar law affecting creditors' rights, or a petition is presented for its winding-up or liquidation, and, in the case of any such proceeding or petition instituted or presented against it, such proceeding or petition (A) results in a judgment of insolvency or bankruptcy or the entry of an order for relief or the making of an order for its winding-up or liquidation or (B) is not dismissed, discharged, stayed or restrained in each case within 30 days of the institution or presentation thereof; (5) has a resolution passed for its winding-up, official management or liquidation (other than pursuant to a consolidation, amalgamation or merger); (6) seeks or becomes subject to the appointment of an administrator, provisional liquidator, conservator, receiver, trustee, custodian or other similar official for it or for all or substantially all its assets; (7) has a secured party take possession of all or substantially all its assets or has a distress, execution, attachment, sequestration or other legal process levied, enforced or sued on or against all or substantially all its assets and such secured party maintains possession, or any such process is not dismissed, discharged, stayed or restrained, in each case within 30 days thereafter; (8) causes or is subject to any event with respect to it which, under the applicable laws of any jurisdiction, has an analogous effect to any of the events specified in clauses (1) to (7) (inclusive); or (9) takes any action in furtherance of, or indicating its consent to, approval of, or acquiescence in, any of the foregoing acts; or

(viii) ***Merger Without Assumption***. The party or any Credit Support Provider of such party consolidates or amalgamates with, or merges with or into, or transfers all or substantially all its assets to, another entity and, at the time of such consolidation, amalgamation, merger or transfer:—

(1) the resulting, surviving or transferee entity fails to assume all the obligations of such party or such Credit Support Provider under this Agreement or any Credit Support Document to which it or its predecessor was a party by operation of law or pursuant to an agreement reasonably satisfactory to the other party to this Agreement; or

(2) the benefits of any Credit Support Document fail to extend (without the consent of the other party) to the performance by such resulting, surviving or transferee entity of its obligations under this Agreement.

(b) ***Termination Events***. The occurrence at any time with respect to a party or, if applicable, any Credit Support Provider of such party or any Specified Entity of such party of any event specified below constitutes an Illegality if the event is specified in (i) below, a Tax Event if the event is specified in (ii) below or a Tax Event Upon Merger if the event is specified in (iii) below, and, if specified to be applicable, a Credit Event

Upon Merger if the event is specified pursuant to (iv) below or an Additional Termination Event if the event is specified pursuant to (v) below:—

(i) ***Illegality.*** Due to the adoption of, or any change in, any applicable law after the date on which a Transaction is entered into, or due to the promulgation of, or any change in, the interpretation by any court, tribunal or regulatory authority with competent jurisdiction of any applicable law after such date, it becomes unlawful (other than as a result of a breach by the party of Section 4(b)) for such party (which will be the Affected Party):—

(1) to perform any absolute or contingent obligation to make a payment or delivery or to receive a payment or delivery in respect of such Transaction or to comply with any other material provision of this Agreement relating to such Transaction; or

(2) to perform, or for any Credit Support Provider of such party to perform, any contingent or other obligation which the party (or such Credit Support Provider) has under any Credit Support Document relating to such Transaction;

(ii) ***Tax Event.*** Due to (x) any action taken by a taxing authority, or brought in a court of competent jurisdiction, on or after the date on which a Transaction is entered into (regardless of whether such action is taken or brought with respect to a party to this Agreement) or (y) a Change in Tax Law, the party (which will be the Affected Party) will, or there is a substantial likelihood that it will, on the next succeeding Scheduled Payment Date (1) be required to pay to the other party an additional amount in respect of an Indemnifiable Tax under Section 2(d)(i)(4) (except in respect of interest under Section 2(e), 6(d)(ii) or 6(e)) or (2) receive a payment from which an amount is required to be deducted or withheld for or on account of a Tax (except in respect of interest under Section 2(e), 6(d)(ii) or 6(e)) and no additional amount is required to be paid in respect of such Tax under Section 2(d)(i)(4) (other than by reason of Section 2(d)(i)(4)(A) or (B));

(iii) ***Tax Event Upon Merger.*** The party (the "Burdened Party") on the next succeeding Scheduled Payment Date will either (1) be required to pay an additional amount in respect of an Indemnifiable Tax under Section 2(d)(i)(4) (except in respect of interest under Section 2(e), 6(d)(ii) or 6(e)) or (2) receive a payment from which an amount has been deducted or withheld for or on account of any Indemnifiable Tax in respect of which the other party is not required to pay an additional amount (other than by reason of Section 2(d)(i)(4)(A) or (B)), in either case as a result of a party consolidating or amalgamating with, or merging with or into, or transferring all or substantially all its assets to, another entity (which will be the Affected Party) where such action does not constitute an event described in Section 5(a)(viii);

(iv) ***Credit Event Upon Merger.*** If "Credit Event Upon Merger" is specified in the Schedule as applying to the party, such party ("X"), any Credit Support Provider of X or any applicable Specified Entity of X consolidates or amalgamates with, or merges with or into, or transfers all or substantially all its assets to, another entity and such action does not constitute an event described in Section 5(a)(viii) but the creditworthiness of the resulting, surviving or transferee entity is materially weaker than that of X, such Credit Support Provider or such Specified Entity, as the case may be, immediately prior to such action (and, in such event, X or its successor or transferee, as appropriate, will be the Affected Party); or

(v) ***Additional Termination Event.*** If any "Additional Termination Event" is specified in the Schedule or any Confirmation as applying, the occurrence of such event (and, in such event, the Affected Party or Affected Parties shall be as specified for such Additional Termination Event in the Schedule or such Confirmation).

(c) ***Event of Default and Illegality.*** If an event or circumstance which would otherwise constitute or give rise to an Event of Default also constitutes an Illegality, it will be treated as an Illegality and will not constitute an Event of Default.

6. Early Termination

(a) ***Right to Terminate Following Event of Default.*** If at any time an Event of Default with respect to a party (the "Defaulting Party") has occurred and is then continuing, the other party (the "Non-defaulting Party") may, by not more than 20 days notice to the Defaulting Party specifying the relevant Event of Default, designate a day not earlier than the day such notice is effective as an Early Termination Date in respect of all outstanding Transactions. If, however, "Automatic Early Termination" is specified in the Schedule as applying to a party, then an Early Termination Date in respect of all outstanding Transactions will occur immediately upon the occurrence with respect to such party of an Event of Default specified in Section 5(a)(vii)(1), (3), (5), (6) or, to the extent analogous thereto, (8), and as of the time immediately preceding the institution of the relevant proceeding or the presentation of the relevant petition upon the occurrence with respect to such party of an Event of Default specified in Section 5(a)(vii)(4) or, to the extent analogous thereto, (8).

(b) ***Right to Terminate Following Termination Event.***

(i) ***Notice.*** If a Termination Event occurs, an Affected Party will, promptly upon becoming aware of it, notify the other party, specifying the nature of that Termination Event and each Affected Transaction and will also give such other information about that Termination Event as the other party may reasonably require.

(ii) ***Transfer to Avoid Termination Event.*** If either an Illegality under Section 5(b)(i)(1) or a Tax Event occurs and there is only one Affected Party, or if a Tax Event Upon Merger occurs and the Burdened Party is the Affected Party, the Affected Party will, as a condition to its right to designate an Early Termination Date under Section 6(b)(iv), use all reasonable efforts (which will not require such party to incur a loss, excluding immaterial, incidental expenses) to transfer within 20 days after it gives notice under Section 6(b)(i) all its rights and obligations under this Agreement in respect of the Affected Transactions to another of its Offices or Affiliates so that such Termination Event ceases to exist.

If the Affected Party is not able to make such a transfer it will give notice to the other party to that effect within such 20 day period, whereupon the other party may effect such a transfer within 30 days after the notice is given under Section 6(b)(i).

Any such transfer by a party under this Section 6(b)(ii) will be subject to and conditional upon the prior written consent of the other party, which consent will not be withheld if such other party's policies in effect at such time would permit it to enter into transactions with the transferee on the terms proposed.

(iii) ***Two Affected Parties.*** If an Illegality under Section 5(b)(i)(1) or a Tax Event occurs and there are two Affected Parties, each party will use all reasonable efforts to reach agreement within 30 days after notice thereof is given under Section 6(b)(i) on action to avoid that Termination Event.

(iv) ***Right to Terminate.*** If:—

(1) a transfer under Section 6(b)(ii) or an agreement under Section 6(b)(iii), as the case may be, has not been effected with respect to all Affected Transactions within 30 days after an Affected Party gives notice under Section 6(b)(i); or

(2) an Illegality under Section 5(b)(i)(2), a Credit Event Upon Merger or an Additional Termination Event occurs, or a Tax Event Upon Merger occurs and the Burdened Party is not the Affected Party,

either party in the case of an Illegality, the Burdened Party in the case of a Tax Event Upon Merger, any Affected Party in the case of a Tax Event or an Additional Termination Event if there is more than one Affected Party, or the party which is not the Affected Party in the case of a Credit Event Upon Merger or an Additional Termination Event if there is only one Affected Party may, by not more than 20 days notice to the other party and provided that the relevant Termination Event is then continuing, designate a day not earlier than the day such notice is effective as an Early Termination Date in respect of all Affected Transactions.

(c) ***Effect of Designation.***

(i) If notice designating an Early Termination Date is given under Section 6(a) or (b), the Early Termination Date will occur on the date so designated, whether or not the relevant Event of Default or Termination Event is then continuing.

(ii) Upon the occurrence or effective designation of an Early Termination Date, no further payments or deliveries under Section 2(a)(i) or 2(e) in respect of the Terminated Transactions will be required to be made, but without prejudice to the other provisions of this Agreement. The amount, if any, payable in respect of an Early Termination Date shall be determined pursuant to Section 6(e).

(d) ***Calculations.***

(i) ***Statement.*** On or as soon as reasonably practicable following the occurrence of an Early Termination Date, each party will make the calculations on its part, if any, contemplated by Section 6(e) and will provide to the other party a statement (1) showing, in reasonable detail, such calculations (including all relevant quotations and specifying any amount payable under Section 6(e)) and (2) giving details of the relevant account to which any amount payable to it is to be paid. In the absence of written confirmation from the source of a quotation obtained in determining a Market Quotation, the records of the party obtaining such quotation will be conclusive evidence of the existence and accuracy of such quotation.

(ii) ***Payment Date.*** An amount calculated as being due in respect of any Early Termination Date under Section 6(e) will be payable on the day that notice of the amount payable is effective (in the case of an Early Termination Date which is designated or occurs as a result of an Event of Default) and on the day which is two Local Business Days after the day on which notice of the amount payable is effective (in the case of an Early Termination Date which is designated as a result of a Termination Event). Such amount will be paid together with (to the extent permitted under applicable law) interest thereon (before as well as after judgment) in the Termination Currency, from (and including) the relevant Early Termination Date to (but excluding) the date such amount is paid, at the Applicable Rate. Such interest will be calculated on the basis of daily compounding and the actual number of days elapsed.

(e) ***Payments on Early Termination.*** If an Early Termination Date occurs, the following provisions shall apply based on the parties' election in the Schedule of a payment measure, either "Market Quotation" or "Loss", and a payment method, either the "First Method" or the "Second Method". If the parties fail to designate a payment measure or payment method in the Schedule, it will be deemed that "Market Quotation" or the "Second Method", as the case may be, shall apply. The amount, if any, payable in respect of an Early Termination Date and determined pursuant to this Section will be subject to any Set-off.

(i) ***Events of Default.*** If the Early Termination Date results from an Event of Default:—

(1) *First Method and Market Quotation.* If the First Method and Market Quotation apply, the Defaulting Party will pay to the Non-defaulting Party the excess, if a positive number, of (A) the sum of the Settlement Amount (determined by the Non-defaulting Party) in respect of the Terminated Transactions and the Termination Currency Equivalent of the Unpaid Amounts owing to the Non-defaulting Party over (B) the Termination Currency Equivalent of the Unpaid Amounts owing to the Defaulting Party.

(2) *First Method and Loss.* If the First Method and Loss apply, the Defaulting Party will pay to the Non-defaulting Party, if a positive number, the Non-defaulting Party's Loss in respect of this Agreement.

(3) *Second Method and Market Quotation.* If the Second Method and Market Quotation apply, an amount will be payable equal to (A) the sum of the Settlement Amount (determined by the

Non-defaulting Party) in respect of the Terminated Transactions and the Termination Currency Equivalent of the Unpaid Amounts owing to the Non-defaulting Party less (B) the Termination Currency Equivalent of the Unpaid Amounts owing to the Defaulting Party. If that amount is a positive number, the Defaulting Party will pay it to the Non-defaulting Party; if it is a negative number, the Non-defaulting Party will pay the absolute value of that amount to the Defaulting Party.

(4) *Second Method and Loss.* If the Second Method and Loss apply, an amount will be payable equal to the Non-defaulting Party's Loss in respect of this Agreement. If that amount is a positive number, the Defaulting Party will pay it to the Non-defaulting Party; if it is a negative number, the Non-defaulting Party will pay the absolute value of that amount to the Defaulting Party.

(ii) ***Termination Events.*** If the Early Termination Date results from a Termination Event:—

(1) *One Affected Party.* If there is one Affected Party, the amount payable will be determined in accordance with Section 6(e)(i)(3), if Market Quotation applies, or Section 6(e)(i)(4), if Loss applies, except that, in either case, references to the Defaulting Party and to the Non-defaulting Party will be deemed to be references to the Affected Party and the party which is not the Affected Party, respectively, and, if Loss applies and fewer than all the Transactions are being terminated, Loss shall be calculated in respect of all Terminated Transactions.

(2) *Two Affected Parties.* If there are two Affected Parties:—

(A) if Market Quotation applies, each party will determine a Settlement Amount in respect of the Terminated Transactions, and an amount will be payable equal to (I) the sum of (a) one-half of the difference between the Settlement Amount of the party with the higher Settlement Amount ("X") and the Settlement Amount of the party with the lower Settlement Amount ("Y") and (b) the Termination Currency Equivalent of the Unpaid Amounts owing to X less (II) the Termination Currency Equivalent of the Unpaid Amounts owing to Y; and

(B) if Loss applies, each party will determine its Loss in respect of this Agreement (or, if fewer than all the Transactions are being terminated, in respect of all Terminated Transactions) and an amount will be payable equal to one-half of the difference between the Loss of the party with the higher Loss ("X") and the Loss of the party with the lower Loss ("Y").

If the amount payable is a positive number, Y will pay it to X; if it is a negative number, X will pay the absolute value of that amount to Y.

(iii) ***Adjustment for Bankruptcy.*** In circumstances where an Early Termination Date occurs because "Automatic Early Termination" applies in respect of a party, the amount determined under this Section 6(e) will be subject to such adjustments as are appropriate and permitted by law to reflect any payments or deliveries made by one party to the other under this Agreement (and retained by such other party) during the period from the relevant Early Termination Date to the date for payment determined under Section 6(d)(ii).

(iv) ***Pre-Estimate.*** The parties agree that if Market Quotation applies an amount recoverable under this Section 6(e) is a reasonable pre-estimate of loss and not a penalty. Such amount is payable for the loss of bargain and the loss of protection against future risks and except as otherwise provided in this Agreement neither party will be entitled to recover any additional damages as a consequence of such losses.

7. Transfer

Subject to Section 6(b)(ii), neither this Agreement nor any interest or obligation in or under this Agreement may be transferred (whether by way of security or otherwise) by either party without the prior written consent of the other party, except that:—

(a) a party may make such a transfer of this Agreement pursuant to a consolidation or amalgamation with, or merger with or into, or transfer of all or substantially all its assets to, another entity (but without prejudice to any other right or remedy under this Agreement); and

(b) a party may make such a transfer of all or any part of its interest in any amount payable to it from a Defaulting Party under Section 6(e).

Any purported transfer that is not in compliance with this Section will be void.

8. Contractual Currency

(a) ***Payment in the Contractual Currency.*** Each payment under this Agreement will be made in the relevant currency specified in this Agreement for that payment (the "Contractual Currency"). To the extent permitted by applicable law, any obligation to make payments under this Agreement in the Contractual Currency will not be discharged or satisfied by any tender in any currency other than the Contractual Currency, except to the extent such tender results in the actual receipt by the party to which payment is owed, acting in a reasonable manner and in good faith in converting the currency so tendered into the Contractual Currency, of the full amount in the Contractual Currency of all amounts payable in respect of this Agreement. If for any reason the amount in the Contractual Currency so received falls short of the amount in the Contractual Currency payable in respect of this Agreement, the party required to make the payment will, to the extent permitted by applicable law, immediately pay such additional amount in the Contractual Currency as may be necessary to compensate for the shortfall. If for any reason the amount in the Contractual Currency so received exceeds the amount in the Contractual Currency payable in respect of this Agreement, the party receiving the payment will refund promptly the amount of such excess.

(b) ***Judgments.*** To the extent permitted by applicable law, if any judgment or order expressed in a currency other than the Contractual Currency is rendered (i) for the payment of any amount owing in respect of this Agreement, (ii) for the payment of any amount relating to any early termination in respect of this Agreement or (iii) in respect of a judgment or order of another court for the payment of any amount described in (i) or (ii) above, the party seeking recovery, after recovery in full of the aggregate amount to which such party is entitled pursuant to the judgment or order, will be entitled to receive immediately from the other party the amount of any shortfall of the Contractual Currency received by such party as a consequence of sums paid in such other currency and will refund promptly to the other party any excess of the Contractual Currency received by such party as a consequence of sums paid in such other currency if such shortfall or such excess arises or results from any variation between the rate of exchange at which the Contractual Currency is converted into the currency of the judgment or order for the purposes of such judgment or order and the rate of exchange at which such party is able, acting in a reasonable manner and in good faith in converting the currency received into the Contractual Currency, to purchase the Contractual Currency with the amount of the currency of the judgment or order actually received by such party. The term "rate of exchange" includes, without limitation, any premiums and costs of exchange payable in connection with the purchase of or conversion into the Contractual Currency.

(c) ***Separate Indemnities.*** To the extent permitted by applicable law, these indemnities constitute separate and independent obligations from the other obligations in this Agreement, will be enforceable as separate and independent causes of action, will apply notwithstanding any indulgence granted by the party to which any payment is owed and will not be affected by judgment being obtained or claim or proof being made for any other sums payable in respect of this Agreement.

(d) ***Evidence of Loss.*** For the purpose of this Section 8, it will be sufficient for a party to demonstrate that it would have suffered a loss had an actual exchange or purchase been made.

9. Miscellaneous

(a) ***Entire Agreement.*** This Agreement constitutes the entire agreement and understanding of the parties with respect to its subject matter and supersedes all oral communication and prior writings with respect thereto.

(b) ***Amendments.*** No amendment, modification or waiver in respect of this Agreement will be effective unless in writing (including a writing evidenced by a facsimile transmission) and executed by each of the parties or confirmed by an exchange of telexes or electronic messages on an electronic messaging system.

(c) ***Survival of Obligations.*** Without prejudice to Sections 2(a)(iii) and 6(c)(ii), the obligations of the parties under this Agreement will survive the termination of any Transaction.

(d) ***Remedies Cumulative.*** Except as provided in this Agreement, the rights, powers, remedies and privileges provided in this Agreement are cumulative and not exclusive of any rights, powers, remedies and privileges provided by law.

(e) ***Counterparts and Confirmations.***

(i) This Agreement (and each amendment, modification and waiver in respect of it) may be executed and delivered in counterparts (including by facsimile transmission), each of which will be deemed an original.

(ii) The parties intend that they are legally bound by the terms of each Transaction from the moment they agree to those terms (whether orally or otherwise). A Confirmation shall be entered into as soon as practicable and may be executed and delivered in counterparts (including by facsimile transmission) or be created by an exchange of telexes or by an exchange of electronic messages on an electronic messaging system, which in each case will be sufficient for all purposes to evidence a binding supplement to this Agreement. The parties will specify therein or through another effective means that any such counterpart, telex or electronic message constitutes a Confirmation.

(f) ***No Waiver of Rights.*** A failure or delay in exercising any right, power or privilege in respect of this Agreement will not be presumed to operate as a waiver, and a single or partial exercise of any right, power or privilege will not be presumed to preclude any subsequent or further exercise, of that right, power or privilege or the exercise of any other right, power or privilege.

(g) ***Headings.*** The headings used in this Agreement are for convenience of reference only and are not to affect the construction of or to be taken into consideration in interpreting this Agreement.

10. Offices; Multibranch Parties

(a) If Section 10(a) is specified in the Schedule as applying, each party that enters into a Transaction through an Office other than its head or home office represents to the other party that, notwithstanding the place of booking office or jurisdiction of incorporation or organisation of such party, the obligations of such party are the same as if it had entered into the Transaction through its head or home office. This representation will be deemed to be repeated by such party on each date on which a Transaction is entered into.

(b) Neither party may change the Office through which it makes and receives payments or deliveries for the purpose of a Transaction without the prior written consent of the other party.

(c) If a party is specified as a Multibranch Party in the Schedule, such Multibranch Party may make and receive payments or deliveries under any Transaction through any Office listed in the Schedule, and the Office through which it makes and receives payments or deliveries with respect to a Transaction will be specified in the relevant Confirmation.

11. Expenses

A Defaulting Party will, on demand, indemnify and hold harmless the other party for and against all reasonable out-of-pocket expenses, including legal fees and Stamp Tax, incurred by such other party by reason of the enforcement and protection of its rights under this Agreement or any Credit Support Document to which the Defaulting Party is a party or by reason of the early termination of any Transaction, including, but not limited to, costs of collection.

12. Notices

(a) ***Effectiveness.*** Any notice or other communication in respect of this Agreement may be given in any manner set forth below (except that a notice or other communication under Section 5 or 6 may not be given by facsimile transmission or electronic messaging system) to the address or number or in accordance with the electronic messaging system details provided (see the Schedule) and will be deemed effective as indicated:—

(i) if in writing and delivered in person or by courier, on the date it is delivered;

(ii) if sent by telex, on the date the recipient's answerback is received;

(iii) if sent by facsimile transmission, on the date that transmission is received by a responsible employee of the recipient in legible form (it being agreed that the burden of proving receipt will be on the sender and will not be met by a transmission report generated by the sender's facsimile machine);

(iv) if sent by certified or registered mail (airmail, if overseas) or the equivalent (return receipt requested), on the date that mail is delivered or its delivery is attempted; or

(v) if sent by electronic messaging system, on the date that electronic message is received,

unless the date of that delivery (or attempted delivery) or that receipt, as applicable, is not a Local Business Day or that communication is delivered (or attempted) or received, as applicable, after the close of business on a Local Business Day, in which case that communication shall be deemed given and effective on the first following day that is a Local Business Day.

(b) ***Change of Addresses.*** Either party may by notice to the other change the address, telex or facsimile number or electronic messaging system details at which notices or other communications are to be given to it.

13. Governing Law and Jurisdiction

(a) ***Governing Law.*** This Agreement will be governed by and construed in accordance with the law specified in the Schedule.

(b) ***Jurisdiction.*** With respect to any suit, action or proceedings relating to this Agreement ("Proceedings"), each party irrevocably:—

(i) submits to the jurisdiction of the English courts, if this Agreement is expressed to be governed by English law, or to the non-exclusive jurisdiction of the courts of the State of New York and the United States District Court located in the Borough of Manhattan in New York City, if this Agreement is expressed to be governed by the laws of the State of New York; and

(ii) waives any objection which it may have at any time to the laying of venue of any Proceedings brought in any such court, waives any claim that such Proceedings have been brought in an inconvenient forum and further waives the right to object, with respect to such Proceedings, that such court does not have any jurisdiction over such party.

Nothing in this Agreement precludes either party from bringing Proceedings in any other jurisdiction (outside, if this Agreement is expressed to be governed by English law, the Contracting States, as defined in Section 1(3) of the Civil Jurisdiction and Judgments Act 1982 or any modification, extension or re-enactment thereof for the time being in force) nor will the bringing of Proceedings in any one or more jurisdictions preclude the bringing of Proceedings in any other jurisdiction.

(c) ***Service of Process.*** Each party irrevocably appoints the Process Agent (if any) specified opposite its name in the Schedule to receive, for it and on its behalf, service of process in any Proceedings. If for any reason any party's Process Agent is unable to act as such, such party will promptly notify the other party and within 30 days appoint a substitute process agent acceptable to the other party. The parties irrevocably consent to service of process given in the manner provided for notices in Section 12. Nothing in this Agreement will affect the right of either party to serve process in any other manner permitted by law.

(d) ***Waiver of Immunities.*** Each party irrevocably waives, to the fullest extent permitted by applicable law, with respect to itself and its revenues and assets (irrespective of their use or intended use), all immunity on the grounds of sovereignty or other similar grounds from (i) suit, (ii) jurisdiction of any court, (iii) relief by way of injunction, order for specific performance or for recovery of property, (iv) attachment of its assets (whether before or after judgment) and (v) execution or enforcement of any judgment to which it or its revenues or assets might otherwise be entitled in any Proceedings in the courts of any jurisdiction and irrevocably agrees, to the extent permitted by applicable law, that it will not claim any such immunity in any Proceedings.

14. Definitions

As used in this Agreement:—

"Additional Termination Event" has the meaning specified in Section 5(b).

"Affected Party" has the meaning specified in Section 5(b).

"Affected Transactions" means (a) with respect to any Termination Event consisting of an Illegality, Tax Event or Tax Event Upon Merger, all Transactions affected by the occurrence of such Termination Event and (b) with respect to any other Termination Event, all Transactions.

"Affiliate" means, subject to the Schedule, in relation to any person, any entity controlled, directly or indirectly, by the person, any entity that controls, directly or indirectly, the person or any entity directly or indirectly under common control with the person. For this purpose, "control" of any entity or person means ownership of a majority of the voting power of the entity or person.

"Applicable Rate" means:—

(a) in respect of obligations payable or deliverable (or which would have been but for Section 2(a)(iii)) by a Defaulting Party, the Default Rate;

(b) in respect of an obligation to pay an amount under Section 6(e) of either party from and after the date (determined in accordance with Section 6(d)(ii)) on which that amount is payable, the Default Rate;

(c) in respect of all other obligations payable or deliverable (or which would have been but for Section 2(a)(iii)) by a Non-defaulting Party, the Non-default Rate; and

(d) in all other cases, the Termination Rate.

"Burdened Party" has the meaning specified in Section 5(b).

"Change in Tax Law" means the enactment, promulgation, execution or ratification of, or any change in or amendment to, any law (or in the application or official interpretation of any law) that occurs on or after the date on which the relevant Transaction is entered into.

"consent" includes a consent, approval, action, authorisation, exemption, notice, filing, registration or exchange control consent.

"Credit Event Upon Merger" has the meaning specified in Section 5(b).

"Credit Support Document" means any agreement or instrument that is specified as such in this Agreement.

"Credit Support Provider" has the meaning specified in the Schedule.

"Default Rate" means a rate per annum equal to the cost (without proof or evidence of any actual cost) to the relevant payee (as certified by it) if it were to fund or of funding the relevant amount plus 1% per annum.

"Defaulting Party" has the meaning specified in Section 6(a).

"Early Termination Date" means the date determined in accordance with Section 6(a) or 6(b)(iv).

"Event of Default" has the meaning specified in Section 5(a) and, if applicable, in the Schedule.

"Illegality" has the meaning specified in Section 5(b).

"Indemnifiable Tax" means any Tax other than a Tax that would not be imposed in respect of a payment under this Agreement but for a present or former connection between the jurisdiction of the government or taxation authority imposing such Tax and the recipient of such payment or a person related to such recipient (including, without limitation, a connection arising from such recipient or related person being or having been a citizen or resident of such jurisdiction, or being or having been organised, present or engaged in a trade or business in such jurisdiction, or having or having had a permanent establishment or fixed place of business in such jurisdiction, but excluding a connection arising solely from such recipient or related person having executed, delivered, performed its obligations or received a payment under, or enforced, this Agreement or a Credit Support Document).

"law" includes any treaty, law, rule or regulation (as modified, in the case of tax matters, by the practice of any relevant governmental revenue authority) and ***"lawful"*** and ***"unlawful"*** will be construed accordingly.

"Local Business Day" means, subject to the Schedule, a day on which commercial banks are open for business (including dealings in foreign exchange and foreign currency deposits) (a) in relation to any obligation under Section 2(a)(i), in the place(s) specified in the relevant Confirmation or, if not so specified, as otherwise agreed by the parties in writing or determined pursuant to provisions contained, or incorporated by reference, in this Agreement, (b) in relation to any other payment, in the place where the relevant account is located and, if different, in the principal financial centre, if any, of the currency of such payment, (c) in relation to any notice or other communication, including notice contemplated under Section 5(a)(i), in the city specified in the address for notice provided by the recipient and, in the case of a notice contemplated by Section 2(b), in the place where the relevant new account is to be located and (d) in relation to Section 5(a)(v)(2), in the relevant locations for performance with respect to such Specified Transaction.

"Loss" means, with respect to this Agreement or one or more Terminated Transactions, as the case may be, and a party, the Termination Currency Equivalent of an amount that party reasonably determines in good faith to be its total losses and costs (or gain, in which case expressed as a negative number) in connection with this Agreement or that Terminated Transaction or group of Terminated Transactions, as the case may be, including any loss of bargain, cost of funding or, at the election of such party but without duplication, loss or cost incurred as a result of its terminating, liquidating, obtaining or reestablishing any hedge or related trading position (or any gain resulting from any of them). Loss includes losses and costs (or gains) in respect of any payment or delivery required to have been made (assuming satisfaction of each applicable condition precedent) on or before the relevant Early Termination Date and not made, except, so as to avoid duplication, if Section 6(e)(i)(1) or (3) or 6(e)(ii)(2)(A) applies. Loss does not include a party's legal fees and out-of-pocket expenses referred to under Section 11. A party will determine its Loss as of the relevant Early Termination Date, or, if that is not reasonably practicable, as of the earliest date thereafter as is reasonably practicable. A party may (but need not) determine its Loss by reference to quotations of relevant rates or prices from one or more leading dealers in the relevant markets.

"Market Quotation" means, with respect to one or more Terminated Transactions and a party making the determination, an amount determined on the basis of quotations from Reference Market-makers. Each quotation will be for an amount, if any, that would be paid to such party (expressed as a negative number) or by such party (expressed as a positive number) in consideration of an agreement between such party (taking into account any existing Credit Support Document with respect to the obligations of such party) and the quoting Reference Market-maker to enter into a transaction (the "Replacement Transaction") that would have the effect of preserving for such party the economic equivalent of any payment or delivery (whether the underlying obligation was absolute or contingent and assuming the satisfaction of each applicable condition precedent) by the parties under Section 2(a)(i) in respect of such Terminated Transaction or group of Terminated Transactions that would, but for the occurrence of the relevant Early Termination Date, have been required after that date. For this purpose, Unpaid Amounts in respect of the Terminated Transaction or group of Terminated Transactions are to be excluded but, without limitation, any payment or delivery that would, but for the relevant Early Termination Date, have been required (assuming satisfaction of each applicable condition precedent) after that Early Termination Date is to be included. The Replacement Transaction would be subject to such documentation as such party and the Reference Market-maker may, in good faith, agree. The party making the determination (or its agent) will request each Reference Market-maker to provide its quotation to the extent reasonably practicable as of the same day and time (without regard to different time zones) on or as soon as reasonably practicable after the relevant Early Termination Date. The day and time as of which those quotations are to be obtained will be selected in good faith by the party obliged to make a determination under Section 6(e), and, if each party is so obliged, after consultation with the other. If more than three quotations are provided, the Market Quotation will be the arithmetic mean of the quotations, without regard to the quotations having the highest and lowest values. If exactly three such quotations are provided, the Market Quotation will be the quotation remaining after disregarding the highest and lowest quotations. For this purpose, if more than one quotation has the same highest value or lowest value, then one of such quotations shall be disregarded. If fewer than three quotations are provided, it will be deemed that the Market Quotation in respect of such Terminated Transaction or group of Terminated Transactions cannot be determined.

"Non-default Rate" means a rate per annum equal to the cost (without proof or evidence of any actual cost) to the Non-defaulting Party (as certified by it) if it were to fund the relevant amount.

"Non-defaulting Party" has the meaning specified in Section 6(a).

"Office" means a branch or office of a party, which may be such party's head or home office.

"Potential Event of Default" means any event which, with the giving of notice or the lapse of time or both, would constitute an Event of Default.

"Reference Market-makers" means four leading dealers in the relevant market selected by the party determining a Market Quotation in good faith (a) from among dealers of the highest credit standing which satisfy all the criteria that such party applies generally at the time in deciding whether to offer or to make an extension of credit and (b) to the extent practicable, from among such dealers having an office in the same city.

"Relevant Jurisdiction" means, with respect to a party, the jurisdictions (a) in which the party is incorporated, organised, managed and controlled or considered to have its seat, (b) where an Office through which the party is acting for purposes of this Agreement is located, (c) in which the party executes this Agreement and (d) in relation to any payment, from or through which such payment is made.

"Scheduled Payment Date" means a date on which a payment or delivery is to be made under Section 2(a)(i) with respect to a Transaction.

"Set-off" means set-off, offset, combination of accounts, right of retention or withholding or similar right or requirement to which the payer of an amount under Section 6 is entitled or subject (whether arising under this Agreement, another contract, applicable law or otherwise) that is exercised by, or imposed on, such payer.

"Settlement Amount" means, with respect to a party and any Early Termination Date, the sum of:—

(a) the Termination Currency Equivalent of the Market Quotations (whether positive or negative) for each Terminated Transaction or group of Terminated Transactions for which a Market Quotation is determined; and

(b) such party's Loss (whether positive or negative and without reference to any Unpaid Amounts) for each Terminated Transaction or group of Terminated Transactions for which a Market Quotation cannot be determined or would not (in the reasonable belief of the party making the determination) produce a commercially reasonable result.

"Specified Entity" has the meaning specified in the Schedule.

"Specified Indebtedness" means, subject to the Schedule, any obligation (whether present or future, contingent or otherwise, as principal or surety or otherwise) in respect of borrowed money.

"Specified Transaction" means, subject to the Schedule, (a) any transaction (including an agreement with respect thereto) now existing or hereafter entered into between one party to this Agreement (or any Credit Support Provider of such party or any applicable Specified Entity of such party) and the other party to this Agreement (or any Credit Support Provider of such other party or any applicable Specified Entity of such other party) which is a rate swap transaction, basis swap, forward rate transaction, commodity swap, commodity option, equity or equity index swap, equity or equity index option, bond option, interest rate option, foreign exchange transaction, cap transaction, floor transaction, collar transaction, currency swap transaction, cross-currency rate swap transaction, currency option or any other similar transaction (including any option with respect to any of these transactions), (b) any combination of these transactions and (c) any other transaction identified as a Specified Transaction in this Agreement or the relevant confirmation.

"Stamp Tax" means any stamp, registration, documentation or similar tax.

"Tax" means any present or future tax, levy, impost, duty, charge, assessment or fee of any nature (including interest, penalties and additions thereto) that is imposed by any government or other taxing authority in respect of any payment under this Agreement other than a stamp, registration, documentation or similar tax.

"Tax Event" has the meaning specified in Section 5(b).

"Tax Event Upon Merger" has the meaning specified in Section 5(b).

"Terminated Transactions" means with respect to any Early Termination Date (a) if resulting from a Termination Event, all Affected Transactions and (b) if resulting from an Event of Default, all Transactions (in either case) in effect immediately before the effectiveness of the notice designating that Early Termination Date (or, if "Automatic Early Termination" applies, immediately before that Early Termination Date).

"Termination Currency" has the meaning specified in the Schedule.

"Termination Currency Equivalent" means, in respect of any amount denominated in the Termination Currency, such Termination Currency amount and, in respect of any amount denominated in a currency other than the Termination Currency (the "Other Currency"), the amount in the Termination Currency determined by the party making the relevant determination as being required to purchase such amount of such Other Currency as at the relevant Early Termination Date, or, if the relevant Market Quotation or Loss (as the case may be), is determined as of a later date, that later date, with the Termination Currency at the rate equal to the spot exchange rate of the foreign exchange agent (selected as provided below) for the purchase of such Other Currency with the Termination Currency at or about 11:00 a.m. (in the city in which such foreign exchange agent is located) on such date as would be customary for the determination of such a rate for the purchase of such Other Currency for value on the relevant Early Termination Date or that later date. The foreign exchange agent will, if only one party is obliged to make a determination under Section 6(e), be selected in good faith by that party and otherwise will be agreed by the parties.

"Termination Event" means an Illegality, a Tax Event or a Tax Event Upon Merger or, if specified to be applicable, a Credit Event Upon Merger or an Additional Termination Event.

"Termination Rate" means a rate per annum equal to the arithmetic mean of the cost (without proof or evidence of any actual cost) to each party (as certified by such party) if it were to fund or of funding such amounts.

"Unpaid Amounts" owing to any party means, with respect to an Early Termination Date, the aggregate of (a) in respect of all Terminated Transactions, the amounts that became payable (or that would have become payable but for Section 2(a)(iii)) to such party under Section 2(a)(i) on or prior to such Early Termination Date and which remain unpaid as at such Early Termination Date and (b) in respect of each Terminated Transaction, for each obligation under Section 2(a)(i) which was (or would have been but for Section 2(a)(iii)) required to be settled by delivery to such party on or prior to such Early Termination Date and which has not been so settled as at such Early Termination Date, an amount equal to the fair market value of that which was (or would have been) required to be delivered as of the originally scheduled date for delivery, in each case together with (to the extent permitted under applicable law) interest, in the currency of such amounts, from (and including) the date such amounts or obligations were or would have been required to have been paid or performed to (but excluding) such Early Termination Date, at the Applicable Rate. Such amounts of interest will be calculated on the basis of daily compounding and the actual number of days elapsed. The fair market value of any obligation referred to in clause (b) above shall be reasonably determined by the party obliged to make the determination under Section 6(e) or, if each party is so obliged, it shall be the average of the Termination Currency Equivalents of the fair market values reasonably determined by both parties.

IN WITNESS WHEREOF the parties have executed this document on the respective dates specified below with effect from the date specified on the first page of this document.

....	....
(Name of Party)	(Name of Party)
By:	By: ....
Name:	Name:
Title:	Title:
Date:	Date:

(Multicurrency—Cross Border)

ISDA®

International Swap Dealers Association, Inc.

SCHEDULE
to the
Master Agreement

dated as of ....

between .... and ....
("Party A") ("Party B")

Part 1. **Termination Provisions.**

(a) ***"Specified Entity"*** means in relation to Party A for the purpose of:—

Section 5(a)(v), ...

Section 5(a)(vi), ...

Section 5(a)(vii), ...

Section 5(b)(iv), ...

and in relation to Party B for the purpose of:—

Section 5(a)(v), ...

Section 5(a)(vi), ...

Section 5(a)(vii), ...

Section 5(b)(iv), ...

(b) ***"Specified Transaction"*** will have the meaning specified in Section 14 of this Agreement unless another meaning is specified here. ....

....

....

(c) The ***"Cross Default"*** provisions of Section 5(a)(vi) will/will not * apply to Party A
will/will not * apply to Party B

If such provisions apply:—

"Specified Indebtedness" will have the meaning specified in Section 14 of this Agreement unless another meaning is specified here ....

....

* Delete as applicable.

"Threshold Amount" means ....

....

(d) The *"Credit Event Upon Merger"* provisions of Section 5(b)(iv) will/will not * apply to Party A
will/will not * apply to Party B

(e) The *"Automatic Early Termination"* provision of Section 6(a) will/will not * apply to Party A
will/will not * apply to Party B

(f) *Payments on Early Termination.* For the purpose of Section 6(e) of this Agreement:—

(i) Market Quotation/Loss * will apply.

(ii) The First Method/The Second Method * will apply.

(g) *"Termination Currency"* means ...., if such currency is specified and freely available, and otherwise United States Dollars.

(h) *Additional Termination Event* will/will not apply*. The following shall constitute an Additional

Termination Event:— ....

....

....

....

....

....

For the purpose of the foregoing Termination Event, the Affected Party or Affected Parties shall be:— ..

....

Part 2. **Tax Representations.**

(a) *Payer Representations.* For the purpose of Section 3(e) of this Agreement, Party A will/will not* make the following representation and Party B will/will not* make the following representation:—

It is not required by any applicable law, as modified by the practice of any relevant governmental revenue authority, of any Relevant Jurisdiction to make any deduction or withholding for or on account of any Tax from any payment (other than interest under Section 2(e), 6(d)(ii) or 6(e) of this Agreement) to be made by it to the other party under this Agreement. In making this representation, it may rely on (i) the accuracy of any representations made by the other party pursuant to Section 3(f) of this Agreement, (ii) the satisfaction of the agreement contained in Section 4(a)(i) or 4(a)(iii) of this Agreement and the accuracy and effectiveness of any document provided by the other party pursuant to Section 4(a)(i) or 4(a)(iii) of this Agreement and (iii) the satisfaction of the agreement of the other party contained in Section 4(d) of this Agreement, *provided* that it shall not be a breach of this representation where reliance is placed on clause (ii) and the other party does not deliver a form or document under Section 4(a)(iii) by reason of material prejudice to its legal or commercial position.

(b) *Payee Representations.* For the purpose of Section 3(f) of this Agreement, Party A and Party B make the representations specified below, if any:

(i) The following representation will/will not* apply to Party A and will/will not* apply to Party B:—

It is fully eligible for the benefits of the "Business Profits" or "Industrial and Commercial Profits" provision, as the case may be, the "Interest" provision or the "Other Income" provision (if any) of the Specified Treaty with respect to any payment described in such provisions and received or to be received

* Delete as applicable.

by it in connection with this Agreement and no such payment is attributable to a trade or business carried on by it through a permanent establishment in the Specified Jurisdiction.

If such representation applies, then:—

"Specified Treaty" means with respect to Party A ....

"Specified Jurisdiction" means with respect to Party A ....

"Specified Treaty" means with respect to Party B ....

"Specified Jurisdiction" means with respect to Party B ....

(ii) The following representation will/will not* apply to Party A and will/will not* apply to Party B:—

Each payment received or to be received by it in connection with this Agreement will be effectively connected with its conduct of a trade or business in the Specified Jurisdiction.

If such representation applies, then:—

"Specified Jurisdiction" means with respect to Party A ....

"Specified Jurisdiction" means with respect to Party B ....

(iii) The following representation will/will not* apply to Party A and will/will not* apply to Party B:—

(A) It is entering into each Transaction in the ordinary course of its trade as, and is, either (1) a recognised U.K. bank or (2) a recognised U.K. swaps dealer (in either case (1) or (2), for purposes of the United Kingdom Inland Revenue extra statutory concession C17 on interest and currency swaps dated March 14, 1989), and (B) it will bring into account payments made and received in respect of each Transaction in computing its income for United Kingdom tax purposes.

(iv) Other Payee Representations:— ....

....

....

....

N.B. The above representations may need modification if either party is a Multibranch Party.

* Delete as applicable.

Part 3. **Agreement to Deliver Documents.**

For the purpose of Sections 4(a)(i) and (ii) of this Agreement, each party agrees to deliver the following documents, as applicable:—

(a) Tax forms, documents or certificates to be delivered are:—

Party required to deliver document	Form/Document/ Certificate	Date by which to be delivered
....	....	....
....	....	....
....	....	....
....	....	....
....	....	....

(b) Other documents to be delivered are:—

Party required to deliver document	Form/Document/ Certificate	Date by which to be delivered	Covered by Section 3(d) Representation
....	....	....	Yes/No*
....	....	....	Yes/No*
....	....	....	Yes/No*
....	....	....	Yes/No*
....	....	....	Yes/No*

Part 4. **Miscellaneous.**

(a) ***Addresses for Notices.*** For the purpose of Section 12(a) of this Agreement:—

Address for notices or communications to Party A:—

Address: ....

Attention: ....

Telex No.: .... Answerback: ....

Facsimile No.: .... Telephone No.: ....

Electronic Messaging System Details: ....

Address for notices or communications to Party B:—

Address: ....

Attention: ....

Telex No.: .... Answerback: ....

* Delete as applicable.

Facsimile No.: .... Telephone No.: ....

Electronic Messaging System Details: ....

(b) ***Process Agent.*** For the purpose of Section 13(c) of this Agreement:—

Party A appoints as its Process Agent ....

Party B appoints as its Process Agent ....

(c) ***Offices.*** The provisions of Section 10(a) will/will not* apply to this Agreement.

(d) ***Multibranch Party.*** For the purpose of Section 10(c) of this Agreement:—

Party A is/is not* a Multibranch Party and, if so, may act through the following Offices:—

....

....

Party B is/is not* a Multibranch Party and, if so, may act through the following Offices:—

....

....

(e) ***Calculation Agent.*** The Calculation Agent is ...., unless otherwise specified in a Confirmation in relation to the relevant Transaction.

(f) ***Credit Support Document.*** Details of any Credit Support Document:— ....

....

....

....

(g) ***Credit Support Provider.*** Credit Support Provider means in relation to Party A, ...

....

....

Credit Support Provider means in relation to Party B, ...

....

....

(h) ***Governing Law.*** This Agreement will be governed by and construed in accordance with English law/the laws of the State of New York (without reference to choice of law doctrine) *.

---

* Delete as applicable.

(i) ***Netting of Payments.*** Subparagraph (ii) of Section 2(c) of this Agreement will not apply to the following Transactions or groups of Transactions (in each case starting from the date of this Agreement/in each case starting from .... *). ....
....
....

(j) ***"Affiliate"*** will have the meaning specified in Section 14 of this Agreement unless another meaning is specified here ....
....

Part 5. **Other Provisions.**

* Delete as applicable.

ANNEX 2 REPRODUCTION OF 2002 ISDA MASTER AGREEMENT

Please see copy of main text for example

ISDA®

International Swaps and Derivatives Association, Inc.

2002 MASTER AGREEMENT

dated as of ……………………………………………………………

…………………………………………………………………… and ……………………………………………………………………

have entered and/or anticipate entering into one or more transactions (each a "Transaction") that are or will be governed by this 2002 Master Agreement, which includes the schedule (the "Schedule"), and the documents and other confirming evidence (each a "Confirmation") exchanged between the parties or otherwise effective for the purpose of confirming or evidencing those Transactions. This 2002 Master Agreement and the Schedule are together referred to as this "Master Agreement".

Accordingly, the parties agree as follows:—

1. Interpretation

(a) ***Definitions.*** The terms defined in Section 14 and elsewhere in this Master Agreement will have the meanings therein specified for the purpose of this Master Agreement.

(b) ***Inconsistency.*** In the event of any inconsistency between the provisions of the Schedule and the other provisions of this Master Agreement, the Schedule will prevail. In the event of any inconsistency between the provisions of any Confirmation and this Master Agreement, such Confirmation will prevail for the purpose of the relevant Transaction.

(c) ***Single Agreement.*** All Transactions are entered into in reliance on the fact that this Master Agreement and all Confirmations form a single agreement between the parties (collectively referred to as this "Agreement"), and the parties would not otherwise enter into any Transactions.

2. Obligations

(a) ***General Conditions.***

(i) Each party will make each payment or delivery specified in each Confirmation to be made by it, subject to the other provisions of this Agreement.

(ii) Payments under this Agreement will be made on the due date for value on that date in the place of the account specified in the relevant Confirmation or otherwise pursuant to this Agreement, in freely transferable funds and in the manner customary for payments in the required currency. Where settlement is by delivery (that is, other than by payment), such delivery will be made for receipt on the due date in the manner customary for the relevant obligation unless otherwise specified in the relevant Confirmation or elsewhere in this Agreement.

(iii) Each obligation of each party under Section 2(a)(i) is subject to (1) the condition precedent that no Event of Default or Potential Event of Default with respect to the other party has occurred and is continuing, (2) the condition precedent that no Early Termination Date in respect of the relevant Transaction has occurred or been effectively designated and (3) each other condition specified in this Agreement to be a condition precedent for the purpose of this Section 2(a)(iii).

(b) ***Change of Account.*** Either party may change its account for receiving a payment or delivery by giving notice to the other party at least five Local Business Days prior to the Scheduled Settlement Date for the payment or delivery to which such change applies unless such other party gives timely notice of a reasonable objection to such change.

(c) ***Netting of Payments.*** If on any date amounts would otherwise be payable:—

(i) in the same currency; and

(ii) in respect of the same Transaction,

by each party to the other, then, on such date, each party's obligation to make payment of any such amount will be automatically satisfied and discharged and, if the aggregate amount that would otherwise have been payable by one party exceeds the aggregate amount that would otherwise have been payable by the other party, replaced by an obligation upon the party by which the larger aggregate amount would have been payable to pay to the other party the excess of the larger aggregate amount over the smaller aggregate amount.

The parties may elect in respect of two or more Transactions that a net amount and payment obligation will be determined in respect of all amounts payable on the same date in the same currency in respect of those Transactions, regardless of whether such amounts are payable in respect of the same Transaction. The election may be made in the Schedule or any Confirmation by specifying that "Multiple Transaction Payment Netting" applies to the Transactions identified as being subject to the election (in which case clause (ii) above will not apply to such Transactions). If Multiple Transaction Payment Netting is applicable to Transactions, it will apply to those Transactions with effect from the starting date specified in the Schedule or such Confirmation, or, if a starting date is not specified in the Schedule or such Confirmation, the starting date otherwise agreed by the parties in writing. This election may be made separately for different groups of Transactions and will apply separately to each pairing of Offices through which the parties make and receive payments or deliveries.

(d) ***Deduction or Withholding for Tax.***

(i) ***Gross-Up.*** All payments under this Agreement will be made without any deduction or withholding for or on account of any Tax unless such deduction or withholding is required by any applicable law, as modified by the practice of any relevant governmental revenue authority, then in effect. If a party is so required to deduct or withhold, then that party ("X") will:—

(1) promptly notify the other party ("Y") of such requirement;

(2) pay to the relevant authorities the full amount required to be deducted or withheld (including the full amount required to be deducted or withheld from any additional amount paid by X to Y under this Section 2(d)) promptly upon the earlier of determining that such deduction or withholding is required or receiving notice that such amount has been assessed against Y;

(3) promptly forward to Y an official receipt (or a certified copy), or other documentation reasonably acceptable to Y, evidencing such payment to such authorities; and

(4) if such Tax is an Indemnifiable Tax, pay to Y, in addition to the payment to which Y is otherwise entitled under this Agreement, such additional amount as is necessary to ensure that the net amount actually received by Y (free and clear of Indemnifiable Taxes, whether assessed against X or Y) will equal the full amount Y would have received had no such deduction or withholding been required. However, X will not be required to pay any additional amount to Y to the extent that it would not be required to be paid but for:—

(A) the failure by Y to comply with or perform any agreement contained in Section 4(a)(i), 4(a)(iii) or 4(d); or

(B) the failure of a representation made by Y pursuant to Section 3(f) to be accurate and true unless such failure would not have occurred but for (I) any action taken by a taxing authority, or brought in a court of competent jurisdiction, after a Transaction is entered into (regardless of whether such action is taken or brought with respect to a party to this Agreement) or (II) a Change in Tax Law.

(ii) ***Liability.*** If:—

(1) X is required by any applicable law, as modified by the practice of any relevant governmental revenue authority, to make any deduction or withholding in respect of which X would not be required to pay an additional amount to Y under Section 2(d)(i)(4);

(2) X does not so deduct or withhold; and

(3) a liability resulting from such Tax is assessed directly against X,

then, except to the extent Y has satisfied or then satisfies the liability resulting from such Tax, Y will promptly pay to X the amount of such liability (including any related liability for interest, but including any related liability for penalties only if Y has failed to comply with or perform any agreement contained in Section 4(a)(i), 4(a)(iii) or 4(d)).

3. Representations

Each party makes the representations contained in Sections 3(a), 3(b), 3(c), 3(d), 3(e) and 3(f) and, if specified in the Schedule as applying, 3(g) to the other party (which representations will be deemed to be repeated by each party on each date on which a Transaction is entered into and, in the case of the representations in Section 3(f), at all times until the termination of this Agreement). If any "Additional Representation" is specified in the Schedule or any Confirmation as applying, the party or parties specified for such Additional Representation will make and, if applicable, be deemed to repeat such Additional Representation at the time or times specified for such Additional Representation.

(a) ***Basic Representations.***

(i) ***Status.*** It is duly organised and validly existing under the laws of the jurisdiction of its organisation or incorporation and, if relevant under such laws, in good standing;

(ii) ***Powers.*** It has the power to execute this Agreement and any other documentation relating to this Agreement to which it is a party, to deliver this Agreement and any other documentation relating to this Agreement that it is required by this Agreement to deliver and to perform its obligations under this Agreement and any obligations it has under any Credit Support Document to which it is a party and has taken all necessary action to authorise such execution, delivery and performance;

(iii) *No Violation or Conflict.* Such execution, delivery and performance do not violate or conflict with any law applicable to it, any provision of its constitutional documents, any order or judgment of any court or other agency of government applicable to it or any of its assets or any contractual restriction binding on or affecting it or any of its assets;

(iv) *Consents.* All governmental and other consents that are required to have been obtained by it with respect to this Agreement or any Credit Support Document to which it is a party have been obtained and are in full force and effect and all conditions of any such consents have been complied with; and

(v) *Obligations Binding.* Its obligations under this Agreement and any Credit Support Document to which it is a party constitute its legal, valid and binding obligations, enforceable in accordance with their respective terms (subject to applicable bankruptcy, reorganisation, insolvency, moratorium or similar laws affecting creditors' rights generally and subject, as to enforceability, to equitable principles of general application (regardless of whether enforcement is sought in a proceeding in equity or at law)).

(b) *Absence of Certain Events.* No Event of Default or Potential Event of Default or, to its knowledge, Termination Event with respect to it has occurred and is continuing and no such event or circumstance would occur as a result of its entering into or performing its obligations under this Agreement or any Credit Support Document to which it is a party.

(c) *Absence of Litigation.* There is not pending or, to its knowledge, threatened against it, any of its Credit Support Providers or any of its applicable Specified Entities any action, suit or proceeding at law or in equity or before any court, tribunal, governmental body, agency or official or any arbitrator that is likely to affect the legality, validity or enforceability against it of this Agreement or any Credit Support Document to which it is a party or its ability to perform its obligations under this Agreement or such Credit Support Document.

(d) *Accuracy of Specified Information.* All applicable information that is furnished in writing by or on behalf of it to the other party and is identified for the purpose of this Section 3(d) in the Schedule is, as of the date of the information, true, accurate and complete in every material respect.

(e) *Payer Tax Representation.* Each representation specified in the Schedule as being made by it for the purpose of this Section 3(e) is accurate and true.

(f) *Payee Tax Representations.* Each representation specified in the Schedule as being made by it for the purpose of this Section 3(f) is accurate and true.

(g) *No Agency.* It is entering into this Agreement, including each Transaction, as principal and not as agent of any person or entity.

4. Agreements

Each party agrees with the other that, so long as either party has or may have any obligation under this Agreement or under any Credit Support Document to which it is a party:—

(a) *Furnish Specified Information.* It will deliver to the other party or, in certain cases under clause (iii) below, to such government or taxing authority as the other party reasonably directs:—

(i) any forms, documents or certificates relating to taxation specified in the Schedule or any Confirmation;

(ii) any other documents specified in the Schedule or any Confirmation; and

(iii) upon reasonable demand by such other party, any form or document that may be required or reasonably requested in writing in order to allow such other party or its Credit Support Provider to make a payment under this Agreement or any applicable Credit Support Document without any deduction or withholding for or on account of any Tax or with such deduction or withholding at a reduced rate (so long as the completion, execution or submission of such form or document would not materially prejudice the legal or commercial position of the party in receipt of such demand), with any such form or document to be accurate and completed in a manner reasonably satisfactory to such other party and to be executed and to be delivered with any reasonably required certification,

in each case by the date specified in the Schedule or such Confirmation or, if none is specified, as soon as reasonably practicable.

(b) ***Maintain Authorisations.*** It will use all reasonable efforts to maintain in full force and effect all consents of any governmental or other authority that are required to be obtained by it with respect to this Agreement or any Credit Support Document to which it is a party and will use all reasonable efforts to obtain any that may become necessary in the future.

(c) ***Comply With Laws.*** It will comply in all material respects with all applicable laws and orders to which it may be subject if failure so to comply would materially impair its ability to perform its obligations under this Agreement or any Credit Support Document to which it is a party.

(d) ***Tax Agreement.*** It will give notice of any failure of a representation made by it under Section 3(f) to be accurate and true promptly upon learning of such failure.

(e) ***Payment of Stamp Tax.*** Subject to Section 11, it will pay any Stamp Tax levied or imposed upon it or in respect of its execution or performance of this Agreement by a jurisdiction in which it is incorporated, organised, managed and controlled or considered to have its seat, or where an Office through which it is acting for the purpose of this Agreement is located ("Stamp Tax Jurisdiction"), and will indemnify the other party against any Stamp Tax levied or imposed upon the other party or in respect of the other party's execution or performance of this Agreement by any such Stamp Tax Jurisdiction which is not also a Stamp Tax Jurisdiction with respect to the other party.

5. Events of Default and Termination Events

(a) ***Events of Default.*** The occurrence at any time with respect to a party or, if applicable, any Credit Support Provider of such party or any Specified Entity of such party of any of the following events constitutes (subject to Sections 5(c) and 6(e)(iv)) an event of default (an "Event of Default") with respect to such party:—

(i) ***Failure to Pay or Deliver.*** Failure by the party to make, when due, any payment under this Agreement or delivery under Section 2(a)(i) or 9(h)(i)(2) or (4) required to be made by it if such failure is not remedied on or before the first Local Business Day in the case of any such payment or the first Local Delivery Day in the case of any such delivery after, in each case, notice of such failure is given to the party;

(ii) ***Breach of Agreement; Repudiation of Agreement.***

(1) Failure by the party to comply with or perform any agreement or obligation (other than an obligation to make any payment under this Agreement or delivery under Section 2(a)(i) or 9(h)(i)(2) or (4) or to give notice of a Termination Event or any agreement or obligation under Section 4(a)(i), 4(a)(iii) or 4(d)) to be complied with or performed by the party in accordance with this Agreement if such failure is not remedied within 30 days after notice of such failure is given to the party; or

(2) the party disaffirms, disclaims, repudiates or rejects, in whole or in part, or challenges the validity of, this Master Agreement, any Confirmation executed and delivered by that party or any

Transaction evidenced by such a Confirmation (or such action is taken by any person or entity appointed or empowered to operate it or act on its behalf);

(iii) ***Credit Support Default.***

(1) Failure by the party or any Credit Support Provider of such party to comply with or perform any agreement or obligation to be complied with or performed by it in accordance with any Credit Support Document if such failure is continuing after any applicable grace period has elapsed;

(2) the expiration or termination of such Credit Support Document or the failing or ceasing of such Credit Support Document, or any security interest granted by such party or such Credit Support Provider to the other party pursuant to any such Credit Support Document, to be in full force and effect for the purpose of this Agreement (in each case other than in accordance with its terms) prior to the satisfaction of all obligations of such party under each Transaction to which such Credit Support Document relates without the written consent of the other party; or

(3) the party or such Credit Support Provider disaffirms, disclaims, repudiates or rejects, in whole or in part, or challenges the validity of, such Credit Support Document (or such action is taken by any person or entity appointed or empowered to operate it or act on its behalf);

(iv) ***Misrepresentation.*** A representation (other than a representation under Section 3(e) or 3(f)) made or repeated or deemed to have been made or repeated by the party or any Credit Support Provider of such party in this Agreement or any Credit Support Document proves to have been incorrect or misleading in any material respect when made or repeated or deemed to have been made or repeated;

(v) ***Default Under Specified Transaction.*** The party, any Credit Support Provider of such party or any applicable Specified Entity of such party:—

(1) defaults (other than by failing to make a delivery) under a Specified Transaction or any credit support arrangement relating to a Specified Transaction and, after giving effect to any applicable notice requirement or grace period, such default results in a liquidation of, an acceleration of obligations under, or an early termination of, that Specified Transaction;

(2) defaults, after giving effect to any applicable notice requirement or grace period, in making any payment due on the last payment or exchange date of, or any payment on early termination of, a Specified Transaction (or, if there is no applicable notice requirement or grace period, such default continues for at least one Local Business Day);

(3) defaults in making any delivery due under (including any delivery due on the last delivery or exchange date of) a Specified Transaction or any credit support arrangement relating to a Specified Transaction and, after giving effect to any applicable notice requirement or grace period, such default results in a liquidation of, an acceleration of obligations under, or an early termination of, all transactions outstanding under the documentation applicable to that Specified Transaction; or

(4) disaffirms, disclaims, repudiates or rejects, in whole or in part, or challenges the validity of, a Specified Transaction or any credit support arrangement relating to a Specified Transaction that is, in either case, confirmed or evidenced by a document or other confirming evidence executed and delivered by that party, Credit Support Provider or Specified Entity (or such action is taken by any person or entity appointed or empowered to operate it or act on its behalf);

(vi) ***Cross-Default.*** If "Cross-Default" is specified in the Schedule as applying to the party, the occurrence or existence of:—

(1) a default, event of default or other similar condition or event (however described) in respect of such party, any Credit Support Provider of such party or any applicable Specified Entity of such party under one or more agreements or instruments relating to Specified Indebtedness of any of them (individually or collectively) where the aggregate principal amount of such agreements or instruments, either alone or together with the amount, if any, referred to in clause (2) below, is not less than the applicable Threshold Amount (as specified in the Schedule) which has resulted in such Specified Indebtedness becoming, or becoming capable at such time of being declared, due and payable under such agreements or instruments before it would otherwise have been due and payable; or

(2) a default by such party, such Credit Support Provider or such Specified Entity (individually or collectively) in making one or more payments under such agreements or instruments on the due date for payment (after giving effect to any applicable notice requirement or grace period) in an aggregate amount, either alone or together with the amount, if any, referred to in clause (1) above, of not less than the applicable Threshold Amount;

(vii) ***Bankruptcy.*** The party, any Credit Support Provider of such party or any applicable Specified Entity of such party:—

(1) is dissolved (other than pursuant to a consolidation, amalgamation or merger); (2) becomes insolvent or is unable to pay its debts or fails or admits in writing its inability generally to pay its debts as they become due; (3) makes a general assignment, arrangement or composition with or for the benefit of its creditors; (4)(A) institutes or has instituted against it, by a regulator, supervisor or any similar official with primary insolvency, rehabilitative or regulatory jurisdiction over it in the jurisdiction of its incorporation or organisation or the jurisdiction of its head or home office, a proceeding seeking a judgment of insolvency or bankruptcy or any other relief under any bankruptcy or insolvency law or other similar law affecting creditors' rights, or a petition is presented for its winding-up or liquidation by it or such regulator, supervisor or similar official, or (B) has instituted against it a proceeding seeking a judgment of insolvency or bankruptcy or any other relief under any bankruptcy or insolvency law or other similar law affecting creditors' rights, or a petition is presented for its winding-up or liquidation, and such proceeding or petition is instituted or presented by a person or entity not described in clause (A) above and either (I) results in a judgment of insolvency or bankruptcy or the entry of an order for relief or the making of an order for its winding-up or liquidation or (II) is not dismissed, discharged, stayed or restrained in each case within 15 days of the institution or presentation thereof; (5) has a resolution passed for its winding-up, official management or liquidation (other than pursuant to a consolidation, amalgamation or merger); (6) seeks or becomes subject to the appointment of an administrator, provisional liquidator, conservator, receiver, trustee, custodian or other similar official for it or for all or substantially all its assets; (7) has a secured party take possession of all or substantially all its assets or has a distress, execution, attachment, sequestration or other legal process levied, enforced or sued on or against all or substantially all its assets and such secured party maintains possession, or any such process is not dismissed, discharged, stayed or restrained, in each case within 15 days thereafter; (8) causes or is subject to any event with respect to it which, under the applicable laws of any jurisdiction, has an analogous effect to any of the events specified in clauses (1) to (7) above (inclusive); or (9) takes any action in furtherance of, or indicating its consent to, approval of, or acquiescence in, any of the foregoing acts; or

(viii) ***Merger Without Assumption.*** The party or any Credit Support Provider of such party consolidates or amalgamates with, or merges with or into, or transfers all or substantially all its assets to, or reorganises, reincorporates or reconstitutes into or as, another entity and, at the time of such consolidation, amalgamation, merger, transfer, reorganisation, reincorporation or reconstitution:—

(1) the resulting, surviving or transferee entity fails to assume all the obligations of such party or such Credit Support Provider under this Agreement or any Credit Support Document to which it or its predecessor was a party; or

(2) the benefits of any Credit Support Document fail to extend (without the consent of the other party) to the performance by such resulting, surviving or transferee entity of its obligations under this Agreement.

(b) ***Termination Events.*** The occurrence at any time with respect to a party or, if applicable, any Credit Support Provider of such party or any Specified Entity of such party of any event specified below constitutes (subject to Section 5(c)) an Illegality if the event is specified in clause (i) below, a Force Majeure Event if the event is specified in clause (ii) below, a Tax Event if the event is specified in clause (iii) below, a Tax Event Upon Merger if the event is specified in clause (iv) below, and, if specified to be applicable, a Credit Event Upon Merger if the event is specified pursuant to clause (v) below or an Additional Termination Event if the event is specified pursuant to clause (vi) below:—

(i) ***Illegality.*** After giving effect to any applicable provision, disruption fallback or remedy specified in, or pursuant to, the relevant Confirmation or elsewhere in this Agreement, due to an event or circumstance (other than any action taken by a party or, if applicable, any Credit Support Provider of such party) occurring after a Transaction is entered into, it becomes unlawful under any applicable law (including without limitation the laws of any country in which payment, delivery or compliance is required by either party or any Credit Support Provider, as the case may be), on any day, or it would be unlawful if the relevant payment, delivery or compliance were required on that day (in each case, other than as a result of a breach by the party of Section 4(b)):—

(1) for the Office through which such party (which will be the Affected Party) makes and receives payments or deliveries with respect to such Transaction to perform any absolute or contingent obligation to make a payment or delivery in respect of such Transaction, to receive a payment or delivery in respect of such Transaction or to comply with any other material provision of this Agreement relating to such Transaction; or

(2) for such party or any Credit Support Provider of such party (which will be the Affected Party) to perform any absolute or contingent obligation to make a payment or delivery which such party or Credit Support Provider has under any Credit Support Document relating to such Transaction, to receive a payment or delivery under such Credit Support Document or to comply with any other material provision of such Credit Support Document;

(ii) ***Force Majeure Event.*** After giving effect to any applicable provision, disruption fallback or remedy specified in, or pursuant to, the relevant Confirmation or elsewhere in this Agreement, by reason of force majeure or act of state occurring after a Transaction is entered into, on any day:—

(1) the Office through which such party (which will be the Affected Party) makes and receives payments or deliveries with respect to such Transaction is prevented from performing any absolute or contingent obligation to make a payment or delivery in respect of such Transaction, from receiving a payment or delivery in respect of such Transaction or from complying with any other material provision of this Agreement relating to such Transaction (or would be so prevented if such payment, delivery or compliance were required on that day), or it becomes impossible or

impracticable for such Office so to perform, receive or comply (or it would be impossible or impracticable for such Office so to perform, receive or comply if such payment, delivery or compliance were required on that day); or

(2) such party or any Credit Support Provider of such party (which will be the Affected Party) is prevented from performing any absolute or contingent obligation to make a payment or delivery which such party or Credit Support Provider has under any Credit Support Document relating to such Transaction, from receiving a payment or delivery under such Credit Support Document or from complying with any other material provision of such Credit Support Document (or would be so prevented if such payment, delivery or compliance were required on that day), or it becomes impossible or impracticable for such party or Credit Support Provider so to perform, receive or comply (or it would be impossible or impracticable for such party or Credit Support Provider so to perform, receive or comply if such payment, delivery or compliance were required on that day),

so long as the force majeure or act of state is beyond the control of such Office, such party or such Credit Support Provider, as appropriate, and such Office, party or Credit Support Provider could not, after using all reasonable efforts (which will not require such party or Credit Support Provider to incur a loss, other than immaterial, incidental expenses), overcome such prevention, impossibility or impracticability;

(iii) ***Tax Event.*** Due to (1) any action taken by a taxing authority, or brought in a court of competent jurisdiction, after a Transaction is entered into (regardless of whether such action is taken or brought with respect to a party to this Agreement) or (2) a Change in Tax Law, the party (which will be the Affected Party) will, or there is a substantial likelihood that it will, on the next succeeding Scheduled Settlement Date (A) be required to pay to the other party an additional amount in respect of an Indemnifiable Tax under Section 2(d)(i)(4) (except in respect of interest under Section 9(h)) or (B) receive a payment from which an amount is required to be deducted or withheld for or on account of a Tax (except in respect of interest under Section 9(h)) and no additional amount is required to be paid in respect of such Tax under Section 2(d)(i)(4) (other than by reason of Section 2(d)(i)(4)(A) or (B));

(iv) ***Tax Event Upon Merger.*** The party (the "Burdened Party") on the next succeeding Scheduled Settlement Date will either (1) be required to pay an additional amount in respect of an Indemnifiable Tax under Section 2(d)(i)(4) (except in respect of interest under Section 9(h)) or (2) receive a payment from which an amount has been deducted or withheld for or on account of any Tax in respect of which the other party is not required to pay an additional amount (other than by reason of Section 2(d)(i)(4)(A) or (B)), in either case as a result of a party consolidating or amalgamating with, or merging with or into, or transferring all or substantially all its assets (or any substantial part of the assets comprising the business conducted by it as of the date of this Master Agreement) to, or reorganising, reincorporating or reconstituting into or as, another entity (which will be the Affected Party) where such action does not constitute a Merger Without Assumption;

(v) ***Credit Event Upon Merger.*** If "Credit Event Upon Merger" is specified in the Schedule as applying to the party, a Designated Event (as defined below) occurs with respect to such party, any Credit Support Provider of such party or any applicable Specified Entity of such party (in each case, "X") and such Designated Event does not constitute a Merger Without Assumption, and the creditworthiness of X or, if applicable, the successor, surviving or transferee entity of X, after taking into account any applicable Credit Support Document, is materially weaker immediately after the occurrence of such Designated Event than that of X immediately prior to the occurrence of such Designated Event (and, in any such event, such party or its successor, surviving or transferee entity, as appropriate, will be the Affected Party). A "Designated Event" with respect to X means that:—

(1) X consolidates or amalgamates with, or merges with or into, or transfers all or substantially all its assets (or any substantial part of the assets comprising the business conducted by X as of the

date of this Master Agreement) to, or reorganises, reincorporates or reconstitutes into or as, another entity;

(2) any person, related group of persons or entity acquires directly or indirectly the beneficial ownership of (A) equity securities having the power to elect a majority of the board of directors (or its equivalent) of X or (B) any other ownership interest enabling it to exercise control of X; or

(3) X effects any substantial change in its capital structure by means of the issuance, incurrence or guarantee of debt or the issuance of (A) preferred stock or other securities convertible into or exchangeable for debt or preferred stock or (B) in the case of entities other than corporations, any other form of ownership interest; or

(vi) ***Additional Termination Event.*** If any "Additional Termination Event" is specified in the Schedule or any Confirmation as applying, the occurrence of such event (and, in such event, the Affected Party or Affected Parties will be as specified for such Additional Termination Event in the Schedule or such Confirmation).

(c) ***Hierarchy of Events.***

(i) An event or circumstance that constitutes or gives rise to an Illegality or a Force Majeure Event will not, for so long as that is the case, also constitute or give rise to an Event of Default under Section 5(a)(i), 5(a)(ii)(1) or 5(a)(iii)(1) insofar as such event or circumstance relates to the failure to make any payment or delivery or a failure to comply with any other material provision of this Agreement or a Credit Support Document, as the case may be.

(ii) Except in circumstances contemplated by clause (i) above, if an event or circumstance which would otherwise constitute or give rise to an Illegality or a Force Majeure Event also constitutes an Event of Default or any other Termination Event, it will be treated as an Event of Default or such other Termination Event, as the case may be, and will not constitute or give rise to an Illegality or a Force Majeure Event.

(iii) If an event or circumstance which would otherwise constitute or give rise to a Force Majeure Event also constitutes an Illegality, it will be treated as an Illegality, except as described in clause (ii) above, and not a Force Majeure Event.

(d) ***Deferral of Payments and Deliveries During Waiting Period.*** If an Illegality or a Force Majeure Event has occurred and is continuing with respect to a Transaction, each payment or delivery which would otherwise be required to be made under that Transaction will be deferred to, and will not be due until:—

(i) the first Local Business Day or, in the case of a delivery, the first Local Delivery Day (or the first day that would have been a Local Business Day or Local Delivery Day, as appropriate, but for the occurrence of the event or circumstance constituting or giving rise to that Illegality or Force Majeure Event) following the end of any applicable Waiting Period in respect of that Illegality or Force Majeure Event, as the case may be; or

(ii) if earlier, the date on which the event or circumstance constituting or giving rise to that Illegality or Force Majeure Event ceases to exist or, if such date is not a Local Business Day or, in the case of a delivery, a Local Delivery Day, the first following day that is a Local Business Day or Local Delivery Day, as appropriate.

(e) ***Inability of Head or Home Office to Perform Obligations of Branch.*** If (i) an Illegality or a Force Majeure Event occurs under Section 5(b)(i)(1) or 5(b)(ii)(1) and the relevant Office is not the Affected Party's head or home office, (ii) Section 10(a) applies, (iii) the other party seeks performance of the relevant obligation or compliance with the relevant provision by the Affected Party's head or home office and (iv) the Affected Party's head or home office fails so to perform or comply due to the occurrence of an event or circumstance which would, if that head or home office were the Office through which the Affected Party makes and receives payments and deliveries with respect to the relevant Transaction, constitute or give rise to an Illegality or a Force Majeure Event, and such failure would otherwise constitute an Event of Default under Section 5(a)(i) or 5(a)(iii)(1) with respect to such party, then, for so long as the relevant event or circumstance continues to exist with respect to both the Office referred to in Section 5(b)(i)(1) or 5(b)(ii)(1), as the case may be, and the Affected Party's head or home office, such failure will not constitute an Event of Default under Section 5(a)(i) or 5(a)(iii)(1).

6. Early Termination; Close-Out Netting

(a) ***Right to Terminate Following Event of Default.*** If at any time an Event of Default with respect to a party (the "Defaulting Party") has occurred and is then continuing, the other party (the "Non-defaulting Party") may, by not more than 20 days notice to the Defaulting Party specifying the relevant Event of Default, designate a day not earlier than the day such notice is effective as an Early Termination Date in respect of all outstanding Transactions. If, however, "Automatic Early Termination" is specified in the Schedule as applying to a party, then an Early Termination Date in respect of all outstanding Transactions will occur immediately upon the occurrence with respect to such party of an Event of Default specified in Section 5(a)(vii)(1), (3), (5), (6) or, to the extent analogous thereto, (8), and as of the time immediately preceding the institution of the relevant proceeding or the presentation of the relevant petition upon the occurrence with respect to such party of an Event of Default specified in Section 5(a)(vii)(4) or, to the extent analogous thereto, (8).

(b) ***Right to Terminate Following Termination Event.***

(i) ***Notice.*** If a Termination Event other than a Force Majeure Event occurs, an Affected Party will, promptly upon becoming aware of it, notify the other party, specifying the nature of that Termination Event and each Affected Transaction, and will also give the other party such other information about that Termination Event as the other party may reasonably require. If a Force Majeure Event occurs, each party will, promptly upon becoming aware of it, use all reasonable efforts to notify the other party, specifying the nature of that Force Majeure Event, and will also give the other party such other information about that Force Majeure Event as the other party may reasonably require.

(ii) ***Transfer to Avoid Termination Event.*** If a Tax Event occurs and there is only one Affected Party, or if a Tax Event Upon Merger occurs and the Burdened Party is the Affected Party, the Affected Party will, as a condition to its right to designate an Early Termination Date under Section 6(b)(iv), use all reasonable efforts (which will not require such party to incur a loss, other than immaterial, incidental expenses) to transfer within 20 days after it gives notice under Section 6(b)(i) all its rights and obligations under this Agreement in respect of the Affected Transactions to another of its Offices or Affiliates so that such Termination Event ceases to exist.

If the Affected Party is not able to make such a transfer it will give notice to the other party to that effect within such 20 day period, whereupon the other party may effect such a transfer within 30 days after the notice is given under Section 6(b)(i).

Any such transfer by a party under this Section 6(b)(ii) will be subject to and conditional upon the prior written consent of the other party, which consent will not be withheld if such other party's policies in effect at such time would permit it to enter into transactions with the transferee on the terms proposed.

(iii) ***Two Affected Parties.*** If a Tax Event occurs and there are two Affected Parties, each party will use all reasonable efforts to reach agreement within 30 days after notice of such occurrence is given under Section 6(b)(i) to avoid that Termination Event.

(iv) ***Right to Terminate.***

(1) If:—

(A) a transfer under Section 6(b)(ii) or an agreement under Section 6(b)(iii), as the case may be, has not been effected with respect to all Affected Transactions within 30 days after an Affected Party gives notice under Section 6(b)(i); or

(B) a Credit Event Upon Merger or an Additional Termination Event occurs, or a Tax Event Upon Merger occurs and the Burdened Party is not the Affected Party,

the Burdened Party in the case of a Tax Event Upon Merger, any Affected Party in the case of a Tax Event or an Additional Termination Event if there are two Affected Parties, or the Non-affected Party in the case of a Credit Event Upon Merger or an Additional Termination Event if there is only one Affected Party may, if the relevant Termination Event is then continuing, by not more than 20 days notice to the other party, designate a day not earlier than the day such notice is effective as an Early Termination Date in respect of all Affected Transactions.

(2) If at any time an Illegality or a Force Majeure Event has occurred and is then continuing and any applicable Waiting Period has expired:—

(A) Subject to clause (B) below, either party may, by not more than 20 days notice to the other party, designate (I) a day not earlier than the day on which such notice becomes effective as an Early Termination Date in respect of all Affected Transactions or (II) by specifying in that notice the Affected Transactions in respect of which it is designating the relevant day as an Early Termination Date, a day not earlier than two Local Business Days following the day on which such notice becomes effective as an Early Termination Date in respect of less than all Affected Transactions. Upon receipt of a notice designating an Early Termination Date in respect of less than all Affected Transactions, the other party may, by notice to the designating party, if such notice is effective on or before the day so designated, designate that same day as an Early Termination Date in respect of any or all other Affected Transactions.

(B) An Affected Party (if the Illegality or Force Majeure Event relates to performance by such party or any Credit Support Provider of such party of an obligation to make any payment or delivery under, or to compliance with any other material provision of, the relevant Credit Support Document) will only have the right to designate an Early Termination Date under Section 6(b)(iv)(2)(A) as a result of an Illegality under Section 5(b)(i)(2) or a Force Majeure Event under Section 5(b)(ii)(2) following the prior designation by the other party of an Early Termination Date, pursuant to Section 6(b)(iv)(2)(A), in respect of less than all Affected Transactions.

(c) ***Effect of Designation.***

(i) If notice designating an Early Termination Date is given under Section 6(a) or 6(b), the Early Termination Date will occur on the date so designated, whether or not the relevant Event of Default or Termination Event is then continuing.

(ii) Upon the occurrence or effective designation of an Early Termination Date, no further payments or deliveries under Section 2(a)(i) or 9(h)(i) in respect of the Terminated Transactions will be required to be made, but without prejudice to the other provisions of this Agreement. The amount, if any, payable in respect of an Early Termination Date will be determined pursuant to Sections 6(e) and 9(h)(ii).

(d) ***Calculations; Payment Date.***

(i) ***Statement.*** On or as soon as reasonably practicable following the occurrence of an Early Termination Date, each party will make the calculations on its part, if any, contemplated by Section 6(e) and will provide to the other party a statement (l) showing, in reasonable detail, such calculations (including any quotations, market data or information from internal sources used in making such calculations), (2) specifying (except where there are two Affected Parties) any Early Termination Amount payable and (3) giving details of the relevant account to which any amount payable to it is to be paid. In the absence of written confirmation from the source of a quotation or market data obtained in determining a Close-out Amount, the records of the party obtaining such quotation or market data will be conclusive evidence of the existence and accuracy of such quotation or market data.

(ii) ***Payment Date.*** An Early Termination Amount due in respect of any Early Termination Date will, together with any amount of interest payable pursuant to Section 9(h)(ii)(2), be payable (1) on the day on which notice of the amount payable is effective in the case of an Early Termination Date which is designated or occurs as a result of an Event of Default and (2) on the day which is two Local Business Days after the day on which notice of the amount payable is effective (or, if there are two Affected Parties, after the day on which the statement provided pursuant to clause (i) above by the second party to provide such a statement is effective) in the case of an Early Termination Date which is designated as a result of a Termination Event.

(e) ***Payments on Early Termination.*** If an Early Termination Date occurs, the amount, if any, payable in respect of that Early Termination Date (the "Early Termination Amount") will be determined pursuant to this Section 6(e) and will be subject to Section 6(f).

(i) ***Events of Default.*** If the Early Termination Date results from an Event of Default, the Early Termination Amount will be an amount equal to (1) the sum of (A) the Termination Currency Equivalent of the Close-out Amount or Close-out Amounts (whether positive or negative) determined by the Non-defaulting Party for each Terminated Transaction or group of Terminated Transactions, as the case may be, and (B) the Termination Currency Equivalent of the Unpaid Amounts owing to the Non-defaulting Party less (2) the Termination Currency Equivalent of the Unpaid Amounts owing to the Defaulting Party. If the Early Termination Amount is a positive number, the Defaulting Party will pay it to the Non-defaulting Party; if it is a negative number, the Non-defaulting Party will pay the absolute value of the Early Termination Amount to the Defaulting Party.

(ii) ***Termination Events.*** If the Early Termination Date results from a Termination Event:—

(1) *One Affected Party.* Subject to clause (3) below, if there is one Affected Party, the Early Termination Amount will be determined in accordance with Section 6(e)(i), except that references to the Defaulting Party and to the Non-defaulting Party will be deemed to be references to the Affected Party and to the Non-affected Party, respectively.

(2) *Two Affected Parties.* Subject to clause (3) below, if there are two Affected Parties, each party will determine an amount equal to the Termination Currency Equivalent of the sum of the Close-out Amount or Close-out Amounts (whether positive or negative) for each Terminated Transaction or group of Terminated Transactions, as the case may be, and the Early Termination Amount will be an amount equal to (A) the sum of (I) one-half of the difference between the higher amount so determined (by party "X") and the lower amount so determined (by party "Y") and (II) the Termination Currency Equivalent of the Unpaid Amounts owing to X less (B) the Termination Currency Equivalent of the Unpaid Amounts owing to Y. If the Early Termination Amount is a positive number, Y will pay it to X; if it is a negative number, X will pay the absolute value of the Early Termination Amount to Y.

(3) *Mid-Market Events*. If that Termination Event is an Illegality or a Force Majeure Event, then the Early Termination Amount will be determined in accordance with clause (1) or (2) above, as appropriate, except that, for the purpose of determining a Close-out Amount or Close-out Amounts, the Determining Party will:—

(A) if obtaining quotations from one or more third parties (or from any of the Determining Party's Affiliates), ask each third party or Affiliate (I) not to take account of the current creditworthiness of the Determining Party or any existing Credit Support Document and (II) to provide mid-market quotations; and

(B) in any other case, use mid-market values without regard to the creditworthiness of the Determining Party.

(iii) ***Adjustment for Bankruptcy.*** In circumstances where an Early Termination Date occurs because Automatic Early Termination applies in respect of a party, the Early Termination Amount will be subject to such adjustments as are appropriate and permitted by applicable law to reflect any payments or deliveries made by one party to the other under this Agreement (and retained by such other party) during the period from the relevant Early Termination Date to the date for payment determined under Section 6(d)(ii).

(iv) ***Adjustment for Illegality or Force Majeure Event.*** The failure by a party or any Credit Support Provider of such party to pay, when due, any Early Termination Amount will not constitute an Event of Default under Section 5(a)(i) or 5(a)(iii)(1) if such failure is due to the occurrence of an event or circumstance which would, if it occurred with respect to payment, delivery or compliance related to a Transaction, constitute or give rise to an Illegality or a Force Majeure Event. Such amount will (1) accrue interest and otherwise be treated as an Unpaid Amount owing to the other party if subsequently an Early Termination Date results from an Event of Default, a Credit Event Upon Merger or an Additional Termination Event in respect of which all outstanding Transactions are Affected Transactions and (2) otherwise accrue interest in accordance with Section 9(h)(ii)(2).

(v) ***Pre-Estimate.*** The parties agree that an amount recoverable under this Section 6(e) is a reasonable pre-estimate of loss and not a penalty. Such amount is payable for the loss of bargain and the loss of protection against future risks, and, except as otherwise provided in this Agreement, neither party will be entitled to recover any additional damages as a consequence of the termination of the Terminated Transactions.

(f) ***Set-Off.*** Any Early Termination Amount payable to one party (the "Payee") by the other party (the "Payer"), in circumstances where there is a Defaulting Party or where there is one Affected Party in the case where either a Credit Event Upon Merger has occurred or any other Termination Event in respect of which all outstanding Transactions are Affected Transactions has occurred, will, at the option of the Non-defaulting Party or the Non-affected Party, as the case may be ("X") (and without prior notice to the Defaulting Party or the Affected Party, as the case may be), be reduced by its set-off against any other amounts ("Other Amounts") payable by the Payee to the Payer (whether or not arising under this Agreement, matured or contingent and irrespective of the currency, place of payment or place of booking of the obligation). To the extent that any Other Amounts are so set off, those Other Amounts will be discharged promptly and in all respects. X will give notice to the other party of any set-off effected under this Section 6(f).

For this purpose, either the Early Termination Amount or the Other Amounts (or the relevant portion of such amounts) may be converted by X into the currency in which the other is denominated at the rate of exchange at which such party would be able, in good faith and using commercially reasonable procedures, to purchase the relevant amount of such currency.

If an obligation is unascertained, X may in good faith estimate that obligation and set off in respect of the estimate, subject to the relevant party accounting to the other when the obligation is ascertained.

Nothing in this Section 6(f) will be effective to create a charge or other security interest. This Section 6(f) will be without prejudice and in addition to any right of set-off, offset, combination of accounts, lien, right of retention or withholding or similar right or requirement to which any party is at any time otherwise entitled or subject (whether by operation of law, contract or otherwise).

7. Transfer

Subject to Section 6(b)(ii) and to the extent permitted by applicable law, neither this Agreement nor any interest or obligation in or under this Agreement may be transferred (whether by way of security or otherwise) by either party without the prior written consent of the other party, except that:—

(a) a party may make such a transfer of this Agreement pursuant to a consolidation or amalgamation with, or merger with or into, or transfer of all or substantially all its assets to, another entity (but without prejudice to any other right or remedy under this Agreement); and

(b) a party may make such a transfer of all or any part of its interest in any Early Termination Amount payable to it by a Defaulting Party, together with any amounts payable on or with respect to that interest and any other rights associated with that interest pursuant to Sections 8, 9(h) and 11.

Any purported transfer that is not in compliance with this Section 7 will be void.

8. Contractual Currency

(a) ***Payment in the Contractual Currency.*** Each payment under this Agreement will be made in the relevant currency specified in this Agreement for that payment (the "Contractual Currency"). To the extent permitted by applicable law, any obligation to make payments under this Agreement in the Contractual Currency will not be discharged or satisfied by any tender in any currency other than the Contractual Currency, except to the extent such tender results in the actual receipt by the party to which payment is owed, acting in good faith and using commercially reasonable procedures in converting the currency so tendered into the Contractual Currency, of the full amount in the Contractual Currency of all amounts payable in respect of this Agreement. If for any reason the amount in the Contractual Currency so received falls short of the amount in the Contractual Currency payable in respect of this Agreement, the party required to make the payment will, to the extent permitted by applicable law, immediately pay such additional amount in the Contractual Currency as may be necessary to compensate for the shortfall. If for any reason the amount in the Contractual Currency so received exceeds the amount in the Contractual Currency payable in respect of this Agreement, the party receiving the payment will refund promptly the amount of such excess.

(b) ***Judgments.*** To the extent permitted by applicable law, if any judgment or order expressed in a currency other than the Contractual Currency is rendered (i) for the payment of any amount owing in respect of this Agreement, (ii) for the payment of any amount relating to any early termination in respect of this Agreement or (iii) in respect of a judgment or order of another court for the payment of any amount described in clause (i) or (ii) above, the party seeking recovery, after recovery in full of the aggregate amount to which such party is entitled pursuant to the judgment or order, will be entitled to receive immediately from the other party the amount of any shortfall of the Contractual Currency received by such party as a consequence of sums paid in such other currency and will refund promptly to the other party any excess of the Contractual Currency received by such party as a consequence of sums paid in such other currency if such shortfall or such excess arises or results from any variation between the rate of exchange at which the Contractual Currency is converted into the currency of the judgment or order for the purpose of such judgment or order and the rate of exchange at which such party is able, acting in good faith and using commercially reasonable procedures in converting the currency received into the Contractual Currency, to purchase the Contractual Currency with the amount of the currency of the judgment or order actually received by such party.

(c) ***Separate Indemnities.*** To the extent permitted by applicable law, the indemnities in this Section 8 constitute separate and independent obligations from the other obligations in this Agreement, will be enforceable as separate and independent causes of action, will apply notwithstanding any indulgence granted by the party to which any payment is owed and will not be affected by judgment being obtained or claim or proof being made for any other sums payable in respect of this Agreement.

(d) ***Evidence of Loss.*** For the purpose of this Section 8, it will be sufficient for a party to demonstrate that it would have suffered a loss had an actual exchange or purchase been made.

9. Miscellaneous

(a) ***Entire Agreement.*** This Agreement constitutes the entire agreement and understanding of the parties with respect to its subject matter. Each of the parties acknowledges that in entering into this Agreement it has not relied on any oral or written representation, warranty or other assurance (except as provided for or referred to in this Agreement) and waives all rights and remedies which might otherwise be available to it in respect thereof, except that nothing in this Agreement will limit or exclude any liability of a party for fraud.

(b) ***Amendments.*** An amendment, modification or waiver in respect of this Agreement will only be effective if in writing (including a writing evidenced by a facsimile transmission) and executed by each of the parties or confirmed by an exchange of telexes or by an exchange of electronic messages on an electronic messaging system.

(c) ***Survival of Obligations.*** Without prejudice to Sections 2(a)(iii) and 6(c)(ii), the obligations of the parties under this Agreement will survive the termination of any Transaction.

(d) ***Remedies Cumulative.*** Except as provided in this Agreement, the rights, powers, remedies and privileges provided in this Agreement are cumulative and not exclusive of any rights, powers, remedies and privileges provided by law.

(e) ***Counterparts and Confirmations.***

(i) This Agreement (and each amendment, modification and waiver in respect of it) may be executed and delivered in counterparts (including by facsimile transmission and by electronic messaging system), each of which will be deemed an original.

(ii) The parties intend that they are legally bound by the terms of each Transaction from the moment they agree to those terms (whether orally or otherwise). A Confirmation will be entered into as soon as practicable and may be executed and delivered in counterparts (including by facsimile transmission) or be created by an exchange of telexes, by an exchange of electronic messages on an electronic messaging system or by an exchange of e-mails, which in each case will be sufficient for all purposes to evidence a binding supplement to this Agreement. The parties will specify therein or through another effective means that any such counterpart, telex, electronic message or e-mail constitutes a Confirmation.

(f) ***No Waiver of Rights.*** A failure or delay in exercising any right, power or privilege in respect of this Agreement will not be presumed to operate as a waiver, and a single or partial exercise of any right, power or privilege will not be presumed to preclude any subsequent or further exercise, of that right, power or privilege or the exercise of any other right, power or privilege.

(g) ***Headings.*** The headings used in this Agreement are for convenience of reference only and are not to affect the construction of or to be taken into consideration in interpreting this Agreement.

(h) ***Interest and Compensation.***

(i) ***Prior to Early Termination.*** Prior to the occurrence or effective designation of an Early Termination Date in respect of the relevant Transaction:—

(1) *Interest on Defaulted Payments.* If a party defaults in the performance of any payment obligation, it will, to the extent permitted by applicable law and subject to Section 6(c), pay interest (before as well as after judgment) on the overdue amount to the other party on demand in the same currency as the overdue amount, for the period from (and including) the original due date for payment to (but excluding) the date of actual payment (and excluding any period in respect of which interest or compensation in respect of the overdue amount is due pursuant to clause (3)(B) or (C) below), at the Default Rate.

(2) *Compensation for Defaulted Deliveries.* If a party defaults in the performance of any obligation required to be settled by delivery, it will on demand (A) compensate the other party to the extent provided for in the relevant Confirmation or elsewhere in this Agreement and (B) unless otherwise provided in the relevant Confirmation or elsewhere in this Agreement, to the extent permitted by applicable law and subject to Section 6(c), pay to the other party interest (before as well as after judgment) on an amount equal to the fair market value of that which was required to be delivered in the same currency as that amount, for the period from (and including) the originally scheduled date for delivery to (but excluding) the date of actual delivery (and excluding any period in respect of which interest or compensation in respect of that amount is due pursuant to clause (4) below), at the Default Rate. The fair market value of any obligation referred to above will be determined as of the originally scheduled date for delivery, in good faith and using commercially reasonable procedures, by the party that was entitled to take delivery.

(3) *Interest on Deferred Payments.* If:—

(A) a party does not pay any amount that, but for Section 2(a)(iii), would have been payable, it will, to the extent permitted by applicable law and subject to Section 6(c) and clauses (B) and (C) below, pay interest (before as well as after judgment) on that amount to the other party on demand (after such amount becomes payable) in the same currency as that amount, for the period from (and including) the date the amount would, but for Section 2(a)(iii), have been payable to (but excluding) the date the amount actually becomes payable, at the Applicable Deferral Rate;

(B) a payment is deferred pursuant to Section 5(d), the party which would otherwise have been required to make that payment will, to the extent permitted by applicable law, subject to Section 6(c) and for so long as no Event of Default or Potential Event of Default with respect to that party has occurred and is continuing, pay interest (before as well as after judgment) on the amount of the deferred payment to the other party on demand (after such amount becomes payable) in the same currency as the deferred payment, for the period from (and including) the date the amount would, but for Section 5(d), have been payable to (but excluding) the earlier of the date the payment is no longer deferred pursuant to Section 5(d) and the date during the deferral period upon which an Event of Default or Potential Event of Default with respect to that party occurs, at the Applicable Deferral Rate; or

(C) a party fails to make any payment due to the occurrence of an Illegality or a Force Majeure Event (after giving effect to any deferral period contemplated by clause (B) above), it will, to the extent permitted by applicable law, subject to Section 6(c) and for so long as the event or circumstance giving rise to that Illegality or Force Majeure Event continues and no Event of Default or Potential Event of Default with respect to that party has occurred and is continuing, pay interest (before as well as after judgment) on the overdue amount to the other party on demand in the same currency as the overdue amount, for the period from (and including) the date the party fails to make the payment due to the occurrence of the relevant Illegality or Force Majeure Event (or, if later, the date the payment is no longer deferred pursuant to Section 5(d)) to (but excluding) the earlier of the date the event or circumstance giving rise to that Illegality or Force Majeure Event ceases to exist and the date during the period upon which an Event of Default or Potential Event of Default with respect to that party occurs (and excluding any period in respect of which interest or compensation in respect of the overdue amount is due pursuant to clause (B) above), at the Applicable Deferral Rate.

(4) *Compensation for Deferred Deliveries.* If:—

(A) a party does not perform any obligation that, but for Section 2(a)(iii), would have been required to be settled by delivery;

(B) a delivery is deferred pursuant to Section 5(d); or

(C) a party fails to make a delivery due to the occurrence of an Illegality or a Force Majeure Event at a time when any applicable Waiting Period has expired,

the party required (or that would otherwise have been required) to make the delivery will, to the extent permitted by applicable law and subject to Section 6(c), compensate and pay interest to the other party on demand (after, in the case of clauses (A) and (B) above, such delivery is required) if and to the extent provided for in the relevant Confirmation or elsewhere in this Agreement.

(ii) ***Early Termination.*** Upon the occurrence or effective designation of an Early Termination Date in respect of a Transaction:—

(1) *Unpaid Amounts.* For the purpose of determining an Unpaid Amount in respect of the relevant Transaction, and to the extent permitted by applicable law, interest will accrue on the amount of any payment obligation or the amount equal to the fair market value of any obligation required to be settled by delivery included in such determination in the same currency as that amount, for the period from (and including) the date the relevant obligation was (or would have been but for Section 2(a)(iii) or 5(d)) required to have been performed to (but excluding) the relevant Early Termination Date, at the Applicable Close-out Rate.

(2) *Interest on Early Termination Amounts.* If an Early Termination Amount is due in respect of such Early Termination Date, that amount will, to the extent permitted by applicable law, be paid together with interest (before as well as after judgment) on that amount in the Termination Currency, for the period from (and including) such Early Termination Date to (but excluding) the date the amount is paid, at the Applicable Close-out Rate.

(iii) ***Interest Calculation.*** Any interest pursuant to this Section 9(h) will be calculated on the basis of daily compounding and the actual number of days elapsed.

10. Offices; Multibranch Parties

(a) If Section 10(a) is specified in the Schedule as applying, each party that enters into a Transaction through an Office other than its head or home office represents to and agrees with the other party that, notwithstanding the place of booking or its jurisdiction of incorporation or organisation, its obligations are the same in terms of recourse against it as if it had entered into the Transaction through its head or home office, except that a party will not have recourse to the head or home office of the other party in respect of any payment or delivery deferred pursuant to Section 5(d) for so long as the payment or delivery is so deferred. This representation and agreement will be deemed to be repeated by each party on each date on which the parties enter into a Transaction.

(b) If a party is specified as a Multibranch Party in the Schedule, such party may, subject to clause (c) below, enter into a Transaction through, book a Transaction in and make and receive payments and deliveries with respect to a Transaction through any Office listed in respect of that party in the Schedule (but not any other Office unless otherwise agreed by the parties in writing).

(c) The Office through which a party enters into a Transaction will be the Office specified for that party in the relevant Confirmation or as otherwise agreed by the parties in writing, and, if an Office for that party is not specified in the Confirmation or otherwise agreed by the parties in writing, its head or home office. Unless the parties otherwise agree in writing, the Office through which a party enters into a Transaction will also be the Office in which it books the Transaction and the Office through which it makes and receives payments and deliveries with respect to the Transaction. Subject to Section 6(b)(ii), neither party may change the Office in which it books the Transaction or the Office through which it makes and receives payments or deliveries with respect to a Transaction without the prior written consent of the other party.

11. Expenses

A Defaulting Party will on demand indemnify and hold harmless the other party for and against all reasonable out-of-pocket expenses, including legal fees, execution fees and Stamp Tax, incurred by such other party by reason of the enforcement and protection of its rights under this Agreement or any Credit Support Document to which the Defaulting Party is a party or by reason of the early termination of any Transaction, including, but not limited to, costs of collection.

12. Notices

(a) ***Effectiveness.*** Any notice or other communication in respect of this Agreement may be given in any manner described below (except that a notice or other communication under Section 5 or 6 may not be given by electronic messaging system or e-mail) to the address or number or in accordance with the electronic messaging system or e-mail details provided (see the Schedule) and will be deemed effective as indicated:—

(i) if in writing and delivered in person or by courier, on the date it is delivered;

(ii) if sent by telex, on the date the recipient's answerback is received;

(iii) if sent by facsimile transmission, on the date it is received by a responsible employee of the recipient in legible form (it being agreed that the burden of proving receipt will be on the sender and will not be met by a transmission report generated by the sender's facsimile machine);

(iv) if sent by certified or registered mail (airmail, if overseas) or the equivalent (return receipt requested), on the date it is delivered or its delivery is attempted;

(v) if sent by electronic messaging system, on the date it is received; or

(vi) if sent by e-mail, on the date it is delivered,

unless the date of that delivery (or attempted delivery) or that receipt, as applicable, is not a Local Business Day or that communication is delivered (or attempted) or received, as applicable, after the close of business on a Local Business Day, in which case that communication will be deemed given and effective on the first following day that is a Local Business Day.

(b) ***Change of Details.*** Either party may by notice to the other change the address, telex or facsimile number or electronic messaging system or e-mail details at which notices or other communications are to be given to it.

13. Governing Law and Jurisdiction

(a) ***Governing Law.*** This Agreement will be governed by and construed in accordance with the law specified in the Schedule.

(b) ***Jurisdiction.*** With respect to any suit, action or proceedings relating to any dispute arising out of or in connection with this Agreement ("Proceedings"), each party irrevocably:—

(i) submits:—

(1) if this Agreement is expressed to be governed by English law, to (A) the non-exclusive jurisdiction of the English courts if the Proceedings do not involve a Convention Court and (B) the exclusive jurisdiction of the English courts if the Proceedings do involve a Convention Court; or

(2) if this Agreement is expressed to be governed by the laws of the State of New York, to the non-exclusive jurisdiction of the courts of the State of New York and the United States District Court located in the Borough of Manhattan in New York City;

(ii) waives any objection which it may have at any time to the laying of venue of any Proceedings brought in any such court, waives any claim that such Proceedings have been brought in an inconvenient forum and further waives the right to object, with respect to such Proceedings, that such court does not have any jurisdiction over such party; and

(iii) agrees, to the extent permitted by applicable law, that the bringing of Proceedings in any one or more jurisdictions will not preclude the bringing of Proceedings in any other jurisdiction.

(c) ***Service of Process.*** Each party irrevocably appoints the Process Agent, if any, specified opposite its name in the Schedule to receive, for it and on its behalf, service of process in any Proceedings. If for any reason any party's Process Agent is unable to act as such, such party will promptly notify the other party and within 30 days appoint a substitute process agent acceptable to the other party. The parties irrevocably consent to service of process given in the manner provided for notices in Section 12(a)(i), 12(a)(iii) or 12(a)(iv). Nothing in this Agreement will affect the right of either party to serve process in any other manner permitted by applicable law.

(d) ***Waiver of Immunities.*** Each party irrevocably waives, to the extent permitted by applicable law, with respect to itself and its revenues and assets (irrespective of their use or intended use), all immunity on the grounds of sovereignty or other similar grounds from (i) suit, (ii) jurisdiction of any court, (iii) relief by way of injunction or order for specific performance or recovery of property, (iv) attachment of its assets (whether before or after judgment) and (v) execution or enforcement of any judgment to which it or its revenues or assets might otherwise be entitled in any Proceedings in the courts of any jurisdiction and irrevocably agrees, to the extent permitted by applicable law, that it will not claim any such immunity in any Proceedings.

14. Definitions

As used in this Agreement:—

"Additional Representation" has the meaning specified in Section 3.

"Additional Termination Event" has the meaning specified in Section 5(b).

"Affected Party" has the meaning specified in Section 5(b).

"Affected Transactions" means (a) with respect to any Termination Event consisting of an Illegality, Force Majeure Event, Tax Event or Tax Event Upon Merger, all Transactions affected by the occurrence of such Termination Event (which, in the case of an Illegality under Section 5(b)(i)(2) or a Force Majeure Event under Section 5(b)(ii)(2), means all Transactions unless the relevant Credit Support Document references only certain Transactions, in which case those Transactions and, if the relevant Credit Support Document constitutes a Confirmation for a Transaction, that Transaction) and (b) with respect to any other Termination Event, all Transactions.

"Affiliate" means, subject to the Schedule, in relation to any person, any entity controlled, directly or indirectly, by the person, any entity that controls, directly or indirectly, the person or any entity directly or indirectly under common control with the person. For this purpose, "control" of any entity or person means ownership of a majority of the voting power of the entity or person.

"Agreement" has the meaning specified in Section 1(c).

"Applicable Close-out Rate" means:—

(a) in respect of the determination of an Unpaid Amount:—

(i) in respect of obligations payable or deliverable (or which would have been but for Section 2(a)(iii)) by a Defaulting Party, the Default Rate;

(ii) in respect of obligations payable or deliverable (or which would have been but for Section 2(a)(iii)) by a Non-defaulting Party, the Non-default Rate;

(iii) in respect of obligations deferred pursuant to Section 5(d), if there is no Defaulting Party and for so long as the deferral period continues, the Applicable Deferral Rate; and

(iv) in all other cases following the occurrence of a Termination Event (except where interest accrues pursuant to clause (iii) above), the Applicable Deferral Rate; and

(b) in respect of an Early Termination Amount:—

(i) for the period from (and including) the relevant Early Termination Date to (but excluding) the date (determined in accordance with Section 6(d)(ii)) on which that amount is payable:—

(1) if the Early Termination Amount is payable by a Defaulting Party, the Default Rate;

(2) if the Early Termination Amount is payable by a Non-defaulting Party, the Non-default Rate; and

(3) in all other cases, the Applicable Deferral Rate; and

(ii) for the period from (and including) the date (determined in accordance with Section 6(d)(ii)) on which that amount is payable to (but excluding) the date of actual payment:—

(1) if a party fails to pay the Early Termination Amount due to the occurrence of an event or circumstance which would, if it occurred with respect to a payment or delivery under a Transaction, constitute or give rise to an Illegality or a Force Majeure Event, and for so long as the Early Termination Amount remains unpaid due to the continuing existence of such event or circumstance, the Applicable Deferral Rate;

(2) if the Early Termination Amount is payable by a Defaulting Party (but excluding any period in respect of which clause (1) above applies), the Default Rate;

(3) if the Early Termination Amount is payable by a Non-defaulting Party (but excluding any period in respect of which clause (1) above applies), the Non-default Rate; and

(4) in all other cases, the Termination Rate.

"Applicable Deferral Rate" means:—

(a) for the purpose of Section 9(h)(i)(3)(A), the rate certified by the relevant payer to be a rate offered to the payer by a major bank in a relevant interbank market for overnight deposits in the applicable currency, such bank to be selected in good faith by the payer for the purpose of obtaining a representative rate that will reasonably reflect conditions prevailing at the time in that relevant market;

(b) for purposes of Section 9(h)(i)(3)(B) and clause (a)(iii) of the definition of Applicable Close-out Rate, the rate certified by the relevant payer to be a rate offered to prime banks by a major bank in a relevant interbank market for overnight deposits in the applicable currency, such bank to be selected in good faith by the payer after consultation with the other party, if practicable, for the purpose of obtaining a representative rate that will reasonably reflect conditions prevailing at the time in that relevant market; and

(c) for purposes of Section 9(h)(i)(3)(C) and clauses (a)(iv), (b)(i)(3) and (b)(ii)(1) of the definition of Applicable Close-out Rate, a rate equal to the arithmetic mean of the rate determined pursuant to clause (a) above and a rate per annum equal to the cost (without proof or evidence of any actual cost) to the relevant payee (as certified by it) if it were to fund or of funding the relevant amount.

"Automatic Early Termination" has the meaning specified in Section 6(a).

"Burdened Party" has the meaning specified in Section 5(b)(iv).

"Change in Tax Law" means the enactment, promulgation, execution or ratification of, or any change in or amendment to, any law (or in the application or official interpretation of any law) that occurs after the parties enter into the relevant Transaction.

"Close-out Amount" means, with respect to each Terminated Transaction or each group of Terminated Transactions and a Determining Party, the amount of the losses or costs of the Determining Party that are or would be incurred under then prevailing circumstances (expressed as a positive number) or gains of the Determining Party that are or would be realised under then prevailing circumstances (expressed as a negative number) in replacing, or in providing for the Determining Party the economic equivalent of, (a) the material terms of that Terminated Transaction or group of Terminated Transactions, including the payments and deliveries by the parties under Section 2(a)(i) in respect of that Terminated Transaction or group of Terminated Transactions that would, but for the occurrence of the relevant Early Termination Date, have been required after that date (assuming satisfaction of the conditions precedent in

Section 2(a)(iii)) and (b) the option rights of the parties in respect of that Terminated Transaction or group of Terminated Transactions.

Any Close-out Amount will be determined by the Determining Party (or its agent), which will act in good faith and use commercially reasonable procedures in order to produce a commercially reasonable result. The Determining Party may determine a Close-out Amount for any group of Terminated Transactions or any individual Terminated Transaction but, in the aggregate, for not less than all Terminated Transactions. Each Close-out Amount will be determined as of the Early Termination Date or, if that would not be commercially reasonable, as of the date or dates following the Early Termination Date as would be commercially reasonable.

Unpaid Amounts in respect of a Terminated Transaction or group of Terminated Transactions and legal fees and out-of-pocket expenses referred to in Section 11 are to be excluded in all determinations of Close-out Amounts.

In determining a Close-out Amount, the Determining Party may consider any relevant information, including, without limitation, one or more of the following types of information:—

(i) quotations (either firm or indicative) for replacement transactions supplied by one or more third parties that may take into account the creditworthiness of the Determining Party at the time the quotation is provided and the terms of any relevant documentation, including credit support documentation, between the Determining Party and the third party providing the quotation;

(ii) information consisting of relevant market data in the relevant market supplied by one or more third parties including, without limitation, relevant rates, prices, yields, yield curves, volatilities, spreads, correlations or other relevant market data in the relevant market; or

(iii) information of the types described in clause (i) or (ii) above from internal sources (including any of the Determining Party's Affiliates) if that information is of the same type used by the Determining Party in the regular course of its business for the valuation of similar transactions.

The Determining Party will consider, taking into account the standards and procedures described in this definition, quotations pursuant to clause (i) above or relevant market data pursuant to clause (ii) above unless the Determining Party reasonably believes in good faith that such quotations or relevant market data are not readily available or would produce a result that would not satisfy those standards. When considering information described in clause (i), (ii) or (iii) above, the Determining Party may include costs of funding, to the extent costs of funding are not and would not be a component of the other information being utilised. Third parties supplying quotations pursuant to clause (i) above or market data pursuant to clause (ii) above may include, without limitation, dealers in the relevant markets, end-users of the relevant product, information vendors, brokers and other sources of market information.

Without duplication of amounts calculated based on information described in clause (i), (ii) or (iii) above, or other relevant information, and when it is commercially reasonable to do so, the Determining Party may in addition consider in calculating a Close-out Amount any loss or cost incurred in connection with its terminating, liquidating or re-establishing any hedge related to a Terminated Transaction or group of Terminated Transactions (or any gain resulting from any of them).

Commercially reasonable procedures used in determining a Close-out Amount may include the following:—

(1) application to relevant market data from third parties pursuant to clause (ii) above or information from internal sources pursuant to clause (iii) above of pricing or other valuation models that are, at the time of the determination of the Close-out Amount, used by the Determining Party in the regular course of its business in pricing or valuing transactions between the Determining Party and unrelated third parties that are similar to the Terminated Transaction or group of Terminated Transactions; and

(2) application of different valuation methods to Terminated Transactions or groups of Terminated Transactions depending on the type, complexity, size or number of the Terminated Transactions or group of Terminated Transactions.

"Confirmation" has the meaning specified in the preamble.

"consent" includes a consent, approval, action, authorisation, exemption, notice, filing, registration or exchange control consent.

"Contractual Currency" has the meaning specified in Section 8(a).

"Convention Court" means any court which is bound to apply to the Proceedings either Article 17 of the 1968 Brussels Convention on Jurisdiction and the Enforcement of Judgments in Civil and Commercial Matters or Article 17 of the 1988 Lugano Convention on Jurisdiction and the Enforcement of Judgments in Civil and Commercial Matters.

"Credit Event Upon Merger" has the meaning specified in Section 5(b).

"Credit Support Document" means any agreement or instrument that is specified as such in this Agreement.

"Credit Support Provider" has the meaning specified in the Schedule.

"Cross-Default" means the event specified in Section 5(a)(vi).

"Default Rate" means a rate per annum equal to the cost (without proof or evidence of any actual cost) to the relevant payee (as certified by it) if it were to fund or of funding the relevant amount plus 1% per annum.

"Defaulting Party" has the meaning specified in Section 6(a).

"Designated Event" has the meaning specified in Section 5(b)(v).

"Determining Party" means the party determining a Close-out Amount.

"Early Termination Amount" has the meaning specified in Section 6(e).

"Early Termination Date" means the date determined in accordance with Section 6(a) or 6(b)(iv).

"electronic messages" does not include e-mails but does include documents expressed in markup languages, and ***"electronic messaging system"*** will be construed accordingly.

"English law" means the law of England and Wales, and ***"English"*** will be construed accordingly.

"Event of Default" has the meaning specified in Section 5(a) and, if applicable, in the Schedule.

"Force Majeure Event" has the meaning specified in Section 5(b).

"General Business Day" means a day on which commercial banks are open for general business (including dealings in foreign exchange and foreign currency deposits).

"Illegality" has the meaning specified in Section 5(b).

"Indemnifiable Tax" means any Tax other than a Tax that would not be imposed in respect of a payment under this Agreement but for a present or former connection between the jurisdiction of the government or taxation authority imposing such Tax and the recipient of such payment or a person related to such recipient (including, without limitation, a connection arising from such recipient or related person being or having been a citizen or resident of such jurisdiction, or being or having been organised, present or engaged in a trade or business in such jurisdiction, or having or having had a permanent establishment or fixed place of business in such jurisdiction, but excluding a connection arising solely from such recipient or related person having executed, delivered, performed its obligations or received a payment under, or enforced, this Agreement or a Credit Support Document).

"law" includes any treaty, law, rule or regulation (as modified, in the case of tax matters, by the practice of any relevant governmental revenue authority), and ***"unlawful"*** will be construed accordingly.

"Local Business Day" means (a) in relation to any obligation under Section 2(a)(i), a General Business Day in the place or places specified in the relevant Confirmation and a day on which a relevant settlement system is open or operating as specified in the relevant Confirmation or, if a place or a settlement system is not so specified, as otherwise agreed by the parties in writing or determined pursuant to provisions contained, or incorporated by reference, in this Agreement, (b) for the purpose of determining when a Waiting Period expires, a General Business Day in the place where the event or circumstance that constitutes or gives rise to the Illegality or Force Majeure Event, as the case may be, occurs, (c) in relation to any other payment, a General Business Day in the place where the relevant account is located and, if different, in the principal financial centre, if any, of the currency of such payment and, if that currency does not have a single recognised principal financial centre, a day on which the settlement system necessary to accomplish such payment is open, (d) in relation to any notice or other communication, including notice contemplated under Section 5(a)(i), a General Business Day (or a day that would have been a General Business Day but for the occurrence of an event or circumstance which would, if it occurred with respect to payment, delivery or compliance related to a Transaction, constitute or give rise to an Illegality or a Force Majeure Event) in the place specified in the address for notice provided by the recipient and, in the case of a notice contemplated by Section 2(b), in the place where the relevant new account is to be located and (e) in relation to Section 5(a)(v)(2), a General Business Day in the relevant locations for performance with respect to such Specified Transaction.

"Local Delivery Day" means, for purposes of Sections 5(a)(i) and 5(d), a day on which settlement systems necessary to accomplish the relevant delivery are generally open for business so that the delivery is capable of being accomplished in accordance with customary market practice, in the place specified in the relevant Confirmation or, if not so specified, in a location as determined in accordance with customary market practice for the relevant delivery.

"Master Agreement" has the meaning specified in the preamble.

"Merger Without Assumption" means the event specified in Section 5(a)(viii).

"Multiple Transaction Payment Netting" has the meaning specified in Section 2(c).

"Non-affected Party" means, so long as there is only one Affected Party, the other party.

"Non-default Rate" means the rate certified by the Non-defaulting Party to be a rate offered to the Non-defaulting Party by a major bank in a relevant interbank market for overnight deposits in the applicable currency, such bank to be selected in good faith by the Non-defaulting Party for the purpose of obtaining a representative rate that will reasonably reflect conditions prevailing at the time in that relevant market.

"Non-defaulting Party" has the meaning specified in Section 6(a).

"Office" means a branch or office of a party, which may be such party's head or home office.

"Other Amounts" has the meaning specified in Section 6(f).

"Payee" has the meaning specified in Section 6(f).

"Payer" has the meaning specified in Section 6(f).

"Potential Event of Default" means any event which, with the giving of notice or the lapse of time or both, would constitute an Event of Default.

"Proceedings" has the meaning specified in Section 13(b).

"Process Agent" has the meaning specified in the Schedule.

"rate of exchange" includes, without limitation, any premiums and costs of exchange payable in connection with the purchase of or conversion into the Contractual Currency.

"Relevant Jurisdiction" means, with respect to a party, the jurisdictions (a) in which the party is incorporated, organised, managed and controlled or considered to have its seat, (b) where an Office through which the party is acting for purposes of this Agreement is located, (c) in which the party executes this Agreement and (d) in relation to any payment, from or through which such payment is made.

"Schedule" has the meaning specified in the preamble.

"Scheduled Settlement Date" means a date on which a payment or delivery is to be made under Section 2(a)(i) with respect to a Transaction.

"Specified Entity" has the meaning specified in the Schedule.

"Specified Indebtedness" means, subject to the Schedule, any obligation (whether present or future, contingent or otherwise, as principal or surety or otherwise) in respect of borrowed money.

"Specified Transaction" means, subject to the Schedule, (a) any transaction (including an agreement with respect to any such transaction) now existing or hereafter entered into between one party to this Agreement (or any Credit Support Provider of such party or any applicable Specified Entity of such party) and the other party to this Agreement (or any Credit Support Provider of such other party or any applicable Specified Entity of such other party) which is not a Transaction under this Agreement but (i) which is a rate swap transaction, swap option, basis swap, forward rate transaction, commodity swap, commodity option, equity or equity index swap, equity or equity index option, bond option, interest rate option, foreign exchange transaction, cap transaction, floor transaction, collar transaction, currency swap transaction, cross-currency rate swap transaction, currency option, credit protection transaction, credit swap, credit default swap, credit default option, total return swap, credit spread transaction, repurchase transaction, reverse repurchase transaction, buy/sell-back transaction, securities lending transaction, weather index transaction or forward purchase or sale of a security, commodity or other financial instrument or interest (including any option with respect to any of these transactions) or (ii) which is a type of transaction that is similar to any transaction referred to in clause (i) above that is currently, or in the future becomes, recurrently entered into in the financial markets (including terms and conditions incorporated by reference in such agreement) and which is a forward, swap, future, option or other derivative on one or more rates, currencies, commodities, equity securities or other equity instruments, debt securities or other debt instruments, economic indices or measures of economic risk or value, or other benchmarks against which payments or deliveries are to be made, (b) any combination of these transactions and (c) any other transaction identified as a Specified Transaction in this Agreement or the relevant confirmation.

"Stamp Tax" means any stamp, registration, documentation or similar tax.

"Stamp Tax Jurisdiction" has the meaning specified in Section 4(e).

"Tax" means any present or future tax, levy, impost, duty, charge, assessment or fee of any nature (including interest, penalties and additions thereto) that is imposed by any government or other taxing authority in respect of any payment under this Agreement other than a stamp, registration, documentation or similar tax.

"Tax Event" has the meaning specified in Section 5(b).

"Tax Event Upon Merger" has the meaning specified in Section 5(b).

"Terminated Transactions" means, with respect to any Early Termination Date, (a) if resulting from an Illegality or a Force Majeure Event, all Affected Transactions specified in the notice given pursuant to Section 6(b)(iv), (b) if resulting from any other Termination Event, all Affected Transactions and (c) if resulting from an Event of Default, all Transactions in effect either immediately before the effectiveness of the notice designating that Early Termination Date or, if Automatic Early Termination applies, immediately before that Early Termination Date.

"Termination Currency" means (a) if a Termination Currency is specified in the Schedule and that currency is freely available, that currency, and (b) otherwise, euro if this Agreement is expressed to be governed by English law or United States Dollars if this Agreement is expressed to be governed by the laws of the State of New York.

"Termination Currency Equivalent" means, in respect of any amount denominated in the Termination Currency, such Termination Currency amount and, in respect of any amount denominated in a currency other than the Termination Currency (the "Other Currency"), the amount in the Termination Currency determined by the party making the relevant determination as being required to purchase such amount of such Other Currency as at the relevant Early Termination Date, or, if the relevant Close-out Amount is determined as of a later date, that later date, with the Termination Currency at the rate equal to the spot exchange rate of the foreign exchange agent (selected as provided below) for the purchase of such Other Currency with the Termination Currency at or about 11:00 a.m. (in the city in which such foreign exchange agent is located) on such date as would be customary for the determination of such a rate for the purchase of such Other Currency for value on the relevant Early Termination Date or that later date. The foreign exchange agent will, if only one party is obliged to make a determination under Section 6(e), be selected in good faith by that party and otherwise will be agreed by the parties.

"Termination Event" means an Illegality, a Force Majeure Event, a Tax Event, a Tax Event Upon Merger or, if specified to be applicable, a Credit Event Upon Merger or an Additional Termination Event.

"Termination Rate" means a rate per annum equal to the arithmetic mean of the cost (without proof or evidence of any actual cost) to each party (as certified by such party) if it were to fund or of funding such amounts.

"Threshold Amount" means the amount, if any, specified as such in the Schedule.

"Transaction" has the meaning specified in the preamble.

"Unpaid Amounts" owing to any party means, with respect to an Early Termination Date, the aggregate of (a) in respect of all Terminated Transactions, the amounts that became payable (or that would have become payable but for Section 2(a)(iii) or due but for Section 5(d)) to such party under Section 2(a)(i) or 2(d)(i)(4) on or prior to such Early Termination Date and which remain unpaid as at such Early Termination Date, (b) in respect of each Terminated Transaction, for each obligation under Section 2(a)(i) which was (or would have been but for Section 2(a)(iii) or 5(d)) required to be settled by delivery to such party on or prior to such Early Termination Date and which has not been so settled as at such Early Termination Date, an amount equal to the fair market value of that which was (or would have been) required to be delivered and (c) if the Early Termination Date results from an Event of Default, a Credit Event Upon Merger or an Additional Termination Event in respect of which all outstanding Transactions are Affected Transactions, any Early Termination Amount due prior to such Early Termination Date and which remains unpaid as of such Early Termination Date, in each case together with any amount of interest accrued or other compensation in respect of that obligation or deferred obligation, as the case may be, pursuant to Section 9(h)(ii)(1) or (2), as appropriate. The fair market value of any obligation referred to in clause (b) above will be determined as of the originally scheduled date for delivery, in good faith and using commercially reasonable procedures, by the party obliged to make the determination under Section 6(e) or, if each party is so obliged, it will be the average of the Termination Currency Equivalents of the fair market values so determined by both parties.

"Waiting Period" means:—

(a) in respect of an event or circumstance under Section 5(b)(i), other than in the case of Section 5(b)(i)(2) where the relevant payment, delivery or compliance is actually required on the relevant day (in which case no Waiting Period will apply), a period of three Local Business Days (or days that would have been Local Business Days but for the occurrence of that event or circumstance) following the occurrence of that event or circumstance; and

(b) in respect of an event or circumstance under Section 5(b)(ii), other than in the case of Section 5(b)(ii)(2) where the relevant payment, delivery or compliance is actually required on the relevant day (in which case no Waiting Period will apply), a period of eight Local Business Days (or days that would have been Local Business Days but for the occurrence of that event or circumstance) following the occurrence of that event or circumstance.

IN WITNESS WHEREOF the parties have executed this document on the respective dates specified below with effect from the date specified on the first page of this document.

....	....
(Name of Party)	(Name of Party)
By:	By: ....
Name:	Name:
Title:	Title:
Date:	Date:

ISDA®

International Swaps and Derivatives Association, Inc.

SCHEDULE
to the
2002 Master Agreement

dated as of ....

between .... ("Party A") and .... ("Party B")

("Party A")	("Party B")
[*established as a [COUNTERPARTY TYPE]*]	[*established as a [COUNTERPARTY TYPE]*]
[*with company number [NUMBER]*]	[*with company number [NUMBER]*]
[*under the laws of [JURISDICTION]*]	[*under the laws of [JURISDICTION]*]
[*acting through its [BRANCH]*]*	[*acting through its [BRANCH]*]*

Part 1. **Termination Provisions.**

(a) ***"Specified Entity"*** means in relation to Party A for the purpose of:—

Section 5(a)(v), ...

Section 5(a)(vi), ...

Section 5(a)(vii), ...

Section 5(b)(v), ...

and in relation to Party B for the purpose of:—

Section 5(a)(v), ...

Section 5(a)(vi), ...

Section 5(a)(vii), ...

Section 5(b)(v), ...

* Include if applicable.

(b) ***"Specified Transaction"*** [will have the meaning specified in Section 14 of this Agreement.][means ....

....

....]*

(c) The ***"Cross-Default"*** provisions of Section 5(a)(vi) [will][will not]* apply to Party A
[will][will not]* apply to Party B

[***"Specified Indebtedness"*** [will have the meaning specified in Section 14 of this Agreement.][means ....

....]*

"Threshold Amount" means ....

....]**

(d) The ***"Credit Event Upon Merger"*** provisions of Section 5(b)(v) [will][will not]* apply to Party A
[will][will not]* apply to Party B

(e) The ***"Automatic Early Termination"*** provision of Section 6(a) [will][will not]* apply to Party A
[will][will not]* apply to Party B

(f) ***"Termination Currency"*** [will have the meaning specified in Section 14 of this Agreement.][means ....

....]*

(g) ***Additional Termination Event*** [will][will not]* apply. [The following will constitute an Additional Termination Event:— ....

....

....

....

For the purpose of the foregoing Termination Event, the Affected Party or Affected Parties will be:— ....

....]***

Part 2. **Tax Representations.******

(a) ***Payer Representations.*** For the purpose of Section 3(e) of this Agreement[, Party A and Party B do not make any representations.][:—

[[(i)] [Party A] [and] [Party B] [each] make[s] the following representation:—

It is not required by any applicable law, as modified by the practice of any relevant governmental revenue authority, of any Relevant Jurisdiction to make any deduction or withholding for or on account of any Tax from any payment (other than interest under Section 9(h) of this Agreement) to

---

* Delete as applicable.

** Include if Cross-Default will apply to either Party A or Party B.

*** Include if Additional Termination Event will apply.

**** N.B.: the following representations may need modification if either party is a Multibranch Party.

be made by it to the other party under this Agreement. In making this representation, it may rely on (i) the accuracy of any representations made by the other party pursuant to Section 3(f) of this Agreement, (ii) the satisfaction of the agreement contained in Section 4(a)(i) or 4(a)(iii) of this Agreement and the accuracy and effectiveness of any document provided by the other party pursuant to Section 4(a)(i) or 4(a)(iii) of this Agreement and (iii) the satisfaction of the agreement of the other party contained in Section 4(d) of this Agreement, except that it will not be a breach of this representation where reliance is placed on clause (ii) above and the other party does not deliver a form or document under Section 4(a)(iii) by reason of material prejudice to its legal or commercial position.]*

[[(ii)] [Party A] [and] [Party B] [each] make[s] the following representation[s]:— ....

....

....

....]]*

(b) ***Payee Representations.*** For the purpose of Section 3(f) of this Agreement[, Party A and Party B do not make any representations.][:—

[[(i)] [Party A] [and] [Party B] [each] make[s] the following representation:—

It is fully eligible for the benefits of the "Business Profits" or "Industrial and Commercial Profits" provision, as the case may be, the "interest" provision or the "Other Income" provision, if any, of the Specified Treaty with respect to any payment described in such provisions and received or to be received by it in connection with this Agreement and no such payment is attributable to a trade or business carried on by it through a permanent establishment in the Specified Jurisdiction.

"Specified Treaty" means with respect to Party A ....

"Specified Jurisdiction" means with respect to Party A ....

"Specified Treaty" means with respect to Party B ....

"Specified Jurisdiction" means with respect to Party B ....]*

[[(ii)] [Party A] [and] [Party B] [each] make[s] the following representation:—

Each payment received or to be received by it in connection with this Agreement will be effectively connected with its conduct of a trade or business in the Specified Jurisdiction.

"Specified Jurisdiction" means with respect to Party A ....

"Specified Jurisdiction" means with respect to Party B ....]*

[[(iii)] [Party A] [and] [Party B] [each] make[s] the following representation:—

It is a "U.S. person" (as that term is used in section 1.1441-4(a)(3)(ii) of United States Treasury Regulations) for United States federal income tax purposes.]*

* Delete as applicable.

[[(iv)] [Party A] [and] [Party B] [each] make[s] the following representation:—

It is a "non-U.S. branch of a foreign person" (as that term is used in section 1.1441-4(a)(3)(ii) of United States Treasury Regulations) for United States federal income tax purposes.]*

[[(v)] [Party A] [and] [Party B] [each] make[s] the following representation:—

With respect to payments made to an address outside the United States or made by a transfer of funds to an account outside the United States, it is a "non-U.S. branch of a foreign person" (as that term is used in section 1.1441-4(a)(3)(ii) of United States Treasury Regulations) for United States federal income tax purposes.]*

[[(vi)] [Party A] [and] [Party B] [each] make[s] the following representation:—

It is a "foreign person" (as that term is used in section 1.6041-4(a)(4) of United States Treasury Regulations) for United States federal income tax purposes.]*

[[(vii)] [Party A] [and] [Party B] [each] make[s] the following representation[s]:—

....

....

....]]*

Part 3. **Agreement to Deliver Documents.**

For the purpose of Sections 4(a)(i) and 4(a)(ii) of this Agreement, each party agrees to deliver the following documents, as applicable:—

(a) Tax forms, documents or certificates to be delivered are[: none][:—

Party required to deliver document	Form/Document/ Certificate	Date by which to be delivered
....	....	....
....	....	....
....	....	....
....	....	....
....	....	....]*

* Delete as applicable.

(b) Other documents to be delivered are[: none][:—

Party required to deliver document	**Form/Document/ Certificate**	**Date by which to be delivered**	**Covered by Section 3(d) Representation**
....	....	....	[Yes][No]
....	....	....	[Yes][No]
....	....	....	[Yes][No]
....	....	....	[Yes][No]
....	....	....	[Yes][No]]*

Part 4. **Miscellaneous.**

(a) ***Addresses for Notices.*** For the purpose of Section 12(a) of this Agreement:—

Address for notices or communications to Party A:—

Address: ....

Attention: ....

Telex No.: .... Answerback: ....

Facsimile No.: .... Telephone No.: ....

E-mail: ....

Electronic Messaging System Details: ....

Specific Instructions: ....

Address for notices or communications to Party B:—

Address: ....

Attention: ....

Telex No.: .... Answerback: ....

Facsimile No.: .... Telephone No.: ....

E-mail: ....

Electronic Messaging System Details: ....

Specific Instructions: ....

* Delete as applicable.

(b) ***Process Agent.*** For the purpose of Section 13(c) of this Agreement:—

Party A appoints as its Process Agent: [not applicable][....]*

Party B appoints as its Process Agent: [not applicable][....]*

(c) ***Offices.*** The provisions of Section 10(a) [will][will not]* apply to this Agreement.

(d) ***Multibranch Party.*** For the purpose of Section 10(b) of this Agreement:—

Party A [is not a Multibranch Party.][is a Multibranch Party and may enter into a Transaction through any of the following Offices:—

....

....]*

Party B [is not a Multibranch Party.][is a Multibranch Party and may enter into a Transaction through any of the following Offices:—

....

....]*

[(e) ***Calculation Agent.*** The Calculation Agent is ...., unless otherwise specified in a Confirmation in relation to the relevant Transaction.]**

[(f)] ***Credit Support Document.*** Details of any Credit Support Document:— [none][....

....

....

....]*

[(g)] ***Credit Support Provider.*** Credit Support Provider means in relation to Party A, [none][..............................

....

....]*

Credit Support Provider means in relation to Party B, [none][..

....

....]*

[(h)] ***Governing Law.*** This Agreement will be governed by and construed in accordance with [English law][the laws of the State of New York (without reference to choice of law doctrine)]*.

* Delete as applicable.

** Include if applicable.

[(i)] ***Netting of Payments.*** "Multiple Transaction Payment Netting" [will not apply for the purpose of Section 2(c) of this Agreement.][will apply for the purpose of Section 2(c) of this Agreement to [all Transactions][the following Transactions or groups of Transactions:— ....
....]
(in each case starting from [the date of this Agreement][....])]*

[(j)] ***"Affiliate"*** [will have the meaning specified in Section 14 of this Agreement.][means ....
....]*

[(k)] ***Absence of Litigation.*** For the purpose of Section 3(c):—

"Specified Entity" means in relation to Party A, ...

"Specified Entity" means in relation to Party B, ...

[(l)] ***No Agency.*** The provisions of Section 3(g) [will][will not]* apply to this Agreement.

[(m)] ***Additional Representation*** [will][will not]* apply. [For the purpose of Section 3 of this Agreement, the following will constitute an Additional Representation:—

[[(i)] ***Relationship Between Parties.*** Each party will be deemed to represent to the other party on the date on which it enters into a Transaction that (absent a written agreement between the parties that expressly imposes affirmative obligations to the contrary for that Transaction):—

[(1)] *Non-Reliance.* It is acting for its own account, and it has made its own independent decisions to enter into that Transaction and as to whether that Transaction is appropriate or proper for it based upon its own judgment and upon advice from such advisers as it has deemed necessary. It is not relying on any communication (written or oral) of the other party as investment advice or as a recommendation to enter into that Transaction, it being understood that information and explanations related to the terms and conditions of a Transaction will not be considered investment advice or a recommendation to enter into that Transaction. No communication (written or oral) received from the other party will be deemed to be an assurance or guarantee as to the expected results of that Transaction.

[(2)] *Assessment and Understanding.* It is capable of assessing the merits of and understanding (on its own behalf or through independent professional advice), and understands and accepts, the terms, conditions and risks of that Transaction. It is also capable of assuming, and assumes, the risks of that Transaction.

[(3)] *Status of Parties.* The other party is not acting as a fiduciary for or an adviser to it in respect of that Transaction.]]*

[[(n)] ***Recording of Conversations.*** Each party (i) consents to the recording of telephone conversations between the trading, marketing and other relevant personnel of the parties in connection with this Agreement or any potential Transaction, (ii) agrees to obtain any necessary consent of, and give any necessary notice of such recording to, its relevant personnel and (iii) agrees, to the extent permitted by applicable law, that recordings may be submitted in evidence in any Proceedings.]**

---

* Delete as applicable.
** Include if applicable.

Part 5. **Other Provisions.**

....	....
(Name of Party)	(Name of Party)
By:	By: ....
Name:	Name:
Title:	Title:
Date:	Date:

ANNEX 3 AMENDMENT: CLOSE-OUT AMOUNT

MARCH 2003

ISDA®

International Swaps and Derivatives Association, Inc.

AMENDMENT[1]

dated as of ....

to the

ISDA MASTER AGREEMENT

dated as of ....

between

.... and ....

(the "Agreement")

The parties have previously entered into the Agreement and have now agreed to amend the Agreement by the terms of this Amendment (this "Amendment").

The International Swaps and Derivatives Association, Inc. ("ISDA") has published the 2002 Master Agreement. The parties wish to modify the Agreement to reflect certain provisions of the 2002 Master Agreement. The specific modifications that the parties wish to incorporate in the Agreement are set forth in the Attachment to this Amendment (the "Attachment"). The purpose of this Amendment is to amend the Agreement on the terms set forth in the Attachment.

Accordingly, in consideration of the mutual agreements contained in this Amendment, the parties agree as follows:

1. Amendment of the Agreement

The Agreement is amended in accordance with the amendments set forth in the Attachment.

---

[1] PARTIES SHOULD CONSULT WITH THEIR LEGAL ADVISERS AND ANY OTHER ADVISERS THEY DEEM APPROPRIATE PRIOR TO USING THIS FORM OF AMENDMENT. BECAUSE OF THE RANGE OF MODIFICATIONS THAT PARTIES MAY HAVE MADE TO THE MASTER AGREEMENT, MODIFICATIONS TO THIS FORM OF AMENDMENT MAY BE NECESSARY OR AN ENTIRELY DIFFERENT FORM OF AMENDMENT MAY BE APPROPRIATE IN REGARD TO A PARTICULAR AGREEMENT.

2. Representations

Each party represents to the other party in respect of the Agreement, as amended pursuant to this Amendment, that all representations made by it pursuant to the Agreement are true and accurate as of the date of this Amendment.

3. Miscellaneous

(a) ***Entire Agreement; Restatement.***

(i) This Amendment constitutes the entire agreement and understanding of the parties with respect to its subject matter and supersedes all oral communication and prior writings (except as otherwise provided herein) with respect thereto.

(ii) Except for any amendment to the Agreement made pursuant to this Amendment, all terms and conditions of the Agreement will continue in full force and effect in accordance with its provisions on the date of this Amendment. References to the Agreement will be to the Agreement, as amended by this Amendment.

(b) ***Amendments.*** No amendment, modification or waiver in respect of the matters contemplated by this Amendment will be effective unless made in accordance with the terms of the Agreement.

(c) ***Counterparts.*** This Amendment may be executed and delivered in counterparts (including by facsimile transmission), each of which will be deemed an original.

(d) ***Headings.*** The headings used in this Amendment are for convenience of reference only and are not to affect the construction of or to be taken into consideration in interpreting this Amendment.

(e) ***Governing Law.*** This Amendment will be governed by and construed in accordance with [English law][the laws of the State of New York (without reference to choice of law doctrine)].[2]

IN WITNESS WHEREOF the parties have executed this Amendment on the respective dates specified below with effect from the date specified first on the first page of this Amendment.

.... (Name of Party)	.... (Name of Party)
By:	By: ....
Name:	Name:
Title:	Title:
Date:	Date:

---

[2] Delete as applicable.

2

ATTACHMENT
Amendments to Master Agreement

1. The terms of Section 6(d)(i) of the Agreement are amended in their entirety as follows:

"(d) ***Calculations; Payment Date.***

(i) ***Statement.*** On or as soon as reasonably practicable following the occurrence of an Early Termination Date, each party will make the calculations on its part, if any, contemplated by Section 6(e) and will provide to the other party a statement (1) showing, in reasonable detail, such calculations (including any quotations, market data or information from internal sources used in making such calculations), (2) specifying (except where there are two Affected Parties) any Early Termination Amount payable and (3) giving details of the relevant account to which any amount payable to it is to be paid. In the absence of written confirmation from the source of a quotation or market data obtained in determining a Close-out Amount, the records of the party obtaining such quotation or market data will be conclusive evidence of the existence and accuracy of such quotation or market data."

2. The terms of Section 6(e) of the Agreement are amended in their entirety as follows[3]:

"(e) ***Payments on Early Termination.*** If an Early Termination Date occurs, the amount, if any, payable in respect of that Early Termination Date (the "Early Termination Amount") will be determined pursuant to this Section 6(e) and will be subject to any Set-off.

(i) ***Events of Default.*** If the Early Termination Date results from an Event of Default, the Early Termination Amount will be an amount equal to (1) the sum of (A) the Termination Currency Equivalent of the Close-out Amount or Close-out Amounts (whether positive or negative) determined by the Non-defaulting Party for each Terminated Transaction or group of Terminated Transactions, as the case may be, and (B) the Termination Currency Equivalent of the Unpaid Amounts owing to the Non-defaulting Party less (2) the Termination Currency Equivalent of the Unpaid Amounts owing to the Defaulting Party. If the Early Termination Amount is a positive number, the Defaulting Party will pay it to the Non-defaulting Party; if it is a negative number, the Non-defaulting Party will pay the absolute value of the Early Termination Amount to the Defaulting Party.

(ii) ***Termination Events.*** If the Early Termination Date results from a Termination Event:?

(1) *One Affected Party*. Subject to clause (3) below, if there is one Affected Party, the Early Termination Amount will be determined in accordance with Section 6(e)(i), except that references to the Defaulting Party and to the Non-defaulting Party will be deemed to be references to the Affected Party and to the Non-affected Party, respectively.

(2) *Two Affected Parties*. Subject to clause (3) below, if there are two Affected Parties, each party will determine an amount equal to the Termination Currency Equivalent of the sum of the Close-out Amount or Close-out Amounts (whether positive or negative) for each Terminated Transaction or group of Terminated Transactions, as the case may be, and the Early Termination Amount will be an amount equal to (A) the sum of (I) one-half of the difference between the

[3] Those parties who selected First Method as their payment method should note that this Amendment eliminates First Method and imposes Second Method as the sole payment method.

3

higher amount so determined (by party "X") and the lower amount so determined (by party "Y") and (II) the Termination Currency Equivalent of the Unpaid Amounts owing to X less (B) the Termination Currency Equivalent of the Unpaid Amounts owing to Y. If the Early Termination Amount is a positive number, Y will pay it to X; if it is a negative number, X will pay the absolute value of the Early Termination Amount to Y.

(iii) ***Adjustment for Bankruptcy.*** In circumstances where an Early Termination Date occurs because "Automatic Early Termination" applies in respect of a party, the Early Termination Amount will be subject to such adjustments as are appropriate and permitted by applicable law to reflect any payments or deliveries made by one party to the other under this Agreement (and retained by such other party) during the period from the relevant Early Termination Date to the date for payment determined under Section 6(d)(ii).

(iv) ***Pre-Estimate.*** The parties agree that an amount recoverable under this Section 6(e) is a reasonable pre-estimate of loss and not a penalty. Such amount is payable for the loss of bargain and the loss of protection against future risks and except as otherwise provided in this Agreement neither party will be entitled to recover any additional damages as a consequence of the termination of the Terminated Transactions."

3. The term "Termination Currency Equivalent" in Section 14 of the Agreement is hereby amended by replacing "Market Quotation or Loss (as the case may be)" with "Close-out Amount".

4. The following terms are added to Section 14 of the Agreement in the appropriate alphabetical position:

""Close-out Amount" means, with respect to each Terminated Transaction or each group of Terminated Transactions and a Determining Party, the amount of the losses or costs of the Determining Party that are or would be incurred under then prevailing circumstances (expressed as a positive number) or gains of the Determining Party that are or would be realised under then prevailing circumstances (expressed as a negative number) in replacing, or in providing for the Determining Party the economic equivalent of, (a) the material terms of that Terminated Transaction or group of Terminated Transactions, including the payments and deliveries by the parties under Section 2(a)(i) in respect of that Terminated Transaction or group of Terminated Transactions that would, but for the occurrence of the relevant Early Termination Date, have been required after that date (assuming satisfaction of the conditions precedent in Section 2(a)(iii)) and (b) the option rights of the parties in respect of that Terminated Transaction or group of Terminated Transactions.

Any Close-out Amount will be determined by the Determining Party (or its agent), which will act in good faith and use commercially reasonable procedures in order to produce a commercially reasonable result. The Determining Party may determine a Close-out Amount for any group of Terminated Transactions or any individual Terminated Transaction but, in the aggregate, for not less than all Terminated Transactions. Each Close-out Amount will be determined as of the Early Termination Date or, if that would not be commercially reasonable, as of the date or dates following the Early Termination Date as would be commercially reasonable.

Unpaid Amounts in respect of a Terminated Transaction or group of Terminated Transactions and legal fees and out-of-pocket expenses referred to in Section 11 are to be excluded in all determinations of Close-out Amounts.

In determining a Close-out Amount, the Determining Party may consider any relevant information, including, without limitation, one or more of the following types of information:?

(i) quotations (either firm or indicative) for replacement transactions supplied by one or more third parties that may take into account the creditworthiness of the Determining Party at the time the quotation is provided and the terms of any relevant documentation, including credit support documentation, between the Determining Party and the third party providing the quotation;

4

(ii) information consisting of relevant market data in the relevant market supplied by one or more third parties including, without limitation, relevant rates, prices, yields, yield curves, volatilities, spreads, correlations or other relevant market data in the relevant market; or

(iii) information of the types described in clause (i) or (ii) above from internal sources (including any of the Determining Party's Affiliates) if that information is of the same type used by the Determining Party in the regular course of its business for the valuation of similar transactions.

The Determining Party will consider, taking into account the standards and procedures described in this definition, quotations pursuant to clause (i) above or relevant market data pursuant to clause (ii) above unless the Determining Party reasonably believes in good faith that such quotations or relevant market data are not readily available or would produce a result that would not satisfy those standards. When considering information described in clause (i), (ii) or (iii) above, the Determining Party may include costs of funding, to the extent costs of funding are not and would not be a component of the other information being utilised. Third parties supplying quotations pursuant to clause (i) above or market data pursuant to clause (ii) above may include, without limitation, dealers in the relevant markets, end-users of the relevant product, information vendors, brokers and other sources of market information.

Without duplication of amounts calculated based on information described in clause (i), (ii) or (iii) above, or other relevant information, and when it is commercially reasonable to do so, the Determining Party may in addition consider in calculating a Close-out Amount any loss or cost incurred in connection with its terminating, liquidating or re-establishing any hedge related to a Terminated Transaction or group of Terminated Transactions (or any gain resulting from any of them).

Commercially reasonable procedures used in determining a Close-out Amount may include the following:?

(1) application to relevant market data from third parties pursuant to clause (ii) above or information from internal sources pursuant to clause (iii) above of pricing or other valuation models that are, at the time of the determination of the Close-out Amount, used by the Determining Party in the regular course of its business in pricing or valuing transactions between the Determining Party and unrelated third parties that are similar to the Terminated Transaction or group of Terminated Transactions; and

(2) application of different valuation methods to Terminated Transactions or groups of Terminated Transactions depending on the type, complexity, size or number of the Terminated Transactions or group of Terminated Transactions."

"***"Determining Party"*** means the party determining a Close-out Amount."

"***"Early Termination Amount"*** has the meaning specified in Section 6(e)."

"***"Non-affected Party"*** means, so long as there is only one Affected Party, the other party."

5. The following terms in Section 14 of the Agreement are deleted in their entirety: *"Loss"*, *"Market Quotation"*, *"Reference Market-makers"* and *"Settlement Amount"*[4].

If any of these terms are used in any Annex or Schedule to the Agreement or a Confirmation, the 1994 ISDA Equity Option Definitions, the 1996 ISDA Equity Derivatives Definitions, the 2002 ISDA Equity Derivatives Definitions, the 1997 ISDA Government Bond Option Definitions, the 1998 FX and Currency Option Definitions, the 1999 ISDA Credit Derivatives Definitions or any other ISDA document incorporated by reference or executed by the parties hereto, the terms will have the respective meanings ascribed to them in the standard form 1992 ISDA Master Agreement (Multicurrency-Cross Border).

---

6. Part 1(f) of the Schedule is deleted in its entirety and the subsequent paragraphs are renumbered sequentially. In case the parties have used another designation for the paragraph of the Schedule specifying the selection of Market Quotation or Loss and First Method or Second Method, the reference herein to Part 1(f) of the Schedule shall be deemed a reference to that paragraph.

ANNEX 4 LIST OF JURISDICTIONS WHERE ISDA HAS OBTAINED NETTING OPINIONS ON THE 1992 AGREEMENT (as at OCTOBER 2003)

Australia	Mallesons Stephens Jaques
Austria	Schonherr Bartuss Torggler & Partners
Bahamas	Higgs & Johnson
Belgium	Coudert Brothers Coppens Van Ommeslaghe
	Horsmans & Faures
Bermuda	Appleby Spurling & Kempe
British Virgin Islands	Walker Smiths
Canada	Stikeman, Elliott
Cayman Islands	Maples & Calder
Denmark	Gorrissen Federspiel Kierkegaard
England	Allen & Overy
Finland	Hannes Snellman
France	Gide Loyrette Nouel
Germany	Hengeler Mueller Weitzel Wirtz
Hong Kong	Allen & Overy
Hungary	Allen & Overy
Indonesia	Ali Budjiardo, Nugroho, Reksodiputro
Ireland	McCann Fitzgerald
Italy	Ughi e Nunziate
Japan	Mitsui, Yasuda, Wani & Maeda
Luxembourg	Beghin & Feider
Malaysia	Shearn Delamore & Co
Mexico	Ritch Heather y Mueller
Netherlands	De Brauw Blackstone Westbroek
Netherlands Antilles	Clifford Chance
New Zealand	Bell Gully
Norway	Wiersholm, Mellbye & Bech
Philippines	Sy Cip Salazar Hernandez Gatmaitan
Portugal	Abreu & Marques, Vinhas
Scotland	Dundas & Wilson
Singapore	Allen & Gledhill
South Africa	Webber Wentzel Bowens
South Korea	Kim & Chang
Spain	Allen & Overy
Sweden	Wistrand
Switzerland	Prof. Dr. Dieter Zobl and Dr. Thomas Werlen
Taiwan	Lee & Li
Thailand	Baker & McKenzie
Turkey	Pekin & Pekin
United States	Cravath, Swaine & Moore

LIST OF JURISDICTIONS WHERE ISDA HAS OBTAINED NETTING OPINIONS ON THE 2002 AGREEMENT (as at OCTOBER 2003)

Australia	Mallesons Stephens Jaques
Austria	Schonherr Bartuss Torggler & Partners
Bahamas	Higgs & Johnson
Belgium	Coudert Brothers Coppens Van Ommeslaghe Horsmans & Faures
Bermuda	Appleby Spurling & Kempe
Canada	Stikeman, Elliott
Cayman Islands	Maples & Calder
Denmark	Gorrissen Federspiel Kierkegaard
England	Allen & Overy
Finland	Hannes Snellman
France	Gide Loyrette Nouel
Germany	Hengeler Mueller Weitzel Wirtz
Hong Kong	Allen & Overy
Indonesia	Ali Budjiardo, Nugroho, Reksodiputro
Ireland	McCann Fitzgerald
Italy	Ughi e Nunziate
Japan	Mitsui, Yasuda, Wani & Maeda
Luxembourg	Beghin & Feider
Malaysia	Shearn Delamore & Co
Mexico	Ritch Heather y Mueller
Netherlands	De Brauw Blackstone Westbroek
Netherlands Antilles	Clifford Chance
New Zealand	Bell Gully
Norway	Wiersholm, Mellbye & Bech
Philippines	Sy Cip Salazar Hernandez Gatmaitan
Portugal	Abreu & Marques, Vinhas
Scotland	Dundas & Wilson
Singapore	Allen & Gledhill
South Africa	Webber Wentzel Bowens
South Korea	Kim & Chang
Spain	Allen & Overy
Sweden	Wistrand
Switzerland	Dr. Thomas Werlen
Taiwan	Lee & Li
Thailand	Baker & McKenzie
United States	Cravath, Swaine & Moore

ANNEX 5 NEW YORK LAW GUARANTEE CONTENTS CHECKLIST

PROVISION	TICK IF PRESENT
1. Guarantee a. Reference to ISDA Master Agreement between parties. b. Guarantor absolutely, unconditionally and irrevocably guarantees as primary obligor and not merely as a surety. c. Prompt payment of all present and future obligations of the counterparty when due subject to any grace period. d. Due and punctual performance of all the counterparty's obligations under the Agreement. e. Guarantee is a Credit Support Document under the Agreement.	
2. Nature of Guarantee a. Guarantee is one of payment *not* collection. b. Beneficiary *not* obliged to proceed against counterparty first. c. Beneficiary not to file any bankruptcy claim against the counterparty before calling on the Guarantor. d. Guarantor remains liable if any payment made on account has to be returned. e. Liability of Guarantor absolute and unconditional and Guarantor waives all illegality or insolvency defences. f. Has right to assert counterparty's payment defences.	
3. Continuing Guarantee Guarantee in full force and effect until all Obligations fully satisfied.	
4. Consents, Waivers and Renewals a. Beneficiary can grant any consents, waivers or renewals to the counterparty without impairing Guarantee. b. Guarantor waives promptness, diligence and all notices required by law (except notice of counterparty's default).	
5. Subrogation All rights of Guarantor against counterparty junior and subordinate to those of Beneficiary until counterparty's obligations met in full.	

PROVISION	TICK IF PRESENT
6. Representations and Warranties a. Duly organised and in good standing under its laws. b. Power to execute and deliver guarantee, perform obligations and all necessary action taken to authorise these. c. Such execution, delivery or performance not in violation of any law, constitutional documents, judgment of court or government agency. d. All consents obtained and are in full force and effect. e. Guarantee obligations legal valid, binding and enforceable. f. No Event of Default (actual or potential) or Termination Event has or would occur or is continuing as a result of giving the Guarantee. g. No material litigation pending. h. All information from Guarantor to Beneficiary true and accurate.	
7. Taxes a. No deduction or withholding of tax on payments. b. Outline of procedure if it is as per Section 2(d) of Agreement. c. Definition of "Tax" and "Indemnifiable Tax".	
8. Currency Conversion Provisions in Section 8 of the Agreement re normal and judgment payments to apply to the Guarantor.	
9. Transfer a. No transfer allowed by Guarantor without Beneficiary's prior written consent. b. Any transfer without it will be void.	
10. No Waiver: Cumulative Rights Usual wording.	
11. Expenses a. Reimbursement of expenses on demand. b. Beneficiary held harmless against all reasonable expenses arising from enforcement or protection of Guarantee rights.	

PROVISION	TICK IF PRESENT
12. Notices Usual wording.	
13. Governing Law a. Laws of the State of New York. b. Without reference to choice of law doctrine.	
14. Consent to Jurisdiction a. Guarantor irrevocably submits to non-exclusive jurisdiction of the courts of the State of New York and the United States District Court located in the Borough of Manhattan. b. Guarantor waives any objection to laying of venue of Proceedings. c. Guarantor waives any inconvenient forum claim. d. Waives objections to court's jurisdiction over Guarantor. e. Beneficiary can bring proceedings in other jurisdictions. f. Guarantor waives immunity. g. Guarantor's Process Agent details and provision for appointing a substitute Process Agent if Guarantor is not resident in New York State.	
15. Termination a. Guarantor may give 5 days' notice of termination to the Beneficiary. b. Guarantee remains in full force and effect for all Transactions entered into before notice becomes effective.	

ANNEX 6 ENGLISH LAW GUARANTEE CONTENTS CHECKLIST

PROVISION	TICK IF PRESENT
1. Guarantee	
a. Reference to ISDA Master Agreement between parties.	
b. Guarantor unconditionally and irrevocably guarantees as primary obligor and not merely as a surety.	
c. Prompt payment of all present and future obligations of the counterparty when due subject to any grace period.	
d. Due and punctual performance of all the counterparty's obligations under the Agreement.	
e. Guarantee is a Credit Support Document under the Agreement.	
2. Nature of Guarantee	
a. Guarantee is in addition to and not in substitution for any other security held by the Beneficiary from time to time.	
b. Beneficiary *not* obliged to proceed against counterparty first.	
c. Beneficiary not to file any bankruptcy claim against the counterparty before calling on the Guarantor.	
d. Guarantor remains liable if any payment made on account has to be returned.	
e. Liability of Guarantor absolute and unconditional and Guarantor waives all illegality or insolvency defences.	
f. Has right to assert counterparty's payment defences.	
g. Guarantor may not prove in competition with Beneficiary unless the counterparty is insolvent and then any moneys must be held in trust for the Beneficiary.	
3. Continuing Security Guarantee is a continuing security and will remain in full force and effect until all Obligations fully satisfied.	

PROVISION	TICK IF PRESENT
4. Payments a. Payments must be made without set off or deduction. b. Interest to accrue at specified rate on all sums demanded under the Guarantee from the date of demand. c. Beneficiary can place sums received to the credit of a suspense account. d. Guarantor cannot direct Beneficiary to appropriate or apply sums received to any particular liability.	
5. Consents, Waivers and Renewals a. Beneficiary can grant any consents, waivers or renewals to the counterparty without impairing Guarantee. b. Guarantor waives promptness, diligence and all notices required by law (except notice of counterparty's default).	
6. Subrogation a All rights of Guarantor against counterparty junior and subordinate to those of Beneficiary until counterparty's obligations met in full. b. Any moneys received will be held on trust for the Beneficiary and applied to discharge Guarantor's liabilities under the Guarantee.	
7. Representations and Warranties a. Duly organised and in good standing under its laws. b. Power to execute and deliver guarantee, perform obligations and all necessary action taken to authorise these. c. Such execution, delivery or performance not in violation of any law, constitutional documents, judgment of court or government agency. d. All consents obtained and are in full force and effect. e. Guarantee obligations legal valid, binding and enforceable. f. No Event of Default (actual or potential) or Termination Event has or would occur or is continuing as a result of giving guarantee. g. No material litigation pending. h. No material adverse change in Guarantor's financial condition since last audited accounts.	

PROVISION	TICK IF PRESENT
8. Taxes a. No deduction or withholding of tax on payments. b. Outline of gross up procedure. c. Definition of "Tax" and "Indemnifiable Tax".	
9. Currency Conversion Provisions in Section 8 of the Agreement re normal and judgment payments to apply to the Guarantor.	
10. Transfer No transfer allowed by Guarantor without Beneficiary's prior written consent.	
11. No Waiver: Cumulative Rights Usual wording.	
12. Expenses Guarantor to pay costs and expenses on a full indemnity basis.	
13. Notices Usual wording.	
14. Set Off Set Off permitted by beneficiary against Guarantor.	
15. Severability language If one or more Guarantee provisions become illegal, invalid or unenforceable, the remaining provisions remain unimpaired.	
16. Governing Law Laws of England.	

PROVISION	TICK IF PRESENT
17. Consent to Jurisdiction a. Guarantor irrevocably submits to non-exclusive jurisdiction of the English courts. b. Guarantor waives any objection to laying of venue of Proceedings. c. Guarantor waives any inconvenient forum claim. d. Waives objections to court's jurisdiction over Guarantor. e. Beneficiary can bring proceedings in other jurisdictions. f. Guarantor waives immunity. g. Guarantor's Process Agent details and provision for appointing a substitute Process Agent if Guarantor is not resident in England.	
18. Termination a. Guarantor may give 5 days' notice of termination to the Beneficiary. b. Guarantee remains in full force and effect for all Transactions entered into before notice becomes effective.	

ANNEX 7 LIST OF LONG-TERM CREDIT RATINGS FROM THREE MAJOR CREDIT RATINGS AGENCIES

The higher ratings are best:

Moody's	*S&P*	*Fitch IBCA*
Aaa	AAA	AAA
Aa1	AA+	AA+
Aa2	AA	AA
Aa3	AA–	AA–
A1	A+	A+
A2	A	A
A3	A–	A–
Baa1	BBB+	BBB+
Baa2	BBB	BBB
Investment Grade Baa3	BBB–	BBB–
Ba1	BB+	BB+
Ba2	BB	BB
Ba3	BB–	BB–
B1	B+	B+
B2	B	B
B3	B–	B–

ANNEX 8 SAMPLE BOARD RESOLUTION FOR UK COMPANY

Rollerblade plc
(the "Company")

Minutes of a meeting of the Board of Directors of Rollerblade plc held at [*Insert address*] on [*Insert date*]

Present: Gunther Schmidt, Chairman
Olaf Higgins
Martha Greenwood

In attendance: Justin O'Brien Secretary

IT WAS RESOLVED:

1. that (after full and careful consideration of the terms of the agreement detailed hereunder; the nature and scale of the liabilities to be undertaken thereby; and of the commercial and financial consequences, direct and indirect, of the execution of such agreement so far as they affect the Company) it is in the best interests of and to the advantage and further benefit of the Company to enter into the agreement detailed hereunder which was approved; and

2. that the Company should further enter into an ISDA Master Agreement dated as of [*Insert date*] with X Bank AG in the form annexed hereto and that Olaf Higgins and Martha Greenwood are authorised to sign the same on behalf of the Company.

CHAIRMAN'S SIGNATURE

Certified as a true copy of the original
SECRETARY'S SIGNATURE
Justin O'Brien
Secretary
Date:

ANNEX 9 USEFUL WEBSITES

International Swaps and Derivatives Association, Inc	www.isda.org
Australian Financial Markets Association	www.afma.com.au
British Bankers' Association	www.bba.org.uk
Bank for International Settlements	www.bis.org
Board of Governors of the Federal Reserve Bank	www.bog.frb.fed.us
The Bond Market Association	www.bondmarkets.com
Commodity Futures Trading Commission	www.cftc.gov
Emerging Markets Traders Association	www.emta.org
Financial Services Authority	www.fsa.gov.uk
The Foreign Exchange Committee	www.ny.frb.org/fxc
International Securities Market Association	www.isma.org
International Securities Lenders' Association	www.isla.co.uk
Securities and Exchange Commission	www.sec.gov
World Bank	www.worldbank.com

BIBLIOGRAPHY

Chapters 1–3, and 6–10

Gooch, A. C. and Klein, L. B. (1993) *Documentation for derivatives* (3rd edition, London: Euromoney Publications).

Johnson, C. A. (2000) *Over-the-Counter Derivatives Documentation* (New York: Bowne Publishing).

International Swaps and Derivatives Association, Inc (1993) *User's Guide to the 1992 ISDA Master Agreements.*

Allen & Overy Derivatives Product Group (1992), *1992 ISDA Master Agreement* (London).

International Swaps and Derivatives Association, Inc (2001) *A Retrospective of ISDA Activities in 2000.*

Harding, P. (1999) "The ISDA Master Agreement", *The Treasurer*, June and July 1999.

Walker, G. (2003) *Mastering Finance-Linked Swaps* (Financial Times-Prentice Hall, 2003)

Chapter 4

International Swaps and Derivatives Association, Inc (2003) *User's Guide to the 2002 ISDA Master Agreement.*

Allen & Overy, *Bulletin on the ISDA 2002 Master Agreement* (January 2003).

Tredgett, R. and Berry, J. (2002) "A new Master Agreement for the new Millennium: The development of the 2002 ISDA Master Agreement" (*Butterworths Journal of International Banking and Financial Law*, May).

Chapter 5

Simon Leifer's sources

Abruzzo, C. T. and Cunningham, D. P. (1995) *Multibranch netting – a Solution to the Problems of Cross-Border Bank Insolvencies*, Capital Markets Forum (London: International Bar Association).

Baggallay, R. (1997) Suitability Requirements and Dealer Liability for Selling Derivatives in England (London).

Chitty on Contracts (1994) (28th edition, London: Sweet & Maxwell).

Harding, M. (1995) *Powers of institutions to use derivatives.*

Hudson, A. (1998) *The Law on Financial Derivatives* (2nd edition, London: Sweet & Maxwell).

Hudson, A. (2000) "The Law of Finance", in Birks, P. and Rose, F. (eds) *Lessons of The Swaps Litigation* (Mansfield Press).

Financial Law Panel (1996) *OTC derivatives – banks' obligations to customers. Bankers Trust* v *PT Dharmala Sakti Sejahtera.*

James, S. (1999) *The Law of Derivatives* (London/Hong Kong: LLP).

O'Dell, E. (2000) "Incapacity", in Birks, P. and Rose, F. (eds) *Lessons of The Swaps Litigation* (Mansfield Press).

Picarda, H. (2000) "Contract and Tort", in Birks, P. and Rose, F. (eds) *Lessons of The Swaps Litigation* (Mansfield Press).

Christian Johnson's sources and further reading suggestions

Books

Gooch, A. and Klein, L. (2002) *Documentation for Derivatives* (3rd edition, London: Euromoney Publications).

Harding, P. (2002) *Mastering the ISDA Master Agreement* (Financial Times/Prentice Hall: November).

Harding, P. and Johnson, C. (2002) *Mastering Collateral Management and Documentation* (Financial Times/Prentice Hall)

Johnson, C. (2000) *Over-the-Counter Derivatives Documentation: A Practical Guide for Executives* (New York: Bowne Publishing)

McLaughlin, R. (1999) *Over-the-Counter Derivative Products: A Guide to Business and Legal Risk Management and Documentation* (The McGraw-Hill Co.).

Other Publications

Bernstein, Sol W. of Reed Smith Shaw & McClay LLP, "Interplay Between Swaps and Loan Documentation", American Bar Association, Section of Business Law, Spring Meeting, San Francisco, California, 16 April 1999.

Bloom, D. T., "Derivatives Risk-How it is Being Addressed in the Documentation", 931 Practicing Law Institute/Corp 343 (1996).

Boggiano, K. and Watterson, P. N., "SPVs & ISDA Documentation", *Derivatives Week*, 24 July 2001.

Cohn, J. D., "ISDA Master Agreements: 1992 and 1987 Versions Compared", Practicing Law Institute, 778 PLI/Corp 105 (11–12 June 1992); 959 PLI/Corp 51 (October 1996); 1017 PLI/Corp 77 (October 1997); 1086 PLI/Corp 85 (November 1998).

Crino, B. L. and Dondanville, P., "Pay Attention to Swap Contracts: Contracting for Derivatives", *Corporate Cashflow Magazine*, August 1995, at p. 30.

Cunningham, D. P. and Rogers, W. P., Jr., et al, "An Introduction to OTC Derivatives", Practicing Law Institute, 848 PLI/Corp 121 (34–24 May 1994).

Davis, W. N., *ISDA Master Agreements – When Reciprocal is Neither Wise Nor Fair*, Futures & Derivatives Law Report, 19 No. 11 Futures & Derivatives L. Rep. 7 (February 2000).

Falloon, W., "The Devil in the Documentation", *Risk*, November 1998, at p. 32.

Flanagan, S. M., "The Rise of a Trade Association: Group Interactions Within the International Swaps and Derivatives Association", *Harvard Negotiation Law Review*, 6 Harv. Negotiation L. Rev. 211 (Spring 2001).

Forster, D. M., "ISDA Documentation: Ten Legal Pitfalls", *Treasury Management International*, July/August 1994, at p. 23.

Gauvin, A., "Is ISDA Documentation Reliable in Case of Early Termination of the Master Agreement?", *Banking Law Journal*, 118 Banking L.J. 766 (September 2001).

Gay, G. D. and Medero, J. T., "The Economics of Derivatives Documentation: Private Contracting as a Substitute for Government Regulation", The Journal of Derivatives, Summer 1996, at pp. 78–89.

Grala, B. E., "Swaps Documentation with ERISA Plans", Practicing Law Institute, 339 PLI/Tax 225 (17 May 1993).

Henderson, Schuyler, "ISDA Swap Documentation", *Treasury Management International*, July/August 1994, at p. 19.

Horan, A. J., "International Swap Dealers Association's Master Swap Agreements: Derivative Documentation for Derivative Products", Practicing Law Institute, 638 PLI/Corp 115 (4 May 1989).

International Swap Dealers Association, "ISDA Master Agreement (MultiCurrency – Cross Border", Practicing Law Institute, 1280 PLI/Corp 31 (November 2001).

International Swaps and Derivatives Association, ISDA Year 2000 Review of Standard Documentation, available at *www.isda.org/publications/index.html*, then click on "Other Documentation".

Johnson, C., "OTC Derivatives Risk Can Be Minimized Through Proper Loan Documentation", *The Journal of Lending & Credit Risk Management*, 9/1/99 J. Lending & Credit Risk Mgmt. 72, September 1999, at p. 72.

Johnson, C., "Preview of The 2002 ISDA Master Agreement", *Derivatives Week*, Learning Curves Column, 11 August 2002.

Johnson, C., "Seven Deadly Sins of ISDA Negotiations" (Learning Curve), *Derivatives Week*, 25 March 2002, at p. 6.

Johnson, C., "Payee Tax Representations" (Learning Curve), *Derivatives Week*, 16 July 2001, at p. 6.

Johnson, C., "Liquidity & The ISDA Master Agreement" (Learning Curve), *Derivatives Week*, 30 April 2001, at p. 6.

Johnson, C., "Rehypothecation Risk" (Learning Curve), *Derivatives Week*, 16 April 2001, at p. 5.

Klein, L. B., "Overview of the ISDA Master Agreement (Multicurrency-Cross Border) Form", Practicing Law Institute, 1280 PLI/Corp 59 (November 2001).

Kruft, S. R., "Cross-Default Provisions in Financing and Derivatives Transactions", 113 *The Banking Law Journal*, 216 (1996).

Nolan, F. D., "Documentation: the Key to Containing Derivatives Risk", *Bankers Magazine*, 15 May 1995, at p. 15.

Rahl, Leslie Lynn, "What Makes a Good OTC Counterparty?" in *The Handbook of Derivatives & Synthetics*, (R. A. Klein and Jess Lederman, eds., 1994).

Sutherland Asbill & Brennan, "Legal Issues Arising from Events of September 11, 2001".

Suetens, D., "Collateralization and the ISDA Credit Support Annex", *International Financial Law Review*, August 1995, at pp. 15–16.

Summe, K., "A New ISDA Master Agreement for the OTC Derivatives Industry", Futures & Derivatives Law Report, Vol. 22, No. 5, July/August 2002.

Taylor, B. W., "Swap Covenants in Loan Agreements", Practicing Law Insitute, 638 PLI/Corp 107 (4 May 1989).

Taylor-Brill, B., "Negotiating and Opining on ISDA Masters", Practicing Law Institute, 1215 PLI/Corp 71 (November 2000).

Taylor-Brill, B., "OTC Derivatives: The Contractual Architecture of Private Regulation", Practicing Law Institute, 1147 PLI/Corp 219 (November 1999); 1215 PLI/Corp 93 (November 2000).

Thompson, P., "Collateralization Agreements", *Derivatives Week*, 10 July 1995, at p. 10.

INDEX